The Cambridge Companion to
LEIBNIZ

Edited by Nicholas Jolley
University of California, San Diego

CAMBRIDGE
UNIVERSITY PRESS

To the memory of Albert Heinekamp

PUBLISHED BY THE PRESS SYNDICATE OF THE UNIVERSITY OF CAMBRIDGE
The Pitt Building, Trumpington Street, Cambridge CB2 1RP, United Kingdom

CAMBRIDGE UNIVERSITY PRESS
The Edinburgh Building, Cambridge CB2 2RU, UK   http://www.cup.cam.ac.uk
40 West 20th Street, New York, NY 10011-4211, USA   http://www.cup.org
10 Stamford Road, Oakleigh, Melbourne 3166, Australia

First published 1995
Reprinted 1995, 1996, 1998

Printed in the United States of America

Typeset in Trump Mediaeval

A catalogue record for this book is available from the British Library

Library of Congress Cataloguing-in-Publication Data is available

ISBN 0-521-36588-0 hardback
ISBN 0-521-36769-7 paperback

CONTENTS

v

vi   Contents

CONTRIBUTORS

ROGER ARIEW is Professor of Philosophy at Virginia Polytechnic Institute and State University. He is the translator of Martial Gueroult, *Descartes' Philosophy According to the Order of Reasons* (1984–5) and of Pierre Duhem, *Medieval Cosmology* (1985); the co-translator of *Leibniz: Philosophical Essays* (1989); and the co-editor of *Revolution and Continuity; Essays in the History and Philosophy of Early Modern Science* (1991).

DAVID BLUMENFELD, Professor of Philosophy and department chair at Georgia State University, has published numerous articles on Leibniz, including "Leibniz on Contingency and Infinite Analysis," *Philosophy and Phenomenological Research* (June 1985,) and "Freedom, Contingency, and Things Possible in Themselves," *Philosophy and Phenomenological Research* (September 1988) (reprinted in V. Chappell [ed.], *Essays on Early Modern Philosophers*, vol. 12).

GREGORY BROWN is Associate Professor of Philosophy at the University of Houston. He is the author of a number of articles on Leibniz and Descartes, some of which have recently been reprinted in Georges J.D. Moyal (ed.), *Descartes: Critical Assessments* (1991) and in R.S. Woolhouse (ed.), *Leibniz: Critical Assessments* (1994).

STUART BROWN, Professor of Philosophy at the Open University, Milton Keynes; is the author of *Leibniz* (1984). He is the co-editor of an English edition of *The Discourse on Metaphysics and Related Writings* (1988) and is the editor of *Nicolas Malebranche: His Philosophical Critics and Successors* (1991).

DANIEL GARBER is Professor of Philosophy and Chairman of the Department of Philosophy at the University of Chicago. The author

vii

of *Descartes' Metaphysical Physics* (1992), he is also the co-translator (with Roger Ariew) of *Leibniz: Philosophical Essays* (1989) and the co-editor (with Michael Ayers) of the forthcoming *Cambridge History of Seventeenth-Century Philosophy*. At present he is working on an annotated edition of J.-B. Morin's seminal *Astrologia Gallica*.

NICHOLAS JOLLEY is Professor of Philosophy at the University of California, San Diego; author of *Leibniz and Locke: A Study of the New Essays on Human Understanding* (1984) and *The Light of the Soul: Theories of Ideas in Leibniz, Malebranche, and Descartes* (1990).

ROBERT MCRAE is Professor Emeritus of Philosophy at the University of Toronto, and the author of *The Problem of the Unity of the Sciences: Bacon to Kant* (1961) and *Leibniz: Perception, Apperception, and Thought* (1976).

CHRISTIA MERCER, Assistant Professor of Philosophy at Columbia University, is the author of *Leibniz's Metaphysics: Its Origins and Development* (forthcoming).

G.H.R. PARKINSON is Emeritus Professor of Philosophy at the University of Reading. His numerous books include *Spinoza's Theory of Knowledge* (1954), *Logic and Reality in Leibniz's Metaphysics* (1965), *Leibniz on Human Freedom* (1970), and *Georg Lukacs* (1977). He is also a General Editor of the *Routledge History of Philosophy* (10 vols., 1993–).

DONALD RUTHERFORD, Associate Professor of Philosophy at Emory University, is the author of *Leibniz and the Rational Order of Nature* (forthcoming). He is currently at work on a new edition and translation of the Leibniz–Des Bosses correspondence.

R.C. SLEIGH, JR., is Professor of Philosophy at the University of Massachusetts at Amherst. He is the author of *Leibniz and Arnauld: A Commentary on their Correspondence* (1990) and co-editor (with Daniel Garber) of the Yale Leibniz series.

CATHERINE WILSON, Professor of Philosophy and department chair at the University of Alberta, has published articles on Descartes, Leibniz, and Malebranche, as well as *Leibniz's Metaphysics: A Historical and Comparative Study* (1989) and a forthcoming book on the microscope in early modern science.

ABBREVIATIONS

A critical edition of Leibniz's collected writings is being prepared by the German Academy of Sciences (see A below), but at present it is far from complete. It is thus necessary to cite a number of partial editions of Leibniz. Throughout this book, references to Leibniz's works are made in parentheses in the main body of the text; a reference to a standard edition of the original texts (e.g. G) is generally followed by a reference to an English translation (e.g., L). For additional works by Leibniz, see the Bibliography

For all other works cited in the notes at the end of the chapter, full publication details may be found in the Bibliography

A: German Academy of Sciences (ed.) *G.W. Leibniz: Sämtliche Schriften und Briefe.* Berlin: Akademie Verlag, 1923–. References are to series and volume.

AG: Ariew, R., and Garber, D. *G.W. Leibniz: Philosophical Essays.* Indianapolis: Hackett, 1989.

BB: Bodemann, E. (ed.) *Der Briefwechsel des Gottfried Wilhelm Leibniz in der Königlichen Öffentlichen Bibliothek zu Hannover.* Hannover: Hahn, 1895; reprinted Hildesheim, Olms, 1966.

BH: Bodemann, E. (ed.) *Die Leibniz-Handschriften der Königlichen Öffentlichen Bibliothek zu Hannover.* Hannover: Hahn; reprinted Hildesheim: Olms, 1966.

C: Couturat, L. (ed.) *Opuscules et fragments inédits de Leibniz.* Paris: Alcan, 1903; reprinted Hildesheim: Olms, 1961.

D: Duncan, G.M. (ed. and trans.) *G.W. Leibniz: Works,* 2nd ed. New Haven: Tuttle, Morehouse and Taylor Co, 1908.

Du: Dutens, L.L. (ed.) *G.G. . Leibnitii Opera Omnia,* 6 vols. Geneva, 1768.

ix

E: Erdmann, J.E. (ed.) *God. Guil. Leibnitii Opera philosophica quae existant Latina, Gallica, Germanica omnia.* Berlin: Eichler, 1839–40; reprinted Aalen, Scientia Verlag, 1974.

FC: Foucher de Careil, A. (ed.) *Nouvelles lettres et opuscules de Leibniz.* Paris: Auguste Durand, 1857; reprinted Hildesheim: Olms, 1971.

G: Gerhardt, C.I. (ed.) *Die Philosophischen Schriften von Leibniz,* 7 vols. Berlin: Weidmann, 1875–90; reprinted Hildesheim: Olms, 1965.

GM: Gerhardt, C.I. (ed.) *Leibnizens Mathematische Schriften,* 7 vols. Berlin: A. Asher/Halle: H.W. Schmidt, 1848–63; reprinted Hildesheim: Olms, 1962.

Gr: Grua, G. (ed.) *G.W. Leibniz: Textes inédits d'après des manuscrits de la Bibliothèque provinciale d'Hanovre.* Paris: Presses Universitaires de France, 1948.

Gu: Guhrauer, G.E., *Leibniz's Deutsche Schriften.* 2 vols. Berlin: Veit, 1838–40.

GW: Gerhardt, C.I. (ed.) *Briefwechsel zwischen Leibniz und Christian Wolff.* Halle: H.W. Schmidt, 1860; reprinted Hildesheim: Olms, 1963.

H: Huggard, E.M. (trans.) *G.W. Leibniz: Theodicy: Essays on the Goodness of God, the Freedom of Man, and the Origin of Evil.* LaSalle, Ill.: Open Court, 1985.

K: Klopp, O. (ed.) *Die Werke von Leibniz,* erste Reihe, 11 vols. Hannover: Klindworth, 1864–84.

L: Loemker, L.E. (ed.) *G.W. Leibniz: Philosophical Papers and Letters,* 2nd ed. Dordrecht: Reidel, 1969.

M: Mollat, G. (ed.) *Mittheilungen aus Leibnizens ungedruckten Schriften.* Leipzig: H. Haessel, 1893.

MB: Martin, R., Niall, D., and Brown, S. (trans. and eds.) *G.W. Leibniz: Discourse on Metaphysics and Related Writings.* Manchester: Manchester University Press, 1988.

MP: Mason, H.T. (trans.) and Parkinson, G.H.R. (intro.) *The Leibniz-Arnauld Correspondence.* Manchester: Manchester University Press, 1967.

P: Parkinson, G.H.R. (trans. and ed.) *Leibniz: Philosophical Writings.* London: Dent, 1973.

Pk: Parkinson, G.H.R. *G.W. Leibniz: De Summa Rerum:*

Metaphysical Papers 1675–1676. New Haven and London: Yale University Press, 1992.

PLP: Parkinson, G.H.R. (trans. and ed.) *Leibniz: Logical Papers.* Oxford: Clarendon Press, 1966.

R: Riley, P. (ed. and trans.) *The Political Writings of Leibniz.* Cambridge: Cambridge University Press, 1972.

RB: Remnant, P., and Bennett, J. (trans. and eds.) *G.W. Leibniz: New Essays on Human Understanding.* Cambridge: Cambridge University Press, 1981. The pagination of Remnant and Bennett is identical with that of the Academy edition (A VI.vi); one reference thus serves for both.

S: Schrecker, P. and A.M. (trans.), *Monadology and Other Philosophical Essays* (Indianapolis: Bobbs-Merrill, 1965).

VE: G.W. Leibniz: *Vorausedition zur Reihe VI (Philosophische Schriften)* in der Ausgabe der Akademie der Wissenschaften der DDR. Ed. Leibniz-Forschungsstelle der Universität Münster (Münster, 1982–).

W: Wiener, P.P. (ed.), *Leibniz: Selections* (New York: Scribner's and Sons, 1951).

1 Introduction

Many people first came across the name "Leibniz" when reading Voltaire's *Candide*, and the encounter is not likely to inspire confidence in Leibniz as a great philosopher. In Voltaire's biting satire, the optimism of Doctor Pangloss – whose character is based either on Leibniz himself or on his disciples – appears as a foolish and almost wickedly complacent response to the evils of our world. The reader cannot help but sympathize with Candide's rhetorical question: "If this is the best of all possible worlds, . . . what can the rest be like?"[1] Even initial exposure to Leibniz's own texts is not always encouraging. Perhaps the most widely read of Leibniz's works is the *Monadology*, and although, in many respects, a brilliant summary of his final metaphysical views, it is not the best introduction to his philosophy. It is natural to feel, as Bertrand Russell once did, that we are presented with "a kind of metaphysical fairy tale, coherent perhaps, but wholly arbitrary";[2] part of the problem is that the fairy tale metaphysics is presented to us in a "take it or leave it" manner with little in the way of sustained argument. Initially, then, Leibniz's reputation as a philosophical genius of the first rank may strike us as puzzling.

Deeper acquaintance with Leibniz's work should serve to dispel these doubts. Leibniz did indeed hold that this is the best of all possible worlds, but this thesis is not the complacent nonsense that it appears to be. A little reflection shows that it is a fairly natural position to take up in response to problems of philosophical theology. For if God is essentially good, then it is difficult – but not impossible – to escape the conclusion that the world that he created must be the best of those alternatives available to him. Moreover, and more importantly, Leibniz's apparatus of possible worlds provides a compelling and influential framework for tackling deep prob-

I

lems about necessity, contingency, and free will. Although the interpretation of Leibniz is controversial in this area, it is largely within
this framework that he seeks to do justice to our intuition that
Julius Caesar, for example, might have done otherwise than cross
the Rubicon. Or consider the *Monadology*. Far from being a gratuitous metaphysical fairy tale, the theory of monads is, in fact, a
solution to the problem of determining the fundamental building-
blocks of reality consistent with Leibniz's conviction that matter is
infinitely divisible. Moreover, the theory of monads has remarkable
parallels with modern metaphysical theories such as reductive materialism. The reductive materialist seeks to argue that all that fundamentally exists is matter, and that apparently nonmaterial things,
such as minds, are, in reality, physical items – namely brains. In a
structurally similar way, Leibniz argues that all that fundamentally
exists is minds (strictly, souls), and that bodies can somehow be
reduced to mental entities. Indeed, the theory of monads is a kind of
idealist mirror image of modern reductive materialism. Reductive
materialism may appear today to be more intuitive than the reductive idealism of the *Monadology*, but the underlying debate is very
far from being concluded in the materialist's favor.[3]

Leibniz shares with Descartes and Spinoza the deep conviction
that human reason is competent to discover the ultimate nature of
reality, and, for this reason, he is traditionally classified with them
as a "Rationalist" philosopher. Yet though Leibniz shares their ambitious conception of the philosophical enterprise, in important respects he stands apart from the other two. Descartes and, less explicitly, Spinoza impress the reader by their insistence on the need to
make a clean break with the philosophical past in order to arrive at
the truth: the edifice of knowledge must be reconstructed on new
foundations. As Descartes said, "I realized that it was necessary,
once in the course of my life, to demolish everything completely and
start again right from the foundations if I wanted to establish anything at all in the sciences that was stable and likely to last."[4]
Leibniz, by contrast, is much less of a revolutionary in spirit; he is
far more respectful of the whole philosophical tradition deriving
from the Greeks. Although at times he can be a sharp polemicist, the
entire tendency of his philosophy is to seek synthesis and reconciliation wherever possible. As he himself puts it, "the majority of the
philosophical sects are right in the greater part of what they affirm,

but not so much in what they deny" (Letter to Remond, 10 January 1714, G III 607). Particularly during his earlier career, Leibniz sought to reconcile the new mechanical philosophy of the Scientific Revolution with the Aristotelian-Scholastic tradition which Descartes and Spinoza largely rejected. Leibniz's eirenical habit of mind is not confined to his philosophy; it displays itself further in the various schemes for political and religious reconciliation which occupied him throughout his career.

Leibniz's preoccupation with peace and reconciliation is understandable, for the Germany of his youth had been ravaged by the horrors of the Thirty Years' War – a war in which dynastic and religious rivalries were inextricably involved. Leibniz, born in Leipzig in 1646, was the son of a university professor. After his father's death in 1652, the prodigiously gifted boy had the run of the family library, and he soon showed the tendency towards polymathy which was a hallmark of his whole career. As Roger Ariew notes (see Chapter 2), Leibniz, having taught himself Latin at seven or eight, embarked on a vast reading course of poets, orators, historians, jurists, philosophers, mathematicians, and theologians. Leibniz was later educated at the universities of Leipzig and Jena, but he was, to a large extent, self-taught and retained some of the habits of mind of the autodidact; he never acquired the ability to wear his immense learning lightly.

Although he was offered a university post, Leibniz, like other great thinkers of the seventeenth century, turned his back on an academic career. His contemporaries' reasons for rejecting academic careers are clear; the universities of the age were bastions of the "old" learning, offering little exposure to the ferment of new ideas associated with the Scientific Revolution. Leibniz's motives for rejecting an academic career may have been different and more complex, for he never harbored the contempt for Scholastic learning that is characteristic of Descartes or Hobbes. Leibniz may have been guided at least in part by the feeling that a university setting would not afford him an adequate outlet for his own full range of interests, which included politics, religion, and diplomacy, as well as philosophy and science. Most of Leibniz's life was spent in the service of minor German courts, where he took advantage of the opportunities offered to devote his energies to political and religious projects. For instance, during his employment in the service of the Elector of Mainz, Leibniz conceived the idea of diverting French expansionist ambitions away from Germany towards Egypt, and he was sent on a diplomatic mission to Paris to try to interest Louis XIV in this scheme. (The idea, never actually proposed to Louis' ministers, was later taken up by Napoleon.) After his return from Paris, Leibniz entered the service of the Electors of Hanover – his final employer, Georg Ludwig, ascended the British throne as George I. In addition to his official duties as court librarian and historian, Leibniz busied himself with projects for political and religious reconciliation. One such project was an ambitious scheme for reuniting the Catholic and Protestant churches; as Ariew shows (see Chapter 2), Leibniz displayed great intellectual subtlety in seeking to find doctrinal formulae on which both sides could agree. Many of Leibniz's schemes were no doubt impractical and unrealistic, and despite his extensive network of connections (carried on through a vast correspondence) all over Europe, Leibniz never seems to have had the knack of pulling strings. On the other hand, the recent history of our own time should make us cautious in passing judgment about what is and is not possible in the realm of politics, for some of Leibniz's schemes have an almost eerily prophetic quality. For instance, Leibniz's concern with trying to establish a degree of sovereignty for German princes within the framework of the Holy Roman Empire anticipates current concerns about the place of nation-states within a united Europe.

Leibniz's diplomatic mission took him to Paris in 1672, and he stayed there for four years. At that time, Paris was the intellectual capital of Europe. Leibniz took full advantage of the opportunities it offered; he made great strides in the study of mathematics (discovering the differential calculus, independently of Newton, in 1675) and he immersed himself in the study of the philosophy of the Moderns and of the French Cartesians, in particular. Yet, as Stuart Brown argues (see Chapter 3), despite Leibniz's exposure to the thought of the Moderns, other strands of seventeenth-century thought are no less important for understanding Leibniz. In addition to the Moderns, Brown isolates the Scholastic and Renaissance strands for special attention. Leibniz's links with the Scholastic tradition are evident not just in his characteristic insistence on reconciling Aristotle and the Moderns, but also in the very choice of problems to place on the philosophical agenda. As Brown argues, "many of the problems that particularly exercised Leibniz were Scholastic ones"; his lifelong concern with reconciling free will with divine foreknowledge and predestination is an obvious example. Leibniz's links with Renaissance philosophy are seen not just in the overall eclecticism of his philosophy but also in some of his more esoteric doctrines which suggest the influence of neoPlatonism. The thesis, central to Leibniz's metaphysics, that every individual substance is a microcosm of the whole universe is an idea he would have encountered in Renaissance philosophy. As Brown points out, Renaissance neo-Platonic philosophy exhibited a tendency towards idealism, and idealism is at the heart of Leibniz's final metaphysics.

Although he regarded himself generally as on the side of the moderns, Leibniz sought to incorporate Scholastic and Renaissance ideas in his philosophy. But as Brown notes, he was not unaware of the dangers of these attempts at synthesis, particularly where Scholasticism was concerned. For much of the seventeenth century, the Aristotelian tradition remained relatively vital; textbook accounts have tended to exaggerate the speed of its demise at the hands of the Moderns. But by the end of the seventeenth century the situation had changed. Particularly in France, toleration for Scholastic concepts and vocabulary was diminishing, and Leibniz came to worry that, by sounding like a Scholastic, he might prejudice his chances of gaining a fair hearing for his system. Perhaps the residue of Scholasticism in his philosophy is one reason why, as we shall see, his system was not well received in the country of Voltaire.

Leibniz's philosophical interests were many and varied, but at the center of his philosophy is his metaphysics – his theory of the fundamental nature of reality. When most people think of Leibniz's metaphysics, they are apt to remember his theory of monads – the thesis that the ultimate constituents of reality are "windowless" (i.e. noninteracting) souls or soul-like substances whose states are harmonized by a benevolent God. Although the theory of monads is the most famous version of Leibniz's metaphysics, it makes a relatively late appearance in his philosophical career; even the term "monad," in the sense which became standard for Leibniz, does not appear in his writings before 1695. Much recent scholarly work has been devoted to tracing the evolution of Leibniz's metaphysical thought towards its final flowering in the theory of monads, and in this volume this interest is reflected in two essays which divide Leibniz's metaphysics on chronological lines. Christia Mercer and Robert Sleigh discuss the development of Leibniz's metaphysics up to the *Discourse on Metaphysics* of 1686, generally recognized as Leibniz's first mature work (see Chapter 4); Donald Rutherford in his essay (Chapter 5) concentrates on the later metaphysics of monads.

Mercer and Sleigh argue that although Leibniz was, at an early stage, attracted by the new mechanistic physics, he was also dissatisfied with its metaphysical foundations; neither Epicurean atoms nor Cartesian matter, divisible to infinity, could be the fundamental building blocks of physical reality. Rather, Leibniz believed that the new physical theory needed to be anchored in a metaphysics of substance whose inspiration would be essentially Aristotelian. As Mercer and Sleigh show, certain intuitions about substance which derive from Aristotle remain fairly constant in his philosophy. For example, the Aristotelian principle that a substance must be in some sense explanatorily self-sufficient makes an early appearance in Leibniz's thought and remains until the end. Mercer and Sleigh show how fruitfully Leibniz develops Aristotle's doctrine of substantial self-sufficiency; Leibniz extends this thesis to cover all substantial properties, not just essential ones. Thus, on the basis of Aristotelian principles Leibniz arrives at some of his most familiar metaphysical doctrines: substances are causally independent of everything except God; they are genuine unities; no two are exactly alike (the Identity of Indiscernibles), and they bear marks of their future states and traces of all their past ones. Mercer and Sleigh argue that these teachings are essentially in place in Leibniz's thought by 1676 – ten years before the *Discourse on Metaphysics*. It is important to see, however, that this conclusion is consistent with the view that Leibniz's metaphysics had to go through a further stage of evolution before it reached its final form. For although, at a rather early date, Leibniz was clear about what conditions had to be satisfied by an entity in order to count as substantial, he was much less certain about what entities, in fact, satisfied these conditions; in technical terminology, although the intension of the term "substance" was clear to Leibniz, its extension was not. Leibniz seems never to have believed that a merely extended being, such as Cartesian body, could count as a substance, but at least around the time of the *Discourse on Metaphysics*, he seems to have entertained the idea that organic bodies, or bodies unified by the presence of a substantial form, might indeed satisfy the conditions for substantiality. It is not until around 1700 that Leibniz found a solution to the "extensional" problem with which he could rest satisfied; he finally became convinced that only souls or soul-like entities could qualify as substances.

In a letter written in 1704, Leibniz told his correspondent, De Volder, that strictly speaking "there is nothing in the world except simple substances and, in them, perception and appetite" (30 June 1704, G II 270: L 537). Leibniz thus provided a concise statement of the basic thesis of his final metaphysics, the theory of monads. Rutherford argues that for all its apparent strangeness, the theory of monads is a metaphysics of some power, with attendant difficulties he does not seek to minimize; the major difficulty perhaps is to understand what account Leibniz can give of the status of bodies within an ontology that regards only souls as ultimately real or substantial. On one occasion, Leibniz tells the same correspondent, De Volder, that he does not seek to eliminate body, but only to reduce it to what it is (letter to De Volder, 1704 or 1705, G II 275: AG 181);[5] thus, Leibniz makes it clear that he wishes to offer some kind of reductionist account of bodies, but the problem is to understand the nature of the reduction. Some commentators have supposed that Leibniz, like Berkeley, intends to offer a version of phenomenalism, or in other words, a theory according to which bodies are harmonized sets of the contents of perceptions. Rutherford argues, however, that such an interpretation does not do justice to Leibniz's many statements to the effect that bodies are founded in some mind-independent reality; for Leibniz, bodies are not sets of perceptions, but aggregates of monads. Rutherford also rejects the suggestion that, because of their mental confusion, human minds simply misperceive certain monads as three-dimensional bodies in space; in Rutherford's view, this interpretation fails to capture Leibniz's intention to identify bodies ontologically with pluralities of monads. Although the theory of monads is Leibniz's official metaphysics in his later writings, Rutherford recognizes that there are occasions when Leibniz seems to depart from the strict purity of the theory. Perhaps the most notorious of Leibniz's attempts to modify the doctrine is his introduction of the concept of a substantial bond (vinculum substantiale) over and above monads which somehow accounts for the unity of organic bodies. Leibniz introduced this notion when challenged by a Jesuit to give an account of the miracle of transubstantiation, and Rutherford, like Bertrand

Russell before him, is inclined to dismiss the substantial bond as the concession of a diplomat rather than the creed of a philosopher.

If metaphysics is at the center of Leibniz's philosophy, what we now call epistemology or the theory of knowledge occupies a somewhat peripheral role. Despite the fact that they are grouped together as "Rationalists," Leibniz showed little of Descartes' interest in the project of finding indubitable foundations for human knowledge. Unlike Descartes, Leibniz was never seriously impressed by the challenge of extreme scepticism, and as Robert McRae argues (in Chapter 6), Leibniz seems to have regarded Descartes' hyperbolical doubt in the First Meditation as a kind of flashy, rhetorical trick which served no useful philosophical purpose. Leibniz was similarly unimpressed by Descartes' first positive move in the reconstruction of the edifice of knowledge – namely, the famous *cogito ergo sum*;[6] Leibniz claimed that there are other propositions such as "Various things are thought by me" (*"Varia a me cogitantur"*) of which one can be equally certain (G IV 357). Such a response may suggest a blindness to the fact that the *cogito* is not merely incorrigible but also self-verifying; to deny that one is thinking or that one exists is pragmatically self-defeating in a way that to deny that one is thinking of a plurality of things is not. Yet, as McRae argues, Leibniz's response to Descartes is also vulnerable to criticism from a rather different direction; for Descartes himself sometimes claims that there are other judgments equally as certain as the *cogito*, and Leibniz seems to have forgotten this fact.

If Leibniz was unimpressed by Descartes' epistemological project in the *Meditations*, he nonetheless agreed with Descartes on certain issues; in particular, he sided with Descartes against Locke in approving of the originally Platonic doctrine of innate ideas. Indeed, the agreement between Leibniz and Descartes on this issue is one of the reasons why the two philosophers have traditionally been classified together as "Rationalists" in opposition to "Empiricists" such as Locke, since the theory of innate ideas implies that the human mind is not dependent on experience for all its knowledge. However, philosophers have sometimes found it difficult to see what is at issue between defenders and opponents of innate ideas, and McRae shows that there are ambiguities and complexities in Leibniz's account; not merely does Leibniz offer different arguments for innate ideas, but he seems to use the term "innate" in different senses. McRae

further addresses the difficulty of how Leibniz can say that mathematical knowledge is innate given his theory that mathematics is
the science of the imaginable.

Leibniz's relative lack of interest in the foundations of knowledge is one aspect of his thought that sets him apart from other
philosophers of the early modern period. Leibniz is also out of step
with his leading contemporaries in his attitude towards logic. In an
age when the subject tended to be regarded with suspicion because
of its alleged association with the more barren aspects of Scholasticism, Leibniz was a keen student of logic, and he made important
contributions to its development; indeed, he has traditionally been
seen as one of the early pioneers of symbolic logic. Yet, as G. H. R.
Parkinson points out (see Chapter 7), when modern scholars speak
of Leibniz's logic, it is not so much his technical contributions to
the subject they have in mind but rather his theory of truth and of
the nature of the proposition, for these are highly relevant to
broader philosophical issues. As Parkinson shows, Leibniz propounded a distinctive "intensional" theory of truth in terms of
concept-containment; simplifying somewhat, we can say that for
Leibniz a proposition is true if and only if the concept of the predicate is contained in the concept of the subject. Such a theory raises
important problems which were first identitifed by Leibniz's correspondent Arnauld and have been debated since; the chief problem
is that the theory seems to have the consequence that all truths are
necessary truths. Leibniz certainly did not wish to be committed to
this consequence, since he reasonably regarded the denial of contingency in the world as inconsistent with the freedom of the will
which he wished to uphold against Spinoza's necessitarianism.
Thus, Leibniz was well aware of the problem of accommodating
contingency in his philosophy, and Parkinson examines Leibniz's
various attempts to solve the problem.

In the second of his essays in this volume (see Chapter 8), Donald
Rutherford argues that Leibniz, in his attitude to language, is once
again out of step with his leading contemporaries. According to
Rutherford, other major seventeenth-century philosophers tended to
think of language "as a barrier between the mind and the world that
must so far as possible be overcome"; Leibniz, by contrast, regarded
language "as a lens that necessarily intervenes between the mind
and world and that can, depending on the skill of the optician, either

distort or magnify our apprehension of the world." This conviction that language can, in principle, be a perfect image of reality finds expression in Leibniz's project for a "universal characteristic" or artificial language. Leibniz was not alone in his enthusiasm for such a project; similar schemes were advanced in the seventeenth century by lesser figures such as Wilkins and Dalgarno. Yet, as Rutherford shows, in the case of Leibniz at least, there is a basic ambiguity in the nature and scope of the project. In one interpretation, the universal characteristic is intended to be a truly ideal language which would symbolically represent the content of thought by means of "real characters." In another interpretation, the goal of Leibniz's project is more modest and is concerned only with form, not content; its aim is simply to express the logical relations among concepts and propositions. In this latter reading, the chief interest of the universal characteristic lies in its role as a precursor of modern symbolic logic. Rutherford argues that Leibniz's views on this issue may have changed over time; in his later writings, Leibniz tended to focus more on the formal, logical nature of the project – what he called the *specieuse generale*. Rutherford suggests, however, that Leibniz never wholly abandoned his early ambition to create an ideal artificial language.

Leibniz's interest in language is by no means exhausted by his project, or projects, for a universal characteristic. As Rutherford shows, Leibniz took a typically lively interest in a wide variety of issues having to do with natural languages, ranging from historical inquiries into the origins of languages to more properly philosophical investigations into the semantics of proper names and general terms. Leibniz's historical inquiries are apt to appear badly dated, and certainly his etymological speculations often strike the modern reader as fanciful, but his contributions to semantics – especially the semantics of general terms – are very much alive; indeed, Leibniz arrived at insights into the functioning of "natural kind" terms which have been independently rediscovered in our own time by Saul Kripke and Hilary Putnam. One issue that Rutherford takes up is the relationship between Leibniz's project for a universal characteristic and his inquiries into natural languages – in particular, did Leibniz ever advocate the eventual replacement of natural languages by an artificial language? The ambiguity in Leibniz's conception of the scope of the universal characteristic suggests that there can be no simple answer to this question; Rutherford answers it with a carefully qualified "yes."

One underlying motive for Leibniz's commitment to the project of a universal characteristic was his desire for peace; he believed that an artificial language would help to promote communication and understanding among peoples divided by their different languages. In a different way, Leibniz's eirenical temperament emerges in his physics, a discipline which he did much to advance by clarifying the concept of force. As Daniel Garber shows (see Chapter 9), although Leibniz was a modern physicist who fully accepted the seventeenth-century commitment to mechanical explanations, he was also committed to reconciling the new physics with Aristotelian principles wherever it was possible to do so; in particular, he sought to anchor his dynamics in a quasi-Aristotelian metaphysics of matter and form. One striking way in which Leibniz seeks to retain the Aristotelian legacy is his attempt to find a place for the category of final causes which had been banished from physics by Descartes and Spinoza.

But whereas Leibniz sought accommodation with Aristotle in his physics, he was much less accommodating in his attitude to the physical theories of two of his leading seventeenth-century rivals, Descartes and Newton. Leibniz was a severe and devastating critic of Descartes' conservation principles and laws of impact, which he showed to be seriously at odds with the empirical data. Towards the end of his life, Leibniz was also a severe critic of Newtonian physics and of what he took to be its inadequate metaphysical foundations. By this stage Leibniz's personal relations with Newton had been soured by the "priority dispute" over the discovery of the differential calculus (see Roger Ariew's chapter), and a year before his death in 1716, Leibniz entered into a somewhat bitter exchange of letters with one of Newton's leading disciples, theologian Samuel Clarke. In this important correspondence, Leibniz employed some of his main metaphysical principles – the Principle of Sufficient Reason and the Identity of Indiscernibles – for polemical purposes against the Newtonian theory of absolute space and time. More recklessly perhaps Leibniz further attacked the Newtonian theory of universal gravitation for its supposed commitment to action at a distance. (Newton himself rejected action at a distance, but it was embraced by some of his disciples). As Garber shows, Leibniz's polemic against the Newtonian theory placed some strain on his general willingness to defend the Aristotelian-Scholastic tradition wherever possible. For Leibniz, the Newtonian theory of attractive forces seemed to herald the reintroduction into natural philosophy of those Scholastic 'occult qualities' which his contemporaries prided themselves on having banished; indeed, in Leibniz's eyes this was one of the great achievements of seventeenth-century physics. Here, then, Leibniz appears in the guise of a rather dogmatic defender of the mechanical philosophy against the Aristotelian tradition.

Natural theology – or that part of theology which uses reason to establish the nature and existence of God – was one of Leibniz's lifelong concerns. It was also a concern that was integrated with other areas of his thought. As Leibniz writes in a passage quoted by Garber, 'those beautiful laws of physics are a marvellous proof of an intelligent and free being against the system of absolute and brute necessity' (*Theodicy* Part I, par. 345, G VI 319) which he associates above all with the name of Spinoza. Sometimes, however, Leibniz reverses the direction of the argument; adopting the perspective of an omniscient and benevolent God, he seeks to discover what physical laws would most recommend themselves to such a being, and would thus be instantiated in our world. Such a strategy has no more than a heuristic value for Leibniz, for he would not seek to deny that any hypotheses arrived at in this way would stand in need of empirical verification.

As we have seen, Leibniz thought that there was much of value in the philosophical past, and in view of this attitude we would expect that he would tend to approve of traditional proofs of God's existence. As David Blumenfeld shows in the first of two essays on Leibniz's natural theology (see Chapter 10), this expectation is, indeed, satisfied. Leibniz writes that "almost all the methods which have been used to prove the existence of God are sound and could serve the purpose if they were rendered complete" (*New Essays*, A VI.vi: RB 438). Leibniz offers four main proofs of the existence of God, and all four are traditional ones; in some cases, though, Leibniz gives them a distinctive twist to bring them into line with the special features of his system. Blumenfeld focuses on those two proofs which he believes to be of most enduring philosophical interest: the ontological and the cosmological arguments.

The ontological argument is far from being Leibniz's own invention, having its own long history which goes back to St. Anselm in the eleventh century; in Leibniz's own time versions of the proof had been put forward by both Descartes and Spinoza. Nonetheless, Leibniz makes at least one distinctive contribution of his own. The essence of the argument is that the existence of God is logically implied by his nature; a most perfect being, or (what Leibniz regards as equivalent) a necessary being, must have the perfection of existence and, hence, must exist. Critics of the argument from Aquinas to Kant have tended to focus on the issue of whether existence is indeed a perfection; in the terms of Kant's objection, existence is not a genuine predicate. Leibniz, by contrast, stands apart by insisting that in order to establish the soundness of the argument, it is crucial to show that a most perfect being is logically possible. It is in this sense that Leibniz regards the ontological argument as one of those proofs which need to be rendered complete. Blumenfeld examines Leibniz's attempt to complete the proof, and finds that the attempt is fraught with difficulties arising from other commitments in his philosophy.

Whereas the ontological argument is entirely *a priori*, the cosmological argument is, at least in part, *a posteriori;* it depends on the premise that a contingent series of things exists. Among other important issues, Blumenfeld examines an implicit debate between Leibniz and Spinoza; at least on a standard reading, Spinoza holds that the existence of the world is not contingent but necessary. Central to the debate between Leibniz and Spinoza is the question of whether there are any unactualized possibilities. Leibniz believes that there are: King Arthur of Britain, for example, is a possible being but not an actual one, for he did not exist. Spinoza, by contrast, believes that the actual is co-extensive with the possible and that, since Arthur did not exist, he is not even possible. Blumenfeld adjudicates the debate by arguing that Leibniz's commitment to unactualized possibilities is at least more intuitive than Spinoza's rejection of this thesis.

Leibniz's God, unlike Spinoza's, then, chooses among possible states of affairs; in the Leibnizian terminology, which has been borrowed in contemporary metaphysics of modality, he chooses among "possible worlds," and the world which God chooses is the best. As we saw at the outset of this Introduction, this thesis that Voltaire made notorious is, in fact, a fairly plausible piece of natural theology. Nonetheless, it obviously prompts some questions about its content: by what standard, we may ask, is this the best of all possible worlds? Voltaire's satire in *Candide* focuses on the criterion of human happiness, but, as Blumenfeld shows (see Chapter 11), Leibniz's basic standard for adjudicating possible worlds is different; it is not moral but metaphysical. For Leibniz, the best world is the one that contains the maximum variety of phenomena and the maximum simplicity of laws. How this standard should be interpreted has been the subject of lively debate in the literature, and Blumenfeld canvasses the various possibilities. He rejects the idea that, for Leibniz, variety and simplicity pull in different directions and that God is forced into a trade-off in order to achieve maximum overall perfection. Instead, Blumenfeld argues that our world is the one in which both variety and simplicity are at a maximum.

If the variety/simplicity criterion is Leibniz's basic yardstick for assessing possible worlds, we may wonder whether Voltaire's satire is completely off target. The answer is "not quite," for though philosophers have wished that Leibniz had confined himself to offering an exclusively metaphysical standard for evaluating possible worlds, he does not, in fact, do so; he proceeds to argue that the actual world is not only the best metaphysically, but also the best morally: it is that possible world in which human happiness is at a maximum. Indeed, Leibniz sometimes seems to think that the world's having the most moral perfection can be derived from its having the most metaphysical perfection. As Blumenfeld shows, throughout his career Leibniz remained both a metaphysical and a moral optimist, but as he also shows, in his later works such as the *Theodicy*, Leibniz seems to have retreated from some of the more blatantly anthropocentric claims of his earlier writings.

Unlike Spinoza with whom he otherwise has so much in common, Leibniz was not a moral or political philosopher of the front rank, and some assessments of his contributions in these areas have been distinctly unflattering. But as Gregory Brown argues (see Chapter 12), this dismissive attitude towards Leibniz's achievements in moral philosophy is unjustified; Leibniz offered "a profound and inventive philosophical underpinning for conventional legal wisdom." Perhaps the most striking aspect of Leibniz's moral philosophy is once again its tendency towards the synthesis of apparently opposing views; as Brown shows, Leibniz makes an attempt to reconcile the views of the radical Hobbes and the more traditional natural law theorist Hugo

Grotius. Leibniz rejected Hobbes's voluntarist view that natural law
(considered strictly as law) is morally binding because it expresses the
will of God, and sided instead with Grotius's thesis that natural law
would oblige human beings even if, *per impossibile*, God did not
exist. But despite Hobbes's evil reputation in the seventeenth century, Leibniz was not afraid to follow him on the issue of psychological egoism; in other words, he agrees with Hobbes in holding that all
our actions are directed in some sense towards our own perceived
good. As Brown shows, Leibniz's concept of justice makes his commitment to the thesis of psychological egoism problematic: "By his own
psychological assumptions, no one can act except for his own perceived good; but in order to act in a truly just way, one cannot act on
mercenary motives. It would thus appear that no one can ever act in a
truly just way." Brown shows that Leibniz's notion of disinterested
love is the key to the solution of this problem: the truly just or virtuous person loves others in a disinterested way by finding his or her
happiness in their happiness.

The range of Leibniz's thought is truly astonishing; the relations
between his philosophy and what we would now regard as independent disciplines are complex and fascinating. But many of Leibniz's
ideas discussed by contributors to this volume were not fully accessible either to his contemporaries or to his successors in the eighteenth century. Leibniz published just one philosophical book, the
Theodicy, and a handful of articles in learned journals; otherwise
much of his work did not see the light of day until long after his
death, and indeed the publication of his *Nachlass* continues apace
even in our own time. Leibniz himself remarked that anyone who
knew him only from his published writings did not really know him
(letter to Placcius, 21 February 1696, Du VI i 65). Because of Leibniz's reluctance to publish, his early readers had access to only a
fraction of his total output and therefore acquired a one-sided and
misleading impression of his achievement; the popular, rather unsatisfactory book, the *Theodicy*, came to assume an undue prominence
in Leibniz's corpus. Not surprisingly, Leibniz's reputation as a great
philosopher was slow to develop and was only fully established
when his logical writings began to be published in the last century.
As Catherine Wilson shows (see Chapter 13), given the progressive
tendency of much of his thought, some early readers were puzzled
by Leibniz's willingness in the *Theodicy* to defend such orthodox

doctrines as eternal punishment and wondered about his sincerity in that work. Hence, there sprang up an idea which, misleading though it may be, has proved remarkably enduring and resistant: the view that Leibniz had two philosophies – one, profound and esoteric, and another which was popular, superficial, and written to defend the dogmas of orthodox theology.[7] Moreover, as Wilson also shows, another factor working against the recognition of Leibniz's genius was a profound change in philosophical climate; in the wake of Locke there was a reaction against the kind of speculative metaphysical system-building of which Leibniz seemed a leading representative. The mood of this reaction was expressed in a rather popular fashion in the writings of Voltaire and Condillac, but it received its most sophisticated philosophical defense in the work of Kant. In his *Critique of Pure Reason*, Kant argued that a speculative metaphysical system such as the theory of monads involves an illegitimate extension of reason beyond its proper sphere of application – the limits of possible experience. Whether Kant is right in his critique of speculative metaphysics remains one of the central issues in philosophy; earlier in our century the Logical Positivists went even further than Kant in their attack on metaphysics, but contemporary philosophers are, in general, more sympathetic. It is true that Leibniz's system of monads finds few supporters today, though it remains one of the most impressive examples of revisionary metaphysics, and there is much in its reductionism from which philosophers can learn. But leaving monadology aside, the fertility of Leibniz's mind is truly remarkable, and many of his ideas have exerted a positive influence on contemporary philosophers. His theory of possible worlds, his semantics of proper names and general terms, his relational theory of space and time, his doctrine of innate knowledge – these and countless other ideas represent an enduring legacy to modern philosophy. Certainly it would be facile in the extreme to suppose that Leibniz's philosophy had been simply demolished by Kant.

NOTES

1 Voltaire, *Candide*, trans. Butt, p. 37.
2 Russell, *A Critical Exposition of The Philosophy of Leibniz*, p. xiii.
3 I do not mean to imply that the theory of monads, or indeed any form of idealism, is the leading alternative to reductive materialism. Some form

of dualism is of course a major competitor. It should also be noted that there are other forms of materialism – for example, eliminative materialism which holds that though the mental cannot be reduced to the physical, nothing in the world falls under the former concept.

4 Descartes, Meditation I, Adam and Tannery, *Oeuvres de Descartes* VII 17: Cottingham, Stoothoff, and Murdoch, *Philosophical Writings of Descartes* II 12.

5 The Latin here is ambiguous. Leibniz may also be read as saying that he seeks to reduce body to what is. But in any case, the main point is clear: bodies are to be reduced to simple substances or monads.

6 The phrase *cogito, ergo sum* does not appear in Meditation II; instead Descartes writes: "I must finally conclude that this proposition, *I am, I exist,* is necessarily true whenever it is put forward by me or conceived in my mind." (Adam and Tannery VII 25: Cottingham, Stoothoff and Murdoch II 17.) For Descartes' use of the famous Latin phrase, see Adam and Tannery VII 140: Cottingham, Stoothoff and Murdoch II 100. See also the *Discourse on Method* for the French version: Adam and Tannery X 32: Cottingham, Stoothoff and Murdoch I 127.

7 In modern times this view is associated above all with Bertrand Russell; see his *Philosophy of Leibniz*, p. vi.

2 G. W. Leibniz, life and works

Gottfried Wilhelm Leibniz[1] was born at Leipzig on July 1, 1646 into a noble and academic family, the son of Friedrich Leibniz,[2] Professor of Moral Philosophy and Registrar of the University of Leipzig, and of Friedrich's third wife, Catharina Schmuck, the daughter of a Professor of Law.[3] Leibniz lost his father in 1652 at the age of six, and his mother took charge of his education. He started school at seven, and, as soon as he knew enough Latin (which, Leibniz says, he taught himself at seven or eight), he was allowed into his father's library. There he undertook a vast reading of poets, orators, historians, jurists, philosophers, mathematicians, and theologians – from Livy and Clavisius to Cicero, Quintilian, Seneca, and Pliny, to Herodotus, Xenophon, and Plato, to the histories of the Roman Empire and the Fathers of the Church.[4] His universal and assiduous reading made him knowledgable in almost every field. Leibniz tells us that history, poetry, and logic were among his earliest interests:

Before I reached the school-class in which logic was taught, I was deep into the historians and poets, for I began to read the historians almost as soon as I was able to read at all, and I found great pleasure and ease in verse. But as soon as I began to learn logic, I was greatly excited by the division and order of thoughts I perceived in it. I immediately noticed, to the extent that a boy of 13 could, that there must be a great deal in it. I took the greatest pleasure in the predicaments, which seemed to me the official roll of all the things in the world, and I turned to all kinds of logics to find the best and most detailed form of this list.   (G VII 516)

During his lifetime, Leibniz produced treatises of great value on the widest possible range of subjects.

18

The extent of Leibniz's work can be glimpsed by looking at Louis Dutens' eighteenth-century edition of Leibniz's corpus, still the only complete work to represent all of Leibniz's interests.[5] Dutens' six volumes are as follows: (I) Theology, including essays on the Trinity, original sin, the love of God, the Eucharist, the status of unbaptized children, religious tolerance, piety, the reuniting of Catholics and Protestants, and the problem of evil; (II) philosophy, with treatises on logic, metaphysics, and epistemology,[6] and natural philosophy, including works in general physics (on the barometer, magnets and the generation of ice), chemistry (the history of the invention of phosphorus and the desalination of water), medicine, botany, and natural history; (III) mathematical works, with essays on the differential calculus, optics, Descartes' law of conservation of motion, projectile motion and acceleration, conic sections, various transcendental curves, infinite series and infinitesimals, binary numbers; (IV) Chinese history and philosophy,[7] history and antiquities, including Leibniz's collection of documents for the History of the House of Brunswick, letters on calendar reform, and on the origin of the French and German nations, and jurisprudence; (V) diplomatic correspondence and philological works, including letters on the formation of scientific societies and to various librarians; (VI) philological correspondence and etymological works.

Leibniz's far-reaching interests render the biographer's job extremely difficult. Consequently, some biographers have decided that it is impossible to make sense of his career chronologically. For example, Fontenelle states:

In somewhat the same way that ancients could manage simultaneously up to eight harnessed horses, Leibniz could manage simultaneously all the sciences. Thus we need to split him up here or, speaking philosophically, to analyze him. Antiquity made only one person from several Hercules; we will make several savants from only one Leibniz. Another reason that determines us not to follow the customary chronological order is that he wrote about different matters during the same years and that this almost perpetual jumble, which did not produce any confusion in his ideas, these abrupt and frequent transitions from one subject to another completely opposite subject, which did not trouble him, would trouble and confuse this history.[8]

Difficult as it might seem, the chronological approach is best, since it is most appropriate for presenting the development of his thoughts. It is now standard to divide Leibniz's career into four periods, roughly corresponding to his various employers and his locations: (1) childhood, from 1646 to 1667, with Leibniz residing mostly at Leipzig and Nuremberg; (2) first steps in politics, theology, and philosophy, from 1667 to March 1672, with Leibniz residing in Frankfurt and Mainz; (3) the Paris Period (including trips to London), from March 1672 to November 1676; (4) Hanover, from 1676 to his death in 1716. It should be noted that historians of philosophy tend to concentrate on this last period at Hanover, that is, Leibniz's mature philosophical period, from the *Discourse on Metaphysics* (1686) and the subsequent correspondence with Arnauld, to the *Monadology* and *Principles of Nature and Grace* (1714). This last period can itself be subdivided into five others: (4.1) Hanover, under Duke Johann Friedrich (1676–79); (4.2) Hanover, under Duke Ernst August (1680–87); (4.3) trip to Southern Germany, Austria, and Italy (November 1687–July 1690); (4.4) Hanover, under Elector Ernst August (1690–98); and (4.5) Hanover, under Elector Georg Ludwig (1698–1716). I will consider Leibniz's life and works chronologically according to the above divisions and subdivisions. But since this is a biographical chapter to a book on Leibniz's philosophy, broadly interpreted to include his theology, philosophy of language, physics, psychology, as well as the more traditional areas of metaphysics, theory of knowledge, logic, and ethics and political philosophy, one can expect that philosophy will be given fuller treatment in the chapters that follow. Thus, I intend to pay particular attention to some of Leibniz's more unusual interests.

I. LEIPZIG AND NUREMBERG, 1646–1667

Leibniz attended university from ages fourteen to twenty-one, first at the University of Leipzig in Saxony (1661–66) and then at the University of Altdorf in the territory of Nuremberg (1666–67).[9] His studies were directed toward jurisprudence and philosophy. Apparently, he was refused the doctorate of Law from Leipzig because of his youth, though there is a story that the Doctorate was blocked by the Dean of the Faculty under the influence of his wife whose ill-will Leibniz incurred. Be that as it may, he received a Doctorate the next year at Altdorf. The thesis he defended was entitled *De casibus perplexis in Jure (On Difficult Cases in Law)*. It was published subsequently with two other small Leibnizian treatises on law.[10]

Another story from the same period illustrates much about Leibniz's intellectual milieu in the 1660s; the story is also interesting because of what it reveals about Leibniz, who was willing to repeat it. When he was at Altdorf, Leibniz went to Nuremberg to see some scholars who told him about a secret society of alchemists seeking the philosopher's stone. Leibniz decided to profit from this opportunity and learn alchemy, but it was difficult to become initiated into its mysteries. He proceeded to read some alchemical books and put together the more obscure expressions – those he understood the least. He then composed a letter that was unintelligible to himself and addressed it to the director of the secret society, asking that he be admitted on the basis of his great knowledge, of which the letter was proof. According to the story, no one doubted that the author of the letter was an adept alchemist or almost one; he was received with honor into the laboratory and was asked to take over the functions of secretary. He was even offered a pension.[11]

During this same period, he met the Baron Johann Christian von Boineburg, Minister to Philipp von Schönborn, the Elector of Mainz. According to one story, they met by chance while Leibniz was dining at an inn in Nuremberg; according to another, Leibniz was introduced to Boineburg by one of the alchemists. Boineburg recognized Leibniz as a young man of great promise and talent, and although Leibniz had an invitation to join the faculty at the University of Altdorf, he chose instead to go into public service. Under Boineburg's patronage, Leibniz entered the service of the Elector of Mainz and occupied a number of positions in Mainz and nearby Nuremberg. There he stayed until he was sent to Paris in the spring of 1672 on diplomatic business, a trip that deeply affected his intellectual development.

II. FRANKFURT AND MAINZ, 1667 – 1672

Leibniz's first publications, other than his university theses and dissertations, concerned politics and jurisprudence. In 1669, under the assumed name of Georgius Ulicovius Lithuanius, Leibniz wrote a treatise about the Polish Royal succession.[12] When Johann Casimir, King of Poland, abdicated his crown in 1668, the Palatine Prince, Phillip Wilhelm von Neuburg, was one of the pretenders. Leibniz argued that the Polish Republic could not make a better choice than von Neuburg.

That same year, he dedicated to von Schönborn a new method of learning and teaching jurisprudence, *Nova methodus discendae docendaeque jurisprudentiae*. He appended to the work a list of what was missing in the law, the *Catalogum desideratorum in Jure*, and promised to supply it. He also published a description of his project to reform all of German law, the *Ratio corporis Juris reconcinnandi*. In the latter work, Leibniz claimed that the various topics of law were in great confusion – German law consisting of a mixture of the Roman code, traditional Germanic common law, and the statute and case law of the various German states. Leibniz sought to rearrange and reshape the law, introducing order by defining all legal concepts in terms of a few basic ones and deducing all specific laws from a small set of principles – clearly an enormous and overly optimistic task.

In 1670, Leibniz, aged twenty-four, published his first philosophical work. Marius Nizolius of Bersello (in the state of Modena) had published a treatise, *De veris principiis, et vera ratione philosophandi contra pseudophilosophos* (On true principles, and the true method of philosophizing against the false philsophers) in 1553. Nizolius' "false philosophers" were all Scholastics, past and present. The main theme of the book was that the technical Latin of the Scholastics had corrupted philosophy, that anything incapable of being described in simple terms in the vernacular should be regarded as nonexistent, fictitious, and useless. Nizolius attacked the Scholastics' alleged monstrous ideas and barbarous language, even treating Saint Thomas Aquinas as one-eyed in the land of the blind. According to Nizolius, the centuries of admiration given Aristotle proved only that scholars were fools. By the seventeenth century, the book had fallen into oblivion. Upon Boineburg's instigation, Leibniz published it with a preface and some notes and used the occasion to show off his general erudition and knowledge of philosophy.

In the preface, one sees an unusual kind of editor and commentator, one who does not attempt to praise the work or excuse its deficiencies: "the errors of Nizolius are many and great" wrote Leibniz. He praises Nizolius, but only because of the courage of his enterprise and whatever truths he may have perceived at the time. He points out Nizolius' invalid reasoning and defective doctrines.

Leibniz chastises Nizolius for his excesses and outbursts against Aristotle who, Leibniz claims, is not blameworthy for the faults of his alleged disciples. In the "Letter to Thomasius," which he printed as an appendix to his preface,[13] Leibniz went so far as to say that he approves of more things in Aristotle's book on the *Physics* than in Descartes' *Meditations*. The project must have appealed to Leibniz because of Nizolius' theme of philosophizing in the vernacular and his nominalism, both of which, Leibniz claimed, were virtues to be found in the works of the modern reformers – and Aristotle – but to a lesser degree in the works of the Schoolmen. The subject of nominalism provided Leibniz with the opportunity to expound upon the nature of universals and the general rule, "entities must not be multiplied without necessity."

Leibniz also published his first work in natural philosophy during the same period. In 1671 he published his *Hypothesis physica nova*, a two-part treatise. He dedicated the first part, the *Theoria motus abstracti*, to the Académie des Sciences de Paris and the second, the *Theoria motus concreti*, to the London Royal Society. The former is an abstract theory of motion along the lines described in Leibniz's Letter to Thomasius (appended to the Nizolius edition) and, on the whole, is derived from Cartesian and Hobbesian sources; in the latter Leibniz attempts to apply the abstract theory. In this early work, Leibniz accepts the void and defines matter as simple extension. He argues that there is an actual infinity of parts in the division of the continuum, against the indefinite of Descartes, which he terms an imaginary concept. Leibniz's critique of Descartes' conservation of quantity of motion seems already well developed in the work, but he has not yet arrived at his fundamental concept of force, basing his analysis of motion on *conatus*. That *conatus* is not force seems to be indicated by Leibniz's conclusion that a body cannot be without motion, for it would then be indistinguishable from space.

Leibniz's other activities during the period included his duties as librarian. He put together a catalogue of books, based on Boineburg's library, as a model for other libraries. Moreover, he proposed something he called a *nucleus librarius*, a list of books to help librarians in selecting works, but did not receive a license to proceed with the project.

One of the principal political problems Leibniz set out to resolve was the French threat. Germany had been seriously damaged by the

Thirty Years War. Leibniz came up with various schemes to weaken French power by weakening its economy. He published anonymously a biting satire on Louis xiv called *Mars Christianissimus* (Most Christian Mars), that is, Most Christian War-God, referring to the king's imperialism:

There will be some who will imagine that His most Christian Majesty would do better to begin his beautiful designs by routing the Turks than by afflicting the poor Christians; but those people do not reflect at all that it is the Germans and the Flemish who live on the frontiers of France and not the Turks; that one must pass from one's neighbors to people far away, and move in these matters by solid degrees rather than by vain and perilous leaps.[14]

As part of his overall strategy, he devised a plan to distract Louis away from Northern Europe by enticing him into attempting the conquest of Egypt – a new crusade against the infidels. Boineburg seemed impressed with the plan and sent Leibniz to Paris to present it to the French government. The occasion to do so did not arise, but Leibniz spent some years in Paris and visited London as a consequence.

III. PARIS AND LONDON, 1672–1676

The intellectual world of the late seventeenth century was in great tumult. Aristotelian philosophy had dominated European thought since the thirteenth century when the bulk of the Aristotelian corpus was rediscovered and translated from Greek and Arabic into Latin. But much had happened by Leibniz's time. New doctrines had emerged from Galileo and his students, Torricelli and Cavalieri, from Descartes and his followers, from Gassendi, Pascal, Hobbes, and from countless others. Although Galileo was condemned by Rome in 1632 and Descartes' works were put on the *Index of Prohibited Books* in 1663, a new philosophy was taking hold; the substantial forms and primary matter of the Schoolmen were giving way to a new mechanist world of geometrical bodies or atoms in motion. With this new world came mathematical tools for dealing with the newly conceived geometrical bodies. Old problems were raised anew, including problems of necessity, contingency, and freedom in a world of atoms governed by laws of motion. Other problems concerned the place of the soul and its immortality, and God and his creation, its sustenance, and ends.

Leibniz knew little of the new philosophy before his trip to Paris in 1672. He was originally trained in a tradition of Aristotelian scholasticism, supplemented with liberal doses of Renaissance humanism. He reports converting to the new mechanism and giving up Aristotle for the new philosophy at age 15:

I discovered Aristotle as a youth, and even the scholastics did not repel me; even now I do not regret this. But then Plato too, and Plotinus, gave me some satisfaction, not to mention the other thinkers whom I consulted later. After finishing the schools of the trivium, I fell upon the moderns, and I recall walking in a grove on the outskirts of Leipzig called the Rosenthal, at the age of fifteen, and deliberating whether to preserve substantial forms or not. Mechanism finally prevailed and led me to apply myself to mathematics. It is true that I did not penetrate its depths until after some conversations with Huygens in Paris. (Letter to Remond, 10 January 1716, G III 606).[15]

As Leibniz indicates, the knowledge he had of the Moderns was slim; despite his enthusiasm, the considerable amount of work he did prior to 1672 in what he took to be the new philosophy was the work of an amateur. Leibniz's letter to Simon Foucher, written in 1675, contains this very revealing passage:

When I think of everything Descartes has said that is beautiful and original, I am more astonished with what he has accomplished than with what he has failed to accomplish. I admit that I have not yet been able to read all his writings with the care that I had intended to bring to them, and my friends know that, as it happened, I read almost all the new philosophers before reading him. Bacon and Gassendi were the first to fall into my hands; their familiar and easy style was better adapted to a person who wants to read everything. It is true that I often glanced at Galileo and Descartes, but since I became a geometer only recently, I was soon repelled by their manner of writing, which requires deep meditation. As for myself, though I always liked to meditate, I always found it difficult to read books that cannot be understood without much meditation. For, when following one's own meditation, one follows a certain natural inclination and gains profit along with pleasure; but one is enormously cramped when having to follow the meditations of others. I always liked books that contained some fine thoughts, books that one could read without stopping, for they aroused ideas in me which I could follow at my fancy and pursue as I pleased. This also prevented me from reading geometry books with care, and I must admit that I have not yet brought myself to read Euclid in any other way than one commonly reads novels. I have learned from experience that this method in general is a good one; but I have learned nevertheless that there are authors for whom one must make an exception – Plato and Aristotle among the ancient philosophers, and Galileo and Descartes among ours. Yet what I know of Descartes' metaphysical and physical meditations is almost entirely derived from reading a number of books, written in a more familiar style, that report his opinions.   (A I.ii 245–49; G I 369–74)

When in Paris from 1672 to 1676, Leibniz made his entrance into the learned world and did his best to seek out intellectual luminaries, such as Arnauld and Malebranche, who made Paris an important center of learning. He managed to gain access to the unpublished manuscripts of Pascal and Descartes. (In fact, some of Descartes' papers have survived only through the copies Leibniz made of them.) Most importantly, he came to know Christiaan Huygens, under whose tutelage Leibniz was introduced to the Moderns. He quickly progressed, and in those years he laid the foundations for his calculus, his physics, and the central core of what was to become his philosophy.

In January 1673 Leibniz accompanied the Elector of Mainz's nephew and Boineburg's son, who was sent to Paris to finish his education under Leibniz's tutelage, on a diplomatic mission to London. There he made contact with the Royal Society and its secretary, Henry Oldenburg. The Society had given a mixed reception to his *Theoria motus concreti*, but seemed more impressed with his project of a calculating machine; it encouraged him to construct a working model. The calculating machine was only one of Leibniz's many technological ideas, which included improvements on timekeeping, distance-reckoning, barometry, the design of lenses, carriages, windmills, suction pumps, gearing mechanisms, and many other devices.

Leibniz's trip to London resulted in his election to the Royal Society in 1673. According to Fontenelle, Leibniz was put at the top of the list of foreign associates of the Académie des Sciences de Paris as early as 1669 (though he had to wait until 1700 to be elected an external member). Leibniz could have become a full member of the Académie, with pension, as early as the Paris period; apparently, the only condition on his membership was conversion to Catholicism, which he rejected.[16]

IV. HANOVER, 1676–1716

1. Hanover under Duke Johann Friedrich, 1676–1679

Leibniz returned to Germany in December 1676 and, along the way, stopped in England and Holland where he met Spinoza and the microscopists, Swammerdam and Leeuwenhoek. Both Boineburg and the Elector of Mainz had died while he was in Paris. He returned to the court of Hanover as a counselor. Though he often traveled and took on responsibilities elsewhere, Hanover was to be his primary residence for the rest of his life.

Leibniz took on a wide variety of tasks both for the Court at Hanover and for his numerous other employers. He served as a mining engineer, supervising the draining of the silver mines in the Harz mountains. His plan was to use air power for which he designed windmills, gearing mechanisms, and suction pumps. It all ended in failure, and Leibniz believed that he was undermined by various lower administrators and workers who feared that the technology would cost them their jobs. He also served as head librarian over a vast collection of books and manuscripts, regularly purchasing new and used books and cataloguing them. In 1679 he had to cope with the transfer of the whole library from the Herrenhausen Palace on the outskirts of Hanover to the city itself; in 1681 the collection was moved again to larger rooms, and in 1698 it was moved to its permanent location (with lodging for the librarian) – the Leibniz-Haus (destroyed during World War II but subsequently rebuilt).

Leibniz also served as an advisor and diplomat. One of his diplomatic projects concerned the reconciliation of the Catholic and Lutheran Churches in Germany. The project had its roots in discussions between Leibniz, the Protestant, and Boineburg, a convert to Catholicism. Leibniz had prepared some position papers for Boineburg, including essays on the Trinity and against atheists and materialists.[17] In 1679, Leibniz proposed to write an apologetic work, *Demonstrationes Catholicae*, to serve as a natural theology for both Protestants and Catholics. As a precondition for the work, Leibniz sought assurance from Rome that his interpretations of the decisions of the Council of Trent, an instrument of the Counter-Reformation, contained nothing heretical or contrary to faith. The project was halted by the death of the Duke, though Leibniz continued to seek approval from

Catholics that his views contained nothing contrary to the Catholic faith (as evidenced by his later requests to obtain a declaration from Arnauld to that effect). Reconciliation and religious tolerance was a constant theme throughout Leibniz's life, Leibniz writing many letters attempting to resolve controversies with religious thinkers such as Bossuet and Pellisson.

Another of Leibniz's diplomatic projects concerned the political situation of his time. After the peace governed by the Treaty of Nijmegen, there were ceremonial difficulties in international affairs for the free Princes of the Empire who were not Electors – including Leibniz's employer, Duke Friedrich. The ministers of the free Princes were not accorded the same treatment as those of the Italian Princes, such as the Dukes of Modena or Mantua. Leibniz published a book supporting the position of the free Princes in 1677,[18] under the alias Cesarinus Furstenerius or "Prince as Emperor." His main purpose was to redefine the concept of sovereignty in a way that would allow the free Princes to be treated as sovereigns in international negotiations. Thus, he attempted to make the concept of sovereignty consistent with the allegiance which a lesser sovereign might owe to a universal power such as the Holy Roman Empire or the Papacy. Leibniz claimed that all Christian states make up a single body of which the Pope is the spiritual head and the Emperor the temporal head and that a certain universal jurisdiction belonged to both. The Emperor is the general, defender, and advocate of the church, principally against the infidels, and his title of Sacred Majesty signifies this. Similarly, the title "Holy Roman Empire" applies to the Empire. Leibniz concludes that his position does not amount to the doctrine of divine right but is a species of political system formed by the consent of the people, and it would be desirable for it to subsist as a whole. The doctrine attempts to maintain a delicate balance between some medieval and more modern political philosophies. As a consequence of the doctrine, the free Princes of Germany should no more be subordinated to the Emperor than the Kings themselves; hence, their sovereignty would not be diminished by the kind of dependency in which they existed. Fontenelle asserted, "this Christian Republic headed by the Emperor and the Pope would not be surprising if it were imagined by a Catholic, instead of a Lutheran German. The spirit of system, which Leibniz possessed to the ultimate degree, prevailed very well on the side of religion against the spirit of partisanship."[19]

As already mentioned, Leibniz had a taste for poetry. He boasted that even in his old age he could still recite Virgil almost word for word and once composed a work of three hundred Latin verses in one day without allowing himself any revision. In 1679, Leibniz wrote a Latin poem about the death of Duke Johann Friedrich of Brunswick, his former protector. In a notable section of this poem, he speaks about the discovery of phosphorus by H. Brand. The Duke of Brunswick, prompted by Leibniz, had summoned Brand to display his discovery, and Leibniz wrote about the hitherto unheard of wonder: "Ignotum, Natura, tibi, ni doctior illum/ Nuperus artifici coqueret Vulcanus in antro: ... Immortale animae referens emblema beatae." (This fire unknown to nature itself, that a new and more skillful Vulcan kindled in an artificial cave ... representing an immortal image of the blessed soul).[20] The poem employs every possible allusion to phosphorus as sacred fire, with references to Prometheus, Jeremiah, sepulchral lamps, Moses, and Egyptian and Assyrian priests, among others. Though not great poetry, it is worthy of mention. Fontenelle, who compares it with the poetry of Lucan, praises Leibniz for his verses and their artful order. Of Leibniz's other poems Fontenelle says, "Leibniz wrote French verses as well, but he did not succeed in German poetry. Our prejudice for our language, and even the esteem due to the poet, allow us to believe that it was not altogether his fault."[21]

2. Hanover under Duke Ernst August, 1680–1687

Through a succession of employers at Hanover and elsewhere, Leibniz continued to develop the philosophical system he started in Paris and before in a series of essays, letters, and books. In 1686, he wrote a letter to the Landgrave Ernst von Hessen-Rheinfels saying: "I have lately composed a short discourse on metaphysics about which I would be very happy to have Mr. Arnauld's opinion. For questions on grace, God's concourse with creatures, the nature of miracles, the cause of sin and the origin of evil, the immortality of the soul, ideas, etc. are touched upon in a manner which seems to provide new openings capable of illuminating some very great difficulties" (G II 11). Leibniz did not send out the full "Discourse on Metaphysics," as it came to be known, following his own characterization, though he appended "summaries" of it to his letter, which the Landgrave transmitted to Arnauld; the summaries are preserved as the titles of each article. Arnauld replied with a letter criticizing section 13, and the Leibniz-Arnauld correspondence began. Although Leibniz prepared the "Discourse" and Arnauld correspondence for publication, he did not actually publish them. The first exposition of his metaphysical system, referring to and developing themes from these works, appeared in the *Journal des Savants* in 1695 as "Système nouveau de la nature et de la communication des substances, aussi bien que de l'union qu'il y a entre l'âme et le corps." The "New System of Nature," an interesting piece with an autobiographical flavor, stimulated much discussion, with Simon Foucher, Basnage de Beauval, Pierre Bayle, and others publishing criticisms of it, and Leibniz answering them; Leibniz continued to defend the article up to the time of his death. It ought to rank as one of Leibniz's more important philosophical pieces, along with his other major published philosophical essay, "De ipsa natura" (On Nature Itself), from *Acta Eruditorum* 1698. "On Nature Itself" offered some of the clearest statements of Leibniz's arguments against Decartes, Spinoza, and the Cartesian occasionalists. It articulated the metaphysical view that force, activity, is in the body itself and not merely in God. The term "monad" made its first appearance in Leibniz's published writings in this context.

Leibniz developed the themes from the "New System of Nature" and "On Nature Itself" in some unpublished essays, such as the "De rerum originatione radicali" (On the Ultimate Origination of Things) of 1697 and the popular summaries of his philosophy, the "Principes de la Nature et de la Grace, fondés en raison" (Principles of Nature and Grace, based on Reason) and "Monadologie" (Monadology) of 1714. The latter two were part of Leibniz's attempts, toward the end of his life, to seek a wider audience for his views than that of his scholarly correspondents. He seemed to have looked to Prince Eugene of Savoy in Vienna, and to Nicolas de Remond, the chief counselor of the Duke of Orleans in Paris, for the propagation of his ideas in the circle of powerful and influential persons.

Behind the metaphysics of Leibniz's mature philosophical essays was his program for logic and a universal language, exhibited in a remarkable series of papers from the late 1670s and 1680s. There he explicated the concept of truth which he drew upon in the celebrated characterization of the individual from section 8 of the "Discourse." Leibniz was also deeply involved with the study of physics. The most extensive account of his physics is found in his *Dynamics* (1689–91), in which he set out the basic laws of motion and force. He never published the work, but he was persuaded to publish an essay based on it. The essay, "A Specimen of Dynamics," appeared in 1695 and contained a discussion of the metaphysical foundations of his physics.

3. Southern Germany, Austria, and Italy, 1687–1690

The Princes of Brunswick commissioned Leibniz to write the history of the House of Brunswick. To accomplish this task and to amass sufficient materials, he scoured the whole of Germany, visited all the ancient Abbeys, searched all the town archives, and examined all tombs and other antiquities. He then went to Italy where the Marquis of Tuscany, Liguria, and Este, who shared their origins with the Princes of Brunswick, had their principalities and domains. There is a story from that period, which Leibniz was fond of repeating. While he was crossing alone in a small boat from Venice to Mesola in Ferrara, a violent storm blew up. The ship's pilot proposed to throw Leibniz overboard and keep his possessions and money. As justification, the Italian pilot asserted (since he did not believe he would be understood by Leibniz, a German) that he considered him the cause of the storm because he was a heretic. Whereupon Leibniz brought out a rosary he had taken with him as a precaution and pretended to use it devoutly. This artifice succeeded; a sailor told the pilot that since Leibniz was not a heretic, it would not be right to throw him overboard.

Leibniz never completed the "History of the House of Brunswick." He left a single volume behind, a kind of preface to that history, called the *Protogaea*. In the Preamble to the work he says: "Even a slight notion about great things has its cost. Thus, in order to trace our state back to its first beginnings, we should say something about the first configuration of the earth and about the nature of the soil and what it contains; for our region of lower Saxony is the most remarkable and, above all, the richest in metals."[22] The *Protogaea*, as indicated by its Preamble and subtitle (*A dissertation on the first formation of the globe and the oldest traces of history in the very monuments of nature*), is a work of geology or natural history.

As with many of his writings, the *Protogaea* remained in manuscript form during his lifetime. However, the work was not totally unknown. Leibniz disseminated bits and pieces of it in letters, various articles in learned journals, and inserted a few paragraphs of it in his *Theodicy* of 1710. When it was finally published, it had a considerable influence on geology – on Buffon, for example – in the controversy between those who sought to explain geological phenomena primarily with the action of water and those who thought they needed fire.

The *Protogaea*'s various doctrines required the dual effects of both water and fire. In *Protogaea*, sec. 3, one of the passages repeated in his *Theodicy*, Leibniz asserts that bodies are variously transformed by fires and floods. As support for this view, he indicates that there is agreement on this point among reason, tradition, and the testimony of the Sacred Scriptures. One can see Leibniz's dual effects at work in another of the passages repeated in the *Theodicy*, the explanation of why the sea is salty. There Leibniz forges an analogy between the saltiness of the sea and the way that tartaric oil forms in a damp place. According to Leibniz, "when the earth's surface cooled after the great conflagration, the moisture that the fire had driven into the air fell back upon the earth, washed its surface, and dissolved and absorbed the solid salt that was left in the cinders, finally filling this great cavity in the surface of our globe, to form the ocean filled with salt water," (G VI 262–63).[23]

Of course, the themes of generation and corruption, of the dual effects of fire and water, were not new with Leibniz. Working within what had become a standard genre, Leibniz took the ancient and Biblical themes and merged them with elements of Cartesian philosophy. Leibniz's planetary cosmology in the *Protogaea* is a nice example of Cartesian doctrines set into the framework of ancient themes. According to Leibniz (following Descartes), the earth is a sun whose sunspots have hardened into a crust.[24] Unlike many of his contemporaries in the seventeenth century, instead of rejecting the past, Leibniz seemed pleased to be able to sift and choose from doctrines both old and new. This is evident in Leibniz's discussion of the major topics of the *Protogaea* – indeed the major topics for any premodern geology – fossils and the flood.

Leibniz appears most proud of his account of fossils, having written a letter about fossils, a report to the Académie des Sciences de

Paris about fossils, and *Protogaea*, sec. 18.[25] For Leibniz, fossils are the remains of animals. They are the real products of a natural furnace, the earth, created on analogy with goldsmiths who produce a golden insect by pouring gold into a mold made by covering an insect with some suitable metal and driving away its ashes. Leibniz's thesis was a conscious attempt to oppose the then fashionable views of Athanasius Kircher, Joachim Becher, and others, who held that fossils are mere games of nature (*lusus naturae*) produced by nature's power of making stones (the *vis lapidifica*) and requiring no further explanation.

Another theme of the *Protogaea* and other works of the same genre, such as Thomas Burnet's *Sacred Theory of the Earth*, was the effect of water, as described in accounts of The Flood, which report the belief that at one time everything was submerged by water. As Leibniz says, "The fact is conserved by the monuments of our holy religion, and the most ancient traditions of various peoples are unanimous on this point; and even when this is not in our minds, the *traces left by the sea in the midst of the earth* would settle our uncertainty, for *there are shells scattered upon the mountains.*"[26] Leibniz's answer to the problem of the origin of the shells is that the tops of the mountains were flooded at one time. If the shells were deposited during the flood, the question arose, where did a quantity of water capable of submerging the mountains come from, and how did this water recede in such a way as to leave part of the earth bare? After discussing numerous possible answers, Leibniz accepted the standard answer that the water came from outlets or caverns into which it subsequently receded.

4. Hanover under Elector Ernst August, 1690–1698

Leibniz returned to Hanover in 1690 with an abundance of materials, more than necessary to write the history of Brunswick. He put together a collection from his extra materials, the first volume of which he published in 1692 under the title *Codex Juris Gentium Diplomaticus*. The volume contained the Acts of Nations, declarations of war, manifestos, peace treaties and truces, and marriage contracts of Sovereigns. In his preface, he stated that there are two kinds of histories, public and secret and two corresponding rules for writing history – "to say nothing false" and "to omit nothing true."

Thus, he argued that the kinds of documents he gave are the real sources of history to the extent it can be known, for he claimed, characteristically, that the ends of history escape us.[27] What has produced these public acts and moved men are an infinity of small, hidden, but very powerful springs, sometimes unknown even to those upon which they act, and almost always disproportionate to their effects. Leibniz speculated about the currents of history that the acts allowed him to consider, and he drew from them some conjectures about the origin of the fixed numbers of Electors of the Empire. In another passage, he asserted that the peace treaties so often renewed between the same nations are an indication of their shame and reluctantly agreed with the Dutch merchant, who, having attached to the front of his house a sign which read *Perpetual Peace*, had a cemetery painted below the sign. A supplement to the work appeared in 1700 under the title *Mantissa Codicis Juris Gentium Diplomatici*. Leibniz also wrote a preface for it.

5. Hanover under Elector Georg Ludwig, 1698–1716

In 1707 Leibniz finally began to bring out the materials related to the history of Brunswick. They consisted of a volume (with preface by Leibniz) of *Scriptores rerum Brunsvicensium*, a collection of original pieces almost all of which he had retrieved from oblivion, which made up the foundation of his history.

He claimed to have made two principal discoveries about the history of that time which opposed two well-established opinions. It was thought that the Governors of several large provinces of Charlemagne's vast Empire afterward became hereditary Princes; but Leibniz argued that they had always been so, thus pushing the origins of the great Houses further into the abyss of the past.

The tenth and eleventh centuries were thought to be the most barbarous of Christianity. Leibniz claimed that the most barbarous were the thirteenth and fourteenth and, that in comparison to the latter, the tenth was a golden age, at least for Germany. According to Leibniz, the true was still distinguished from the false during the twelfth century, but afterwards, the fables and legends that were once confined to cloisters became widely accepted. He attributed the principal cause of the malaise to people who were institutionally poor and who made up beliefs by necessity. What interested Leibniz most were the origins of nations, their languages, their customs, their opinions, and above all the history of the human mind and of the succession of ideas that arose in people. Volumes two and three of *Scriptorum Brunsvicensia illustrantium* appeared in 1710 and 1711. The history of Brunswick was supposed to follow but was never published.

Leibniz intended to preface his history with a dissertation on the state of Germany as it was prior to all histories, taking as evidence natural monuments, petrified shells, stones with the imprint of fish or plants, and even fish and plants not from the country itself but bearing incontestable marks of the flood. Next he intended to treat the oldest known people, then the different German peoples that succeeded one another, treating their languages and the mixtures of these languages to the extent known from existing etymologies. The origins of Brunswick would begin with Charlemagne in 769 and continue with the Emperors descended from him and with the five Emperors of the House of Brunswick – Henry I the Fowler, the three Ottos, and Henry II – ending in 1025. This segment of time would encompass the ancient history of Saxony through the House of Witikind, of Upper Germany through the House of the Guelfs, and of Lombardy through the Houses of the Dukes and Marquis of Tuscany and Liguria. The Princes of Brunswick descended from all these ancient Princes. After these origins would come the genealogy of the House of the Guelfs or of Brunswick, with a short history to the present time. This genealogy would be accompanied by those of the other great Houses, including the House of the Ghibellines, ancient and modern Austria, and Bavaria. Leibniz claimed that until his time there was nothing of the kind for the history of the Middle Ages. He proposed to shed a completely new light on these centuries, correct errors, and clarify many uncertainties. For example, he would reject the fable of Joan, the woman Pope, first accepted by some, rejected by others, then reestablished. In the course of his research he claimed to have discovered the true origin of the French and published a dissertation on it in 1716. It was disputed by the noted Jesuit, René-Joseph de Tournemine.

The last period of Leibniz's life was marred by controversy, none more bitter than the debate about the priority of the invention of the calculus. The first public blow in the debate was probably delivered by Fatio de Duillier who, in 1697, wrote an article attributing its invention to Newton and attacking Leibniz. The feud simmered, and in 1711 Leibniz complained to the Royal Society about an accusation by John Keill, another Newtonian, that Leibniz had stolen Newton's calculus. In 1712 the Society pronounced that Leibniz did not know anything of differential calculus before Newton revealed it to him in a letter in 1672; that Newton invented the calculus in 1669, fifteen years before Leibniz published his version in the *Acta Eruditorum* of Leipzig; and that, consequently, Keill had not slandered Leibniz. The Society made its findings public in its *Commercium Epistolicum de Analysi promota*. The episode had many repercussions up to Leibniz's death. Perhaps the most charitable thing one can say about the episode is that it provides good data about the politics of scientific institutions and the psychopathology of the Royal Society during the late seventeenth and early eighteenth centuries. It is clear that the very notion of a first or even single creator of calculus is sufficiently problematic that it should be rejected. Many thinkers, including Leibniz, Newton, and others, contributed substantially to the creation of the calculus.

In the course of articulating and defending his own view, Leibniz also differentiated his conception of physics from that of the Cartesians and the Newtonians, and related his view to that of the Schoolmen; to those ends he maintained an extensive circle of correspondents, including Huygens, De Volder, Des Bosses, and Clarke. Theology was a constant theme; it became central in the *Theodicy* of 1710, one of two philosophical books Leibniz wrote. His other philosophical book was the *New Essays on Human Understanding*, finished in 1704 but not published in his lifetime. The *New Essays* were meant as a response to Locke's *Essay concerning Human Understanding*, but Locke's death in 1704 caused Leibniz to withhold publication. In general, Leibniz read avidly and reacted to the thought of his contemporaries. He copied passages from everything he read and wrote his comments on them. In addition to the *New Essays* and other writings on Locke, Leibniz left detailed essays and notes on Hobbes and Spinoza, Descartes and Malebranche, Newton, and even the very young George Berkeley, to name but a select few of those who caught his attention. Late in life Leibniz told one correspondent, Nicolas Remond, that he has always tried "to uncover and reunite the truth buried and scattered through the opinions of the different sects of philosophers." Leibniz continued, "I have found that most sects are correct in the better part of what they put forward, though not so much in what they deny. . . ." (Letter to Remond, 10 January 1714: GIII 607). In this way Leibniz hoped to unite Catholicism and Protestantism, Hobbesian materialism with Cartesian dualism, and the mechanism of the moderns with the substantial forms of the schoolmen.

Leibniz's interest in the philosophy and theology of the Chinese was also a manifestation of his spirit of reconciliation. In 1716 Leibniz wrote a letter to Nicolas Remond responding to Remond's request for Leibniz's opinion of some works by Catholic missionaries on Chinese religion.[28] In the letter, Leibniz defended the position of Matteo Ricci, the first Chinese missionary, against that of his successor and opponent,Nicholas Longobardi. The issue concerned whether or not Chinese converts to Catholicism should be required to abandon Chinese customs and rituals. Ricci had argued the accommodationist position that Chinese rituals were compatible with the practices of Christianity, and Longobardi had claimed that the materialism of the ancient Chinese religion and the atheism of the moderns required the renunciation of traditional Confucian beliefs. Although Leibniz agreed with Longobardi that modern Chinese religion was atheistic, he attempted to demonstrate that the ancient Chinese religion was based on a *natural* theology, and was therefore compatible with Christianity. Leibniz's standard argument was that a particular aspect of the Chinese religion was compatible with his own thought – and was therefore compatible with Christianity. For example, in the letter, Leibniz worries about whether the Chinese ever recognized spiritual substances. He claims that they did, but that they did not recognize them as separated and existing apart from matter, and argues that the doctrine is harmless for created spirits, reminding his reader that several Church fathers believed angels to have bodies and that he himself holds that the rational soul is never entirely stripped of all matter.[29]

Leibniz's spirit of inquiry is apparent even in his report to the Académie des Sciences about a talking dog. Leibniz describes the dog as a common, middle-sized dog owned by a peasant. According to Leibniz, a young girl who heard the dog make noises resembling German words decided to teach it to speak. After much time and effort, it learned to pronounce approximately thirty words, including *"thé," "caffé," "chocolat,"* and *"assemblée"* – French words which had passed into German unchanged. Leibniz also adds the crucial observation that the dog speaks only "as an echo," that is, after its master pronounced the word; "it seems that the dog speaks only by force, in spite of itself, though without ill-treatment" (Du II 180).

Leibniz did not marry. He considered it at the age of fifty, but the person to whom he proposed wanted time to think about it. That also gave Leibniz time to reconsider the proposal. According to Eckhart, Leibniz was generally in good health, ate well, and seldom drank. He generally ate alone at irregular hours as his studies allowed. In his later years, he had gout and dined only on milk. He allowed himself a large supper and went to bed each night at one or two in the morning, often while reading, and slept the night in a chair; he would wake up at seven or eight in the morning and continue his work. He spent months at a time without leaving his study. He was accused of being miserly, but lived plainly and left a considerable sum for his heirs. He was easily angered but composed himself quickly. Similarly, he reacted badly to criticism but accepted it soon afterwards. He had an excellent memory; the last of his many employers, Georg Ludwig, called him his Living Dictionary.

Leibniz died in his bed in Hanover on November 14, 1716. Georg Ludwig had been in London since succeeding to the throne of England as George I some two years earlier, but Leibniz was not welcome there. The official reason was that he was to stay in Hanover until the history of the House of Hanover was closer to being complete. But there was also great hostility at court to the then elderly counselor. He was often a subject of ridicule, treated as an old fossil, with his enormous black wig and his once-fashionable ornate clothes. The court may also have been embarrassed by the protracted debate between Leibniz and Newton over the discovery of the calculus, which had been going on for some years and had taken on decidedly nationalistic overtones. When Leibniz died in Hanover, what was left of the court failed to attend his otherwise proper funeral. Eckhart hypothesizes that Leibniz's religious views were an important cause of his neglect. Viewed by some as overly sympathetic to Catholicism because of his conservative theological and political views and his association with Papists and Jesuits, Leibniz was also seen by others as an atheist. Eckhart reports that he did not remember Leibniz ever taking communion during the nineteen years he acted as his secretary. Although the Hanover Court may not have appreciated him, he had already become extremely well known and respected by the time of his death. He never founded a school of thought, as Descartes before him had, but even after his death his works continuted to be published and his views discussed, influencing new generations of thinkers on an extremely broad range of topics.[30]

NOTES

1 For a fuller account of Leibniz's life and works, see Aiton, *Leibniz, A Biography*. The standard biography of Leibniz is by Guhrauer, *Gottfried Wilhelm Freiherr von Leibniz: Eine Biographie*, 2 vols.; it should be supplemented by Müller and Krönert, *Leben und Werk von Gottfried Wilhelm Leibniz: eine Chronik*. Mackie's *Life of Godfrey William von Leibnitz* is an English translation of Guhrauer that condenses the work by deleting its biographical documents. Two other biographies, notable because they were published by Leibniz's contemporaries, are "Eloge de Mr. G. G. Leibniz," by Fontenelle, secretary of the Académie Royale des Sciences, *Histoire de l'Académie Royale des Sciences de Paris* (1716), republished in Du I; pp. xix–liv, and Johann Georg von Eckhart, *Lebensbeschreibung des Freyherr von Leibniz* (1779), reprinted in Eberhard and Eckhart, *Leibniz-Biographien*, pp. 125–231. Fontenelle's "Eloge" was based on a copy of Eckhart's biography sent to him by the author, who was Leibniz's secretary during the last nineteen years of his life.

2 The nobility of the family derives from Leibniz's great uncle Paul Leibniz who received his coat of arms in 1600 from the Emperor Rudolph II as a result of his military service in Hungary.

3 Originally Leubnütz or Leibnütz, it was changed by Gottfried Wilhelm to Leibniz (and not to Leibnitz, as it is frequently seen) in his twenties. Friedrich also had a son, Johann Friedrich, by his first wife, and a daughter, Anna Catherina, by his third – that is, Gottfried Wilhelm's mother. Eventually, Anna Catherina's son, Friedrich Simon Löffler, became Gottfried Wilhelm's sole heir.

4 Perhaps that is why he later describes himself as "nearly self-taught," G VII 185 and elsewhere.

5 For Leibniz's publications 1663–1716, see Ravier, *Bibliographie des Oeuvres de Leibniz*, supplemented by P. Schrecker, "Une bibliographie de Leibniz," pp. 324–46. The most complete edition of Leibniz's philosophical works is G. There is a major ongoing project of editing and publishing Leibniz's complete corpus. Since 1923, that has been the task of the Prussian Academy of Sciences (now the Deutsche Akademie der Wissenschaften). To date, the Academy (A) has published about 20 volumes

(mostly juvenilia). Given the magnitude of the task, at the present rate of work, completion is expected to take two more centuries. What the Academy has produced thus far is only the tip of the iceberg. The Academy edition has done well with Leibniz's diplomatic correspondence, but with respect to mathematics and natural philosophy perhaps as little as ten percent of the manuscripts in possession of the Hanover Library exists in any printed edition. Until the completion of the academy edition, the scholar must use G together with GM and his *Briefwechsel zwischen Leibniz und Christian Wolff* (GW). They should be supplemented by the twentieth-century editions of Couturat and Grua: C and Gr; these provide a reasonably good collection of Leibniz's writings on philosophy (taken narrowly), mathematics, and mathematical physics. For Leibniz's other writings, including those on natural philosophy, the most useful collection available is that of Dutens (Du). What should be understood about Du is that it was accomplished even though he was refused access to the manuscripts in Hanover. Oddly, this renders it particularly useful. Although Du is only a fragment of Leibniz's writings, it does attempt to represent all of Leibniz's interests; since it is the collection of the writings of Leibniz that could be most easily gathered from scholarly journals and from the libraries of France and Italy during the early eighteenth century, it can be thought as a kind of random collection of Leibniz's "influential" writings. It does contain these, though it also contains C. L. Sheidt's 1749 edition of the *Protogaea*; however, it is missing R. E. Raspe's 1765 edition of the *New Essays* with some other philosophical essays (Raspe's *Oeuvres philosophiques*).

6 Including such significant philosophical essays, widely available during Leibniz's life as the "Meditationes de cognitiones, veritate & ideis," "Principes de la Nature et de la Grâce," "Système nouveau de la Nature et de la communication des substances" (with the subsequent "Eclaircissements"), and the philosophical correspondence with Foucher, Arnauld, Clarke, and Des Bosses.

7 Including the preface to *Novissima Sinica* (Leibniz's correspondence about China with some Jesuits), a treatise on Chinese religion, and some letters on Chinese philosophy.

8 Fontenelle, "Eloge," p. xx. Fontenelle's difficulty with Leibniz's "perpetual jumble" illustrates the point that Leibniz's interests were extremely broad, even by seventeenth and eighteenth century standards.

9 One should mention that Leibniz spent the summer term of 1663 at the University of Jena, where he came into contact with Erhard Weigel who had published a treatise attempting to reconcile Aristotle and the Moderns – *Analysis Aristotelica ex Euclide restituta* (1658) – surely an important influence on Leibniz.

10 The two juridical treatises Leibniz published in 1669 with the *De casibus perplexis* were the *Specimen encyclopediae in jure, seu Quaestiones philosophicae amoeniores ex jure collectae* and the *Specimen certitudinis seu demonstrationum in Jure exhibitum in doctrina conditionum*. Leibniz also wrote a bachelor's thesis in 1661, the *Disputatio metaphysica de principio individui* (published in 1663), and a Master's dissertation in philosophy, the *Specimen quaestionum philosophicarum ex Jure collectarum*, which was published in 1664. From 1664 on, he worked on early drafts of the *Disputatio de arte combinatoria* (which he published in 1666). In 1665–66, he also published two juridical disputations.

11 Later in his life, Leibniz tried to distance himself from his association with the secret alchemical society of his youth by making fun of it. However, one should point out that Leibniz never lost his initial interest in the properties of minerals and plants. He assisted and collaborated with J. D. Craft, an expert on the manufacture of wool and the preparation of dyes. The latter introduced Leibniz to H. Brand, the discoverer of phosphorus. Leibniz even wrote a report about the properties of phosphorus for the Paris Academy and invited Brand to the Court. Leibniz also wrote reports about and publicized the medicinal qualities of an antidysenteric American plant.

12 The *Specimen demonstrationum politicarum pro eligendo rege polonorum*.

13 The *De Aristotele Recentioribus reconciliabili* or Letter to Jacob Thomasius, April 20/30, 1669, G I 15–27: L 93–104.

14 *Mars Christianissimus*, R 145.

15 The same progression is sketched in the "New System of Nature," G IV 477–78: AG 139: "I had penetrated far into the territory of the scholastics, when mathematics and the modern authors made me withdraw from it, while I was still young. . . . In the beginning, when I had freed myself from the yoke of Aristotle, I accepted the void and atoms, for they best satisfy the imagination."

16 Fontenelle, "Eloge," p. xiviii. It is worth noting that Leibniz founded a scientific society at Berlin in 1700 and was made its President for life. (That academy was later transformed into the Deutsche Akademie der Wissenschaften.)

17 *Defensio Trinitatis per nova reperta logica*, written in 1669 and published posthumously in 1717, and *Confessio naturae contra atheistas*, published anonymously in T. Spitzel's *de Atheismo eradicando ad Virum praeclarissimum Dn. Antonium Reiserum Augustanum*, etc. *Epistola* (1669). There are also some drafts on the Eucharist, the Incarnation, and Divine Grace, from the same period, in the Academy Edition.

18 The book of the pseudo-Cesarinus Furstenerius was entitled *De jure Suprematus ac Legationis Principium Germaniae;* it was published numerous times. Leibniz also published a dialogue on the subject, *Entretien de Philarète et d'Eugène, sur la question du temps agitée à Nimwegue; touchant le droit d'ambassade des electeurs et des princes de l'empire.*

19 Fontenelle, "Eloge," p. xxii.

20 Eckhart, *Lebensbeschreibung,* pp. 153–54.

21 Fontenelle, "Eloge," p. xxi.

22 G. W. Leibniz, Sheidt, ed., *Protogaea,* p. 1. The history of the House of Brunswick was finally published in four volumes during the nineteenth century by G. H. Pertz, a Hanover librarian and editor of Leibniz's works.

23 Leibniz himself seems to regard this explanation as one of his accomplishments, since, on two separate occasions, in letters to his correspondent, Thomas Burnett (not Thomas Burnet, author of *Sacred Theory of the Earth*), it is the only geological thesis he relates – see G III 221, 250.

24 Leibniz specifically attributes the view to Descartes (*Principles of Philosophy* III, art. 94–96) in a letter to Bourguet (G III 566).

25 *Epistola ad autorem dissertationes de figuris animalium quae in lapidibus observantur, & lithozoorum nomine venire possunt,* and *Mémoire sur les pierres qui renferment des plantes & des poissons desséchés.*

26 *Protogaea,* p. 9.

27 The reason I say "characteristically" is that the "infinity of small hidden springs" is a characteristic Leibnizian image – compare with the roar of the sea or *petites perceptions* from the Preface to the *New Essays,* for example.

28 Translated as Rosemont and Cook, eds., *Discourse on the Natural Theology of the Chinese.*

29 *Natural Theology of the Chinese,* pp. 55–56.

30 I wish to thank Peter Barker, Daniel Garber, and Marjorie Grene for their assistance in producing this piece.

3 The seventeenth-century intellectual background

Many of the Modern philosophers, most conspicuously Descartes and his followers, seem to have played down their debt to previous philosophy and left little hint as to their background and influences. Leibniz was not in step with this trend towards setting past philosophy aside. He not only regretted the tendency in others but made a practice of locating his own discussions within a broad tradition of philosophical debate. Although he was in his own eyes a Modern philosopher, Leibniz encouraged the revival of the philosophy of the ancients and the selection from it of what was relevant to contemporary problems.[1] Both in his respect for past philosophers and in his willingness to draw on them in an eclectic manner, Leibniz belonged within the tradition of Renaissance humanism.

Renaissance humanism derived from the fifteenth century but continued right through the seventeenth. It had been stimulated by the discovery of manuscripts and a revival of interest in ancient writings that had long been neglected. The Renaissance philosophers had initially been in reaction against the prevailing academic (Scholastic) philosophy. The Scholastics acknowledged Aristotle simply as "the Philosopher" but, while preserving some Aristotelian terminology, they developed a style of philosophizing that was found to be obscure and unfruitful. Partly in response to Humanist critics, Scholasticism was modified and enjoyed a new lease on life in the late sixteenth century. It continued to be the dominant form of philosophy in the universities of Europe for almost the whole of the seventeenth century.

Leibniz was a student at a time when the advent of Modern philosophy in Germany was the subject of much controversy. He nonetheless received something of a Scholastic training, and throughout his life

43

he retained a respect for the "deeper Scholastics," took many of their problems seriously and, indeed, contributed to ongoing debates about them.[2] This was so even though he largely agreed with the Humanist and Modern critiques of Scholasticism. It would be too simple to say that Leibniz himself was a "Scholastic" – a term he himself seemed to associate with monks in cloisters. Moreover, though his apparently genuine desire to retain the best from past philosophies places him in line with some of the Humanists, his concern with Modern problems makes Renaissance labels equally inappropriate. Nonetheless, his Scholastic and Renaissance background is of much more than marginal importance for understanding his philosophy.[3]

For convenience, the Scholastic, Renaissance, and Modern backgrounds will be treated separately. But they are not mutually exclusive. For instance, Leibniz's teacher, Jacob Thomasius, was concerned with Scholastic problems, and his teaching to some extent mediated the Scholastic influence on his students.[4] Yet he was also a severe critic of the Scholastics in the manner of Renaissance philosophers, arguing that they had perverted Aristotle's meaning.[5] Thus one form of Renaissance revival provided a source of renewal for Aristotelianism as well as for the Scholastic Aristotelian tradition.

Another form of revival was, in Leibniz's view, a direct source of Modern philosophy. He regarded Pierre Gassendi (1592–1655) as one of the five "founders of Modern philosophy" by virtue of the fact that he had "revived the opinions of Democritus and Epicurus" (G IV 343), i.e., classical Greek atomism. For a while, he was inclined to represent all the leading Moderns as "restorers"[6] of some ancient school of thought or other, particularly that of Epicurus.

Some of the universities remained bastions of Scholasticism throughout the seventeenth century, but others were tolerant of and even willing to accommodate the new ideas. There was a whole spectrum of reaction to the ideas of Modern philosophy within the Scholastic tradition. In some universities Modern philosophy was much discouraged and often, particularly in the case of Cartesianism, banned.[7] But elsewhere it was possible for individuals to find what seemed to them a satisfactory harmonisation of the old and the new. Thus, there were many philosophers in the seventeenth century who are not straightforwardly identifiable as either "Modern" or "Scholastic."[8]

Although these three strands of seventeenth-century philosophy are interwoven and some philosophers, Leibniz included, felt able to harmonise them, they are distinguishable and can therefore be treated separately. Scholasticism is the oldest of these traditions and so is usually treated first. This perfectly correct historical procedure has, unfortunately, created one of the most fundamental misunderstandings of the seventeenth century, namely, that Scholasticism was effectively finished. There is also a related misunderstanding about Renaissance philosophy. In order to underscore the continuing vitality of the three strands in the seventeenth century, they will be considered in a different order from that suggested by their earlier history. Since Renaissance revival of the ancients played a pivotal role in the period being studied, it is appropriate to discuss Renaissance philosophies first.

RENAISSANCE PHILOSOPHIES

A distinctive feature of Renaissance philosophers was their enthusiasm for reviving the thought of the ancients. Marsilio Ficino (1433–99) played a leading part in producing Latin translations from the manuscripts of Plato, Plotinus, and others, including the legendary Egyptian sage, Hermes Tresmegistus.[9] An eclectic and occult tradition of what is usually known as "Neoplatonism" was made possible by such translations. An excessive emphasis by the Renaissance Neoplatonists on the magical and mystical at the expense of clear definitions seemed to Leibniz to be untrue to Plato himself.[10] But a number of Neoplatonic notions are retained in his philosophy, for instance the thought that every individual thing is a microcosm of the universe as a whole and that everything emanates from and imitates a single center or Godhead.[11]

Christian Cabbalism

Many Christian Neoplatonists were interested in the Jewish Cabbala, which had a philosophical component strongly reminiscent of Platonism.[12] This interest culminated in a project carried out by friends of Leibniz, particularly Christian Knorr von Rosenruth (1636–89), to translate the classical Cabbalistic writings (known as the Zohar) into Latin.[13] At the center of Cabbalist thought was a problem with a close affinity to that about how minds and bodies could interact: how could God, who is a spirit, unchanging, imperishable and utterly different from the material universe, be its creator? Since nothing can come out of nothing the Cabbalistic philosophers argued,[14] the effect must have something in common with its cause and, indeed, bear the imprint of its cause. Cabbalistic stories about the origin of matter were elaborate, involved many stages, and catered to devotional as well as intellectual needs. But the philosophical point, and the one assimilated into Neoplatonic thought, was that the material world cannot have been created directly by God from whom only spirit-like things or monads emanate,[15] assuming that the cause must have something in common with its effect. Matter is either unreal or at least derivative, resulting from a process of degeneration. Fundamentally, therefore, the world is spiritual. Moreover, according to the Christian Cabbalists, the process of degeneration can be reversed and indeed will be reversed at the end of this world.

The Cabbalistic and Platonistic philosophers were inclined to idealism and insisted that the universe was animated in all its parts.[16] They were therefore opposed to the characteristic claim of the Moderns that everything in the material world was to be explained mechanically.[17] Some of the leading works of the Moderns were attacks on Cabbalistic writers.[18] But not all Renaissance thought was opposed to Modern philosophy. It was, on the contrary, varied and in the seventeenth century produced a number of rival philosophical sects, several of which either seemed in tune with Modern philosophy or could at least be made consistent with it. This was most conspicuous in the case of the atomists like Gassendi – whom Leibniz regarded as one of the founders of Modern philosophy. There was also a tradition with which Leibniz tended to align himself, of reviving an Aristotelian philosophy in a form consistent with Modernism. But mention should first be made of the revivals of Stoicism and of ancient Greek scepticism, both of which interested Leibniz.

Stoicism

Stoicism was an ancient Greek philosophy that had been revived in the sixteenth century by Justus Lipsius (1547–1606) among others.

The Stoics believed that events in the material world were pro-
foundly and necessarily interconnected. They believed there was an
underlying cause of these events but did not identify this first cause
with a Providence. Wise men do not allow themselves to be dependent on the way the world goes but seek to achieve tranquility by
recognising the interconnection of things. Stoicism was highly influential in the seventeenth century and affected Descartes, Spinoza,
and Leibniz in varying degrees.[19]

Scepticism

The arguments of the ancient sceptics were revived in the sixteenth
and seventeenth centuries. Leibniz knew many of these arguments,
but he seems to have been relatively unaware of the sceptical background of Descartes' *Meditations*.[20] He sometimes credited Descartes, though more commonly Simon Foucher (1644–96), with reviving Academic Scepticism, which cast doubt on the reliability of
the senses and sought to put knowledge on a better footing.[21] Leibniz
was sympathetic to Academic Scepticism though not to the Pyrrhon-
ists, whose goal of a suspense of judgement seemed to him neither
desirable nor attainable.[22] In spite of such reservations, he had an
amicable correspondence with Pierre Bayle (1647–1706), whose *Historical and Critical Dictionary* contained some forceful statements
of Pyrrhonistic scepticism that were to influence later figures such
as Berkeley and Hume.[23]

Renaissance Aristotelianism

Some of the Renaissance Humanists, like Lorenzo Valla (1407–57),
associated Aristotle with the Scholasticism they rejected. There
were others, such as Ermolao Barbaro (1454–93), who sought to
revive what they regarded as the true Aristotle, studied in the
Greek, as against the distorted Aristotelian doctrines taught by the
Scholastics. Leibniz owed something to Barbaro[24] but much more
to seventeenth-century Aristotelians who sought to reconcile Aristotle with the mechanical philosophy – in particular to Erhard
Weigel (1625–99), with whom Leibniz had studied in Jena in the
summer of 1663. Weigel instilled in Leibniz his enthusiasm for
demonstration following the method of Euclid in preference to the

Scholastic method of disputation. At the same time, he contributed to Leibniz's view of the late 1660s that the true reformers of philosophy were those who sought to reconcile Modern philosophy with that of Aristotle.[25]

In 1669, Leibniz wrote an important letter to his former teacher Jacob Thomasius in which he outlined how he then thought Aristotle's physics was consistent with the view that "only magnitude, figure and motion are to be used in explaining corporeal properties" (G I 16: L 94). He did not claim to be the only person engaged in showing how the texts of Aristotle himself, as distinct from those of the Scholastics, could be reconciled with Modern philosophy. There were others in France and England, as well as in Germany.[26] Leibniz did not continue to show this kind of concern with the correct interpretation of Aristotle, but he continued to praise those who sought to reconcile Aristotelian and Modern philosophy in the spirit of retaining what is best from the past.[27]

EARLY MODERN PHILOSOPHY

The "revival of letters" paved the way for Modern philosophy in at least three ways. First, it fostered criticism of Scholastic teaching, especially of its aridity, dogmatism, and obscurantism. Second, it gave attention to alternative approaches and ways of thinking about the world that had previously been neglected. The stress on the authority of the ancients led some into intellectual sectarianism, others into professing an eclectic mixture of doctrines, and yet others into scepticism. What was needed was a method or methods for deciding with certainty what is true without reference to authorities. Third and more indirectly, some began to suggest that truth is not to be established by appealing to books but by experimentation and demonstration.[28]

Modern philosophers subscribed to the rule that, in explaining particular phenomena, recourse was to be had only to mechanical explanations, i.e., explanations in terms of the primary qualities of bodies – magnitude, figure, and motion.[29] The Scholastics and other practitioners of "barbaric physics" invoked incorporeal things such as substantial forms and occult qualities.[30] The Modern philosophers shunned such obscurantism and turned instead to mathematical notions in terms of which to explain phenomena.

The founders of modern philosophy

Each of the five "founders of Modern philosophy" contributed to its development in a different way and each had a different impact on Leibniz.[31]

Francis Bacon (1561–1626) initiated the art of experimenting, of putting nature to the test.[32] Leibniz liked his pleasant and easy style and had the highest opinion of his *Advancement of Learning* (1605) and *Novum Organum* (1620) (A VI.i 284: L 89). He saw Bacon as one of the liberators of philosophy from Scholasticism and shared Bacon's stress on the importance of scientific institutions.

Johannes Kepler (1571–1630) made important contributions to mathematical astronomy and also worked on optics and the theory of the composition of motion. Although in some respects a pre-Modern figure, he prepared the way for Descartes' harmonization of the mechanical philosophy with Copernicanism (G IV 301). Leibniz regarded him as "one of the most excellent mathematicians" and made frequent reference to Kepler's belief in a natural inertia in bodies (G VI 341).

Galileo Galilei (1564–1642) enjoyed, together with Descartes, a position of pre-eminence among even the foremost Modern philosophers (G IV 283: L 273), particularly because of his pioneering the science of motion and contributing to the development of Copernican astronomy. After the publication of his *Dialogue Concerning the Two Chief World Systems* (1632), he was tried by the Inquisition and spent the rest of his life under virtual house arrest, unable to publish further.[33] Leibniz made a study of Galileo's *Two New Sciences* (1638) and sought to build on Galileo's work on motion.

René Descartes (1596–1650) had a standing among Modern philosophers that was rivalled only by Galileo (G I 196: L 188). The range of his work in mathematics and the natural sciences was astonishing. He appended to his *Discourse on Method* of 1637 three substantial essays, on *Geometry, Optics,* and *Meteorology.*[34] The work by which he was best known in the seventeenth century, however, was his *Principles of Philosophy* (1644).[35] His claim to have a clear and distinct idea of the essence of matter – as consisting only of extension – was seen as subversive of Catholic belief in transsubstantiation, and his philosophy was seen as tending to a materialistic determinism that threatened other fundamentals of Christian belief. Cartesianism was suppressed in the universities in France and Germany, and it was only later that the more acceptable face of Descartes' philosophy as expressed in his *Meditations on First Philosophy* (1641) became widely known.

Leibniz was led into Modern philosophy through Bacon and Gassendi and had made little study of Descartes prior to his stay in Paris in the early 1670s. He found that Descartes and the Cartesians were at the center of much controversy. He tended to side with those who were appalled by Descartes' dismissal of past philosophy and took pains to identify many of Descartes' intellectual debts: for instance, to Augustine for the *Cogito*, to Anselm for the ontological argument, and to Plato and the Academics for his scepticism about the senses.[36] His references to Descartes exceed those to any other philosopher though they are often critical and even carping. He was in no sense a follower of Descartes, and though he later came to acknowledge that they had much in common, he seems not to have been significantly influenced by his illustrious predecessor.[37]

Pierre Gassendi (1592–1655) was best known both as a critic of other philosophies and as the resuscitator of the atomism of Epicurus, which he sought to make consistent with Christianity.[38] He held a chair in mathematics at the Collège de France and wrote on astronomy. He produced a forceful set of objections to Descartes' *Meditations* to which Descartes replied.[39] Leibniz found his style easy and familiar, and a summary by François Bernier helped to make his work widely known. But it is difficult to account for his reputation as a serious rival to Descartes.[40]

The rise of modern science

The term "Modern philosophy" was often used by Leibniz to refer to the new physics of Galileo and Descartes and, thus, included not only questions of metaphysics but also matters that were properly the subject of experimentation. Leibniz did not confuse metaphysics with the natural sciences, but he thought of them as interconnected and as contributing to a single overall picture of the universe. He was, accordingly, willing to cite and was probably influenced by the existence of what appeared to be well confirmed empirical results, such as those of the Dutch microscopists.[41]

The dividing lines between Modern and Scholastic philosophy

tended to be seen as more sharply drawn towards the end of the century. The reason for this may not have been so much that people came to regard them as incompatible but rather that the Moderns became increasingly taken up with a distinctive agenda and with controversies of their own. In the 1660s, Leibniz had been one of those who attempted to show how the true Aristotle, as opposed to the corrupted Aristotle of the Schoolmen, could be reconciled with Modern philosophy. Such schematic reconciliations may have seemed less and less convincing and more and more irrelevant, so far as the Moderns were concerned. But these changes were gradual and subject to much local variation. Thus, when Leibniz wrote in French for the *Journal des Savants*, he made rather different assumptions about his readers than when he wrote in Latin for German academics, or to one of his Jesuit correspondents. By the end of the century, Leibniz was perceived differently by people of different orientations. In Germany he remained something of a lone beacon of Modernism in an environment that was predominantly Scholastic.[42]

THE SCHOLASTIC TRADITION

One reason why the Scholastic tradition survived in the early Modern period is that many writers in that tradition showed an ability to adapt to new styles, to new problems, and to new ideas.[43] The Spanish Jesuits of the late sixteenth century, for instance, debated questions in political and legal philosophy within a broad Aristotelian/ Thomist framework.[44] Their writings, particularly those of Francisco Suarez (1548–1617),[45] continued to influence Modern philosophers – Leibniz included – in the seventeenth century.

Many of the problems that particularly exercised Leibniz were Scholastic ones. They include what he referred to as the two great labyrinths into which the human mind is drawn: the problem about the composition of the continuum and about free will and divine predestination.[46] The first problem was addressed by one of Descartes' Scholastic critics, Libert Fromond (1587–1653). It is the problem of how anything that is extended in space or time can be real if each of its parts is further divisible *ad infinitum*. The problem of free will was the subject of fierce debate between the Spanish Dominicans and Jesuits such as Luis de Molina (1535–1600).

In his *New Essays*, Leibniz offers a list of topics that received "substantial discussions" from the "deeper Scholastics" such as Suarez (A VI.vi: RB 431).[47] The list includes the infinite, contingency, the nature of the will, and the principles of justice, and mentions the principle of individuation, a topic on which Leibniz had written a student dissertation.[48] It also includes "the origin of forms," a problem that continued to concern a number of seventeenth-century writers (including Leibniz's teacher Thomasius).[49]

It was possible for Modern Philosophers to grapple with many Scholastic problems, but there were points at which it was assumed that they could not. Anyone who accepted the mechanistic philosophy (that the phenomena of Nature are to be explained in terms of size, figure, and motion alone) was bound to reject the use of "substantial forms" for this purpose. The substantial form, as understood by the Scholastics, was the principle within a thing which accounted for its being a substance of that kind. According to this view, the properties of a thing are derived from this principle and, hence, explanations of phenomena are to be referred to substantial forms. The objection of the Moderns to invoking substantial forms in this way was the same as that to "occult qualities" generally, that it takes us no closer to an understanding of how Nature operates.[50]

Leibniz's life spans a period when the standing of Scholastic philosophy changed markedly. By the early eighteenth century, it had ceased to be the dominant philosophy in the majority of universities.[51] The students in these institutions received less and less instruction in Scholasticism and it eventually became known to them only by caricature. By the middle of the seventeenth century, there had been many who were willing to combine Scholastic or at least Aristotelian with Modern approaches: Kenelm Digby (1603–65), Thomas White (1593–1676) and Honoratus Fabri, S.J. (1606–88), to mention three of those whose work was known to Leibniz.[52] Against this background Leibniz thought he could claim to be a restorer of substantial forms, albeit with the qualification that each individual substance was to be taken as a "lowest species" (*Discourse* 9–10, G IV 433–5: MB 47–9). But by the 1690s he became increasingly afraid that to continue to use Scholastic language at all would create obstacles to having his system taken seriously in Modern circles, especially in the French-reading world.[53]

SOME LEADING CONTEMPORARIES

Leibniz took an interest in an exceptionally wide range of topics, including the work of all the other major philosophical figures of the latter half of the seventeenth century. Their influence on him varied, and minor figures such as his teachers Jacob Thomasius and Erhard Weigel, or his friends Francis Mercury van Helmont and Simon Foucher may, in some cases, have been more important influences in his philosophical work.[54] Leibniz benefited greatly in his mastery of mathematics from the help of the great Dutch scientist Christiaan Huygens (1629–95), whom he knew in Paris. There were, however, other leading figures who either influenced Leibniz or to whose philosophy Leibniz responded.

Thomas Hobbes

Hobbes (1588–1679) was best known to Leibniz through a trilogy intended to develop, on the basis of the mechanical philosophy, a connected view of the physical world, of human beings, and of the citizen. The trilogy, called the *Elements of Philosophy*, had already appeared in its separate parts – *De corpore* (1655), *De homine* (1658), and *De cive* (1642) – which were not collected together until 1668. In 1670, Leibniz made a careful study of Hobbes and his early work on motion was influenced by *De corpore*.[55] He was much impressed by Hobbes's suggestion that all thought was a kind of computation (A VI.i 194: PLP 3). But, though positively influenced by Hobbes in some respects, Leibniz was also provoked by his extreme nominalism (G IV 158: L 128),[56] his deterministic materialism[57] and his commitment in politics to equating right with might.[58]

Robert Boyle

Boyle (1627–91) was one of the leading figures of the Royal Society whom Leibniz met during his 1673 London visit. Though there were many differences between them, Leibniz would have been encouraged to meet someone who shared his concern with promoting scientific institutions and with the reconciliation of science and religion. Leibniz made notes on Boyle's *The Origin of Forms and Qualities* and *The Excellency of Theology*.[59] Though he always referred to

Boyle in terms of great respect, his attitude seems to have been one of critical detachment. Boyle, in his *Free Inquiry into the Vulgarly Received Notion of Nature*, proposed that the word "Nature" should be avoided and that the word "mechanism" should be used instead. Leibniz contributed an article to the controversy in which he argued against Boyle that the mechanisms of the physical world had a metaphysical origin and, that from the point of view of metaphysics, it was right to attribute an "inherent force" or "action" to created things.[60]

Benedict de Spinoza

Spinoza (1632–77) was first known to Leibniz as the author of *The Principles of Descartes' Philosophy* (1663). He seemed initially to be just another Cartesian, but once Leibniz had read the *Theologico-Political Treatise* of 1670, he formed an altogether different view. From meetings with disciples of Spinoza in Paris, Leibniz began to form the highest expectations of the demonstrative metaphysics the "master" was undertaking. On his way to Hanover in 1676, he visited Spinoza, spent a considerable time in discussion with him, and was allowed access to the older philosopher's manuscripts. It is clear that Spinoza's ethical views had a certain charm for Leibniz,[61] and it has even been alleged that Leibniz was a secret Spinozist.[62] It is, however, hard to doubt that Leibniz was genuinely disappointed with the lack of perspicuous demonstration in the posthumously published *Ethics*.[63] Leibniz was, on his own account, less drawn to Spinozistic monism, pantheism, and determinism than were other philosophers.[64] As it seemed to him, Spinoza was developing explicitly a tendency of seventeenth-century and particularly Cartesian philosophy[65] that he was more successful in resisting than others.

Nicolas Malebranche

Malebranche (1638–1715) was an Oratorian and, like other members of his order, put some stress on the philosophy and theology of Augustine. His *Search after Truth* (1673–75) was published during Leibniz's stay in Paris. His charming style and his deference to Augustine did much to habilitate Descartes in religious circles. He also seemed to find a way round some of Descartes' specifically philosophical difficulties, for instance over the union of soul and body. According to Malebranche and other Cartesian "occasionalists," nothing strictly acts on us except God alone. Only in the case of God's willing something to happen is there a necessary connection between a cause and its effect. It would be a contradiction to assert that an omnipotent being had willed something to happen, but yet it had not happened. What we usually call causes are really no more than "occasions" on which, in accordance with his own laws, God acts to bring about the effect. There is no *influence*, as Suarez had called it, of any created thing on another. God, in short, is the only true cause.[66]

Related to his occasionalism is Malebranche's most distinctive doctrine, of seeing all things in God. It follows from occasionalism that our knowledge cannot be due to ideas arising in us from our senses. On the contrary it seemed to Malebranche, the ideas which are the immediate object of our perception must be in God. This was one point of disagreement between Malebranche and Arnauld in the controversy between them about ideas.[67]

Leibniz agreed more with Arnauld (and Descartes) about ideas, namely, that ideas are in us and not in God (G IV 426: MB 114f).[68] But Malebranche was a seminal influence on the formation of Leibniz's philosophical system,[69] and Leibniz continued to believe that a good sense could be attached to talk of seeing all things in God (G VI 578: W 503; G I 659: MB 116; G VI 593: AG 268).

Leibniz also agreed with Malebranche, as against Arnauld and Descartes, on another fundamental aspect of the controversy, provoked by the publication of Malebranche's *Treatise of Nature and of Grace* in 1680. Malebranche held that it is in the nature of God's perfection to create a completely orderly universe. However, not only is the universe governed by laws of nature, but God's dealings with his creatures are themselves governed by laws of grace.[70] There is nothing arbitrary, therefore, about God's grace. This seemed to Arnauld and others to subtract from the majesty of God, since God is thus bound by laws of goodness and justice. The problem had been put by Plato in his *Euthyphro*: Does God act the way he does because it is good to do so? Or is it good simply because it is God who does it? Malebranche and Leibniz favored the former alternative, which is incorporated into some versions of Leibniz's principle of sufficient reason. Arnauld favored the latter alternative, sometimes known as voluntarism,[71] and Descartes himself adopted it in an extreme form, even allowing that the laws of mathematics are subject to the will of God.

Malebranche was an extremely influential figure, with a substantial following in Britain as well as in France. Leibniz rejected occasionalism, but he evidently felt much closer to Malebranche than to the philosophers who began to eclipse him in the early eighteenth century, such as Locke and Bayle.[72]

Antoine Arnauld

Arnauld (1612–94) enjoyed a very high reputation, both as a theologian (he was a Jansenist) and as a philosopher. He was one who contributed objections to the *Meditations* of Descartes.[73] He was one of the authors of the *Port-Royal Logic,* and his controversy with Malebranche was the occasion for the publication of his *True and False Ideas.* Leibniz had long had the highest respect for Arnauld's judgement, and it was Arnauld whose opinion he sought of his *Discourse on Metaphysics* in 1686.[74] Once Arnauld had overcome his initial religious revulsion at what had seemed to him to be Leibniz's "fatalism," he proved himself to be a sharp and judicious critic who forced Leibniz to clarify and restate his position, influencing the way in which Leibniz's system was developed.

Isaac Newton

Leibniz's reputation in the eighteenth century suffered because of his rivalry with Newton (1642–1727). They are both now acknowledged as having invented the differential calculus independently of one another. Leibniz had known something of Newton's mathematical work before it was published, through his connections with the English Royal Society, though he did not know of the essential details. Newton's charge of plagiarism was unjustified,[75] but the affair nonetheless damaged Leibniz's reputation in England. The controversy was compounded by the fact that Leibniz, who studied Newton's *Principia* when it was published,[76] joined the Cartesians in objecting to gravitation as an "occult quality" and to his theory therefore as unintelligible. Newton's work, because of its commitment to absolute space and motion, provided a stimulus to the articulation of Leibniz's quite different views. Towards the end of his life Leibniz found himself drawn into a public and confrontational correspondence with Newton's friend and supporter Samuel Clarke.[77]

John Locke

John Locke (1632–1704) seems to have first become known to Leibniz as the author of the *Essay Concerning Human Understanding* (1690). Locke was by this time nearly sixty years old, and Leibniz's own philosophical views had already matured. Leibniz made some headway with the English edition but it was not until the publication of Pierre Coste's French translation of 1700 that he began to study it systematically. He was encouraged in his attention to the *Essay* by his former pupil, by then Queen Sophie Charlotte of Prussia. Although his *New Essays* are the most detailed commentary Leibniz wrote on any philosophical work, he was not influenced by Locke in any way. On the contrary, his *New Essays* would have served at once to advertise his own system and to lessen the influence of Locke on others.[78] Leibniz seems especially to have disapproved of Locke's willingness to contemplate the possibility that the soul was material.

Pierre Bayle

Bayle (1647–1706) was most celebrated as the author of a *Dictionnaire historique et critique* (1696), a rambling work of great erudition in which a wide range of authors and doctrines are discussed. Bayle was the first writer of consequence to take note of Leibniz's system (in his entry on "Rorarius") and his open-minded though sceptical attention led to an amicable exchange between the two men.[79] Leibniz seems to have admired Bayle's ability to state sceptical arguments,[80] but he was provoked by Bayle's divorce between reason and faith in religious matters. He did not approve of Bayle's sympathetic presentation of the Manichean heresy, according to which the world is fundamentally dualistic, with an independent power of evil struggling against the spiritual forces for good. The felt need for a corrective to Bayle gave Leibniz an excuse for publishing his only substantial book, *Theodicy*.[81] This book begins in an early eighteenth-century controversy, but its references reveal that its author was drawing upon traditions of philosophy that originated in the sixteenth century and even earlier.

NOTES

1 In a letter of 1686 to his former Paris friend, Simon Foucher, Leibniz praises him for reviving the ancient academics, as others had revived the Stoics, Epicurus, Pythagoras, and Plato. "I would like it," he added, "if someone would take from the ancients what is most suited to the custom and most in accordance with the taste of our time, without distinction of sect . . ." (G I 380f). Nor did he hesitate to specify what he believed was of value in the philosophies of the ancients (see G VII 153). Leibniz seems to have thought, some years later, that he himself had fulfilled this aspiration. He suggested in one place that consideration of his system led one to see more reason than one would expect in the majority of sects of philosophers (G IV 523). He even went so far as to claim that what he had produced "takes the best from all systems and then goes further than anyone has done do far" (A VI.vi: RB 71). For a fuller statement of Leibniz's attitude to sectarianism in philosophy, see G III 606f.: L 654–55.

2 See A VI.vi: RB 431 for a list of problems that received "substantial discussions" from the "deeper scholastics." Leibniz himself addressed many of these problems, both as a student (see G I 198: L 190) and in his later writings, such as his *Theodicy*.

3 There are many more influences on Leibniz's philosophy than can be acknowledged in a short account of his background. In selecting or giving greater priority to some elements in preference to others, I have tried to take my cue from Leibniz's own remarks about his intellectual background. Value judgments, in so far as they are given in summary appraisals or are implicit in selection, are intended to be those of Leibniz himself. Some of his support for such judgments is indicated in the notes.

4 G IV 156 alludes to the fact that Thomasius wrote a disquisition on the origin of forms, a problem much discussed by the Scholastics. Leibniz himself thought he had a solution in the 1660s (A VI.i 166: L 96) but returned to the problem several times in later life, for instance in *Theodicy* 87ff., G VI 149–53. Thomasius supervised Leibniz's Scholastic dissertation on the principle of individuation.

5 See A VI.i 164: L 95; A VI.i 169: L 99 and G I 196 for evidence of the influence of Thomasius on Leibniz at this point.

6 He was willing to equate "those contemporary philosophers who have revived Democritus and Epicurus" with those Robert Boyle called "cor-

puscular philosophers," "such as Galileo, Bacon, Gassendi, Descartes, Hobbes, and Digby" (G IV 106: L 110).

7 Cartesianism was banned in Paris and was much opposed in the German universities. This may explain the hostile tone of Leibniz's early references to Descartes.

8 Leibniz himself may be regarded as one of them. There were many minor figures in the same position: the German physicians Daniel Sennert (1572–1637) and Jean Sperling (1603–58) were corpuscularians who nonetheless theorised in a Scholastic manner (see A VI.i 163: L 93). Thomas White is an English example. See Mercer, *Leibniz's Metaphysics*, for a fuller treatment of the philosophical reformers who sought to reconcile Modernism with Aristotle.

9 Ficino also translated writings attributed to Pythagoras and the early Greek Neoplatonists, such as Proclus.

10 Leibniz criticised Ficino for launching into extravagant thoughts and abandoning what was more simple and solid. "Ficino speaks everywhere of ideas, soul of the world, mystical numbers, and similar things, instead of pursuing the exact definitions Plato tries to give of notions" (G I 380).

11 See *Discourse* 9, G IV 434: L 308 and G III 429f.: L 633.

12 Leibniz thought it likely that the Jews received the Cabbalistic philosophy from Platonists such as Philo. See Foucher de Careil, *Réfutation inédite*, p. 119.

13 The *Kabbala Denudata* was published in two stages, in 1677 and 1684. Leibniz spent a month as Knorr's guest in 1688 when he studied these Cabbalistic writings and discussed them with their translator. See Foucher de Careil, *Leibniz, la philosophie juive*, pp. 57ff. Leibniz had a high opinion of Knorr, whose book he recommended, though he thought it needed reducing to a system (G III 563).

14 What follows is based on the argument offered by Francis Mercurius van Helmont (1614–98) in his *Cabbalistical Dialogue*. This was one of van Helmont's contributions to the *Kabbala Denudata*, which he helped von Rosenruth to produce. Van Helmont was a friend of Leibniz who made an extended visit to Hanover in 1696, and who, like the Cabbalists, produced many "fine thoughts" even though they were not adequately proved (A I.vi 20).

15 It is possible that Leibniz's adoption of the word "monad" in the late 1690s is due to the influence of van Helmont. But the word was also used by Henry More (1614–87) in some of his Cabbalistic writings that were known to Leibniz. Anne Conway (1631–79), whose *Principia Philosophiae* was edited and published by van Helmont, also belongs to this group of Christian Cabbalists. See Brown, "Leibniz and More's Cabbalistic Circle." Although the word "monadology" was concocted

later by an editor and is not a word Leibniz himself used, he may be seen as belonging to a tradition of monadological writing. Leibniz often writes as if he believed in emanation, a process whereby the world results from an outpouring of the divine nature: for instance, *Discourse* 14, G IV 439: L 311 and G III 429f.: L 633. See MB 146.

16 One of the virtues Leibniz claimed for his system was that it enabled one "to make sense of those who put life and perception into everything" (A VI.vi: RB 72).

17 Leibniz remained strongly committed to the principle that "in explaining corporeal phenomena, we must not unnecessarily resort to any other incorporeal thing, form, or quality . . . but that so far as can be done, everything should be derived from the nature of body and its primary qualities – magnitude, figure, and motion" (G IV 106: L 110). What ought to be sought, in short, was what he and his contemporaries called "mechanical" explanations of natural phenomena.

18 For instance, Gassendi wrote a book attacking the "Mosaic philosophy" of Robert Fludd (1574–1637), a Cabbalistic writer who held that the true philosophy could be extracted from the early books of the Bible. Leibniz knew of Gassendi's book and himself frequently criticised the "fanatical philosophy" of Fludd. (See, for instance, A VI.vi: RB 68 and G VII 340: AG 315.)

19 The extent of this influence is controversial. Leibniz accused Descartes and Spinoza of effectively founding a "new Stoic sect" (G VII 334: MB 104). Leibniz seems, on his own admission (A VI.vi: RB 73), to have been inclined at one time to just such a Stoicism. But he eventually rejected the "forced patience" of the Stoics as inconsistent with Christian hope. He wanted to retain "the Stoic connectedness" without rejecting freedom (G IV 523: L 496). He seems to have appropriated and adapted the Stoic thought that only the wise man is truly free (A VI.vi: RB 175).

20 See Popkin, *History of Scepticism*, for the sceptical background to Descartes. Leibniz was familiar with the arguments of Zeno, Sextus Empiricus, and Carneades but not with the tradition of French scepticism associated with figures like Michel de Montaigne or Pierre Charron.

21 Leibniz went so far as to write, in one of many letters, that the "laws" of the Academics as stated by Foucher were those of "the true logic" (G I 390). But he did not think that Foucher adhered strictly to the methodological rule requiring that new knowledge should be sought. Foucher distanced himself from Leibniz's system as much as he had previously from that of Malebranche.

22 He seems to have thought that we were naturally disposed to put trust in the senses (C 514: P 8) and this trust was well placed (G VII 296: P 15), affording "moral certainty." To attempt to suspend belief where absolute

certainty could not be attained would be to risk substituting one prejudice for another, as he claimed Descartes did as a result of his method of
universal doubt (G IV 356–57: L 384–85).

23 See separate subsection on Bayle below.

24 In *Monadology* section 48 (G VI 615: L 647), Leibniz appeals to Barbaro's
translation of Aristotle's word "entelechies" as *"perfectihabiae"* in order
to support his claim that the attributes of the Monads (or entelechies) are
imitations of the perfections of God. In *Theodicy* 87 (G VI 150), he invokes Barbaro's translation of the very same word in order to make the
rather different point that actions are realisations of potency. This suggests that Leibniz may have been using a Humanist rhetoric at these
points to persuade his reader. That, in turn, suggests that he was still
assuming in the early eighteenth century that his readers would be impressed by such an appeal to the supposedly true meaning of Aristotle's
Greek.

25 Leibniz paid tribute to Weigel in these regards. See, for instance, C 179f.:
W 55 and *Theodicy* 384, G VI 343. In a letter to Jacob Thomasius (G I 23)
Leibniz made a comparison between the reformation of theology and the
reformation of philosophy. Just as the theological reformers were divided
into three categories (heretics, schismatics, and true reformers, who
went back to the Bible and the Church Fathers) so too the philosophical
reformers were divided into three: the uncultivated (like Paracelsus)
who rejected Aristotle; the rash (like Descartes) who rejected all past
philosophy; and the true reformers who regarded Aristotle as "a great
man in whom there was much truth" (G I 24). Weigel was one of the
"true reformers" as, of course, Leibniz thought he himself was.

26 These included Jean de Raey (d. 1702), Kenelm Digby (1603–65), Thomas
White (1593–1676), and Erhard Weigel.

27 See note 1 above.

28 Leibniz wrote of "that horrible mass of books that keeps on growing" and
of how, in contrast to the oblivion to which authors of books are rightly
destined: "A single observation or demonstration of consequence is
enough to make one immortal and deserving of posterity" (G VII 160f.: W
30f.). I interpret these remarks as intended to assure his readers, whose
influence might have secured support for a research project, of Leibniz's
Modern credentials. I take them therefore as evidence of what Leibniz
thought was involved in being a Modern. Leibniz himself was a voracious
reader and valued books much more than these remarks imply.

29 Leibniz endorsed this view. See, for instance, G IV 106: L 110. See also
note 20.

30 Late on in life Leibniz wrote a tract entitled *Anti-barbarus physicus* in
which he attacked not only the Scholastics and neo-Platonists but also

Newton, whose notion of gravitation he regarded as unintelligible. See G VII 337–44: AG 312–20.

31 This is Leibniz's phrase and his list. See G IV 343.

32 See A VI.vi: RB 454f. Leibniz may have inherited from Bacon his stress on scientific organisation and on the utility of science.

33 Leibniz wrote a diplomatic piece on this sensitive issue during a visit to Italy (C 590–93: AG 90ff.) but was elsewhere outspoken in his condemnation of the Church in Italy and Spain for continuing to suppress the Copernican doctrine. See A VI.vi: RB 515.

34 These works are published together in a modern English edition. See Olscamp, ed., *Descartes: Discourse on Method.*

35 Leibniz did not study Descartes carefully as a young man (G I 371) but was content to read expositions of his thought by others. He later produced a large number of works on Descartes, the most substantial being his "Critical Thoughts Concerning the General Part of Descartes' *Principles of Philosophy*" (G IV 350–92: L 383–410).

36 On Descartes' debt to Anselm for the ontological argument, see G IV 358f.: L 386. On Descartes as a renewer of Plato's doubts about the senses and of Academic scepticism, see G IV 468: L 432.

37 In the 1690s Leibniz was accused of trying to build his own reputation on the ruins of that of Descartes. See G IV 333ff. Whether that was true or not, his acknowledgements of Descartes' genius had tended to be vague, his criticisms extensive and his sympathy confined to aspects of Descartes' philosophy, like the distinction between soul and body, that reminded him of Plato. Later on he stopped writing critiques or assessments of Descartes' contributions in various areas. One of the reasons for this might have been that by the early eighteenth century Leibniz began to feel that he had more in common with Descartes than with the new figures of consequence, like Locke. See note 40.

38 See note 18 and "Renaissance Philosophies" above. Leibniz found Gassendi easy reading as a young man (G I 371: AG 2) and for a while adopted his atomism. See, for instance, G III 620: L 657.

39 Gassendi's are the Fifth Set of Objections. See Cottingham, Stoothoff and Murdoch, eds., *Philosophical Writings of Descartes*, II 179ff. Leibniz agreed with a number of Gassendi's objections (G III 621: L 657) and he seems to have drawn on them in his own critique of Descartes. But see note 40.

40 Leibniz's *New Essays* (A VI.vi: RB 70) make something of the opposition between Gassendi and Descartes. The dialogue is between someone (the Locke disciple) who agrees more with Gassendi and Leibniz's own follower, who is more in sympathy with Descartes. In spite of his youthful enthusiasm for Gassendi and his ambivalent attitude to Descartes, Leib-

niz tended in later life to emphasize the many points at which he and Descartes agreed.

41 These include Antoni van Leeuwenhoek (1632–1723) and Jan Swammerdam (1637–80). Leibniz met Swammerdam during his visit to the Netherlands in 1671. Leibniz thought his claim that living things do not perish when they die but are only transformed was confirmed by the evidence of the microscopists. See G IV 480: P 118.

42 See Petersen, *Geschichte der Aristotelischen Philosophie*.

43 See Schmitt, "Towards a Reassessment."

44 The tradition of "natural law," though not unrivalled, continued to flourish in the seventeenth century and was drawn on, for instance, by John Locke in his *Two Treatises of Government* (1690). Leibniz himself belonged to this tradition. See R. He was influenced by the writings of Hugo Grotius (1583–1645).

45 Suarez's *Metaphysical Disputations* (1597) and *De legibus* (1612) were read by leading Moderns such as Descartes, Malebranche, and Leibniz. It was Suarez who formulated what Leibniz takes as the Scholastic theory of "influence" to account for the communication between mind and body. Although he was dismissive of this theory (G IV 148: L 126), Leibniz regarded Suarez as one of the "deeper Scholastics" whose works contained "substantial discussions" (A VI.vi: RB 431).

46 For a more detailed account, see Brown, *Leibniz*, pp. 24ff. The labyrinth metaphor was one Leibniz probably owed to the title of Fromond's book. He refers to the two labyrinths in his *Theodicy* (Prelim. 24, G VI 65) and gives his own account of the debate between the Dominicans and the Jesuits in the Essays themselves (*Theodicy* 39, G VI 124).

47 Although itself considerable, the list does not exhaust the Scholastic problems Leibniz thought worth discussing. There are others, such as the origin of evil (see *Theodicy* 20ff., G VI 114–15), the immortality of the soul, and many of the arguments for the existence of God.

48 His *Disputatio metaphysica de principio individui* (G IV 15–26, A VI.i 9–19) of 1663 is striking evidence of the importance of Leibniz's Scholastic background. The problem was ultimately dissolved so far as Leibniz was concerned by the principle of the Identity of Indiscernibles. See Brown, *Leibniz*, pp. 19ff. When a student Leibniz also studied "the composition of the continuum" and "the concourse" of God, i.e., God's concurrence in what is done by his creatures. See G I 198: L 190.

49 Leibniz frequently alluded to the "origin of forms" without explanation but he himself discussed the controversy in the *Theodicy* (87ff., G VI 149–53).

50 Hence Leibniz writes: "It is as if we were to content ourselves with saying that a clock has the horodictic quality deriving from its form

without considering what that consists in" (*Discourse* 10, G IV 434: L 308).

51 The continued vitality of Aristotelian-based scholasticism in the post-Renaissance period had been widely overlooked prior to the important researches of the late Charles Schmitt. His judgement was that "scholasticism generally lost its hold on the more progressive and up-to-date universities during the fifty years around 1700" (Schmitt, "Towards a Reassessment," p. 179).

52 See A VI.i 168: L 97 for references to the reconciling activities of Digby, White, and others. In a letter to his Jesuit correspondent Bartholomew des Bosses in 1706, Leibniz expresses approval of the fact that not a few outstanding men, including Jesuits, had sought to reconcile the old and new philosophy (G II 294). Fabri is the only Jesuit mentioned in this connection, and it is perhaps significant that Leibniz did not cite anyone who was then still alive.

53 John Bernoulli advised Leibniz in 1698 that, since the language of "forms" was objectionable (*odiosum*) to the Cartesians and other Moderns, it would be better not to use it (GM III 547). Leibniz (GM III 552) indicated his willingness to take this advice and he appears to have done so, at any rate in his Modern writings, even though he thought it "more a matter of fashion than of reason" (A VI.vi: RB 317).

54 There are many more minor influences, such as John Bisterfeld (1605–55) on whose work the young Leibniz wrote some notes (A II.i 151–61), than can be traced in a short chapter. The best source is Moll, *Der junge Leibniz*. See also Loemker, "Leibniz and the Herborn Encyclopedists."

55 See Aiton, *Leibniz: A Biography*, pp. 32–3. The strikingly Hobbesian language used in parts of Leibniz's *New Physical Hypothesis* of 1671 has led some to conjecture that Hobbes was a significant influence on Leibniz's philosophy. But it seems more likely, as is argued by Wilson, *Leibniz's Metaphysics* (p. 56), that Leibniz's purpose was to transform notions like Hobbes's "momentary mind" from being a mainstay of materialism so that they could be used among his "confessions of nature" (against the atheists).

56 Leibniz wrote a dialogue against the view of truth implied by Hobbes's nominalism. See G VII 190–93: AG 269–72.

57 See G II 563 for the charge that Hobbes denies freedom (and Providence). See G VI 333: AG 282 for the charge of materialism.

58 See M 43: L 562.

59 See Loemker, "Boyle and Leibniz," for an account of Boyle's influence on Leibniz and for a transcription into English of these notes.

60 The paper, entitled *De ipsa natura (On Nature Itself)* was inserted in the *Acta eruditorum* in 1698. See G IV 504–16: L 498–507.

61 It seems to have been the Stoicism of Spinoza that both attracted him (A VI.vi: RB 73, 175) and, perhaps by way of reaction, became the chief target of his criticism. See G VII 334f.: MB 104f. See note 19.

62 The influence of Spinoza on Leibniz has been a matter of considerable controversy. See Stein, *Leibniz und Spinoza*, and Friedmann, *Leibniz et Spinoza*.

63 For Leibniz's notes on Spinoza's *Ethics*, see G I 139–50: L 196–205. He later remarked that this work was "so full of lacunae that I am amazed" (G VII 166: W 37).

64 For Leibniz's perception of the tendencies to monism in late seventeenth-century philosophy, see G VI 529–38: L 554–60.

65 For his remark that what Spinoza did was only to "cultivate certain seeds of the philosophy of Descartes" see G II 563. Leibniz later expressed the view that Spinozism was a corrupt blend of Cartesianism and Cabbalism (G III 545).

66 See Lennon and Olscamp, trans., *Malebranche: The Search After Truth*, p. 448 for an argument of Malebranche along these lines.

67 Malebranche's arguments in *The Search After Truth* for his doctrine of seeing all things in God are highly complex and involve arguing that the other explanations of how we see things are wholly unsatisfactory.

68 The importance of the controversy as a background to the development of Leibniz's system is brought out in Loemker, "A Note on the Origin."

69 See Robinet, *Malebranche et Leibniz*, and Brown, *Leibniz*, chap. 7.

70 Leibniz was clearly responding to Malebranche's *Treatise of Nature and of Grace* in his *Discourse on Metaphysics*, and particularly so in the early sections. See Robinet, *Malebranche et Leibniz*, p. 140, for a comparison of the contents of the two works.

71 Leibniz's attacks on voluntarism and its arbitrary despotic god are unusually passionate. See *Discourse* 2, G IV 427–28: L 304 and G VII 334: MB 104.

72 He wrote to Malebranche that he was trying to combat superficial philosophers like Locke, who lacked (what Leibniz and Malebranche must have thought they had in common) a knowledge of the mathematical sciences and an understanding of eternal truths (G I 361). His reasons for thinking that he had to combat Bayle were rather different.

73 He was the author of the "Fourth Set of Objections." See Cottingham, Stoothoff, and Murdoch, eds., *Philosophical Writings of Descartes*, II 138–53.

74 G. H. R. Parkinson has added a valuable introduction on Leibniz's relations with Arnauld (see MP).

75 Aiton, *Leibniz: A Biography*, gives particular attention to this controversy and generally to Leibniz's dealings with other mathematicians.

76 For Leibniz's notes on his copy of Newton's *Principles*, see Fellmann, *Leibniz: Marginalia*.

77 AG contains a selection from Leibniz's comments on Newton, including parts of the Clarke correspondence and his polemical "Against Barbaric Physics" (translated from G VII 337–44). See also Alexander, *Leibniz-Clarke Correspondence*.

78 See Jolley, *Leibniz and Locke*, for an account of the relation between the two philosophers and of Leibniz's *New Essays*.

79 See Popkin, "Leibniz and the French Sceptics," for an account of Leibniz's relations wtih Bayle and other French sceptics.

80 Leibniz found particular pleasure in studying the articles on the Paulicians, Origen, Pereira, Rorarius, Spinoza, and Zeno, according to his own account G IV 566f.: L 582.

81 Leibniz was encouraged by his former pupil, Sophie Charlotte, by then Queen of Prussia, to put his objections to Bayle's opposition between faith and reason in writing. Leibniz's system had also been mentioned in passing in the controversy between Bayle and others. He felt, as he explained in the Preface (G VI 38ff: H 62ff.), he was therefore justified in producing a book on the subjects (like the origin of evil) under discussion.

4 Metaphysics: The early period to the *Discourse on Metaphysics*

The *Discourse on Metaphysics* of 1686 is generally regarded as the first complete presentation of Leibniz's mature metaphysics. In this chapter, we trace the development of that philosophy from Leibniz's youth, through his years in Paris, to his time in Hanover. Because the metaphysics of the 1680s has lately received so much attention and because the importance of the earlier philosophy has generally not been recognized, we concentrate on Leibniz's thought prior to 1680. In section 1, we present the intellectual context in which his youthful metaphysics is most easily understood and summarize both his original metaphysical principles and his first conception of substance. We claim that these metaphysical principles, all of which concern substance, form the bedrock of Leibniz's philosophy for years to come. In section 2, we unearth an inconsistency that Leibniz discovered between his first account of substance and the principles, and trace the steps he took in revising the former. In section 3, we argue that this concept of substance, combined with certain theological commitments, led Leibniz to develop most of the central doctrines of his mature thought. For example, we claim that by April, 1676, Leibniz has arrived at his doctrine of preestablished harmony. In section 4, we discuss the relationship between his concept containment theory of truth, which grew out of intensive work on logic in 1679, and his theory of substance. We finally give a brief summary of the central doctrines of the metaphysics of the *Discourse*.[1]

I THE ORIGINAL METAPHYSICS

In 1668, Leibniz began work on an ambitious theological project under the encouragement of his friend and patron, Baron Johann

Christian von Boineburg. The motivation behind this project, entitled "Catholic Demonstrations," was to effect a reconciliation between Roman Catholics and Protestants. Leibniz hoped to solve certain theological problems in a way that would satisfy members of both faiths and would remain consistent with the pronouncements of the Council of Trent. Although each of the essays in this collection treats a traditional Christian theological question (e.g., transubstantiation, incarnation), Leibniz's answers lay the foundations of his metaphysics. These works are especially valuable for what they reveal about the motivations behind Leibniz's first account of substance. As we shall see, Leibniz soon revises his original theory, but the concerns and principles first articulated in these early theological essays continue to guide his philosophical reasoning for years to come.

That Leibniz had a metaphysics at this time will come as a surprise to many. It has not been previously recognized and is discernible only if one approaches the early works with a sufficiently broad textual and historical perspective.[2]

1.1 Intellectual background and textual difficulties

The intellectual culture of seventeenth-century Protestant Germany is enormously interesting and complicated but cannot be adequately discussed here. Two of its features are worth mentioning because they form the background against which Leibniz's early metaphysics is most easily discerned. Over the long expanse of Leibniz's philosophical career, many of the details of his thought change and the arguments for them evolve, but he never abandons certain core assumptions and concerns that he acquired during his youth and that are firmly rooted in the intellectual climate of seventeenth-century Germany.

However odd it may seem to us that Leibniz's first attempt at systematic metaphysics was directed towards an ecumenical goal, such a project was not at all unusual in the mid-seventeenth century. Whether motivated by political, millenarian, or other religious concerns, the period is full of intellectuals in search of peace among the faithful and of natural philosophers attempting to forge a synthesis between Christian doctrine and the new science. Throughout his life, many of Leibniz's most important metaphysical projects are motivated by theological questions, and he frequently criticizes other philosophers for not having the proper concern for such theological matters. We will see in what follows that some of the central doctrines of the *Discourse on Metaphysics* were developed at least partly in an attempt to solve specific theological problems.[3]

The second feature of Leibniz's intellectual culture worth discussing here is particularly difficult to appreciate, given our twentieth-century sensibilities. From Renaissance humanists in Germany, Leibniz acquired an intellectual goal and accompanying philosophical method which, however peculiar they may seem to us now, were well respected and widely used throughout early modern Europe.[4] Johann C. Sturm (1635–1703), a German philosopher with whom Leibniz corresponded, presents an account of both the goal and its method in his *Eclectic Philosophy*.[5] According to Sturm, the goal of philosophy "is the Truth, as Aristotle taught" (p. 127), and the proper way to find what is "most true" is to rid oneself of the dogma of any particular philosophical sect and to acquire knowledge of all the significant intellectual traditions: "all of Nature and Reason" is available to those "few people" who practice the proper critical eclecticism (pp. 5ff.). In order to discover the truth one must understand the philosophy of Aristotle, Plato, Gassendi, Descartes, and the "other geniuses"; once a proper understanding of the thought of such philosophers is acquired, their views can be combined into a coherent and true system (pp. 189f.).

For German eclectics like Sturm, the resulting system was fundamentally based in the philosophy of Aristotle. The assumption was that Aristotle had been systematically misinterpreted by the scholastics and that, once his philosophy was seen in light of the new science, it could be accurately understood. During the period, it was common for people to call themselves Aristotelians and yet borrow heavily from non-Aristotelian ideas and even from the new science.[6] Leibniz learned this lesson well from his two most important teachers. Jacob Thomasius of Leipzig and Erhard Weigel of Jena both believed that the thought of Aristotle had been perverted by his uncomprehending Scholastic followers and, that once the philosophy of the ancient was disentangled from that of the incompetent Schoolmen, it would form the basis for the "true philosophy."[7]

Unless Leibniz's first metaphysical reflections and his subsequent philosophical development are seen against the background of this eclectic Aristotelianism, they are nearly impossible to discern. Therefore, in studying Leibniz's texts it is important to keep in mind that by the time he had finished his formal studies, he had acquired a goal, a method, and a set of assumptions that would persist for years to come. The goal was to uncover the truth that was presumed to lie hidden beneath the various conflicting philosophical schools; the method was to study carefully all the prominent philosophical sects and, in Sturm's words, not "to cut ourselves off from any source of knowledge" (p. 20); the assumptions were that the philosophy of Aristotle does not conflict with the new science and could be made to cohere with other philosophical traditions (e.g., Platonism); the result was a system firmly based in the philosophy of Aristotle, somewhat imaginatively interpreted.[8] It should not be surprising therefore that throughout his life Leibniz studies a wide range of authors, that he is inclined to force comparisons between his own views and those of other thinkers, and that he often uses terms and philosophical jargon from an odd collection of sources to express his own ideas (see, e.g., A VI.ii 279f.: W 90f.; A VI.i 516: L 117f.; G IV 479f.: AG 140: G IV 451ff.: AG 58).

In order to discover Leibniz's earliest metaphysical ideas it is not only important to understand something about the complications of his intellectual culture, it is also necessary to appreciate the difficulty posed by his philosophical corpus. Although this energetic German wrote thousands of pages of notes and hundreds of letters, he published very little, and there is no single systematic text in which he explicates his philosophy. One has to piece together Leibniz's metaphysics from his abundant letters and short, mostly unedited essays. This by itself would not be so difficult if it were not for the fact that Leibniz is often both imprecise and incomplete in the articulation of his ideas. His notes – replete with cross-outs, arrows, and reformulations – reveal an impatient intellect hurrying to express its ideas as quickly as possible. As Leibniz himself wrote about his papers in 1676: "instead of treasure . . . , you will only find ashes; instead of elaborate works, a few sheets of paper and some poorly expressed vestiges of hasty reflections, which were only saved for the sake of my memory" (A VI.iii 533). One might expect more from the letters that he sent to the great philosophers of Europe, often with the expressed intention of revealing his ideas. But there is a problem even here: Leibniz neither states his most fundamental assumptions nor explains how he arrived at his conclusions. In an uncharacteristically frank moment of 1676 Leibniz writes:

A metaphysics should be written with accurate definitions and demonstrations, but nothing should be demonstrated in it apart from that which does not clash too much with received opinions. For in that way this metaphysics can be accepted; and once it has been approved then, *if people examine it more deeply later, they themselves will draw the necessary consequences.* Besides this, one can, as a separate undertaking, show these people later the way of reasoning about these things. In this metaphysics, it will be useful for there to be added here and there the authoritative utterances of great men, who have reasoned in a similar way; especially when these utterances contain something that seems to have some possible relevance to the illustration of a view. (A VI.iii 573f.: Pk 95; our emphasis)

There is one especially important lesson to be learned here: as students of Leibniz, we must not be satisfied with the definitions and demonstrations that he offers, nor should we accept at face value his proclamations about other philosophers. Rather, we must be willing to dig beneath these definitions and comments in an attempt to discover the more fundamental assumptions beneath. Only when we have unearthed these assumptions will we have arrived at his real "way of reasoning about these things."

Given the scant help Leibniz gives his reader about his underlying concerns and deep motivations, it is no wonder that it has been so difficult to make out his most fundamental views. It is in an attempt to discover these views that we turn to Leibniz's early metaphysics where his most basic assumptions are closest to the surface and easiest to discern.

1.2 The original metaphysical principles

When Leibniz begins work on the theological project in 1668, he is both a mechanist and an Aristotelian and maintains that the philosophy of Aristotle "can be conformed easily" to that of the mechanists (A II.i 10). He is a mechanist in the sense that he accepts mechanical explanations in physics: "I maintain the rule which is common to all these moderns, [namely that] nothing ought to be explained in bodies except through magnitude, figure, and motion" (A II.i 15: L*94; cf. A VI.i 490: L 110).[9] He is an

Aristotelian in his basic metaphysical commitments, especially his robust sense of the self-sufficiency of individual corporeal substances. That is, Leibniz sides with "the Moderns" in that he wants to explain corporeal properties in terms of matter in motion, but he rejects what he considers to be the metaphysical foundations of that physics. In his opinion, mechanists like Hobbes, Gassendi, and Descartes were mistaken in assuming that they could ground their physics in a notion of body that included only the material and excluded the immaterial. Leibniz's original metaphysics is an attempt to replace that wholly material (and hence "atheistic") foundation with his own Aristotelian conception that combines the corporeal with the incorporeal. By forging a synthesis of Aristotelian metaphysics and mechanical physics, he hopes to show "that the very views which the moderns are putting forth so pompously flow from Aristotelian principles" (A II.i 16: L* 95).[10]

Both Leibniz's argument against the mechanical concept of corporeal substance and his reasons for replacing it with his own conception are easily lost in the obscurity and complications of the texts. They become apparent only when seen against the background of his basic metaphysical assumptions. Leibniz is rarely explicit about these assumptions, but they are discernible as the implicit premises and unstated assumptions of his arguments in the texts of 1668–69. Each exposes a slightly different aspect of the robust self-sufficiency that Leibniz requires of substances; together they form the bedrock of his metaphysical thinking. They may be summarized as follows.

The *Principle of Self-sufficiency* (PS): a being S is self-sufficient if and only if the complete reason for its properties can be discovered in the nature of S.[11]

The *Principle of Substantial Self-sufficiency* (PSS): a being S is a substance if and only if S is self-sufficient.[12]

The *Principle of Causal Self-sufficiency* (PCS): for any being S, strictly speaking, S can be said to have a property p and p can be said to exist in S just in case the complete reason for p can be found in the nature of S.[13]

The *Principle of Substantial Activity* (PSA): a being S is a substance if and only if it subsists per se and S subsists per se if and only if it has a principle of activity within its own nature.[14]

The *Principle of Sufficient Reason* (PSR): for everything there is there is a complete reason.[15] A *complete reason* for some state of affairs *s* (1) constitutes the necessary and sufficient condition for *s;* (2) is perspicuous in that, in those cases where one can understand it, one sees exactly why *s* as opposed to some other state of affairs came about; (3) is such that in those cases when a full account of it can be given, that account constitutes a complete explanation of *s;* and (4) the reason itself does not require a reason of the same type.[16] This notion of complete reason along with the Principle of Sufficient Reason implies two other assumptions.

The *Logical Assumption:* for any state of affairs *s*, the logically necessary and sufficient conditions of *s* exist and in theory can be articulated; the *Intelligibility Assumption:* those conditions are in theory intelligible.

These original metaphysical principles and assumptions imply a good deal about both the universe and its maker. They yield a world of active, self-sufficient substances whose natures constitute the cause and explanation of their properties. Since all the events of the natural world are ultimately reducible to these substantial natures, the world is rendered both explicable and intelligible. It is significant that Leibniz does not think it is necessary to argue for these claims: the intelligibility of the world seems to follow from his belief in the wisdom and rationality of God; the self-sufficiency of essentially active substances from his acceptance of the philosophy of Aristotle, as he interpreted it.

The importance that these metaphysical commitments have for the development of Leibniz's thought cannot be overemphasized: they guide his metaphysical reasoning for years to come. The precise role they play in the development of his original conception of substance is perhaps most apparent in the criticisms Leibniz offers of the standard metaphysical foundations of mechanism.

1.3 The original concept of substance

Leibniz and the Moderns agree that all the properties of bodies are reducible to the motion of matter and that motion itself cannot be derived from corporeal nature alone. That is, however the standard mechanist defined body (e.g., as extended stuff or as extended, impenetrable stuff), they agreed with Leibniz that motion could not be derived from it. Because corporeal nature needed an outside source of motion, each philosopher had some way of bringing God, as a source of motion, to body. For example, Descartes maintains that God adds motion to body by continual creation, while Gassendi thinks that God infuses motion into atoms at their creation.[17]

But this is where the agreement between Leibniz and the Moderns ends. The latter maintained that God was in some sense the cause of the motion in bodies and yet they were perfectly happy to make motion a fundamental property of body. For instance, Descartes maintains that motion is a mode *of* extension, even though it has to be added *to* extension by God. The important point here is that, for the standard mechanist, regardless of how motion comes into the picture, two things were taken to be true about it: (1) it is not reducible to or caused by the nature or essence of body and yet (2) it is a fundamental feature of body. Leibniz finds this position unacceptable and offers (1) as a reason for denying (2). For Leibniz, the Moderns made two crucial mistakes, one made evident by the PCS, the other by the PSS. First, they attributed motion to body as a fundamental property or mode despite the fact that the cause of motion did not reside in the nature of body. According to Leibniz and the PCS, if the cause of motion is not in corporeal nature, then strictly speaking motion cannot be said to belong to that nature (see, for instance, A II.i 23f, L 101f). Second, they intended to construct a substance out of corporeal nature alone despite the fact that it is was not "self-sufficient" and could "not subsist without an incorporeal principle." According to Leibniz and the PSS, any substance worth the name ought to be self-sufficient at least with regard to its essential properties (A VI.i 490: L 110). In other words, for Leibniz, the standard mechanical conception of corporeal substance was unacceptably insubstantial.

Leibniz's original notion of substance grew out of his attempt to make corporeal substance properly substantial while retaining mechanical physics. His commitment to the metaphysical principles listed above required that such a substance be both causally and substantially self-sufficient in the appropriate way; his commitment to mechanical physics demanded it be constituted of extended stuff in motion; his commitment to the philosophy of Aristotle implied that the substance would have both a passive and active principle.

In constructing the proper passive principle, Leibniz distinguished between matter and body: the former is nothing other than impenetrability and extension, matter without mind, inert stuff without a principle of activity, and hence without motion; the latter is a combination of matter and a principle of activity that can cause motion.[18] As Leibniz explains: "It must be demonstrated against Descartes that space and extension are really different from body because otherwise motion would not be a real thing [in body]" (A VI.i 510). Matter is basically inert stuff and does not have motion while body is constituted of matter in motion.[19]

Mind functions as the active principle and plays the role of the Aristotelian substantial form. According to Leibniz, because only something incorporeal can act as a source of activity, it follows from the PSA that a substance is that which has an incorporeal principle. Because of the fundamental connection between substance and activity, a body will be a substance if and only if it is in union with something incorporeal that can function as its principle of activity. Leibniz writes: "Something when taken together with concurring mind is substance," otherwise it is not. A mind makes the body substantial by constituting its principle of activity: "the substance of the body is union with sustaining mind" (A VI.i 508–9: L 115–16).[20] There are two sorts of minds and hence two sorts of substances. Leibniz writes: "the substance of the human body is union with human mind, and the substance of bodies which lack reason [i.e., nonhuman substances] is union with the universal mind, or God" (A VI.i 509: L 116). For both human and nonhuman substances, mind is the active principle, that which informs matter with motion and thereby makes it into a corporeal substance. Human substances have their own minds and hence their own source of activity. Nonhuman substances have God, the "universal mind," as their active, determining principle. In his role as "primary form" (e.g., A II.i 20: L 99), God individuates matter and thereby produces an individual substance, or what Leibniz sometimes describes as "an organized arrangement of parts" of matter (A II.i 16f.: L 96).[21] According to Leibniz, in devising his conception of substance, he has followed Aristotle: the individual corporeal substance is composed of indeterminate matter and a determining form; the substantial nature, here a composite of matter in motion, acts as the cause and explanation of its properties (A II.i 11; A II.i 21f.: L 100).

We noted above that, when Leibniz began work on the theological project in 1668, he was both a mechanist and an Aristotelian and maintained that the philosophy of Aristotle "can be conformed easily" to that of the mechanists (A II.i 10). We have just described the motivation behind his original notion of substance: he found what he considered to be serious flaws in the foundations of mechanical physics and attempted to construct his own, more secure Aristotelian foundation.[22] There are two points to make about the results of this, Leibniz's first attempt at original metaphysics. First, Leibniz does forge a synthesis of mechanical and Aristotelian elements. By demoting the mechanical conception of body to prime matter and hence to a mere constituent of corporeal substance and by defining corporeal substance as the *union* of matter and mind, Leibniz makes his conception more appropriately self-sufficient and more consistent with Aristotelian metaphysics. Matter and mind combine as passive and active elements to form a union that constitutes the cause and explanation for the properties of substances and hence for everything else there is. But Leibniz's original notion of corporeal substance is also consistent with mechanical physics: by making substance a union of mind and matter, he has all the necessary ingredients for a proper mechanical physics. As Leibniz happily proclaims in 1669, "the explanation of all qualities must be found in magnitude, figure, motion, etc." (A II.i 23f.: L 102).

The second point to emphasize about Leibniz's original account of substance is that it is very much a tentative solution to the difficult philosophical and theological issues with which he was grappling in 1668–69. By April, 1669, Leibniz has decided both that the Moderns were seriously mistaken in their materialist conception of corporeal substance and that the only way to correct their mistake and to solve certain difficult theological problems (e.g., transubstantiation) was to put something incorporeal into substance.[23] But he was undecided about the details of his solution. Most importantly, he was unclear about how to conceive the relations between God and matter. His second conception of substance evolved out of an attempt to solve this problem.

2 THE ORIGINS OF THE MATURE THEORY OF SUBSTANCE, 1669–1672

Leibniz was proud of his original account of substance. In his writings of 1668–69 he frequently emphasizes the several advantages that he thinks it has both in solving theological problems (e.g., A II.i

11, 24; A VI.i 508, 492, 494) and in revealing the true sophistication of the philosophy of Aristotle (e.g., A II.i 15, 18; A VI.i 510). He probably would have maintained this conception if not for a problem he found lurking beneath the surface, one that he considered significant enough to require a dramatic shift in his thinking. The problem is due to the fact that, while each nonhuman corporeal substance has a nature (i.e., an organized arrangement of parts of matter) in terms of which its properties can be explained, that nature is itself *caused* by a substance that stands wholly outside of it. What Leibniz came to consider problematic is that, although corporeal properties follow from the combination of matter and motion, motion is itself caused by something substantially distinct from that nature. It follows from the PCS and the fact that God is the cause of motion in body that, strictly speaking, the motion neither belongs to the body nor really exists in it. And, if motion is not really in the body, it becomes unclear how the *nature* of body is supposed to be constituted of matter in motion. Since God causes the nature (by moving the matter), it follows from the PCS that the motion does not really belong to the nature and hence that the nature does not strictly speaking belong to the body.

Nor is it clear how the properties of a body that are supposed to be caused by this nature really belong to it. For example, according to the mechanical physics to which Leibniz is committed, the shape of a body is reducible to and explainable in terms of the arrangement of the parts of the body. But, since the cause of motion is God, it is not clear in what sense the shape belongs to the body. Because God causes the shape by moving the matter, it would seem to follow from the PCS that the shape belongs as much to God as to the body. In other words, it is not clear whether the shape of the shoe is strictly in God or in the object.

Because Leibniz was concerned to formulate an account of nonhuman substance that would be both substantially and causally self-sufficient, the fact that his original conception turns out *not* to be self-sufficient in just these ways constitutes a serious flaw. Leibniz's second conception of substance grew out of his attempt to solve exactly this problem. Between the spring of 1669 and the winter of 1670, he realized that the only justifiable way to attribute corporeal properties to individual bodies, given his PCS, and to make nonhuman corporeal substances properly self-sufficient, given his PSS, was to give each body its own incorporeal principle, one that could be part of corporeal nature in the way God was not. Leibniz makes the point succinctly in the mid-1670s when he explains that "in order to *complete* the concept of Body . . . [a principle of] action . . . has to be added to the concept of extension" (A VI.iii 158: W 64; our emphasis).

In 1669, Leibniz had his work cut out for him. First, he had to decide upon an incorporeal principle to put into body so that its nature would be the cause of its own motion and hence of its properties. Second, Leibniz had to find a way to make this incorporeal principle part of the *nature* of the substance: otherwise, he would not have escaped the problem facing his first conception. Following the PSS, if the corporeal and incorporeal principles were not unified into a single nature, the problem with the original account would remain, i.e., the motion would belong only to the incorporeal principle that directly caused it and not to the substance as a whole. To avoid this problem, the corporeal and incorporeal elements in substance had to form one nature so that the motion strictly speaking could be attributed to the substance and not just to the incorporeal cause of motion within the substance.

There is straightforward evidence that Leibniz's development took exactly these steps, and for precisely these reasons, i.e., that once he discovered the problem with his original concept of substance, he decided to solve it by giving each body its own incorporeal principle and then worked out the details of how to form a substantial union out of two things, each with its own nature.[24] The steps that Leibniz took in devising his full solution are as follows.

In April, 1669, Leibniz wrote a letter to his revered teacher, Jacob Thomasius, presenting for the first time in detail his original conception of substance. In early 1670, Leibniz published an edition of a text by the Renaissance humanist, Marius Nizolius. Besides writing a preface to the text, Leibniz attached to it a slightly altered version of his letter to Thomasius. Although the actual additions and deletions in the second, published version of the letter are few, they represent a fundamental shift in Leibniz's views about substance: Leibniz adds an incorporeal principle, namely thought (*cogitatio*), to extension as an element in corporeal substance and deletes the reference to God as the cause of the motion in bodies.[25] That is, within months of composing his original letter to Thomasius, Leibniz had recognized not only the problem with his first account of substance but also what was required to solve it.

The changes Leibniz makes in the letter do not constitute any thing like a fully worked out solution to the problem, but they do reveal both Leibniz's recognition of the problem and the form his solution would take. Leibniz is searching for some kind of incorporeal principle that can take the place of God as the cause of motion. It is not surprising then that within weeks of revising his letter to Thomasius, Leibniz is hard at work constructing a new conception of substance. The first explicit revision of Leibniz's original conception of substance occurs in a theological essay entitled *On the Incarnation of God or Hypostatic Union*. In this paper, Leibniz faces the problem of hypostatic union, here understood to be the problem of how there can be a union of the divine and human natures of Christ. Given Leibniz's philosophical concerns at the time, the theological problem of hypostatic union seems an especially appropriate context for a discussion of how an immaterial and a material principle (each with its own nature) are to be related so as to form one substance. Although Leibniz's discussion in this unfinished essay is enormously complicated, the points relevant to the present discussion may be summarized as follows. Leibniz describes an hypostatic union between two things, A and B, in the following way: "If A is [that which does] the unifying and B is that which is said to be unified, then, in the first place, A is a thing subsisting per se; in the second, A acts through B . . . ; and thus, A acts immediately in B or [*seu*] not through another" (A VI.i 534). Here we find the three crucial features of an hypostatic union: the union is made out of two elements, one active, one passive; the active element subsists *per se*, but can only act through the other; the passive element need not subsist *per se*, but is the means by which the active element acts. Moreover, according to Leibniz, although God does not need a passive element through which to act, created mind does. This means that in order for there to be any activity in the created world, hypostatical unions are required. Further, it is not enough that the active element acts some of the time, it must act constantly on the passive element. The idea seems to be that when the acting stops, so does the union. Thus, according to Leibniz, A and B are hypostatically unified if and only if the active element acts constantly on the passive element and the latter is its "immediate instrument" of acting.

Leibniz's pronouncements here represent a significant step towards solving the problem with his original account of substance and constitute the foundations of a new conception. By focusing on the necessary conditions for an hypostatic union, the essay squarely faces the problem with the first account. According to the PCS, a property p will belong to an object b if and only if the full account of p is found in the *nature* of b. The crucial flaw with the original view was that the cause of the motion of body *qua* substance (namely, divine mind) stood outside it and, hence, remained wholly distinct from the nature of the corporeal substance. The key to Leibniz's new position is that he inserts created mind between God and body qua matter and withdraws the claim that God causes the motion in the corporeal substance. Instead, God creates mind so that it may act as "God's instrument." By such means, created mind becomes the principle of activity in the body *qua* substance; it thereby constitutes, along with its matter, the nature of the substance and the cause and explanation of its properties.

Nor is it problematic that mind, the incorporeal element in the substance, is the efficient cause of the activity in the substance. While the mind is the source of activity, the motion or action must occur *through* matter. By combining mind and body *qua* matter in the way he does, Leibniz has cleverly managed to create a single unit out of corporeal and incorporeal elements. His strategy is fairly simple: a real substantial union between elements of two different natures (one active, one passive) depends on the constant activity of the active principle on the passive principle because the constancy of the union of the two depends on the constancy of the connection between them. Since the two elements will cease to be a union when they cease to be connected, and since constant activity assures constant connection, Leibniz's account of substantial union requires constant activity. In other words, the hypostatic union of incorporeal and corporeal natures crucially depends upon two features of the principle of activity: first, that it constantly acts and, second, that it cannot act except through the matter in which it is rooted.

A comparison to organic unities may be helpful at this point. If one understands an organic unity to be composed of a mind and some portion of matter, then it is easy to understand why the unity requires the constant activity of the one on the other. With any organic unity, however simple or complex, its survival depends on the maintenance of its organization: if the mind or organizing principle in either an amoeba or rhododendron desists in acting, then the organization ceases and the union dissolves; there is no longer an organized arrangement of matter, but a heap of decaying flesh. On this model the active element or mind cannot act outside itself except through the passive element, because in order to act externally it has to do so through the matter that it organizes.

Despite the fact that *On the Incarnation of God* presents the fundamental structure of Leibniz's second account of substance, it leaves crucial questions unanswered. Most of these cluster around the issue of the nature of mind and its relation to body. It is not surprising, therefore, that upon completing this essay, Leibniz turned his attention to topics concerning mind. According to his own account, it was during the winter of 1669–70, that Leibniz was able "to penetrate" into the "deepest nature of mind" (A II.i 65) and to grasp that the motion of bodies cannot be explained "without invoking incorporeal beings" (A II.i 64–65). The results of this study were significant: not only did Leibniz produce the most important publication of his early years, he summarized his new views in a series of letters that he sent to some of the most prominent philosophers of Europe. These writings contain the original formulations of what would become Leibniz's mature metaphysics. Although there is not space here to go into their details, the most significant metaphysical conclusions of these texts follow.

Leibniz published two major works in 1671: the *New Physical Hypothesis*, which he dedicated to the Royal Society of London and the *Theory of Abstract Motion*, which he dedicated to the Royal Academy of Paris. It is in the latter that he presents his new idea: "I demonstrated that the true locus of mind is a certain point or center" that is unextended and indivisible (A II.i 173: L 149) and thereby showed that "mind itself actually exists in a point as opposed to body [which] occupies space" (A II.i 108). By conceiving of a point as that which is unextended and indivisible, Leibniz gave himself the conceptual means to distinguish neatly between the "place" of mind and that of body and hence a way of putting mind into body.[26]

The second crucial discovery during this period concerns the precise relation between the mind and the substance of which it is part.

Leibniz is especially explicit about this in a letter to Duke Johann Friedrich of May 1671. He asserts that "there is a kernel of [every] substance" that can either "spread throughout" the body or "draw itself into an invisible center" and that is like the source and "fount of the substance." According to Leibniz the mind or kernel of every corporeal substance causes and maintains its organization, which can be more or less expansive. The mind does not literally spread throughout the body (for then it would exist in space), but the organization that it causes does. That is, the incorporeal principle causes and maintains an organization of matter that can be more or less "spread out." Making explicit use of an organic model, Leibniz asks us to conceive the relation between substance and mind as that between an organism and its organizing principle: just as it is the organizing principle that causes the organism to grow from an acorn to a tree and then, say, to survive the removal of several limbs, it is the mind that produces and sustains the organized arrangement of matter in every body (A II.i 108f.).[27]

Along with his letter to the Duke, Leibniz enclosed an essay on a "most difficult" theological problem, the resurrection of the body. Drawing upon the same organic model, Leibniz offers a neat solution to the problem. He explains that the soul resides in "a certain center" of a corporeal substance which is the "fountain of life" of the substance and that, even in fire or other drastic physical changes, this center survives in the ashes or some small part of the original body. Resurrection occurs when "the flower of the substance of the same body [that died], through excretions and emissions, transforms itself into something new." Moreover, according to Leibniz, this "flower of substance" explains "the generation of plants from seeds," the development of "the seed in the uterus," and even "the essences of chemicals" (A II.i 116). Thus, human beings, animals, plants, and even chemical elements are all substances in the sense that they are constituted of mind and matter, where the former constantly acts on the latter and in doing so produces a single unified thing. This unity of mind and matter can expand (as when a plant grows from a seed) or recede (as when a tree burns away to ash), but through all such changes the mind and some bit of matter persist.

An obvious question arises at this point: how do the minds in chemical elements and plants differ from those in human beings? Leibniz was enormously proud of the fact that in studying "the innermost nature of mind" he had developed an answer to just this question. He writes: "I demonstrated that the true locus of mind is a certain point or center, and from this I deduced some remarkable conclusions about . . . the true innermost difference between motion and thought" (A II.i 173: L 149). The key to understanding the difference is to appreciate the importance of the fact that, although "mind in its very nature acts" (A II.i 162) and "the actions of mind consist in conatuses" which are infinitesimal motions "in a point" (A II.i 108), only the actions of "true minds" persist and thereby produce "a harmony of conatuses." It is the persistence of the actions of true minds that allows them "to think, to compare diverse things, to perceive" (A II.i 113). The minds in bodies do not persist; during the period Leibniz sometimes describes them as momentary (e.g., A II.i 102; A VI.ii 266: L 141).

In the development of his second account of substance, Leibniz did not focus exclusively on the topic of mind. He also deliberated upon the nature of matter, the other constituent in corporeal substance. Sometime in 1670/71 Leibniz wrote an important fragment "On Prime Matter" in which he reveals the full force of his eclecticism. He argues that "the prime matter of Aristotle is the same as the subtle matter of Descartes: each is infinitely divisible, each lacks form and motion per se, each receives form through motion, and each receives motion from mind." Moreover, Leibniz praises those Scholastics who believed that "prime matter has [its] existence from form," which he understands to mean that without motion there is no variety and without variety "matter is nothing." In other words, prime matter becomes some thing when mind organizes it into a body. What he considers one of his contributions to these views is that "matter is actually divided into infinite parts" so that "there are infinite creatures in any given body" (A VI.ii 279f: W* 90f).

With this said, the materials are in place to explicate Leibniz's second theory of substance. Interestingly enough, its structure is fundamentally the same as the first conception. Matter plays the role of Aristotelian prime matter, i.e., it is indeterminate and must be made some *thing* through activity: "particulars or bodies arise" only when matter is activated by mind (A VI.ii 280: W 91). The principle of activity is something incorporeal that plays the role of the Aristotelian substantial form, the determining principle, that which makes the thing what it is. When the incorporeal principle individuates matter, the result is an individual corporeal substance. And once again the resulting physics is fundamentally mechanical in that all corporeal properties are reducible to and explainable in terms of the movements of the parts of body.

The crucial difference between the two theories is that in the second each substance has its own principle of activity or substantial form that is so related to the corporeal principle as to form a single nature with it. Although mind exists in a point, it constantly acts through the matter to which it is attached and, as Leibniz writes, it can "act upon" a larger or smaller extent of matter. It is important to emphasize the fact that every activity is the result of mind's acting *through* matter: the mind does the moving, but the matter is what is moved. Thus, mind and matter are constitutive parts of any activity. Since the mind and the matter are constantly joined in the activity of the one on the other, the substance is an hypostatic union of mind and matter; each substance is constituted by mind and matter in constant relation. By so combining mind and matter to form an hypostatic union, Leibniz renders substance self-sufficient in a way consistent with the PSS and PCS. He thereby solves the problem with his original theory and lays the groundwork for his mature metaphysics.

3 THE EVOLUTION OF THE MATURE PHILOSOPHY, 1672 – 1676

For decades, core features of the philosophy of the *Discourse on Metaphysics* have baffled scholars. Despite extensive analysis and study, its deep motivations and the precise relations among some of its central doctrines have remained largely mysterious.[28] We will argue in this section that most of the fundamental tenets of Leibniz's mature thought are already in place in 1676 and that they grew naturally out of Leibniz's early metaphysics.

During the four years Leibniz spent in Paris (1672–76), his intellectual energies were focused primarily on mathematical and technical problems. The results include the construction of a calculating machine that was successfully demonstrated in early 1675 and the invention of the calculus in the autumn of that year. But he did not wholly neglect the metaphysical ideas that he worked so hard to develop during the period of 1669–71. In Paris, he found time to enlarge upon key elements of the earlier metaphysical system.[29] At the most general level, his metaphysical investigations concern four areas of study: God as the cause of the universe (sec. 3.1) and created minds as the source of the activity (3.2), plenitude (3.3), and harmony (3.4) in that world.[30]

3.1   God and the importance of being harmonious

In March, 1673 Leibniz wrote a letter to Duke Johann Friedrich in which he describes his intellectual activities during his first year in Paris: "I have made important demonstrations in the difficult areas of religion and the true philosophy," and also contributions concerning "the inner nature of things" (A II.i 232). That God stands at the center of this "true philosophy" and that the evolution in Leibniz's thinking about mind and matter during the period is encouraged by his reflections on the nature of God is clear from his notes. Leibniz arrived in Paris with the basic outline of his theory of substance; the next step in his metaphysical investigations was to examine the precise relationship between such creatures and their creator.

Leibniz's analysis of this relationship is best seen in the context of the PSR and its notion of a complete reason. The PSR implies that God as the cause of the world is its sufficient reason. As Leibniz defined it just before his departure for Paris, "a sufficient reason is that which having been given the thing is" (A VI.ii 483). The notion of complete reason demands an intimate and intelligible relation between a cause and its effect so that an examination of the divine sufficient reason would in theory render the effect intelligible. When Leibniz arrived in Paris he assumed that the world would have features that reflect or express this divine cause. Before moving ahead in his metaphysical enquiries, it was necessary to identify the relevant features of the world as a product of God. Only after a careful inventory of those features had been made could Leibniz proceed to construct the "true philosophy."

In his Philosophers Confession of 1672, Leibniz identifies harmony as the dominant feature of the world that God had sufficient reason to create. He writes: "God is the ultimate reason of things, i.e., the sufficient reason of the universe" which itself is "most rational" and "most supreme in beauty and universal harmony" (A VI.iii 126). Harmony is the most supreme unity within the greatest variety and is that feature of the world that follows from God's nature (A VI.iii 122f). In an important essay of 1676, entitled "On the Secrets of the Sublime" he proclaims: "After due consideration I take as a principle the harmony of things: that is, that the greatest amount of essence that can exist does exist" (A VI.iii 472: Pk 21). In order to attribute as much goodness as possible to the universe, Leibniz assumes that essences are good and then reasons that the more (compatible) essences in the world the better. It is important that Leibniz is not just after the greatest possible number of essences, he wants to make every positive aspect of the world as full as possible. He states: "It follows from this principle that there is no vacuum among forms; also that there is no vacuum in place and time. . . . From which it follows that there is no assignable time in which something did not exist, nor is there a place which is not full" (A VI.iii 473: Pk 23). Although he is uncertain about the exact consequences of this "plenitude of the world," he thinks that "it is true that any part of matter, however small, contains an infinity of creatures, i.e., is a world" (A VI.iii 474: Pk 25). It becomes clear in the course of the essay that this commitment to plenitude is only one part of the principle of harmony and that proper maximization will occur only within the context of a divinely arranged elegant simplicity. God is the kind of "intelligent substance" and "perfect mind" who finds what is "most harmonious" to be "most pleasing" and who "arranged all things from the beginning" such that "all things are in general good" (A VI.iii 474ff.: Pk* 25ff.). The suggestion is that God's creation combines the greatest possible elegance with the greatest possible variety. Leibniz emphasizes the harmonious simplicity of the universe in an essay written a few months later: "Harmony is just this: a certain simplicity in multiplicity. Beauty and pleasure also consist in this. So for things to exist is the same as for them to be understood by God to be the best, i.e., the most harmonious" (A VI.iii 588: Pk 113).

From these and related texts it is clear that by 1676 Leibniz has committed himself to a principle of harmony according to which the world is as full as possible while also being rational, elegant, and good. In such a way the universe reflects the "divine wisdom" of its cause.

3.2 *Mind and activity*

While Leibniz was deciding upon harmonious plenitude as the dominant feature of God's creation, he was also concerned with developing his theory of substance along consistent lines. It was surely of immediate importance to explain how the principles of activity in substances could accommodate such harmony. In section 2, we argued that the success of Leibniz's second account of substance depended on two specific innovations: first, that the principle of activity or mind in substance could create with its matter, by the constant activity of the one on the other, a single substantial nature; second, that the organization created by mind acting on matter could be more or less expansive. In 1672–76, Leibniz develops these points in ways consonant with harmony.

During the period, Leibniz emphasizes the connection (explicit in the PSA) between activity and substantiality: he emphasizes the fact that a substance is "a thing that acts" and acknowledges that minds insofar as they act are themselves "incorporeal substances" (e.g., A VI.iii 78ff.). But he is also explicit about the fact that there are no disembodied or spiritual substances. According to Leibniz, "God alone" is a substance "separate from matter" (A VI.iii 395: Pk 49). He puts his view succinctly in 1673–75:

> once we hold that every substance is active and every active thing is called a substance . . . we can show from the inner truths of metaphysics that what is not active is nothing . . . [and] that, in fact, every finite soul is embodied, even the angels are not excepted.   (A VI.iii 158: W*64f.)[31]

The ontology is clear. There is an infinite number of active incorporeal substances. Of these, only God does not form an hypostatic union with some portion of matter. Created reality therefore consists of an infinity of individual corporeal substances and their modifications.

Leibniz also expands upon the connection (implied by the conjunction of the PSS and PSA) between the activity and self-sufficiency of substances: mind produces an indestructible and indivisible unit with the matter it organizes and it constitutes both the source of identity and individuation of that organization.[32] Each of these new characterizations of mind depends on its constant activity, each is at least partly motivated by theological concerns, and each becomes an important tenet in his mature philosophy.

For Leibniz, the activity of mind renders it naturally indestructible: "whatever acts cannot be destroyed" (A VI.iii 521: Pk 81), nor "can [it] be dissolved naturally" (A VI.iii 393: Pk 47). That is, once God creates a mind, it is naturally unstoppable and hence indestructible. But what about the proposed indestructibility and indivisibility of the organization or unit it forms with matter? Since matter is divisible and since "whatever is divided is destroyed" (392: Pk 45), it is not immediately clear how the union of matter and mind is supposed to avoid divisibility and destruction. Once again, however, the activity of mind guarantees survival. According to Leibniz, whatever has one mind will be indivisible: "there comes into existence a body which is one and unsplittable, i.e., an atom, of whatever size it may be, whenever it has a single mind" (393: Pk 47). Mind takes some portion of matter, acts as the "cement" of "the parts of matter," and thereby produces a "naturally indestructible" atom (A VI.iii 474ff.: Pk 25ff.). Nor should the term *atom* mislead us: for Leibniz, an atom is indestructible, but it is not invariable; it is the fundamental unit of the physical world, but it is constituted of mind and matter. Mind functions as the metaphysical glue or "cement" of an atom or corporeal substance by persistently producing an organization with some chunk of matter; exactly which chunk it organizes is unimportant. When Wanda cuts her hair, her organization remains constant however much matter she sheds. The indivisibility and indestructibility of her unity follows from the organizational persistence of her mind. The organization will persist as long as her mind continues to act, as it always will, through some matter. Thus, the natural indivisibility and indestructibility of the union formed by mind and matter follow from two features of mind: that it is naturally unstoppable and that it will organize some matter as long as it acts.

Two other functions of mind are closely related to its role as the metaphysical "cement" or organizational principle in the world. As the active principle in substance, mind constitutes both the identity of the substance whose cement it is and the source of its individuation. Leibniz is most explicit about the importance of this dual function of mind in his comments about resurrection. In some important notes from the winter of 1675–76, he claims that one can easily solve the theological problem by offering a proper account of the identity of the body. Because "all bodies" are made from "the same matter," it is not difficult "for the very same thing to be reproduced"; all that is required is that the same mind cause the reproduction (A VI.iii 240). That is, since the soul "is firmly planted in a flower of substance" which "subsists perpetually in all changes" and which can be "diffused" through the entire body or only some small part of it, it follows that "in the same way that individual salts" become reconstituted after being dissolved in water, so "any human individual" can be reconstituted after death (A VI.iii 478f). Because substantial identity depends wholly on the mind, as long as the mind remains the same so will the body or corporeal substance, regardless of which particular bits of matter come and go. There is then a very straightforward explanation of what occurs at resurrection: the flower of substance or soul, which at death shrank down to some minute portion of the original body, diffuses itself through an appropriate amount of matter (as it did during the individual's original growth from fetus to adulthood, only faster) and thereby becomes the same body it was at death. The same body or atom exists both before and after the resurrection; it has merely changed significantly in size. The transformation that occurs at resurrection is a model (however dramatic) of what happens constantly among the bodies in the world.

In the Paris years, Leibniz attaches increasingly greater metaphysical importance to the activity of created minds and thereby makes substances increasingly more self-sufficient: by acting constantly on the matter to which it is attached, the mind or the principle of activity renders the resultant union a single, unstoppable, and naturally unsplittable thing such that, however much the matter may vary, the thing remains the same as long as its mind does. In short, the activity of mind is the source of the indestructibility, indivisibility, individuality, and identity of corporeal substance. These are important developments in Leibniz's theory of substance; it is now time to explore the precise relevance they have for his conception of harmonious plenitude.

3.3 Mind and plenitude

One of the striking things about Leibniz's notes on physics of 1672–73 is the theological importance attached to the activity of mind. An argument that recurs throughout the period is one that proves the existence of minds from the diversity and harmony of things in the world. Its basic structure is as follows: because matter is everywhere the same, if there were only matter in the world, there would be no activity, diversity, or harmony; the world has such features: therefore, there must be minds (e.g., A VI.ii: 57, 67, 72, 79, 100, 146). Leibniz thinks that this argument from diversity and harmony has far-reaching consequences: "all the most beautiful truths" concerning the universe, such as the variety of things and "the greatest of all truths," namely, harmony, depend on mind (A VI.iii 67). Because the world, as a product of God, has the greatest possible harmony and because mind is "the unique efficient cause of things," it follows that mind is the cause of the activity, diversity, and harmony of the world (146). It also follows that God, as the creator of mind, exists (see A VI.iii 67, 101). According to Leibniz, "nothing else demonstrated by me has greater significance" (A VI.iii 67).

We have seen that between 1672 and 1676 Leibniz increases the metaphysical work of minds: they act constantly on the matter to which they are attached and thereby produce an indestructible corporeal substance. It is significant that in his notes on physics of 1672 Leibniz replaces the momentary minds of the pre-Paris years with eternal ones and that in 1676 he claims that harmonious plenitude entails the eternity of minds. According to Leibniz, "every mind is of endless duration" and "is indissolubly implanted in matter. . . . There are innumerable minds everywhere" which "do not perish" (A VI.iii 476f.: Pk* 31).[33]

It is one thing for minds to be indestructible and quite another for them to be eternal: the constant activity of minds guarantees the natural indestructibility of substances, but it does not by itself guarantee their eternity. Once created, such substances will persist forever only if God deems their survival harmonious. But this is problematic: it is not at all obvious exactly how the eternity of substances is supposed to *increase* harmonious plenitude. For example, if God were to replace one infinite set of substances with a new one (say, one every millenium), would the universe not be rendered fuller?

Leibniz explains his position in 1676. At the same time he reveals the motivation behind his doctrine of marks and traces and part of the motivation behind his hypothesis of expression.[34] He writes:

"There are beautiful discoveries and ingenious images with regard to the harmony of things" (A VI.iii 476: Pk 29). One of the most ingenious images of his mature philosophy is presented in his essay "On the Secrets of the Sublime" of February, 1676, in which Leibniz first proclaims his commitment to harmony as a principle. He writes: "Particular minds exist, in sum, simply because the supreme being judges it harmonious that there should exist somewhere that which understands, or, is a kind of intellectual mirror or replica of the world" (A VI.iii 474: Pk 25).[35] Leibniz explains his intention when he applies this metaphor to God: "A most perfect being is that which *contains the most.* Such a being is capable of ideas and thoughts, *for this multiplies the varieties of things,* like a mirror" (475, Pk 29; our emphasis). Created minds cannot contain all perfections, but they can reflect them all. That is, the image of a mirror, a prominent fixture of Leibniz's later philosophy, is motivated by a desire to increase the variety and content of the world as much as possible. It allows Leibniz to go beyond the maximization of objects to that of their images and ideas. He greatly increases the multitude and variety of things by giving each indestructible mind at every moment of its eternal existence a perception or idea of the entire world.

Within a few weeks of exhibiting this picture of the mind as a mirror, Leibniz expands upon it. He writes in March, 1676 that all minds have thoughts, each one of which is an action of mind; that each mind "senses all the endeavors" or activities of all the other minds; and that no activity of any mind "is ever lost" (A VI.iii 393: Pk 47). That is, minds not only sense all the activities of all the minds in the world, they also retain a memory or trace of them as well. In Leibniz's words, "[i]t is not credible that the effect of all perceptions should vanish in the future" (A VI.iii 510: Pk 61), rather they must be "stored up in the mind" (A VI.iii 393: Pk 47). In April he presents the original version of what comes to be his doctrine of marks and traces: "there is present in any matter something which retains the effect of what precedes it, namely a mind"; but also "there is in it a quality of such a kind as to bring this [state of substance or effect] about" (A VI.iii 491: Pk 51). We will have the opportunity to talk about the significance of the doctrine of marks and traces for Leibniz's theories of expression and causation in the next section. In the present context its importance is that it adds significantly to the plenitude of the world: each mind at every moment includes an effect or trace of all it has done and sensed as well as a quality or mark of all it will do and sense. According to Leibniz, "no endeavor in the universe is lost; they are stored up in the mind, not destroyed" (A VI.iii 393: Pk 47). By making minds eternal, by allowing them to sense all endeavors, and by giving them traces of all that has gone before and marks of all that will occur, Leibniz has made each mind a mirror of the entire course of the world at every moment in time. Each mind reflects or expresses the entire world – past, present and future – at every moment of the mind's existence.

But it is not enough for minds to be eternal, they must also be diverse. That is, harmonious plenitude requires not just that substances eternally express the entire world, it demands that each does so from its own point of view. Leibniz writes:

It seems to me that every mind is omniscient in a confused way; that any mind perceives simultaneously whatever happens in the entire world. . . . But time is infinitely divisible, and it is certain that at any moment the soul perceives various things. . . . Again, it is not surprising that any mind should perceive what is done in the entire world, since there is no body that is too small to sense all other things, given the plenitude of the world. And so a wonderful variety arises in this way, for there are as many different relations of things as there are minds, just as when the same town is seen from various places. So God, by the creation of many minds, willed to bring about with respect to the universe what is willed with respect to a large town by a painter, who wants to display delineations of its various aspects or projections. The painter does on canvas what God does on the mind.

(A VI.iii 524: Pk* 85)

The image here is a powerful one. Each mind mirrors every aspect of the world from its own point of view so that there is not merely an infinity of substances and an infinity of complete pictures or reflections of the world, there are infinitely many *different* pictures or expressions as well.

The difference among perspectives is worth emphasizing. The desired pictorial fecundity requires that each substance be distinctive: in order to maximize the variety of images, each substance must have a perspective that is different from every other. This means that no two perspectives will be similar and, hence, that no two substances will be the same. We will have more to say about Leibniz's principle of the identity of indiscernibles below, but it is worth noting here that within a month of formulating this idea of minds as eternal mirrors he gives the first articulation of this principle (see A VI.iii 491: Pk 51).

3.4 Mind and harmony

Substances not only express the world in their own diverse ways, they do so in harmony with one another. As early as 1673–75, Leibniz is prepared to write: "once we hold that every substance is active . . . we can show from the inner truths of metaphysics . . . that all forces act for the highest mind whose will is the final reason for all things, the cause being the universal harmony." Leibniz maintains that "it is the task of Metaphysics to examine the continuous temporal modifications in the universe" and that the truths about these modifications will follow "once the true and inevitable concept of substance is understood" (A VI.iii 156f.: W* 62ff.).

In early 1676 Leibniz was prompted to consider exactly how his theory of substance could fully explain "these continuous modifications" and act toward universal harmony. The results of his ruminations include some of the central tenets of the metaphysics of the *Discourse*, namely, the doctrine of preestablished harmony, the principle of the identity of indiscernibles, and the idea that each substance expresses the entire universe. We propose that the combination of the original metaphysical principles and the newly proposed principle of harmony encouraged the development of these doctrines in the spring of 1676.[36] Since Leibniz maintains his characteristic silence about his deep motivations, the case for this proposal must be circumstantial, based on clues that Leibniz leaves along the way.

Much of the progress Leibniz made in his account of the harmony among minds is inspired by his original principles; it therefore will be helpful to review some of the relevant implications of those principles. It follows from the PCS that p is a property of a substance S if and only if the nature of S is the cause of p. Given the PSR and the notion of a complete cause, this means that every property of S is caused by the nature of S in the sense that the nature of S constitutes the necessary and sufficient conditions of p. Given the PSR and the PSA, it follows that all the events in the world reduce to modifications of substances. This consequence is important: when coupled with the Logical Assumption it implies that there are necessary and sufficient conditions for every state of the world and that these conditions reside in the nature of substances; when combined with the Intelligibility Assumption it implies that these conditions are in theory both intelligible and discoverable in those natures. Thus, substances are the ultimate subjects of predication and in theory can offer an intelligible explanation for every event of the world. Moreover, once Leibniz gives each substance its own active principle or mind so that it is the mind of S that constitutes its active principle, it follows that every property of S must originate in that mind in the sense that it is the mind of S that begins the process that produces the property. For instance, the property of Wanda walking is one that originated in some action in Wanda's mind although the complete reason for that property involves both the mind and the matter or passive principle through which it acts.

There are two problems or tensions which the implications of these principles make evident but which are not resolved in Leibniz's original metaphysics. According to the PSS and the PCS, the relation between a substance and property is such that the complete cause and explanation of the property is supposed to be discoverable in the nature of the substance to which it belongs. However, a problem lurks here due to a slight tension between the PCS and the PSR: on the one hand, the PSR demands that there be a sufficient explanation for a property; on the other, the PCS claims that a property cannot be said to belong to a substance unless that explanation lies in the nature of the substance. What this means is that if the PCS extends only to some properties (say, essential ones) and not to others (say, accidental ones), then the latter cannot strictly be said to exist in the substance. In the early writings, Leibniz does not explain exactly how far the PCS extends. While he clearly believes, for instance, that Wanda's walking down the street is caused by her nature, it is unclear what he thinks about the mud on her boots. Since the complete cause and explanation of the mud would seem to involve substances other than just Wanda, it is not at all clear to whom or what the property belongs.

The second problem arises from an epistemological asymmetry in the relation between a cause and its effect in Leibniz's original principles. The notion of complete reason maintains that the understanding of a cause entails full knowledge of its effect: one sees exactly why the effect and no other occurred. But the principles are silent about any such entailment from effect to cause. Since the Intelligibility Assumption implies that a property p of a substance S is rendered intelligible (at least in theory) by a consideration of S's nature, one would think that a full understanding of p requires that one know enough about S to see exactly how S caused p. In other words, the principles suggest that a thorough understanding of p would involve S in fairly significant ways. It is therefore odd that neither in the principles nor in his articulation of the early metaphysics does Leibniz say anything explicit about the epistemological work that an effect does for its cause.

We have argued that Leibniz's conception of harmony influenced his investigations about the activity of substances; in particular, we have suggested that some important doctrines (e.g., that minds have marks and traces) were developed in response to that conception's demand for plenitude and variety. The principle of harmony also prodded him to think a bit harder about the precise relationship between substantial natures and the properties they cause. In particular, its demand for mutual coordination among substances led Leibniz to develop a more thoroughgoing account of the relationship between the actions of minds and the production of substantial properties. As we shall see, in 1676 he developed solutions to the problems just noted. We will now trace the steps that Leibniz took toward those solutions.

On 11 February 1676, in the same essay in which he first explicitly states his principle of harmony, Leibniz articulates his assumptions about the harmonious activities of minds. He ends "On the Secrets of the Sublime" by noting that "God arranged things from the beginning" so that minds can "understand their function" and accordingly attain the "wonderful uses" to which they "are destined by providence" (A VI.iii 477: Pk* 31).[37] In an essay of early 1676 he offers a definition crucial to his account of how God might so arrange things: "A rule [*regula*] is an instrument of action, determining the form of the action by the perpetual and successive application of the agent to the parts of the instrument." From the examples he gives it is clear that a rule not only specifies what the actor does, but the order in which she does it. According to Leibniz a footpath across a plain is a rule, but a compass is not. He explains: "The instruction which an emperor gives to a deputy . . . is a rule if it is written so that the deputy, in his action, can only follow it in order" (483: Pk 39). With this conception of a rule as an instrument of action, Leibniz was in a position to articulate a production rule for the activities of minds.

In a series of essays written in March and April, he analyzes the relationship between God and the universe. These essays are both important and obscure: they offer critical insight into the evolution of Leibniz's ideas on our topic, but they also depend on certain difficult neo-Platonic and Aristotelian doctrines. Fortunately we need not bother with the complicated details of the latter.[38] What is significant about these texts is that they offer two somewhat different characterizations of God's relation to the world. Each of these provides a clue to Leibniz's underlying assumptions about how minds function as the source of the world's harmony.

Leibniz defines God as "the subject of all absolute simple forms – absolute, that is affirmative" (A VI.iii 519: Pk 79). "Form" here refers to a kind of Platonic form or essence, so that God contains all positive essences. Thus, God can be thought of as "the conjunction in the same subject of all possible absolute forms or perfections (521: Pk 81)." Particular substances arise when the combinations or modifications of these forms are instantiated in a subject: "The various results of forms, combined with a subject, bring it about that particulars result" (523: Pk 85). Each subject is distinct, although each expresses both the world and the essence of God. The difficult details of this account of creation are extraneous to our topic. What is important for our present purpose is that in describing the relationship between the creator and its creation Leibniz reveals a good deal about how the individual creatures function in that world. He writes:

since the ultimate reason of things is unique, and contains by itself the aggregate of all the requisites of all things, it is evident that the requisites of all things are the same. So also is their essence. . . . Therefore the essence of all things is the same, and things differ only modally, just as a town seen from a high point differs from the town seen from a plain.

(A VI.iii 573: Pk 93f.)[39]

We need to proceed cautiously here. In this passage Leibniz explains that God (the ultimate reason of things) is unique and contains the necessary and sufficient conditions for the existence of all things. It is supposed to follow that the essence of all things is the same. But this seems problematic since it appears to conflict with his view that each substantial nature differs from every other. Leibniz offers the crux of a solution in a related text:

It seems to me that the origin of things from God is of the same kind as the origin of properties from an essence; just as $6 = 1+1+1+1+1+1$, therefore $6 = 3+3$, $= 3 \times 2$, $= 4+2$, etc. Nor may one doubt that the one expression differs from the other. . . . So just as these properties differ from each other and from essence, so do things differ from each other and from God.

(A VI.iii 518f.: Pk 77)

With this material in hand we can resolve the apparent tension and discern the first significant evidence of Leibniz's production rule for the activities of mind.

According to Leibniz, each created substance is an expression of God's essence and in this sense each has the same essence. But each nonetheless differs from every other because it is a *different* expression of that essence or, as Leibniz suggests in the previous quotation, it is a modification of that essence. An analogy may help to grasp Leibniz's point. We can think of the essence expressed in the world as a series of true propositions and each modification of that essence as a corresponding series of sentences in a language. Following this analogy, each substance expresses the same series of propositions, but each does so in a different language. Because the sentences in, say, Italian will be different from those in Arabic which will be different again from those in Russian, each series will be a different way of expressing the same thing. According to Leibniz, then, there is an essence (of infinite complexity) that God has chosen to instantiate in the world by means of an infinite number of different expressions. On this account, God creates each substance so that it will express that essence in its own way. As each series of sentences is a different expression of the same propositions, so each substance is a different expression of the same essence.

There is good textual evidence to support this interpretation of the relation between the essence of God and the expression of substances. The analogies used by Leibniz during the period offer particularly vivid support. In the comparison to arithmetical expressions (examples of which we have already seen), there is an essence, say 6, that God intends to express in different ways, say, $3+3$, $2+4$, $1+5$, etc. In the analogy to ideal representations of a town (an example of which occurs in the long quotation on p. 92), the point seems to be that in order to represent or express the essence of the town, the best one can do is to represent it from a variety of perspectives. An important use of the town analogy appears in December, 1676:

There is no doubt that God understands how we perceive things; just as someone who wants to provide a perfect conception of a town will represent it in several ways. And this understanding of God, in so far as it understands our way of understanding, is very like our understanding. Indeed our understanding results from it, from which we can say that God has an understanding that is in a way like ours. For God understands things as we do but with this difference: that he understands them at the same time in infinitely many ways, whereas we understand them in one way only.

(A VI.iii 400: Pk 115)

As in the arithmetical case, in creating the world, God creates different perspectives or expressions of the same thing. It is in this sense that our understanding or perspective "results from" God. Each substance is created by God so as to be a unique expression of the divine essence; and it is the nature of the individual substance to be that unique expression.[40]

The second way in which Leibniz characterizes the relation between God and the world in the relevant essays provides another important clue to his views about the the means by which minds act harmoniously. Elaborating on the Aristotelian notion of active intellect, Leibniz defines God as "the primary intelligence, in so far as he is omniscient." This same omniscience is "ascribed in a limited way to other things which are said to perceive something," i.e., to minds (A VI.iii 520: Pk 79). Leibniz also maintains that there are "infinitely many" perceptions of mind which "are not explicable in terms of each other," but which follow from mind "as properties result from essence" (521: Pk 81). He writes:

it can be shown that the mind is continually changed, with the exception of that in us which is divine, or, comes from outside. In sum, . . . there is something divine in mind, which is what Aristotle used to call the active intellect, and this is the same as the omniscience of God.

(A VI.iii 391: Pk 43)

It is important that this divine, omniscient element in mind comes "from the outside," remains the same through its constant changes, and acts as the cause of those changes. Leibniz distinguishes between mind and its actions by noting that the former "remains always the same during change," while the latter are discrete productions of the soul or mind (A VI.iii 326; see also A VI.iii 524: Pk 85).

But what precisely is it about mind that is both omniscient and divine? We propose that these features apply to a mind insofar as God has given it a production rule in terms of which it can act in harmony with all other minds and express the entire universe. The production rule is a kind of blueprint for the continuous production of the discrete states of the substance so that each mind is a principle of activity replete with its own set of instructions that tells it how to act and what to perceive at every moment of its existence. Following Leibniz's definition of a rule, we assume that the production rule for substantial properties is something that the mind "can only follow . . . in order." So, if S lives from $t1$ to tn and is in a different state at each moment of its existence, then at every moment of S's life there will be some instruction about what to do or what to express next. The present state q occurring at t together with the instructions will determine what S does at $t+1$. In this case, the complete cause and full explanation of $q+1$ will be found in the nature of S. In other words, the *complete* cause of each state of the substance is the conjunction of the principle of activity, the production rule, and the previous state.[41]

That in early 1676 Leibniz needed a way to explain the coordination and harmony among substances is clear, as is the fact that the explanation had to be simple and had to accommodate the other features of substance (e.g., their indestructibility and eternity). With the development of the production rule for the activities of mind Leibniz had procured an elegant way to achieve these ends. As Leibniz puts it in December, 1676:

The harmony of things requires that there should be in bodies beings that act on themselves [*quae agerent in se ipsa*]. On the nature of a being that acts on itself: it acts by the simplest means, for in that there is harmony. Once it has begun, it is eternal. There are ideas in it of those things it has sensed and done, as there are in God; the difference is that in God the ideas are of all things and are simultaneous. . . . Thought [*cogitatio*] or the sensation of oneself, i.e., action on oneself, is necessarily continued.
(A VI.iii 588: Pk 113)

By means of a divinely arranged production rule, each mind acts simply and eternally on itself expressing the divine essence from its own perspective but in perfect harmony with the infinite number of other eternal representations of that essence.

The evolution of Leibniz's production rule for the activities of mind is a dramatic achievement. But how dramatic? We propose that it gave Leibniz the conceptual means to construct the original version of the doctrine of preestablished harmony. This doctrine, which is one of the central tenets of Leibniz's mature thought, claims that God created finite substances so that they do not causally interact, but harmonize with one another in virtue of their internal nature. The doctrine is interpreted in various ways, but is usually understood to include the following three claims: (1) that each state of an individual substance is caused by something internal to its nature, (2) that the states of substances correspond perfectly with one another, and (3) that substances do not causally interact or, more precisely, that no state of a substance has as a real cause some state of another substance.

Because of the central role this doctrine plays in his mature thought, it is important to proceed with care. The production rule for the activities of mind is equivalent to (1), but Leibniz's acceptance of (1) does not by itself entail commitment to either (2) or (3). We will now argue, however, that by April, 1676 Leibniz was committed to these three doctrines, although he did not yet call their conjunction *preestablished* harmony.[42]

During the same two months in which Leibniz was so intensely examining the relation between God and the world and the means by which minds act, he was analyzing what explains the coherence of our sensations. On 15 April, in an important essay entitled "On Truths, the Mind, God, and the Universe," he writes:

On due consideration, only this is certain: that we sense, and that we sense in a consistent way [*congruenter*], and that a certain rule [*regulam*] is observed by us in sensing. For something to be sensed in a consistent way is for it to be sensed in such a way that a reason can be given for everything and everything can be predicted.   (A VI.iii 511: Pk* 63)

According to Leibniz here, on the basis of the consistency of our sensations we can infer that there is a reason for everything, that everything can be predicted, and that in sensing we observe a rule. Two questions arise at this point: what exactly is the cause of the consistency of sensations and how is that cause a rule? From the text so far quoted, the consistency of sensations could be caused either by something internal to the mind, like a production rule, or by something external to it, like the physical world. Leibniz clarifies matters in what follows. He continues:

This is what existence consists in – namely, in sensation that follows certain laws [*leges*]. . . . Further, it consists in the fact that several people sense the same, and sense consistently [*consentientia*]; and that diverse minds sense themselves and their own effects. From this it follows that there is one and the same cause that causes our own and others' sensations. Nevertheless it is not necessary either that we act on them or that they act on us, but only that we sense with such conformity; and necessarily so, on account of the sameness of the cause. . . . Therefore there is no reason why we should ask whether there exist certain bodies outside us. . . . [I]t does not follow that there exists anything but sensation, and the cause of this sensation and its consistency.   (A VI.iii 511: Pk* 63f.)

This text makes clear that, in order to explain existence, it is unnecessary to resort to outside bodies. Leibniz proposes that we reduce existence to the consistency of sensations, where the latter includes both the consistency of the sensation within a mind and the coordination among minds. There is no reason to ask whether bodies exist outside us because the consistency of sensations and coordination among minds can be explained elsewhere. Although Leibniz is not explicit about what this cause is, he offers some details about what it does: the cause produces the consistency of sensations within a mind and the coordination of sensations among minds; it offers a reason for everything and a means of predicting everything; and it somehow involves diverse minds sensing "themselves and their own effects" in a way that does not require that they act on one another. That is, assuming that the cause is somehow internal, what the cause does is produce preestablished harmony.[43] Leibniz writes:

the mind will be created by God, since it will exist and remain by the will of God, that is, by the will of the good intellect. For to exist is simply to be understood to be good. Existence is stated equivocally of bodies and of our mind. We sense or perceive that we exist; when we say that bodies exist, we mean that there exist certain consistent sensations, having a particular constant cause. Just as 3 is one thing, and 1,1,1 is another – for 3 is 1+1+1. In such a way, the form of 3 is different from all its parts; so creatures differ from God, who is all things. Creatures are certain things.
                                                      (A VI.iii 512: Pk* 65f.)

We noted in section 1 that Leibniz describes his papers of the period as "poorly expressed vestiges of hasty reflections" (A VI.iii 533), and his essays of March/April, 1676 are surely obscure. But large sections of these texts are rendered transparent once we see them as describing a world in which each substance expresses the essence of God from its own perspective and does so *because* of its production rule (Cf. A VI.iii 508f.: Pk 57ff.; 514: Pk 69; and esp. 588: Pk 113).[44] For example, once we realize that the missing "single cause" in "On Truth, the Mind, God, and the Universe" is the essence of God and once we grasp that the notion of rule employed there is that of a production rule for the activity of mind (the instantiation of that essence in a single substance), we are able to make out the full significance of the text. In short, once we understand that the notes of March/April, 1676 assume the production rule, we can discern the doctrine of preestablished harmony.

Other texts offer further evidence for the acceptance of claims (2) and (3). In an essay of December, 1676 Leibniz maintains: "We have no idea of existence, other than that we understand things to be sensed. . . . Without sentient beings, nothing [in the created world] would exist. Without one primary sentient being, which is the same as the cause of all things, nothing would be sensed" (A VI.iii 588: Pk 113). We sense things not because there are external objects acting on us, but because God has given each mind a "certain rule." It is because of this rule that there is a reason for everything and everything can be predicted.

We have already noted that in "On Truth, the Mind, God, and the Universe" Leibniz proposes that there is a rule that "several people sense the same, and sense consistently." In the same work he talks about the coherence "among minds" (A VI.iii 512: Pk 67). The implication is that the states of substances correspond perfectly because each state of an individual substance is caused by something internal to its nature and because those internal natures have been coordinated. Leibniz makes this point explicit in the same essay in which he first presents his definition of a rule. He writes: "if we were perfectly knowing, i.e., if we were gods, we would easily see that those things which, because of our ignorance, now appear to exist at the same time by accident, co-exist by their very nature, i.e., by the necessity of the divine intellect" (A VI.iii 484: Pk 41).

Nor should we be surprised that Leibniz develops his doctrine of preestablished harmony during this period: in a fairly straightforward way it follows from the second conception of substance, the PSR, and the PCS when the latter is extended to all substantial properties. As we noted earlier, there is a tension between the PSR and PCS. The unresolved problem of the pre-Paris years was whether or not to extend the PCS to all substantial properties or only some (say, the essential ones). Leibniz's production rule for the activities of mind gave him a way to extend the PCS to all substantial properties and his desire for harmony demanded that the activities of created minds be harmonized so as to reflect God's goodness. The result is a world of substances whose self-sufficient natures extend to all their properties, both essential and accidental.

In 1676, Leibniz also managed to solve another problem left over from his pre-Paris years. His solution constitutes another important advancement in his thought; and it offers further evidence of his acceptance of preestablished harmony. As noted at the beginning of this section, there is an epistemological asymmetry between a cause and its effect in his original metaphysical principles. While the principles suggest that a thorough understanding of a property p would require significant knowledge of the substantial nature to which p belongs (or at least the part of that nature that caused p), Leibniz is silent on this matter. He breaks this awkward silence in April, 1676 when he first begins to claim that "[a]n effect is conceived through its cause" (A VI.iii 514: Pk 71). Nor should Leibniz's sudden interest in the epistemological connection between an effect and its cause come as a surprise: given his Logical and Intelligibility Assumptions, his newly developed production rule for the activities of minds entails that the necessary and sufficient conditions of any state (or effect) of a substance S would exist in S and in theory be intelligible.

Leibniz argues at length for just this sort of relation between a substance and its states in one of the most important essays of the period. He begins "A Meditation on the Principle of the Individual" of 1 April 1676 by writing: "We say that the effect involves its cause; that is, in such a way that whoever understands some effect perfectly will also arrive at knowledge of its cause. For it is necessary that there is a certain connection between a complete cause and the effect" (A VI.iii 490: Pk* 51). Leibniz then poses an apparent counterexample to this theory: in some cases "different causes can produce an effect that is perfectly the same." His immediate response to this potential problem is important. He denies that there could ever be such a case and claims that "we are certain, from some other source, that the effect does involve its cause," and therefore that "it is necessary that the method of production must always be discernible" in the effect.[45] It is "impossible" that two effects could be perfectly similar "for they will consist of matter" which "will have a mind" such that "the mind will retain the effect of its former state." He does not explain what this "other source" of certainty is, but attempts to demonstrate his claim by means of a *reductio ad absurdum*. He argues that if any two individuals were perfectly similar, three unacceptable conclusions would result: "the effect would not involve its cause"; "the principle of individuation" would be "outside the thing, in its cause"; and "one individual would not differ from another in itself." It is important that Leibniz does not feel the need to explain why these results are absurd. He seems to have taken their untenability to be obvious. And of course it is obvious given his newly developed ideas: since each mind has its own production rule of the sort articulated above and since harmonious plenitude requires that each substance expresses God's essence from its *own* perspective, it follows that each substance has its own *distinct* production rule. That is, because a rule would make each substance distinct from every other, the principle of individuation of the substance would have to be in the thing itself and because no two rules could be the same, no two individuals could be the same either.

So far so good. But how exactly does the effect involve its cause? Leibniz continues his discussion:

But if we admit that two different things always differ in themselves in some respect as well, it follows that there is present in any matter something that retains the effect of what precedes it, namely, a mind. And from this it is also proved that the effect involves the cause. For it is true of it that it was produced by such a cause; therefore right up to the present there is in it a quality of such a kind as to bring this about, and this quality . . . has about it something that is real. It is evident what great consequences follow from such little premises.   (A VI.iii 491: Pk 51)

Great consequences indeed: the effect involves its cause because, for any effect, it is caused by the mind in the substance from which it results and that mind not only has traces of all it has done, it has a quality that acts as the real cause of that effect. If we understand this quality to be conjoined with a production rule, then it would seem to follow, as Leibniz put it at the first of the essay, that "the effect involves its cause . . . in such a way that whoever understands some effect perfectly will also arrive at knowledge of its cause." But what is it one knows when one knows the cause? Our notion of a production rule reveals Leibniz's point: since a complete cause includes the necessary and sufficient conditions of an effect, through a perfect understanding of the effect one would acquire knowledge of at least the previous state of the substance and the relevant part of the production rule. That is, for some effect or state q of a substance S, a perfect understanding of $q+1$ would lead to knowledge of q and the part of the production rule that would entail $q+1$ given q. One of the "great consequences" of Leibniz's essay is that it assumes something quite like our notion of a production rule in an attempt to show that every effect involves its cause. Moreover, an effect would not involve its cause in the way Leibniz's argument demands, if claims (1) and (3) were not both assumed.

We propose that Leibniz's sudden desire to show that "whoever understands some effect perfectly will also arrive at the knowledge of its cause" grew out of his newly evolved conception of a production rule. Once Leibniz had decided upon the latter and decided that substances do not causally interact, he was free to reform the epistemological asymmetry of his original principles. Before an effect could lead back to its cause, there had to be only one way to produce an effect. Or, to put it another way, once Leibniz decided to extend the PCS to all the properties of a substance (i.e., once he came to accept claims (1) and (3)), it would follow that an effect could be produced in only one way and hence that every effect would have to be "conceived through its cause."[46]

We are now prepared to return to a point we made in section 3.3 about plenitude and the original version of the principle of the identity of indiscernibles, which first appears in "A Meditation on the Principle of the Individual." We suggested there that Leibniz's desire for both substantial and pictorial fecundity may have been part of the motivation behind the development of that principle. We can now see that the principle constitutes one of the fundamental assumptions of the essay. Leibniz assumes from the outset that no two individuals can be exactly similar. It would seem that once Leibniz had developed the idea of a production rule, he had a neat way of making each individual distinct: each substance has its own unique "instrument of action."

But there was another important result of Leibniz's newly evolved preestablished harmony. In the winter and spring of 1676, Leibniz was making great strides in the development of his views about the activities of mind. He was not as successful on the topic of matter. In an essay of March, 1676 he poses a number of problems for which he does not have answers.[47] One of the most pressing of these concerns the precise relation between body and mind. According to Leibniz: "As mind is something which has a certain relation to some portion of matter, then it must be stated why it extends itself to this portion and not to all adjacent portions; or why it is that some body, and not every body, belongs to it in the same way" (A VI.iii 392: Pk 45). It was not until late 1676 that we find a solution to this problem. His solution, which constitutes an important development in Leibniz's views about body, might well have been inspired by the development of his original version of preestablished harmony, especially claims (1) and (2). For the first time Leibniz makes a distinction between bodies as aggregates and bodies as elements. He writes: "Every body which is an aggregate can be destroyed. There seem to be elements, i.e., indestructible bodies, because there is a mind in them" (A VI.iii 521: Pk 81). Atoms are "the fundamental elements" out of which "cohering bodies arise" so that "all things come from" them (A VI.iii 585: Pk 109). In other words, there are bodies whose parts are separable and bodies whose parts are not; the latter make up the former (A VI.iii 473f.: Pk 23f.). One of the most explicit statements of this position appears in December 1676. Leibniz writes:

A substance or complete Being is for me that which alone involves all things, or for the perfect understanding of which, no other thing needs to be understood. A figure [figura] is not of this kind, for in order to understand from what a figure [figura] of such and such a kind has arisen, there must be a recourse to motion. Each complete being can be produced in only one way: that figures [figurae] can be produced in various ways is enough to indicate that they are not complete Beings.   (A VI.iii 400: Pk* 115)[48]

Once Leibniz has conceived of the minds in corporeal substances as capable of perceiving and sensing everything else in the world in a harmonized fashion, it is not difficult to think of a collection of such atoms forming an aggregate among themselves. Such an entity would not be a substance, but would be formed of substances; and, as a collection of atoms, it could be produced in any number of ways. It would not be a complete being itself because it would not have its own principle of activity to which it owed its being; rather it would owe its being to the activity of the minds in the atoms which make it up.

A final point to make about the evolution of Leibniz's thought during 1672–76 is that the materials are in place for the development of his complete concept theory of substance. According to that theory, *S* is an individual substance just in case its concept contains all and only the concepts of those properties that may be attributed to it. According to Leibniz in the quotation above, "[a] substance or complete Being is for me that which alone involves everything, or for the perfect understanding of which, no other thing needs to be understood" (A VI.iii 400: Pk 115). Such a position would follow fairly straightforwardly from Leibniz's notion of a production rule for the activities of minds: to understand perfectly the production rule would be to understand "everything" about the substance. As we shall now see, it would not take Leibniz long to characterize substance as that which has a complete concept.

4 1679 TO THE *DISCOURSE ON METAPHYSICS*

In April, 1679 Leibniz formulated an original series of logical systems for testing formal validity (C42–92). It is in these papers that Leibniz put front and center the concept containment account of truth, which he then presented as the source of his metaphysics of individual substance in *The Discourse on Metaphysics*, and the subsequent correspondence with Antoine Arnauld. Indeed, the systems developed in the April, 1679 papers are all based on the concept containment account of truth, i.e., put somewhat loosely, the thesis that an affirmative categorical proposition is true just in case the concept of its predicate is contained in the concept of its subject. In the second of the papers in the series Leibniz said as much.

> In order to make evident the use of characteristic numbers in propositions it must be considered that every true categorical affirmative universal proposition signifies nothing other than some connection between predicate and subject (in the non-oblique case, which is always meant here), so that the predicate is said to be in the subject, or contained in the subject, either absolutely and regarded in itself, or at any rate in some instance, i.e., the subject is said to contain the predicate in the fashion stated. That is to say that the concept of the subject, either in itself or with some addition, involves the concept of the predicate.   (C 51: PLP 18–19)

Note that in this passage Leibniz began with a version of the concept containment account of truth restricted to universal propositions. But in the closing sentence of the passage, with the phrase "or with some addition," Leibniz prepared the way for a generalization of the concept containment account of truth to all categorical affirmative propositions. Leibniz's logical papers from this period make it plausible to ascribe to him the view that an adequate theory of truth for categorical affirmative propositions will settle the truth conditions for all propositions. Hence, although a full statement of Leibniz's concept containment account of truth would be quite complex, the idea that truth is a matter of relations among concepts is surely its basis.

Numerous problems arise for the student of Leibniz by virtue of ascribing the concept containment account of truth to him, including these two crucial questions: (1) what tempted him to accept it, and (2) what did he take to be its relevance for his metaphysics of substance? The first question is surely burning, since the concept containment account of truth seems to imply that a proposition is true just in case it is conceptually true, and, hence, to imply that a proposition is true just in case it is necessarily true. Yet we know from a number of papers written during our time period that Leibniz rejected the thesis that if a proposition is true then it is necessarily true.[49] So why on earth did Leibniz accept an account of truth that, as he himself noted, exacerbates the problem of establishing that there are contingent truths? In his seminal work, *La Logique de Leibniz*, Couturat suggested that Leibniz saw the concept containment account of truth as a consequence of the principle of sufficient reason, a thesis that he took as an axiom in his system.[50] Fabrizio Mondadori has recommended an alternative account, again utilizing the bedrock character of the principle of sufficient reason in Leibniz's system. His idea is this: the fact is that given Leibniz's sharpest characterizations of the truth definition and the principle of sufficient reason, the latter is a consequence of the former. Hence, Mondadori suggests, Leibniz accepted the former because it has the latter as a consequence.[51]

There is a lot to be said for these efforts, especially Mondadori's subtle account. We want to recommend consideration of an alternate strategy in which the concept containment of truth is viewed as motivated, at least in part, by what Leibniz considered to be its consequences for the metaphysics of individual substances. It is well to have a number of alternative explanations for Leibniz's intellectual motivations for accepting the concept containment account of truth, since all answers to our first question seem underdetermined by the textual evidence currently available. And there is no reason to expect the discovery of a "smoking gun" text on this matter; here we have a question that probably will not receive a definitive answer.

Let us look at the second question. Paragraphs 8 and 9 of the *Discourse on Metaphysics* surely suggest this answer: Leibniz claimed that the concept containment account of truth, when applied to singular propositions, has the consequence that the concept of an individual substance is complete, i.e., "is sufficient . . . to allow the deduction from it of all the predicates of the subject to which this concept is attributed." And in Paragraph 9 Leibniz seems to have claimed that the thesis that an entity is an individual substance if and only if its concept is complete has the following weighty metaphysical consequences: the identity of indiscernibles, the thesis that substances begin only by creation and perish only by annihilation, and the thesis that each substance expresses every other and, hence, is quasi-omniscient and quasi-omnipotent since each substance perceives every other and is such that every other substance accommodates, in some measure, to it.

When we examine relations among the concept containment account of truth, the complete concept theory of individual substance, and various Leibnizian theses about individual substances (including those just noted from *Discourse* 9), the conclusion just has to be that matters are vastly more complicated than Leibniz's easy prose in these paragraphs would suggest and that versions of the deep metaphysical principles unearthed in section 1.2 are at work once again. Indeed, we suggest that the following description of Leibniz's reasoning provides at least as plausible an account as does the more traditional one limned above. First, we propose that the original metaphysical principles conjoined with the decision to extend the PSS and PCS to all substantial properties entails that each of a substance's properties is related to it in such fashion as to imply that the concept of an individual substance is complete. We then note that this result makes plausible the claim that the concept containment account of truth holds for affirmative categorical singular propositions whose singular subject terms refer to individual substances. Next we note that in the traditions in which Leibniz worked "individual substance" was code for a basic individual in one's ontology, so that once truth conditions were set for affirmative categorical singular propositions whose singular subject terms refer to individual substance, truth conditions are set for propositions of the same variety about individuals, basic or nonbasic. The general structure of Leibniz's proposal for extending the truth definition may be gleaned from the April 1679 logical papers previously noted.

Various authors have attempted explanations of Leibniz's reasoning along lines similar to those just recommended.[52] It is not our purpose here to offer the details of such an explanation, but rather to note Leibniz's use of the deep metaphysical principles in formulating and refining his ideas about individual substances in the seminal period from the April, 1679 logic papers through *The Discourse on Metaphysics* and the ensuing correspondence with Antoine Arnauld. It is in this period that Leibniz solidified his thinking concerning the intension of the term "individual substance," characterizing it in terms of his various metaphysical theses about the nature of complete entities. Among the relevant metaphysical theses are these: where S is an individual substance, Leibniz held in this period that S remains genuinely numerically the same over time; each state of S contains traces of all that S has been and marks of all that S will be (the doctrine of marks and traces); the identity of indiscernibles holds of S; each state of S, other than its initial state and any of its states caused miraculously, is caused by preceding states of S (the doctrine of spontaneity); S is incorruptible and ingenerable; S expresses the entire universe; S is indivisible; and S has true, substantial unity.[53]

While Leibniz was confident in the time period under consideration that an entity must satisfy the conditions just noted in order to be an individual substance, a complete entity, i.e., a basic individual, he was less secure than he was to become about what sorts of entities satisfy those conditions. We know that his final position is that only monads satisfy all the requisite conditions; we know that in our period he held that only entities with substantial forms satisfy all the requisite conditions. A disputed question is whether he held in our period that there are extended entities informed by substantial forms that satisfy all the requisite conditions, which are basic individual entities. In part, resolution of this question of interpretation turns on obtaining proper perspective on Leibniz's attitude toward the attribute of extension in the time period under consideration.[54]

Leibniz's early metaphysical writings are brilliant and original, indeed, idiosyncratic. In his metaphysical writings in the period from 1679 through 1686, Leibniz made a genuine effort to connect his views with traditional metaphysical offerings. In particular, he emphasized a connection he envisaged between his own idiosyncratic principles concerning individual substances, and the traditional notion that, in order to be a genuine individual substance, an entity must possess strict numerical identity over time. In a piece entitled "*De Mundo Praesenti*," contained in the *Vorausedition*, but otherwise unpublished, Leibniz provided a taxonomy of the kinds of being he was prepared to discuss, first distinguishing between real and imaginary beings, and then, within the class of real beings, between beings *per se*, and beings *per accidens*, arguing that beings through aggregation are instances of beings *per accidens*, and that in order to reach the level of a being *per se*, an individual must possess a substantial form (LH IV 7 C Bl 111–14; VE 416–23). These ideas are repeated in numerous places in *The Discourse on Metaphysics* and the correspondence with Arnauld. They are connected with the requirement of strict numerical identity over time in the important paper "Notationes Generales," part of which was published by Grua, all of which is contained in the

Vorausedition (Gr 322–34; VE 184–90). There Leibniz took a human person as a paradigm of an individual substance – a being *per
se*, and an army as a paradigm of a nonbasic individual – a being *per
accidens*. He wrote:

It is worth investigating in what way a being through aggregation, such as
an army or even a disorganized multitude of men, is one; and in what way
its unity and reality differ from the unity and reality of a man. . . . The
chief point is this: an army accurately considered is not the same thing
even for a moment, for it has nothing real in itself that does not result
from the reality of the parts from which it is aggregated; and since its
entire nature consists in number, figure, appearance and similar things,
when these change it is not the same thing, but the human soul has its
own special reality so that it can not come to an end by any change in the
parts of the body.
    A thing can remain the same, even if it is changed, if it follows from its
own nature that one and the same thing must have diverse, successive
states. Without doubt, I am said to be the same as he who was before
because my substance involves all my states, past, present and future.
                                                    (Gr 323; VE 188–89).

In this passage Leibniz not only affirmed the metaphysical principle that an entity is an individual substance only if its properties
are a consequence of its nature, but he connected the latter requirement with the traditional requirement that an entity is an individual substance only if it remains numerically identical over time in
the strictest sense. Thus, in this passage Leibniz affirmed the conjunction of the Principle of Self-sufficiency and the Principle of
Substantial Self-sufficiency and connected their conjunction with
strict numerical identity.[55] In a number of texts in our time period
Leibniz made use of these ideas without explicitly affirming them
in order to argue that an entity whose essence is extension and
which, therefore, lacks a substantial form, cannot satisfy the conditions requisite to being an individual substance. Thus, contemplat-
ing the supposition that the essence of body is extension, Leibniz
wrote in paragraph 12 of *The Discourse on Metaphysics:* "if there
were no other principle of identity in bodies than what we have
just said, a body would never subsist more than a moment." While
amplifying on the point made in this passage, Leibniz wrote the
following in a letter to Arnauld: "Extension is an attribute that can
not make up a complete entity: no action or change can be deduced

from it – it expresses only a present state, not at all the future and past as the concept of a substance must do" (G II 72: MP 86). Here Leibniz claimed that any individual whose essence is extension will not satisfy the doctrine of marks and traces and, hence, will not be a substance. It is presupposed that any entity that lacks an internal principle of activity is no substance and that possession of an internal principle of activity of sufficient complexity to satisfy the doctrine of marks and traces and the doctrine of spontaneity yields an individual substance. These are but articulations of the ideas implicit in PSA.

Suppose we put aside problems generated by God's miraculous intervention and formulate the doctrine of spontaneity as follows: if x is an individual substance, then for any noninitial state S of x, there is some state S' of x such that x's being in S' provides a causal explanation for x's being in S. Given this simplified version of the doctrine of spontaneity, we may attribute the following account of substantial persistence to Leibniz, an account which, in the absence of the doctrine of spontaneity, would be unacceptable: finite substance x at t is strictly numerically identical with finite substance y at t' (with t' later than t) just in case some state of x at t is a causal ancestor of some state of y at t'.

We may conclude that much of Leibniz's mature metaphysics of substance consists in an elaboration of the deep metaphysical principles discussed earlier in this essay. Still, it is important not to exaggerate the interpretive progress these conclusions permit. A decent question is this: what induced Leibniz to think that possession of a substantial form by an individual x brought it about that x, unlike some entity whose essence is extension, satisfied the various doctrines and principles that constitute his metaphysics of substance? A tempting answer is that it is a matter of the definition Leibniz employed of the term "substantial form." That answer may be a beginning, but it is no more than that. Leibniz drew conclusions about substances and substantial forms, based on the conception of substantial form standard in the traditions he inherited. It would be important to make sure that the inferences he drew from the tradition are warranted given his own, perhaps idiosyncratic, use of the term.

Note that it is understandable why Leibniz would think that a substantial form itself satisfies the conditions required in order for an entity to be an individual substance. But the texts in our time period suggest that Leibniz seriously considered the thesis that an extended entity with a substantial form may satisfy the relevant conditions and, hence, constitute a substance – a corporeal substance.[56] If we suppose that this is Leibniz's considered view in our period, then an important and difficult problem of interpretation arises: namely, what considerations induced Leibniz to come to a quite different conclusion in the final theory, i.e., the monadology? In Leibniz's final theory the only entities said to satisfy all the conditions required for possessing substantial unity are the monads. In the final theory Leibniz recognized various kinds of entities that may be treated usefully as individuals, although members of that kind do not possess substantial unity. Furthermore, in the final theory Leibniz made room for various levels of approximation toward substantial unity with so-called corporeal substances, for example, offering a closer approximation than mere aggregates thereof.

In our period Leibniz was already committed to many of these ideas. In particular, he recognized the usefulness of treating certain entities as individuals even though they lack the substantial unity required of individual substances. (See letter to Arnauld, 30 April 1687, G II 100–102: MP 126–28.) Furthermore, he was prepared to recognize various levels of approximation to full substantial unity. Moreover, the same candidates were under consideration with essentially the same ordering as in the final theory: "mere aggregates" (e.g., a flock of sheep, a pile of sand), followed by bodies (e.g., a grain of sand), and animate bodies (e.g., a sheep). The difference is that in our period Leibniz gave the appearance of being in a genuine quandary about whether animate bodies satisfy the strictest standards of substantial unity.

One element that is common to the texts from our period and the final theory is Leibniz's commitment to the idea that these non-substantial individuals need not be admitted into one's ontology, not "in metaphysical rigor."[57] In the correspondence with Arnauld, after noting the utility in some cases of treating nonsubstances as individuals, Leibniz concluded:

But one must not let oneself be deceived and make of them so many substances or truly real beings; that is only for those who stop at appearances, or those who make realities out of all the abstractions of the mind. . . . Whereas I maintain that philosophy can not be better established, and reduced to something precise, than by recognizing the only substances or

complete beings endowed with a true unity with their different states following one another. All the rest are nothing but phenomena, abstractions,
or relations. (G II 101: MP 126–27)

Leibniz's way with individuals that do not amount to individual substances in metaphysical rigor is to treat them as logical constructions.
In the passage from "Notationes Generales" previously quoted, employing an army as an example of an aggregate and its soldiers as
examples of substances, Leibniz noted that whatever is true of the
aggregate, the army, may be restated utilizing propositions predicat-
ing properties of its component soldiers. Many of Leibniz's short,
private pieces are exercises in logical construction.

The questions raised in this section are difficult ones. But we
should not lose sight of the fact that the notion of substance employed here is a direct descendent of the metaphysical principles
assumed by Leibniz in the 1660s. We have argued that those original
principles prompted Leibniz to construct a theory of substance in
1670 that provides the framework for his metaphysical investigations through the period of the *Discourse on Metaphysics*. We propose that a closer study of the principles elaborated and a fuller
analysis of the difficult texts surveyed will provide a more complete
picture of Leibniz's mature philosophy. We have made a start here,
but there is plenty of room for progress.

NOTES

1 Mercer is the author of sections 1–3; Sleigh of section 4. Most of the
material of sections 1 and 2 appears in Mercer's Ph.D. thesis "The Origin
and Development of Leibniz's Conception of Substance," Princeton
(1989); section 3 is derived from a much expanded version of that work
entitled *Leibniz's Metaphysics: Its Origins and Development*. The
notes in the present chapter are truncated. For further argumentation
and citation in support of the material presented in secs. 1–3, see Mercer's book. For a more detailed account of the metaphysics of the *Discourse on Metaphysics* and some of the issues of sec. 4, see Sleigh,
Leibniz and Arnauld: A Commentary on Their Correspondence. We
have greatly benefited from advice and criticism offered by Daniel
Garber, Stephen Grover, Daniel Fouke, Nicholas Jolley, Ohad Nachtomy,
and Donald Rutherford.
2 There has been little scholarly work done on the 1660s. The most
complete studies remain Kabitz, *Die Philosophie des jungen Leibniz,*

and Hannequin, "La Première Philosophie de Leibnitz." For recent
work that is helpful on some details, see Belaval, *Leibniz: Initiation à
sa philosophie;* Moll, *Der junge Leibniz,* Vol. I & II; Garber, "Motion
and Metaphysics in the Young Leibniz," pp. 160–84; Robinet, *Architectonique disjonctive automates systémiques et idéalité transcend-
antale dans l'oeuvre de G.W. Leibniz,* 3.1–4.6; Catherine Wilson, *Leibniz's Metaphysics: A Historical and Comparative Study,* pp. 7–58;
Fouke, "Metaphysics and the Eucharist in the Early Leibniz."

3 For one of the most explicit, relatively early statements of Leibniz's
conception of the close connections among metaphysics, "Natural Theology," and "the mysteries of the faith," see A VI.iii 155ff; W 58ff. This
provocative essay dates from 1673–75 and not the mid-1680s as Wiener
claims. See A VI.iii 154. One recent scholar who has been concerned to
explore the relationship between Leibniz's theological interests and his
metaphysical development is Daniel C. Fouke whose excellent papers
shed light on these and other important topics. See his "Metaphysics
and the Eucharist," "Dynamics and Transubstantiation in Leibniz's *Systema Theologicum,*" "Spontaneity and the Generation of Rational Beings in Leibniz's Theory of Biological Reproduction."

4 The nature and significance of humanism has been much discussed. For
the most important recent discussions and references to the vast literature
on humanism and the humanists, see Grafton, *Defenders of the Text: The
Tradition of Scholarship in an Age of Science, 1450–1800; The Transmission of Culture in Early Modern Europe,* eds., Grafton and Blair; and *The
Impact of Humanism on Western Europe,* eds., Goodman and Mackay.

5 *Philosophia Eclectica* (Altdorf, 1686). Sturm's works were widely read.
Leibniz refers to them throughout his life (e.g., A VI.i 186 and G IV 399,
504), although he does not refer specifically to *Philosophia eclectica.* For a
discussion of the role and use of Aristotle by Protestant German philosophers, see Bohatec, *Die cartesianische Scholastik in der Philosophie und
reformierten Dogmatik des 17. Jahrhunderts;* Wundt, *Die Philosophie an
der Universitaet Jena* and *Die Deutsche Schulmetaphysik des 17.
Jahrhunderts;* and Petersen, *Geschichte der aristotelischen Philosophie
im protestantischen Deutschland.*

6 Motivated by the ground-breaking work of Charles Schmitt, there has
recently been a re-evaluation of the role of Aristotelianism in the early
modern period. See Schmitt, *Aristotle and the Renaissance* and his *John
Case and Aristotelianism in Renaissance England;* Brockliss, *French
Higher Education in the Seventeenth and Eighteenth Centuries* and
"Aristotle, Descartes, and the new Science: Natural Philosophy at the
University of Paris, 1600–1740," 33–69; and Mercer, "The Vitality and
Importance of Early Modern Aristotelianism."

7 For a discussion of the eclectic Aristotelians who had the greatest influence on Leibniz, see Mercer, "The Seventeenth-Century Debate between the Moderns and the Aristotelians: Leibniz and *Philosophia Reformata.*"

8 For some of Leibniz's most explicit accounts of his method, both early and late, see A VI.iii 155ff: W 58ff.; G III 606: L 654; GM VI 234ff.: AG 118ff., L 435ff.; G VII 127ff. For Leibniz's early commitment to the philosophy of Aristotle, see A II.i 57, L 107; A II.i 64; A VI.i 85; and esp. A VI.ii 434f.: L 94f. Mercer discusses the method in greater detail in her "Mechanizing Aristotle."

9 An asterisk (*) indicates a deviation from the translation cited.

10 See also A II.i 22, A II.i 10, and especially A VI.i 489ff: L 109ff. When Leibniz argues against the Moderns, he has standard mechanists like Hobbes, Descartes, and Gassendi in mind. When he claims that most of the philosophy of Aristotle is "certain and demonstrated" (A II.i 15: L 94), he has in mind his own eclectic brand of Aristotelianism, which can comfortably accommodate heavy doses of Platonism, about which we will say more below.

11 The PS first appears in 1668 (A VI.i 490: L 110). Loemker is mistaken about the date of the *Confession of Nature against the Atheists:* it was written in 1668 and not 1669.

12 The PSS first occurs in 1668 (A VI.i 508: L 115).

13 The PCS first appears in 1668 (A VI.i 492: L 112) and is first explicitly stated in 1669 (A II.i 23: L 101–2). During the late 1660s, the scope of the PS, PSS, and PCS appears to extend only to essential properties. By 1676, it has been extended to all properties. See sec. 3.4.

14 The PSA first appears in 1668 (A VI ii 508: L 115) but occurs frequently thereafter. It is most often used as the core of a definition of substance, but it is also combined with the PSS in discussions about the characteristics of substance.

15 The PSR is used in 1668 (A VI.i 492: L 112), but its first explicit statement occurs in the winter of 1668–69 (A VI.i 494). Leibniz's first demonstration of it appears in the winter of 1671–72; see A VI.ii 483.

16 The notion of complete reason is used in several places (A VI.i 95; A VI.i 176: L 80; A II.i 117: L 146), but its first appearance in an essay of metaphysical importance occurs in 1668 (A VI.ii 490f.: L 111). Its first explicit formulation, where it is presented as the necessary and sufficient conditions for a thing, occurs in a note written in the winter of 1671–72 (A VI.ii 483).

17 For example, Gassendi writes in 1658: "It may be supposed that individual atoms received from God . . . the force [*vis*] requisite for moving, [and for] imparting motions to others. . . . All this to the degree that he

foresaw what would be necessary for every purpose . . . he had destined them for." See Bush, *The Selected Works of Pierre Gassendi*, pp. 400–401. Descartes is also clear about the original source of motion (although the precise relation between God and the motion of a body at a particular time is less easy to discern). He writes, for example, in the *Principles of Philosophy*, "God is the primary cause of motion. . . . Thus, God imparted various motions to the parts of matter when he first created them, and he now preserves all this matter in the same way, and by the same process by which he originally created it." See *The Philosophical Writings of Descartes*, trans., Cottingham, Stoothoff, Murdoch, Vol. I, p. 240. It is important to note that Hobbes is the exception. Unlike the other standard mechanical philosophers, he seems to think that motion does not need an immaterial cause.

18 Aristotle's notion of principle (the Greek is *archē*, the Latin translation for it became *principium*) has been much discussed. Suffice it to say here that a principle is the origin or source of something; a principle of activity therefore is the origin or source of activity. This sense of the term persisted throughout the early modern period, but is obviously different from what we think of as a principle today: a sort of basic truth or law. For a helpful introduction to the notion of principle and some related issues in Aristotle, see Witt, *Substance and Essence in Aristotle: An Interpretation of Metaphysics VII–IX*, pp. 15–19; for an excellent discussion of the notion among medieval philosophers, see Gracia, *Introduction to the Problem of Individuation in the Early Middle Ages*, p. 37, *passim*.

19 One feature of the theological essays which makes them so difficult is their imprecise terminology. Especially in the essays of 1668, Leibniz obscures the distinction between matter and body by often using "corpus" to refer to each. The distinction is however discernible, especially at A VI.i 502ff. and A II.i 10f.

20 It follows from the PSA that insofar as mind is a source of activity it is itself a substance, i.e., it follows that mind is both a substance and a constituent of the substance that it creates with body *qua* matter. We will say more about this in sec. 3.2. It is worth noting that, in the theological writings of 1668–69, Leibniz uses both "substantial form" and "mind" to designate the incorporeal principle or active element in substance, often in the same essay. See for instance A VI.i 508–12: L 115ff.

21 This is not occasionalism, but a kind of Platonized Aristotelianism in which God sustains the corporeal nature (by activating its matter through an Idea) so that the nature is able to act as the efficient cause of motion in other bodies (A VI.ii 511–12: L* 118). For further discussion of these details, see Mercer's forthcoming book. For a fascinating discus-

sion of neo-Platonic elements in the account that Leibniz and other scholastic philosophers (e.g., Aquinas) give of God's relation to the created world, see Fouke, "Emanation and the Perfection of Being: Divine Causation and the Autonomy of Nature in Leibniz."

22 In 1668 Leibniz gives both his first systematic argument against the mechanists (A VI.i 489ff.: L 109ff.) and his first presentation of his original conception of substance (A II.i 10f.).

23 Leibniz was especially concerned to treat satisfactorily "the mystery of the Eucharist," a topic on which he wrote a number of papers in connection with the "Catholic Demonstrations." See A VI.i 501ff. For an interesting discussion of the importance which the problem of the Eucharist had for early Leibniz, see Fouke, "Metaphysics and the Eucharist."

24 For someone in search of such a principle in the seventeenth century, the most obvious candidates were mind, soul, and substantial form (as some Aristotelians had defined it). Leibniz uses all three terms to designate the incorporeal principle in substances, though he favors "mind" (*mens*) in the theological essays.

25 There are four important changes which Leibniz makes to the published version of his April, 1669 letter to Thomasius. Compare (1) A II.i 20, line 34 with A VI.ii 440, line 20; (2) A II.i 22, line 24 with A VI.ii 442, line 5; (3) A II.i 23, line 32 with A VI.ii 443, line 18; and (4) A II.i 23–24 with A VI.ii 443, line 19. In his edition of Leibniz's 1670 letter (VI, pp. 162–74) Gerhardt's list of changes is significantly incomplete. Garber mentions change (3) in his "Motion and Metaphysics in the Young Leibniz," p. 171. For a commentary on this letter, which includes an analysis of the changes, see Mercer, *Leibniz's Metaphysics.*

26 He also gave himself a more dramatic way of demonstrating the immortality of the soul: given that "mind consists in a point" and that "a point is indivisible and therefore cannot be destroyed," it follows that the mind or soul is immortal (A II.i 113). He presents this argument throughout the period.

27 The notion of cause here is obscure. That there is a causal relation between the mind and the matter is obvious; what is not obvious is how exactly to conceive that relation. The most likely causal model is the neo-Platonic *influxus* one. For an excellent discussion of this model in the seventeenth century, see O'Neill, "Influxus Physicus," pp. 27–55. For further details about Leibniz's notion of intrasubstantial causation in his philosophical development, see Mercer's forthcoming book.

28 For a good introduction to the difficulties and tensions in the philosophy of the *Discourse* and for a survey of the literature about them, see C. Wilson, *Leibniz's Metaphysics,* chapter III.

29 Leibniz arrived in Paris in March, 1672 and left in October, 1676. Between early 1673 and late 1675, Leibniz applied most of his energies to mathematics; nearly all of his philosophical work falls on either side of this period.

30 None of the relatively few studies of the Paris years has recognized its full importance. For the most helpful recent work see Catherine Wilson, *Leibniz's Metaphysics*, chapter II; Fouke, "Leibniz's Opposition to Cartesian Bodies during the Paris Period (1672–76)"; Parkinson, "Introduction," *De Summa Rerum* and "Leibniz's *De Summa Rerum*: A Systematic Approach," pp. 132–51; Kulstad, "Causation and Preestablished Harmony in the Early Development of Leibniz's Philosophy"; pp. 93–117. Wilson and Kulstad include references to the preceding literature.

31 Between 1668 and 1676 there is no mention of any disembodied incorporeal substances other than God. Cf. A VI.iii 74; 518: Pk 76.

32 A mind is the source of the individuation of a substance in that it renders the substance the individual it is; it is the source of the identity of a substance in that it makes the substance the same thing over time. The distinction, often blurred in contemporary discussions, has been important in the history of philosophy. For an excellent discussion of these and related topics, see Gracia, *Introduction to the Problem of Individuation in the Early Middle Ages*, chapter 1.

33 According to Leibniz, nonhuman substances exist from the creation of the world and never cease to be. Human substances, on the other hand, are created by God in the course of the world, but then exist eternally.

34 The doctrine of expression as it appears in the mature philosophy is notoriously difficult to articulate. There has been a good deal of discussion in the literature both about what exactly the doctrine is and what motivated it. See, e.g., Mates, *Philosophy of Leibniz*, pp. 37ff; Sleigh, *Leibniz and Arnauld*, pp. 170ff; Kulstad, "Causation and Preestablished Harmony," pp. 93ff. We address only the latter topic here and side-step the former altogether.

35 Leibniz compares a mind to a mirror in some of his pre-Paris notes, but he does not develop the image. See, e.g., A VI.i 438; 464; 482.

36 Although scholars agree that Leibniz's doctrines of expression and preestablished harmony stand at the center of the metaphysics of the *Discourse*, there has been a good deal of disagreement about when the doctrines first emerge, about what might have motivated their development, and about their interrelation. The earliest date that has been given for the emergence of either is 1678–79 and most commentators have placed their development at the time of the *Discourse*. For a summary and analysis of the most important secondary literature on these topics, see Kulstad, "Causation and Preestablished Harmony, pp. 93–117.

37 In his pre-Paris papers, Leibniz refers to the harmony among substances, but he does not develop the notion. See A II.i 79, 174; A VI.i 492: L 112; A VI.ii 283.

38 Scholars have noted Leibniz's many references to Plato, and a few French scholars have argued convincingly for Platonic elements in Leibniz's thought, but there has not yet been a careful study of this difficult topic. For a helpful bibliography and an excellent introduction to Platonic elements in Leibniz's conception of the relation between God and creation, see Fouke, "Emanation and the Perfection of Being."

39 Just before departing for Paris, Leibniz claims that a requisite is a necessary condition and "all the requisites are the sufficient reason" for the existence of a thing (A VI.ii 483).

40 For the arithmetical analogy, see A VI.iii 512: Pk 67; 523: Pk 83. For the town analogy, see A VI.iii 573: Pk 95; A VI.iii 523: Pk 83. Leibniz soon ceases to use the former analogy, but uses the latter in some of his most important later works. See, e.g., *Discourse* par.9; G IV 434: AG 42; *Monadology*, par. 57, G VI 616: AG 220; *First Truths*, C 521: AG 33, L 269. Note that previous datings of the latter paper have been incorrect: the editors of the Akademie edition assign this much discussed text to 1689. See *Vorausedition*, Faszikel 8, p. 1998.

41 The development of this interpretation of Leibniz's production rule for the activities of mind was much aided by discussions with Ohad Nachtomy. For more details about how the production rule works, see Mercer's book.

42 Scholars have often wondered about the precise relationship between the philosophy of Spinoza and that of Leibniz. There are striking resemblances and it has been proposed that the former influenced the latter. It is a consequence of our interpretation that the philosophy of the *Ethics* could have had no extensive influence on the development of preestablished harmony and the related doctrines articulated in sec. 4 since Leibniz neither saw a copy of the *Ethics* nor talked with its author about it until November, 1676. However, Leibniz had been made aware of some of Spinoza's doctrines earlier in that year. See A VI.iii 380, 384f; A VI.iii 580; A VI.iii 510: Pk 61; A II.i 304. For some recent literature on this topic, see Catherine Wilson, *Leibniz's Metaphysics*, pp. 69, 85ff.; Kulstad, "Causation and Pre-established Harmony," pp. 110ff.

43 We saw in sec. 3.2 that, according to Leibniz, minds cannot act except through the matter to which they are attached and hence that the only active things in the created world are corporeal substances. Therefore, Leibniz's denial that "we act on them" and that "they act on us" is an explicit denial of intersubstantial causality.

44 It is not surprising that most of the commentators who have considered these passages have attributed to Leibniz a form of scepticism. See Brown *Leibniz*, pp. 39ff.; Catherine Wilson *Leibniz's Metaphysics*, pp. 66ff.

45 We assume that this would not be true of aggregates of substances since an aggregate is not strictly an individual. For a discussion of the development of Leibniz's view of aggregates, see below.

46 Late in 1676 (after his meeting with Spinoza) Leibniz pushed the relation between cause and effect a bit further and developed a principle that became important to his work on physics. In December, 1676 he writes: "*There is nothing without a cause*, because there is nothing without all the requisites for existing. *The entire effect is equipollent to the full cause*, since there must be some equality between cause and effect, passing from one to the other" (A VI.iii 584: Pk 107). In the same month he explains more precisely what he means: "the cause is equipollent to the effect not in perfection but in expression" (A VI.iii 584: Pk 109). For the importance of this principle to Leibniz's physics, see Garber (this volume), sec I.

47 By far the most important of these was the problem of the continuum: "One must unravel, with the greatest rigour, the entire labyrinth concerning the composition of the continuum" (A VI.iii 475: Pk 27). Leibniz wrote a dialogue on this and related issues in the fall of 1676, see A VI.iii 528–71.

48 The Latin word "*figura*" is ambiguous in an important way. It can mean figure or shape, but also nature, kind, or species. When talking about the stuff of which bodies are made, Leibniz employs the latter sense where the idea is that the matter is an organized arrangement that makes up the nature of the body. See A II.i 10f., 18; A VI.i 502.

49 See, for example, "De Libertate," (FC 178–85: P 106–11) written in 1689, in which, Leibniz wrote: "Once I had recognized the contingency of things, I then began to consider what a clear notion of truth would be; for I hoped, not unreasonably, to derive from it some light on the problem of distinguishing necessary from contingent truth." Then, having summarized the concept containment account of truth, he added "But this only seemed to increase the difficulty for if, at a given time, the concept of the predicate is in the concept of the subject, then how, without contradiction and impossibility, can the predicate not be in the subject at that time . . . ?" (FC 179: P107).

50 Couturat, *La Logique de Leibniz*, pp. 208–18.

51 Mondadori, "Reference, Essentialism, and Modality in Leibniz's Metaphysics."

52 See, for example, Adams, "Predication, Truth, and Transworld Identity in Leibniz," pp. 235–83; and Sleigh, *Leibniz and Arnauld*, pp. 126–32.

53 All of these doctrines are to be found in *The Discourse on Metaphysics* and the correspondence with Arnauld. For details, see Sleigh, *Leibniz and Arnauld*, chapter 5.

54 For a brilliant defense of the thesis that in this period Leibniz took extended entities to be basic individual substances, see Garber's seminal essay "Leibniz and the Foundations of Physics: the Middle Years" pp. 27–30. For doubts about Garber's view, see Sleigh, *Leibniz and Arnauld*, pp. 110–15. For doubts about Sleigh's doubts, see Garber's review, *The Journal of Philosophy*, 1992, especially pp. 52–55.

55 Aside from "Notationes Generales" and "De Mundo Praesenti," the following texts from the *Vorausedition* are worth consulting on this matter: "Definitiones," pp. 411–12; and "Mira de natura substantiae corporeae," p. 294.

56 This is particularly true of the Arnauld correspondence, see Garber, op. cit.

57 When Leibniz was about to place his ontological cards on the table he often said that he was speaking "in metaphysico rigore" or "dans la precision metaphysique," or "à la rigueur metaphysique."

5 Metaphysics: The late period

Leibniz's late metaphysics is dominated by his theory of monads, a doctrine that posits that the only fully real beings are unextended, soul-like substances.[1] Since the seventeenth century, this theory has perplexed Leibniz's readers. Not only is the notion of the monad itself – a substance that is in his description "windowless" and "like a world of its own" – hard to fathom, but it is difficult to see how Leibniz means to integrate the doctrine of monads with a plausible account of the nature of matter and with his famous hypothesis of the preestablished harmony of soul and body.

I begin by looking briefly at the relationship of Leibniz's late metaphysics to his earlier thought from the vantage point of his *New System* (I), a transitional work that will also serve to introduce us to the issues most central to his later period. Subsequent sections examine the details of the theory of monads (II), his reduction of matter to monads (III), and the status accorded by his late philosophy to the notions of soul-body union and corporeal substance (IV).

I. THE NEW SYSTEM

The first published statement of Leibniz's mature metaphysics, the *New System of the Nature and Communication of Substances, and of the Union of the Soul and the Body*, appeared in the Paris *Journal des Savants* in June 1695.[2] For Leibniz, this essay marked something of a philosophical coming of age. In its opening paragraph, he recounts how he had conceived his new system some years ago and had communicated its contents to a number of learned men, including Antoine Arnauld.[3] However, he was reluctant at that time to make his views public, either for want of complete confidence in

124

them or for fear of the consequences that might ensue. The course of prudence was to test their reception by a few respected thinkers like Arnauld, and only then to make them available to a wider audience. By 1695, Leibniz evidently felt confident that the time had come. As a result of their correspondence, he reports, Arnauld had dropped his initial objections to the system, accepting some of its propositions and withdrawing his censure of those with which he still disagreed. Now, with some important persons desiring to see his opinions further clarified, Leibniz was prepared to commit his views to print, "even though they are not at all popular, nor able to be appreciated by all sorts of minds" (G IV 477: AG 138).

Leibniz's opening remarks in the *New System*, as well as comments he makes elsewhere, strongly suggest a continuity between its concerns and those of his writings of the 1680s.[4] This conclusion has been challenged, however, regarding his treatment of substance.[5] While Leibniz appears most directly occupied during the 1680s with developing an account of substance that grows out of questions about predication and identity (his so-called "complete concept" theory), such considerations are nowhere to be found in the *New System*. Instead, he begins his discussion by stressing substance's foundational role as a principle of force and of "true unity." It being impossible to explain the laws of nature in terms of extended mass alone, Leibniz argues, it is necessary to introduce a notion of force, "despite the fact that it belongs in the domain of metaphysics" (G IV 478: AG 139). Similarly, the impossibility of finding "the principles of a true unity in matter alone, or in what is merely passive," entails the need for certain "formal atoms," since "a material thing cannot be both material and, at the same time, perfectly indivisible, that is, endowed with a true unity" (G IV 478: AG 139). Leibniz goes on to suggest that the demand for grounding principles of force and unity can only be met by returning to something like the substantial forms of Aristotle and the Scholastics:

Hence, it was necessary to restore, and, as it were, to rehabilitate the *substantial forms* which are in such disrepute today, but in a way that would render them intelligible, and separate the use one should make of them from the abuse that has been made of them. I found then that their nature consists in force, and from this there follows something analogous to sensation and appetite, so that we must conceive of them on the model of the notion we have of *souls*.   (G IV 478–79: AG 139)

Distinguishing his position from that of some Scholastics, Leibniz cautions that such forms are not to be used to explain "the particular details of the economy of the animal's body," or the particular phenomena of nature. The soul-like substances he defends are instead only "true general principles." As "first entelechies" or "primitive forces," they supply nature with an original activity; as indivisible forms, "which can only begin by creation and end by annihilation," they provide the true unities from which all other things must be constituted.

The account of substance that appears in the *New System* is superficially quite different from that of the *Discourse on Metaphysics*, particularly the complete concept theory advanced in §8 of that essay. It is important, however, that we not exaggerate this difference. From the 1680s onward, Leibniz remains committed to a set of basic assumptions about substance. To be a substance is, minimally, to be an individual principle of action, which persists through change and which serves as a ground for the existence and properties of all other things.[6] The latter requirement, which sees substance as an ultimate explanatory principle, implies for Leibniz that whatever is true of a substance must be true in virtue of its own nature, and not the nature of something else. It follows that for something to be a substance it is not enough simply for it to be, as Leibniz stresses in the *New System*, a source of action. It must be a principle of force that it is sufficient to produce all and only those modifications that are predicable of that substance. In Leibniz's terminology, the nature of any substance must be *spontaneous*, or causally self-sufficient, such that it is dependent for the production of its states on no other created being.[7]

This conception of the essential properties of substance is a fixed point in Leibniz's mature metaphysics. This is not to say, however, that he remains wedded to a single way of representing the *individual* natures of substances, i.e., that by which they are determined as this or that substance. During the 1680s, he invests considerable energy in developing the idea of a "complete concept" as an appropriate means of articulating God's knowledge of a substance's individual nature. By the early 1690s, the period following his Italian journey, his enthusiasm for this view has clearly waned. The reason for this change can be traced to his increasing preoccupation with the science of dynamics, a theory devoted to explaining the forces and actions of material things.[8] From the start, Leibniz sees an important connection between this science and his general understanding of substance. Characteristic is a passage from his 1694 essay *On the Improvement of First Philosophy, and on the Notion of Substance:*

I will say for the present that the concept of *forces* or *powers*, which the Germans call *Kraft* and the French *la force*, and for whose explanation I have set up a distinct science of *dynamics*, brings the strongest light to bear on our understanding of the true concept of *substance*. Active force differs from the mere power familiar to the Schools, for the active power or faculty of the Scholastics is nothing but a near possibility of acting, which needs an external excitation or stimulus, as it were, to be transferred into action. Active force, by contrast, contains a certain act or entelechy and is thus midway between the faculty of acting and the act itself and involves conatus. It is thus carried into action by itself and needs no help but only the removal of an impediment. . . . I say that this power of acting inheres in all substance and that some action always arises from it. (G IV 469–70: L 433)

The theory of substance that figures most prominently in Leibniz's post-1690 writings stresses the nature of substance as an entelechy or spontaneous principle of action: not simply a capacity or faculty to act, but that which does act provided that nothing impedes it. As in the *New System*, there is little sign of the complete concept theory.[9]

At the same time that this shift is underway, there appears an idea, not completely new to Leibniz's thought, that effectively supplants the device of a complete concept. This is the notion of a substance's individual "law of the series."[10] Leibniz's insistence on the need for some such principle to determine the individual nature of a substance testifies to the underlying continuity of his concerns. To De Volder, he suggests that "we should seek no other notion of power or force than that it is an attribute from which follows change, whose subject is substance itself" (G II 170). But to say no more than that substance is "the subject of change," he argues, is to give only a "nominal" account of its nature (G II 182: L 520). It may allow us to pick out all and only those beings that are substances, but it does not convey what it is to be an *individual* substance. For this, it is necessary to appeal to the principle that defines the series of its particular modifications and hence makes it *that* substance rather than any other. A substance, therefore, is not simply a being that is active or subject to change: it is a "primitive entelechy . . . whose nature consists in a certain perpetual law of the series of the changes through which it runs unhindered" (G II 171: L 517).[11]

A substance's "law of the series" is conceived by Leibniz as playing much the same theoretical role as is played by a complete concept in his 1680s theory. It offers, however, at least one crucial advantage over the earlier theory. It is arguably a significant weakness of the complete concept theory that it attempts to model the nature of substance, an inherently active being, in a manner that is essentially static. A complete concept is defined as "containing" all that can be predicated of the same subject; yet it gives no hint of the order and causal dependence of the successive states of a substance. What we can surmise is that as the focus of Leibniz's interests began to shift away from the more traditional logical and metaphysical concerns of the 1680s to the project of dynamics, an opportunity arose for him to rethink his treatment of substance. All of the essential features of substance remained in place. What emerged, however, was his explicit recognition that if the nature of substance in general is to be an entelechy or principle of action, then the most appropriate device for representing the individual nature of a substance is not a complete concept, but rather the law of the series of its operations.

Leibniz's emphasis in the *New System* on substance as a true unity also repeats a theme prominent in his earlier writings. In works from the 1680s, he stresses that it is only substance's nature as a form, or spontaneous principle of action, that guarantees its identity through change, and hence makes it truly one. No simple material thing has this property.[12] We likewise find considerable attention paid in the 1680s to the *New System*'s grounding argument for true unities. As Leibniz summarizes his position for Arnauld: "I deduce that many beings do not exist where there is not one that is genuinely one being, and that every multitude presupposes unity" (G II 118: MP 151).[13] Although the notion of substance as a principle of unity thus figures as a constant in Leibniz's thinking from the 1680s onward, some change can be observed in his opinion concerning what sorts of things count as true unities. In the Arnauld correspondence, it is plausible to read him as defending the existence of "quasi-Aristotelian" corporeal substances, as well as immaterial substances – souls and soul-like forms.[14] According to the view he develops there, the unities presupposed by the existence of bodies are themselves corporeal beings: composites formed from an organic body and an immaterial substantial form.[15] By the time he composes the *New System*, Leibniz appears to have rejected this position. He instead holds that the only true unities are soul-like forms and that any multitude presupposes these for its existence:

> Only metaphysical points or points of substance (constituted by forms or souls) are exact and real, and without them there would be nothing real, since without true unities there would be no multitude.
>
> (G IV 483: AG 142)

While some changes do occur in Leibniz's view of substance between the 1680s and the *New System*, our overall impression is one of continuity. Throughout this period, he remains committed to the thesis that to be a substance is to be a spontaneous principle of action, which persists through change and is a true unity. The most significant development in his position is undoubtedly his increasing confidence in the idea that the only entities that answer to this description are immaterial souls or forms.

As important as the opening sections of the *New System* are for our understanding of Leibniz's conception of substance, the essay is best known for its exposition of his novel solution to the Cartesian problem of soul-body communication. Descartes himself, Leibniz argues, had simply given up on this problem, limited as he was to conceiving how two completely distinct substances, *res cogitans* and *res extensa*, might nonetheless exert a mutual influence on one another. In response to this puzzle, post-Cartesian philosophers such as Malebranche turned to the "system of occasional causes," thereby relegating all causal power to God, who initiates sensations in the soul on the occasion of motions in matter and movements of the body on the occasion of volitions of the will. To the extent that it denies a real causal influence of one created substance on another, Leibniz is sympathetic to the occasionalist position. Nevertheless, he remains unsatisfied with occasionalism's insistence that God alone is the source of all causal activity in the world:

> It is quite true that, speaking with metaphysical rigor, there is no real influence of one created substance on another, and that all things, with all their reality, are continually produced by the power of God. But in solving problems it is not sufficient to make use of the general cause and to invoke what is called a *Deus ex machina*. For when one does that without giving any other explanation derived from the order of secondary causes, it is, properly speaking, having recourse to miracle. (G IV 483: AG 143)[16]

In meditating on the impossibility of one created substance affecting another, Leibniz recalls, he was finally led to a position that incorporated this occasionalist insight while at the same time preserving the activity of substance. This theory, his "hypothesis of agreement" or "preestablished harmony," maintains that "God originally created the soul (or any other real unity) in such a way that everything must arise for it from its own depths, through a perfect *spontaneity* relative to itself, and yet with a perfect *conformity* relative to external things" (G IV 484: AG 143).

In the *New System*, Leibniz advances the doctrine of preestablished harmony as a consequence of his general understanding of substance.[17] It is in the first place substance's nature as a self-sufficient principle of action that supports the claim that the soul is responsible for producing all its own states, with no need of influence from the body. The second idea integral to Leibniz's theory is that every substance naturally "expresses" or "represents" everything that occurs within the world, with the result that there is an immediate correlation between its states and those of all external things:

Every substance represent[s] the whole universe exactly and in its own way, from a certain point of view, and . . . the perceptions or expressions of external things occur in the soul at a given time, in virtue of its own laws, as if in a world apart, and as if there existed only God and itself. (G IV 484: AG 143)[18]

This picture of the universe as composed of an infinity of independent soul-like substances, each of which mirrors in its activity the states of all the rest, has its roots in some of Leibniz's earliest philosophical reading.[19] A major development of his mature works is his elaboration of this picture through a recognition of the special role played by the soul-body relationship. In his later writings, the soul is depicted not simply as a substance that is naturally expressive of the universe, but as one that expresses the universe from the "point of view" of its associated organic body. The latter, in turn, is itself conceived by Leibniz as acting in a spontaneous manner, in accordance with the mechanical laws of motion.[20] The result is a harmony in which the soul perceives itself as acting through its organic body and as being affected by those things that affect its body, although no real interaction occurs between the two.

Leibniz's *New System* raises one further issue that resonates through his later writings. Both the title and text of the essay advance the theory of preestablished harmony as an explanation not only of the apparent communication of the soul and the body, but also of their *union*, or of why it is reasonable to think of the soul and its body as together forming one entity: a single human being, plant, or animal. Repeating an account sketched in the *Discourse on Metaphysics*, Leibniz suggests that a soul can be regarded as united to a particular organic body to the extent that it expresses most distinctly the operations of that body, i.e., that it perceives itself as having a presence in that body and as interacting with other bodies through the instrumentality of that body. The union of the soul and the body thus consists of nothing more than the fact that the perceptions of the soul occur in a perfect harmony with the states of its body.[21]

It is difficult to say how much Leibniz thought he could conclude from this rather modest account of soul-body union – whether in particular he felt that such an account was sufficient to support the thesis that the soul and its body together form an *unum per se* or corporeal substance. There is evidence that during the 1680s he was inclined to believe that this was in fact the case. In the Arnauld correspondence, he claims that the soul is "the form of its body because it is an expression of the phenomena of all other bodies in accordance with their relation to its own" (G II 58: MP 65–66), and that such a form is capable of bestowing a "substantial unity" on what is otherwise only an *unum per accidens* (G II 76: MP 94) or "unity of aggregation" (G II 100: MP 125).[22] This does not, however, seem to be his view in the *New System*. What we find there is instead an open admission that the only true unities are unextended, soul-like forms. To be sure, Leibniz continues to speak in this work of "corporeal substances," by which he means creatures composed of a soul or soul-like form and an organic body; and he even goes so far as to maintain that it is not just the soul "but the animal itself and its organic machine" that is conserved through all change, including the appearance of death (G IV 481: AG 141). However, there is no indication that he regards such soul-body composites as full-fledged substances. His position, fairly clearly, is that a soul or soul-like form, which is a true unity, unites the plurality that is its organic body simply by representing that plurality of things as a single entity that is subordinated to it.[23] As we shall see, at least by the standards of his later philosophy, such a union cannot suffice to transform a plurality of distinct things into a true unity. Consequently, while Leibniz maintains that nature has the appearance of being everywhere composed of organic creatures enveloped within organic creatures, his deepest metaphysics holds that these creatures, too, are ultimately the product of soullike substances alone.

II. THE THEORY OF MONADS

Leibniz's theory of monads is in all essential respects consistent with the account of substance advanced in the *New System*. For several reasons, however, it warrants a separate treatment here. First, the doctrine of monads is the culmination of Leibniz's thinking about substance. Once he has settled on his definition of a monad, his views about substance remain fixed until his death.[24] Second, as it is developed in late texts such as the *Monadology* and the *Principles of Nature and of Grace*, the doctrine of monads amounts to a more precise and systematic presentation of Leibniz's conception of substance than he had previously achieved. In no earlier writings does he exhibit so clearly the relationship between the different components of his theory. Finally, the doctrine of monads provides the basis for a powerful reductionist metaphysics that Leibniz asserts with increasing surety during the early 1700s. Having arrived at a stable conception of substances as monads, he comes to defend forcefully the view that reality consists solely of monads and that all other beings are merely "results" of them.

Leibniz's fullest exposition of the properties of monads is contained in the essay entitled *Monadology*.[25] In §1 of that work he defines a monad as "nothing but a simple substance that enters into composites – simple, that is, without parts" (G VI 607: AG 213). Simplicity is demanded of monads, since without simples there would be no composites; composites, by their very nature, are nothing but "collections" or "aggregates" of simples (§2, ibid.).[26] However, in order to qualify as genuine simples, monads must be without parts, and hence without extension, shape or divisibility (§3, ibid.).[27] From this initial definition, Leibniz draws two important consequences. First, a monad is subject to neither generation nor corruption. Insofar as it lacks parts, "there is no conceivable way in which a simple substance can perish naturally" (§4, ibid.), and no way in which it "can begin naturally, since it cannot be formed by composition" (§5, ibid.). Instead, a monad can only begin by creation and end by annihilation (§6, ibid.). Second, there is no conceivable way in which one monad can be affected by another:

There is . . . no way of explaining how a monad can be altered or changed internally by some other creature, since one cannot transpose anything in it, nor can one conceive of any internal motion that can be excited, directed, augmented, or diminished within it, as can be done in composites, where there can be change among the parts. (§7, G VI 607: AG 213–14)[28]

Although monads are by definition "simple," in the sense of lacking parts, Leibniz insists that such simplicity is consistent with their having internal complexity, in the form of a multitude of simultaneous modifications.[29] Indeed, he holds that it is necessary that monads be distinguished in this way. As the "true atoms" of nature (§3, G VI 607: AG 213), monads must provide a ground for the qualitative differences observed in composite things. They must therefore possess at least some qualities, for if there were no differences among monads "one state of things would be indistinguishable from another" (§8, G VI 608: AG 214). Leibniz, however, draws an even stronger conclusion than this. It follows from the principle of the identity of indiscernibles not simply that there must be some differences among monads, but that "each monad must be different from every other. For there are no two things in nature that are perfectly alike, two beings in which it is not possible to discover an internal difference, that is, one founded on an intrinsic denomination" (§9, ibid.). It is thus ruled out that any two monads could in principle share all their modifications.

In §10 of the *Monadology*, Leibniz offers it as an axiom that "every created being, and consequently the created monad as well, is subject to change," and "that this change is continual in each thing." On the basis of the points already established, he infers that a "monad's natural changes come from an *internal principle*, since no external cause can influence it internally" (§11, ibid.); and that "besides the principle of change, there must be *diversity in that which changes*, which produces, so to speak, the specification and variety of simple substances" (§12, ibid.). These conclusions set the stage for his description of the modifications of monads. Taking the second point first, he argues that "there must be a plurality of affections and relations in the simple substance, although it has no parts" (§13, ibid.). These he identifies with a monad's "perceptions":

The passing state which involves and represents a multitude in the unity or in the simple substance is nothing other than what one calls *perception*.
(§14, ibid.)

Subsequently, he designates a monad's "appetition" as the "action of the internal principle which brings about the change or passage from one affect to another" (§15, G VI 609: AG 215). Together, these two types of modification – perceptions and appetitions – exhaust the intrinsic properties of monads:

This is all one can find in simple substance – that is, perceptions and their changes. It is also in this alone that all the *internal actions* of simple substances can consist.
(§17, ibid.)

This completes Leibniz's preliminary account of monads. Any simple substance or monad, he claims, is a principle of action. Its state at any moment is defined in terms of "a plurality of affections and relations," which are its perceptions; and these affections and relations are subject to continual change, as a consequence of its appetitions – the tendencies of its states to proceed towards new perceptions. While this theory is on the face of it clear enough, a number of complexities emerge when we examine it more closely.

We may begin with a monad's perceptions. Conceived in themselves, perceptions are nothing more than the plurality of modifications that constitute the state of a simple substance at a given moment. In addition to their status as modifications of substance, however, such perceptions also possess a certain content. According to Leibniz, "perception is nothing other than the representation of external variation in internal variation" (G VII 329–30).[30] Thus, the modifications that he identifies with a monad's perceptions must include some reference to external things. It is here that we find the significance of his claim that there exists a plurality of affections *and* relations within any monad. When Leibniz says that there is a plurality of relations within any monad what he seems to mean by this is that there are within any monad perceptual states that involve a representation of the relatedness of that monad to the other monads in its world.[31]

In order to understand this point, we must turn briefly to Leibniz's

account of intermonadic relations. As a condition of their belonging
to a single world, he argues, all created beings are united by a certain
"connection."[32] In a late study, he suggests that this connection is
the product of three types of intermonadic relations: relations of
position [situs], relations of duration [duratio], and relations of intercourse [commercio] or reciprocal action (G II 438: AG 199). The first
two of these determine what he calls the "order of coexistence" and
the "order of succession," or space and time. For the moment, we
shall restrict our attention to these; later we shall return to monadic
relations of intercourse.

It is well known that Leibniz denies that monads are in any literal
sense located within space or time.[33] He nonetheless maintains that
analogues of spatiotemporal relations are predicable of monads. In
general, for any two monads that belong to the same world, it must
be possible to locate their actions relative to one another within a
common spatiotemporal framework.[34] Such relations are designated
by what he calls "extrinsic denominations."[35] Now, notoriously,
Leibniz also asserts that there exist no *purely* extrinsic denominations, on account of the "real connection" or "universal sympathy"
of all things.[36] There has been much debate as to how this claim is to
be interpreted.[37] For our purposes, we may sidestep this controversy
and turn directly to one of Leibniz's most informative statements on
this topic. Our text is a short essay that Parkinson has dated ca.
1696. It begins with a general statement of the "no purely extrinsic
denominations" thesis:

A consideration which is of the greatest importance in all philosophy, and in
theology itself, is this: that there are no purely extrinsic denominations,
because of the interconnection of things, and that it is not possible for two
things to differ from one another in respect of place and time alone, but that
it is always necessary that there shall be some other internal difference.

(C 8: P 133)

According to Leibniz, spatial and temporal position (place and time)
are "mere results, which do not constitute any intrinsic denomination *per se*," but instead "demand a foundation derived from the
category of quality, that is, from an intrinsic accidental denomination" (C 9: P 134). In this text, the crux of the no purely extrinsic
denominations thesis emerges as the claim that, while genuine, the
connection of monads within a world is not an irreducible fact about

them, but merely a result of their "intrinsic accidental denominations." These intrinsic accidents are subsequently identified as states of the monad that have the property of expressing its position vis-à-vis the positions of other monads:

To be in a place seems, abstractly at any rate, to imply nothing but position. But in actuality, that which has a place must express place in itself; so that distance and the degree of distance involves also a degree of expressing in the thing itself a remote thing, either of affecting it or of receiving an affection from it. So, in fact, position [situs] really involves a degree of expression.

(C 9: P 133)[38]

The doctrine that Leibniz advances here affirms that to be conceived as connected within a world monads must possess accidents that have a relational content: accidents that express the spatiotemporal relatedness of that monad with respect to the other things in its world. Thus, monads' being, as it were, spatiotemporally related is derivative from their *expressing* themselves as standing in spatiotemporal relations.[39]

A full explanation of this last claim – that a monad is capable of expressing its spatiotemporal relatedness to the other monads in its world – requires the introduction of one further thesis. Until the end of his life, Leibniz defends the view that no monad ever exists completely detached from an organic body.[40] As we shall see, the ontological status of these bodies remains problematic. On one interpretation, they are nothing more than phenomenal entities, or what a soul-like substance perceives as its body. Nevertheless, Leibniz argues that monads can only be conceived as related to one another, via the orders of space and time, if we assume that each is endowed with its own organic body.[41] Given this, we can say that each monad expresses the universe as a whole insofar as it represents itself as located in a body that is situated vis-à-vis the body of every other monad:

Since every organic body is affected by the entire universe through relations which are determinate with respect to each part of the universe, it is not surprising that the soul, which represents to itself the rest in accordance with the relations of its body, is a kind of mirror of the universe, which represents the rest in accordance with (so to speak) its point of view – just as the same city presents, to a person who looks at it from various sides, projections which are quite different.

(C 15: P 176)

Under this scheme, a space-like order of coexistence is determined among monads via the apparent spatial relations of their bodies. While monads are not themselves extended, Leibniz writes,

They nevertheless have a certain kind of position [*situs*] in extension, that is, they have a certain ordered relation of coexistence with others, through the machine which they control. I do not think that any finite substances exist apart from every body, or, therefore, that they lack a position or an order relative to the other things coexisting in the universe.

(G II 253: L 531)[42]

Although it has not often been remarked, there is a close connection between Leibniz's theory of monads and his doctrine of the preestablished harmony of soul and body. It would not be going too far to suggest that the latter doctrine, which maintains that the soul naturally represents itself as acting in concert with an organic body, supplies the basis for his general account of intermonadic relations. We may summarize this account as follows. As a condition of their belonging to a single world, relations of connection must be predicable of monads. These intermonadic relations are not, in Leibniz's view, irreducible facts about monads, but rather "results" of their intrinsic accidents, in particular, perceptions which express their relatedness to the other monads in their world. This expression is made possible by a monad's representation of itself as an embodied creature that stands in spatiotemporal and causal relations to every other body in the universe, and hence to every body that is represented by another monad as *its* body. While there remain gaps to be filled in this picture, we can see it as a remarkable attempt on Leibniz's part to merge intuitions about the independence and spontaneity of monads with the assumption that they together make up one world.[43]

In his descriptions of the properties of monads, Leibniz often distinguishes, as we have seen, two different kinds of modification: perceptions and appetitions. At times, however, he appears to suggest that monads in fact possess only one type of modification, perceptions, which themselves include an inherent tendency towards new perceptions. In his reply to the second edition of Bayle's *Dictionary*, he writes:

The soul ... though entirely indivisible, involves a composite tendency, that is a multitude of present thoughts, each of which tends to a particular change according to what it involves and what is found in it at the time by virtue of its essential relationship to all the other things in the world.

(G IV 562: L 579)

Whether we regard appetitions as modifications in their own right or merely as properties of perceptions, Leibniz makes it clear that two different types of intrinsic denomination are required in order to specify fully the state of a monad: denominations that designate both "a power of transition and that to which the transition is made" (C 9: P 134). Thus, we can at least distinguish conceptually the perceptions of a monad, which are individuated in terms of their content or what they represent, and the tendency of those perceptions to give way to new perceptions. For Leibniz, this latter "appetition" or "endeavor" is an intrinsic feature of any monadic state. He conceives of it on analogy with the *conatus* of a moving body. While motion is expressed in a body's path through space during a finite interval of time, conatus is expressed in its momentary tendency to move in a certain direction. Monadic appetition is thus to be thought of not as the actual change that occurs in a monad, but as the tendency of a given perception to give way to a new perception. As in the case of perceptions themselves, the state of any monad at a given time is characterized by an infinity of such appetitions. The result of their action is the continual progression of the monad to new perceptions.[44]

Although every monad is by nature a principle of change, insofar as its states naturally tend towards new states, in the strictest sense change itself is not an intrinsic denomination of monads. It is instead merely an aggregate or "result" of two contradictory states of a monad. So understood, monadic changes can be divided into two types. A monad's *actions* are those changes by which it passes from a less perfect state to a more (or equally) perfect state; its *passions* are those changes by which it passes from a more perfect state to a less perfect state.[45] In each case, the degree of perfection of a monad's state is defined in terms of the relative distinctness of its perceptions, or its proportion of distinct to confused perceptions.[46] Thus, a monad can be said to "act" insofar as its perceptions are becoming more distinct, and to "suffer" insofar as they are becoming more confused:

If we take "action" to be an endeavor toward perfection, and "passion" to be the opposite, then genuine substances are active only when their perceptions . . . are becoming better developed and more distinct, just as they are passive only when their perceptions are becoming more confused.

(*New Essays* II, xxi, 72; A VI.vi: RB 210)[47]

We observed earlier that Leibniz includes relations of "intercourse" as one of the basic types of intermonadic relation. Given his insistence on the absence of any interaction among monads, it is at first glance puzzling that he should do so. When we examine what he means by this intercourse, however, the puzzle quickly dissolves. While there is a clear sense for him in which every monad is "the true immediate cause of all its internal actions and passions" (G VI 354: H 362), Leibniz also holds that there is a sense in which a monad may be thought of as acting or suffering with respect to other monads. As he describes his view in the *Monadology* (§§49–52, G VI 615: AG 219–20), one monad may be thought of as "acting" on another insofar as it is more perfect than the latter, or, what is equivalent, insofar as there are found in it distinct perceptions that explain a priori what happens in the latter. Conversely, one monad "suffers" with respect to another insofar as the latter's distinct perceptions provide an *a priori* explanation for the change that occurs within it. Putting these two ideas together, we find that within any world there is a complex "reciprocity" between the perceptual states of every monad and those of every other:

Actions and passions among creatures are mutual. For God, comparing two simple substances, finds in each reasons that require him to adjust the other to it; and consequently, what is active in some respects is passive from another point of view: *active* insofar as what is known distinctly in one serves to explain what happens in another; and *passive* insofar as the reason for what happens in one is found in what is known distinctly in another.

(G VI 615: AG 219–20)

The explanation Leibniz offers of the intercourse of monads is of a piece with his account of monads' spatiotemporal relations. In both cases, we are to see these intermonadic relations as supervening on the intrinsic accidents of individual monads: whether one monad "acts" on another is determined entirely by correlations among their respective perceptions.

In Leibniz's view, every created monad is subject to both actions and passions. As such, it must be regarded as possessing both a "primitive active power," its entelechy or principle of force, and a "primitive passive power," its "primary matter."[48] In a sense, therefore, a monad can be characterized as a hylomorphic substance, or a composite of form and matter. It is important, though, that we not be misled by this description. Under no circumstances should we think of monads as material substances. Leibniz, on the contrary, explicitly describes them as "incorporeal automata":

> One can call all simple substances or created monads "entelechies," for they have in themselves a certain perfection; they have a sufficiency that makes them the sources of their internal actions, and, so to speak, incorporeal automata.   (§18, G VI 609–10: AG 215)

The identification of monads with entelechies, the principles of action which Leibniz elsewhere designates as "forms," makes it clear that monads themselves are not corporeal substances. They are instead soul-like beings, which unite with an organic body to form an organism or living creature.[49]

If this is so, however, the question of the source of the passivity of monads, or their "primary matter," becomes especially pressing. Leibniz characteristically associates this aspect of a monad's nature with its resistance to change and with its confused perceptions:

> As monads are subject to passions (excepting the primitive one [God]), they are not pure forces; they are the foundation not only of actions, but also of resistances or passivities [passibilités], and their passions are in confused perceptions.   (G III 636)

But how, we must ask, are the confused perceptions of a monad specifically linked with its resistance to change and with its tendency to suffer or to pass from more perfect to less perfect states? The resolution of this problem requires that we distinguish two different senses in which a monad can be said to "act." As an entelechy or spontaneous source of change, a monad acts continuously to produce whatever changes occur in its own states:

> Anything which occurs in what is strictly speaking a substance must be a case of "action" in the metaphysically rigorous sense of something which occurs in the substance spontaneously, arising out of its own depths; for no created substance can have an influence upon any other, so that everything comes to a substance from itself (though ultimately from God).
> (New Essays II, xxi, 72; A VI.vi: RB 210)

According to Leibniz, any changes that occur in the states of a monad are entirely the product of its own appetitions, or the momentary tendencies of its states to give way to new states; and every such appetition can be regarded as a modification of the intrinsic force or primitive active power of that monad. While any change within the state of a monad thus results from the same source – the exercise of monadic appetition – we can nonetheless distinguish between those changes that terminate in states of increased perfection (a monad's actions) and those that terminate in states of decreased perfection (its passions). Whether the total appetition of a monad at a given moment results in an action or a passion will be determined by its corresponding resistance to change at that moment, i.e., its primary matter or confused perceptions.

We can best understand how this resistance arises by appealing to Leibniz's basic model of action (both human and divine) as the joint product of wisdom and volition. For Leibniz, will or appetite is naturally good: it tends toward any end in proportion to its apparent degree of goodness. What impedes the attainment of the good is thus not the character of an agent's will but its associated degree of wisdom: its capacity to assess the relative goodness of competing ends.[50] With this, we can clarify the respective roles played by primitive active force and primary matter in the operations of a monad. A monad is conceived by Leibniz as a combination of volitional and cognitive elements – of a faculty of appetite and a faculty of perception. By nature a monad is a spontaneous principle of action, which tends toward change unless it is in some way impeded; and it tends toward change in accordance with the law of final causes, i.e., it aims to attain the greatest possible good.[51]

To the extent that a monad is impeded in its striving for states of greater perfection, it must itself be the source of the impediment. Leibniz rejects the influence of any finite substance on another, and he is committed to denying that God is in any way responsible for what is passive or limited in created beings. The only explanation for the resistance to the progressive strivings of a monad, then, is that monad's limited apprehension of the good towards which its appetitions are directed. This limited apprehension is the product of its confused perceptions, which are identified by Leibniz with the primary matter or passive power of the monad.

Before concluding this section, a few words must be said about the divisions Leibniz recognizes within the class of monads. To the extent that it exemplifies the properties of unity, activity, and perception, a monad is essentially soul-like. In §19 of the *Monadology*, Leibniz suggests that in a sense it might be proper even to identify monads with souls:

If we wish to call *soul* everything that has *perceptions* and *appetitions* in the general sense I have just explained, then all simple substances or created monads can be called souls.   (GVI 610: AG 215)

He retreats from this conclusion, however, in the interest of distinguishing between three different grades of monads based on the relative quality of their faculty of perception. Leibniz assumes that all monads at every moment are endowed with an infinity of *petites perceptions*.[52] As a condition of its being in a world in which "all is connected," every monad must possess modifications that express its relatedness to everything else in the infinite universe. We know, however, that not even the most elevated created monads are aware of their relatedness to everything else. It follows, then, that the majority of a monad's perceptions must be unconscious ones. At any moment, only a fraction of them become sufficiently distinct for the monad to be aware of them.[53]

Leibniz regards monads as varying greatly in the degree to which their perceptions are distinct, or admit of discernible differences. At the lowest level in the hierarchy of monads are those substances that possess the basic properties of perception and appetition, but whose perceptions themselves have no appreciable degree of distinctness. For such simple monads, there is no sensory awareness and no self-conscious reflection on the contents of their perceptions. Their mental life is identified with the quality of our own "when we faint or when we are overwhelmed by a deep, dreamless sleep" (§20, G VI 610: AG 215). At the stage above this one, Leibniz locates "souls": substances whose perceptions are more distinct, sufficient for the purposes of sensation, and accompanied by memory (§19, ibid.). He assigns souls of this sort to animals and judges that they provide them with the ability to reason "like an Empiric," i.e., according to the lessons of experience and habit (§§26–28, G VI 611: AG 216–17). The highest level of monads, finally, is composed of "spirits" or "rational minds," which are distinguished from the souls of animals by their knowledge of necessary truths, acquired through reflection on the nature of their own minds:

In thinking of ourselves, we think of being, of substance, of the simple and of the composite, of the immaterial and of God himself, by conceiving that that which is limited in us is limitless in him. And these reflective acts furnish the principal objects of our reasonings.   (§30, G VI 612: AG 217)[54]

While a variety of pressures push Leibniz in the direction of claiming that there are sharp divisions to be drawn between simple monads and animal souls, on the one hand, and animal souls and rational minds, on the other, it is doubtful whether his metaphysics can support such divisions. It is a fundamental tenet of the latter that whatever differences are claimed to exist among monads, it must be possible to conceive of the powers of higher monads as emerging through a gradual incrementation of those of lower monads, and indeed of the lowest bare monads.[55] Where this seems least plausible is in the case of the distinctive capacity for self-reflection and rational thought that Leibniz assigns to human minds.

III. THE REALITY OF MATTER

Leibniz's late writings defend the thesis that, at the deepest level, the created world is composed solely of monads and their individual modifications.[56] On this account, material things do not form part of his fundamental ontology. Their existence is, instead, to be explained in terms of the existence and properties of monads alone. Yet how exactly such an explanation might work remains one of the most difficult problems in the interpretation of Leibniz's philosophy. At various times Leibniz refers to bodies as "well-founded phenomena," as "results" of monads, and as "aggregates" of monads. Initially, at least, it is unclear how we are to understand these expressions and whether they all point towards the same theory of matter.[57]

Prompted by Leibniz's statements that reality consists solely of monads and their perceptions, many commentators have read him as propounding a version of phenomenalism. By this they have typically meant that for Leibniz bodies are nothing over and above the harmonious perceptions of monads, or that all truths about bodies are reducible to truths about the perceptions of monads. This interpretation is supported by considerable textual evidence. Representative is a much quoted passage from a letter to De Volder of 30 June 1704:

> Considering the matter carefully, it may be said that there is nothing in the world except simple substances and, in them, perception and appetite. Matter and motion, however, are not so much substances or things [res], as they are the phenomena of percipient beings, whose reality is located in the harmony of the percipient with himself (at different times) and with other percipient beings.   (G II 270: L 537)[58]

In attempting to assess the strength of Leibniz's commitment to phenomenalism, we may pass over the question of whether we find in his writings even the seeds of a modern phenomenalist reduction of body. Consistent with the usage of most authors, I shall take "phenomenalism" to refer simply to that view of matter according to which the reality of bodies is to be explained solely in terms of the agreement or harmony among the phenomena perceived by different monads.[59] If Leibniz is committed to a version of phenomenalism, he must believe that the content of a monad's perceptions corresponds to no external reality. Although such perceptions appear to indicate the existence of mind-independent entities, they are in truth *mere* phenomena, indistinguishable from dreams or illusions save for the fact that they cohere in a law-like manner and harmonize with the perceptions of other monads.[60] Such a view might seem a natural consequence of Leibniz's assertion that the only real beings are soul-like monads. However, it is important to see that it is not the only option available to him. While embracing the doctrine of monads, he might simultaneously defend a nonphenomenalistic account of matter by arguing that veridical perceptions of bodies are, indeed, grounded in a mind-independent reality – namely, that of other monads. Thus, he might claim that a monad's perceptions of bodies do not merely agree with the perceptions of other monads; in addition, there is a way of understanding the content of those perceptions that reveals them to be the appearances of other soul-like substances.[61]

Leibniz's sympathy for this sort of position can be discerned in his letter to De Volder of 30 June 1704. On the basis of the passage already quoted, it has been argued that this letter offers decisive proof of his movement towards phenomenalism.[62] This claim, however, must be squared with the fact that the rest of the letter suggests a very different view of the reality of matter. Leibniz begins his letter by reviewing an argument offered in a previous letter for the claim that substantial unities "are in" (insunt) bodies. He criticizes De Volder for misinterpreting the position he had defended there:

You actually substitute a conclusion different from mine, which I do not understand how you wish to infer from what I say, namely the proposition that from this "it is rightly concluded that indivisible unities cannot be designated in the matter of bodies." But I think that the contrary follows, namely that in corporeal matter, or in the things constituting corporeal things, we must return to indivisible unities as though to primary constituents [prima constitutiva].   (G II 267)

Leibniz's designation of the "primary constituents" of bodies as "indivisible unities" makes it clear that these are to be understood as monads. He arrives at the conclusion that monads "are in" bodies by a version of his grounding argument: because of its division ad infinitum, matter is essentially a multitude of things; whatever is a multitude must be constituted from true unities; the only true unities are monads; hence, bodies must be constituted from monads.[63] Elaborating on the relation between matter and monads, he continues:

And granted that these divisions [of matter] proceed to infinity, they are nonetheless all the results of fixed primary constituents or real unities, though infinite in number. Accurately speaking, however, matter is not composed of these constitutive unities but results from them, since matter or extended mass is nothing but a phenomenon grounded [fundatum] in things, like a rainbow or a mock-sun, and all reality belongs only to unities. . . . Substantial unities are in fact not parts but foundations [fundamenta] of phenomena.   (G II 268: L 536)

Leibniz maintains that monads are not the spatial parts of bodies, but that bodies "result" from monads and that monads are the reality in which the phenomenon of matter is "grounded." These remarks suggest a decidedly nonphenomenalistic view of matter. They imply that bodies are not simply the content of the harmonious perceptions of monads, but also the appearances of a mind-independent reality of other substances.

This account is further developed in Leibniz's remarks to De Volder on the correct analysis of physical concepts. The extension of matter, he writes,

expresses nothing but a certain nonsuccessive . . . but simultaneous diffusion or repetition of some particular nature, or what amounts to the same thing, a multitude of things of this same nature which exist together with some order between them. . . . But this nature which is said to be diffused, repeated, and continued is that which constitutes a physical body, and it can be found in no other principle but that of acting and enduring, since no other principle is suggested to us by the phenomena.   (G II 269: L 536)

According to Leibniz, a complete analysis of the concept of matter shows that bodies are to be understood as constituted from a multitude of things having the nature of a "principle of acting and enduring." This is supported both by the analysis of the notion of an extended thing (as in the above passage) and by the analysis of the notion of physical force, since a principle of action and passion is presupposed as the foundation [fundamentum] of the phenomenal derivative forces exerted by bodies in motion (G II 269–70: L 537). Again, it is reasonable to conclude that the reality represented in corporeal phenomena is that of a plurality of external monads.[64]

Commentators who have acknowledged Leibniz's commitment to the position that bodies are phenomena which are grounded in monads have generally tried to make sense of it in terms of a thesis about monadic perception. According to them, when Leibniz says that bodies are "well-founded phenomena," he means simply that certain monads give the appearance of being extended bodies when "misperceived" (or confusedly perceived) by other monads.[65] Yet this approach fails to account for what is arguably the most significant feature of Leibniz's position: his intention to identify bodies ontologically with pluralities of monads. His method of establishing the well-foundedness of matter via an analysis of the content of corporeal phenomena indicates that he is, in fact, advancing a thesis about the essence of matter, or what it is to be a material thing. His claim is that certain properties of bodies could only exist under the condition that material things are pluralities of monads. Thus, the appearances of bodies are confused representations of other monads for Leibniz, but these representations are not so confused that they are not amenable to further analysis. In his view, such an analysis is sufficient to demonstrate that bodies are, despite their appearances, constituted from monads.[66]

If this is correct, then Leibniz defends a position that is at odds with the doctrine of phenomenalism. Bodies are not, as the phenomenalist interpretation maintains, simply the way things appear to monads, but are in reality pluralities of other monads. It remains, however, to reconcile this reading with the passage quoted earlier, in which Leibniz asserts to De Volder that matter is a phenomenon whose reality is "located in" the harmony of monadic perceivers. Against the interpretation I have advanced, this text would seem to suggest that bodies are appearances that harmonize or agree with the perceptions of other monads but that do not themselves refer to any external reality. One response to this apparent tension in Leibniz's position would be to say that he is just not very careful about his terminology and that he equivocates on the meaning of key terms like "reality." The drawback of this move, however, is that it leaves us on the verge of ascribing a deep, and rather obvious, incoherence to his late writings. We are left to conclude that he simply has two incompatible accounts of the reality of body and that he advances them simultaneously.[67] In order to avoid this conclusion, we require some further explanation of why Leibniz might have thought it harmless (and even defensible) to employ in tandem two different notions of the reality of matter: one that explains the reality of bodies in terms of their being pluralities of monads, the other that locates their reality in the agreement among the phenomena perceived by monads.

For this, we must look more closely at Leibniz's technical notions of "result" and "well-founded phenomenon," and their relation to his view, expressed elsewhere, that bodies are "aggregates" or "collections" of monads. That he sees a close connection between these terms is unquestionable:

We can therefore conclude that a mass of matter is not truly a substance, that its unity is only ideal, and that (leaving the understanding aside) it is only an aggregate, a collection, a multitude of an infinity of true substances, a well-founded phenomenon. (G VII 564)

Many authors have been reluctant to accept that Leibniz actually holds that bodies are aggregates *of* monads, as opposed to aggregates which *result* from monads – a claim that avoids any hint of bodies being spatial collections of monads.[68] Although references to bodies as "results" probably occur more frequently in his later writings, numerous texts, including the one just quoted, demonstrate that he also advances the stronger thesis.[69] Moreover, there is reason to think that these two expressions are closely linked in meaning. In a 1703 letter to De Volder, Leibniz makes it clear that in his terminology an aggregate of substances is a "result" of a plurality of individuals, whose unity as a composite is determined by the mind:

And so when it is asked what we understand by the word "substance," I warn that above all aggregates should be excluded. For an aggregate is nothing other than all those things taken at the same time from which it results, [i.e., those things] which surely have their union from the mind alone on account of what they have in common, like a flock of sheep.   (G II 256)

Besides establishing a firm link between the notions of aggregate and result, this passage suggests a close relation between these notions and Leibniz's conception of a phenomenon. In general, he applies the label "phenomenon" to any "being through aggregation" (*ens per aggregationem*), for aggregated beings, he claims, can only exist to the extent that a plurality of individuals are co-perceived, or otherwise apprehended by a mind, as forming a single entity.[70] The roots of this characteristic Leibnizian position are ontological. For Leibniz, the created world is composed solely of monads and their individual modifications. Relations, therefore, are not *in* the world, but are rather "modes of conceiving," or what a mind imposes *on* the world in apprehending the agreement and connection of singular things. Abstracted from their *relata*, relations are merely "beings of reason" (*entia rationis*), whose reality is limited to their expression of the ideas and eternal truths constitutive of God's understanding.[71] A simple line of reasoning leads to the conclusion that beings through aggregation are without exception phenomena, which exist "by convention" rather than "by nature."[72] Since relations are only supplied by a mind, and since the designation of any group of individuals as an aggregate depends upon their being related in specific ways such that if those relations cease to hold the identity of the aggregate is also destroyed, it follows that aggregates can only exist as things which are perceived or thought. We cannot conclude from this, however, that aggregates are merely mental or imaginary things. As "well-founded phenomena," aggregates have a foundation in certain individuals, which together determine the existence of a single composite being insofar as they are apprehended as standing in certain relations with respect to one another. The identity of a being through aggregation thus depends in an essential way both on its individual constituents and on the relations apprehended among them.

All of this is consistent with Leibniz's description of aggregates as entities which "result" from monads. In a study from the 1680s, he offers the following definition of this term:

I understand that to result [*resultare*], which can immediately be understood when those things from which it results have been posited.

(LH IV 7C Bl. 108 [VE 415])[73]

It is apparent from this definition that resulting is not a physical or causal relation. It is instead best understood as a relation of ontological determination. To say that a given being "results" from certain other beings is to say that its existence can be conceived as being immediately determined by the existence of those prior beings. For Leibniz, the principal class of entities determined in this way are those whose existence is dependent upon relations holding among certain individuals. The reason for this is again his insistence that relations are merely ideal: they are not themselves created beings, but merely ways the world is capable of being known (perceived, thought) by minds. Relational facts, and relational entities such as aggregates, are thus things that immediately exist for a mind insofar as it apprehends a certain sameness or connection among a plurality of individuals.

With these preliminaries out of the way, we can turn to the specifics of Leibniz's account of bodies as aggregates of monads. Here we face three main questions: (1) What are the particular relations upon which the aggregation of monads depends? (2) To what mind are these relations owed? (3) Under what conditions do there result aggregates of monads identifiable with the phenomenal bodies perceived by us?

We have already charted an answer to the first of these questions. In Leibniz's view, monads stand in no external relations to one another; each is rather "like a world of its own" (G II 436:L 600). Nevertheless, certain relations of connection are predicable of monads. The basis for these relations, we have seen, is a monad's capacity to express its relatedness to other monads via its representation of the spatiotemporal and causal relations of its organic body. Now to this point, we have restricted ourselves to the perspective of a single monad. We have claimed that a monad's perceptual states express its relatedness to the world and that these states provide the foundation for intermonadic relations, but we have not yet confronted the question of how these relations are in fact determined. Given Leibniz's insistence that every monad is "like a world of its own," it is unsurprising that he holds that such relations can only result from correlations among the phenomena of different monads.[74] Obviously, such correlations are not directly accessible to finite minds. They are, however, known to God, who has chosen to create the totality of monads that is the world precisely so that a particular harmony is realized among their perceptions.[75] Consistent with Leibniz's definition of the term, then, we can conclude that aggregates of monads *result* from individual monads insofar as the divine mind apprehends certain objective relations among those monads' phenomenal representations of the world.[76]

The relations most relevant to monadic aggregation are closely associated with a monad's representation of itself as an embodied creature. On the basis of what we have already established, we may see Leibniz as conceiving of this body in two complementary ways: on the one hand, as a mere appearance or what a monad perceives as its organic body; on the other hand, as what that body is in itself, some aggregate of monads. The problem we face is how to fit these two conceptions of body together: how to make sense of the idea that what a monad perceives as its body (or what it perceives as the body of another monad) is – provided that that perception is veridical – really some aggregate of monads. In his late writings, Leibniz equates the embodiment of a monad with its being "dominant" with respect to a plurality of lesser monads.[77] A promising way to approach our problem, then, is to ask under what conditions such a plurality of monads can be said to result in the organic body of its dominant monad or soul.

We may assume that a monad characteristically represents an

organic body as its body to the extent that it represents that body
as where it is and as the instrument through which it acts. An
organic body is thus in this sense subordinate to its soul: it only
persists as the body of that soul, or as the same organic body,
insofar as the soul represents it as defining its dimensions in space
and time and its immediate capacity for action. Now, it is reasonable to suppose that if certain monads are to be conceived as
grounding a soul's perception of its body, they must be monads that
provide a ground for the body's characteristic relation to the soul.
They must, in other words, be monads that reciprocally express
themselves as subordinate to the soul. We have found, however,
that monads are only able to express their relatedness via what
they represent as the relations of their organic bodies. It follows,
therefore, that if certain monads are to be conceived as grounding
the reality of a soul's body, they must be monads that characteristically represent their own organic bodies as subordinate to the
soul's body.

The paradigm of this sort of bodily subordination for Leibniz is
that which exists between a living body and its separate organs,
cells, and subcellular components. In this case, the latter are conceived not simply as spatial parts of the body, but as parts whose
activities are adapted to the activity of the body as a whole. Working from this example, we may infer that the monads that ground
the reality of a soul's organic body will be those whose bodies are
represented (by themselves and by the soul) as the functional components of the soul's body. To conceive of all the monads that share
this characteristic will be to conceive of those monads that collectively determine (via their representations of their bodies) a complete conception of the soul's organic body.[78] It is important to
recognize the dual role played by these grounding monads. On the
one hand, these monads are themselves identified with the soul's
body: they are the reality that the soul confusedly represents as its
extended body. At the same time, what is special about these monads is that they share the property of representing themselves as
the organic constituents of the soul's body. Hence, to the extent
that a mind is able to comprehend these monads in relation to each
other – a relatedness that can only be conceived in terms of their
representations of their embodiment – it would be led from a conception of the mutual relationship of their bodies to a conception

of the organic body they ground, i.e., the body of their dominant monad or soul. It is just this idea of the conception of one thing being immediately determined by the conception of certain prior things that is conveyed in Leibniz's definition of "result." Thus, for a plurality of monads to result in an aggregate that is identifiable with the organic body of a dominant monad is for there to be a specific correlation among their perceptions, such that a mind that had access to each monad's representation of the relatedness of its body to the universe would judge that the bodies of the lesser monads indeed exhausted the organic components of the body of the dominant monad.

The claim that these correlations among monadic perceptions are ones that are apprehended by God alone is clearly crucial. Still, it might be wondered whether monadic perceptions contain the information that would allow even God to establish such correlations among their perceptions. Human souls are not, in general, aware of the minute components of their bodies, nor is it plausible to think that monads that perceive themselves (however obscurely) as commanding the body's cells are aware of their containment in the body. Thus, how could God possibly apprehend the relatedness of monads according to the scheme described above? Here we must pay careful attention to the limits Leibniz places on monadic perception. In his view, these limits come not in the completeness of a monad's representation of the universe, but in its capacity to extract meaningful information – in the form of distinct perceptions – from that representation.[79] He thus leaves it open that an unlimited intelligence could "read" in the perceptions of any created monad a complete account of the relatedness of its body to the rest of the universe, and would thereby have the information needed to establish the correlations that determine the aggregation of monads.[80]

While complicated, the above account supports Leibniz's own understanding of his philosophy as involving a *reduction* of matter to monads:

In truth, I do not do away with body but reduce [*revoco*] it to that which is, for I show that corporeal mass ... is not a substance, but a phenomenon resulting from simple substances, which alone have a unity and absolute reality.   (G II 275)[81]

The reduction Leibniz propounds contains elements of a phenomenalist view of matter. Since the relations that determine the aggregation of monads are limited to correlations among those monads' phenomenal representations of the world, aggregates can only come to be as a result of the agreement apprehended by God among their perceptions. There is thus a sense in which Leibniz can legitimately claim that the reality of material things is "located in" the harmony that exists among the perceptions of monads. Granting this, however, does not entail that his theory is best understood as a version of phenomenalism. Although an agreement among the perceptions of monads is presupposed in defining the relations on which aggregation depends, matter is reduced on his theory to a plurality of simple substances, not a plurality of their perceptions. In Leibniz's view, a distinct understanding of the essential properties of matter – its multiplicity, force and resistance – reveals bodies to be multitudes of unextended, active substances. Thus, the corporeal phenomena perceived by monads are rendered intelligible as appearances of a supersensible reality of other monads.[82]

Significantly, Leibniz maintains that we can gain this type of understanding of matter only at the level of general concepts: we can know distinctly that any body must be constituted from monads, but we cannot thereby identify the particular monads from which it results. To even conceive of an answer to this sort of question, we are forced to appeal to the phenomena that would be perceived by those monads. The reason for this is that in Leibniz's philosophy all monads share the generic nature of being simple substances that are principles of action and passion; they are individuated by their intrinsic denominations, in particular their unique perceptual representation of the universe. In attempting to specify the ground in reality for a particular phenomenal body, therefore, even God has no alternative but to identify the grounding monads in terms of the phenomena they would perceive under the assumption of universal harmony. As I have reconstructed Leibniz's position, these would be monads that represented their organic bodies as comprising collectively the functional components of the phenomenal body in question. Under this circumstance, we can speak of that body as "resulting" from those monads, since it is in this way conceivable as the body that is determined by those monads' mutual relations.

IV. THE PROBLEM OF CORPOREAL SUBSTANCE

During the 1680s, Leibniz appears to believe that although the soul and the body are related only by a preestablished harmony, the soul *qua* substantial form is capable of endowing its body with the *per se* unity of a substance. Already in the *New System*, we found evidence of his retreat from this conclusion. Although he continues to speak of animated organic bodies as "corporeal substances," there is no indication that he regards these as ontologically basic. He instead defends the thesis that the only true unities are unextended, soul-like forms. And this is a position that is reaffirmed by his theory of monads. While Leibniz preserves in this theory the role of organisms as units of natural order, he is clear that at a fundamental level we are to conceive of such organisms as mere results: aggregates composed of a single dominant monad and a plurality of lesser, bodily monads.[83] While the relation of a dominant monad to the monads of its body must be distinguishable in some way from the relations of other monads, it too for Leibniz is merely a relation of harmony or correspondence and hence results in no more than the accidental unity of a being through aggregation. Thus, if the only union uniting a dominant monad with the enmassed monads of its body is that determined by their preestablished harmony, we must conclude that a dominant monad does not endow its body with the *per se* unity of a substance.[84]

In a sense, we might still see this dominant monad as playing the role of a substantial form. Assuming that it defines the point of view from which an organism represents the world, it serves as that organism's principle of unity and identity: regardless of how its body (or the monads constituting its body) change, the dominant monad will continue to represent it (them) as the same persisting body. Likewise, assuming the subordination of the body's monads to the dominnte monad, it is the latter that defines the characteristic activity of the organism: the lesser monads of the body necessarily represent the actions of their bodies as commanded by those of the dominant monad, i.e., by the body as a whole. These correlations among the perceptions of monads provide a basis for saying that, in a manner of speaking, the dominant monad of an organism serves as the substantial form of its body. Nevertheless, this explanation of the monadic reality underlying the phenomena makes it clear that in the strictest sense there is no unitary organism, if this is understood as the *composite* of a soul-like monad and its associated corporeal mass. Consequently, if Leibniz accepts the theory of monads, he is committed to the rejection of organic creatures as genuine corporeal substances: animated bodies that possess the property of being an *unum per se*. At the deepest level, the unity of the organism resides in the soul alone, which merely represents itself as a persistent embodied creature.[85]

I suggest that this conclusion defines the central thrust of Leibniz's late metaphysics. Because it is a view that runs contrary to both ordinary experience and orthodox Christianity, it is unsurprisingly not a position for which he was able to find many ready adherents. Consequently, during the last two decades of his life, Leibniz was forced to devote considerable attention to responding to critics of his metaphysics, as well as simply to explaining it to those who found its details bewildering. In the course of these efforts to bring his views more in line with common opinions, we sometimes find signs of what seem to be retreats from the more extreme consequences of his position. This is especially so as regards his rejection of corporeal substance. It remains for us, then, to look more closely at these hesitations and to offer some conclusions concerning the steadfastness of Leibniz's commitment to the theory of monads.

One of the most significant challenges to Leibniz's late metaphysics was initiated by Father René-Joseph de Tournemine,, editor of the Jesuit journal *Mémoires de Trévoux*, in an article published in May 1703. While praising the doctrine of preestablished harmony as an improvement over the "Cartesian" (i.e., occasionalist) account of the agreement of the soul and its body, Tournemine disputed Leibniz's claim to have offered an adequate explanation of their *union*. Seeing to the heart of Leibniz's position, he observed that no simple harmony between the operations of the soul and the body could make it the case that the two together formed one substance, a single human being.[86]

Leibniz's reply to Tournemine, published in the same *Mémoires* in 1708, is a masterly exercise in diplomacy. Respectful of the political influence of the Jesuits, he has no interest in appearing overly innovative. He is thus careful to insist that he does not deny the possibility of a "metaphysical" union between the soul and the body, although at the same time he does not explicitly allow that he believes such a union exists:

I must admit that it would have been very wrong of me to object to the Cartesians that the agreement God immediately maintains, according to them, between the soul and the body does not bring about a true union, since, to be sure, my preestablished harmony would do no better than it does. My intent was to explain naturally what they explain by perpetual miracles, and I tried to account for the phenomena, that is, for the relation that is perceived between the soul and the body. But since the metaphysical union one adds is not a phenomenon, and since no one has ever given an intelligible notion of it, I did not take it upon myself to seek a reason for it. However, I do not deny that there is something having this nature.

(G VI 595: AG 196–97)

On the surface at least this passage sees Leibniz recanting his strong claim, in the *New System* and elsewhere, to have provided a solution to the problem of soul-body union. Surely he is being disingenuous when he writes in the same reply that he does not remember having claimed that his preestablished harmony accounts for soul-body union in a way that the Cartesian position does not. In any case, he adds, "I declare that if I did ever make [this claim], I renounce it from now on"; and he goes on to offer the preceding statement in its place. A second important point is that Leibniz acknowledges here, in contrast to his position of the 1680s, that by itself the preestablished harmony of soul and body is insufficient to render their composite an *unum per se*. For this, some additional metaphysical union is required.

It remains an open question how much Leibniz actually commits himself to in his reply to Tournemaine. Is he really prepared to make room in his philosophy for a metaphysical union between the soul and the body, or is he merely engaged in a philosophical sleight of hand designed to placate his Jesuit critic? The cynical reading of Leibniz's recantation would be that while he does not rule out a metaphysical union as logically impossible, he not only recognizes no grounds for believing that such a union exists, but he positively discourages us from supposing its existence, since it has no phenomenal effects and no intelligible notion can be formed of it.[87] Support for this reading can be found in his contemporary correspondence with De Volder. In his last letter to De Volder, dated 19 January 1706, Leibniz writes:

You rightly despair of obtaining from me what I can give you no hope of receiving and what I neither hope nor desire to find for myself. The Scholastics commonly sought things which were not only ultramundane but utopian. The brilliant French Jesuit Tournemaine recently gave me an excellent example of this. He gave general approval of my preestablished harmony, which seemed to him to supply a reason for the agreement which we perceive between soul and body, but said that he still desired one thing – to know the reason for the *union* between the two, which he held to differ from their agreement. I replied that this mysterious [*nescio quam*] metaphysical union which the School assumes in addition to their agreement is not a phenomenon, and that there is no concept [*notionem*] or notion [*notitiam*] of it. So neither could I think of a reason that might be given for it.

(G II 281: L 538–39)

While again not absolutely ruling out the possibility of a metaphysical union, Leibniz is clearly much less sanguine here about its prospects. In effect, he tells De Volder: assume such a union if you want to engage in pointless speculation; I who am interested in founding my metaphysics on intelligible concepts alone will have no truck with it. The contents of the De Volder correspondence strongly suggest that while Leibniz is not prepared to deny outright the existence of a metaphysical union, he also recognizes no positive grounds for asserting it. Seen from this perspective, his reply to Tournemaine must seem somewhat contrived: an attempt to blunt the full force of his philosophy for the sake of his Jesuit critics.[88]

This conclusion is, I believe, essentially correct. Nevertheless, it does not quite represent the full story, for in certain contexts Leibniz acknowledges truths that, while not contrary to reason, are nonetheless "above reason."[89] The Creation, the Holy Trinity, the Incarnation, and the Eucharist all represent religious "mysteries" that surpass human reason, yet are not contrary to reason, since they do not contradict "absolutely certain and indispensable truths." In this respect, they are acceptable as dogmas of religion: they are not demonstrated by reason, but they also do not oppose reason. Now, the critical question is whether Leibniz believes that the situation is the same for the metaphysical union of soul and body. Can this be described as a "mystery" that surpasses reason, yet is acceptable on the basis of faith? In both his reply to Tournemaine and in the *Theodicy*, Leibniz associates the union of the soul and the body with the religious mysteries in that in both cases we are

capable of only a partial, analogical understanding of the relevant
notions. At no time, however, does he explicitly claim the union of
the soul and the body as a religious mystery.[90] Still, it must be
acknowledged that in the *Theodicy* he comes very close to asserting their metaphysical union:

> We also mean something when we speak of the union of the soul with the
> body to make thereof one single person. For although I do not hold that the
> soul changes the laws of the body, or that the body changes the laws of the
> soul, and I have introduced the preestablished harmony to avoid this de-
> rangement, I nevertheless admit a true union between the soul and the body,
> which makes a *suppositum* of them. This union belongs to the metaphysi-
> cal, whereas a union of influence would belong to the physical.
>
> ("Preliminary Discourse," §55; G VI 81: H 104)

On the basis of the *Theodicy* alone, we would have to conclude that
Leibniz is, in fact, quite sympathetic to the idea of a metaphysical
union, and hence to the idea of the human being as an *unum per se*
or corporeal substance.[91] But we must remember that this is the
Theodicy: a book that Leibniz was prepared to release to the general
public and for which he craved the widest possible support. Working
on the assumption that a strong sense of caution directs all of Leibniz's actions, I would suggest that this text is not the best guide to
his deepest thoughts. Some of these thoughts are, however, expressed in his correspondence with another Jesuit, Bartholomew Des
Bosses, the Latin translator of the *Theodicy*.

Leibniz's correspondence with Des Bosses spans a ten-year period
(1706–16) and comprises over 130 letters.[92] At the outset, it is worth
citing one passage in support of the claim that these letters provide a
more dependable guide to Leibniz's late metaphysical views than
published works such as the *Theodicy* or his reply to Tournemine :.
Fairly early on in their correspondence, he offers Des Bosses the
following admonition:

> I do not think that those things we have discussed concerning philosophical
> matters are suited for communication in any public way. . . . I have written
> these things for you, namely for the wise, not for any one at all. And thus
> they are hardly appropriate for the *Mémoires de Trévoux*, which is intended
> more for a popular audience; I hope that you, by virtue of your goodwill
> towards me, would not allow them to appear in such an unsuitable place.
>
> (G II 328)

This is as explicit a statement as one could hope for of Leibniz's conviction that there are certain things that are suited for communication in a public forum and certain things that are not: philosophical matters that are only safely discussed with the "wise." If this is so, then we should be able to count on the Des Bosses correspondence to offer us some insight into Leibniz's most considered views concerning the union of soul and body.

The issue of substantial union first acquires prominence in the correspondence in September 1709, when Des Bosses raises the question of how the doctrine of the real presence of Christ's body in the Eucharist can be defended on Leibniz's principles (G II 388). Leibniz's response to this query is revealing. As a Lutheran, he writes, he is personally committed to neither transubstantiation (the orthodox Catholic position), nor consubstantiation; that is, he himself believes neither that the substance of the bread is transformed into the substance of the body of Christ, nor that the substance of Christ's body comes to coexist with that of the bread. All that he is prepared to accept is that Christ's body is "present" in the sense that it is perceived (by God and the blessed) at the time that the bread is received. While disengaging himself in this way from Catholic orthodoxy, Leibniz nonetheless goes on to suggest how transubstantiation might be accounted for within his philosophy. Addressing the Catholic doctrine of "real accidents," he hypothesizes that the monads of the bread may be destroyed with respect to their substantial natures – i.e., primitive active and passive powers – while preserving their accidents or derivative forces, and that the monads of Christ's body may be substituted for them, with those new monads exhibiting the phenomena of the bread by virtue of the preservation of its accidents (G II 390–91).

Des Bosses is heartened by this response, yet raises an important objection. He points out that unlike accidents, which are "absolute," Leibniz's derivative forces are modifications of primitive forces. Hence their being is wholly dependent on that of the primitive forces and with these destroyed the derivative forces will also be destroyed (G II 396). When Leibniz comes to reply to this criticism, he adopts a completely different tack. Now, instead of maintaining that it is the constitutive monads of the bread which are destroyed at the consecration, he claims that it is a certain "superadded union" which is destroyed, in order to be replaced by "some divinely substituted equivalent" union:

Since bread is not in fact a substance, but a being through aggregation [ens per aggregationem] or a substantiatum resulting from innumerable monads through some superadded union, its substantiality resides in this union; thus it is not necessary for your view that those monads be destroyed or changed by God, but only that there be removed that through which they produce a new being [ens novum], namely that union. In this way, the substantiality residing in them will cease, although there will remain the phenomenon, which now will not arise from those monads, but from some divinely substituted equivalent for the union of those monads. Thus no substantial subject will in fact participate. However, those of us who reject transubstantiation have no need of such things.   (G II 399)

Although it is not identified by name, there appears here the first hint of Leibniz's doctrine of the *vinculum substantiale* or "substantial chain." Two years later, he provides Des Bosses with a more complete statement of this theory in the letter which introduces the term itself:

If a corporeal substance is something real over and above monads, just as a line is held to be something over and above points, then we will have to say that corporeal substance consists in a certain union, or better, in a real unifying thing that God superadds to monads. . . . And so we must say one of two things: either bodies are mere phenomena, and so extension too will be only a phenomenon and monads alone will be real, but the union will be provided by the operation of the perceiving mind on the phenomena, or, if faith compels us to accept corporeal substances, we must say that the substance consists in that unifying [unionalis] reality that adds *something absolute* (and therefore substantial), though in flux, to those things that are to be united. Your transubstantiation must be located in its change, for monads are not really ingredients of this thing which is added, but requisites for it, although they are required not by absolute and metaphysical necessity, but things merely needed for it. And so the monads can remain, as well as the sensible phenomena grounded in them, even if the substance of the body is changed. . . . To speak candidly, however, I should prefer to explain the accidents of the Eucharist through phenomena; then we will not need nonmodal accidents, for which I care very little.

(G II 435–37: AG 198–89: L 600–601)

The first thing to note about these last two letters is the way in which Leibniz explicitly distances himself from the position he is describing. "Those of us who reject transubstantiation have no need of such things," he says at the end of the first passage; and at the end of the second: "To speak candidly ... I should prefer to explain the accidents of the Eucharist through phenomena." Nevertheless, he goes on for several years discussing with Des Bosses the details of this account of substantial union and its implications for the doctrine of transubstantiation. Very briefly, his conclusions are these.[93]

(1) A plurality of monads which together constitute an organism (i.e., a plurality which includes a dominant monad to which the remaining monads are subordinated) will qualify as an *unum per se* or corporeal substance if and only if its members are united by a substantial chain; otherwise, they will form only an *ens per aggregationem* and the body will be no more than a phenomenon.

(2) A substantial chain is itself a substantial thing, not a mode or accident; it is responsible for the substantiality of a corporeal substance. In Leibniz's terms, the addition of a substantial chain "realizes" the phenomenon of a body.

(3) A given set of monads is naturally required by the substantial chain that unifies them, but they are not essentially required by it. The monads can continue to exist without that chain (although they will then form only an *ens per aggregationem*); and, conversely, that chain can through a miracle be united with a completely different set of monads.

(4) The phenomenal accidents of bodies are grounded in (or results of) their constitutive monads; nevertheless, in a secondary sense these accidents are also modifications of the substantial chain, which naturally receives its modifications from the monads it unites "as an echo."

(5) While bread is not itself a corporeal substance, it is nonetheless an aggregate of corporeal substances. Transubstantiation can now be explained as follows. At the moment of the consecration, God destroys the substantial chains of the monads constitutive of the bread and substitutes for them the chain definitive of the substantiality of Christ's body. Since the monads of the bread remain, the same phenomena will remain. However, those phenomena now miraculously become modifications of the substantial chain of Christ's body. A substantial change thus occurs without any change occurring in the monads themselves or in the phenomena which result from them.

This does not cover all the intricacies of the theory Leibniz presents to Des Bosses, but it is sufficient for our purposes. It is, to say the least, a theory of baroque complexity. It is also a theory that never completely convinces Des Bosses, who persistently presses Leibniz on the need for real accidents. Most importantly of all, the theory strikes one as being little more than an academic exercise for Leibniz, as he himself at one point all but admits to Des Bosses.[94] From the start of their correspondence, Leibniz makes it clear that he does not accept the doctrine of transubstantiation. Thus, he can hardly be held responsible for a theory of substantial union that is only introduced for the purposes of accounting for that doctrine. On its own, the theory of substantial chains is something of an embarrassment. Leibniz is adamant that the addition of a substantial chain to an aggregate of monads has no effect on the phenomena which result from that aggregate. It can be added or removed by God at will without any discernible change. At the same time, however, corporeal accidents are claimed as modifications of substantial chains, which they receive "as an echo" from the monads they unite.

It is little wonder that Leibniz periodically comes back to reassert his own preference for the theory of monads. Midway through the correspondence he writes: "I consider the explanation of all phenomena solely through the perceptions of monads functioning in harmony with each other, with corporeal substance rejected, to be useful for a fundamental investigation of things" (G II 450: L 604).[95] He presses Des Bosses to suggest a way in which transubstantiation can be reconciled with "the hypothesis of bodies reduced to phenomena" (G II 452). Yet at bottom he seems to realize that such a reconciliation is impossible. For his own part, Leibniz remains satisfied to explain the miracle of the Eucharist in terms of the perceived presence alone of Christ's body.[96]

The Des Bosses correspondence is of critical importance for the emphasis it gives to the point that, within the theory of monads, composite corporeal substance is only conceivable on the condition that we admit a real union among monads, in the form of something like a *vinculum substantiale*. While a handful of passages show Leibniz seriously pondering such a device, the most dependable texts come down firmly on the side of monads alone with real union and composite substance rejected. And indeed, this is exactly what we should expect given his deep and abiding commitment to the ideality of relations.[97]

When presented with challenges to this conclusion we can only proceed on a case by case basis, paying careful attention to context. I end with one such case. A passage that seems on the surface to acknowledge the existence of composite substances is §3 of the *Principles of Nature and of Grace:*

Each distinct simple substance or monad, which makes up the center of a composite substance (an animal, for example) and is the principle of its unity, is surrounded by a *mass* composed of an infinity of other monads, which constitute the body belonging to this central monad.

(G VI 598–99: AG 207)

In order to assess the significance of this passage we need to be aware of three things.[98] First, the reference to "composite substance" does not appear in the first draft of the *Principles.* There Leibniz writes simply: "each simple substance or monad is surrounded by a mass composed of an infinity of other monads, which constitute its organic body."[99] Second, the *Principles* were specifically prepared for a group of prominent statesmen: on the one hand, Prince Eugen in Vienna, on the other, the circle of the Duc d'Orléans in Paris. Third, at the same time that he was preparing the *Principles,* Leibniz composed another summary of his system, which was intended for Nicolas Remond, chief counselor to the Duc d'Orléans, who had been pleading for a further elaboration of his views. The document Leibniz prepared is remarkable in being one of the most explicit statements extant of his reduction of matter to monads; it contains no mention of real union or corporeal substances.[100] It ends with this cautionary remark to Remond:

But I fear that this letter so full of abstract thoughts far removed from what is commonly imagined may repel you. I would ask that you not meditate on it for too long at one time; it would be better to return to it. I want you to note, however, how I value you and honor you in writing to you what I would not readily write to others. Thus, this letter must be only for you. Many others would find it absurd or unintelligible.   (G III 624)

Leibniz in fact never sent this document to Remond. He instead forwarded a copy of the less abstract *Principles of Nature and of Grace,* now emended to include a mention of "composite substance." Evidently, on reflection he decided that Remond was not among the "wise."[101]

NOTES

1 The material in this chapter appears in a fuller form in my book *Leibniz and the Rational Order of Nature* (Cambridge University Press, forthcoming). For their helpful comments on earlier drafts, I would like to thank David Blumenfeld, Nicholas Jolley, and Christia Mercer. This work was supported by a grant from the University Research Committee of Emory University and by an Emory College Faculty Development Award.

2 I emphasize "published." The first presentation of Leibniz's mature philosophy is generally taken to be his 1686 *Discourse on Metaphysics* (see Mercer and Sleigh, this volume). As Leibniz suggests in the *New System*, the contents of this earlier work were shared with a number of correspondents but were not advanced publicly.

3 For the background to his famous exchange with Arnauld, see Sleigh, *Leibniz and Arnauld*, chaps, 1–2.

4 See his letter to Thomas Burnett of 8/18 May 1697: "I changed my mind again and again after new insights, and it is only for about twelve years that I have been satisfied . . ." (G III 205); and his 1696 reply to Foucher (G IV 493–94: P 125–26).

5 See, in particular, C. Wilson, *Leibniz's Metaphysics*, chap. 5.

6 In addition to these features, Leibniz recognizes at least one other essential property of substance, that of universal expression. This commitment has a different origin from those cited in the text. While the latter articulate substance's traditional role as an ontological and explanatory primitive, the property of universal expression is related to the Leibnizian thesis that in every possible world "all is connected." The significance of this idea will become apparent in what follows.

7 As we shall see, the doctrine of the spontaneity of substance appears explicitly in the *New System*, where it serves to ground the hypothesis of preestablished harmony. It is likewise a view that is prominent in the *Discourse on Metaphysics*: "We also see that every substance has a perfect spontaneity (which becomes freedom in intelligent creatures), that everything that happens to it is a consequence of its idea or of its being, and that nothing determines it, except God alone" (§32; G IV 458: AG 64). As Mercer and Sleigh (this volume) show, a version of the doctrine can also be found in Leibniz's earlier metaphysical writings.

8 See Garber's chapter in this volume.

9 One of the few texts in which this idea does resurface is a draft of a 1701 letter to De Volder. There Leibniz inscribes the following marginal note: "A substance is an *atomon autoploroun*, an atom complete in itself or completing itself [*per se completum seu se ipsum complens*]. From this

it follows that it is a vital atom or an atom having an entelechy. That which is an atom is identical to that which is truly one" (G II 224). Although this definition employs the vocabulary of completeness, a subtle shift has by this time occurred in Leibniz's understanding of the term. The completeness of a substance is now directly linked to its character as a "vital atom," rather than to the logical condition of being an ultimate subject of predication. A substance is not merely complete in itself: it is actively *completing* itself.

10 This idea, which derives from Leibniz's mathematical work, can already be found in texts from his Paris period. In a set of notes from 1676, he writes: "The author is right to say that thought is not the essence of the soul. For a thought is an action, and since one thought succeeds another it is necessary that what persists during this change is rather the essence of the soul, since it remains always the same. The essence of substance consists in the primitive force of acting, or in the law of the series of its changes . . ." (A VI.iii 326).

11 Cf. G II 136: MP 170; G II 258: L 533; G III 58, 464–65, 657; G IV 506–7: AG 158; G IV 512: AG 162–63; G IV 553–54.

12 See, e.g., his letter to Arnauld of 28 November/8 December 1686 (G II 76: MP 93–95).

13 For more on this argument, see Garber, "Leibniz and the Foundations of Physics: The Middle Years," pp. 31ff; Sleigh, *Leibniz and Arnauld*, chap. 6; Rutherford, "Leibniz's 'Analysis of Multitude and Phenomena into Unities and Reality'."

14 See Garber, "Leibniz and the Foundations of Physics," p. 63. Others supporting this interpretation include Broad, *Leibniz*, pp. 75ff.; C. Wilson, *Leibniz's Metaphysics*, pp. 98ff. For a contrasting view, see Sleigh, *Leibniz and Arnauld*, chap. 5.

15 See his letter to Arnauld of 30 April 1687: "You say you do not see what leads me to admit these substantial forms or rather these bodily substances endowed with true unity; but it is because I cannot conceive of any reality without true unity" (G II 97: MP 122).

16 For further discussion of Leibniz's charge that occasionalism transforms the communication of soul and body into a "perpetual miracle," see Rutherford, "Natures, Laws and Miracles: The Roots of Leibniz's Critique of Occasionalism."

17 See also his 1696 reply to Foucher (G IV 494: P 126).

18 For more on Leibniz's doctrine of expression, see Kulstad, "Leibniz's Conception of Expression"; Sleigh, *Leibniz and Arnauld*, pp. 170ff.

19 In particular, the writings of Johann Heinrich Bisterfeld. See Leibniz's notes (ca. 1663) in A VI.i, 151–61; Loemker, "Leibniz and the Herborn Encyclopedists"; Mugnai, "Der Begriff der Harmonie."

20 As we shall see in sec. III, the spontaneity of a body's action is ultimately
    explained in terms of its constitution from soul-like entelechies.

21 In a July 1694 letter to Bossuet, which enclosed a draft of the *New
    System* for his approval, Leibniz writes confidently: "I believe I have
    resolved the great problem of the union of the soul and the body. My
    explanation will be presented as a hypothesis, but I take it to be demon-
    strated" (*Correspondance de Bossuet*, vol. 6, p. 348). Cf. A I.x 143.

22 For the most part, Leibniz prefers to advance his position as a dis-
    junction: either there are corporeal substances or bodies are mere phe-
    nomena. See his letter to Arnauld of 28 November/8 December 1686:
    "[I]f I am asked for my views . . . on the sun, the globe of the earth, the
    moon, trees and similar bodies, and even about animals, I cannot declare
    with absolute certainty whether they are animated, or even whether
    they are substances, or indeed whether they are simply machines or
    aggregates of many substances. But at least I can say that if there are no
    corporeal substances such as I maintain, it follows that bodies will be
    only true phenomena, like the rainbow. . . . [And] apart from man there
    would be nothing substantial in the visible world" (G II 77: MP 95).
    Why, we might ask, is Leibniz so confident that "man" is an exception?
    The answer is perhaps found in a remark he makes earlier in the same
    letter: "Besides, the last Lateran Council asserts that the soul is truly
    the substantial form of our body" (G II 75: MP 93). Later in the correspon-
    dence, he is more confident in affirming the existence of an infinity of
    lesser substantial forms. See his letter to Arnauld of 9 October 1687 (G II
    118: MP 151–52).

23 This, I take it, is the significance of his statement that "the soul has its
    seat in the body by an immediate presence which could not be greater,
    since the soul is in the body as unity is in the resultant of unities, which
    is a multitude" (G IV 485: AG 144).

24 It has often been claimed that Leibniz first uses the term "monad" to
    refer to his own conception of substance in a letter to Fardella of 3/13
    September 1696 (FC 326). Consistent with this, Merchant ("The Vi-
    talism of Anne Conway") argues that he appropriated the term from van
    Helmont during the latter's visit to Hanover in March 1696, and that the
    immediate sources for his usage are van Helmont's *Cabbalistical Dia-
    logue* (1682) and Anne Conway's *Principles of the Most Ancient and
    Modern Philosophy* (1690). Parkinson (P 255) has noted, however, that
    there is at least one earlier text, an unfinished letter to the Marquis de
    l'Hospital dated 22 July 1695, in which Leibniz uses the term *monas* to
    designate whatever is a "real unity" (GM II 295).

25 G VI 607–23. The title is not Leibniz's own, but that of an early editor.
    Unless otherwise indicated, the parenthetical references that follow are

to sections of this essay. I follow the translation of Ariew and Garber (AG 213–25).

26 Here again we find evidence of Leibniz's grounding argument. Cf. *Principles of Nature and of Grace*, §1 (G VI 598: AG 207).

27 Cf. G II 239: L 526.

28 The claim that monads cannot affect one another involves more than their supposed simplicity or lack of parts. Also relevant is Leibniz's dismissal of the possibility of the migration of accidents from one substance to another, a point summarized in his assertion that "monads have no windows through which something can enter or leave" (§7, G VI 607: AG 214).

29 Cf. *Principles of Nature and of Grace*, §2 (G VI 598: AG 207); G VI 628: AG 228–29.

30 Cf. G VII 528.

31 Mugnai refers to these as "intramonadic relations" ("A Systematical Approach to Leibniz's Theory of Relations," p. 78). They are not to be confused with what others have called "relational properties," i.e., properties such as fatherhood that are predicable of an individual only insofar as there exists some other individual to which it stands in relation (see Ishiguro, *Leibniz's Philosophy of Logic and Language*, p. 132). "Intramonadic relations" are merely monadic accidents that have a relational content. They do not, therefore, imply the existence of irreducible relational facts about monads.

32 See *Theodicy*, §9: "all things are connected [*tout est lié*] in each one of the possible worlds: the universe, whatever it may be, is all of one piece, like an ocean" (G VI 107: H 128).

33 See G II 450–51: L 604.

34 See his letter to De Volder of 20 June 1703: "every change, both spiritual and material, has its proper place [*sedes*], so to speak, in the order of successions, or in time, as well as its proper place [*locus*] in the order of coexistents, or in space" (G II 253). Loemker's translation at L 531 omits the words "in the order of successions."

35 Strictly speaking, an extrinsic denomination is not a relation, but a term that designates an individual as being related to something else. By contrast, an intrinsic denomination designates the individual in terms of its own modifications (e.g., a monad's perceptions and appetitions).

36 See *New Essays* II, xxv, 5 (A VI.vi: RB 227); G VII 311: P 78.

37 See, among others, Parkinson, *Logic and Reality in Leibniz's Metaphysics*; Ishiguro, *Leibniz's Philosophy of Logic and Language*; Kulstad, "A Closer Look at Leibniz's Alleged Reduction of Relations"; Mates, *The Philosophy of Leibniz*; G. Brown, "Compossibility, Harmony, and Perfection in Leibniz"; Cover, "Relations and Reduction in Leibniz."

38 To De Volder, Leibniz writes: "Things which differ in place [*loco*] must express their place, that is, their surroundings [*ambientia*], and thus differ not only in place or an extrinsic denomination" (G II 250: L 529). Cf. G II 240: L 526–27.

39 This account is consistent with interpretations that ascribe to Leibniz a doctrine of the reducibility of intermonadic relations. Specifically, it supports the conclusion that the relations of monads supervene on, or "result" from, their individual accidents: perceptual states that express their relatedness to the rest of the world. For a development of this view, see Cover, "Relations and Reduction in Leibniz."

40 See *Theodicy*, "Preliminary Discourse," §10 (G VI 56: H 80); ibid. §124 (G VI 179: H 198); *New Essays*, Preface, (A VI.vi: RB 58).

41 Cf. *Metaphysical Consequences of the Principle of Reason*, §7: "[E]very simple substance has an organic body which corresponds to it – otherwise it would not have any kind of orderly relationship to other things in the universe, nor would it act or be acted upon in an orderly way . . ." (C 14: P 175). See also, ibid. §13; *Considerations on Vital Principles and Plastic Natures* (G VI 545: L 590); *Theodicy*, §§120, 200 (G VI 172–73: H 192, G VI 235: H 252).

42 Cf. *New Essays*, II, xv, 11: "Every finite spirit is always joined to an organic body, and represents other bodies to itself by their relation to its own body. Thus it is obviously related to space as bodies are" (A VI.vi: RB 155). For further discussion of this point, see Rutherford, "Leibniz and the Problem of Monadic Aggregation."

43 We shall return to some further consequences of this picture in the next section.

44 Cf. G VII 330; G IV 562: L 579.

45 "Change [*mutatio*] is an aggregate of two contradictory states. . . . A passion is a change which decreases perfection. An action is a change which increases or conserves perfection" (Gr 323). Cf. C 9: P 134.

46 Cf. *Principles of Nature and of Grace*, §13 (G VI 604: AG 211).

47 Cf. G III 347.

48 "God alone is a substance truly separated from matter, since he is pure act, endowed with no passive power, which, wherever it is, constitutes matter" (G VII 530).

49 We shall return to this point in sec. IV.

50 See, e.g., *Causa Dei*, §18 (G VI 441).

51 See *Principles of Nature and of Grace*, §3 (G VI 599: AG 207).

52 See *New Essays*, Preface (A VI.vi: RB 53); II, ix, 1 (A VI.vi: RB 134); II, xix, 4 (A VI.vi: RB 161–62).

53 Leibniz offers several other arguments on behalf of the doctrine of *petites perceptions*. See Jolley, *Leibniz and Locke*, pp. 110–12.

54 For detailed discussions of monadic reflection and its relation to apperception and consciousness, see McRae, *Leibniz: Perception, Apperception, and Thought*; Kulstad, *Leibniz on Apperception, Consciousness,
   and Reflection*.

55 This follows from the principle of continuity. See *New Essays* IV, xvi, 12
   (A VI.vi: RB 473–74).

56 See his 1716 letter to Dangicourt: "I believe that there are only monads
   in nature, the rest being only phenomena which result from them" (E
   745). Cf. G II 256; G II 265: L 535; G II 269: L 537; G II 281–82: L 539; G
   II 451: L 604; G II 473, 504; G III 545; G III 606: L 655; G III 636: L 659; G
   VI 590: L 625; G VII 501.

57 Unless otherwise noted, the term "matter" is used to refer to what
   Leibniz calls "secondary matter" (*materia secunda*), i.e., the matter of
   existing bodies, as opposed to "primary matter" or the primitive passive
   power of monads. Parts of this section are based on my paper, "Phenomenalism and the Reality of Body in Leibniz's Later Philosophy."

58 Other passages suggestive of phenomenalism include G II 264: L 535; G
   II 281; G II 435–36: L 600; G II 451–52: L 605; G III 567.

59 Furth is one of the few authors to ascribe to Leibniz a modern version
   of phenomenalism: "a reductive explication of statements about material things as translations or abbreviations of statements about perceptions" ("Monadology," p. 184). There is a long tradition of commentators who claim for Leibniz a weaker phenomenalism that does not
   stress the issue of translation. See Dillmann, *Eine neue Darstellung der
   Leibnizschen Monadenlehre*; Cassirer, *Leibniz' System*; Martin, *Leibniz: Logic and Metaphysics*; Earman, "Perceptions and Relations in the
   Monadology"; Adams, "Phenomenalism and Corporeal Substance in
   Leibniz."

60 Another way of making this point is to say that the being of material
   things consists solely in the fact that they are perceived, a claim that
   echoes Berkeley's famous thesis. The best discussion of the relationship
   between Leibniz and Berkeley is that of Margaret Wilson, "The Phenomenalisms of Leibniz and Berkeley."

61 This point is emphasized by Jolley, "Leibniz and Phenomenalism."

62 Loeb, *From Descartes to Hume*, pp. 303–5.

63 I defend this reading in Rutherford, "Leibniz's 'Analysis of Multitude
   and Phenomena into Unities and Reality'."

64 This is corroborated by his subsequent letters to De Volder of 25 January
   1705 (G II 275–78) and 19 January 1706 (G II 281–83: L 538–39). Cf.
   Jolley, "Leibniz and Phenomenalism," pp. 50–51.

65 See Erdmann, *Versuch einer wissenschaftlichen Darstellung der Geschichte der neuren Philosophie*, vol. 4, sec. 6; Russell, *A Critical Exposi-*

tion of the Philosophy of Leibniz, p. 105; Rescher, *The Philosophy of Leibniz*, chap. 7; Broad, *Leibniz*, pp. 91–92; McGuire, " 'Labyrinthus Continui': Leibniz on Substance, Activity and Matter," p. 306; Jolley, "Leibniz and Phenomenalism," pp. 47–48.

66 In a 1705 letter to the Electress Sophie, Leibniz writes: "[A]n analysis of the matter which is now found in space leads us demonstratively to substantial unities, to simple, indivisible, enduring substances, and consequently to souls, which can only be immortal and are dispersed throughout nature," (G VII 565). Cf. *New Essays* IV, iii, 6 (A VI.vi: RB 378–79). It is crucial not to fall into the trap of thinking that because Leibniz holds that bodies are pluralities of monads, he is committed to conceiving of them as *spatial* aggregates of monads. From the 1670s onward, he is deeply critical of this mistake, which he associates with the labyrinth of the continuum. His solution is to recognize that matter can be *understood* to be constituted from monads without our having to conceive of this constitution in spatial terms (see G II 436: L 600; G II 451: L 605). In the same vein, he criticizes Cartesians for remaining at the level of appearances in their treatment of matter: "It is really not surprising that the Cartesians have failed to understand the nature of corporeal substance and to arrive at true principles, since they consider extension as something absolute, irresolvable, ineffable, or primitive. For trusting their sense perceptions, and perhaps also seeking the applause of men, they were content to stop where their sense perceptions stopped, even though they also boasted elsewhere that they had distinguished sharply between the sensible and intelligible realms" (G II 269: L 536–37).

67 See C. Wilson, *Leibniz's Metaphysics*, pp. 190–96.

68 See Jolley, "Leibniz and Phenomenalism," p. 42; Mates, *The Philosophy of Leibniz*, p. 204; C. Wilson, *Leibniz's Metaphysics*, p. 192. We have already seen (n. 66) that this worry is unfounded, since Leibniz believes that bodies can be understood to be constituted from monads, and hence "aggregates" of those monads, without this implying that they are spatial collections of monads. For further discussion of this point, see Rutherford, "Leibniz's 'Analysis of Multitude and Phenomena into Unities and Reality'."

69 For references to bodies as "results," see G II 184: L 520; G II 187; G II 250–51: L 529; G II 306; G III 636: L 659; E 745. For references to "aggregates" or "collections" of monads, see G II 282: L 539; G II 444: L 602; G III 367, 545, 622; G VII 561.

70 Cf. A VI.vi: RB 146, 328–29; G II 101; G II 517; G VI 598: L 623; G VI 625: AG 227.

71 Cf. G II 486: L 609; A VI.vi: RB 145, 227, 265.

72 Cf. G II 252: L 531; G III 69.

73 A related definition occurs in the *Metaphysical Foundations of Mathe-matics* (GM VII 21–22: L 669).

74 "Monads have no position with respect to each other, that is, no real order that reaches beyond the order of phenomena. Each is like a sepa-rate world, and they correspond to each other through their own phe-nomena and not by any other intercourse and connection" (G II 444: L 602). Cf. G II 436: L 600; G II 451: L 604. This point is stressed by Earman ("Perceptions and Relations in the Monadology"), who defends a phenomenalist interpretation of Leibniz.

75 Cf. *Monadology*, §§53–59, G VI 615–16: AG 220.

76 See the notes composed by Leibniz for his letter to Des Bosses of 5 Febru-ary 1712: "God considers not only single monads and the modifications of every possible monad, but also their relations; and the reality of relations and truths consists in this" (G II 438: AG 199). Leibniz goes on to suggest that the composite beings determined in this way are "simple results," which "consist solely in true or real relations." For an elaboration of this view, see Rutherford, "Leibniz and the Problem of Monadic Aggregation."

77 In his 1702 response to Bayle, Leibniz writes: "There is no soul or entelechy which is not dominant to an infinity of others which enter into its organs, and the soul is never without an organic body which fits its present state" (G IV 564: L 580).

78 According to Leibniz, every organic body is composed of an infinity of lesser organisms, each of whose bodies is in turn composed of an infinity of lesser organisms, *ad infinitum*. Thus, the functional components of any organic body will include an infinity of subordinate organisms. See *Monadology*, §§64–70 G VI 618–19: AG 221–22; *Considerations on Vital Principles and Plastic Natures* (G VI 539: L 586–90).

79 See *Monadology*, §60, G VI 616–17: AG 220–21.

80 In this way God overcomes the limited perspective of created monads: "[B]etween the appearances of bodies given to us and the appearances given to God there is as much of a difference as between a perspectival projection [*scenographia*] and a ground plan [*ichnographia*]. For perspec-tival projections differ according to the position [*situs*] of the viewer, [while] a ground plan or geometrical representation is unique. God natu-rally sees things exactly such as they are according to geometrical truth, although at the same time he also knows how anything appears differ-ently to someone else, and thus all other appearances are contained in him eminently" (G II 437: AG 199). See again Rutherford, "Leibniz and the Problem of Monadic Aggregation."

81 Cf. G VI 590: L 625; and G III 430: L 633, where Leibniz speaks of Shaftesbury as overlooking his "reduction of matter or multitude to unities or simple substances."

82 This is the point at which my account diverges most sharply from that of Adams ("Phenomenalism and Corporeal Substance in Leibniz"). According to Adams, a mind indirectly perceives the members of an aggregate of monads insofar as it directly perceives bodies that are correlated in a lawlike way with the bodies that those monads perceive as theirs. Yet there is no basis for regarding any of these bodies as anything more than appearances apprehended by monadic perceivers. Adams' theory is thus genuinely phenomenalistic: it reduces to an account of how the perceptions of certain monads are harmonized with those of other monads. The crucial claim that the content of corporeal phenomena can be analyzed in such a way as to demonstrate the grounding of matter in monads is not upheld.

83 "Any mass contains innumerable monads, for although any one organic body in nature has its corresponding monad, it nevertheless contains in its parts other monads endowed in the same way with organic bodies subservient to the primary one; and the whole of nature consists of nothing else, for it is necessary that every aggregate result from simple substances as if from true elements" (Letter to Bierling, 12 August 1711; G VII 502). Cf. *Metaphysical Consequences of the Principle of Reason*, §7 (C 13–14: P 175); Letter to Dangicourt, August 1716 (E 745–46), quoted in n. 101.

84 In a manuscript fragment, Leibniz cites preestablished harmony as an example of a relation from which there results an *ens per aggregationem*: "Beings through aggregation, such as a herd, a pool full of fish, a machine, are only semi-beings [*semientia*], whose reality consists in the union that a mind makes or in an extrinsic denomination or relation. Such is distance or the preestablished harmony, which makes it that one thing seems to influence another; these are therefore mental or relational results" (LH IV, 3, 5e, Bl. 23).

85 Nevertheless, throughout this period, Leibniz continues to speak of animated creatures as "corporeal substances." A good example is his letter to De Volder of 20 June 1703: "If you think of mass as an aggregate containing many substances, you can still conceive of one preeminent substance, or a thing animated by a primary entelechy, in it. On the other hand, in the monad or complete simple substance, I unite with an entelechy only a primitive passive force which is related to the whole mass of the organic body. The remaining subordinate monads placed in the organs do not make up a part of it, though they are immediately required for it, and they combine [*concurrunt*] with the primary monad to make the organic corporeal substance, or the animal or plant. I therefore distinguish: (1) the primitive entelechy or soul; (2) primary matter or primitive passive power; (3) the complete monad formed by these

two; (4) mass or secondary matter, or the organic machine in which innumerable subordinate monads combine; and (5) the animal or corporeal substance which the dominant monad makes into one machine" (G II 252: L 530). There are two reasons for thinking that when Leibniz refers here to "corporeal substance" he is speaking loosely. First, he is clear in both this letter and the rest of the correspondence that, strictly speaking, the only true substances are monads (see the texts cited in n. 56). Second, the language he uses to describe how a mass of monads "combines" with a dominant monad is very weak (*concurrunt* = "run together" or "coincide") and need not be taken to imply anything more than an accidental unity.

86 For a statement of Tournemine's objection, see AG 196. In criticizing Leibniz's position, Tournemine is defending Church doctrine (cf. Leibniz's reference in n. 22 to the declaration of the Fifth Lateran Council), as well as the standard position of Jesuit scholastic philosophy. Concerning the latter, see Boehm, *Le "Vinculum Substantiale" chez Leibniz*.

87 Cf. his letter to the Electress Sophie of May 1706: "With regard to the relation between the different unities, and in particular between the mind and matter, I have conceived the system of preestablished harmony. . . . But if in addition to the relation between the mind and the body, by which what happens in one corresponds by itself to what happens in the other, I am still asked in what consists their union, I am not in a position to answer. For this union is not a phenomenon that makes itself known by any sensible effects beyond those of this relation, and we cannot here go above and beyond the phenomena" (Klopp, ed., *Correspondenz*, vol. 3, pp. 174–75).

88 Garber ('Leibniz and the Foundations of Physics," p. 110) recognizes the above passage as less supportive of the idea of a metaphysical union, but suggests that this is because it was written before Leibniz's reply to Tournemine. There is good evidence, however, that although this reply did not appear in the *Mémoires de Trévoux* until 1708, it was submitted to Tournemine prior to Leibniz's last letter to De Volder in January 1706. In this letter, Leibniz clearly says that he has replied (*respondi*) to Tournemine : Further evidence that he had already submitted his reply to the *Mémoires* and that it had been lost along the way is found in the first letters he exchanged with Des Bosses in February 1706 (G II 296, 301). It appears that his reply eventually reached Tournemine through the intercession of Des Bosses (see G II 354). If this is correct, then the rather more negative tone of his letter to De Volder tells us something about Leibniz's true attitude towards a metaphysical union.

89 See *Theodicy*, "Preliminary Discourse," §23 (G VI 64: H 88).

90 This might seem to be contradicted by his letter to Des Bosses of 5 February 1710: "If faith compels us to accept corporeal substances, we must say that the substance consists in that unifying reality that adds *something absolute* (and therefore substantial), though in flux, to those things that are to be united" (G II 435: AG 198). This passage, however, must be read with the knowledge that Leibniz's Lutheran faith did not compel *him* to accept the grounds being offered here for a real union (namely, transubstantiation). We shall return to this point shortly.

91 Interestingly, the same view is defended in the *New Essays* II, vi, 24, 42 (A VI.vi: RB 317–18, 328–29).

92 I am currently preparing a new critical edition of this correspondence for Felix Meiner Verlag. There I plan to deal with its contents in greater detail.

93 See Leibniz's letters of 5 February 1712 (G II 435–36: AG 198–99; G II 438–39: AG 199–200); 26 May 1712 (G II 444: AG 200–201); 16 July 1712 (G II 450–51: L 604–605); 20 September 1712 (G II 457–61: L 605–607); 24 January 1713 (G II 473–75: L 608); 23 August 1713 (G II 481–83); 21 April 1714 (G II 485–86: L 609); 29 April 1715 (G II 495–96: L 610–11); 19 August 1715 (G II 502–505: L 613–15).

94 "I fear that the things I have written you at different times on the subject do not sufficiently agree among themselves, since I have certainly treated this argument concerning the raising of phenomena to reality or composite substances only on the occasion of your letters" (30 June 1715; G II 499).

95 See also his letter of 19 August 1715 (G II 504: L 614). It should be noted, however, that in two of Leibniz's last letters from 1716, he speaks unreservedly of *mea doctrina de substantia composita,* and aligns himself openly with the position of the Schools. Cf. G II 510–11, G II 519–20, and the ontological table appended to his letter of 19 August 1715 (G II 506: L 615).

96 "If . . . composite beings are mere phenomena, it would have to be said that the substance of bodies consists in true phenomena, namely, those which God himself perceives in them through *scientia visionis,* as do also angels and the blessed, to whom it is given to see things truly. So God and the blessed would perceive the body of Christ where only bread and wine appear to us" (G II 474: L 607–8; cf. G II 482).

97 In notes ca. 1715, Leibniz argues that a real union would require an additional act of divine will over and above that which issues in the creation of monads and their preestablished harmony: "If there are real unions which not do result from the simple positing of unities, these do not exist through the divine understanding alone, like mere relations, but in addition through his will, which produces a new entity. Such

unions are necessary for corporeal masses to be true beings and they add to monads something besides a mere relation" (LH IV 8 Bl. 60 [VE 1083]). Cf. G II 438: AG 199–200.

98 See Robinet's introduction to his critical edition of the *Principles* (*G. W. Leibniz. Principes de la nature et de la grâce fondés en raison*, ed., Robinet). My quotation from Leibniz's first draft of the *Principles* is taken from this text.

99 Significantly, the only union mentioned in any version of the text is the "physical" union, determined by the "perfect *harmony* between the perceptions of the monad and the motions of bodies" (G VI 599: AG 208).

100 The following is an excerpt from this text: "I believe that the entire universe of creatures consists only of simple substances or monads and their collections [*assemblages*]. . . . The collections are what we call 'body'. . . . However, all these bodies and all that we attribute to them are not substances, but only well founded phenomena, or the foundations of appearances, which are different in different observers, but which are related and come from the same foundation, like different appearances of the same city viewed from several sides" (G III 622).

101 Leibniz later forwarded to Remond a letter, dated 4 November 1715, that includes an explicit acknowledgement of composite substances: "*Secondary matter* (as, for example, the organic body) is not a substance, but . . . a mass [*amas*] of many substances, like a pool of fish or like a herd of sheep; and consequently it is what is called an *unum per accidens*, in a word, a phenomenon. A true substance (such as an animal) is composed of an immaterial soul and an organic body, and it is the composite of these two that is called an *unum per se*. . . . [S]ouls agree with bodies, and among themselves, by virtue of the preestablished harmony, and not at all by mutual physical influence, save for the metaphysical union of the soul and its body, which makes them compose an *unum per se*, an animal, a living being" (G III 657–58). This passage should be compared with his letter to Dangicourt September 1716: "I am also of the opinion that, to speak exactly, there is no extended substance. . . . The true substances are only simple substances or what I call 'monads.' And I believe that there are only monads in nature, the rest being only phenomena which result from them. Each monad is a mirror of the universe according to its point of view and is accompanied by a multitude of other monads which compose its organic body, of which it is the dominant monad" (E 745–46).

6   The theory of knowledge

THE REACTION TO DESCARTES

On the basis of their theories of knowledge, early modern philosophers are customarily divided between rationalists and empiricists, with Leibniz following Descartes among the Rationalists, primarily because of his espousal of innate ideas. Whatever one may think of this division of philosophers, Leibniz asserts something very like it. When confronting Locke's *Essay Concerning Human Understanding*, he remarks:

Our disagreements concern points of some importance. There is the question whether the soul in itself is completely blank like a writing tablet on which nothing has yet been written – a *tabula rasa* – as Aristotle and the writer of the Essay maintain, and whether everything which is inscribed there comes solely from the senses and experience; or whether the soul inherently contains the source of various notions and doctrines, which external objects merely rouse up on suitable occasions, as I believe and as do Plato and even the schoolmen.   (*New Essays*, Preface, A VI.vi, RB 48)

Leibniz wrote an extensive commentary on and critique of Parts I and II of Descartes' *Principles of Philosophy*, but he has nothing in it to say about innate ideas because in the *Principles* neither does Descartes. Leibniz, in criticizing the theory of knowledge contained in Part I, of which he is in general highly contemptuous, has no occasion to mention them. Indeed, there is only one thing in the *Principles* for which he expresses approval: the "I think therefore I am." This he considers to be "excellent" and relates it to his own distinction between truths of reason and truths of fact. Both kinds have their primitive truths. The first truth of reason is the principle of identity or contradiction. Among the primitive truths of fact, there is the "I think that," for of what I am thinking I am immediately conscious, i.e., certain. Leibniz considers these latter truths to be an important addition to Descartes' *cogito ergo sum* as primitive truths of fact. He had, however, apparently forgotten that just as he maintained that there exists the appearance of a golden mountain or a centaur when dreaming of these, so Descartes, following on the *cogito*, had maintained that a she-goat or a chimera in the imagination, *qua* objects of thought, are exactly as they appear to consciousness and share the indubitability of the *cogito*.

The tone of Leibniz's anti-Cartesianism is immediately apparent in his reaction to the opening principle that in the search after truth one must, once in a lifetime and as far as possible, doubt everything. Leibniz sees in this a mere stunt to attract attention and Descartes' preference for applause to that certainty he was allegedly seeking. Leibniz considered the proof of nonidentical axioms a greatly superior alternative to Cartesian doubt for achieving certainty in the sciences.

Descartes' dictum that everything in which there is the least uncertainty is to be doubted might have been better and more exactly formulated in the precept that we must . . . look into the reasons for every doctrine. . . . If Descartes [like Apollonius, Proclus, and more recently Roberval who had sought to prove axioms in geometry] had wished to carry out what is best in his rule, he should have worked on the demonstration of scientific principles . . . [that is, reduce them, if they are necessary truths, to identicals].

(G IV: 354: L 383)

In Principle IV Descartes says, "our initial doubts will be about the existence of objects of sense-perception and imagination."[1] Knowing that Descartes is, in the end, going to come up with a proof for the existence of sensible or material things, Leibniz's immediate reaction is to assert that his skepticism is inescapable. There is no way in which it can be refuted. The whole of life could be a well-ordered, coherent dream in which we are to some extent able to predict the future from past experience. "To seek any other truth or reality than what this contains is vain, and skeptics ought not to demand any other, nor dogmatists promise it" (G IV 356: L 384).

However, the most fundamental differences between Leibniz and Descartes with regard to knowledge arise in connection with "clear and distinct ideas." In the *Discourse on Method*, after arriving at the *cogito ergo sum*, Descartes then considered in general what is required of a proposition in order for it to be true and certain; for since I had just found one that I knew to be such, I thought that I ought also to know what this certainty consists in. I observed that there is nothing at all in the proposition "I am thinking, therefore I exist" to assure me that I am speaking the truth except that I see very clearly that in order to think it is necessary to exist. So I decided that I could take it as a general rule that the things we conceive very clearly and very distinctly are all true.[2]

Leibniz considers this rule useless unless criteria of clearness better than those proposed by Descartes are given. For Leibniz, it is by the logical analysis or definition alone of ideas that they are rendered distinct.

For the rest, the *rules of common logic*, of which also the geometricians make use, are not to be despised as criteria of the truth of judgements. . . . A demonstration is sound when it observes the form prescribed in logic, although it need not always follow the form of syllogisms arranged in the scholastic manner . . . ; it is merely necessary that the argument be conclusive by virtue of its form [for example, "any valid calculation"].

(G IV 425–26: L 294)

Descartes on the other hand firmly rejected "the precepts of the dialecticians" who suppose that it is by the form of argument alone that we are able to arrive at conclusions which are certain; "truth often slips through these fetters, while those who employ them are left entrapped in them."[3] In place of argument which is valid by virtue of form, Descartes puts intuition and deduction – the latter consisting solely in a succession of intuitions. He defines intuition as "the conception of a clear and attentive mind, which is so easy and distinct that there can be no room for doubt about what we are understanding . . . [it] proceeds solely from the light of reason."[4] There is only one mode of cognition, a direct seeing, a mental vision or intuition. For Leibniz on the other hand most of our thinking is "blind or symbolic; we use it in algebra and arithmetic and indeed almost everywhere" (G IV 423: L 292).[5]

THREE LEVELS OF OBJECTS: THE SENSIBLE, THE
IMAGINABLE, AND THE INTELLIGIBLE

A major factor in determining the character of Leibniz's theory of knowledge is his solution of the problem of the composition of the continuum – one of the two great labyrinths in which the mind gets trapped, the other being freedom. The solution consists in distinguishing between phenomena or appearances and substances. The former are infinitely divisible and comprise such continua as space and time and the extended mass of a body, while the latter must necessarily be indivisible unities. The principle of the identity of indiscernibles, or "that there is no perfect similarity anywhere" ("On Nature Itself," par. 13) requires that these simple substances must be distinguished by their internal qualities and that there must then be a plurality of affections and relations within the unity of the simple substance. The only way in which this plurality in unity can be conceived is as we find it in our own experience, namely the plurality in unity which characterizes a perception (*Monadology*, pars. 16, 17, G VI 609: L 644). "One cannot doubt the possibility of many things in one, for our soul provides us with an example of it" (G II 112). The terms "perception," "representation," and "expression" are equivalent. Another psychological term which enters into the concept of a simple substance or monad is that of appetition, the internal principle of change, i.e., the tendency of a perception to a succeeding perception. This does not mean, however, that all these perceiving and appetitive beings are minds. To be a mind or spirit is to be able to think, to form concepts, to reason, and to discover necessary truths. And what makes this possible in the simple substance is the possession of consciousness or apperception. "It is well to make the distinction between perception, which is the internal state of the monad representing external things, and *apperception*, which is *consciousness* or the reflexive knowledge of this internal state itself and which is not given to all souls, nor at all times to the same soul"(*Principles of Nature and Grace*, par. 4, G VI 600: L 637).

Apperception, as consciousness of the internal states, is always at the same time consciousness of the I or the self, the subject of these states. It is by virtue of this consciousness that we become persons, beings accountable for our actions, members of a moral world. Besides apperception there is one other necessary condition of the possibility of thought, namely sensation. "The most abstract thoughts are in need of some *sense perception*" (G IV 563), and that in turn makes it essential that the simple substance which is a mind or spirit be related to a body with sense organs. The body consists of an infinitude of subordinate monads under a dominant

monad, or substantial form, and comprising with it a living substance or organism.

Together with a particular body, each monad makes a living substance. . . .
But when the monad has organs so adjusted that by means of them the
impressions which are received, and consequently the perceptions which
represent these impressions, are heightened and distinguished (as, for example, when rays of light are concentrated by means of the shape of the hu-
mours of the eye and act with greater force), then this may amount to
sensation.   (*Principles of Nature and Grace*, par. 4, G VI 599: L 637)

It is as sufficiently heightened and distinct that perceptions are
noticed, that is, become objects of apperception or consciousness. It
is at this point in our experience that ideas or concepts come into
play. Ideas are distinguished by two principal characteristics: first,
they are dispositions or capacities for thought, and, two, they have
as objects the possible, including the actual as possible. This can be
seen if we consider the clear idea of sensible qualities such as
colors, sounds, tastes, odors. We are said to have a clear idea of blue
if we are able to recognize this object as blue, recognition here
being the act of thought of which the clear idea is the power or
capacity. Second, the idea is the recognition that *this* blue is the
bearer of resemblance to other possibles, whether or not we have
ever seen another blue, i.e., the clear idea is of possibles, including
as possible this actual blue.

Besides the idea of sensible qualities which comes to us from one
or other of the particular external senses, there are some which
come from more than one sense, such as number, magnitude, space,
figure, and motion. These are attributed to the common sense and,
unlike the proper sensibles, they are susceptible of definition. As
such they are not only clear, they are also distinct.

There must be an *internal sense* where the perceptions of these different
external senses are found united. This is called the *imagination*, which
comprises at once the *concepts of particular senses*, which are *clear* but
confused, and the *concepts of the common sense*, which are clear and distinct. And these clear and distinct ideas which are subject to the imagination are the objects of the *mathematical sciences*, namely arithmetic and
geometry, which are the *pure* mathematical sciences, and their applications
to nature, which make up *mixed* mathematics [such as optics, astronomy
and phoronomy].
                 ("On What is Independent of Sense and Matter," G VI 501: L 548)

The possibility of these mathematical sciences rests on more than sense and imagination. The intellect is also involved. Besides the objects of the particular senses and those of the common sense, or imagination, there are some which are intelligible only, for example, the concept of the I who perceives and acts. The I is neither sensible, nor imaginable, but intelligible only.

> And since I conceive that there are other beings who also have the right to say "I," or for whom this can be said, it is by this that I conceive what is called *substance* in general. It is the consideration of myself, also, which provides me with other concepts in *metaphysics*, such as those of cause, effect, action, similarity, etc., and even with those of *logic* and *ethics*. . . . There are thus three levels of concepts: those which are *sensible* only, which are produced by each sense in particular; those which are at once *sensible* and *intelligible*, which appertain to the common sense; and those which are *intelligible* only, which belong to the understanding. The first and second together are imaginable but the third lie beyond the imagination. The second and third are intelligible and distinct, but the first are confused, although they may be clear and recognizable.   (Ibid., G VI 502: L 549)

In this letter to the Queen of Prussia, Leibniz does not indicate where physics comes into the ordering of the sciences, but elsewhere he indicates that physics rests on a conjunction of two classes of concepts – those of mathematics and those of metaphysics. Here he is consciously attacking the Cartesian notion of extension as constituting the nature of corporeal substance with its consequence as stated by Descartes at the conclusion of his *Principles of Material Things*, which contain his laws of motion. Descartes writes, "The only principles which I accept, or require, in physics are those of geometry and pure mathematics; these principles explain all natural phenomena, and enable us to provide quite certain demonstrations regarding them."[7] In the *Specimen Dynamicum*, in which Leibniz offers an explanation of his "new science of dynamics," he claims to show that "if the body is understood in mathematical terms alone – magnitude, figure, and their change," then certain absurdities arise in "the bare laws of motion derived from geometry." What is required is something additional to the geometrical, namely the concept of force which is metaphysical. "I concluded, therefore, that besides purely mathematical principles subject to the imagination, there must be admitted certain metaphysical principles perceptible only by the mind," such as those of cause and effect, action and passion, in short the concept of forces (G M VI 241–42: L 440–41). A similar reference is made to the imagination in the *Tentamen Anagogicum,* where he refers to the errors of those whose "thinking stops at what imagination can supply, namely at magnitudes and figures and their modifications. But when one pushes forward this inquiry into reasons it is found that the laws of motion cannot be explained through purely geometrical principles or by the imagination alone" (G VII 271: L 478). The following statements will serve to indicate the essential relation of mathematics to the imagination for Leibniz:

Mathematics is the science of imaginable things.   (C 556)

Universal mathematics should treat of the method of determining exactly that which falls under the imagination or that which I call the logic of the imagination.   (C 348)

Geometry or the science of universal imagination.   (GM III 243)

THE IMAGINARY, THE ABSTRACT, AND THE IDEAL IN MATHEMATICS AND NATURAL SCIENCE

We can better understand Leibniz's use of the term "imagination" if we consider two other terms that appear in the same contexts: "abstraction" and "the ideal" or "mental" in the discussion of continua. The concept of the continuum or of "the repetition and diffusion of the same nature" has its origin in the senses, as, for example, the yellow color in gold, or whiteness in milk, or weight in a body. This appearance of continuity is the result of a deficiency in our senses, which are incapable of revealing the little inequalities and differences in actual things. "Things which are uniform, containing no variety, are always mere abstractions, for instance, time, space and the other entities of pure mathematics (*New Essays,* II.1.2, A VI.vi: RB 110). Or again, "In actual bodies there is only discrete quantity . . . But a continuous quantity is something ideal which pertains to possibles and to actuals only insofar as they are possible" (G II 282: L 539).

The imaginary, the abstract, and the ideal are contrasted by Leibniz with the actual or real, and they give rise to the following seeming paradox – "that though continuity is something ideal and there is never anything in nature with perfectly uniform parts, the real, in turn, never ceases to be governed perfectly by the ideal and the abstract . . . this is because everything is governed by reason; otherwise there would be no science and no rule" (GM IV 93–4: L 544). Those perfectly straight and circular lines which are drawn by the imagination, for example the line joining the centers of two globes, or the axes and circles in a sphere, though they are nothing actual, nevertheless can be clearly and distinctly conceived, that is to say, can be defined. And it is definitions together with the axiom of identity which make possible the knowledge of eternal truths and the demonstrative sciences. In speaking of space and time, which, as continua, are ideal, Leibniz says, "Continuity uniformly regulated, although only something supposed and an abstraction, forms the foundation of eternal truths and the necessary sciences: it is the object of the divine understanding as are all truths" (G VII 564).

How then does the mind make the transition from the extension it initially encounters in physical bodies to the extension in purely mathematical bodies? Extension is always the extension or diffusion of something. In the case of space, its subject is the diffusion of place, just as in a physical body its subject is the diffusion of antitypia (mass or resistance). Leibniz calls space, or diffusion of place, the primary subject of extension. By virtue of it we are able to speak of physical bodies as being situated in space. But what then is place? The concept of place is an ideal thing, a being of the imagination formed by abstraction. Physical bodies have relations of "situation" to one another. But in nature there are no two things that are exactly the same and no two things could have successively the same relations of situation, however similar, to other things taken to be at rest.

For two different subjects, as A and B, cannot have precisely the same individual affection, it being impossible that the same individual accident should be in two subjects or pass from one subject to another. But the mind, not contented with an agreement, looks for an identity, for something that should be truly the same, and conceives it as being extrinsic to the thing, containing a certain order, wherein the mind conceives the application of relations.   (G VII 400: L 704)

The concept of time, or the temporal continuum, is formed in a way analogous to the formation of the concept of space, that is, with times like places being formed by abstraction. "*Space* is nothing but the order of the existence of things possible at the same time, while *time* is the order of existence of things possible successively" (G II 269: L 536). *Number*, the subject of arithmetic, has the same mental or imaginary status as space and time. It is an abstraction from numbered things. "The concepts [of number and time] are only orders or relations pertaining to possibility and to the eternal truths of the world, and are then further applicable to actual events" (G II 268: L 536). In commenting on Locke's classification of objects of thought into substances, modes, and relations, Leibniz says that while qualities are only modifications of substances, "the understanding adds the relations. . . . It may be that *dozen* and *score* are merely relations and exist only with respect to the understanding" (*New Essays* II. 12.3 and 5, A VI.vi: RB 145). Numbers are in the same case as space and the surfaces, lines and points that are conceived in it, that is, they are nothing but relations or order and have no ultimate components (G IV 491). They are extrinsic denominations, indifferent to the things that can be enumerated, and as such are beings of the imagination.

One of Leibniz's main criticisms of Locke in the *New Essays* is that he confuses an idea with an image. He remarks "how essential it is to distinguish *images* from *exact ideas*, which are composed of definitions"(*New Essays* II, 9.8, A VI.vi: RB 137). Leibniz was writing the *New Essays* in the same period as when in his correspondence with the Queen of Prussia he speaks of "the clear and distinct ideas of the common sense which are subject to the imagination" as being "the objects of the *mathematical sciences*, namely arithmetic and geometry." It is probably for tactical reasons that Leibniz, in making his case against Locke, is silent about his own conception of the essential connection between mathematics and the imagination. There is, of course, no confusion in Leibniz's own treatment of ideas and the imaginable. When he defines mathematics as "the science of imaginable things," he is saying, in effect, the objects of the mathematical ideas are imaginable things. The very space of the geometers is an ideal thing, a being of the imagination, and the clear and distinct ideas of space, of figures, of numbers, etc., are definitions of these imaginable things.

Another function of the imagination is that of bestowing unity on a set of data of sense so that they can be conceived as together comprising   *one* thing or *one* body. Among the metaphysical concepts which arise from reflection on the I or self are those of being and unity. "I hold as axiomatic," says Leibniz, "the identical proposition which varies only in emphasis; that which is not truly *one* entity is not truly one *entity* either. It has always been thought that 'one' and 'entity' are interchangeable" (G II 97). There are for Leibniz two kinds of entities and correspondingly two kinds of unity: substance, which is *unum per se* or a true unity, and entity by aggregation or *unum per accidens*, "an entity of the imagination or perception" (G II 96). "A body is not a true unity; it is only an aggregate, which the Scholastics call a being *per accidens*, a collection like a herd. Its unity comes from our perception. It is a being of *reason*, or rather, of *imagination*, a phenomenon" (G VI 586: L 623).

As we have noted, Leibniz maintained that besides the purely mathematical principles subject to the imagination it is necessary in physics to admit certain metaphysical principles, i.e., forces. The concept of force, like all other metaphysical concepts, is got by reflection on the self. In his metaphysics Leibniz makes a distinction between primitive forces, which are permanent and are the monadic substances themselves, defined as "beings capable of action," and derivative forces which are the changing modifications of the primitive forces. It is the derivative forces which are diffused through a phenomenon or aggregate of monads. Active derivative force is the cause of motion and is measured by mass and the square of velocity.

I regard substance itself, being endowed with primary active and passive power, as an indivisible or perfect monad – like the ego, or something similar to it – but I do not so regard the derivative forces, which are found to be changing continuously. . . . The forces which arise from mass and velocity are derivative and belong to aggregates or phenomena. . . . [But] derivative forces are in fact nothing but the modifications and echoes of primitive forces.   (G II 251: L 530)

Taken metaphysically, derivative forces are modifications of primitive forces, but when *a* force is attributed to *a* body, it has the *unity* of an aggregate of modifications of primitive forces. It is a phenomenon, and like all phenomena a product of abstraction, in this case abstraction from the monadic substances which are its foundation, with the consequence that the consideration of monads "serves no purpose in the details of physics and . . . they ought not to be used to explain particular phenomena" (G IV 434: L 308).

As we have seen, Leibniz defines mathematics in terms of its objects, namely imaginable things. There are no actual determinate figures, or circles, or ellipses in nature, but they can be drawn in the imagination if one has their concepts or definitions. To have a real as opposed to a merely nominal definition is to know the possibility of the thing. In geometry, this possibility can be known in either of two ways: by an analytical definition showing that the concept contains no contradiction or logical incompatibility of terms, or by a causal definition showing the method by which the thing can be produced. "Hence," says Leibniz, "causal definitions are more useful than others" (G IV 425: L 293).[8] Euclid's concept of the circle, for example, namely that of a figure described by the motion of a straight line in a plane about a fixed end, provides a real definition, i.e., shows that such a figure is possible (G VII 294: L 230). Or we may take the definition of parallel straight lines which states that the two lines in the same plane will never meet. This, says Leibniz, is only a nominal definition because we can still doubt its possibility.

But once we understand that we can have a straight line in a plane, parallel to a given straight line, by ensuring that the point of the stylus drawing the parallel line remains at the same distance from the given line, we see at once that the thing is possible, and why they have the property of never meeting, which is their nominal definition.   (*New Essays* III. 3. 18, A VI.vi: RB 295)

THE ROLE OF FICTIONS IN SCIENCE

But while Leibniz defines mathematics as the science of imaginables, or as things which come under the imagination, we must take account of such a statement as that made to Lady Masham that she should not be astonished that there are things which are beyond extension and the changes which take place in it and which are therefore not imaginable, "for even mathematics furnishes us with an infinity of things which cannot be imagined" (G III 357). The reason that they cannot be imagined, i.e., constructed in the imagination, is that their concepts contain a contradiction. For example, the law of continuity takes "rest as infinitely small motion (that is, as equivalent to a particular instance of its own contradictory), coincidence as infinitely small distance, equality as the limit of inequalities" (GM IV 93: L 544). Or, to take other examples, we might conceive of a space with more than three dimensions, or powers whose exponents are not ordinary numbers, to shorten our reasoning (GM IV 92–93: L 543). The reason that four dimensions in space are unimaginable is that they cannot be constructed in the imagination, that is to say, they are not possible. Consider the following constructions.

A *surface* is the path of a line. A *filled space* [*amplum*] or what is commonly called a *solid* is the path of a surface. The magnitudes of the paths in which points describe lines, lines surfaces and surfaces solids are called *length*, *breadth* and *depth*. These are called dimensions, and in geometry it is shown that there are only three.   (GM VII 20–21: L 668)

That space can have only three dimensions is a necessary truth, "because," Leibniz says in the *Theodicy*, "the geometricians have been able to prove that there are only three straight lines perpendicular to one another which can intersect at one and the same point" (*Theodicy*, par. 351, G VI 323). If the three-dimensionality of space is a necessary truth then the conceptions of four- or five-dimensional spaces will contain a contradiction, i.e., are not possible, but, nevertheless, just by virtue of that it is possible that they could perform a methodological function in the discovery of truth and shorten our reasoning. It is true that Leibniz uses the same expression for such unimaginable concepts as he does for the concepts of imaginable things like straight lines, circles and ellipses, namely that they are "ideal or abstract" concepts (GM IV 92–93: L 543–44). But he also has another name for them, "useful fictions." The notions of infinite wholes and infinitesimals imply a contradiction, and there can be none in nature (*New Essays* II. 17.3, A VI.vi: RB 158).

I regard both of them as fictions of the mind, useful for calculation as are imaginary roots in algebra. In the meantime I have shown that these expressions have great use for the abbreviating of thought and thus for invention, and that they cannot lead to error for it is sufficient to substitute for the infinitely small as small a thing as one may wish, so that the error may be less than any given amount.   (G II 305; cf. GM IV 98; G VI 629)

These unimaginables do not, however, conflict with Leibniz's definition of mathematics as the science of imaginable things, for their utility lies precisely in establishing truths about imaginable things, as, for example, in the cases of concepts involved in the law of continuity, where truths can be determined about rest, coincidence or equality, which are possible properties of imaginable things, and properties also of physical phenomena to the extent that they are subject to the imagination and that mathematics is accordingly applicable to them.

It was inevitable that in his dispute with Locke over innate ideas Leibniz should have invoked mathematics and stated approvingly that Plato in the *Meno* had shown that "all arithmetic and geometry are innate." The question arises, in what sense are they innate if one takes into account that these sciences are both sensible, i.e., imaginable and intelligible, and that without the senses they would not exist. It has already been noted that the concept of the continuum has its origin in the senses. It is a pure appearance, arising from the mind's incapacity to discern or distinguish the actual parts. What appears is a continuum or diffusion of the same, as, for example, in a color or the hardness of a body. The primary characteristic of a continuum for Leibniz is that it is indeterminate as to parts or contains the pure possibilities of division to infinity.

Space, time, mathematical motion, the intension or continual increase one conceives in velocity and other qualities, in short all that gives rise to the thought of possibilities, is in itself a continuous and indeterminate possibility of dividing as one will.   (G VII 562)

An entire realm of possibles, the objects of the concepts of geometry, is recognized by the understanding in the idea of space. It is the concepts of these possibles which the understanding adds to what is furnished by the common sensibles. As he says to Locke's spokesman, "they are from the mind itself" (*New Essays* II. 5, A VI.vi: RB 128). In that sense, they are innate.

The objects of arithmetic, like those of geometry, belong to the realm of the possibles, for the concepts of number, like those of space and time, "are only orders or relations pertaining to possibility" (G II 268). But does number as an order of possibilities arise out of common sense and the imaginable as do the concepts of geometry? While it is only sensible or imaginary things which have continuous quantity, it might be argued that it is not sensible things alone which are numberable. Leibniz himself raises this point in the early *Cum Deo* in speaking of arithmetic as "the science of quantity or numbers." He continues, "But the Scholastics falsely believed that number arises only from the division of the continuum and cannot be applied to incorporeal beings. For number is a kind of incorporeal figure, as it were, which arises from the union of any beings whatever; for example, God, an angel, a man, and motion taken together are four" (G IV 35: L 76–7). It would appear, however, that Leibniz, like Descartes, derives number as a concept of arithmetic from extension. Thus, when Descartes examines his ideas of external things, he remarks that he is able "distinctly to imagine continuous quantity, or the breadth, and depth that is in this quantity. . . . Moreover I am able to *number* in it many different parts, and attribute to each of its parts many sorts of size, figure, situation, and local motion. . . . I discover an infinitude of particulars respecting *numbers*, figures, motions and other such things" (author's emphasis).[9] Leibniz says, "Whenever one tries to explain sensible qualities distinctly one always falls back on mathematical ideas, and these ideas always include *magnitude* or multitude of parts" (G VI 501: L 548). Just because of its divisibility into parts continuous quantity involves number.

In the three levels of concepts distinguished in the letter to the Queen of Prussia, the third consists of those concepts which lie beyond the imagination and are intelligible only, those of metaphysics, logic, and ethics. Like the concepts of the mathematical sciences they are innate, but in a different way, or, rather, in two different ways. In the first of these, the concepts have their origin in apperception, consciousness of, or reflection on, the self. The self is conscious of itself as being, as one, as acting, as possessing the power to act. Here, Leibniz presents an important parallel with his account of the origin of the concepts of the proper sensibles, like colors and sounds, where, for example, on encountering the color blue for the first time I recognize this blue as the bearer of similarity to other possibles which I may have not yet encountered. Apperception of the self and its actions is conceived by Leibniz as *like* immediate sense experience. He conveys this by such expressions as *"le sens interne"* (G V 23), *"le sentiment du moi"* (G V 218), *"les experiences internes immediates"* (G V 221). Directly involved in the experience of the self and its attributes is the concept of other possible beings possessing similar attributes. It is in this way that I acquire the general concepts of those properties common to all classes of beings. These concepts are innate in that the possibles which are their objects are discovered in the self. But the metaphysical concepts are innate also in another way closely related to Leibniz's definition of substance as a being capable of action. In the present case this active substance is the mind. Ideas or concepts are specific powers or dispositions to acts of thought, and these powers of the mind are never without acts. They are constitutive of the nature of the mind as mind, and those who speak of the mind as "a 'blank page' cannot say what is left over of it once the ideas have been taken away – like the Scholastics who leave nothing in their 'prime' matter" (*New Essays* II.1.2, A VI.vi: RB 110). Leibniz refers to ideas as "functions of the soul." Thus he says, "I have shown that there are in truth certain materials of thought or objects of the understanding in the soul which have not been furnished by the external senses, namely the soul itself and its functions (*nihil est in intellectu quod non fuerit in sensu, nisi ipse intellectus*) (G VI 532: L 556). In response to Locke's assertion of the absurdity of supposing the ideas of *impossibility* and *identity* (terms in the principle of identity) to be innate since children and many adults have never heard of them, Leibniz says, "The ideas of *being, of possible,* and *same* are so thoroughly innate, that they enter into all our thoughts and reasoning, and I regard them as essential to our minds. But I have already said that we do not always pay particular attention to them, and that it takes time to sort them out" (*New Essays* I.3.3, A VI.vi: RB 102).

THE CONCEPT OF AN INDIVIDUAL

A further type of Leibnizian concept is that which he calls *complete* and which he contrasts with *incomplete and abstract* concepts, the latter being such as "thought supports but which nature does not know in their bare form; such notions as that of time, also of space, or that which is extended only mathematically, of merely passive mass, of motion considered mathematically, etc" (G II 249: L 529). A complete concept is the concept of the individual in its pure individuality. It is impossible that the human understanding should ever have such concepts; only the divine understanding can. "It is impossible for us to know individuals or to find any way of precisely *determining* the individuality of anything. . . . Individuality involves infinity, and only someone who is capable of grasping the infinite could know the principle of individuation of a given thing" (*New Essays* III.3.6, A VI.vi: RB 289–90). That there must be such concepts of individuals is a consequence of the nature of truth according to which in all true propositions, necessary or contingent, universal or particular, the concept of the predicate is contained in that of the subject – "otherwise I do not know what truth is" (G II 56: L 337). Each individual substance expresses the entire infinite universe in its own way and is therefore the subject of an infinitude of predicates. For each of these to be truly asserted of the individual substance there must be "a concept of it so complete that it is sufficient to make us understand and deduce from it all the predicates of the subject to which the concept is attributed" (G IV 433: L 307). Not only must there be such concepts of actual individuals, but there must be such concepts for all *possible* individuals for it is among these that God chooses those which are to be made actual. "Lying springs from the Devil's own nature . . . because it is written in the book of eternal truths, which contains things possible before any decree of God that this creature would freely turn towards evil if he were created (*Theodicy*, par. 275, G VI 280).

The nature of the inclusion of the predicate in the subject differs, however, for the concept of an individual man, e.g., Adam and his historic act of sinning, and the general concept of "man" which, on analysis, might be found to contain "rational" and "animal." The concept of an individual takes the form of a law, the law of a series, differing from a mathematical series, however, in that its successive terms are ordered in time. This law constitutes the individuality of each substance. Given the law and the beginning of the series it would be possible to deduce all the successive predicates of the individual.

Besides the concept of the individual, Leibniz speaks also of the concept of the world which contains its individual members. And this concept of the world too is a law. Moreover, the law of each individual in it is only a variation of the general law of the world differing from it as a city appears differently from different points of view. Leibniz refers to the concept of the world as the "primary concept" and whatever occurs in the history of the individuals in it is a consequence of this general law. This, nevertheless, conflicts with some very deeply held views of Leibniz. To say that there is "a concept of the world so complete . . ." etc. is to say that the world is an individual substance; for there to be such a concept constitutes the very definition of an individual substance (G IV 433: L 307). To think of the world as a super-individual, embracing all other individuals in it as having an organic unity like Adam's soul in relation to his body is either to identify the world with God or to think of God as the soul of the world and the world as his body. "The world cannot be regarded as an animal or as a substance" (*Theodicy*, par. 195, G VI 232). The world is not an individual substance but an aggregate of substances.

> It is true that there is sometimes more, sometimes less basis for assuming many things to be forming a single thing, according to the degree of connection between these things, but that is useful only for abridging our thoughts and representing phenomena. It seems too that what makes the essence of a being by aggregation is only a state of being of those of which it is composed; for instance what constitutes the essence of an army is only a state of being of the men who compose it.   (G II 96–7)

No matter how strong the reasons for regarding the world as a single entity and the integration of all its parts to a common end, the law of the universe would be only a compendium of the laws of its individual members.

THE EPISTEMIC STATUS OF THE PRINCIPLES OF CONTRADICTION AND SUFFICIENT REASON

With concepts there comes the recognition of truths and knowledge of the reasoning by which truths are arrived at. Reasoning is based on two great principles: the Principle of Contradiction or Axiom of Identity, according to which what involves a contradiction is false, and the Principle of Sufficient Reason, according to which nothing can be true or existent for which there is not a sufficient reason or cause why it is so. Leibniz does not give a consistent account of the epistemological status of these two principles. Sometimes the Principle of Contradiction is given the status of a necessary *assumption*, one which we must make if we are to reason at all, let alone be able to affirm or deny anything (GV 14–15).

> One cannot go to infinity in his proofs and therefore some things must be assumed without proof . . . after the example of the geometricians who acknowledge at the very outset the assumed axioms they are to use, so that they may be sure that all conclusions are proved at least hypothetically. First of all, I assume that every affirmation or negation is either true or false and if the affirmation is true the negation is false.   (G VII 299: L 225)

There then follows a long list of different formulations of the Principle of Contradiction (ibid.). But sometimes Leibniz regards the

principle of contradiction and other principles as native to the mind
and determining how it works.

For general principles enter into our thoughts, serving as their inner core
and as their mortar. Even if we give no thought to them, they are necessary
for thought, as muscles and tendons are for walking. The mind relies on
these principles constantly; but it does not find it so easy to sort them out
and to command a distinct view of each of them separately, for that requires
great attention to what it is doing, and the unreflective majority are hardly
capable of that.   (*New Essays* I.1.20, A VI.vi: RB 84)

He also refers to the principles of reasoning being employed by "a
natural instinct" (*New Essays* I.2.3, A VI.vi: RB 90). We have here,
then, an argument for the innateness of the principles of reasoning
similar to that, as we saw, for the innateness of metaphysical concepts, "being," "possible," "the same," namely that they are essential to the mind as "entering" into all our thoughts and reasoning.

But Leibniz has another quite different argument for innateness
based on the nonempirical nature of necessary truths – "for the
senses can indeed help us after a fashion to know what is, but they
cannot help to know what must be or what cannot be otherwise." For
us to know these truths there must be "a light which is born with us"
(G VI 505: L 551). Necessary truths are either identical propositions or
reducible to identities by definitions or the analysis of their terms or
concepts. Identical axioms which are the indemonstrable foundations of necessary truths are merely different embodiments or exem-
plifications of *the* axiom of identity or principle of contradiction –
"We can really count *A is A* and *B is B* as a single principle variously
garbed" (*New Essays* IV.7.10, A VI.vi: RB 414). Because all necessary
truths are reducible to identities, and all identities are simply *the*
principle of contradiction or axiom of identity itself, and because all
necessary truths must be innate because not drawn from the senses
and by induction, then so must the principle of contradiction be innate. But to say that "*A is A*" or "*AB is A*" is innate because these
statements are not drawn from the senses and by induction is hardly
likely to be a compelling argument for the many who think that there
are necessary truths and that, as does Leibniz, they are "analytic" – to
use the terminology of a later period.

As for the principle of sufficient reason there is no consistent
account of its status because of differences of meaning which Leib-

niz gives to the expression "sufficient reason." At one point he puts
it on the same basis as the principle of contradiction; these two basic
truths are assumptions (G II 62). Elsewhere he makes it the first and
immediate consequence of the principle that in every true proposition the predicate is contained within the concept of the subject,
whether the proposition is universal or singular, necessary or contingent. "At once this gives rise to the accepted axiom that *there is
nothing without a reason or no effect without a cause*. Otherwise
there would be truth that could not be proved a priori or resolved
into identities – contrary to the nature of truth, which is always
expressly or implicitly identical" (C 519: L 268).[10] The difference
between a necessary and a contingent truth is that in the case of the
former the proof can be achieved by a finite analysis, but the latter
requires an infinite analysis, and that, of course, can never be accomplished by the human mind, nor, Leibniz admits, can it be accomplished by the divine mind either, for not even God can perform the
contradictory or complete an infinite analysis. Nevertheless he can
know the contingent truths, if not by proof, by "an infallible vision."

In other versions of the principle of sufficient reason, Leibniz is
concerned not with the logical relation of the predicate with the
subject, but with the cause of events and the existence of things.
Sometimes the cause referred to is the efficient cause, but more generally the final cause. In the latter case the principle is also called the
principle of perfection or of the best. In his exchange with Clarke over
the nature of space and time, Leibniz makes very extensive use of the
principle of sufficient reason or principle of perfection to undermine
Newton's theory of absolute space and time. Finally in frustration,
Clarke complains that Leibniz always "supposes" the principle but
gives no proof of it. Leibniz was deeply disturbed at this charge.

He pretended, that I have been guilty of a *petitio principii*. But of what
principle, I beseech you? Would to God, less clear principles had never been
laid down. The principle in question, is the principle of the want of a sufficient reason; in order to anything's existing. In order to any event's happening. In order to any truth's taking place. Is this principle that wants to be
proved? . . . Has not everybody made use of this principle, upon a thousand
occasions? . . . I have often defied people to allege an instance against that
great principle, to bring any one uncontested example wherein it falls. But
they have never done it, nor *ever* will.

(Fifth Paper to Clarke, pars. 125–29, G VII 419–20: L 717)

It would appear that when Leibniz expresses surprise that the principle should be thought to need any proof, and asserts that everyone
has made use of it a thousand times, he is referring to the very
general principle that every event has a cause rather than specifically to the principle of perfection. But how does Leibniz himself
make use of the principle of the best? In two ways. First, negatively,
to show the impossibility of "absolute real time or space, a vacuum,
atoms, attraction in the Scholastic [i.e., Newtonian] sense, a physical influence of the soul over the body, and a thousand other fictions" (Fifth Paper to Clarke, par. 127, G VII 420: L 717). Second, he
uses the principle of the best to establish scientific laws such as the
laws of motion or those of optics. In the *Discourse on Metaphysics*
(sections 5 and 6) Leibniz states "of what the rules of the divine
action consist." There are two rules: first, "that the simplicity of the
means is in balance with the richness of the effects," and second,
"that God does nothing which is disorderly."

In relation to physics, these two rules give rise to three architectonic principles or principles expressive of final causes: the law of
continuity, which is a principle of order; the principle of determination by maxima and minima; and finally, the principle of the easiest
and most determined action, this third consisting in a conjunction
of the first two. These principles are specifications of the two "rules
of divine action" insofar as they are applied to actions *in space*, for it
is with these that physics is concerned. They therefore have a special relation to geometry. In the case of the principle of continuity
Leibniz says,

I certainly hold that this principle is a general one and holds not only in
geometry but also in physics. Since geometry is but the science of the
continuous, it is not surprising that the law is observed everywhere in
it. . . . The universality of this principle in geometry soon informed me
that it could not fail to apply also to physics, since I see that for there to be
any regularity and order in nature, the physical must constantly be in
harmony with the geometrical, and that the contrary would happen if
whenever geometry requires some continuation physics would allow a
certain interruption.[11]

In geometry discontinuities are logically impossible, not so for
physics. That the law of continuity holds in physics is a contingent truth to be accounted for by the divine wisdom. The prin-

ciple can be put to work to show the bizarre discontinuities entailed by Descartes' laws of motion, and it is by the elimination of these discontinuities that Leibniz arrives at the true laws of motion. As for the method of analysis by maximum and minimum quantities, which, Leibniz says, goes back to the ancient geometers, it will be found that the principle of determination by maxima and minima operates in nature also. Leibniz combines it with the law of continuity to form the principle of the most determined action and then uses this in turn to find the laws of reflection and refraction in optics (*Tentamen Anagogicum,* G VII 270–79: L 477–84).

HOW THE TRUTH OF THE "NEW SYSTEM" IS TO BE DETERMINED

What kind of knowledge claims does Leibniz put forward for the truth of his system – "the new system of pre-established harmony"? The name itself gives some initial indications. From the beginning he puts the system forward as a hypothesis. The terms "system," "hypothesis," "harmony," are all borrowed from the language of the astronomers, and so also is the notion that it is the function of a hypothesis "to save appearances." Further the new system is a cosmology of immaterial monadic substances conceived to some degree by analogy with the cosmologies of the astronomers. Speaking of his own system, Leibniz says, "All hypotheses are made with a special view . . . i.e., to save appearances. . . . It is usually enough if a hypothesis is proved a posteriori, but where there are in addition other reasons for it, and these a priori, it is so much the better" (G IV 496). With respect to his first presentation of the system, he says, "I can prove all of this, but for the present it is enough to maintain it as a possible hypothesis suitable for explaining phenomena" (G IV 518: L 493). In the history of his accounts of the system, there is a tendency to move from the *a priori* reasons for it to the *a posteriori* justification, i.e., as the saving of appearances. In the first but unpublished statement of it in *First Truths* (1680–84), where it is called the "hypothesis of concomitance," it is given in a logically ordered list of what "follows from" the principle of sufficient reason, which, in turn, is given as a consequence of the inherence of the predicate in the subject. In the first published account, *A New*

System of the Nature and the Communication of Substances, as well as the Union of the Soul and the Body (1695), the principal claim for the hypothesis resides in the extent of what it can explain, i.e., it is given an *a posteriori* justification. "This hypothesis is entirely possible.... As soon as one sees the possibility of this hypothesis of agreement one sees that it is the most reasonable one." There then follows a list of its explanatory advantages and he concludes, "In addition to all these advantages which recommend this hypothesis, we can say that it is something more than a hypothesis, since it seems hardly possible to explain things in any other intelligible way, and since a number of serious difficulties which have heretofore troubled thinkers seem to disappear of themselves when we rightly understand it" (G IV 486: L 458–59). The fullest and ultimate justification of the new system is to be found at the beginning of the *New Essays* (1704), and it is entirely *a posteriori*. Where in *First Truths* the hypothesis is but one of the consequences of the principle of the inherence of the predicate in the subject, it now embraces in its explanatory scope the whole of Leibniz's philosophy, including the elements of his theory of knowledge, which has been the subject of this essay (*New Essays* I.1, A VI.vi: RB 71–73).

NOTES

1 Adam and Tannery, eds., *Oeuvres de Descartes*, VIII–A 5–6; Cottingham, Stoothoff, and Murdoch, trans., *The Philosophical Writings of Descartes*, I 193–94.

2 Adam and Tannery VI 33; Cottingham, Stoothoff, and Murdoch I 127.

3 Adam and Tannery X 405–6; Cottingham, Stoothoff, and Murdoch I 36.

4 Adam and Tannery X 368; Cottingham, Stoothoff, and Murdoch I 14.

5 In his *Leibniz critique de Descartes*, Belaval's first chapter is a very thorough study of what he calls Leibniz's *"formalisme"* as opposed to Descartes' *"intuitionisme."* On p. 53 he aptly remarks, *"L'ordre des raisons pour Descartes est une chaine d'intuitions; il devient pour Leibniz catena definitionum"* (G I 174).

6 In Ishiguro's *Leibniz's Philosophy of Logic and Language*, there is a valuable study of "Ideas of sensible qualities," pp. 52–70.

7 *The Principles of Philosophy*, pt. II, art. 64, Adam and Tannery IX 101; Cottingham, Stoothoff, and Murdoch I 247.

8 A third way of knowing possibility is by experiencing the actual existence of the thing, for whatever exists is possible. This will not help, however, with circles and ellipses for there are none existing in nature.

9 Adam and Tannery IX 50–1.

10 The same claim is made also for the principle of contradiction. "These two principles are contained in the definition of the True and the False." *Theodicy*, Appendix IV, par. 14, G VI 414.

11 Cassirer, ed., and Buchenau, trans., *G.W. Leibniz Hauptschriften zur Gruendung der Philosophie*, II 556.

7 Philosophy and logic

Problems about the relations between Leibniz's philosophy and his logic have exercised scholars ever since Bertrand Russell's book on the philosophy of Leibniz, first published in 1900. The thesis of that book, as Russell expressed it later,[1] was that "Leibniz's philosophy was almost entirely derived from his logic." Russell's argument was that Leibniz derived from his logic his distinctive views about the nature of substance – that each substance is a genuine unity, a "monad"; that each created substance expresses the entire universe, and, strictly speaking, does not act on any other substance; that each substance is a soul, or at any rate soul-like; and that no substance resembles any other substance entirely. Russell also discussed Leibniz's views about contingency, about possible worlds, and about freedom. In this volume, Leibniz's views about logic and substance are discussed by Professor Sleigh in a separate chapter;[2] I shall restrict myself to the topics of contingency, possible worlds, and freedom. This is not a haphazard group; there are close connections between Leibniz's discussions of these topics. Nor are the issues raised merely marginal; on the contrary, they take us to the very heart of Leibniz's philosophy.

Before one can usefully discuss the relations between Leibniz's philosophy and his logic, one must clarify the sense which the word "logic" has in this context. Russell was not thinking of logic in the sense of the study of the structure of valid reasoning; rather, he had in mind theories about the nature of the proposition and of truth. In Leibniz, such theories are closely connected in that his theory of truth presupposes a certain view about the nature of the proposition: namely, that all propositions are (either expressly or implicitly) of the subject-predicate form.

199

I. LEIBNIZ'S THEORY OF TRUTH

From Leibniz's many statements of his theory of truth, we may select the following as an example: "In every affirmative true proposition, necessary or contingent, universal or singular, the concept of the predicate is included in that of the subject, *praedicatum inest subjecto*" (letter to Arnauld, 14 July 1686, G II 56: P 62).[3] This mentions affirmative truths only; but Leibniz notes that negative propositions can easily be adapted to fit what he has said: "Thus when I say, 'No scoundrel is happy' it is the same as if I were to say 'Every scoundrel is non-happy,' or, 'Non-happiness is in the scoundrel' " (C 86).[4]

My primary concern here is with Leibniz's theory of contingent truths; but before this theory can be discussed, there is much to be said by way of clarification of his theory of truth in general. When Leibniz speaks of a "subject" and a "predicate," he means respectively that about which something is said (in the sense of asserted or denied) and that which is said of it. So, when it is said that Leibniz will go on a journey, Leibniz is the subject and the making of a journey the predicate (G II 52: P 61). These are still standard senses of the terms; so, too, is the sense in which Leibniz uses the term "concept" (*conceptus, notio, la notion*). In modern usage, a concept might be defined roughly as the meaning of a word.[5] So, when a philosopher investigates "the concept of mind," he is investigating the meaning of the word "mind"; and if one says of a dictator that he had no concept of justice, one is in effect saying that he simply did not know what the word "justice" meant. For Leibniz, too, a meaningful word is the sign of a concept, and a meaningless word is a sign without a concept.[6]

The examples of concepts just given – mind, justice – were general terms. But Leibniz believed that not only is there a concept of, for example, kingship, but that there is an individual concept of *this* king – Alexander the Great, for example. The merits and defects of Leibniz's views about individual concepts cannot be argued here, but it is worth noting that his critic Arnauld did not object to the idea of a concept of Adam, or indeed of Arnauld himself (G II 27, 30). Nor is such a use restricted to Leibniz's contemporaries; a modern writer would find such a phrase as "different concepts of Alexander the Great" (held, for example, by different historians) quite natural.

But there is an important point to be noted here. Take the true proposition "Alexander the Great was a king." In such a case, Leibniz would say that the concept of kingship is in the concept of the subject, Alexander. But he does not mean by the latter, *any* concept of Alexander that might be had by anyone at any time – a concept that might well change over time. Rather he means what one might call *the* concept of Alexander: that is, the concept of Alexander possessed by someone who understands the term "Alexander" perfectly. In short, to have a concept of this sort is to have a "God's-eye" view of the subject.

After discussing subjects, predicates, and their concepts, we come finally to Leibniz's notion of inclusion or containment: to what he means when he says that in the case of a true proposition, the concept of the predicate is *included in* that of the subject. For Leibniz, to say that the concept of P is included in the concept of S is to say that the concept of P is among those concepts that constitute the concept of S. So, for example, it is true to say that all gold is metal because the concept of metal is one of the concepts that constitute the concept of gold (C 53: PLP 20). Leibniz knew that in treating propositions in this way he was diverging from a common practice. He notes that for him, the concept of gold is "greater than" the concept of metal in that it includes both the concept of metal and other concepts as well – e.g., that of being the heaviest among metals. He continues:

The Scholastics speak differently; for they consider, not concepts, but instances which are brought under universal concepts. So they say metal is wider than gold, since it contains more species than gold, and if we wish to enumerate the individuals made of gold on the one hand and those made of metal on the other, the latter will be more than the former, which will therefore be contained in the latter as a part in the whole.   (C 53: PLP 20)

Leibniz is here contrasting his own "intensional" approach to the proposition with the "extensional" approach. His reason for preferring the former is that concepts "do not depend on the existence of individuals." So if, for example, gold were a purely mythical metal, it would still be true to say that all gold is metal (C 53: PLP 20).

Leibniz does not define truth in terms of inclusion or containment alone; he also says that a true proposition is one which is either an identical proposition or reducible to one (see, e.g., C 513: P 7; C 519:

P 87; G VII 196: P 14). Superficially, this may seem quite different from the previous definition, but the only difference is that in the present definition, Leibniz is calling attention to the fact that the inclusion of the concept of the predicate in that of the subject is not always obvious, but often has to be shown. To understand what Leibniz is saying here, it is necessary first of all to realize that when he speaks of an identical proposition, he does not mean only propositions of the form "*A* is *A*" – e.g., "A man is a man"; he also means propositions of the form "*AB* is *A*" – e.g., "A white man is white" (C 11: P 172). This is obviously related to what Leibniz has said about truth in terms of inclusion; e.g., he could have said that in the case of the proposition "A white man is white" the concept of the predicate, whiteness, is included in that of the subject. In such a case, the inclusion is manifest or evident (C 11: P 172); however, there are many cases in which the inclusion is concealed or implicit. Such implicit inclusion is "shown by the analysis of terms, by substituting for one another definitions and what is defined" (G VII 309: P 79. Cf. *Discourse*, par. 8, G IV 443: P 18; C 11: P 172; C 519: P 87). Leibniz means that in the case of the true proposition "Every man is rational" the inclusion of the concept of rationality in that of man is only implicit; however, it can be made explicit by substituting for "man" its definition "rational animal," so that we get the identical proposition "Every rational animal is rational." It is in this way that a true proposition is "reduced" to an identical proposition. This way of defining truth is of particular importance in Leibniz's account of contingent truth, which is our next topic.

II. TRUTH AND CONTINGENCY

Many would disagree about the answer to the question, "What are the fundamental propositions of Leibniz's philosophy?" But there would probably be general agreement that among these is the proposition that there are objective contingent truths and falsehoods. By "objective" I mean that to ascribe contingency to truths and falsehoods is not just a mark of human ignorance. For Spinoza, it was. In his view, someone who understands how things really are knows that whatever exists, exists necessarily, and that what does not exist cannot exist. For Leibniz, such a view is clearly false.[7] It is, for example, absurd to suppose that "it is impossible, from all eternity, that Spinoza should not die at the Hague" (*Theodicy*, par. 173, G VI 217). Again, Spinoza claimed that whatever is possible necessarily exists (for otherwise God would not be both a necessary and an absolutely infinite being). Leibniz replies that this is refuted by the fact that one can think of unfulfilled possibilities. He makes this point forcibly in an illuminating paper on freedom, written about 1689 (FC 178–85: P 106–11). Take, he says, the legends about King Arthur of Britain. It is false that there was a King Arthur of the kind portrayed by the story-tellers. Now, this falsehood is a contingent one; there *could have been* such a king, i.e., his existence is not an impossibility. So "if certain possibles never exist, then existing things are not always necessary; otherwise it would be impossible for other things to exist instead of them, and so all things that never exist would be impossible" (FC 179: P 106).

Leibniz's views about unfulfilled possibilities will meet us again, when we consider his views about possible worlds (Section IV below). For the present, I wish to concentrate on a difficulty that is presented by Leibniz's own theory of truth. As he himself saw, this theory seemed to imply that there are no truths that are not necessary. It was pointed out in the last section that Leibniz defines a true proposition as one which is either an identical proposition or is reducible to an identical proposition. The problem is, that he offers exactly the same definition of a necessary truth (FC 181: P 108; G VII 300; C 17: P 96; Gr 303). An alternative definition of a necessary truth – namely, that a necessary truth is one whose opposite implies a contradiction (C 17: P 96) – also causes difficulties, this time in connection with Leibniz's theory of truth as it is stated in terms of containment. For, as Leibniz saw (FC 179: P 107), "If, at a given time, the concept of the predicate is in the concept of the subject, then how, without contradiction and impossibility, can the predicate not be in the subject at that time?"

Speaking of this problem and his attempts to solve it, Leibniz says that (FC 180: P 107) "A new and unexpected light finally arose in a quarter where I least hoped for it – namely, out of mathematical considerations of the nature of the infinite." The solution, which dates from 1686,[8] was this: in the case of necessary truths, the inclusion of the concept of the predicate in that of the subject is something that we human beings can prove. That is, we can show *in a finite number of steps* that the concept of the predicate is included in that of the subject; or (what is the same) we can, in a finite number of steps, reduce to an identical proposition the proposition whose truth is to be established. But in the case of contingent truths, we cannot do this. The concept of the predicate is indeed in that of the subject; but "this can never be demonstrated, nor can the proposition ever be reduced to an equation or identity. Instead, the analysis proceeds to infinity" (FC 182: P 109). It is only God who can see "the connection of terms or the inclusion of the predicate in the subject, for he sees whatever is in the series" (ibid. cf. C 17: P 97; C 2; G VII 200).

This solution, however, raises problems of its own. First, what exactly was the light that arose "out of mathematical considerations of the nature of the infinite?" To answer this question, one needs to take a wider view of Leibniz's thought during and around 1686. At this time, not only was Leibniz working out the relations between his logic and his metaphysics in the *Discourse on Metaphysics* and associated writings; he was also criticising Descartes' physics. In particular, he was involved in a controversy with Malebranche, who tried to defend some of Descartes' laws of motion against Leibniz's attacks (G III 46). In the course of this controversy, Leibniz published a letter in reply to Malebranche, in the *Nouvelles de la République des Lettres* of July 1687. A passage from this letter,[9] to which Leibniz often referred, is worth quoting at length. In it, Leibniz expounds what he calls a "principle of general order," though elsewhere the same principle is called, perhaps more helpfully, a "law of continuity" (e.g., *New Essays*, Preface, A VI.vi: RB 56). This principle, Leibniz says,

derives its origin from the infinite; it is absolutely necessary in geometry, but it is also valid in physics, because the sovereign wisdom, which is the source of all things, acts as a perfect geometer, following a harmony to which nothing can be added. . . . One can state it as follows: "When the difference between two cases can be diminished beyond any given magnitude in the data (or, in that which is given) it must be possible to find it also diminished beyond every given magnitude in that which is sought (or, in that which results from it)." Or, to speak less technically: "When cases (or, that which is given) approach each other continuously and eventually vanish into one another, the consequences or outcome (or, that which is sought) must also do the same." This depends, in turn, on a more general principle, namely: "When the data are ordered, the things which are sought are also ordered." But to understand this, one needs examples. It is known that the case or supposition of an ellipse can approach the case of a parabola as much as one wishes, such that the difference between the ellipse and the parabola can become less than any given difference. . . . Consequently, all the geometrical theorems which are found to be true of the ellipse in general can be applied to the parabola, considering the latter . . . as a figure which differs from some ellipse by less than any given difference. The same principle holds in physics: for example, rest can be considered as a speed which is infinitely little, or as an infinite slowness. This is why everything which is true with regard to slowness or speed in general must also be found to be true of rest taken in the same way, such that the rule applying to rest must be regarded as a particular case of the rule applying to motion. Otherwise, if this does not hold, it will be a sure sign that the rules are badly drawn up. Similarly, equality can be considered as an inequality which is infinitely small, and one can make inequality approach equality as much as one wishes.   (G III 52–53)

This, I suggest, is the light that dawned upon Leibniz when he puzzled over the problem of reconciling his views about truth in general with his view that some truths are contingent. To put the point simply: what, at first sight, could appear to be more different from each other than motion and rest? Yet, as we have seen, Leibniz holds that rest can be considered as a special case of motion – motion which is infinitely little, or which vanishes into rest. Similarly, a contingent truth can be regarded as a special case of the inclusion of the concept of the predicate in that of the subject – namely, where the analysis of concepts that would be necessary to provide a proof is infinite.

It is noteworthy that Leibniz does not say that his thesis about the nature of contingent truth *springs from* the law of continuity. Indeed, there is a fundamental difference between "motion which is infinitely little is rest" and "a truth whose analysis is infinite is contingent." In the case of motion and rest, Leibniz is saying that one of an apparent pair of opposites (rest) is a special case of the other (motion). But he does not say that necessary and contingent truths are an apparent pair of opposites, one of which is really a special case of the other. It is *not* the case, in his view, that contingent truths are really necessary truths; the distinction between them is a real one. So when Leibniz said that mathematical considerations of the infinite shed light on the problem of contingent truth, he meant no more than that they *suggested* a solution.

But is the solution a genuine one? Leibniz says that mathematics suggested the solution; but he also knew that it suggested an objection to it. The difficulty in question involves the irrational numbers. Leibniz often compares the distinction between necessary and contingent truths with that between rational and irrational numbers, or, as he says, between numbers that are commensurable and those that are incommensurable or "surd" (e.g., C 388: PLP 77; G VII 309: P 75; FC 183–84: P 110; C 1–2). He explains his difficulty by reference to incommensurable ratios or proportions.[10] He says (C 2) that an incommensurable ratio is not "expressible" (*effabilis*), which is to say that it cannot be expressed by a finite series of numbers; the series required is infinite. Correspondingly, the analysis of a contingent truth is infinite. None of this is new; however, Leibniz also points out (and this raises the problem) that in mathematics, "we can . . . establish demonstrations, by showing that the error involved is less than any assignable error" (C 18: P 97).[11] As this is so, it may seem that "human beings also will be able to comprehend contingent truths with certainty" (C 388: PLP 78). Leibniz, however, says that this is beyond our powers. We can indeed establish proofs of the kind described – i.e., proofs in which the error involved is less than any assignable error – in the case of incommensurable ratios. But "in the case of contingent truths, not even this is conceded to a created mind" (C 18: P 97).

But what entitles Leibniz to be sure about this? After all, there was doubtless a time when it was thought that human beings could not give mathematical proofs of the kind to which Leibniz refers; yet such proofs were found. Why, then, should it be beyond human powers to find comparable proofs of contingent truths? In seeking Leibniz's answer, it is necessary to go further into his logic.

III. CONTINGENT TRUTHS AND THE PRINCIPLE OF SUFFICIENT REASON

What is necessary is to examine another way in which Leibniz distinguishes necessary from contingent truths – a way which he was following at the same time as he offered his solution in terms of infinite analysis. In paragraph 13 of the *Discourse on Metaphysics* (1686) Leibniz says that necessary truths "are based on the principle of contradiction and on the possibility or impossibility of essences themselves." By this he means that if P is a property of the circle, then the proposition that the circle has the property P is a necessary truth in that to deny it would involve a contradiction. In such a proposition, the connection between the subject and the predicate (ibid.) is "based . . . on ideas pure and simple"; that is, it is based simply on the essences of geometrical figures. But the reasons that one can bring for a contingent truth "are based only on . . . that which is or appears the best among several things which are equally possible"; such truths (unlike necessary truths) are based on "the free will of God or of creatures." Leibniz adds that "It is true that their choice always has its reasons; but these incline without necessitating" (*Discourse on Metaphysics*, par. 13, G II 12: L 310).

This last phrase will meet us again (sec. V); the point to be emphasised at present, however, is that Leibniz is distinguishing between necessary and contingent truths by reference to the different *reasons* that can be brought for them. This way of distinguishing between these two types of truth is a theme that runs through much of Leibniz's philosophical thought. It is emphasised repeatedly in the correspondence with Arnauld, which is linked with the *Discourse on Metaphysics* (G II 39, 46, 49, 52), and Leibniz was still making use of it in the last year of his life in the course of his fifth and last paper for Samuel Clarke (5.8–10, G VII 390–91: P 221–22). In that paper, Leibniz calls the principles involved those of contradiction and sufficient reason respectively, and says that "What is necessary is so by its essence because the opposite implies a contradiction; but the contingent which exists owes its existence to the principle of what is best, the sufficient reason for things" (to Clarke, 5.9, G VII 390: P 221–22).

Leibniz's use of terms here is confusing, in that he often (even in the nearly contemporary *Monadology*, par. 32) uses the term "principle of sufficient reason" in such a way as to apply to absolutely all truths, necessary as well as contingent. In this use, he says that the principle of sufficient reason is that by which we consider that (my emphasis) "*no* fact can be real or existing and *no* proposition can be true unless there is a sufficient reason, why it should be thus and not otherwise" (*Monadology*, par. 32. G VI 612: P 184).[12] Leibniz does not advance this principle as an axiom of which no proof can be given; on the contrary he argues for its truth, and his argument rests on purely logical considerations. The principle of sufficient reason,

he says in an appendix to the *Theodicy*, is "contained in the definition of truth and falsity" (G VI 414). From the many passages which
explain what this means (e.g., *Discourse*, par. 13, G IV 436–39: P 25;
G II 56: P 62; G VII 295: P 15; C 11: P 172; C 513: P 8), I select one
from a paper entitled *Primary Truths*, written about 1686 (C 519: P
87–88). Leibniz begins by stating his views about the nature of truth
in general – namely, that in a true proposition the predicate is in the
subject. He next explains the nature of proof, saying that "In identities this . . . inclusion of the predicate in the subject is express,
whereas in all other truths it is implicit and must be shown through
the analysis of concepts, in which *a priori* demonstration consists."
From this, he says,

> There at once arises the accepted axiom, "There is nothing without a rea-
> son", or, "There is no effect without a cause." For otherwise there would be
> a truth which could not be proved *a priori*, i.e. which is not analysed into
> identities; and this is contrary to the nature of truth, which is always, either
> expressly or implicitly, identical.   (C 519: P 87–88)[13]

This version of the principle of sufficient reason, which applies
both to necessary and contingent truths, adds little to what has already been seen of Leibniz's theory of truth. We have seen already,
towards the end of section I, that there are cases in which the inclusion of the concept of the predicate in that of the subject is implicit,
and has to be shown by the analysis of terms. All that Leibniz has
added to this is the statement that to do so is to give a reason for the
truth of a proposition. However, earlier in the present section we also
saw that Leibniz uses something that he calls the principle of sufficient reason to *distinguish* contingent truths (whose principle it is)
from necessary truths (whose principle is that of contradiction). In
this sense of the principle of sufficient reason, the reasons that one
can bring for a contingent truth are based on "that which is or appears
the best among several things which are equally possible" (*Discourse*,
par. 13, G IV 438: P 25), and they are related to "the free will of God or
of creatures" (*Discourse*, par. 13, G IV 439: P 25). Or, as Leibniz says
elsewhere (C 402: P 94) the connection between the predicate and the
subject of a contingent truth is not a necessary one, but "depends on
an assumed divine decree and on free will."

One may illustrate Leibniz's meaning as follows. Suppose that
someone rolls a large stone down a slope, with the intention of

crushing an enemy who is below. The proposition, "This stone is rolling down a slope" is a contingent truth in that its truth depends on the will of the person in question. No self-contradiction would have been involved if the man had not rolled the stone; the proposition is true because the man willed freely to roll the stone, and actually did roll it. Suppose, next, that a stone rolls down a slope as a result of a volcanic eruption. Here, one might think, no act of will is involved; the stone rolls because of the laws of nature and because of the state of the universe before the event. Leibniz would reply that these laws, and the state of the universe at any time, do depend on a will – the will of God.

What is involved in each case is not a mere act of will, but something which "is or appears the best." The man rolled the stone down the slope because it appeared to him to be the best thing to do in the circumstances ("appeared" because it may not actually have been the best course of action). In the case of God – a being who is omniscient, omnipotent, and perfectly good – that which is aimed at and which comes about *is* the best (cf. *Monadology*, par. 55, G VI 616: P 187). This is doubtless why Leibniz often refers to the principle of sufficient reason, taken in the sense which now concerns us, as "the principle of the best."[14] To avoid confusion, we will in what follows always refer to the principle of sufficient reason in the sense in which it differentiates contingent from necessary truths, as "the principle of the best." The term "principle of sufficient reason" will henceforward be used to refer exclusively to the proposition that *every* truth has a reason, i.e., that it is, in principle, possible to say of any true proposition *why* it is true. We will also, to simplify exposition of the principle of the best, ignore those contingent truths which depend on human beings and concentrate on those which depend on the will of God – a will which is always for the real good, as opposed to a merely apparent good.

It is obvious that, whereas the principle of sufficient reason depends on purely logical considerations, the principle of the best does not: it involves metaphysical views about the nature of God, and more specifically about God's freedom. These views were controversial. In saying that contingent truths depend on the free will of God and necessary truths do not, Leibniz was opposing Descartes, who said that the will of God is involved even in necessary truths, and also Spinoza, who took the view that God cannot be said to act from freedom of will.[15] Leibniz's reasons for rejecting Spinoza's views about necessity have already been discussed at the beginning of section II, but it will be worthwhile to consider here what Leibniz says about Descartes, as this helps to bring his own position into sharper focus.

In his reply to the Sixth Objections, Descartes argues that because God is omnipotent, we are logically bound to say that his will is in no way constrained; rather, it was from all eternity "indifferent" to everything that has happened or will happen.[16] This means, for example, that God did not will to create the world in time (as opposed to creating it from all eternity) because he saw that it would be better thus; rather, it is because he willed to create the world in time that it is better thus. The same can be said of the truths of mathematics. God did not will the interior angles of a triangle to be equal to two right angles because he recognised that it could not be otherwise. Rather, it is because he willed them to be necessarily equal to two right angles that this is true and cannot be otherwise.

Clearly, this is radically different from Leibniz's position. Leibniz insists that the good does not depend on God's will; the good is the sufficient reason of what God wills to do. That is, God wills to create this rather than that *because* this is the best. As to truths such as those of mathematics – eternal truths, as Leibniz calls them – we saw at the beginning of this section that these are "based upon the principle of contradiction and on the possibility or impossibility of essences themselves" (*Discourse on Metaphysics*, par. 13, G IV 438–39: P 25). Leibniz concedes that there is a sense in which God can be called the source of essences in so far as the understanding of God is the region of eternal truths or of the ideas on which they depend (*Monadology*, par. 43, G VI 614: P 185). But this is not to say that the eternal truths are arbitrary and depend on God's will. It is only contingent truths that depend on God's will; necessary truths "depend solely on his understanding, of which they are the internal object" (*Monadology*, par. 46, G VI 614: P 186; cf. G II 49).

Leibniz's reasons for rejecting these Cartesian views are stated clearly in a letter of January 1680 written to a certain Christian Philipp (G IV 284–85), who was in the service of the Elector of Saxony and who had a taste for philosophy. Leibniz cannot, of course, use the principle of the best against Descartes, for that principle is itself at issue. When discussing Descartes' views about God's will and the good, he appeals to the principle of sufficient reason. He says that if things are good or bad only by virtue of being an effect of the will of God, then the good is not a motive of God's will, which will be a kind of absolute decree, without reason. So "the will of God will be a mere fiction." As to Descartes' views about the relation between God's will and the eternal truths, Leibniz replies that these views imply that God does not have an understanding. The understanding, Leibniz says, is necessarily prior in nature to the will – the point being that, as he says elsewhere, an act of will presupposes a belief or judgement about good and bad(Gr. 513).[17] So if truth depends on the will of God and not on the nature of things, "the understanding of God will be prior to the truth of things and consequently will not have the truth as its object." Such an understanding, Leibniz says, is an absurdity.

In sum, Leibniz holds (against Spinoza) that there are contingent truths which depend on the free will of God and of creatures. He also holds (against Descartes) that God's free will is not arbitrary; God acts for the sake of the good which is independent of his will, and his actions are in accordance with eternal truths which his will does not produce. It is now time to complete this exposition of Leibniz's theory of contingent truth by seeing how his two accounts – that in terms of God's will and that in terms of infinite analysis – are related to each other. Leibniz himself saw them as closely linked. For example, in his paper On Freedom (FC 182: P 109), he follows an account of contingent truth in terms of infinite analysis with the remark that "this very same [contingent] truth has arisen in part from his [God's] own intellect and in part from his will, and expresses in its own way the infinite perfection and the harmony of the whole series of things."

In establishing a connection between his two accounts, Leibniz relies in part on a thesis which is derived from the principle of the best: namely, that the best world is that which contains an infinity of substances (G II 460). He connects this with a thesis about the nature of an individual substance, which is derived from his logic. This thesis, which is discussed elsewhere in this book, is that each substance "expresses" the whole universe, i.e., that the complete concept of each substance is such that every state of the universe can, in principle, be derived from it. But since the universe is infinite, any such concept must be of infinite complexity, and its full analysis must surpass human powers.

We are now in a position to attempt an answer to the question posed at the end of section II, namely, how Leibniz can be sure that no human being will ever discover a way of demonstrating a contingent truth. What has just been said about the connection between contingent truths and the will of God might suggest one answer, namely, that no contingent truth can ever be proved because the will of God is too profound for us to grasp. Leibniz, however, would not answer in this way. First, we have seen already that the free will involved in contingent truths is not just that of God but is also, in some cases, that of human beings. Second, Leibniz insists that Descartes is wrong in saying that the will of God is entirely beyond our grasp (G IV 299; G IV 360–61: L 387). The laws of motion, which are based on the principle of the best, are such that we can have an *a priori* knowledge of them (*Principles of Nature and Grace*, par. 11, G VI 603: P 200; G VII 303: P 138).[18]

Perhaps Leibniz's answer to the problem would be this. We shall never be able to demonstrate contingent truths precisely because the will on which such truths depend – whether it be the will of God or of one of his creatures – is a *free* will, and that means that its acts are not logically necessary. This naturally raises the question, whether there really is free will. Leibniz gave an affirmative answer, and that answer will concern us in the final section of this chapter. But first there is another topic to be considered.

IV. POSSIBLE WORLDS

At the beginning of section II, I mentioned Leibniz's disagreement with Spinoza's thesis that everything possible exists, and I said that Leibniz objects to this view on the grounds that there are unfulfilled possibilities. Leibniz also expresses this objection in terms of the notion of possible universes, or, more commonly, possible worlds. Leibniz's view is stated concisely in the *Monadology*, pars. 53–55 (G VI 615–16: P 187). There is, he says, an infinity of possible universes, of which only one can exist; God, in creating the universe, chooses among these, bringing into existence the one which is the best.

The assertion that the world that God creates is the best of all possible worlds forms the climax of Leibniz's *Theodicy* (par. 416, G VI 364). This view was mocked by Voltaire in *Candide* – and, incidentally, has not been accepted by all Christian theologians.[19] However, the notion of a possible world, divorced from any reference to a *best* possible world, has aroused interest recently, because philosophers have found the notion useful in their attempts to elucidate the logic of modal terms such as "possible" and "necessary." In this section, I will examine what Leibniz meant by a "possible world," and the use that he made of the concept.

Leibniz explains that by the term "world" (*monde*) or "universe" (*univers*) he means "the entire sequence and the entire collection of all existing things" (*Theodicy*, par. 8, G VI 107). That is, he means by "the world" all the things that there have been, or will be. By "possible" he means that which does not involve a contradiction (C 513: P 7; C 261, 371–72; Gr 324, 390, 392, 396). We have just seen that Leibniz holds that out of an infinity of possible worlds, only one can exist (*Monadology*, par. 53, G VI 615–16: P 187). He also puts this in terms of a distinction between the "possible" and the "compossible." Briefly, *A* and *B* are "compossible" if each is not only possible in isolation, but each is consistent with the other, so that they are what we might call "co-possible." This distinction is applied in a letter which Leibniz wrote in December 1714 to Louis Bourguet, who had raised some difficulties about the *Theodicy*. Bourguet had objected that if the universe is regarded as a collection, then there cannot be several universes – the point being that the universe is all that there is, and there cannot be several such totalities. Leibniz replies:

That would be true, if the universe were the collection of all possibles; but that is not the case, since all possibles are not compossible. So the universe is only the collection of a certain sort [*façon*] of compossibles, and the actual universe is the collection of all existent possibles, i.e. those which form the most rich composite. And as there are different combinations of possibles, some better than others, there are several possible universes, each collection of compossibles constituting one.   (G III 573)

In sum, Leibniz is saying that God, in deciding to create the world, chooses between possible worlds which are not compossible, i.e., are not compatible with one another.[20] But what exactly *is* a possible world, according to Leibniz? One might perhaps think that he would agree with a contemporary philosopher who has made much use of the concept of possible worlds, David Lewis. Lewis has argued that not only is the notion of a possible world a useful conceptual tool, but that it has to be granted that such worlds *exist*.[21] There are passages from Leibniz's works which might seem to imply that he took the same view. For example, in his paper *On the Ultimate Origination of Things*, written in 1697, he says that there is in all things a certain demand (*exigentia*) for existence, or, so to speak, a claim (*praetensio*) to exist. From this it follows, Leibniz says, that "all things which are possible . . . tend by equal right towards existence in proportion to . . . the degree of perfection which belongs to them" (G VII 303: P 137–38). Here, and in other passages, possibles are viewed as claimants.[22] The question is whether this is a metaphor, or whether Leibniz thought that possibles really exist. The answer is that the language is metaphorical. Possible universes, Leibniz says, are in the ideas of God (*Monadology*, par. 53, G VI 615: P 187; cf. G VII 305, P 140; *Principles*, par. 10 G VI 603: P 200; *Theodicy*, par. 201 G VI 236); that is, they have a merely conceptual existence. To be more precise: Leibniz says that a world is an aggregate of several substances (Gr 396), from which it follows that a possible world is a set of the concepts of a number of substances, each of which concepts is possible and each of which is compatible with the rest of the set.

Although Leibniz would have rejected Lewis's thesis about the existence of possible worlds, there is one technical term introduced by Lewis that is useful in the exposition of Leibniz's views. In one of his letters, Arnauld criticised the view (which he ascribed to Leibniz) that God chose one possible Adam in preference to other possible Adams (to Leibniz, 13 May 1686, G II 29–30). One of his criticisms was that one cannot conceive of many possible Adams. To do this would be like trying to conceive of

several possible "mes," which is certainly inconceivable. . . . The reason is that these different "mes" would be different from each other, otherwise there would not be several "mes." There must therefore have been one of these "mes" which was not me, which is an evident contradiction.

Leibniz replied (G II 41–42: P 55–56) that what Arnauld said was in a sense true, but that this did not affect the point that he wanted to make. If Adam is taken to be an individual nature (*une nature singulière*) – in other words, if the concept of Adam is taken to be a complete concept, i.e., the concept of an individual substance – then indeed there cannot be many Adams. However, in speaking of several Adams, Leibniz was not taking Adam as a determinate individual; rather, he was speaking of a *vague* Adam (cf. G II 19: P 50; G II 37). In such a case, the concept of Adam which is entertained is not complete. Leibniz explains himself as follows:

> When in considering Adam we consider a part of his predicates, as for instance that he is the first man, set in a pleasure garden, out of whose side God took a woman, and similar things considered *sub ratione generalitatis* (i.e. without naming Eve, Paradise, or other circumstances which fix individuality), and we give the name "Adam" to the person to whom these predicates are attributed, all this is not sufficient to determine the individual; for there might be an infinity of Adams, that is to say of possible persons, different from one another, to whom all that is appropriate.
>
> (G II 42: P 55)

In this passage, Leibniz takes the view that there might have been an infinity of Adams, but that of these only one is *our* Adam (G II 42: P 56). Sometimes, however, he seems to want a proper name to refer to just one individual – the one who actually existed – and not to a collection of possible individuals as well. So, for example, in the *Theodicy* (par. 414, G VI 363) he distinguishes between the real Sextus Tarquinius and other possible individuals of the same name who are thought of as acting differently from the real Sextus, by calling the latter *"des Sextus approchants"* – "approximations to Sextus" or "near-Sextuses." Here, David Lewis's notion of a "counterpart"[23] would be appropriate; so, for example, a Sextus who did not rape Lucretia would be a "counterpart" of the Sextus who did.

What Leibniz says about several "vague" Adams, or several different approximations to Adam, has a paradoxical consequence which has often been noted. It seems evident, on the face of it, that one and the same Adam could have done many things that he did not do. He could, for example, have rejected the apple proffered by Eve; he could have had a different progeny, and so on. In considering these possibilities it seems obvious that one is referring to the same individual; or, putting the point in terms of possible worlds, one is talking about an individual who preserves his identity over a number of

possible worlds. This thesis, termed the thesis of trans-world identification, or trans-world identity, has been powerfully defended by
Saul Kripke.[24] Leibniz, however, would reject such a view. For him,
to talk of Adam *is to talk of* an individual who ate the apple proffered by Eve, whose sons were Cain, Abel, and Seth. An Adam who
did not eat the apple would not be Adam; he would be an approximation to Adam.

Leibniz often makes this point in connection with the doctrine of
predestination. He says that:

God does not decide whether Adam should sin, but whether that series of
things in which there is an Adam whose perfect individual concept involves
sin should nevertheless be preferred to others. This was also seen by Hugh of
St. Victor, who answered the question why God chose Jacob and not Esau by
simply saying: because Jacob is not Esau. For in the perfect concept of an
individual substance, considered in a pure state of possibility before every
actual decree of existence, there is already whatever will happen to it if it
exists, and indeed the whole series of things of which it forms a part.

(G VII 311: P 78; cf. *Discourse*, par. 30, G IV 454–56: P:. 38–41; Gr 314; A
VI.iii 148)

To put this in terms of possible worlds: Leibniz is saying that we
are not to think of one and the same individual as a member of a
number of possible worlds. The complete concept of Adam is tied to
one possible world, the possible world of which that concept is a
member.

V. CONTINGENCY, HYPOTHETICAL NECESSITY, AND FREEDOM

Leibniz often speaks of contingent truths as "truths of fact," opposing
them to "truths of reason," i.e., to what he calls elsewhere "necessary
truths" (*Monadology*, pars. 33, 35, G VI 612: P 184; *New Essays* IV.2.1,
A VI.vi: RB 361; G IV 357; Gr 514). It must be stressed that, for
Leibniz, a truth of fact is simply a true proposition whose opposite is
possible (*Monadology*, par. 33, G VI 612: P 184); it does not state what
one might call a brute fact – that is, something which one just has to
accept as being the case, and of which no explanation can be given. For
Leibniz, the principle of sufficient reason covers every fact and every
truth; "No fact can be real or existing and no proposition can be true

unless there is a sufficient reason, why it should be thus and not otherwise" (*Monadology*, par. 32, G VI 612: P 184). In the case of truths of fact, explanation terminates in the necessary being – that is, a being which *must* exist, and so contains within itself the explanation of its own existence (*Principles*, par. 8, G VI 602: P 199; cf. C 13: P 174). It has already been seen that, for Leibniz, this necessary being is a creative deity, and so it can be said that the sufficient reason for truths of fact is the will of God, which brings into existence the best possible world. This leads Leibniz to describe contingent truths in a way which, superficially at any rate, is quite unlike anything which has met us so far. Instead of distinguishing between necessary and contingent truths, he regards contingent truths as necessary truths *of a certain kind*. What are described elsewhere simply as necessary truths are now said to have "absolute" or "metaphysical" necessity (*Theodicy*, par. 37, G VI 123; cf. G VI 441); this sort of necessity, Leibniz adds, is also called "logical" or "mathematical" (to Clarke, 5.4, G VII 389: L 696). Contingent truths, on the other hand, are said to have "hypothetical" necessity – also termed by Leibniz "consequential," "moral" or "physical" necessity.[25]

The idea of hypothetical necessity goes back as far as Aristotle. In the *Physics*, Aristotle says:

Why is a saw such as it is? To effect so and so for the sake of so and so. This end, however, cannot be realised unless the saw is made of iron. It is, therefore, necessary for it to be of iron, *if* we are to have a saw and perform the operation of sawing. What is necessary, then, is necessary *on a hypothesis*.[26]

Here the notion of hypothetical necessity is connected with the *function* of a saw, and so with the purposes or ends of those who use saws. For Leibniz, similarly, the connection between contingent truths and hypothetical necessity comes by way of the link that he finds between contingency and the purposes of either God or his creatures (Cf. *Discourse*, par. 13 G IV 436–39: P 23–25, discussed in sec. III). The notion of hypothetical necessity also plays an important part in Leibniz's attempt to establish the freedom of the will, and this use of the notion will concern us later in this section.[27] For the moment, however, our concern is with Leibniz's account of contingent truths.

The way in which hypothetical necessity enters into this account may be introduced by a passage from *On the Ultimate Origination of Things* in which (G VII 303: P 137) Leibniz asserts that the present state of the world is not absolutely necessary, but is only hypothetically necessary. "In other words, granted that it is once such and such, it follows that such and such things will come into being." Here one asks: precisely how, i.e., in accordance with what laws, does it follow that the present state of the universe must be such and such? One possible answer would be that the laws in question are those of logic; that is, that some previous state of the universe is contingent, and that the present state of the universe follows logically from it. In such a case, the present state of the universe is not absolutely necessary; it is necessary given only that a previous, contingent state of the universe was such and such. This would be analogous to an example of hypothetical necessity given by Leibniz, namely that "It is impossible for Codrus to have money taken from him, given that he has no money" (C 271). This involves the logically necessary truth that if x does not possess y, then y cannot be taken from x. However, this is not the way in which Leibniz would answer the question just posed. For him, the laws in accordance with which the present state of the universe follows from a previous state are themselves only hypothetically necessary. This is made clear in a paper on necessary and contingent truths, written in about 1686 (C 19: P 99–100). Here, Leibniz distinguishes between (i) "the first essential laws of the series," which are true without exception and so include even miracles, (ii) "subordinate laws of nature, which have only physical necessity and which are not repealed except by a miracle," and (iii) "others whose universality is even less, . . . and of which a part constitutes physical science."[28] Leibniz insists that all these laws are only hypothetically necessary. For "since the fact that the series itself exists is contingent and depends on the free decrees of God, its laws also will be contingent in the absolute sense; but they will be hypothetically necessary and will only be essential *given the series.*" In sum, the laws of nature are not absolutely or logically necessary. Their necessity is hypothetical only, in that they depend on God's will to create the best possible world.

It is obvious from what has already been said that Leibniz's belief that there is freedom of the will plays an important part in his theory of contingent truth. Leibniz's theory of the will and of its freedom is too complex to be discussed fully here; however, it is possible to give some account of the part that the concept of hypothetical necessity plays in this theory. Let us return to Leibniz's assertion, quoted early in section III, that contingent truths are "based on the free will of God and of creatures. It is true that their choice always has its reasons, but these incline without necessitating" (*Discourse*, par. 13, G II 12: P 23). The phrase "incline without necessitating" is often used by Leibniz,[29] and indeed is widely quoted. But it can easily mislead. It may suggest that Leibniz means that when someone – whether God or a finite being – makes what would commonly be called a free choice, the reasons or motives for the decision exercise, as it were, some kind of influence on the agent but do not determine the decision reached. Suppose, for example, that a man has a reason for going on strike; he is a member of a trade union, and the union has called for strike action. Suppose further that the man thinks that to go on strike on this occasion would be morally wrong, since innocent people would be harmed. Then one might think that this is a case in which there are reasons or motives for action, each of which inclines a man to act in a certain way, but neither of which compels him to act in this way. However, this is not what Leibniz means when he says that reasons "incline without necessitating." He makes clear (*Theodicy*, par. 45, G VI 127; *New Essays* II.21.8, A VI.vi: RB 175; cf. to Clarke, 5.15, G VII 392: P 222–23) that what he has in mind is the "prevailing" or "strongest" reason. So, for example, if the man just described decides not to go on strike, then it is his reason for not going on strike which "inclines" (though it does not necessitate) him to make this decision. What, then, does Leibniz mean? Not that a choice is in no sense necessitated, but only that it is not *absolutely* necessary (to Clarke, 5.8–9, G VII 390: P 221–22; *Theodicy*, par. 53, G VI 131–32). The man who decides not to go on strike *could have* decided to strike, in that such a decision would not have involved a logical contradiction. But *given that* the motive of not harming innocent people was the strongest of his motives, then it was necessary – hypothetically necessary – that he should decide not to go on strike.

One may doubt, however, whether Leibniz has done enough to establish the freedom of the will, as this is normally understood. He would claim to have shown that, when a rational agent makes a decision, it is always possible for that agent to have decided otherwise. But, as Stuart Hampshire has forcefully argued,[30] the sense of "possibility" which Leibniz has in mind here is "merely that in which it *makes sense* to suppose that . . . [someone] does act other-wise, that this does not contain a contradiction." But this, Hamp-shire argues, is not enough to establish freedom; what is required is something that Hampshire calls "actual" possibility. Suppose, for example, that a man is bound and gagged by intruders and so cannot prevent his house from being robbed. Now, it makes sense (in the sense of not involving a logical contradiction) to suppose that the man could have prevented the burglary. But, Hampshire argues, "No one would suppose that such a man was *free* to prevent the burglary. We need for freedom more than the mere logical possibility of the alternative, which is all that Leibniz gives us."

Hampshire's objection is sound as far as it goes; certainly, more is required for freedom than the mere logical possibility of acting in a way different from that in which one does act. But it must be made clear that Leibniz would not have denied this. Freedom, he says, involves both spontaneity and choice (e.g., *Theodicy*, par. 34, G VI 122; *Theodicy*, par. 288, G VI 288; G VI 441).[31] By "spon-taneity," Leibniz means that the principle of action is within the agent; a free agent is not "compelled," is not the mere plaything of external forces (G VII 108). But Leibniz also insists that spon-taneity, though necessary for human freedom, is not sufficient. As he points out in the *New Essays on Human Understanding*, a ball which moves smoothly in a straight line acts without any hin-drance, and yet it is not a free agent (II.21.9, A VI.vi: RB 176). For freedom, there must not only be spontaneity; there must also be choice.

Let us now apply this to Hampshire's example of the householder. It may seem obvious that the householder does not satisfy Leibniz's first condition of freedom in that he is clearly subject to compulsion – crude physical compulsion. But there is a complication here raised by Leibniz's metaphysical views. For Leibniz, the householder's soul would be a single individual substance, and his body (e.g., G II 119) a vast, but unified collection of substances. But it is one of the best-known theses of Leibniz's metaphysics that each substance is the principle of its own actions. So it seems that Leibniz's philosophy again leads him into paradox; the householder, whether viewed as soul or as body, is free. This is not so, however: the householder does not satisfy Leibniz's second condition of freedom in that it is assumed that he does not *choose* to be tied up.

One may readily agree with Leibniz that human beings exercise choice; the question is whether they are also spontaneous beings in Leibniz's sense of the term. Leibniz rejects the idea, which he ascribes to Descartes, that the mind's spontaneity is known by a "lively internal sentiment" (*Theodicy*, par. 50, G VI 130). Instead, he offers arguments for this conclusion. At the time of the *Discourse on Metaphysics*, the arguments are based on the thesis that each substance has a complete concept (e.g., pars. 9, 13, G IV 433–44, 436–39: P. 19–20, 23–35); later, the argument rests on the simplicity of substance (e.g. *Monadology*, pars. 1, 7, G VI 607, 607–8: P 179). But it is not the purpose of this chapter to go further into Leibniz's views about freedom; the point made here is simply that Leibniz has an answer to what may seem to be a powerful objection. Yet the objection has some force; if Leibniz is to produce a successful defense of free will he must do more than draw a purely logical distinction between two kinds of necessity.

NOTES

1 Russell, *The Philosophy of Leibniz*, v.

2 My own views on this topic can be found in Parkinson, *Logic and Reality in Leibniz's Metaphysics*.

3 For similar formulations, see, e.g., G VII 309: P 75; C 518–19: P 87–88; C 401–2: P 93; C 16: P 96.

4 Unless otherwise specified, translations from Leibniz are my own. For a fuller account of negative truths, see Parkinson, *Logic and Reality*, pp. 23–37.

5 Cf. J. L. Austin, *Philosophical Papers*, p. 12: "To ask 'whether we possess a certain concept' is the same as to ask whether a certain word – or rather, sentences in which it occurs – has any meaning."

6 C 512: P 6. To be more exact (C 432) it is nouns (*nomina*) that are the signs of concepts; other parts of speech are ways of conceiving (*modi concipiendi*). It should be added that Leibniz does not mean that only language-users have concepts. God has concepts (e.g., *Discourse on Metaphysics*, par. 8, G IV 433: P 19), but God does not use language.

7 Leibniz does not express his disagreement with Spinoza alone on this issue. In *Theodicy*, pars. 170–73 (G VI 212–17) he mentions, as also taking the view that nothing can happen apart from what does happen, Diodorus the Megarian, Abelard, Wyclif, and Hobbes. I draw attention to Spinoza here because Leibniz's relations with Spinoza's philosophy are often discussed.

8 It is announced as a discovery in par. 137 of Leibniz's *General Inquiries about the Analysis of Concepts and of Truths* (C 389: PLP 78), a work which was written in 1686.

9 For references made by Leibniz to this passage, see, e.g., G II 104–5; *New Essays*, Preface, A VI.vi: RB 56; G IV 375–76.

10 Such ratios were known to the ancient Greeks, and indeed Leibniz (C 2) quotes the tenth book of Euclid's *Elements* in this connection. Put succinctly, the Greeks discovered that "lengths exist which are not any exact fraction of the original length. For example, the diagonal of a square cannot be expressed as any fraction of the side of the same square; in our modern notation the length of the diagonal is $\sqrt{2}$ times the length of the side. But there is no fraction which exactly represents $\sqrt{2}$" (Whitehead, *Introduction to Mathematics*, p. 50).

11 Leibniz does not give examples of this, but we may take as an example the square root of 2. The continued fraction $1 + \cfrac{1}{2 + \cfrac{1}{2 + \cfrac{1}{2} \ldots}}$ converges upon $\sqrt{2}$. Incidentally, the use of continued fractions was described by Rafael Bombelli, whose *Algebra* (1st ed., 1572) was known to Leibniz. See, e.g., A III.i 271, 277; C 148.

12 For other, similar formulations of the principle, see Parkinson, *Logic and Reality*, pp. 63–66.

13 One problem which arises from this argument for the principle of sufficient reason is that, here and elsewhere (e.g., C 513: P 7–8; G VII 199, 309), Leibniz seems to restrict the principle to propositions which have to be proved, i.e., which are not expressly identical propositions. Yet there are many passages, such as *Monadology*, par. 32, quoted earlier, in which the principle is said to apply to all truths without exception (cf. G II 62; G VI 413; G VII 295: P 15; G VII 301; to Clarke 5.125, G VII 419: L 717; C 402). A way of reconciling the two positions is suggested by G VII 295: P 15, namely, that although an explicitly identical proposition cannot be proved, it has a *reason* for its truth, and this reason is the very fact that it is an identical proposition.

14 E.g., to Clarke, 5.19, G VII 393, L 698–99; *Theodicy*, G VI 44. The principle is also called "the principle of fitness" (*convenance*, *convenientia*), (*Monadology*, par. 46, G VI 614: P 186; *Principles of Nature and Grace*, par. 11, G VI 603: P 201; C 528) and "the principle of perfection" (Gr 288).

15 *Ethics* I Prop. 32, Coroll. 1.

16 Cottingham, Stoothoff, and Murdoch, *Philosophical Writings of Descartes* II, pp. 291–92.

17 Cf. Parkinson, *Leibniz on Human Freedom*, p. 19.

18 See Parkinson, *Logic and Reality*, pp. 113–14.

19 See, e.g., Kenny, *The God of the Philosophers*, pp. 114–17.

20 Cf. G VII 289 (also C 534): P 145–46. For other uses of the concept of compossibility, see C 530 (also A VI.iii 581) and *New Essays* III.6.12, A VI.vi: RB 307.

21 See, e.g., Lewis, *On the Plurality of Worlds*.

22 G VII 195n.; G VII 289–90: P 145–46; *Theodicy*, par. 7, G VI 106; Gr 285.

23 Lewis, "Counterpart Theory and Quantified Modal Logic," 113–26. For the application of the theory to the philosophy of Leibniz see, e.g., Mates, *The Philosophy of Leibniz*, pp. 137–51.

24 *Naming and Necessity*, pp. 15–20, 42–53, 76–77.

25 The many references to hypothetical necessity include G VI 123; to Clarke, 5.4, G VII 389: L 696; G VII 303: P 137; *Discourse on Metaphysics*, par. 13, G IV 437: P 24. For "consequential necessity" see C 271, G III 400; for "moral necessity," G VI 441, G II 419; for "physical necessity" see G VII 303.

26 Aristotle, *Physics* II 9, 200 a10–14, trans. R. P. Hardie, Oxford, Clarendon Press, 1930.

27 Leibniz also uses the concept (as did earlier philosophers such as Boethius and Aquinas) to explain how God's foreknowledge can be reconciled with contingency. See *Leibniz on Human Freedom*, p. 7, and William and Martha Kneale, *The Development of Logic*, p. 237.

28 For examples of such laws of physics, see *Logic and Reality*, p. 113, which cites G IV 318, 340; G VII 295, 304; *Discourse on Metaphysics*, par. 22, G IV 447–48: L 317–18; *New Essays* II.21.9, A VI.vi: RB 176.

29 See *Leibniz on Human Freedom*, p. 50 n. 3. Leibniz says that he borrowed the phrase from the "famous dictum": "*astra inclinant, non necessitant*" (*Theodicy*, par. 43, G VI 126). On this dictum, which is to be found in the Scholastics, see *Leibniz on Human Freedom*, p. 52 n. 36.

30 *The Age of Reason*, p. 167.

31 Cf. *Leibniz on Human Freedom*, pp. 57–58.

8   Philosophy and language in Leibniz

Leibniz's views on language, and on the relationship of language to philosophy, constitute a rich and, until recently, little explored area of his thought. Unlike some of his seventeenth-century contemporaries, Leibniz was conscious of a deep connection between the human capacity for language and the capacity to comprehend reality. Language is less a barrier between the mind and the world that must so far as possible be overcome than a lens that necessarily intervenes between mind and world and that can, depending on the skill of the optician, either distort or magnify our apprehension of the world.[1] Accordingly, a careful study of language forms an essential part of the method of philosophy.

It is helpful at the outset to distinguish two primary focal points of Leibniz's interest in language.[2] Within his writings these are represented, on the one hand, by the many sketches and plans associated with the notion of an ideal, artificial language – the "universal characteristic"; and, on the other, by numerous historical and philological investigations of natural languages, many of them directed towards uncovering the common roots of a multitude of human languages. On the face of it, there seems to be a tension between the aims and assumptions of these two very different approaches to the subject of language.[3] In Leibniz's view, one of the principal objectives of the universal characteristic is to rectify a serious deficiency in natural languages by providing a symbolism in which it would be possible to represent more accurately and more effectively the structure of rational thought. Basic to this approach, then, is a critical attitude toward the powers of natural language, which is judged to be almost as successful at confounding the human capacity for reason as it is at securing everyday communication between human beings.[4] By contrast, the universal characteristic would enable us to construct linguistic characters which are transparent representations of intelligible thoughts, something the signs of natural languages typically fail to be, and to reduce logical reasoning to a mechanical procedure relying solely on the substitution of formal characters.

To the extent that this conception of a universal characteristic forms the core of Leibniz's understanding of language, there is every reason to suspect that he would find little of philosophical value in the study of natural languages. However, such a conclusion is at odds with the evidence of his writings. These suggest that while natural language may indeed be criticized as a medium for scientific reasoning and the representation of knowledge, its study is nevertheless of prime importance for what it can tell us about the foundations of linguistic meaning and the operations of the human mind. In his investigations of natural language, Leibniz appears to opt for an approach that is relatively independent from that adopted in the case of the universal characteristic, treating natural language as a distinctive form of linguistic phenomenon which results from the innate capacity of human beings for speech and the variety of their interactions with their environment. It follows that if Leibniz's ideal of language is the complete and perfect representation of thought, and thus reality, in a formal characteristic, he nevertheless recognizes that in practice language must be seen as grounded in the contingency of human needs, capacities, and interests. This, in turn, explains the potential value of a study of natural languages which focuses on the specific pattern of their historical and cultural development.

This sketch of Leibniz's twofold approach to the topic of language, artificial and natural, forms the background for the rest of this chapter. In section I, I examine his various schemes for a universal characteristic, the connection between the universal characteristic and rival seventeenth-century plans for a universal language, and the general importance of the universal characteristic within the overall framework of Leibniz's philosophy. In section II, I turn to natural languages, paying particular attention to Leibniz's view of the origin of linguistic meaning and the evidence he finds in comparative linguistic studies for the hypothesis of a common original language. In section III, I bring these two concerns together in order to consider whether the universal characteristic and natural languages, in fact, represent wholly disparate forms of language for Leibniz, or whether certain common assumptions about the nature of meaning, and the relationship of language to thought and reality, might be found to underlie both.

The final issue I examine is the language of philosophy itself. A once popular conclusion of positivist theories of meaning was that philosophical discourse must, strictly speaking, be meaningless insofar as it routinely formulates theses about matters that transcend the possibility of empirical verification. Surprising as it may seem, Leibniz's view of meaning has at least one important point of contact with the positivist's position: his claim that all linguistic expressions originally acquire their meaning through reference to some sensible state of affairs. In section IV, we will see how he manages to render this view consistent with the significance of his own metaphysics through an interesting theory of the analogical extension of meaning from the domain of the sensible to that of the supersensible.

I. THE UNIVERSAL CHARACTERISTIC

It has become almost a commonplace to associate Leibniz's name with the idea of a "universal characteristic," although widespread disagreement has persisted about the nature, scope, and significance of this project.[5] For some, the interest of the universal characteristic is limited to its role as the earliest precursor of twentieth-century projects for formal languages capable of representing and verifying modes of valid inference. Those who favor such an interpretation see the key to the universal characteristic in the idea that it is possible to represent the logical relations among concepts (or propositions) while ignoring the actual content of the concepts themselves, by substituting arbitrary symbols for them.[6] For others, the philosophical significance of the universal characteristic is found outside its connection to formal logic in its role as a *lingua philosophica:* an ideal, philosophical language composed of "real characters" which would, on the contrary, precisely express the content of an encyclopedic knowledge of reality.[7]

Within the large and heterogeneous collection of Leibniz's writings relating to the universal characteristic, there is evidence supporting both interpretations. Indeed, it seems likely, as Pombo has argued, that a basic ambiguity underlies his conception of this scheme.[8] In different writings Leibniz characterizes the universal characteristic both as a type of ideal language, although one far more powerful than any devised by his contemporaries, and as a general symbolic method, "by means of which the relations of things are suitably represented in characters" (GM VII 159). Under the first of these descriptions, primary emphasis is laid on the universal characteristic as a system of real characters, i.e., signs which possess a determinate content and exactly correspond in their structure to the analysis of thoughts.[9] Under the second description, the universal characteristic is identified with a plan for a general science of forms, the *spécieuse générale:* a symbolic calculus (or collection of calculi) whose principal object would be the formalization of patterns of inference in different domains of knowledge. Such a symbolism could be constructed without definitive results having been obtained in any of the sciences, by using variables to represent arbitrary concepts and formal rules to express valid patterns of inference.

From the perspective of Leibniz's philosophy, it is the first of these projects which would represent the full culmination of the universal characteristic, since only in this case would there be realized the pansophic ideal of a language which transparently expressed the totality of all possible human knowledge.[10] However, insofar as this project appears as a more or less unattainable goal, presupposing as it does a complete and final analysis of all concepts and the devising of characters which would exactly convey the content of these concepts, it is arguably the second approach which bears the greater fruit. In the rest of this section, I will consider in more detail the development of these two related projects and try to show how, beginning from an early enthusiasm for the universal characteristic as a system of philosophical writing, Leibniz gradually retreats to the more limited design of his "general science of forms." Although he never completely gives up his hope that a philosophical language will one day be realized, in practice it is the latter project which best reveals his accomplishment.

The roots of Leibniz's interest in the idea of a universal characteristic can be traced at least as far back as his 1666 dissertation *On the Art of Combinations.* For our purposes, *On the Art of Combinations* is of greatest importance for the model of conceptual thought that it presupposes and develops. In it we meet full-blown the theory of the combinatorial nature of concepts – the doctrine that all complex concepts are composed from, and analyzable into, simpler concepts – a constant feature of all of Leibniz's later writings. It is evident that he regards this theory of concepts as following from more general metaphysical principles. In his view, *all* things, and thus all concepts, are defined in terms of the parts they contain (their "matter") and the specific arrangement of these parts (their "form"). Differences in parts (when these parts are conceived as belonging to some larger whole) are differences of "complexion"; differences in the arrangement of parts are differences of "situation" or "disposition."

> Since all things which exist or can be thought of are in the main composed of parts, either real or at any rate conceptual, it is necessary that those things which differ in species differ either in that they have different parts – and here is the use of complexions – or in that they have a different situation – and here is the use of dispositions.   (A VI.i 177: PLP 3)

In keeping with the Aristotelian tradition, concepts are defined by the division of more comprehensive concepts; for example, the concept *man* is defined as the product of the concept *animal* and the concept *rational*. In Leibniz's scheme, however, the species-genus hierarchy of Aristotelian logic is subordinated to a more basic principle: the concept *man* is composed of the concepts *animal* and *rational* as a whole from parts; and these constituent concepts (which together comprise a definition of the original concept) are in turn conceived as complex wholes composed of other conceptual parts (A VI.i 195: PLP 5). The principal application of this theory of concepts in *On the Art of Combinations* is in the service of what Leibniz calls the "inventive logic." Granted that any proposition can be regarded as a "combination" of two concepts (its subject and predicate terms),[11] this logic is charged with the task of establishing via analysis all the true combinations of concepts, and subsequently all the valid forms of the syllogism. This requires determining in every case whether the concept expressed by the predicate term can be obtained through an analysis of the concept expressed by the subject term; and to obtain a complete enumeration of truths such a procedure will have to be carried out until a complete analysis of the concepts into their simplest components has been accomplished. Leibniz then proposes reversing this procedure and, starting from a class of simple, indefinable terms, constructing all the possible true propositions *a priori* (A VI.i 195–96: PLP 4–5).

As a corollary to this inventive logic, Leibniz goes on to advance a plan for a system of universal writing which would be "intelligible to anyone who reads it, whatever language he knows" (A VI.i 201: PLP 10). After briefly noting the shortcomings of several contemporary schemes, he describes the sort of symbolism that will be possible once a class of basic terms or categories has been established.

Let the first terms, of the combination of which all others consist, be designated by signs; these signs will be a kind of alphabet. . . . If these are correctly and ingeniously established, this universal writing will be as easy as it is common, and will be capable of being read without any dictionary; at the same time, a fundamental knowledge of all things will be obtained. The whole of such a writing will be made of geometrical figures, as it were, and of a kind of pictures – just as the ancient Egyptians did, and the Chinese do today. Their pictures, however, are not reduced to an alphabet, i.e., to letters, with the result that a tremendous strain on the memory is necessary, which is the contrary of what we propose. (A VI.i 202: PLP 11)

Although it is difficult to know what exactly Leibniz has in mind in this brief passage, two points stand out concerning the requirements of his proposed system of universal writing. First, given the existence of a class of primitive terms or categories, it will be necessary to construct a corresponding class of pictorial characters (or "geometrical figures"), which will exactly represent the content of the primitive terms. Second, in order to avoid too great a strain on the memory (as happens in existing character languages like Chinese), it will be necessary to give an order to these simple characters and rules for their combination, thereby reducing them to the letters of an alphabet. With this done, we will possess a system of writing in which every simple idea is immediately evoked by the character assigned to it, and every complex idea is designated by a complex character whose formation from simple characters exactly parallels the formation of the complex idea from its simpler conceptual parts. Such a system will constitute a truly universal writing, since its pictorial representations will be intelligible to speakers of any language and its compositional rules will be completely regular and easily memorized.

Within Leibniz's later thought, this plan for a universal writing survives as the key to his conception of the universal characteristic as a philosophical language or writing.[12] Three points remain central to this scheme:

(1) The resolution of all concepts into a set of unanalyzable primitive concepts, the elements of the "alphabet of human thoughts";

(2) The devising of signs or characters suitable for representing each of these primitive concepts;

(3) The formulation of rules for the combination of these characters which exactly parallel the logical relations among the corresponding concepts.[13]

As we shall see, these requirements form the core of the analytic and symbolic method that Leibniz recommends throughout his career as essential for the advancement of knowledge.[14]

In developing his plan for a philosophical writing, Leibniz was acting in concert with a widespread movement in the seventeenth century. This movement suggests the existence of a strong contemporary need both for some variety of universal language capable of bridging the gulf between disparate linguistic groups in the service of peace and commerce, and for languages or symbolisms that might be useful in rendering more rigorous the process of logical and mathematical reasoning and advancing the pace of scientific discoveries.[15] To what extent Leibniz's own project for a universal characteristic merely elaborates the themes of his contemporaries, and to what extent it offers something truly novel, is a matter of some contention. The tendency of recent scholars has been to emphasize the similarities between his plan and the works of earlier authors such as Dalgarno and Wilkins. In the view of one commentator: "It is only in thinking of a logical calculus as an ancillary to his universal character which would be useful in eliciting implications that Leibniz seems to have had no precursor."[16] Whatever the merit of this claim, it is clear that Leibniz's own view of the value of his characteristic over those of his predecessors is quite different. The charge he levels repeatedly against the schemes of such authors as Dalgarno and Wilkins is that they have neglected the role of the universal characteristic as an "instrument of reason" in order to highlight its function as an effective medium for communication. "For their language or writing achieves only this: convenient communication between those sundered by language; but the true real characteristic, such as I conceive it, must be thought one of the most apt instruments of the human mind, with an invincible power for discovery, memory and judgment" (G VII 7; cf. G III 216, VII 16–17). Even if, as seems probable, Leibniz was at times prone to underestimate his debt to the universal language schemes of his predecessors, it is fair to say that he saw far more clearly than anyone had before the potential connection between symbolic systems and the logic of conceptual thought. It was just his innovation to emphasize the need for a characteristic in which the order and relations of signs would so mirror the order and relations of ideas that all valid reasoning could be reduced to an infallible, mechanical procedure involving only the formal substitution of characters.[17] Such a characteristic would, moreover, supersede the scope of modern systems of formal logic; for it would be the task of the universal characteristic not only to express the formal structure of valid deductive inferences, but also to express the *content* of the ideas being reasoned about. Such is the difference between a mere calculus and a real characteristic or philosophical writing.

Leibniz considered his plan for a universal characteristic to be among the most important of his inventions; and, particularly in his early years, he endowed it with extraordinary powers. In a letter to Oldenburg, ca. 1673, he writes: "To anyone who wanted to speak or write about any topic, the genius of this language will supply not only the words but also the things. The very name of any thing will be the key to all that could reasonably be said or thought about it or done with it."[18] Again, in a 1679 letter to his first Hanoverian patron Johann Friedrich, he describes his characteristic as "the great instrument of reason, which will carry the forces of the mind further than the microscope has carried those of sight" (A II.i 557; cf. A II.i 239; C 158). During the same period, he cites its need in the creation of an encyclopedic compendium of human knowledge, the *Plus Ultra*, in which truths from every branch of learning would be gathered together and arranged according to their deductive order.[19] Finally, many of Leibniz's statements concerning the universal characteristic emphasize the point that by this means it will become possible to reason in ethics and metaphysics with a degree of certainty hitherto found only in mathematics (A II.i 380, 384).

But could such a characteristic ever be realized? Arguably not. To carry out the aims that Leibniz foresees for it, its characters would, from the start, have to be constructed such that they exactly express the composition of the concepts they are meant to replace. This implies that rather than aiding the philosophical analysis of concepts, the formulation of a universal characteristic, in fact, *presupposes* a complete analysis of concepts into their simplest parts.[20] This is a problem that had already been recognized by Descartes. Replying in 1629 to a query by Mersenne, he suggests that the invention of a universal language, "a language in which the primitive words and symbols mirrored an ordering of all the thoughts which can come into the human mind in an order like the order of natural numbers," would require the "true philosophy."

> For without that philosophy it is impossible to number and order all the thoughts of men or even to separate them out into clear and simple thoughts, which in my opinion is the great secret for acquiring true scientific knowledge. If someone were to explain correctly what are the simple ideas in the human imagination out of which all human thoughts are compounded, and if his explanation were generally received, I would dare to hope for a universal language very easy to learn, to speak, and to write.[21]

While acknowledging the possibility of such a language, Descartes is skeptical that it, or the true philosophy on which it depends, will be realized, since "[f]or that, the order of nature would have to change so that the world turned into a terrestrial paradise; and that is too much to suggest outside of fairyland" (ibid.). Descartes' remarks suggest an imposing problem for any scheme for a universal characteristic in Leibniz's sense. It is only reasonable to conceive of such a characteristic once we are in possession of the "true philosophy": a complete analysis of ideas into their simplest components.

When Leibniz came across Descartes' letter sometime after the composition of *On the Art of Combinations,* he was already prepared with a reply. While accepting the essential truth of Descartes' observation, he denies that the construction of the universal characteristic need wait for the completion of the "true philosophy" (C 28).[22] Instead, once the principles of the latter have been established, the two endeavors can, and must, proceed in parallel. The construction of suitable characters will aid the analysis of concepts, which in turn will instruct us in the formation of better characters. Whether or not this serves as an adequate response to the problem raised by Descartes, it is clear that by this time Leibniz had already begun to hesitate on the central issue of whether an analysis of all concepts into logically simple components lies within the power of the human mind.[23] He is certain that such an analysis must be possible in principle and that genuinely primitive concepts must exist (C 429–30: P 2). Yet, in practice, he appears to give up the search for primitives and instead focuses on devising definitions of important terms (whether or not these definitions are framed in terms of primitives) as a first step towards the demonstration of various metaphysical theorems (C 176, 220–21).

The critical importance of a large number of studies devoted by Leibniz to the definition of key philosophical terms was for many years overlooked, in part due to their unavailability in published form.[24] The recent appearance of these studies, many of them written during the decade 1675–85, has revealed a crucial background to the *Discourse on Metaphysics,* the unpublished essay widely accepted as the first articulation of Leibniz's mature philosophy.[25] On the basis of the evidence that is now available, we may venture two revisionary hypotheses about the place of this essay in the development of his thought. First, for at least five years prior to the composition of the *Discourse on Metaphysics* Leibniz was intensely engaged in perfecting definitions of the terms needed for the formulation of the central theses of this work.[26] Second, the *Discourse* (along with Leibniz's subsequent published writings) is at bottom no more than a popularized or "exoteric" expression of his metaphysical doctrines.[27] In his own view, an adequate statement of his metaphysics would only be achieved when its theorems had been arranged in a strict demonstrative order, beginning with the definitions of basic terms and a small number of axiomatic principles. Numerous comments made by Leibniz in his later writings suggest that from about 1686 onwards he was confident that it would be only a matter of time before his philosophy could be presented in this form. Crucial to this enterprise would be the construction of characters capable of expressing the analytic relations among metaphysical concepts such that theorems could be established mechanically, via the substitution of characters. He writes in a letter to Foucher:

I once composed an essay of demonstrations using the calculus of containment in which I demonstrated by means of characters (almost in the manner of algebra and numbers) certain propositions. I could give demonstrations not only of magnitude, but also of quality, form, relation, and many other things, which are demonstrated entirely hypothetically from a few suppositions by the simple substitution of equivalent characters. The most important would be of cause, effect, change, action, [and] time, in which I find that the truth is very different from what is imagined.   (G I 390–91)[28]

According to Leibniz, progress in every branch of rational knowledge (including philosophy) is linked to the development of suitable signs or characters.[29] He conceives of the class of signs in general as being very broad. It includes:

Words, letters; chemical, astronomical, and Chinese figures; hieroglyphs; musical, cryptographic, mathematical, algebraic notations; and all other symbols which in our thoughts we use for the signified things. When the signs are written, drawn, or carved, they are called characters.

(G VII 204: S 18)

Not all of these signs, however, are useful in the discovery of truths of reason. For this we need characters which adequately represent their subject matter and support our reasoning about it.[30] Alchemical and astrological symbols, Egyptian hieroglyphs, and Chinese characters are all deemed unsuitable for this purpose. Instead, the future progress of the rational sciences depends on their adopting the kinds of symbols used in arithmetic and algebra.

It is obvious that if we could find characters or signs suited for expressing all our thoughts as clearly and exactly as arithmetic expresses numbers or geometrical analysis expresses lines, we could do in all matters *insofar as they are subject to reasoning* all that we can do in arithmetic and geometry. For all investigations which depend on reasoning would be carried out by the transposition of these characters and by a species of calculus.

(C 155; emphasis in the original)[31]

Leibniz is regrettably brief in his accounts of the basic relation of "expression" or "representation" that unites a character and what it signifies. Typical of his statements on the matter is the following definition from a 1679 essay:

I call whatever represents some other object of thought a *character*. But that is said to *represent* which corresponds in such a way that from it something else can be thought, [and this] even if they are not similar, provided that all the things which occur in the one are referred, according to some definite rule or relation, to certain corresponding things in the other

(LH XXXV 1, 27 Bl. 3–10 [VE 1364])[32]

As this passage suggests, a necessary condition for an adequate characteristic is that any character representing a complex concept should be constructed from simple characters in a way that exactly corresponds to the composition of the complex concept from its simpler conceptual parts. In the late 1670s, Leibniz discovered a type of characteristic which nicely illustrates this principle.[33] He proposes representing simple concepts by prime numbers and the composition of concepts by numerical multiplication. Since any integral number can be uniquely factored as a multiple of primes, this scheme offers a way of exactly representing the relations among concepts in a simple numerical symbolism. At the same time, however, this characteristic also highlights what would seem to be a second serious obstacle to the realization of Leibniz's original plan for a philosophical language. Although it promises a method for accurately representing the relations among concepts, and thus a formal framework for logical inference, it relies throughout on the assumption of a conventional relation between hypothetical primitive concepts and prime numbers. For this reason, it cannot be expected that the simple characters of this system will naturally evoke in the mind the elements of the "alphabet of human thoughts."[34] While this issue is connected with the problem of the resolution of concepts into true primitives, it also raises an independent question about how the basic signs of the universal characteristic are meant to signify their objects. Can these simple signs themselves be assumed to "represent" the basic elements of reality with which they are associated? Or must we be content with a purely conventional relation between simple characters and the ideas they signify? And if the latter, can Leibniz continue to hope for a truly universal and philosophical language of the sort first projected in *On the Art of Combinations?*

To fully address these questions would require some discussion of Leibniz's account of the origin of meaning in natural languages, a topic we will take up in section II. For the moment it is enough to note that in the present context he generally opts for the position that there need be only a conventional relation between the simple signs of his characteristic and primitive concepts.[35] This position seems to be consistent, moreover, with the idea that, from a semantic point of view, it is the notion of "representation" or "expression" which is of fundamental importance for the universal characteristic.

According to Leibniz's most explicit definitions, "expression" is a purely structural notion, i.e., it depends solely on an isomorphism of relations between an expression and what it expresses. What a character and the concept it expresses have in common is a certain shared order among their simpler components, such that from our knowledge of the former, conclusions can be drawn about the composition of the latter.[36] If this is correct, it implies that in this sense it is impossible for truly simple signs to express primitive concepts, for it is a necessary condition of their simplicity that they lack the structure on which the requisite relations of order are to be defined. To a large extent, then, Leibniz seems committed to there being only a conventional relation between the simplest signs of his universal characteristic and primitive concepts. Nevertheless, it is hard not to think that he at times hoped for something more than this, for some sort of ideal natural or pictorial relationship between sign and signified.[37] For without the latter, his philosophical language could directly convey only the formal structure of reality, and not its content. For the rest we would be dependent on our knowledge of the conventional assignments of simple signs to primitive concepts.

Leibniz's later writings offer few clues as to how this problem is to be resolved. However, two particular proposals deserve mention. In the *New Essays*, he describes a "universal symbolism" very similar to that advanced in *On the Art of Combinations*, in which "in place of words we used little diagrams which represented visible things pictorially and invisible things by means of the visible ones which go with them" (IV.vi 2; A VI.vi: RB 398–99). This system appears to capture much of the flavor of at least one version of his philosophical language. Its characters would be like "inherently significant pictures," as opposed to ordinary letters and Chinese characters which signify only conventionally, or "through the will of men [*ex instituto*]." Consequently, "this way of writing would be of great service in enriching our imagination and giving us thoughts which were less blind and less verbal than our present ones are" (ibid.). Unfortunately, Leibniz says too little about this symbolism for us to draw any solid conclusions about its philosophical significance.[38]

Of considerably greater interest is a plan for a universal characteristic based on the analogy of binary arithmetic. In the domain of mathematics, Leibniz regarded binary notation as intrinsically superior to decimal notation (C 284; GM III 661). Over and above this advantage, however, he believed that it contained the key to resolving both the problem of conceptual primitives and the problem of adequate characters. If it could be established, as Leibniz speculated from about 1679 onwards, that the only truly primitive concepts were those of God and Nothingness (or Being and Privation),[39] then the symbols I and o would form the basis for an adequate characteristic, whose simplest signs would stand in an immediate relation to the two conceptual primitives.[40] Later, when he had learned of the similarity between his binary notation and the figures of the *I Ching*, Leibniz wrote to the French Jesuit Bouvet that he had discovered

a new characteristic which will appear as a successor to that of FoHi and will give a beginning to the analysis of ideas and to that wonderful calculus of reason which I have projected. This secret and sacred characteristic would also give us the means of insinuating into the Chinese the most important truths of philosophy and natural theology.   (Du IV.ii 6)[41]

There is no indication in Leibniz's later writings that this plan was ever realized in any detail, presumably because he was stopped by the problem of showing how all concepts can be constructed as complex combinations of the concepts of God and Nothingness. Again, there are signs of a deep ambivalence on his part concerning the possibility of any endeavor of this sort. While never ceasing to project optimistic plans for the future, he was, as early as 1679, prone to express skepticism about the chances of an *a priori* philosophical language, which would exactly articulate the conceptual structure of reality.

Since it is not in our power to demonstrate completely the possibility of things *a priori*, that is, to reduce them to God and Nothingness, it will suffice for us to reduce the multitude of them to some few, the possibility of which can either be supposed and postulated, or proven by experience.
                    (C 431: P 3; cf. C 514: P 8)

I suggested earlier that in a number of studies from the 1680s and 1690s Leibniz endeavors to analyze and define a selection of key philosophical concepts, without attempting to determine how they are constituted from the ultimate simples. Consistent with the hypothetical nature of this enterprise, i.e., with its acceptance of nonprimitive conceptual starting points, Leibniz lays no emphasis in these studies on the need for characters which would immediately evoke the simplest elements of thought. Instead, he seems to give up the hope of establishing a characteristic which has this property and limits himself to one in which conceptual relations are expressed by relations among purely conventional marks, such as the letters of the alphabet.[42] As he explains in an essay from the late 1680s:

Since no definite result has yet been reached as to the way these signs [i.e., real characters] must be formed, we shall meanwhile follow the example of mathematics for their future formation, and use the letters of the alphabet, or any other arbitrary notation which in the course of our progress will suggest itself as most convenient.   (G VII 205: S 19)

In most of Leibniz's later writings, the plan for an *a priori* philosophical language – a language composed of "real characters" capable of expressing the content of well-defined concepts – is replaced by the project of the *spécieuse générale*, or general science of forms.[43] This latter scheme is explicitly linked to the concerns of his earliest work in this area: "The art of combinations . . . signifies in my view just the science of forms, or indeed of variations in general. In a word, it is the *spécieuse universelle* or the characteristic" (C 531: VE 1335; cf. G VII 297–98: P 17). By the time these words are written, sometime after 1690, an evolution has obviously occurred in Leibniz's understanding of the universal characteristic: it is now primarily associated with the combinatorial method itself rather than with a philosophical language that might, as in his early scheme, develop out of it.

An essay from the early 1680s gives a good idea of the scope of Leibniz's mature view of the combinatory:

Combinatory treats of calculus in general, or of general signs or characters (such as *A, B, C*, where any one could be taken for another at will), and of the various laws of arrangement and transition, or of formulas in general. The algebraic calculus is a certain species of the general calculus, [in which], for example, there is a law of multiplication. . . . Not all formulas signify quantity, and an infinite number of ways of calculating can be conceived.
                    (C 556: VE 1354)

The above passage brings to light several important features of Leibniz's conception of the *spécieuse générale*. First, the *spécieuse générale* is conceived as a general theory of the possible combinations of symbolic forms, without regard to what in particular the forms signify. Second, the only restriction on the possible modes of combination is that they should represent *formal* relations among the symbols in question, that is, relations which can be represented within a calculus in which transitions between symbols are governed by rules which depend only on their form, and not their content. Third, depending on the intended signification of the symbols and the allowed relations among them, numerous different calculi can be conceived, all of which fall within the scope of the *spécieuse générale.* Some of these will be algebraic calculi, in which the symbols signify quantities or numbers; others logical calculi, in which the symbols signify qualities or ideas (G VII 245: L 380). As these points suggest, Leibniz's writings on the *spécieuse générale* reveal an understanding of the concept of formal method that goes well beyond that of any philosopher prior to the nineteenth century. As Hacking has observed, his conception of a formal calculus based on the substitutivity of signs according to determinate rules essentially captures the modern notion of logical proof (cf. G VII 206: S 18–19).[44]

The movement of Leibniz's thought in the mid-1680s and 1690s in the direction of an investigation of the general properties of formal systems signals a weakening of his interest in the idea of a philosophical language. There is no indication, however, that he ever gives up completely his hopes for this farsighted plan. Although in his later years he seems to focus more on the universal characteristic as a "general science of forms," he persists in his claim that a universal language would follow as an immediate by-product of it.

I should venture to add that if I had been less distracted, or if I were younger or had talented young men to help me, I should still hope to create a kind of *spécieuse générale,* in which all truths of reason would be reduced to a kind of calculus. At the same time this could be a kind of universal language or writing, though infinitely different from all such languages which have thus far been proposed, for the characters and the words themselves would give directions to reason, and the errors (except those of fact) would be only mistakes in calculation. It would be very difficult to form or invent this language or characteristic but very easy to learn it without any dictionaries.
(Letter to Remond, 1714; G III 605: L 654)[45]

While Leibniz continued to conceive of the universal characteristic as finding its final form in an ideal philosophical language, he was able to advance little beyond brief descriptions of its most general features and requirements. We have considered several problems intrinsic to this project which help to explain why this might have been so. These were not, however, problems which were fully evident to Leibniz himself. On the contrary, until the very end of his life, he spoke as if his failure to realize the universal characteristic was due solely to the burdens that had been imposed upon him by his Hanoverian employers.[46]

II. NATURAL LANGUAGES

Leibniz's views on natural language have attracted considerably less attention from philosophers than his project for a universal characteristic.[47] This may in part be due to the fact that the universal characteristic has much in common with modern formal theories, whereas Leibniz's studies of natural language are seen as being of primarily historical interest. Or it may just be that philosophers are less acquainted with the wide range of his research in this area. Whatever the reason for this neglect, Leibniz's writings on natural language address a number of issues of philosophical importance. Among these are questions of the origin and diversity of human languages; the natural or conventional basis of meaning; and the semantics of natural language expressions.

A convenient starting point for a consideration of Leibniz's views on these issues is the influential doctrine that all human languages trace their roots to a single Adamic language, i.e., the language ascribed to Adam in *Genesis* when he named the animals that God had created. One prominent example of this theory, advanced by the early seventeenth-century German philosopher Jacob Boehme, held that the names chosen by Adam for each species contained the key to the essence or nature of that species, and that they thus formed the vocabulary of a so-called *Natur-Sprache*. As a consequence of the Fall and the dispersion of tongues at the Tower of Babel, this *Natur-Sprache* has been lost to human beings; present-day languages are corrupt forms in which there is missing any direct connection between words and the nature of the things they denote. Many thinkers like Boehme nevertheless believed that traces of the Adamic language could still be discerned in existing languages (for some, in Hebrew), and that via intuition there might be had an immediate knowledge of the Adamic vocabulary that would at the same time supply a perfect knowledge of the natures of things.[48]

Although Leibniz tentatively accepts the hypothesis of a single original human language, he rejects the idea of an Adamic language in its literal form.[49] He instead defends this hypothesis on the grounds of its consistency with the assumption of a common origin for all human beings and, most importantly, with the available philological evidence.[50] To the collection and analysis of the latter, he devoted an enormous amount of attention. Comparative studies of a large number of widely separated languages supported him in the belief that a common origin, followed by successive migration, isolation, and linguistic shifts due to different climates and conditions best explained the present diversity of languages. Leibniz's view of the origin of natural language is thus plainly antitheological; it is likely that all natural languages arose from a single source, but this source is in no way recoverable and is equally obscured in the roots of all human tongues (cf. C 151).

A related issue on which Leibniz's position bears some resemblance to the Adamic thesis, but ultimately diverges from it, concerns the origin of linguistic meaning. Do words naturally signify the objects they denote, as is supposed for the expressions of Boehme's *Natur-Sprache?* Or are the meanings of words imposed by human beings through arbitrary conventions? The latter view is forcefully defended by Locke in his *Essay Concerning Human Understanding;* however, it is rejected by Leibniz.[51] In the *New Essays,* he argues on the contrary that there is "something natural in the origin of words – something which reveals a relationship between things and the sounds and motions of the vocal organs" (III.ii.1; A VI.vi: RB 283). Leibniz's approach to the question of how linguistic expressions acquire meaning is strongly influenced by his commitment to the principle of sufficient reason.[52] In rejecting the doctrine that words acquire meaning in an arbitrary or conventional manner, he does not claim that the relationship between words and things is immediate in the sense of Boehme's *Natur-Sprache,* but only that meaning is "settled by reasons – sometimes natural ones in which chance plays some part, sometimes moral ones which involve choice" (ibid.; A VI.vi: RB 278). Words are "not so arbitrary and accidental in origin as some suppose," he writes, "for there is nothing accidental in the world except owing to our ignorance, when the causes are hidden to us" (Du VI.ii 28).

Consistent with this assumption, Leibniz proceeds by advancing a series of tentative conjectures about the origin of meaning in natural languages which are aimed at drawing out the causal roots of the signification of linguistic expressions. Originally, he suggests, language arises in the form of interjections – simple cries and groans – which express an immediate agreement between uttered sounds and human emotions. Furthermore, even in derivative languages like our own, a consonance of sound and perception is the natural root of meaning.[53] A paradigm for Leibniz in this context is the phenomenon of onomatopoeia, i.e., the naming of things or actions by imitation of sounds associated with them, as in "crack" or "buzz." This principle, and related assumptions about the natural origin of meaning, are subsequently employed by him as starting points in etymologies such as the following:

> The Latin coaxare, applied to frogs, corresponds to the German couaquen or quaken. It would seem that the noise these animals make is the primordial root of other words in the Germanic language. Since these animals make a great deal of noise, we connect it with chatterers and babblers, whom we call by the diminutive quakler. . . . And since those sounds or noises of animals testify to the presence of life, and tell us that something living is there before we can see it, in old German quek signified life or living. . . . In Low German certain weeds are called Quaken, that is, alive and running, as they say in German, spreading and seeding themselves easily in the fields to the detriment of the grain; and in English quickly means promptly and in a lively manner.   (New Essays III.ii.1; A VI.vi: RB 282)

To the modern reader, derivations such as these must inevitably seem overly speculative and even rather bizarre. We should, however, be lenient in our criticism of Leibniz on this count, for he goes out of his way to distance himself from contemporary writers who were far less cautious in their etymological claims (ibid.; A VI.vi: RB 285). He is insistent that etymologies always retain the status of hypotheses subject to revision on the condition of additional evidence, and further, that the interpretation of this evidence must always be guided by the law of continuity:

> One must interrelate the languages of various peoples, and one should not make too many leaps from one nation to another remote one unless there is

sound confirming evidence, especially evidence provided by intervening peoples. In general, one should put no trust in etymologies unless there is a great deal of concurrent evidence.   (Ibid.)[54]

Leibniz thus intends his etymologies as empirical hypotheses, whose purpose is to trace the varied and complicated routes by which the meanings of natural language expressions have evolved. Grounding these etymologies is the principle of sufficient reason: words have not acquired their meanings arbitrarily, but always as a consequence of some identifiable cause. In the first place, he speculates, meanings arise, in a pattern common to all languages, as the result of a natural harmony between human emotion or perception and uttered sounds. Thereafter, however, we must look to explain the evolution of meaning as the product of a complex array of environmental and linguistic factors. In mature languages, "various accidents and transformations have left most words greatly changed and far removed from their original pronunciation and signification" (*New Essays* III.ii.1; A VI.vi: RB 283). Thus, no single account will suffice to explain how words ultimately acquire the meaning they possess. At most, through the careful gathering of evidence and the cautious formation of hypotheses, we can attempt to explain "how words have passed by means of metaphors, synecdoches, and metonymies from one signification to another, without our always being able to follow the trail" (ibid.). In all of this, we see Leibniz advocating a scientific approach to the study of language. The connection between words and things is not to be explained by an appeal to theological dogma: the Adamic language is at most a suggestive metaphor for the natural processes by which language originates and evolves in human culture.[55]

In addition to his speculations on the origin of language and the historical evolution of meaning, Leibniz offers a number of theoretical observations concerning the function and structure of natural language. With Locke, he agrees that the basis of language is the use of sounds or marks as signs of our "internal conceptions," so as to make ourselves understood to others (*Essay*, III.i.2; cf. ii 2). In order for communication to occur, however, it is not necessary that a person consciously intend to transfer his thoughts to another. For signs are often used "blindly," without explicit awareness of the ideas they signify, and still a speaker "always does mean something of a general sort by what he says" (*New Essays* III.ii.2; A VI.vi: RB 286). In Leibniz's view, this possibility of "blind" or "symbolic" thought, where the use and exchange of signs takes the place of a conscious apprehension of ideas, opens the door on another critical function of language.[56] Leibniz writes,

[Language] once created also enables man to reason to himself, both because words provide the means for remembering abstract thoughts and because of the usefulness of symbols and blind thoughts in reasoning, since it would take too long to lay everything out and always replace terms by definitions.

(Ibid.; A VI.vi: RB 275)

The capacity of linguistic symbols to stabilize logical reasoning and to expand the scope of its application lies at the heart of Leibniz's project of a universal characteristic. It is important to recognize, however, that with regard to their ability to support the function of blind or symbolic thought he sees no essential difference between the signs of natural and artificial languages. Both serve as counters in rule-governed exchanges of symbols, whose results may, if properly coordinated, express the conclusions of logical reasoning. There nevertheless remains some uncertainty about the status Leibniz assigns to "blind" thought. Although almost all authors agree that he accords some cognitive role to language as an "instrument of reason," it has been argued that this function is necessarily parasitical on a prior, nonlinguistic mode of thought. Thus, linguistic signs may take the place of concepts in reasoning, but the significance of this reasoning depends on these signs ultimately being "cashed out" in favor of the concepts they represent. Recently, this view has been challenged by those who argue for a more basic role for language within Leibniz's theory of knowledge. According to these authors, Leibniz largely anticipates the modern doctrine that language and conceptual thought are necessarily coextensive: to think and reason is just to operate with the signs of some language.[57] A number of important texts suggest that this second reading may be closest to the truth: so far as human beings are concerned at least, Leibniz regards all conceptual thought as essentially symbolic.[58]

Within the class of natural language expressions, Leibniz recognizes a basic twofold division between terms and particles, or what he sometimes calls the "matter" and "form" of language.[59] By "terms" he understands "general terms," i.e., words signifying general or indeterminate ideas (species or essences). Particles, by contrast, include conjunctions, prepositions, and some adverbs; in general, they are those words which

> connect not only the component propositions of a discourse, and the component ideas of a proposition, but also the parts of an idea made up of other ideas variously combined. This last sort of connection is signified by *prepositions*, whereas *adverbs* govern affirmation, and negation when it occurs in the verb, and *conjunctions* govern the connections between various affirmations and negations. (*New Essays* III.vii.2; A VI.vi: RB 330)

The distinction Leibniz draws between terms and particles reflects his understanding of the different roles these two types of expression play in discourse. Terms serve to convey content and, when joined as subject and predicate within a proposition, to make assertions and denials. Particles serve, as the above passage suggests, to relate terms and complex combinations of terms in a variety of different ways. Leibniz's choice of this particular division of linguistic duties is clearly motivated by theory, namely, an *a priori* conception of what is required by the very idea of language. If language is primarily concerned with the transmission of thought via words from the mind of the speaker to the mind of the hearer, then the only necessary resources of language are expressions capable of conveying or signifying basic thoughts (terms) and expressions capable of ordering the expressions of these thoughts among themselves (particles).[60] As we shall see in the next section, this assumption about the essential resources of language supports Leibniz in a project for refining the grammatical structure of natural language which is closely associated with his univeral characteristic.

Before concluding this section, it is worth touching on two further points made by Leibniz in his discussion of terms in the *New Essays*. The first concerns his treatment of proper names. Leibniz is adamant that a language could not function if it contained only proper names and no general terms. This is because "new individuals and accidents and (what we talk about the most) actions" are being discovered all the time, and we could never keep up with (or make sense of) the task of assigning each one a unique proper name (III.i.3; A VI.vi: RB 275). Furthermore, insofar as proper names do occur in present-day natural languages it is certain that they were "originally appellative or general" (ibid.; A VI.vi: RB 276).

We know that the first Brutus was given this name because of his apparent stupidity, that Caesar was the name of a child delivered through an incision in his mother's abdomen, that Augusta was a name expressing reverence, that Capito and Bucephalus both mean big-headed, that Lentalus, Piso and Cicero were names originally given to those who grew only certain kinds of vegetables. . . . In fact, I would venture to say that almost all words were originally general terms, since it will very rarely happen that a name will be invented just for one given individual without any reason for it. So we can say that individual names used to be names of species that were given to some individual either as a prime example of the species or for some other reason. (III.iii.5; A VI.vi: RB 288–89)

On the face of it, Leibniz here seems to be making a purely historical claim about the origin of proper names that might be judged fairly plausible, yet at the same time inconsequential from the point of view of semantics. For even if proper names have arisen as appellative expressions, there is no reason why they could not have subsequently acquired an independent status within language as singular referring expressions. However, this is not a development that Leibniz foresees. Within his scheme no provision is made for a primitive relation of reference, whereby a proper name directly "designates" or "stands for" its bearer. Instead, all terms immediately signify concepts which, in turn, pick out certain individuals. Thus, apart from particles there are only terms of greater or lesser scope, i.e., terms whose associated concepts are instantiated by more or fewer individuals. Proper names are distinguished solely by the fact that they signify *complete* concepts which are sufficiently complex that they pick out a single individual.[61] In contrast to the position of Mill, then, Leibniz maintains that proper names, as much as general terms, do possess a determinate sense or meaning. In this, he agrees with Frege, who associates with each proper name a content sufficient to determine the bearer or reference of that name. Unlike Frege, however, Leibniz does not explicitly draw on the notion of reference as a distinct semantic relation uniting proper names with their bearers.

A second point at which Leibniz's views come into contact with modern work in the philosophy of language is in connection with his account of the meaning of natural-kind terms. In the *New Essays*, he argues strongly against Locke's claim that natural-kind terms signify only "nominal essences": abstract ideas which the mind forms from its observation of particular things and thereafter uses to classify those things into sorts or kinds (*Essay*, III.iii.12–17). Leibniz's disagreement with Locke over the meaning of natural-kind terms rests on a deeper, metaphysical division concerning the status of natural kinds themselves. In Leibniz's view, the "boundaries of species are fixed by the natures of things"; i.e., things possess real essences or natures which are the basis for our partitioning them into particular classes or species (*New Essays* III.v.3; A VI.vi: RB 302).[62] Locke, by contrast, is skeptical whether any such essences exist; and even if they do, he is certain that they cannot be known by us and have nothing to do with the classification and naming of things (*Essay*, III.iii.17, 20).[63] Instead,

The *sorting* of [things] under Names, *is the Workmanship of the Understanding, taking occasion from the similitude* it observes amongst them, to make abstract general *Ideas*, and to set them up in the mind, with Names annexed to them, as Patterns, or Forms, . . . to which, as particular Things existing are found to agree, so they come to be of that Species.

(Essay, III.iii.13)

A consequence of Locke's position is that a term like "gold" can, strictly speaking, mean different things to different people, depending on the set of observable properties that each associates with the term (*Essay*, III.iii 14). This is a view which Leibniz strongly rejects, both in its limitation of the meaning of natural-kind terms to observable properties and in its implication that meanings are idiosyncratic to a speaker. Against it, he argues:

The name "gold" . . . signifies not merely what the speaker knows of gold, e.g., something yellow and very heavy, but also what he does not know, which *may* be known by someone, namely: a body endowed with an *inner constitution* from which flow its colour and weight, and which also generates other properties which he acknowledges to be better known by the experts.   (*New Essays* III.xi.24; A VI.vi: RB 354)[64]

In this passage, Leibniz anticipates in a striking way recent arguments of Putnam concerning the "division of linguistic labor" and the relevance of hidden structure or essence in determining the meaning of natural-kind terms.[65] Like Putnam, he claims that it is not what any one person conceives in connection with a term like "gold" which fixes the meaning of the word, but rather the collective beliefs of a linguistic community, including experts with the latest knowledge and techniques available for distinguishing what is and is not gold. Furthermore, like Putnam, Leibniz maintains that underlying structure is a crucial factor in determining the meaning of natural kind terms. Roughly, "gold" signifies whatever has the same essence or nature as some paradigmatic example of this metal, where it is allowed both that expert knowledge may be needed to decide whether a word has been used correctly in a given instance and that in some cases speakers may be mistaken in their beliefs about the signification of a term insofar as they lack this crucial knowledge.[66]

III. THE UNITY OF LEIBNIZ'S PHILOSOPHY OF LANGUAGE

A number of philosophers have argued that there is a fundamental conflict between Leibniz's treatments of natural and artificial language. At least implicitly, this seems to be the opinion of Cassirer, who emphasizes Leibniz's conception of language "purely as a means of cognition, an instrument of logical analysis," and concludes that with him "the specific character of language as a language of sounds and words seems not so much acknowledged and explained, as ultimately negated."[67] This interpretation of Leibniz's view of language has crystallized into what has been dubbed (fairly or not) the "Cassirer thesis."[68] In the view of its critics, this thesis maintains (i) that at a conceptual level Leibniz draws a fundamental distinction between the character of natural language and artificial languages like his universal characteristic; and (ii) that it is Leibniz's ultimate aim to advocate the replacement of the former by the latter, insofar as the universal characteristic is specifically designed to fulfill the most significant function of language: the precise fixing of thought in sensible characters for the purposes of reasoning and (to a lesser extent) communication.

The majority of recent authors on this topic have strongly opposed the Cassirer thesis and have instead taken pains to stress the continuity between Leibniz's accounts of natural and artificial language. While acknowledging an apparent shift in Leibniz's interests away from the universal characteristic and toward the empirical study of natural languages (a shift that would in fact contradict the second part of the Cassirer thesis), these authors have for the most part held that he remains committed to both linguistic approaches until the very end of his life.[69] Whether or not the universal characteristic was intended eventually to replace natural language as the only reliable "instrument of reason," Leibniz's writings clearly show that he assigns considerable importance to the investigation of existing human languages. The question now before us is whether these writings also support the contention that a common set of principles grounds his understanding of natural language and the universal characteristic.

The best evidence for the underlying unity of Leibniz's view of language is the fact that he draws no definitive line between the categories of natural and artificial language.[70] This lack of a clear boundary is most fully revealed in his many studies of what he calls a "philosophical" or "rational" grammar.[71] According to Couturat, Leibniz embarks on this project in the late 1670s after losing faith in the plan for an *a priori* philosophical language which he had pursued since *On the Art of Combinations*.[72] In response to the obstacles which confront the completion of the universal characteristic, he lights on the idea of reversing his procedure and constructing an ideal language by gradually refining the resources of an existing natural language such as Latin.[73] Presupposed in this project is the idea that a common grammatical structure underlies all human language, or, what amounts to the same thing for Leibniz, that the grammar of any language can be refined and simplified so as to reveal the essential structure of language as such (cf. *New Essays* III.v.8; A VI.vi: RB 301–2).[74]

Beginning in 1678, Leibniz advances a three-part program for the analysis and regimentation of Latin.[75] First, it is necessary to render the language systematic from a semantic point of view, by eliminating through paraphrase all ambiguities and any colloquial expression whose meaning is determined solely through use (C 352–53). The result is a language in which the meaning of every complex expression (term or sentence) conforms to the principle of compositionality: its semantic value is a determinate function of the semantic values of its component parts. Next, or perhaps concurrently, our base language must be rendered completely uniform from a syntactic point of view: all grammatical categories are to be identified and all irregularities (i.e., exceptions to grammatical rules) eliminated (C 353; G VII 28).

Finally, in order to produce a "rational" or "philosophical" grammar, it is necessary to remove all the superfluous features of this regularized Latin grammar. Here Leibniz adopts a very rigorous approach, advocating the elimination of all unnecessary distinctions of gender, case, number, tense, person, and mood.[76] The result of this reductive analysis is a grammar of exceedingly simple structure: "Everything in discourse can be analyzed into the noun substantive, *Ens* or *Res*, the copula or substantive verb *est*, adjectives and formal particles" (C 289: PLP 16). As Leibniz sees it these are all the resources that are needed to express any intelligible proposition. For any simple proposition is a complex of two terms united by the copula *est;* and any meaningful term can be expressed as a combination of the substantive *Ens* or *Res* and an adjectival or participial expression. Particles, finally, will serve the role of modifying and relating simple propositions so as to express more complicated forms of thought.[77]

Leibniz's plan for a rational grammar, a grammar which would involve only the essential resources of language, clearly derives from a prior philosophical view about the legitimate scope of conceptual thought. The rational grammar is taken to define the fundamental form of language precisely because it best accords with his commitment to a version of nominalism, whereby the only actual or existing things in the world are concrete particulars (substances and their singular accidents). Accordingly, in his reconstructed philosophical language there appear only concrete terms: i.e., terms referring to particular things (e.g., human beings, wise beings, hot beings), and not to abstract entities (humanity, wisdom, heat).[78] This general opposition to abstractions of all kinds is made evident in his early "Preface to Nizolius" (1670),[79] and remains a constant feature of all of his later writings.[80]

Leibniz's project of a rational grammar appears to demonstrate in a fairly conclusive way the falsity of the first half of the Cassirer thesis: there is no fundamental conflict between his conception of a man-made philosophical language and natural language. Indeed, the backbone of a philosophical language can be arrived at through the progressive refinement of the grammatical structure of a natural language like Latin. This result, however, also seems to go a long way toward confirming the truth of the second half of the thesis. To the extent that Leibniz's rational grammar is better suited than the grammars of natural language for representing the fundamental structure of reality, there is every reason to think that he would ultimately advocate the replacement of the latter by the former. At least in the context of what is, broadly speaking, scientific discourse (and what discourse for Leibniz isn't ultimately best framed in these terms?) natural language should be rejected in favor of the greater precision and expressive power of his rational language.

Of recent authors, Heinekamp has gone the furthest in denying this conclusion and emphasizing instead the independent authority of natural language.[81] His interpretation focuses not on the grammar of natural language but on its vocabulary and contends that on the issue of word meaning there is a basic, ineliminable difference between natural and artificial languages.[82] We observed in section I that Leibniz seems committed to the position that the simple signs of his universal characteristic signify only conventionally. They are merely arbitrary marks through whose relations alone meaning is conveyed via expression. As we saw in section II, this is not the case with the signs of natural language. Whatever arbitrariness there may be in the choice of a written symbol to stand for a given sound, each phoneme, syllable, or word has, in Leibniz's view, a natural origin, on account of "the relationship between things and the sounds and motions of the vocal organs" (*New Essays* III.ii.1; A VI.vi: RB 283). Thus, there is a fundamental difference between the way in which the signs of natural and artificial languages acquire meaning.[83]

Leibniz's remarks on the origins of natural language make it clear that the meaning of root words is always originally grounded in some sensory experience, whereafter these meanings are transformed and elaborated through metaphor, metonymy, synecdoche, etc.[84] Now, as Heinekamp points out, it is consistent with this that, in Leibniz's view, "natural language does not represent things directly, but only insofar as reality is reflected in the consciousness of human beings."[85] That is, natural language is not a transparent expression of the natures of things (the claim of Boehme's *Natur-Sprache* and perhaps of Leibniz's earliest plans for a philosophical language), but only of the impression or effect of things on the human mind.[86] At a basic level, this effect is one that is common to all human beings; nevertheless, human beings experience the world under very different circumstances, and these differences (of climate, material conditions, and history) are responsible for the differential evolution of the common root words into a multiplicity of human languages.[87] Given these points, Heinekamp argues that it is a mistake to think of Leibniz as recommending the eventual replacement of natural language by an artificial, philosophical language. Even if, in the context of scientific reasoning, there is an important role for artificial languages, this does not mean that we could ever do without natural language. Leibniz's philosophical language is conceived as a language of pure reason: its aim is to express the content and inferential relations of concepts, insofar as they are purely intelligible. However, we are creatures who, in spite of our intellectual capacities, are bound to a world of sense and emotion – a world that is immediately communicable through, and only through, the resources of natural language. According to Heinekamp, Leibniz's theory of human language reflects very clearly his understanding of this dual nature of humanity, the fact that human beings are inescapably creatures of both sense and reason. We cannot aspire to the standpoint of pure reason, and hence the original ideal of a rational or philosophical language is necessarily a limited one.[88]

Heinekamp's application of the sense/reason division to the interpretation of Leibniz's view of language is in many ways compelling. It is worth emphasizing, however, that within this framework there remains a basis for upholding the theoretical primacy of a philosophical language of reason over the natural language of sense experience. In proposing his doctrine of the two kingdoms of sense and reason (or the material and the intelligible), Leibniz is always careful to indicate that the realm of sense is naturally subordinated to the realm of reason; the operation of the former is governed by the principles of the latter (cf. BH 62–63; C 341–42). Thus, while it is impossible for us ever to elude the world of sensory experience and the natural languages that are its complement, our ability to function successfully within this world depends upon our capacity to comprehend the intelligible order of nature, an order that can only be accurately expressed through the medium of a rational language. Given Leibniz's steady support for the ideal of a rational understanding of nature over the brute experience of "empirics," it should come as no surprise that he also favors wherever possible the progress of a language grounded in reason.[89] It therefore seems that at least a limited version of the second part of the Cassirer thesis can be upheld.

First-time readers of Leibniz's popular works such as the *Monadology* are often struck by the vivid imagery of his philosophical writing. We read that every monadic substance is a "mirror" of the universe, and the "center" of a bodily mass; moreover, soul-like monads are located everywhere "within" matter, with the result that nature is everywhere "alive." It is easy to be misled by language like this and to conclude that Leibniz's metaphysics is far stranger, and far less credible, than it actually is. Now and then we are given signs to indicate that expressions such as these are not to be taken literally; but for the most part, in Leibniz's more popular writings, we are left to interpret them as we will. His confidence that we will treat them solely as helpful indicators of a deeper underlying truth has all too seldom been borne out by the habits of his readers. They have misread the figurative for the literal, and in so doing have tranformed a metaphysics of reason into an implausible fantasy.[90]

In several important passages, Leibniz addresses this error explicitly. In a letter composed shortly before his death, he writes:

> To say that souls are "intelligible points" is not a sufficiently exact expression. If I call them "centers" or "concentrations" of external things I speak by analogy. Points, to speak exactly, are limits of extension, and not at all the constitutive parts of things.   (G VI 627)

Similarly, he allows that in his theory of the monad the term "mirror" supplies only "a figurative expression, but one that is appropriate enough and that has already been employed by philosophers and theologians when they have wanted to speak of a mirror infinitely more perfect, namely the mirror of the divinity" (G VI 626).[91] In both cases, Leibniz concludes, we will have misunderstood his philosophy if we take these expressions according to their literal meaning. Instead, they are to be interpreted as spatial and sensory metaphors for purely intelligible ideas.[92]

Behind these several examples of Leibniz's distinctive use of philosophical language lies an intriguing theory, never fully developed, of the relationship between philosophical truth and the linguistic means available for its expression. Throughout his career, Leibniz maintains that philosophical truths are truths of reason, or truths founded on innate ideas of the intellect. At the same time, however, he is aware that human cognition is intimately bound up with language, and that to a large extent we are able to think distinctly only what we are capable of expressing in symbolic terms.[93] On this latter view, the items of thought – human concepts – are not ghostly forms, but signs bearing sense; and it is legitimate to inquire under what circumstances these signs have acquired significance for us. As we have seen, Leibniz's position seems to be that the words of natural language only acquire meaning in the first place through their association with certain perceptions or emotions; they are natural expressions of our causal interaction with the environment. Now if it is possible, I think we should read Leibniz as attempting to harmonize these two apparently conflicting commitments within a single theory of philosophical discourse. On the one hand, it is correct to see philosophical truths as truths of pure reason; on the other hand, for the expression of such truths, we humans have available only signs which have originally acquired meaning through reference to sensible states of affairs. The key to overcoming this tension is to suppose another mode of meaning, whereby terms which refer literally to some perceivable spatial situation can acquire an extended, figurative sense which allows them to convey a content expressive of a nonsensible or intelligible state of affairs.[94]

In a number of passages, Leibniz indicates his support for a theory of this sort. In the *New Essays*, he agrees with Locke that "the terms of theology, moral philosophy and metaphysics are originally derived from earthly things" on account of the "analogy between sensible and insensible things" (III.i.5; A VI.vi: RB 277).[95] Of special importance in this context are the various functions of prepositions.[96] Expressions such as "to," "with," "of," "before," and "in," Leibniz writes, "are all derived from place, distance and motion and subsequently transferred to all kinds of changes, orders, sequences, differences, and conformities" (ibid.). The significance of such analogical extensions of meaning is perhaps clearest in the case of the preposition "in," the root of the metaphysical notions of "being in" [*inesse*] and "inherence."[97] At work here, however, is a general principle of meaning, which Leibniz makes explicit in an essay from the 1680s:

It seems that all [prepositions] in natural languages originally signify with respect to spatial position, and from there they are transformed by some figure into certain metaphysical notions less subject to the imagination. And this is not surprising, since men try to explain things which cannot be imagined through things subject to the imagination.

(C 290: VE 361; cf C 287: VE 351)

It is a basic principle of Leibniz's thought that being and truth are comprehended solely through intelligible concepts (G VI 502: L 549). To this point, too little attention has been paid to his view of how such thought is possible for human beings and how it is related to our use of metaphysical language. In Leibniz's fragmentary studies of prepositions, we see the vague glimmerings of an answer. In the first place, he seems to suggest, all prepositions originally signify some perceivable spatial relation. Thereafter, through a combination of abstraction and analogy, we are able to refine that literal meaning to express something quite different: a logical relation among ideas or concepts. Thus, from perceiving what it is for one thing (a part) to be spatially in another (a whole), we infer that the latter relies for its existence on the former: there are no wholes without parts. Then, isolating this purely intelligible idea of the dependency of one existence on another, we are able to apply it in the context of metaphysics.[98] Leibniz's meditations on the metaphysical significance of prepositions signal a profound line of thought which has yet to be fully explored. Like all of his investigations in this field, his speculations are far from definitive. Nevertheless, they once again confirm his deep appreciation of the intimate connection between language and philosophy.[99]

NOTES

1 As Leibniz writes in a May 1678 letter to Tschirnhaus: "But no one can be afraid that the contemplation of characters will lead us away from things; on the contrary, it will lead us into the secrets of things" (A II.i 413: L 193). Cf. Dascal, "Language and Money," pp. 207–8.

2 Cf. Heinekamp, "Ars characteristica und natürliche Sprache bei Leibniz," pp. 446–47.

3 This tension is discussed in section III.

4 "Although natural languages may offer many things for reasoning, they are nevertheless guilty of innumerable equivocations and cannot perform the work of calculation, such that errors of reasoning could be uncovered from the very form and construction of words like solecisms and barbarisms" (G VII 205: S 18). Cf. G VII 27.

5 Couturat, *La Logique de Leibniz*, remains the best overall source for Leibniz's efforts in this area. A recent study that challenges him on several points is Pombo, *Leibniz and the Problem of a Universal Language*.

6 Russell, *Critical Exposition of the Philosophy of Leibniz*, pp. 169–71; Cohen, "On the Project of a Universal Character."

7 Heinekamp, "Natürliche Sprache und allgemeine Charakteristik bei Leibniz," p. 267.

8 Pombo, *Leibniz and the Problem of a Universal Language*, pp. 168–70.

9 Cf. G III 216: "genuinely real and philosophical characters must correspond to the analysis of thoughts." Leibniz borrows the expression "real character" from John Wilkins, *Essay Towards a Real Character and a Philosophical Language* (1668), who in turn derives it from Bacon's *Advancement of Learning* (1605). According to Bacon, "characters real" are ideographic signs which "express neither letters nor words in gross, but things or notions," and hence may be understood by speakers of different languages. However, unlike "hieroglyphics and gestures," which have "some similitude or congruity with the notion," real characters signify conventionally, "having force only by contract or acceptation" (II.xvi.2–3). Missing from Bacon's account of real characters is the emphasis laid by later authors such as Wilkins and Leibniz on the requirement that the characters exactly express the structure of concepts, which in turn express the natures of things. Slaughter, *Universal Languages and Scientific Taxonomy in the Seventeenth Century*, p. 127, argues that this is the main difference between early seventeenth-century advocates of real characters as the components of a universal language and later proponents of a "philosophical language."

10 "Whoever learns this language," Leibniz writes in an early letter to Oldenburg, "at the same time also learns the encyclopedia which is the true entrance to things" (A I.i 240). In his pursuit of this goal Leibniz was influenced by, among others, the seventeenth-century Czech philosopher and reformer Jan Amos Comenius. Cf. Couturat, *La Logique*, pp. 100, 571–72; Coudert, "Some Theories of Natural Language from the Renaissance to the Seventeenth Century," pp. 95ff.

11 Leibniz defines a "combination" or "com2nation" as a complexion of degree 2, i.e., a complex of 2 things or concepts. This is to be contrasted with a "conternation" or complexion of degree 3, and so on (A VI.i 172: PLP 2).

12 For Leibniz, the difference between a "characteristic" or system of writing and a full-fledged "language" is that in the latter there is given the means of pronouncing each of the language's signs (G VII 26). In what

follows, I ignore this distinction (as Leibniz himself often does: cf. A II.i 380, 413, 555, 557) and use "language" in places where what is in question is only a system of written characters. As always, there is considerable variation in Leibniz's terminology. What I am here calling his "philosophical language" (G VII 11, 198–99, 269; C 152, 288) is also described as a "rational language" or "rational writing" (A II.i 380), and as a "universal language" (A II.i 384; G III 605; G VII 12, 17, 25; C 176, 279, 283). Cf. Heinekamp, "Ars characteristica," p. 462; Pombo, *Leibniz and the Problem*, p. 123.

13 Cf. Pombo, *Leibniz and the Problem*, p. 171, and Rossi, "The Twisted Roots of Leibniz' Characteristic," p. 276. It is evident that a set of more basic assumptions about the relationship between language, thought, and reality underlies Leibniz's project of a universal characteristic. For this project to make sense it must be supposed from the start that reality has an intelligible structure that can be expressed in terms of combinations of atomic concepts, and that this structure is in principle accessible to the human intellect. On Hegel's critique of Leibniz's conception of a philosophical language, see Cook, "Leibniz and Hegel on the Philosophy of Language," pp. 235–36.

14 Leibniz's confidence in the method of *On the Art of Combinations* is apparent in an early letter (*ca.* 1671–72) to Duke Johann Friedrich: "In philosophy, I have found a means of accomplishing in all the sciences what Descartes and others have done in arithmetic and geometry through algebra and analysis, by the art of combinations, which Lullius and Father Kircher indeed cultivate, although without having seen further into some of its secrets. By this means, all composite notions in the whole world are reduced to a few simple ones as their alphabet; and by the combination of such an alphabet a way is made of finding, in time by an ordered method, all things with their theorems and whatever it is possible to investigate concerning them" (G I 57–58).

15 Knowlson, *Universal Language Schemes in England and France, 1600–1800*, is a good general survey of this topic; cf. also Dascal, "Comments on James Knowlson"; Slaughter, *Universal Languages*; and Singer, "Hieroglyphs, Real Characters, and the Idea of a Natural Language in English Seventeenth-Century Thought." Different authors take the notion of a universal language to support different combinations of the above objectives, as well as others more obscure. Leibniz alludes to the mystical significance that some authors attribute to it at G VII 184: L 221; G VII 204–5: S 18. For an excellent account of the Renaissance background to this movement, and its connections with neo-Platonic and Christian Kabbalist thought, see Coudert, "Some Theories."

16 Cohen, "On the Project."

17 As Pombo, "Leibnizian Strategies" pp. 753–54, emphasizes, Leibniz makes two principal criticisms of previous attempts at a universal characteristic: (1) the authors of such schemes have failed to base their symbolisms on a complete analysis of concepts into their simplest parts; (2) they have relied on characters (astrological signs, geometrical figures) which fail to convey the structure of the corresponding concepts. Consequently, such schemes cannot succeed in realizing Leibniz's goal of reducing conceptual reasoning to the mechanical manipulation of signs. As he writes in a 1678 letter to Tschirnhaus: "[W]ith the aid of characters, we will easily have the most distinct notions, for we will have at hand a mechanical thread of meditation, as it were, with whose aid we can very easily resolve any idea whatever into those of which it is composed. In fact, if the character expressing any concept is considered attentively, the simpler concepts into which it is resolvable will at once come to mind. Since the analysis of concepts thus corresponds exactly to the analysis of characters, we need merely to see the characters in order to have adequate notions brought to our mind freely and without effort" (A II.i 413: L 193). See also his 1678 letter to the Princess Elizabeth (?) (A II.i 437). Leibniz frequently describes his characteristic as a sensible "thread of meditation" (A II.i 247, 384; C 351) or a "thread of Ariadne" (A II.i 381, 525), which would serve as an infallible guide for reasoning.

18 The passage continues: "For my own part I admit (and the facts also proclaim) that certain chemical phenomena which time and opportunity reveal cannot now be derived from the name which we impose on (for example) gold, until we have obtained phenomena sufficient for determining the rest. It belongs to God alone in the first place to impose names of this intuitive sort on things. Nevertheless, the name which will be imposed on gold in this language will be the key to all those things which can be humanly, i.e. by reason and method, known about gold" (A II.i 240). The language that Leibniz here envisages will have powers equal to those of Boehme's divinely-inspired *Natur-Sprache* (see sec. II). Nevertheless, it is tempting to think that what he calls the "name" of gold would be nothing more or less than a symbolic expression of the atomic structure of gold. On the relation between the universal language movement and Lavoisier's development of modern chemical notation, see Knowlson, *Universal Language Schemes*, p. 173.

19 Cf. Couturat, *La Logique*, chaps. IV–V.

20 Ibid., p. 117.

21 Descartes, *Philosophical Letters*, ed., Kenny, p. 6.

22 The claim is contradicted, however, by a 1697 letter to Burnett in which Leibniz writes: "It is true that these [genuinely real and philosophical]

characters would presuppose the true philosophy, and it is only now that I would dare undertake to construct them" (G III 216).

23 Thus he writes in an essay *ca.* 1679: "An analysis of concepts by which we are enabled to arrive at primitive notions, i.e. at those which are conceived through themselves, does not seem to be in the power of man" (C 514: P 8). Cf. the 1684 essay, *Meditations on Knowledge, Truth, and Ideas* (G IV 425: L 293); and Couturat, *La Logique,* pp. 198–200.

24 An exception to this are the pioneering studies of Schepers, "Leibniz' Arbeiten zu einer Reformation der Kategorien," "Begriffsanalyse und Kategorialsynthese"; and Couturat, *La Logique,* chap. V.

25 Rescher writes that "for the long interval 1675–1685 Leibniz devoted himself mainly to his official duties and to mathematics, logic, and physics. His ideas in metaphysics lay fallow, apart from his continued intensive assimilation of ideas. . . . During the winter of 1685–1686 he returned to philosophy and, in a concentrated period of thought, worked out the details of his philosophical system" (*Leibniz: An Introduction to his Philosophy,* p. 7). Papers published in the *Vorausedition* to series VI, volume 4 of the *Akademie* edition demonstrate that the development of Leibniz's thought in the decade 1675–85 is far more gradual and continuous than Rescher here allows.

26 Cf. Rutherford, "Truth, Predication, and the Complete Concept of an Individual Substance." A good example of these definitional studies is the piece *Definitiones Notionum Metaphysicarum atque Logicarum,* G. W. Leibniz: *Fragmente zur Logik,* pp. 478–84. Watermark evidence shows it to date from June 1685 (VE 1251).

27 Leibniz's employment of the exoteric/esoteric distinction can be traced to his 1670 "Preface to Nizolius" (A VI.ii 416). A clear statement of it appears in a 1704 letter to Fontenelle: "The true metaphysics, or philosophy if you will, appears to me no less important than geometry, particularly if there is also a means of introducing into it demonstrations, which until now have been completely banned from it along with the calculus which will be needed in order to give them the complete entry they need. However, it is necessary to prepare readers for this through exoteric writings" (FC 234). Cf. *New Essays* II.xxix.12, A VI.vi: RB 260–61, and a 1696 letter to Placcius (Du VI.i 65). Wohrmann, "Die Unterscheidung von Exoterik und Esoterik bei Leibniz," offers a similar interpretation of Leibniz's use of the distinction to that sketched here, although he does not specifically refer to the definitional studies of the 1680s. A rather different reading is defended by Ross, "The Demarcation Between Metaphysics and Other Disciplines in the Thought of Leibniz."

28 Leibniz goes on to cite further conclusions relating to his theory of substance, which he also takes to be demonstrable. Similar claims are made at A I.xiii 657; G II 134; G III 205, 302–3; G VII 199–200: S 12–13.

29 In an essay *ca.* 1688–89, he writes: "All human reasoning is perfected through the use of signs or characters. For not only the things themselves, but also the ideas of things cannot and should not always be distinctly perceived in the soul; and thus, for the sake of brevity, signs are used in place of them" (G VII 204: S 17). The dating of this piece is taken from a newly-edited version of it which will appear in series VI, vol. 4 of the *Akademie* edition (VE 1203).

30 "[Characters] are the more useful the more they express the concept of the signified thing, so that they can serve not only for representation, but also for reasoning" (G VII 204: S 18).

31 The watermark dating of this essay places it around 1677–78 (VE 311). Cf. G VII 205: S 18; GM V 216, VII 17; C 256–57.

32 "I call a visible sign representing thoughts a *character*. The *characteristic art* is thus the art of forming and ordering characters, so that they may register thoughts or have among themselves the relation which the thoughts have among themselves. An *expression* is a collection of characters representing the thing which is expressed. The *law of expression* is this: just as an idea of the thing to be expressed is formed from the ideas of certain things, so an expression of the thing is formed from characters of those things" (BH 80–81). Cf. G VII 198, as well as the well-known definition of "expression" which appears in the Arnauld correspondence (G II 112: L 339). In what follows, I assume that in his linguistic writings Leibniz uses the terms "expression" and "representation" interchangeably.

33 This characteristic is announced in a Latin essay, *ca.* 1677–79 (G VII 184–89: VE 669–75: L 221–25), and developed into a complete logical system in a series of essays dated April 1679 (C 42ff: PLP 17ff).

34 Walker, "Leibniz and Language," p. 296.

35 Cf. C 151; G VII 192: L 184; G VII 264: L 208.

36 Cf. *What is an Idea?* (1678): "That is said to express a thing in which there are relations [*habitudines*] which correspond to the relations of the thing expressed. But there are various kinds of expression; for example, the model of a machine expresses the machine itself, the projective delineation on a plane expresses a solid, speech expresses thoughts and truths, characters express numbers, and an algebraic equation expresses a circle or some other figure. What is common to all these expressions is that we can pass from a consideration of the relations in the expression to a knowledge of the corresponding properties of the thing expressed. Hence it is not necessary for that which expresses to be similar to the

thing expressed, provided that a certain analogy is maintained between the relations" (G VII 263–64: L 207–8). See also the "Dialogue on the Relation Between Words and Things," 1677 (G VII 191–93: L 184–85), and Kneale, "Leibniz and the Picture Theory of Language," p. 208–9. For the importance of this point in the context of seventeenth-century English efforts at a universal language, see Coudert, "Some Theories," pp. 102–4; and Singer, "Hieroglyphs, Real Characters," pp. 59–61.

37 It is worth noting that Leibniz does think that some relations of expression are natural; however, by 1678 he denies that this is so in the case of characters: "It is also clear that some expressions have a basis in nature, while others are arbitrary, at least in part, such as the expressions which consist of words or characters. Those which are founded in nature either require some similarity, . . . or require some connection" (G VII 264: L 208). Cf. G II 112: L 339.

38 Cf. Couturat, *La Logique*, pp. 108–9.

39 Cf. C 430: P 2; GM VII 239. On the face of it, it is unclear whether this scheme is reconcilable with Leibniz's claim elsewhere that a "perfect analysis of concepts" terminates in "first possibles" [*prima possibilia*], which are identified with the "absolute attributes of God" (G IV 425: L 293). Perhaps it is enough to say that "we do not understand distinctly enough the way in which the natures of things flow from God, nor the ideas of things from the idea of God. This would constitute ultimate analysis, i.e. the adequate knowledge of all things through their cause" (C 513: P 7).

40 Even here, however, Leibniz cannot completely elude some measure of conventionality in the sign/signified relation. There is at most a suggestive analogy between the simple signs of the binary characteristic (1 and 0) and the primitive concepts (God/Being and Nothingness/Privation). This is made clear in the "Dialogue on the Relation Between Words and Things": "A. But what similarity do you think there is between ten and the character *10*? B. There is some relation or order in the characters which is also in the things, especially if the characters are well invented. A. That may be, but what similarity do the first elements themselves have with things; for example, *O* with nothing, or *a* with a line? You will have to admit, therefore, that in these elements at least, there is no need of similarity to things" (G VII 192: L 184).

41 Cf. G II 383–84; Couturat, *La Logique*, pp. 109, 473–78; Pombo, *Leibniz and the Problem*, p. 268; Walker, "Leibniz and Language," pp. 305–6.

42. Cf. here in particular the 1687 study *Definitiones, Notiones, Characteres* (LH IV 7B, 2 Bl. 73–74 [VE 1228–35]).

43 In Latin: *speciosa generalis*; in French, Leibniz also refers to this science as the *spécieuse universelle*.

44 Hacking, "Leibniz and Descartes: Proof and Eternal Truths."
45 See also his 1708 letter to Rodeken (G VII 32).
46 Cf. his letter to Biber of March 1716: "My great historical work prevents
    me from carrying out the idea I have of displaying philosophy in the
    form of demonstrations . . . for I see that it is possible to invent a general
    characteristic, which could do in all inquiries capable of certainty what
    algebra does in mathematics" (BB 15–16).
47 The best recent studies on this topic are Aarsleff, "The Study and Use of
    Etymology in Leibniz," "Schulenburg's Leibniz als Sprachforscher," and
    "The Eighteenth Century, Including Leibniz"; Heinekamp, "Ars charac-
    teristica," "Natürliche Sprache," and "Sprache und Wirklichkeit bei
    Leibniz"; and Schulenburg, Leibniz als Sprachforscher. Aarsleff, "The
    Study and Use," gives a helpful overview of Leibniz's main writings on
    natural language. These include the Unvorgreiffliche Gedancken, be-
    treffend die Ausübung und Verbesserung der Teutschen Sprache ("Some
    Unanticipated Thoughts Concerning the Practice and Improvement of
    the German Language," after 1697; Du VI.ii 6ff: Gu I 449ff); Book III of
    the New Essays, ca. 1704 ("Of Words"); Brevis designatio meditationum
    de Originibus Gentium, ductis potissimum ex indicio linguarum ("Brief
    Exposition of Thoughts Concerning the Origins of Nations, Principally
    Drawn from the Evidence of Languages," 1710; Du IV.ii 186–98); the as
    yet unpublished Epistolaris de Historia Etymologica Dissertatio (unfin-
    ished at Leibniz's death); as well as extensive correspondence.
48 On Boehme, see Koyré, La Philosophie de Jacob Böhme; Kayser, "Böhmes
    Natursprachenlehre und ihre Grundlagen," and Coudert, "Some Theo-
    ries." Coudert provides a good account of the importance of these ideas for
    Leibniz's friend F. M. van Helmont, who, unlike Boehme, regarded He-
    brew as uniquely expressive of the Adamic language.
49 See Brevis designatio, quoted below, n. 55. For Leibniz's rejection of
    Hebrew as the original language, see his letter to Tenzel of July 1697 (Du
    VI.ii 232), and New Essays III.ii.1, A VI.vi: RB 281; for his rejection of
    Boehme's Natur-Sprache, see Epistolaris, sec. 14 (quoted in Aarsleff,
    "The Study and Use," p. 178, n. 13)
50 Cf. New Essays III.ii.1: "Now all these Scythian languages have many
    roots in common with one another and with ours; even Arabic (in which
    Hebrew, ancient Punic, Chaldean, Syriac, and the Ethiopian of the Abys-
    sinians should be included) has so many roots in common with our
    languages and shows such a striking agreement with them, that this
    cannot be attributed to mere chance or even to mere interaction, but
    rather to the migration of people. Thus, in all of this there is nothing
    which conflicts with – indeed there is nothing which does not support –
    the belief in the common origin of all nations and in a primitive root-

language" (A VI.vi: RB 281). See also the "Conjectures de M. Leibniz sur l'origine du mot Blason," 1692: "It indeed seems to me that nearly all languages are only variations, though often much confused, of the same roots; but it is difficult to recognize this, short of comparing many languages with one another" (Du VI.ii 185); and Leibniz's letter to Ludolf of September 5/15, 1691 (A I.vii 366; trans., Waterman, *Leibniz and Ludolf on Things Linguistic*, p. 22.)

51 Aarsleff, "Leibniz on Locke on Language," argues that this is the central issue separating the views of Leibniz and Locke on language.

52 Cf. Aarsleff, "The Study and Use," pp. 179f; Heinekamp, "Ars characteristica," pp. 474–75; and Walker, "Leibniz and Language," p. 295.

53 Leibniz's view of the natural origin of linguistic meaning is perhaps best expressed in a brief, undated essay (*ca.* 1677–85): "It cannot be said that there is a certain and determinate connection between things and words, yet the matter is not purely arbitrary; rather it is necessary that causes be present which explain why certain words are assigned to certain things. It cannot be said that the connection has arisen by convention, except in the case of certain artificial languages . . . such as Dalgarno, Wilkins and others have devised. . . . [L]anguages have a certain natural origin, on account of the agreement of sounds with the affects which the images of things excite in the mind. And I think that this origin has a place not only in the primal language, but also in languages that developed later, partly from the primal language and partly from the new practices of peoples scattered throughout the Earth" (C 151: VE 497).

54 On the application of the law of continuity to comparative linguistics, see Aarsleff, "The Study and Use."

55 The thought is clearly expressed in the *Brevis Designatio:* "But in languages born little by little, words have arisen as occasion arose from the analogy of a sound with the affect that accompanies the perception of the thing. I am inclined to believe that Adam did not impose names in any other fashion" (Du IV.ii 187). Hacking, "Locke, Leibniz, Language and Hans Aarsleff," challenges Aarsleff's reading on this point, accusing him of making Leibniz a "residual Adamicist," but it is unclear how much ground really separates them. Aarsleff makes it plain that Leibniz rejects the Adamic thesis in its literal form: "Leibniz dismissed the Natur-Sprache doctrine as utterly meaningless," ("The Study and Use," p. 178).

56 One of Leibniz's fullest discussions of "blind thought" is in the essay *Meditations on Knowledge, Truth, and Ideas*, G IV 424: L 292.

57 As Dascal (*La Sémiologie de Leibniz* and *Leibniz: Language, Signs and Thought*) forcefully argues, the role of signs in thinking is not just "auxil-

iary" but "constitutive." For a criticism of this view, see McRae, "Leibniz and Locke on Linguistic Particles", pp. 130–31.

58 This position is clearly stated in the "Dialogue on the Relation Between Words and Things": "B. I notice that no truth is ever known, discovered, or proved by me except by the use of words and other signs presented to the mind. A. In fact, if there were no characters, we could neither think of anything distinctly nor reason about it" (G VII 191: L 183–84). Cf. *New Essays* I.i.5, A VI.vi: RB 77; C 351–52; G VII 31: "All our reasoning is nothing but the connection and substitution of characters. These characters are either words, or marks, or finally images."

59 Cf. C 288: "Vocables are either words [i.e., terms] or particles. Words constitute the matter, particles the form of discourse" Cf. C 432–34. Leibniz's distinction between terms and particles follows fairly closely the medieval distinction between categorematic and syncategorematic terms. See Spade, "The Semantics of Terms."

60 In the case of particles in particular, Leibniz conceives of an extremely close connection between the workings of language and the workings of the mind. In a much-quoted passage from the end of Bk. III, chap. vii of the *New Essays* ("Of Particles"), he writes: "I really believe that languages are the best mirror of the human mind, and that a precise analysis of the significations of words would tell us more than anything else about the operations of the understanding" (A VI.vi: RB 333; cf. A VI.vi: RB 330 and Du VI.ii 6). At C 434, Leibniz identifies particles with "modes of conceiving."

61 "The difference between proper names [*propria*] and appellatives can also be set aside, for not only were the names of individuals originally appellatives, acquired from some distinction, but also it is of no consequence whether we say that the thing of which we speak is alone in the nature of things or whether there elsewhere exists something similar to it" (C 433). Cf. Du IV.ii 186; LH IV 7C Bl. 105–6 (VE 1299); C 360: PLP 51.

62 Cf. *New Essays* III.vi.4,13, A VI.vi: RB 305,309–10. This is consistent, in Leibniz's view, with the idea that there is also a continuum of species. See *New Essays* III.vi.12,27; A VI.vi: RB 307,321.

63 Locke distinguishes two senses of "real essence," only one of which he takes to be defensible. The "more rational Opinion, is of those, who look on all natural Things to have a real, but unknown Constitution of their insensible Parts, from which flow those sensible Qualities, which serve us to distinguish them one from another, according as we have Occasion to rank them into sorts, under common Denominations." Indefensible is the opinion (close to Leibniz's) "which supposes these *Essences*, as a certain number of Forms or Molds, wherein all natural Things, that exist, are cast, and do equally partake" (*Essay*, III.iii.17).

64 Cf. *New Essays* III.x.18, A VI.vi: RB 345.

65 Putnam, "The Meaning of 'Meaning'."

66 Thus, Leibniz writes at *New Essays* III.vi.38: "we speak . . . conjecturally, when it is a question of the inner truth of things, with the presumption that they have some essential and unchangeable nature" (A VI.vi: RB 325). Cf. *New Essays* III.vi.17, A VI.vi: RB 311–12. For a fuller discussion of these issues, see Jolley, *Leibniz and Locke*, chap. 8, and Duchesneau, "Leibniz on the Classificatory Function of Language."

67 Cassirer, *Philosophy of Symbolic Forms*, pp. 130, 132. Cf. Aarsleff, "The Eighteenth Century, Including Leibniz," p. 386.

68 See Aarsleff, "Schulenburg's *Leibniz*", p. 130; "The Eighteenth Century," pp. 399–401, but cf. p. 386 where Aarsleff offers a more balanced view of Cassirer's relation to the thesis which bears his name.

69 Cf. Heinekamp, "Ars characteristica," p. 449; Aarsleff, "The Eighteenth Century," p. 400; Dascal, "Language and Money," pp. 207ff; Gensini, "Variety and Unity of Linguistic Inquiries: Leibniz's Theory of Meaning"; Pombo, "Leibnizian Strategies for the Semantic Foundations of a Univeral Language."

70 Cf. Heinekamp, "Ars characteristica," p. 469. By Leibniz's own admission some natural languages (in one passage he cites Coptic and Chinese) are already close to being "philosophical languages" in their present form (Aarsleff, "The Study and Use," p. 182). This does not seem to be a status he extends to German, although he does claim that it is more primitive than Hebrew (*New Essays,* III.ii.1: A VI.vi: RB 285). In his "Preface to Nizolius" (1670) and the *Unvorgreiffliche Gedancken* (post-1697), Leibniz praises German not as a philosophical language (in his sense), but as a language ideally suited for detecting philosophical nonsense, on account of its concrete vocabulary. Thus he writes in the latter work: "I am accustomed to boast to Italians and Frenchmen that we Germans have a peculiar touchstone, which is unknown to others; and, when they are eager to know something about this, I tell them that it is our language; for what can be said in it intelligibly without loaned or unusual words is really something solid; but empty words, with nothing at the back of them, which are only the light froth of idle thoughts, these the pure German language will not accept" (Gu I, 452–53; quoted in Walker, "Leibniz and Language," pp. 301–2). Cf. A VI.ii, 414–15: L 125, and Cook, "Leibniz and Hegel," pp. 232–33.

71 Or "rational language." Again, there is much variation in terminology. For "rational grammar," see C 35, 286, 287; for "philosophical grammar," G VII 28; C 221, 511; for "rational language," G VII 28–30; C 243, 280–81, 289; for "philosophical language," C 152, 288. With regard to the latter two designations, an obvious ambiguity arises in

Leibniz's technical vocabulary at this point, given the difference between this project and the plans for a "philosophical language" discussed in sec. I.

72 It is tempting to see an abrupt transition here, as Couturat (*La Logique*,
pp. 63–64) appears to, between the essay *Lingua generalis* (C 277–79),
which was written in February 1678 and employs the numerical characteristic discussed in section I, and the essay *De grammatica rationali* (C
280–81), which is dated April 1678 and is concerned with the analysis
and refinement of natural language. Such a conjecture, however, is
surely an oversimplification, and it would seem that Leibniz instead
pursues both approaches for some time. Cf. Pombo, *Leibniz and the
Problem*, p. 156.

73 Cf. the essay *Lingua rationalis* (ca. 1680–85): "The first thing to be done
is to show how discourse can be translated from other languages into
this [rational language]. For this purpose, there should be established a
general grammar of languages, and in particular of Latin. For since Latin
is today the language of science in Europe, it will suffice if anything can
be translated from Latin into the rational language" (G VII 28: VE 795).

74 As he writes in a 1678 essay: "Everything else must be reduced to those
things which are absolutely necessary for expressing the soul's thoughts"
(C 281: VE 921). For a discussion of the relationship between Leibniz's
views and Chomsky's theory of grammar, see Brekle, "Die Idee einer
generativen Grammatik in Leibnizens Fragmenten zur Logik," and
Dascal, "About the Idea." It is worth emphasizing that Leibniz's project
for a rational grammar largely focuses on a different aspect of language
than the attempts at a universal characteristic discussed in section I. The
latter for the most part concentrates on the analysis of concepts and their
symbolic representation. In order to create a complete rational *language*
from the grammar discussed here, this part of Leibniz's scheme would
presumably still have to be pursued.

75 Pombo, *Leibniz and the Problem*, pp. 152ff.

76 "Distinction of gender is not relevant to a rational grammar; neither
do distinctions of declensions and conjugations have any use in a
philosophical grammar. For we vary gender, declensions and conjugations without any benefit, without any gain in brevity – unless perhaps the variation pleases the ear; and this consideration does not
concern philosophy" (C 286: PLP 13). "It is superfluous to have in-
flexions in adjectives, for it is enough to have them in the substantive
to which the adjective is attached. In the same way, number is unnecessary in the verb, for this is sufficiently understood from the noun to
which it is attached" (C 290: PLP 16). Cf. C 286: PLP 13; C 244: PLP
13; C 281; C 287: PLP 14–15; C 290: PLP 16; C 357. For further

discussion of this reduction of grammatical structure, see Couturat, *La Logique*, pp. 65–71; Mates, "Nominalism and Evander's Sword"; Pombo, *Leibniz and the Problem*, pp. 162–65; McRae, "Locke and Leibniz," p. 158.

77 Thus, a relational sentence such as "Paris loves Helen" can be reduced to the following: "Paris is a lover and *eo ipso* Helen is a loved one" (C 287). Cf. Mates, "Nominalism" and *The Philosophy of Leibniz*.

78 For more on this aspect of Leibniz's theory of terms, see Rutherford, "Truth, Predication," and Mates, "The Lingua Philosophica," pp. 64ff; "Nominalism," pp. 214–15; and *The Philosophy of Leibniz*, chap. X.

79 There he writes: "Yet it appears certain that the passion for devising abstract words has almost obfuscated philosophy for us entirely; we can well enough dispense completely with this procedure in our philosophizing" (A VI.ii 417: L 126).

80 Cf. *New Essays*, II.xxiii.1, A VI.vi: RB 217; C 243, 354, 435, 512–13; LH IV 7C Bl. 101 (VE 182); LH IV 7C Bl. 109–10 (VE 191); LH IV 7B, 3 Bl. 40–49 (VE 357).

81 Heinekamp, "Ars characteristica," "Natürliche Sprache," "Sprache und Wirklichkeit."

82 Heinekamp, "Ars characteristica," p. 469; "Natürliche Sprache," p. 279.

83 As Leibniz says explicitly at C 151 (quoted, n. 53.) See also the *Brevis Designatio*: "Languages neither originate by convention nor are established like laws, but arise by some natural impulse of human beings, accommodating sounds to affects and motions of the soul. I make an exception, however, for *artificial languages*, such as that of Wilkins" (Du IV.ii 187). Cf. Heinekamp, "Ars characteristica," p. 476.

84 See Heinekamp, "Ars characteristica," pp. 480–81. For more on this point, see sec. IV.

85 Ibid., p. 484.

86 Heinekamp, "Ars characteristica," pp. 475–81.

87 Thus, in Leibniz's view, natural languages are "the oldest monuments of peoples, earlier than writing and the arts, [and] best indicate their origins, kinship and migrations" (*New Essays* III.ii.1, A VI.vi: RB 285). Cf. above nn. 50 and 53 and Heinekamp, "Ars characteristica," pp. 471–72.

88 Heinekamp, "Ars characteristica," pp. 487–88. In support of his position, Heinekamp, "Natürliche Sprache," cites the following passage from the *New Essays*: "The situation is such that [specifically human] needs have forced us to abandon the natural order of ideas, for that order would be common to angels and men and to intelligences in general. It would be the one for us to follow if we had no concern for our own interests. However, we have had to hold fast to the order which was provided by the incidents and accidents to which our species is subject;

this order represents the history of our discoveries, as it were, rather than the origin of notions" (III.i.5; A VI.vi: RB 276).

89 This is observed both in the emphasis Leibniz places on the substitution of distinct concepts for confused ones (see, e.g., G IV 422–26: L 291–94; G VII 292–98: P 10–17), and, as we saw above, in his efforts to reduce the grammar of natural languages to a "rational" grammar.

90 Here Leibniz may deceive himself, for he evidently believes (with some qualification) that figurative language will aid his less able readers in penetrating to the heart of his philosophy: "M. Descartes speaks with exactitude, Father Malebranche has clothed his thoughts in the manner of an orator, for which I do not blame him; for when one has once thought rightly, figurative expressions are useful for winning over those for whom abstract meditations are painful. However, when one indulges oneself with metaphors, it is necessary to take care lest they give rise to illusions" (BH 56–57). See also his comments to Remond (G III 624).

91 As he elaborates in another work, "any monad is a mirror not only of its body, but also of the whole universe, since the whole universe is also expressed in the motions of its body: not in the sense that it is similar to it, but as a circle is expressed by a parabola and a straight line by a cone in gnomonic projections – namely, when from any part the whole could be known (like the lion from its claw) by an omniscient being" (quoted in Gerhardt, "Über neu gefundene Manuscripte von Leibniz." Cf. C 15: P 176–77.

92 Another example of this confusion involves Leibniz's thesis that monads "are in" ([*inesse*]) bodies, where it is clear that he is using the idea of one thing's being "in" another not in its literal sense of spatial inclusion, but in an extended figurative sense of one thing's being a conceptual prerequisite of another. I discuss this case at length in Rutherford, "Leibniz's 'Analysis of Multitude and Phenomena into Unities and Reality'." Yet another example is diagnosed by Blumenfeld, "Leibniz's Theory of Striving Possibles."

93 See the discussion of "blind thought" in sec. III.

94 Cf. Strange, "Plotinus, Porphyry, and the Neoplatonic Interpretation of the 'Categories' ", pp. 972–74, who attributes a related view to Plotinus.

95 Cf. the *Epistolaris*, sec. 23: "But the names of all natural, sensible, and frequently occurring things were prior to those of rare, artificial, moral and metaphysical ones. Thus '*pneuma*,' 'spirit,' and 'soul,' words which now signify incorporeal things, originally denoted gases, from which they were transferred to other invisible, albeit also active things, such as souls and spirits (quoted in Heinekamp, "Ars characteristica," p. 481).

96 Cf. C 287, 291; LH IV 7D, 1 Bl. 15 (VE 1318–19). For discussions of this topic, see Aarsleff, "Leibniz on Locke," p. 186; Walker, "Leibniz and Language"; McRae, "Locke and Leibniz."

97 Thus, Leibniz writes in the *New Essays:* "just as what is shut up somewhere or is *in* some whole, is supported by it and goes where it goes, so accidents are thought of similarly as *in* the subject – *sunt in subjecto, inhaerent subjecto*" (III.i.5; A.VI.vi: RB 278). This particular example of an analogical extension of meaning is anticipated by Aristotle, *Physics* IV.iii (210a14–24).

98 This is only a rough sketch of what Leibniz may have in mind. It is suggested by the following brief passage from the 1686 essay *Elements of Reason:* "notions abstracted from the matter of images are the most important and hold the explanation [*ratio*] of everything. They contain the origins, and even the connections, of imaginable things and, as it were, the soul of human thought" (C 351).

99 For helpful comments on an earlier draft of this chapter, I would like to thank D. Blumenfeld, A. Heinekamp, N. Jolley, R. N. McCauley and G. H. R. Parkinson. Receipt of an Emory College Summer Faculty Development Award is gratefully acknowledged.

9 Leibniz: physics and philosophy

Understanding the physical world was one of Leibniz's central interests. Earlier chapters of this *Companion* have explored aspects of Leibniz's metaphysics as they developed, his account of substance in general, and corporeal substance in particular. But Leibniz's interest in the physical world did not stop with metaphysics. Among his writings are numerous letters, notes, essays, and more extended treatments of questions in physics that show his deep engagement with the science of his day. Leibniz was one of the most important physicists of the late seventeenth century; other than Sir Isaac Newton, there is probably no other physicist of his generation who contributed more to the new mathematical physics. Thus, to understand the history of science in this crucial period, we must understand Leibniz's thoughts on physics. For Leibniz, as for many of his contemporaries, there was no clear boundary between philosophy and physics; understanding the world was at issue, and often those involved in what we would call philosophical projects to understand the world were also deeply involved in what we would consider scientific projects as well. Descartes, for example, the great philosopher of the earlier seventeenth century, made important contributions in his writings to mathematics and physics, as did Bacon, Hobbes, Gassendi, and later, Berkeley. Leibniz's physics and his philosophy were deeply intertwined; to try to study the one without the other is to get only a partial and inadequate picture of his thought.

In this essay, I shall outline the foundations and main features of Leibniz's thoughts on physics. After discussion of the state of physics in the late seventeenth century and of the historical development of Leibniz's thought, I shall discuss his science of dynamics and the self-consciously metaphysical notion of force central to that science.

I shall then turn to physics proper and discuss Leibniz's conception of space, motion, and the laws of motion, ending with a discussion of the relations between the domain of physics and other domains of Leibniz's concern.[1]

I. ARISTOTELIANISM, MECHANISM, AND LEIBNIZ'S EARLY PHYSICS

The seventeenth century was a period of rapid development in the sciences, the period in which the Aristotelian science that dominated the Middle Ages and the Renaissance schools was replaced with what was soon to become classical physics. In the beginning of the century, every student learned physics from Aristotle; only one hundred years later, Newton was the new master.

Aristotelian physics was a matter of some complexity, but to understand the intellectual transformation in which Leibniz participated, we must understand something of its starting place. For the Aristotelian physics, the basic explanatory principles were matter and form. Together, matter and form were taken to compose body. Matter is what remained constant in change, while form is what changed when a body changed its properties; accidental form explained changes in accidents (from brown to yellow hair, from hot to cold), while substantial form explained changes in substance, from air to water, or from prince to frog. Thus, for the Aristotelian physicist, the characteristic properties of bodies were explained in terms of these forms and were thought of as innate tendencies bodies have to behave in one way or another; stones were thus thought to fall, and fire to rise, fire to heat, and water to cool by virtue of the forms that the bodies in question have.[2]

While Aristotelian natural philosophy was controversial from its first reintroduction into Western Europe in the late twelfth and early thirteenth centuries, by the beginning of the seventeenth century it had become the orthodoxy in the schools.[3] But early in the seventeenth century, it came under a new kind of attack from proponents of the new mechanical philosophy. According to this new philosophy, the only explanatory principles in physics were size, shape, and motion. It was held that the properties of bodies are to be explained, not in terms of form, accidental or substantial, but in terms of the broadly geometrical properties of the tiny particles that make up larger bodies, in terms of the motion of tiny corpuscles of different sizes and shapes, whose motion changed through collision alone. And so, heat and cold are to be explained not in terms of form, but of the shape of the particles that make up a body or the speed with which they move; heaviness is to be explained not in terms of an innate tendency to fall, but in terms of the collision between a falling stone and the particles in the atmosphere that push it downward. This new billiard-ball world was the work of many in that century, including Galileo, Descartes, Hobbes, Huygens, Gassendi, and others. For some it was linked to the doctrines of the ancient atomists with their unsplittable atoms swimming in a void, while others saw infinitely divisible material substance swimming in a plenum; for some it was linked with the framing of precise mathematical laws, while others were content with more general and less precise descriptions of the behavior of bodies; for some it was experimental, while for others it was largely *a priori*. There was also profound disagreement about just how new this new mechanical philosophy really was. While some adherents represent it as quite revolutionary, many, including Leibniz in some parts of his career, represent it as continuous with Aristotelian thought, consistent with either medieval Aristotelianism or with what Aristotle himself originally intended, however much Aristotle's thought may have been distorted by later thinkers.[4]

It is against this background that we must view Leibniz's thought in physics. Leibniz's earliest reading and education was certainly in the Scholastic tradition, and it is no doubt Aristotelian physics that he first learned.[5] But when he was only fifteen, if his own testimony is to be trusted, Leibniz turned toward the Moderns.[6] Nothing survives from this very earliest mechanist period which would have commenced in 1661. By the mid- and late 1660s, there is ample evidence of Leibniz's interest in the new mechanical philosophy.[7] Most important in these very early years are two letters that Leibniz wrote, in 1668 and 1669, to his mentor, Jacob Thomasius, in which he discusses the new mechanists (A II.i no. 9 and 11). Like many of the new mechanists, Leibniz saw the nature of body as consisting of its broadly geometrical properties, extension and antitypy (impenetrability) (see A II.i 23: L 101). Like many mechanists, particularly the Cartesians, Leibniz also seems to have flirted with occasionalism at this stage, and told Thomasius that only God has the ability to move bodies by continually recreating them in different places at different times (see A II.i 23–4: L 101–2).[8] Referring to such new philosophers as Descartes, Bacon, Gassendi, Hobbes, and Digby, Leibniz declares: "I maintain the rule which is common to all of these renovators of philosophy, that only magnitude, figure, and motion are to be used in explaining corporeal properties" (A II.i 15:L 94).

Though Leibniz was clearly an adherent of the new mechanical philosophy by the late 1660s, there is no reason to believe that he thought that his brand of mechanism was in any way inconsistent with an adherence to Aristotelian philosophy. Indeed, in the April 1669 letter to Thomasius, Leibniz emphasizes over and over again that while the new philosophy may be inconsistent with the teachings of the Schoolmen, it is fully consistent with the teachings of Aristotle himself; when properly understood, Leibniz argues, Aristotle too was a mechanist of sorts (A II.i no. 11: L 93–103). Recent studies of these texts have also suggested that Leibniz's concept of substance in these years is best thought of in Aristotelian terms, in terms of matter and form. As noted earlier, during this period Leibniz held that the essence of body is extension and impenetrability, as many mechanists did. However, unlike run-of-the-mill mechanists, Leibniz combined this view with an Aristotelian view of substance, holding that bodies only constitute substances when taken together with concurrent minds, in particular, the mind of God, who is the source of activity in the world.[9] All in all, it seems best to view Leibniz in the context not of the radical mechanists, but of the renovators or reformers, of the seventeenth century thinkers who were attracted to the new mechanical philosophy while at the same time thinking that it could be reconciled with the old Aristotelian physics. For Leibniz in this period – and, as we shall see, for the rest of his career as a physicist – the view was that the true physics must somehow be a blend of the old and the new, a physics that was at the same time Aristotelian and mechanist.[10]

Early indications of Leibniz's interest in the new mechanical physics are programmatic and unsystematic. The first indication of any serious and systematic interest in physics on Leibniz's part isn't found until late 1669. Then begins a series of notes on questions in physics, mainly the theory of motion, that lead to Leibniz's first substantial writings in physics, the *Hypothesis physica nova* (HPN) or *Theoria motus concreti*, presented to the Royal Society of London in 1671, and the *Theoria motus abstracti* (TMA), presented to the French Academy of Sciences that same year.[11]

Together these works constitute an interesting system of physics. In the TMA, Leibniz gives an abstract account of motion, as the title suggests, an account of motion that is grounded purely in reason, so Leibniz claims. But such an account of motion is radically in contradiction with the everyday experience of bodies and with the more exact experiments of other investigators. Leibniz's solution to this apparent inconsistency between reason and the world is a hypothesis about the state of the universe God created, which, together with the abstract laws, yields something close to what it is that we observe in the world; this is the task of the HPN, or the theory of concrete motion, as the subtitle suggests, a theory of motion for *our* world (A VI.ii 223).[12]

The heart of Leibniz's abstract theory of motion in the TMA is an account of the collision of two bodies; for Leibniz, as for other mechanists, collision is the only way in which the motion of a body can be changed naturally. The account of impact is given in terms of the notion of a *conatus*, an indivisible, nonextended part of motion, the beginning or end of motion, as he puts it (A VI.ii 264–65: L 139–40).[13] Leibniz constructs his abstract theory of motion on the conviction that the outcomes of collisions are determined by simply combining the instantaneous motions (*conatus*) of the two bodies at the moment of collision; body as such offers no resistance to motion and so the mass or size of the bodies in question plays *no role whatsoever* in the outcome of a collision. As Leibniz put it in the HPN, "all power in bodies depends on the speed" (A VI.ii 228). If two bodies with unequal speed collide, then, Leibniz argues, the two will move together after the collision with a speed which is the difference between the two, and in the direction of the faster. In particular, if a moving body A hits a body B at rest, then they both move off in the direction the body A has, no matter how small A is, and no matter how large the resting B might be; in this case, the body B offers no resistance whatsoever to being set into motion. When the two speeds are equal, then "the directions of both will be destroyed, and a third will be chosen intermediate between the two, the velocity of the *conatus* being conserved," a conclusion that Leibniz argues is "the peak of rationality in motion." He justifies his conclusion by an appeal to the principle that "there is nothing without reason." This is very likely the first time that Leibniz appealed in print to this most fruitful of his principles.[14] An interesting special case occurs when two bodies with the same speed collide directly. In this case, both come to a halt, in violation of the Cartesian conservation principle, in accordance with which the total quantity of motion (size times speed) is conserved in the world in general and in every individual collision.[15]

These laws of motion, reasonable as they might be in the abstract, fit very poorly with the world we see around us, as Leibniz knew; in particular, the bodies of our world do seem to offer resistance to being set into motion. In the HPN these abstract laws are reconciled with experience through an hypothesis about the makeup of the world. As his earlier writings might suggest, the spirit behind the HPN is thoroughly mechanistic. Leibniz writes:

I agree completely with the followers of those excellent gentlemen, Descartes and Gassendi, and with whomever else teaches that in the end, all variety in bodies must be explained in terms of size, shape, and motion.
(HPN sec. 57; A VI.ii 248; cf. A VI.ii 249–50)

Leibniz's procedure in the HPN is very reminiscent of the creation story that Descartes told some years earlier.[16] Descartes' strategy was to derive the present state of the world from an initial creation and the laws of motion. Leibniz, too, starts at the beginning with an assumed first state, a solar and a terrestrial globe (he ignores the other planetary bodies, large and small), which are set into motions of various sorts and result in these two bodies rotating, each around its own axis, and revolving around each other, with light streaming from the sun to the earth (HPN secs. 1–10; A VI.ii 223–36). Leibniz argues that the impact of the light against the surface of the earth results in the production of tiny balls of matter. This is a crucial step in the theory. For, Leibniz argues, "these . . . balls are the seeds of things, . . . the foundation of bodies, and the ground of all of the variety that we admire in things, and all of the impetus we find in motions" (HPN sec. 12; A VI.ii 226). The project, then, is to explain the main phenomena of the world in terms of these tiny balls or corpuscles. For example, Leibniz discusses the Aristotelian four elements (earth, water, air, and fire), showing how each can be generated from his theory (HPN secs. 13–14); gravity (HPN secs. 15f.); color, sound, and heat (HPN secs. 30f.); the magnet (HPN secs. 33bis f.); chemical reactions (HPN secs. 37f.); density and rarity (HPN sec. 56); and others.

Of most interest to us in this context is the exact way the abstract laws of motion concerning bodies in impact are affected by the new hypothesis of the HPN. According to the abstract theory of the TMA, size or mass can play no role in the determination of the outcome of a collision. Furthermore, since at the moment of impact, the two bodies in impact will have exactly the same *conatus*, they will always move in the same direction at the same speed. But experience shows that bodies in the real world don't behave in that way; in every circumstance, the size or mass *does* play a role, and in most circumstances, bodies rebound in collision. Leibniz frames his hypothesis in such a way that in the world of the HPN, bodies acting in accordance with the laws of motion outlined in the TMA will behave as we see them behave. In the world of the HPN, the bodies of ordinary experience are made up of a multitude of tiny corpuscles. Imagine, now, a horizontal row of n tiny discrete balls, a_1, a_2, etc., colliding with a single ball, B, moving in the opposite direction. Let us further suppose that B moves faster than the balls in row A. Consider, for example, the first ball, a_1, hitting B. According to the laws of the TMA, the post-collision speed of B will be its precollision speed, minus the speed of a_1, and the two balls will go off in the same direction at the same speed after the collision, i.e., the direction in which B originally moved. The pair of balls, a_1 and B will then hit a_2, and the same thing will happen, that is, the speed of B will be further reduced. In this way, the speed of B will be reduced in the collision; if there are a sufficient number of balls, it can even be reversed. And so, in a discontinuous body, size (or, at least, the number of particles in the line of direct collision) *can* play a role in the outcome of a collision.[17] Similarly, Leibniz can appeal to his physical hypothesis (here the discontinuity of bodies, together with the ether that flows around their parts) to introduce elasticity in the world, thus enabling bodies to reflect from one another on occasion.[18] He wrote in the HPN:

But by means of the wonderful handiwork of the creator, or through his gift, necessary for life, on our hypothesis all sensible bodies are elastic, due to the circulation of the ether, and therefore all sensible bodies reflect or refract. . . . Everything is discontinuous, from which it follows that other things equal, the greater mass accomplishes more; everything is elastic, that is, when compressed, and left to itself, it soon restores itself to its prior state on account of the circulating ether.   (HPN sec. 22; A VI.ii 229, 230)

Indeed, Leibniz thought that together his abstract laws and his physical hypothesis yielded the Huygens/Wren laws of impact, recently discovered and widely discussed. Writing on 13/23 July, 1670 to Henry Oldenburg, secretary of the Royal Society, which had published the Huygens/Wren laws and to which the HPN had been dedicated, Leibniz noted:

> For I have established certain elements of the true laws of motion, demonstrated in the geometrical method from the definitions of terms alone, . . . and this has also shown that those rules of motion, which the incomparable Huygens and Wren have established, are not primary, not absolute, not clear but, no less than gravity, follow from a certain state of the ter-aqueous globe, not demonstrable by axiom or theorem, but from experience, phenomena, and observation, however fertile and admirable . . . they might be.
>
> (A II.i 59. See also HPN sec. 23; A VI.ii 231–32)[19]

And so, the laws bodies appear to obey in our world are are the result of abstract and geometrical laws, very different from what we experience in day-to-day life, operating in a complex world that God created for his ends.

The TMA and HPN are very important as the first systematic treatises in physics that Leibniz composed. But also of interest in these writings is an important metaphysical change from just a few years earlier. In the Thomasius letter of 1669, the nature of body is extension and impenetrability, but by the publication of the TMA, Leibniz's thinking is a bit different. Writing to Arnauld in November, 1671, announcing to him his new publications, Leibniz declares that the essence of body consists not in extension, or in extension and impenetrability, but in *motion* (A II.i 172:L 149). Furthermore, with the TMA and HPN, Leibniz seems to give up the occasionalism of his earlier writings. As noted above, in the letters to Thomasius from 1668 and 1669, Leibniz held that God is the only real source of activity in the world and the real cause of motion in the physical world. But in these writings, this occasionalism is rejected and the cause of motion is moved from God to bodies themselves; bodies are, it seems, the sources of their own motion, which derives from their own minds, and these minds together with their bodies constitute genuine substances.[20] The rejection of occasionalism together with an unambiguous attribution of activity to substances in the world itself will be central to Leibniz's mature thinking about the physical world.

Leibniz's writings show continued interest in questions of physics throughout the decade, both during and after his important visit to Paris in 1672.[21] Though his intellectual world was rapidly expanding, his ideas in physics remain constant for a few years. In a long manuscript from 1672 that Leibniz entitled "Propositiones quaedam physicae" (A VI.iii 4–72), one can find an attempt to present the basic theory of the HPN in a systematic and geometrical fashion, an enterprise that is repeated in an important letter to Honoratus Fabri in late 1676 (A II.i 286–301). The Leibniz of 1671 can also be discerned in a fascinating set of notes that he wrote on Descartes' *Principles of Philosophy* in late 1675 or early 1676 (see A VI.iii 213–17).[22] There he denies the Cartesian conservation law and substitutes his own view that it is *conatus* which is conserved, a view found in the writings of 1671. Similarly, against Descartes, he denies that bodies in and of themselves have any tendency to remain in the state in which they are, or resist the acquisition of new motion, repeating perhaps the most audacious claim made in the HPN and TMA, that the laws of collision are independent of size or mass (A VI.ii 215–6). As Yvon Belaval put it, "it is, above all, the author of the *Hypothesis Physica Nova* who wrote these first reflections on the *Principles*."[23]

Starting in 1676 Leibniz seems to have undertaken some serious rethinking of his views on the foundations of physics. The physics of 1671 recognizes no inherent resistance in bodies; size or mass play no role in determining the outcome of a collision between two bodies. It is evident that at the most basic level, the Cartesian law of the conservation of quantity of motion, size times speed, must be violated. But while the Cartesian conservation principle is not a *basic* law, Leibniz argues in a piece from December 1675 that in *this* world (i.e., the world of the HPN), full of matter, it is satisfied (A VI.iii 466ff).[24]

There is reason to believe that Leibniz found a fatal flaw in Descartes' basic law less than a year later. In what is quite clearly a reference to his meeting with Spinoza in late 1676, Leibniz reports having set Spinoza right about the Cartesian laws of motion:

Spinoza did not see the mistakes in Descartes' rules of motion; he was surprised when I began to show him that they violate the equality of cause and effect.[25]

For Leibniz the principle of the equality of cause and effect is the principle in accordance with which there must be exactly as much in the effect as there was in the cause, a principle that, as we shall see, has a crucial role to play in Leibniz's mature physics.[26] While the remark about what he showed Spinoza may be a bit cryptic, later writings suggest what Leibniz almost certainly meant: the Cartesian collision laws, governed by the principle of the conservation of quantity of motion, are inconsistent with the principle of the equality of cause and effect; if Cartesian quantity of motion is conserved in collision, then the ability the bodies had to do work before the collision can simply be lost after impact (see, e.g., letter to Theodor Craanen, June 1679, A II.i 469–71).[27] And so, Leibniz implies, the Cartesian conservation principle must be wrong.

By January 1678, Leibniz seems to have gone a step further and replaced the Cartesian conservation law with one of his own. It was a consequence of Huygens' laws of impact that, in impact, the product of mass (size) and the square of the speed are the same, before and after the collision; indeed, Leibniz duly noted this in his own notes on Huygens on collision from late 1669, though it seems not to have made much of an impression on him at that time (see AVI.ii 158). But in a manuscript that can be dated precisely to January 1678, Leibniz takes this observation Huygens makes about bodies in impact and turns it into something central to his thought.[28] Leibniz came to hold in these years that in collision between bodies, the force or power of action must be conserved.[29] What he discovered in January 1678 was that this force or power of action must be measured by mv^2.

As Leibniz later emphasizes, the replacement of the earlier physics of the TMA and HPN with a new physics grounded in the conservation of mv^2 was imbued with the greatest philosophical significance. Leibniz wrote a few years later in the *Discourse on Metaphysics* of 1686:

This consideration, the distinction between force and quantity of motion, is rather important, not only in physics and mechanics, in order to find the true laws of nature and the rules of motion, . . . but also in metaphysics, in order to understand the principles better.

(*Discourse*, par. 18., G IV 444: AG 51)

In particular, Leibniz argues that understanding the new conservation principle will lead us to appreciate that body and motion are to be grounded in what he calls force, something distinct from the notions of extension and motion that ground the Cartesian world (ibid.).[30]

Later we shall examine this claim more carefully. But it is worth pointing out that the new conservation law was not the only important change in Leibniz's views in these years. More generally, the abandonment of the basic strategy physics of the HPN and TMA, very likely in this same period, resulted in very basic changes in the way Leibniz thought about physics and its principles. Leibniz gives an account of this in the "Specimen Dynamicum" (SD) some years later, in 1695. As he characterizes his earlier thought in the SD, the view of the HPN was that body contains only "mathematical notions, size, shape, place, and their change," and that, as a result, the outcome of a collision is determined by the "geometrical composition of conatus alone," resulting in the consequence that the smallest body can move the largest without any resulting loss in speed. And so, Leibniz tells his later readers, he held that "the Wisest Author of things had avoided the consequences that follow *per se* from the bare laws of motion derived from geometry" through the organization of things in the world, the hypothesis of the HPN (SD part I, par. 10, GM VI 241: AG 124).[31] He then continues:

But after I examined all of this more deeply, I saw what a systematic explanation of things consists in, and noticed that my earlier hypothesis about the notion of body was imperfect.... [B]ecause we cannot derive all truths concerning corporeal things from logical and geometrical axioms alone ... , and because we must appeal to other axioms pertaining to cause and effect, action and passion, in terms of which we can explain the order of things, we must admit something metaphysical, something perceptible by the mind alone over and above that which is purely mathematical and subject to the imagination, and we must add to material mass a certain superior and, so to speak, formal principle. Whether we call this principle form or entelechy or force does not matter, as long as we remember that it can only be explained through the notion of forces.   (SD part I, par. 11, GM VI 241: AG 124–25)

Physical hypotheses about various phenomena will continue to be important for Leibniz, as they were for any orthodox mechanical philosopher of the seventeenth century. But what is important here is that by the end of the 1670s, much of the behavior of bodies that Leibniz attributed to the state of the world now becomes basic to bodies as such; the sort of conservation principle that appears at best as a derivative principle in Leibniz's physics in the 1670s now appears basic to body, as we shall develop in more detail below. Leibniz represents this as a move from a geometrical conception of body and its laws to a metaphysical conception. This cannot be exactly right. As we saw earlier, the principle of sufficient reason has an important role to play in the early physics of the TMA and HPN. Furthermore, even in that early physics, body is not "purely mathematical" and composed of "material mass" alone. But it is the case that a number of metaphysical principles, like the equality of cause and effect, now enter into the determination of the ground-level laws of nature in ways that they didn't earlier, and, as a consequence, Leibniz claims, the nature of body cannot be extension or motion, but must be force.

2. THE MATURE PHYSICS: AN OVERVIEW

Leibniz's notes and correspondence in the late 1670s and early 1680s show considerable interest in questions of motion, physics, and, more generally, natural philosophy.[32] But the foundations of Leibniz's new physics were not publicly revealed until 1686, when Leibniz published his brief but important "Brevis Demonstratio Erroris memorabilis Cartesii et aliorum circa Legem Naturalem" (BD) in the *Acta Eruditorum*.[33] In this work, Leibniz presented for the first time in public what he had been telling friends and correspondents in private for some years – that the Cartesian law of the conservation of quantity of motion (size times speed) is false and leads to paradox. We shall discuss this argument in more detail in section 4.3. An enormous controversy followed among the many who still followed Descartes in holding the conservation principle, a controversy that continued well into the 1690s.[34]

While the BD emphasized what is wrong with Descartes' physics, it gave only a hint of what Leibniz intended to replace it with. But shortly after the appearance of that essay, perhaps goaded by the appearance of Isaac Newton's *Principia Mathematica* in 1687, Leibniz began to work out the details of his own positive program in physics.[35] Most important from the point of view of the foundations of the new science that Leibniz dubbed "dynamics" is the massive *Dynamica de Potentia et Legibus Naturae corporeae*, written during Leibniz's trip to Italy in 1689–90 with the intention of publication, but unpublished during his lifetime.[36] This work is a systematic treatise on motion and its laws, presenting in a systematic and rigorous fashion the conclusions of the new science. While Leibniz never published the *Dynamica*, he did publish an essay that presents what he takes to be the foundations of the dynamics. This essay was entitled "Specimen Dynamicum" (SD), and was published in the *Acta Eruditorum* in 1695.[37] Though its title suggests a summary of, or selection from, the earlier work and Leibniz's opening words suggest that the new work will present some hint of what the *Dynamica* contained, little of the highly technical material from the *Dynamica* is found in the SD; instead, what we have is a careful exposition of the metaphysical foundations of the new science, something that is hard to find in the old *Dynamica*, and no less valuable than the more technical physics of the *Dynamica*.

Also important in the writings of this period is the "Tentamen de Motuum Coelestium causis," published in the *Acta Eruditorum* in 1689. In this essay Leibniz offers an account of the motion of the planets, using a complex scheme of vortices, a more explicitly mechanist alternative to the account in terms of the theory of universal gravitation that Newton presented in his *Principia*.[38] While Newton does not deny that there may be an underlying mechanical explanation of the force of gravity he discovered and the motion of the planets that follows from that force on his theory, his *Principia* offers no such account. Leibniz's essay, on the other hand, is intended specifically to offer such an account; it is a most visible tribute to the depths of Leibniz's continuing commitment to the mechanist program of a physics grounded in size, shape, and motion.

These by no means exhaust Leibniz's scientific interests in this period, from which numerous other notes and publications date.[39] But what is especially interesting is the way in which Leibniz's new program for physics penetrates the more philosophical writings, particularly in the 1680s and 1690s. In Leibniz's mind, as we shall later see in more detail, the new program for physics is intimately linked with his more philosophical programs, and so Leibniz's enthusiasm for his new physics spills over into works like the *Discourse on Metaphysics*, his philosophical correspondence, particularly the letters with Arnauld in the late 1680s, essays like the "Correction of Metaphysics . . ."of 1694, and the "New System" of 1695. Most interesting here is an essay Leibniz published in 1698, "On Nature Itself," which, Leibniz announces in the subtitle, is "on the inherent force and actions of created things, toward confirming and illustrating their dynamics."

It is in the 1680s and 1690s that Leibniz is most actively interested in working out his physics and the metaphysical questions connected with it. His interest in physics by no means disappears in later writings; he continues to discuss his ideas in physics and its foundations with his correspondents, as is shown, for example, by his correspondence with DeVolder, Des Bosses, and, especially, the correspondence he conducted at the very end of his life with Samuel Clarke, who acted as a stand-in for the great Sir Isaac Newton.[40] But by the late 1690s, it is fair to say that Leibniz's basic views on physics and its foundations are well settled. Without ignoring those later writings, I shall try to give an overview of Leibniz's thought on matters of physics in these two crucial decades. Before turning to the details, though, it will be helpful to introduce a distinction implicit in Leibniz's writings about the natural world, a distinction that will help to organize the discussion to follow.

Throughout his mature writings, Leibniz sides with the mechanists against both the philosophy of the schools and against the Newtonian attempt to extend the mechanical philosophy through the introduction of gravity, a force that some Newtonians, if not Newton himself, thought was inexplicable in mechanical terms. But, Leibniz held, the mechanical physics is not fundamental in a very important sense. Leibniz writes in a characteristic passage from the *Discourse on Metaphysics of* 1686:

> Although all the particular phenomena of nature can be explained mathematically or mechanically by those who understand them, nevertheless the general principles of corporeal nature and of mechanics itself are more metaphysical than geometrical, and belong to some indivisible forms or natures as the causes of appearances, rather than to corporeal mass or extension.
> (*Discourse*, par. 18, G IV 444: AG 51–52)[41]

These "indivisible forms or natures" pertain to corporeal substances, which, as we shall see below, are characterized in the physical writings in terms of the notion of force. This suggests that there are at least two levels in Leibniz's natural philosophy. At the surface, as it were, is the mechanical philosophy, in which everything is explained in terms of the notions of size, shape, and motion, assuming that motion satisfies certain laws. This, I think, is what Leibniz often thought of as physics proper. But below physics proper stands the science that treats force and the metaphysical entities, the corporeal substances to which force, properly speaking, pertains and from which motion and its laws derive. This science is what Leibniz called dynamics.[42] Leibniz clearly thinks that dynamics is closely connected to metaphysics, but the relation between the corporeal substances, characterized in terms of force, and the individual substances, later monads, that dominate his more directly metaphysical writings is obscure, as we shall later see.[43] In the remainder of this essay, I would like to focus on the more straightforward categories of physics and dynamics. The two levels are difficult to separate completely and treat entirely independently. I will begin by discussing the dynamical level in Leibniz's natural philosophy, the notion of force, before turning to the notions of space, shape, and motion that constitute Leibniz's notion of physics proper.

3. FORCE: THE DYNAMICAL LEVEL

3.1 The refutation of the Cartesian doctrine of body

Cartesian physics was still very much alive when Leibniz began to work out his own ideas about physics in the 1670s and 1680s. A reasonable place to begin our account of Leibniz's views on the physical world is with an account of his rejection of the Cartesian doctrine of the nature of body, and his advocacy of a conception of body grounded in the notion of force; in this is grounded his dynamics.

Basic to Descartes and his many followers was the view that the essence of body is extension; bodies, for Descartes, were the objects of geometry made real. As a consequence, Descartes held that all of the bodies' properties are broadly geometrical, including size, shape, position with respect to other bodies, and motion. This was central to Cartesian mechanism; because all there is in body is extension and its modes everything in physics must be explicable in those terms.[44]

Leibniz shared the mechanical philosophy of the Cartesians; for him, too, everything was explicable in terms of size, shape, and motion. But though he shared the physics, he did not share the metaphysics on which Descartes had grounded his mechanism. While bodies may be extended, Leibniz held that this was not their essence.

Leibniz offers a number of interesting arguments against the

Cartesian conception of body, from a number of different premises, and leading to a number of different conclusions.

First, there are arguments showing the insufficiency of the notion of extension for defining body. Leibniz argues that extension cannot be the essence of body, as Descartes and his followers claim, because extension is not the sort of thing that *can* constitute the essence of *anything*; it is a relative concept, he claims, and is comprehensible only with respect to some quality or other that is extended (see, e.g., G IV 467; letter to Malebranche, 1693–94?. G I 352; to De Volder, 24 March /3 April 1699, G II 169–70: AG 171–72; G IV 393–94: AG 251; G VI 584: AG 261). Leibniz also offers a somewhat puzzling argument to the effect that insofar as bodies in the real world are actually divided to infinity, strictly speaking they have no shape. Since one cannot have an extended thing that has no shape, extension cannot constitute the essence of body.[45] These arguments, interesting as they are, lead us away from the Cartesian position, but don't lead clearly toward anything else.

Other arguments, though, give us more insight into Leibniz's own position. One of the most important such arguments is what might be called the aggregate argument. This is the main argument he uses against the mechanist ontology in the letters he wrote to Arnauld in the late 1680s. There he focuses on the fact that for most Cartesian mechanists, body is infinitely (or, to use Descartes' phrase, indefinitely) divisible.[46] In writing to Arnauld, Leibniz announces: "I hold this basic proposition, differentiated only by the emphasis to be an axiom, namely, that *what is not truly* one *being* is *not truly one* being *either*" (letter to Arnauld, 30 April 1687:G II 97: AG 86). So, Leibniz concludes, the ultimate existents in his world must be things that are genuinely one, genuine unities. Thus, Leibniz claims that the reality of aggregates must depend on the reality of the individuals that make up those aggregates: "I do not agree that *there are only aggregates of substances,* and if there are aggregates of substances, there must also be true substances from which all the aggregates result" (letter to Arnauld, 30 April 1687, G II 96: AG 85). Now, Leibniz claims that extended things, at least inanimate extended things, are by their nature aggregates; *any* body, taken by itself is only an aggregate of the parts into which one can divide it (see the discussion in letter to Arnauld, 28 November/8 December 1686, G II 76: AG 79). And so, Leibniz concludes:

We must then necessarily come down either to mathematical points of which some authors constitute extension, or to the atoms of Epicurus or Cordemoy (which things you reject along with me), or else we must admit that we do not find any reality in bodies; or finally we must recognize some substances that have a true unity.

(Letter to Arnauld, 30 April 1687, G II 96: AG 85)

That is, for extended bodies to be real, they must ultimately be composed of things that are genuine unities, something that cannot be found in extension alone.[47]

The aggregate argument turns on the fact that in the infinitely divisible bodies of the Cartesians there are no genuine individuals, and thus no reality, properly speaking. Another argument Leibniz gives goes even a step further. In sec. 13 of the important essay "On Nature Itself" (1698), Leibniz presented a general argument intended to show that if the world is full, and full of matter uniform in its nature (both of which follow from the doctrine of body as extension Descartes held), then change is impossible. Leibniz argues:

For if no portion of matter whatsoever were to differ from equal and congruent portions of matter, . . . and furthermore, if one momentary state were to differ from another in virtue of the transportation of equal and interchangeable portions of matter alone, portions of matter in every way identical, then, on account of this perpetual substitution of indistinguishables, it obviously follows that in the corporeal world there can be no way of distinguishing different momentary states from one another.   (G IV 513: AG 163–64)

The problem Leibniz has in mind here is not merely epistemological, a matter of our not being able to *tell* whether or not the world is changing (though given our evident experience of change, this would be problem enough for the mechanist); the problem is deeper, that given the common mechanist conceptions of body, it doesn't even make *sense* to talk about same and different with respect to body: "under the assumption of perfect uniformity of matter, one cannot in any way distinguish one place from another, or one bit of matter from another bit of matter in the same place" (G IV 513–14: AG 164).

These arguments establish that bodies must be grounded not in bare geometrical extension but in some sort of unities; genuine individuals. Leibniz's conception of these individuals is further fleshed out in another series of arguments against the Cartesian doctrine of body that emphasize the notions of force and activity.

First, there is a suggestion that the Cartesian view of body is refuted by the very refutation of the Cartesian conservation principle, and that when we substitute the conservation of mv^2 for the Cartesian size times speed, it follows that we must introduce something into body over and above extension. Leibniz writes to Bayle about his new conservation law, shortly after the publication of the BD:

I would like to add a remark of consequence for metaphysics. I have shown that force ought not to be estimated by the product of speed and size, but by the future effect. However, it seems that force or power is something real at present, while the future effect is not. From which it follows *that we must admit in bodies something different from size and speed, at least unless one wants to refuse bodies all power of acting.*

(Letter to Bayle, 9 January 1687, G III 48)

The argument is somewhat obscure, but what Leibniz seems to have in mind is this. For the Cartesian, all there is in body must be geometrical, size and speed. But if the ability to do work is conserved, for example, the ability a body has to raise itself a certain height, then it is not size times speed that is conserved, but size times the square of speed.[48] That is to say that neither size nor speed (nor their product) can represent in a body at a time n the ability that that body has at some future time to do work. But since the body really does have that ability at time n, there must be something it has at time n by virtue of which it has that future ability, something that goes beyond its geometrical properties; this is what Leibniz calls force.[49]

Perhaps more intelligible is another kind of argument Leibniz appeals to, an argument that derives from the claim that Cartesian bodies, the objects of geometry made real, must be completely inert, and indifferent to motion or rest. This argument is used in a wide variety of texts in the late 1680s and throughout the 1690s. Leibniz sketches the argument in the *Discourse on Metaphysics.*:

If there were nothing in bodies but extended mass and nothing in motion but change of place and if everything should and could be deduced solely from these definitions by geometrical necessity, it would follow . . . that, upon contact, the smallest body would impart its own speed to the largest body without losing any of this speed; and we would have to accept a number of such rules which are completely contrary to the formation of a system.   (*Discourse*, par. 21, G IV 446–47: AG 53–54)[50]

The argument is clear enough. If bodies were just extended, as the Cartesians say, then they would have to obey certain absurd laws of motion; in particular, the smallest body in motion could move the largest body at rest without losing any of its own motion, as in Leibniz's own early physics. But this is absurd, in contradiction both with experience, and with metaphysics, since in a world governed by such a law, the mv^2 in a collision could increase or decrease, depending upon circumstances, resulting in violations of the principle of the equivalence of cause and effect. And so Leibniz concludes, there must be something in bodies over and above mere extension, something from which the force of resistance can arise.[51]

   This argument is not entirely fair to Descartes and his followers. The laws Leibniz criticizes in this argument are not Descartes', nor do they belong to any of his followers; Descartes himself certainly recognized a kind of resistance in bodies, something that he traced back to God, the ultimate source of motion in the physical world.[52] But his isn't good enough for Leibniz. In 1702 Leibniz writes:

Though in origin [motions] ought to be attributed to God, the general cause of things, however, directly and in particular cases, they ought to be attributed to the force God placed in things. For to say that, in creation, God gave bodies a law for acting means nothing, unless, at the same time, he gave them something by means of which it could happen that the law is followed; otherwise, he himself would always have to look after carrying out the law in an extraordinary way. But indeed, his law is efficacious, and he did render bodies efficacious, that is, he gave them an inherent force.
(G IV 396–97: AG 253–54; cf. SD part I, par. 11, GM VI 241–42: AG 125;
"On Nature Itself," G IV 508–09: AG 159–60; G IV 568: L 583)

But if force is in the bodies themselves, then they cannot be the inert extended things that they are for the Cartesians.

   These arguments establish that the bodies of the mechanical philosophy are not things merely extended. Rather, Leibniz argues, they are grounded in genuine unities that are the seat of forces in the world. But to fully understand Leibniz's position here, we must understand what exactly he means by "force." It is to this question that we must turn.

3.2 Body and force

The notion of force was important to Leibniz's mature thought from the time of its origins in the late 1670s. It is fair to say that in the early seventeenth century, the notion of force had no single definite meaning, nor did it in Leibniz's own earlier writings.[53] But throughout Leibniz's writings in the 1680s and 1690s, it is in the process of becoming a more precise technical term. The notion of force and the distinctions that Leibniz draws among the different kinds of force do not emerge all at once. But by 1695 everything seems to be in place, and Leibniz's ontology of force and its relation to the notions of body and substance receive a tidy and well-organized presentation in the SD.

In the SD and related writings, Leibniz presents a conception of force that involves two important distinctions, the distinction between primitive and derivative forces, and the distinction between active and passive forces. So in all, there are four principal varieties of force – primitive active and passive force, and derivative active and passive force. Leibniz writes:

Active force [which might not inappropriately be called *power* [*virtus*] as some do] is twofold, that is, either *primitive*, which is inherent in every corporeal substance *per se* . . . or *derivative*, which, resulting from a limitation of primitive force through the collision of bodies with one another, for example, is found in different degrees. Indeed, primitive force (which is nothing but the first entelechy) corresponds to the *soul or substantial form*. . . . Similarly, passive force is also twofold, either primitive or derivative. And indeed, the *primitive* force *of being acted upon* [*vis primitiva patiendi*] or of resisting constitutes that which is called *primary matter* in the schools, if correctly interpreted. This force is that by virtue of which it happens that a body cannot be penetrated by another body, but presents an obstacle to it, and at the same time is endowed with a certain laziness, so to speak, that is, an opposition to motion, nor, further, does it allow itself to be put into motion without somewhat diminishing the force of the body acting on it. As a result, the *derivative force of being acted upon* later shows itself to different degrees in *secondary matter*.

(SD, part I, par. 3, GM IV 236–7: AG 119–20)[54]

Let us begin by examining the notions of active and passive force. Leibniz writes in the SD:

[Active] force is . . . twofold. One force is elementary, which I also call *dead force*, since motion does not yet exist in it, but only a solicitation to motion, as with the ball in the tube[55] or a stone in a sling being held in by a rope. The other is ordinary force, joined with actual motion, which I call *living force* [*vis viva*]. An example of dead force is centrifugal force itself, and also the force of heaviness [*vis gravitatis*] or centripetal force, and the force by which a stretched elastic body begins to restore itself. But when we are dealing with impact, which arises from a heavy body which has already been falling for some time, or from a bow that has already been restoring its shape for some time, or from a similar cause, the force in question is living force, which arises from an infinity of continual impressions of dead force.

(SD, part I, par. 6, GM VI 238: AG 121–22.)

This suggests that active force is to be connected with velocity and acceleration, more specifically, dead force with acceleration, and living force with actual motion. But though connected, active forces must not be *identified* with motion or acceleration; motion and change in motion (acceleration) are not forces themselves, as we shall later see in sec. 4.2, but the *effects* of forces. Furthermore, the BD argument shows that what is conserved in nature is not size times speed, but size times the square of speed. And so, if what is conserved in motion is force (living force), then force is not to be identified with motion *simpliciter*, since when the motion (velocity or speed) is doubled, the force is quadrupled.

Passive force is something quite different.[56] As the earlier passage quoted from the SD suggests, passive force is connected not with motion, but with the resistance to motion. This resistance is of two sorts.[57] First there is impenetrability, "that by virtue of which it happens that a body cannot be penetrated by another body." But in addition to that there is a kind of passive force by virtue of which bodies actively oppose the motion other bodies try to impose on it in impact, what Leibniz calls "a certain laziness." This resistance is something quite different from the mere tendency bodies have to remain in a given state, a notion basic to the thought of Descartes, Hobbes, and Spinoza. Leibniz writes to the Cartesian De Volder:

I admit that each and every thing remains in its state until there is a reason for change; this is a principle of metaphysical necessity. But it is one thing to retain a state until something changes it, which even something intrinsically indifferent to both states does, and quite another thing, much more significant, for a thing not to be indifferent, but to have a force and, as it were, an inclination to retain its state, and so to resist changing.

(Letter to De Volder, 24 March/3 April 1699; G II 170: AG 172)[58]

It is this force of resistance that slows the body in motion colliding with the body at rest, allowing Leibniz to avoid the result that so tainted his own early physics. As with the active forces, Leibniz differentiates passive forces from the behavior in bodies that they cause. In the SD Leibniz is careful to characterize passive force as "that by virtue of which it happens" that bodies have impenetrability and resistance; the passive forces are the causes of this behavior in just the way that the active forces are the causes of motion. Passive force also seems to be the cause (in a somewhat extended sense) of a body's extension. Writing to Arnauld, Leibniz discusses the "primitive passive power [i.e., force]" of a substance as its matter, and claims that "in this sense matter would not be extended or divisible, although it would be the principle of divisibility or that which amounts to it in the substance" (letter to Arnauld, 9 October 1687, G II 120; see also G IV 394: AG 251). The view seems to be that the extension of a body is just the diffusion of resistance; extension is, properly speaking, a direct consequence of the property bodies have by virtue of which they resist penetration by other bodies.

Let us now turn to the distinction between primitive and derivative forces. In the passage from the SD quoted above, Leibniz characterizes the primitive active force as corresponding to "the soul or substantial form"; the primitive passive force, on the other hand, is characterized as constituting "that which is called *primary matter* in the schools, if correctly interpreted." Form and matter are, of course, terms of art from the Aristotelian account of substance; as noted earlier in characterizing the Aristotelian conception of substance in section 1, form and matter join together to constitute a substance for Aristotle and his followers. And so for Leibniz as well. Leibniz writes in his essay of May 1702:

Primitive active force, which Aristotle calls first entelechy and one commonly calls the form of a substance, is another natural principle which, together with matter or [primitive] passive force, completes a corporeal substance. This substance, of course, is one *per se*, and not a mere aggregate of many substances, for there is a great difference between an animal, for example, and a flock.   (G IV 395: AG 252)

And so, it seems, the primitive forces, active and passive, come together to make up the corporeal substance, the genuine unity that, Leibniz claims, underlies the extended bodies of physics.

Derivative forces, in contrast, are the forces most of interest to the physicist. Leibniz writes in the SD:

Therefore, by derivative force, namely, that by which bodies actually act on one another or are acted upon by one another, I understand . . . only that which is connected to motion (local motion, of course), and which, in turn, tends further to produce local motion. For we acknowledge that all other material phenomena can be explained by local motion.

(SD, pt. I, par. 4, GM VI 237: AG 120)

Derivative force is, furthermore, that in terms of which we can frame the laws of physics. Leibniz writes, again in the SD:

It is to these notions [i.e., the derivative forces] that the laws of action apply, laws which are understood not only through reason, but are also corroborated by sense itself through the phenomena.

(SD, part I, par. 3, GM VI 237: AG 120)

Leibniz uses a number of terms to describe the relation between primitive and derivative forces. In the SD he talks of derivative force as resulting from "a *limitation* of primitive force through the collision of bodies with one another" (SD, part I, par. 3, GM VI 236: AG 119). In the first draft of the "New System" (ca. 1694) he writes:

[I call form or entelechy] the primitive force in order to distinguish it from the secondary [i.e., derivative force], what one calls moving force, which is a limitation or accidental variation of the primitive force.   (G IV 473)

Similarly, he writes to Bernoulli in 1698:

If we conceive of soul or form as the primary activity from whose modification secondary [i.e., derivative] forces arise as shapes arise from the modification of extension, then, I think, we take sufficient account of the intellect. Indeed there can be no active modifications of that which is merely passive in its essence, because modifications limit rather than increase or add.

(Letter to Bernoulli, 17 December 1698, GM III 552: AG 169)

And finally, Leibniz writes in the essay of May 1702 that "active force is twofold, primitive and derivative, that is, either substantial or accidental (G IV 395: AG 252). These passages suggest that derivative forces are to be understood as modes, accidents or the like, modifications of the primitive forces, which are understood as substances, or, better, as constituents of corporeal substances. Primitive active and passive forces, then, are the substantial ground of the derivative active and passive forces, which are their accidents or modes, as shape is an accident or mode of an extended thing.

The picture of the physical world that emerges out of the SD and related writings is quite interesting for the way in which it joins scholasticism with mechanism. At the metaphysical ground are corporeal substances, unities of form and matter, primitive active and passive forces. These, in turn, ground derivative forces, the modes or accidents of these primitive forces, their momentary states that can change as do shapes in an extended substance. The derivative forces, active and passive, in turn, are the immediate cause of motion, resistance, impenetrability, and even extension in bodies, giving rise to the mechanist's world of extended bodies in motion, following certain laws. In this way Leibniz can say, as we have seen, that everything in the world happens mechanically, but that the world of the mechanical philosophers is grounded in something quite different than extended matter and motion, an Aristotelian metaphysics of substantial form and primary matter; it is the dynamics, the science of force that links the underlying Aristotelian metaphysics with the physics of the mechanists. The final form of this doctrine, with its careful distinction between form and matter, primitive and derivative forces, active and passive forces of different varieties may not appear until the mid 1690s; but the basic picture is integral to Leibniz's thought about the physical world from the 1680s on.[59]

In section 4 of this essay, we shall turn to the mechanist physics that Leibniz builds on the foundations of the dynamics, but we must first take a turn in the other direction, to the metaphysics, and examine the relation between the apparently Aristotelian metaphysics that seems to underlie the SD and the conception of substance that underlies Leibniz's more familiar metaphysical writings.

3.3 Dynamics and the metaphysics of substance

The world of forces Leibniz came to sketch in the SD and related writings is grounded in the active and passive primitive forces he posits, which he interprets as the form and matter of corporeal substance. But, one might ask, what status do these corporeal substances have in Leibniz's complex metaphysics? The answer to this is, unfortunately, not altogether clear. The careful reader can find at least two different strains in Leibniz's writings.[60]

One view is found very prominently in the 1680s and 1690s when Leibniz was most actively working out his physics: it is the corporeal substances of the dynamical writings that form the metaphysical grounding of Leibniz's system. This view falls naturally out of the aggregate argument, discussed in section 3.1, as developed particularly in the correspondence with Arnauld. The point of the argument is to show that extension is not, by itself, sufficient to constitute body, and that underlying the extension there must be genuine substances. These substances are quite clearly the corporeal substances that constitute the foundations of the dynamics. Leibniz is quite clear that the human being is one, both body and soul. He writes:

Man . . . is an entity endowed with a genuine unity conferred on him by his soul, notwithstanding the fact that the mass of his body is divided into organs, vessels, humors, spirits, and that the parts are undoubtedly full of an infinite number of other corporeal substances endowed with their own entelechies.

(Letter to Arnauld, 9 October 1687, G II 120; see also letter to Arnauld, 28 November/8 December 1686, G II 75: AG 78)

Here the body is regarded as a collection of corporeal substances, united by a soul, which gives them true unity. Each of the corporeal substances that make up the body of the human being is itself a body (a collection of smaller corporeal substances), united by its own soul. In general, his view seems to be that all genuine substances are to be understood as living creatures of a sort, on analogy with the human being, unities of soul and body, and that the world is filled with an infinity of such genuine substances, nested in one another to infinity. Leibniz writes to Arnauld:

I am very far removed from the belief that animate bodies are only a small part of the others. For I believe rather that everything is full of animate bodies, and to my mind there are incomparably more souls than there are atoms for M. Cordemoy, who makes a finite number of them, whereas I maintain that the number of souls or at least of forms is quite infinite, and that since matter is endlessly divisible, one cannot fix on a part so small that there are no animate bodies within, or at least bodies endowed with a basic entelechy or (if you permit one to use the word "life" so generally) with a vital principle, that is to say corporeal substances, about which it may be said in general of them all that they are living.

(Letter to Arnauld, 9 October 1687, G II 118)

These corporeal substances, conceived on analogy with animals, are, I believe, the basic constituents of the world for Leibniz. While he does recognize souls and forms here, he is quite unsure whether or not they deserve the status of substances. In a very interesting document from March 1690, comments on some remarks by Michel Angelo Fardella, Leibniz remarks:

The soul, properly and accurately speaking, is not a substance, but a substantial form, or the primitive form existing in substances, the first act, the first active faculty.   ("Notes on Fardella, March 1690," FC 322: AG 105)

And even if the soul or form were a substance, Leibniz is clear that it never actually exists without being attached to a body (see, e.g., G IV 395–96: AG 252–53). Particularly significant are Leibniz's first uses of the term "monad," which enters Leibniz's philosophical vocabulary in the late 1690s. Writing to Johann Bernoulli in September 1698, Leibniz notes:

What I call a complete monad or individual substance is not so much the soul, as it is the animal itself, or something analogous to it, endowed with a soul or form and an organic body.
     (Letter to Johann Bernoulli, 20/30 September 1698, GM III 542: AG 168)

And so, Leibniz wrote in that same letter:

You ask me to divide for you a portion of mass into the substances of which it is composed. I respond, there are as many individual substances in it as there are animals or living things or things analogous to them.
               (ibid., GM III 542: AG 167)[61]

While the world of physics may be grounded in such substances, tiny animals, not every body is animate, of course. But, Leibniz argues, the inanimate bodies of physics are made up of such substances. Bodies emerge in this picture looking something like a pile of stones, or, better, a flock of sheep or a pool of wriggling fish, to use comparisons Leibniz often used. In this view, bodies, inanimate bodies at least, are phenomenal insofar as it is *we* who put the pieces (animate substances) together to form an individual. As Leibniz explains it to Arnauld:

Our mind notices or conceives some true substances which have certain modes; these modes involve relations to other substances, so the mind takes the occasion to join them together in thought and to make one name account for all these things together. This is useful for reasoning, but we must now allow ourselves to be misled into making substances or true beings of them.   (Letter to Arnauld, 30 April 1687, G II 101: AG 89)

In this view, it is relatively easy to fit the ontology of the SD and other dynamical writings directly into Leibniz's other metaphysical writings. In this view, the active and passive primitive forces of the dynamics correspond reasonably well to the form and matter of the metaphysical writings.[62] The derivative forces, then, emerge as modes of corporeal substance, and their reality in inanimate bodies is grounded in the corporeal substances that make them up.[63]

But this isn't Leibniz's only metaphysical conception of the world, and it isn't the only way he conceives of the metaphysical foundations of his dynamics. Better known is the metaphysics of the *Monadology*, where Leibniz's individual substances, what he comes to call monads, are conceived not on the model of animals but on the model of Cartesian souls (see letter to De Volder, 1699, G II 194: L 522). While traces of this position can be found in virtually every period of Leibniz's mature writings, it is what seems to dominate after 1704 or 1705. In late writings, such as the *Monadology*, Leibniz still holds that the physical world is made up of organisms, and that these organisms are everywhere in apparently lifeless matter, as in the correspondence with Arnauld (see, e.g., *Monadology*, pars. 63ff., G VI 617–18: AG 221–22). However, he holds that what is ultimately real are the mind-like simple substances, and, in general, he holds that the organisms that populate the world are not themselves substances, in the proper sense of the word. The inanimate bodies physics usually treats have a somewhat complex structure, then, and are, in a sense, doubly phenomenal. First of all, they are made up of an infinity of living things, rudimentary organisms. But these organisms are, in turn, phenomenal, aggregates of genuine substances, monads and are not themselves fully real (see, e.g., letters to De Volder, 30 June 1704 G II 268:AG 178–79, 1704 or 1705, G II 275:AG 181; "Antibarbarus Physicus," G VII 344: AG 319–20).[64]

Where do the forces of the SD fit into this metaphysical picture? One answer emerges out of what Leibniz wrote to De Volder in 1704 or 1705:

I don't really eliminate body, but reduce it to what it is. For I show that corporeal mass, which is thought to have something over and above simple substances, is not a substance, but a phenomenon resulting from simple substances, which along have unity and absolute reality. I relegate derivative forces to the phenomena, but I think that it is obvious that primitive forces can be nothing but the internal strivings of simple substances, strivings by means of which they pass from perception to perception in accordance with a fixed law of their nature.

(Letter to De Volder, 1704 or 1705, G II 275: AG 181)[65]

Similarly Leibniz wrote to Des Bosses in 1706:

From a multiplicity of monads results secondary matter, alone with derivative forces, actions, passions, which are only entities through aggregation, and therefore semi-mental, like the rainbow and other well-founded phenomena.   (Letter to Des Bosses, 11 March 1706, G II 306)[66]

This suggests the following picture. The primitive forces, active and passive, now pertain not to corporeal substances, but to the monads; they are now identified with what Leibniz calls appetition, the activity in things by virtue of which a monad passes from one internal state to another. Derivative forces, on the other hand, are relegated to the phenomena. These forces, those that are the direct cause of motion and thus most of interest to the physicist, pertain now to bodies and bodies alone. While grounded in something that is real – the monads or simple substances – they belong to aggregates of monads alone, and thus are irreducibly phenomenal.

But this may not have been Leibniz's considered opinion. The question of the possibility of a genuine composite substance (like the corporeal substances of the correspondence with Arnauld) is one of the main themes of the correspondence with Des Bosses; in these letters Leibniz is trying to figure what would be required for there to be such things in his world of monads.[67] In an appendix to the letter to Des Bosses from 19 August 1715, Leibniz presented a diagrammatic representation of his views on unity and beings by aggregation (G II 506: L 617). He begins with a distinction between things that are genuine individuals, and beings by aggregation. Now, in this scheme, derivative force (here derivative power) appears twice, once as a modification of a composite substance, and once as a "semiaccident," the modification of a "semisubstance," a being by aggregation, which, Leibniz says, derives "from the modifications of [genuine] substances." But primitive active and passive force (here, primitive active and passive power) appears only once in the diagram, in the characterization of a composite substance, which, Leibniz says, "consists in primitive active and passive power, that is, it consists in primary matter, i.e. the principle of resistance, and in substantial form, i.e. the principle of impetus."[68] Interestingly enough, it does not appear on the other side of the chart, in the characterization of semisubstances. In this reading, if there are no genuine composite (corporeal) substances in the world, then all derivative force must be phenomenal. But in that situation, there would be no primitive forces at all in the world, it would seem.[69]

In the end, then, it is not clear exactly how the world of the dynamics, primitive and derivative, active and passive forces is supposed to fit into Leibniz's larger metaphysical picture. But then, what uncertainty there is derives from Leibniz's own uncertainties about the details of that metaphysics, as it evolved from the 1680s to the end of his life.

3.4 Dynamics and the refutation of occasionalism

Leibniz's dynamics was central to his program for physics. In the next section we shall see how his account of force is connected with his conception of the world of the mechanical philosophy and the mathematical laws that govern it. But the dynamics was also connected with an important theme in Leibniz's metaphysics, the rejection of occasionalism.

The doctrine of occasionalism was central to seventeenth-century metaphysics, particularly among the Cartesians. In this widely held view, the changes that one body appears to cause in another upon impact, the changes that a body can cause in a mind in producing a sensation, or a mind can cause in a body in producing a voluntary action are all due directly to God, moving bodies or producing sensations in minds on the occasion of other appropriate events. The doctrine of occasionalism is sometimes presented as having been primarily a solution to the problem of mind/body interaction; since it is inconceivable how minds and bodies can interact, it is argued, seventeenth century philosophers held that it is God who connects the motion of the sensory organs with the sensation in the mind, and the volition in the mind with the voluntary motion of the body. But in reality, the motivation for the doctrine among most seventeenth-century philosophers is somewhat different.[70]

For many of Descartes' later followers, what is central to the doctrine of occasionalism is the denial of the efficacy of finite causes simply by virtue of their finitude. Clerselier, for example, argues for occasionalism by first establishing that only an incorporeal substance can cause motion in body. But, he claims, only an infinite substance, like God, can imprint new motion in the world "because the infinite distance there is between nothingness and being can only be surmounted by a power which is actually infinite."[71] Cordemoy argues similarly. Like Clerselier, he argues that only an incorporeal substance can be the cause of motion in a body, and that this incorporeal substance can only be infinite; he concludes by saying that "our weakness informs us that it is not our mind which makes [a body] move," and so he concludes that what imparts motion to bodies and conserves it can only be "another Mind, to which nothing is lacking, [which] does it [i.e., causes motion] through its will."[72] And finally, the infinitude of God is crucial to the main argument that Malebranche offers for occasionalism in his central work, *De la recherche de la vérité*. The title of the chapter in which Malebranche presents his main arguments for the doctrine is "The most dangerous error in the philosophy of the ancients."[73] And the most dangerous error he is referring to is their belief that finite things can be genuine cause of the effects that they appear to produce, an error that, Malebranche claims, causes people to love and fear things other than God in the belief that they are the genuine causes of their happiness or unhappiness.[74] But why is it an error to believe that finite things can be genuine causes? Malebranche argues as follows:

> As I understand it, a true cause is one in which the mind perceives a necessary connection between the cause and its effect. Now, it is only in an infinitely perfect being that one perceives a necessary connection between its will and its effects. Thus God is the only true cause, and only he truly has the power to move bodies. I further say that it is not conceivable that God would communicate to men or angels the power he has to move bodies.[75]

For these occasionalists, then, God must be the cause of motion in the world because only an infinite substance can be a genuine cause of anything at all.

Leibniz's dynamics is intended as a direct challenge to occasionalism; rather than inert extended bodies shuffled about by a God who is the only source of genuine activity in the world, Leibniz posits genuinely active bodies, bodies that are the source of their own activity, bodies, in short, that genuinely embody forces.

Leibniz offers a number of arguments to this conclusion.[76] One of them was discussed in section 3.1, in connection with the refutation of the Cartesian conception of body as extension. There, Leibniz argues that God gave bodies forces, that is, the ability to act because otherwise he would always have to carry out his commands himself. More generally, Leibniz argues that occasionalism involves a perpetual miracle insofar as on that doctrine, God must carry out his own commands. Leibniz writes to Arnauld:

Properly speaking, God performs a miracle when he does something that surpasses the forces he has given to creatures and conserves in them. . . . Thus . . . we must say . . . that if continuing motion exceeds the force of bodies, then the continuation of the motion is a true miracle. But I believe that corporeal substance has the ability [force] to continue its changes in accordance with the laws God put into its nature and conserves there.
(Letter to Arnauld, 30 April 1687, G II 93: AG 83)

Leibniz also argues that placing force and activity in bodies is necessary for them to exist as genuine entities, independent of God. And so, he writes in section 8 of "On Nature Itself" (1698):

The very substance of things consists in a force for acting and being acted upon. From this it follows that persisting things cannot be produced if no force lasting through time can be imprinted upon them by the divine power. Were that so, it would follow that no created substance, no soul would remain numerically the same, and thus nothing would be conserved by God, and consequently everything would merely be certain vanishing or unstable modifications and phantasms, so to speak, of one permanent divine substance. Or, what comes to the same thing, God would be the very nature or substance of all things, a sort of doctrine of ill repute which a recent writer, subtle indeed, though profane, either introduced to the world or revived.
(G IV 508–9: AG 159–60; cf. G IV 396–97: AG 253–54; G IV 567–68: L 583; SD part I, par. 12, GM 242: AG 125)

The argument is obscure, to be sure. But Leibniz is attempting to argue here that unless we follow him away from the occasionalist and toward the dynamical conception of body that he is arguing for, we will find ourselves in Spinoza's camp, where everything exists only as a mode of God, a doctrine he regarded as both false and dangerous.

It is certainly too much to say that Leibniz's physics constitutes a "scientific" refutation of the doctrine of occasionalism; though connected with his dynamics, the arguments against occasionalism have a definite metaphysical flavor. But it is true that the dynamical world of primitive and derivative forces is deeply intertwined with a central aspect of Leibniz's metaphysical program, returning to the world the activity that the Cartesians had improperly removed.

4. MECHANIST PHYSICS: SPACE, MOTION, AND THE LAWS OF MOTION

In the previous section, we examined Leibniz's conception of force, that which underlies the reality of the world for Leibniz. Now we must turn to the physics proper, the mechanist account of the world of extended bodies moving in space that Leibniz grounds in his dynamics. We begin with an account of space and motion, the basic notions in this mechanistic physics, before turning to Leibniz's account of the laws of motion.

4.1 Space and void

The question as to what space is, and whether a vacuum and empty space is possible, is one of the most vexed questions in early modern science. A full history of those notions as treated in thinkers before Leibniz is impossible in the context of this essay.[77] Briefly, coming into the seventeenth century, there are at least two important strains of thought. For Aristotle and his followers, the notion of space independent of body is incoherent; though certain theological concessions had to be made to accommodate divine freedom – God's ability to move the world as a whole if he so chose – what was basic was body, and space was an abstraction from what really was. For the ancient atomists whose doctrines were being actively revived in the early seventeenth century, and for critics of Aristotelianism, space was a something of a sort, something that had a real existence outside of body, and which could exist without body.[78] This same debate continued into the seventeenth century. Descartes and his followers pursued what was basically an Aristotelian line, denying the independent reality of space and the possibility of a vacuum.[79] Others, including the atomist Pierre Gassendi and Blaise Pascal, bolstered by what they interpreted as new experimental evidence, argued for a space that could exist independently of body, both empty and full.[80] The most formidable adherent of this latter view in the seventeenth century was Sir Isaac Newton. Newton argued for a conception of space that was radically independent of the bodies that it may or may not contain. While he recognized that we normally understand space in terms of the sensible bodies that occupy it, in his *Principia* of 1687 he argued that physics requires what he called absolute space:

Absolute space, in its own nature, without relation to anything external, remains always similar and immovable. Relative space is some movable dimension or measure of the absolute spaces, which our senses determine by its position to bodies, and which is vulgarly taken for immovable space. . . . Because the parts of [absolute] space cannot be seen or distinguished from one another by our senses, therefore in their stead we use sensible measures of them. . . . But in philosophical disquisitions we ought to abstract from our senses, and consider things themselves, distinct from what are only sensible measures of them.[81]

In the second edition of 1713, Newton went so far as to identify this absolute space with God himself:

He endures forever, and is everywhere present, and by existing always and everywhere, he constitutes duration and space. . . . He is omnipresent not only virtually, but also substantially; for virtue cannot subsist without substance. In him are all things contained and moved.[82]

For Newton, then, space is something quite real, something quite independent of the bodies that exist in it.[83]

Leibniz was interested in the notion of space from his earliest writings. Though there is a strong suggestion in some of his earlier writings that he thought of space as something distinct from body[84], in his mature writings he quite clearly denies the independent reality of space, particularly in opposition to the specific form that that doctrine was given in Newton's writings. In a typical passage Leibniz wrote in 1695, the same year as the SD, a reply to Foucher's objections to the "New System" he holds:

Extension or space and the surfaces, lines, and points one can conceive in it are only relations of order or orders of coexistence, both for the actually existing thing and for the possible thing one can put in its place.

(G IV 491:AG 146)

Leibniz explains this at somewhat greater length in his responses to Samuel Clarke, part of the important correspondence between the two at the very end of Leibniz's life, where Leibniz's views are contrasted with those of his great rival, Newton. Leibniz writes:

> The author [i.e., Clarke] contends that space does not depend upon the situation of bodies. I answer: It is true, it does not depend upon such or such a situation of bodies, but it is that order which renders bodies capable of being situated, and by which they have a situation among themselves when they exist together, as time is that order with respect to their successive position. But if there were no creatures, space and time would only be in the ideas of God. (Fourth letter to Clarke, par. 41, G VII 376–77: AG 331)[85]

As was the case with extension, discussed in section 3.1, space is just the order of things, and presupposes the existence of things to be ordered, bodies, ultimately substances, which are the only things that are real in the proper sense for Leibniz. And so, Leibniz holds, space would not exist were there not bodies and the substances which underlie them; as he wrote in an untitled essay from 1689, "space without matter is something imaginary" (C 590: AG 91).

In addition to the general argument against Newton from his own definition of space, Leibniz offers another kind of argument. Responding to Clarke, Leibniz writes:

> I say, then, that if space were an absolute being, something would happen for which it would be impossible that there should be a sufficient reason – which is against my axiom. And I can prove it thus. Space is something absolutely uniform, and without the things placed in it, one point of space absolutely does not differ in anything from another point of space. But, from hence it follows (supposing space to be something in itself, besides the order of bodies among themselves) that it is impossible there should be a reason why God, preserving the same situations of bodies among themselves, should have placed them in space after one certain particular manner and not otherwise – why everything was not placed the quite contrary way, for instance, by changing east into west. But if space is nothing else but this order or relation, and is nothing at all without bodies but the possibility of placing them, then those two states, the one such as it is now, the other supposed to be quite the contrary way, would not at all differ from one another. Their difference therefore is only to be found in our chimerical supposition of the reality of space in itself.
> (Third letter to Clarke, par. 5, G VII 363–64: AG 325)

If Newton is right, Leibniz argues, then there is a real difference between our world, as it is, and another world in which the relations between things are the same, but east and west are reversed, for example. But since Newton's absolute space is completely uniform, and one region interchangeable with every other, there can be no reason for God to prefer one configuration to another. And so, if there is absolute space as Newton supposes, then in creating a world in space, God must violate the Principle of Sufficient Reason. Leibniz's conclusion is that such a space cannot, therefore, exist. Leibniz supplements this argument with another. Suppose God were to reverse everything in the universe, as he could if Newton were right. Then we would have a new state of the universe, distinct from the original one, but entirely indistinguishable from it. Such an action on God's part would, thus, be "a change without any change," and God would have acted without doing anything, something Leibniz finds absurd (Fourth letter to Clarke, par. 13, G VII 373: AG 328–29).[86]

Though he agrees with Descartes and the Cartesian tradition that space is not something independent of the bodies that occupy it, Leibniz takes a position on the void that differs from that of the Cartesians in an interesting way. For Descartes, the essence of body is extension, of course. And, he reasons, since there can be no accident without a subject in which it can inhere, whenever there is extension, there must be extended substance, that is, body. From this it follows that where there are no bodies, there can be no space. Furthermore, he concludes, there can be no vacuum, no space (region of extension) that lacks body.[87] Sometimes Leibniz expresses views on the void very similar to those Descartes held. Leibniz asks Clarke, for example:

If space is a property or attribute, it must be the property of some substance. But of what substance will that bounded space be an affect or property, which the persons I am arguing with suppose to be between two bodies? (Fourth letter to Clarke, par. 8, G VII 372: AG 328; cf fifth letter, par. 48, G VII 402: AG 339)[88]

But elsewhere he takes a different view. As discussed above in section 3.1, extension for Leibniz must be the extension of some quality or other, and cannot constitute the essence of body or anything else. Since extension is a relative notion, and presupposes something that is extended, Leibniz does grant that it is possible to conceive of an extension that is not the extension of force that constitutes body.[89] But while an extended space without body is thus possible for Leibniz in a way in which it isn't for Descartes, it raises other problems. One problem is put succinctly in the "First Truths" paper of 1689:

There is no vacuum. For the different parts of empty space would then be perfectly similar and mutually congruent and could not be distinguished from one another. And so they would differ in number alone, which is absurd.   (C 521–22: AG 33)[90]

Thus, Leibniz argues, the principle of the identity of indiscernibles argues against empty space. Elsewhere, he appeals to the principle of plenitude. Writing to Johann Bernoulli on 13/23 January 1699, he argues:

I don't say that the vacuum, the atom, and other things of this sort are impossible, but only that they are not in agreement with divine wisdom. . . . From an infinity of possibles, God chose, in accordance with his wisdom, that which is most appropriate. However, it is obvious that the vacuum . . . leaves sterile and uncultivated places, places in which something additional could have been produced, while preserving everything else. For such places to remain contradicts wisdom.   (GM III 565: AG 170–71)[91]

And finally, Leibniz argues in the letters to Clarke that were there empty spaces in the world, then there would be a violation of the Principle of Sufficient Reason, his master principle. For, Leibniz asserts, "it is impossible there should be any principle to determine what proportion of matter there ought to be, out of all the possible degrees from a plenum to a void, or from a void to a plenum" (Fourth letter to Clarke, G VII 378: AG 332). For Leibniz's God it must thus be all or nothing, and since there is something, it must be all.

4.2 Motion

"If motion . . . is something real," Leibniz wrote to Huygens in June of 1694, "it must have a *subject*" (Letter to Huygens, 12/22 June 1694, GM II 184: AG 308). But, as Leibniz had explained to Arnauld some years earlier, this is precisely what motion as commonly understood lacks:

Motion, insofar as it is only a modification of extension and a change of neighborhood [i.e., as Descartes defined it] contains something imaginary, so that one doesn't know how to determine to which among the subjects changing it belongs.   (Letter to Arnauld, 30 April 1687, G II 98: AG 86)

The problem that Leibniz is pointing out here is twofold. One problem simply derives from the widely held view that motion, taken by itself, is just the change of spatial relations among various bodies. If this is all that motion is, strictly speaking, then in the case where bodies A and B are in motion with respect to one another, we are free to consider A at rest and B in motion or B at rest and A in motion. "Motion, in all mathematical rigor, is nothing but a change in the positions of bodies with respect to one another," Leibniz wrote in an untitled essay in 1689, "and so, motion is not something absolute, but consists in a relation" (C 590: AG 91). This observation is, of course, not unique to Leibniz, nor is it particularly deep. But Leibniz also holds a deeper and more characteristically Leibnizian view on the matter. Now, motion might be relative in this first, weak sense, and yet one might claim that it is possible to perform an experiment to determine whether it is really A or really B that is in motion. The most celebrated argument of this sort is Newton's bucket experiment. In his *Principia*, Newton argued that the way the water climbs the sides of a twirling bucket shows that it is the bucket that is moving in a universe at rest, and not the universe twirling around a resting bucket of water.[92] And so Newton distinguished between relative motion – motion with respect to an arbitrarily chosen rest point, and absolute motion – motion with respect to absolute space.[93] Leibniz knew of Newton's claim, and just as he rejected absolute space, he rejected Newton's absolute motion. Leibniz wrote to Huygens that:

Mr. Newton recognized the equivalence of hypotheses in the case of rectilinear motions. But with respect to circular motions, he believes that the effort that circulating bodies make to recede from the center or from the axis of circulation allows us to know their absolute motion. But I have reasons that make me believe that nothing disrupts the general law of equivalence.

(GM II 184–85: AG 308)[94]

Leibniz's arguments are difficult and obscure.[95] But the basic idea seems to have been this: everyone grants the equivalence of hypotheses for rectilinear motion, that is, we cannot perform any experiments that will allow us to tell whether we are in uniform rectilinear motion or at rest. But, Leibniz seems to have reasoned, in the billiard-ball world of the mechanical philosophy, all curvilinear and accelerated motion is made up of (very short) segments of uniform rectilinear motion, the direction or speed of which is changed by collision with other bodies. And insofar as he thought that we cannot distinguish between a uniformly moving A colliding with a resting B, and a moving B colliding with a resting A, he seems to have thought that in the real, mechanical world, at least, the equivalence of hypotheses should hold for curvilinear and accelerated motions as much as it does for uniform rectilinear motions. And so he thought that he could give a demonstration that *no* experiments could allow one to distinguish any frame from any other and establish that the one is the true rest frame and the other isn't; this is what he calls the doctrine of the equivalence of hypotheses, stated (and proved) as proposition 19 of part II, section 3 of the *Dynamica* (GM VI 507–8).[96] And so, according to Leibniz's doctrine, not even an angel could discern whether Copernicus is right in holding that the Earth moves, or Ptolemy and Tycho are right in preferring a moving sun. In an interesting piece, written, significantly enough in 1689, during his year in Italy, where the memory of the condemnation of Galileo was still very much alive, Leibniz wrote:

And whether the bodies are moving freely or colliding with one another, it is a wonderful law of nature that no eye, wherever in matter it might be placed, has a sure criterion for telling from the phenomena where there is motion, how much motion there is and of what sort it is, *or even whether God moves everything around it, or whether he moves that very eye itself.*

(C 590: AG 91)[97]

Nothing in the world of physics taken strictly, that is, nothing in the mechanist world of size, shape, and motion can determine whether a given body is in motion or at rest, *mathematico rigore.* And so, Leibniz argues, motion so understood lacks a determinate subject, and lacking a subject, cannot itself really be a constituent of the world. Behind this view, of course, is a metaphysical assumption or two. Leibniz finds it absolutely unintelligible that there could be a property that is not really a property of some one thing, a property that is *irreducibly* relational. What exactly this means is not altogether clear.[98] But, Leibniz inferred, if motion is to be real, it must be grounded in something that is not mere relation, something that is a real property of real things.

Though Leibniz tried a number of solutions,[99] the one he finally settled on was *force:* "One cannot really . . . say to which subject motion belongs, and thus there is nothing real in motion except force and the power [*potentia*] things are endowed with," Leibniz wrote in a characteristic passage from 1683 (VE II 294; cf. *Discourse,* par. 18, G IV 444: AG 51; SD, part II, par. 2, GM VI 247–48: AG 130–1; G IV 369: L 393; G IV 400: AG 256; G IV 523: L 496; VE III 481, 488, 495). The ontology of force we discussed in section 3 gives Leibniz a way of grounding the reality of motion. Though motion or rest taken narrowly, the change of position or the lack thereof, cannot be attributed to individual bodies in a nonarbitrary way, Leibniz claims that there is a real fact of the matter about the force that is the cause of the motion we see, which really can be said to pertain to one body or another. As Leibniz wrote in the *Discourse on Metaphysics* (1686):

Motion . . . is not a thing entirely real. . . . But force or the proximate cause of these changes is something more real, and there are sufficient grounds to attribute it to one body rather than to another. Furthermore, it is only in this way that we can know to which body the motion belongs.

(*Discourse,* par. 18, G IV 444: AG 51)

Though motion understood as change of place is relative, strictly speaking, the appeal beyond the world of extension and its changes to force can break that relativity, Leibniz seems to think, and allow us to talk intelligibly about the *cause* of motion as pertaining to one body rather than another. Motion so grounded can enter the world of physics.

Leibniz's view on motion raises an interesting question, though. Motion is completely relative, and by the doctrine of the equivalence of hypotheses, there are no physical marks to distinguish real motion from apparent; every frame of reference is as good as every other, at least from the point of view of physics proper, that is, if we limit ourselves to the consideration of extended bodies in motion.[100] But, Leibniz argues, underlying motion there must be force, the cause of motion, something that goes beyond the mechanist's world of extension and its modes, something that really pertains to one body rather than another. There is, in this sense, a correct frame for determining motion, the frame in which the motions observed are the effects of real underlying forces which are their causes. *But such a frame could never be identified.* Motion has a foundation, in a sense, but one that makes no real (or apparent) difference in the world of physics; in this way the theory of motion would seem to float free of its foundations in the notion of force.[101]

The fact that we cannot link observed motions to some particular underlying forces should not, by itself, undermine Leibniz's project; Leibniz hadn't intended that force should ground physics in that crude and direct way, I think. What force explains is that the attribution of motion to the world makes sense *at all*. For Leibniz, all real properties of things in the world ultimately reside in genuine individuals. If that is the case, it is evident why mere motion, the mere change of place, just won't do; for it to be intelligible that there is motion at all, there must be something nonrelativistic, something that is an absolute and nonarbitrary property of some individual thing, that is the cause and ground of motion. This is where force comes in. The present state of the world must have a ground in reality, in *some* configuration of forces; *something* must be there, though Leibniz cannot say *what specifically*. Nor does it matter *which* of the infinity of possible configurations of force there are in the world from the point of view of physics; it is only important that there is some one such configuration.

But the appeal to force grounds more than just the reality of motion: it grounds its laws as well. Despite the fact that we cannot determine where the real causes of motion lie in nature, these forces have a crucial role to play in the derivation of Leibniz's laws of motion. This is what we shall see in the following section.

4.3 *The laws of motion*

In discussing Leibniz's views on the laws of motion, it will be useful to begin where Leibniz himself began, with the critique of others, particularly Descartes.

Let us begin with the Cartesian conservation principle. Basic to Descartes' physics was the principle of the conservation of quantity of motion. According to Descartes, God sustains the universe from moment to moment and, in doing so, preserves the same quantity of motion in the world as a whole, as measured by the size times the speed of each of the bodies in the world.[102] While not without challenge, it was still held by many in the 1670s, '80s, and '90s. It was the Cartesian conservation principle that Leibniz had to confront – and refute – in the late 1670s when formulating his own physics, and it was Leibniz's published critique of the Cartesian conservation principle in the BD of 1686 that raised one of the most visible public controversies in Leibniz's career, as Cartesians came out of the woodwork to defend what many took as the foundation of their physics. Leibniz was not the first to attack Descartes' conservation principle, and the specifics of his arguments owe much to others, particularly Huygens.[103] But the liveliness of the exchanges that followed the BD suggests that Leibniz's point was still news to many. This controversy, the so-called *vis viva* (living force) controversy, resulted in numerous refinements and variants on the original argument, as formulated in the late 1670s and published in 1686.[104] But leaving all details aside, the arguments Leibniz developed in this connection sort themselves out into two groups, *a priori*, and *a posteriori*.

Let us begin with the *a posteriori* arguments, which likely date back as early as 1676. This group of arguments shares a common strategy and a number of common assumptions to argue to a number of interconnected conclusions. The basic idea behind these arguments is that bodies in motion have an ability to do work by virtue of being in motion; this is the sensible effect of what Leibniz came to call their living force (*vis viva*). This ability to do work can be compared in different bodies by comparing the actual work they accomplish in consuming that force. What Leibniz chooses to look at is the height to which a body in uniform horizontal motion could raise itself when that horizontal motion is turned to the vertical and consumed in ascent; the height to which a body with a given speed can raise itself from the horizontal is a measure of the force it has by virtue of having that motion, Leibniz argues.[105] Of course, by the equivalence of hypotheses (see section 4.2) we cannot know where the real force is in the world, whether the body moving on a horizontal surface has the force, or whether it is the horizontal surface that does, for instance. But by the same principle of the equivalence of hypotheses, we are also free to attribute the force to the horizontally moving body, if we choose; the laws of physics will come out the same. Certain assumptions, then, allow Leibniz to draw his conclusions. Most basic is the principle of the equality of cause and effect, the principle that "the whole effect has the same power as its full cause, so that one cannot obtain perpetual motion without violating the order of things through an increase in the power of

the effect beyond that of its cause" (*Dynamica*, specimen praeliminare, GM VI 287: AG 106).[106] This metaphysical principle,
whose significance Leibniz first seems to have realized in 1676 at
the time when he first began to move away from his early system,
is central to his derivation of the laws of motion. In the *a posteriori* arguments we are examining, it is used to establish that
force, the ability to do work, must be conserved in a closed system, and that the speed a heavy body in free fall acquires in
falling a distance *d* is sufficient to raise it to that same distance *d*.
In addition to the principle of the equality of cause and effect, in
the *a posteriori* arguments Leibniz assumes the Galilean law of
free fall, that the speed a heavy body falls is proportional to the
square root of the distance fallen, that is, that the distance fallen
is proportional to the square of the velocity acquired through free
fall. This assumption is, of course, *a posteriori*.

These assumptions allow Leibniz to establish that: (1) force (understood as the ability to do work) is not the same as the quantity of
motion of the Cartesians; (2) the quantity of motion of the Cartesians is not conserved in the universe; and (3) what is conserved is
mv^2. That force and quantity of motion are different follows out
directly from the assumptions Leibniz makes. Consider two bodies;
let *A* be one unit in size, and *B* be four. Now, Leibniz reasons, it takes
exactly as much work to raise *A* four feet as it does to raise *B* one
foot, since one can regard the larger body *B* as being made up of four
smaller bodies, each identical to *A*, and each of which is being raised
one foot. (See figure 1.) And so, when *A* and *B* fall through those
respective distances, and their speeds converted to the horizontal,
they should have exactly the same force, that is, ability to do work,
for by the principle of the equality of cause and effect, the velocity
that *A* and *B* acquire in falling is sufficient to raise those bodies to
their original heights, and we have assumed that it takes as much
work to raise *A* four feet as it does to raise *B* one. Now, Leibniz
argues, when *A* falls, by the Galilean law of free fall it will acquire
two degrees of speed, while *B* acquires one. But if that is the case,
then after the fall, *A* will have two units of quantity of motion while
B will have four. So, since *A* and *B* have the same ability to do work
(force), it follows that force and quantity of motion cannot be the
same.[107] As noted above, it follows directly from the principle of the
equality of cause and effect that force, the ability to do work must be

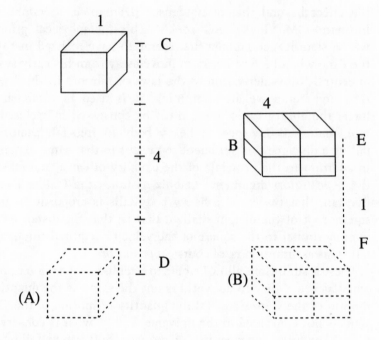

Figure 1

conserved in the universe as a whole.[108] That Cartesian quantity of
motion is not conserved then follows directly from the conservation
of force together with the conclusion that force and quantity of
motion are distinct and different.[109] But the result can also be established directly from the principle of the equality of cause and effect.
For, Leibniz can show, if it is the Cartesian's quantity of motion that
is conserved, one could build a perpetual motion machine, a machine that would create the ability to do work out of nothing at all,
in obvious violation of the the principle of the equality of cause and
effect.[110] That mv^2 is the correct measure of force, and thus that it is
mv^2 that is conserved in the world can also be established using a
variant of this argument. Consider bodies A and B as above. It is
evident that in the case at hand, while A and B have different quantities of motion, their size times the square of their speeds will be
equal. It is easy to generalize this, and show that *whenever* they
have equal force, the size times the square of their speed will be
equal, and that whenever this is violated, the ability to do work will·

either be gained or lost, in violation of the principle of the equality of cause and effect (see, e.g., SD, part I, par. 16, GM VI 244–45: AG 128). Similarly, one can show that a perpetual motion machine can always be constructed unless it is mv^2 that is conserved.

But as striking as the *a posteriori* argument is, it has an obvious imperfection. Insofar as it depends on the behavior of heavy bodies in free fall, it depends on certain contingent features of our world that have nothing to do with the basic laws of physics. This sort of criticism is particularly problematic for Leibniz and many of his contemporaries, who believed that gravity derived from the particular configuration of etherial vortices that surround the earth; were the vortices different, the law of free fall might also be altogether different, resulting in a different quantity conserved, it would appear.[111] In response to such a difficulty, Leibniz attempted to formulate an *a priori* demonstration of his conservation law. The *a priori* demonstration first appears in the *Dynamica* of 1689–90, and in Leibniz's correspondence starting in 1696 (see *Dynamica*, specimen praeliminare, GM VI 291–92: AG 110–11; *Dynamica* GM VI 345–67; letter to De Volder, 24 March/3 April 1699, G II 172–74; letter to Bayle, 1699–1701, G III 59–60; SD, part I, par. 15, GM VI 243–44: AG 127). Leibniz gives a particularly simple exposition of the argument in a letter to Bayle from the late 1690s:

In the uniform motion of a single body (1) the action of traversing two places in two hours is double the action of traversing one place in one hour (since the first action contains the second precisely two times); (2) the action of traversing one place in one hour is double the action of traversing one place in two hours (or better, actions which produce the same effect are proportional to their speeds). And thus (3) the action of traversing two places in two hours is four times the action of traversing one place in two hours. This demonstration shows that a moving body receiving a double or triple motion so as to be able to accomplish a double or triple effect in a given time, receives a quadruple or ninefold action. Thus, actions are proportional to the square of speeds. Thus it turns out, most happily, that this accords with my measure of force derived either from experience, or on the grounds of the avoidance of perpetual mechanical motion.   (G III 60)

Though it is not at all obvious that "action" as understood in this argument is equivalent to force as understood in the *a posteriori* arguments, as the ability to do work, Leibniz clearly identifies the two,[112] and takes this *a priori* argument to establish the same conclusion as some of the *a posteriori* arguments do, that force is measured by mv^2, and not by Cartesian quantity of motion. Once this is established, the conservation of mv^2 follows directly from the principle of the equality of cause and effect, as above with the *a posteriori* arguments. Despite its surface simplicity, this argument hides a tangle of complexity.[113] But nevertheless, it is obvious why such a strategy should be attractive to Leibniz.

Leibniz's most visible attack on Cartesian physics concerned the conservation principle. But Leibniz also set himself against Descartes' account of impact. Much progress had been made in understanding impact in the years since Descartes first set out his rules, and unlike the conservation principle, only the most blindly dedicated Cartesian could follow the master on the question of impact by the time Leibniz was working out his own mature physics.[114] In this way Leibniz's critique of Descartes' rules of impact did not have the kind of topical interest that the critique of the conservation principle had for his contemporaries.[115] But, nevertheless, Leibniz's critique of the Cartesian laws of impact shows another interesting feature of his own physics.

In his *Principles of Philosophy* of 1644, Descartes set out a general law of impact, followed by seven rules that applied the law to specific cases of direct impact, the situation in which two bodies collide on a straight line. Descartes' law is in two parts. First, if a body B collides with another body C that is "stronger" than it is, it will rebound with the same speed it had originally. However, if B is stronger than C, B will set C into motion, and the two bodies will move in such a way that the total quantity of motion, size times speed, is the same before and after the collision. For bodies in motion, the "strength" of a body is measured by its quantity of motion; when B is in motion and C at rest, then the "strength" of C in collision with B is the size of C times the speed of B.[116]

One of Leibniz's criticisms of this supposed law of impact follows directly out of his critique of the conservation principle. Above we discussed Descartes' claim that the total quantity of motion in the world as a whole is conserved. But Descartes also held that the conservation principle is satisfied in collision; on Descartes' law of impact, the final speeds of two bodies in impact are determined in such a way that the total quantity of motion in the system is the same before and after the collision. Leibniz found it very easy to use the sorts of arguments he used against the general conservation principle to show that Descartes' law of impact could result in outcomes in which the ability to do work in two bodies is either greatly increased or greatly decreased after impact, (see e.g., letter to Bayle, 9 January 1687, G III 45–46; GM VI 123–24).[117] But more interesting is another kind of criticism Leibniz offered.

Important to Leibniz's mature physics is the principle of continuity. In its first public statement in 1687, in a short essay responding to Malebranche's attack on the BD, Leibniz presents the principle as follows:

When the differences between two instances in a given series or that which is presupposed can be diminished until it becomes smaller than any given quantity whatever, the corresponding difference in what is sought or in their results must of necessity also be diminished or become less than any given quantity whatever. Or to put it more commonly, when two instances or data approach each other continuously, so that one at last passes over into the others, it is necessary for their consequences or results (or the unknown) to do so also.   ("Letter of Mr. Leibniz . . .", G III 52: L 351)[118]

Or, to put it more commonly still, "no change happens through a leap" (SD, part II, par. 3, GM VI 248: AG 131). Later we shall see some of the positive consequences this principle has for Leibniz's conception of the physical world, how he uses the principle of continuity to establish that all bodies are elastic to some degree. But it also shows the evident falsity of Descartes' law of impact, Leibniz argues. Consider two bodies, B and C, moving with equal speed in opposite directions on the same line. Suppose first that B and C are equal (case 1). Then, according to Descartes' laws, both B and C will rebound in the opposite direction with the same speed they originally had. But if B is even the slightest bit larger than C, then B will be "stronger" than C, and B will continue in its motion, while C will reverse its motion, keeping its original speed.[119] But, Leibniz notes, "this is an enormous leap from one extreme to another," in violation of his principle of continuity; for however small we make the difference between the sizes of B and C, the outcomes will be the same, and will be radically different than if the two bodies were of the same size (see "Letter of Mr. Leibniz . . .", G III 53: L 352). In his 1692 comments on Descartes' *Principles of Philosophy*, Leibniz works the idea out at greater length, and shows the discontinuities in Descartes' rules of impact when we consider two bodies of the same size, and vary the speed and direction of their motion (see G IV 381–84: L 402–3, 412, n. 34).[120]

In this way, Leibniz shows that Descartes' laws of impact cannot be correct. Leibniz's own account of impact is found in the *Dynamica*, as well as in an essay, "Essay de Dynamique sur les Loix du Mouvement . . ." (ED) that probably dates from the early 1690s.[121] Leibniz's account of impact is grounded in a series of conservation laws which, he argues, must be satisfied in impact. Together these laws determine the outcome of a collision between any (elastic) bodies.

First of all, Leibniz holds that the total *absolute force* (living force) in a system of bodies is conserved in an elastic collision; that is, the sum of mv^2 over all of the bodies is the same both before and after a collision. And so the conservation of living force applies not only to the universe as a whole, but to any closed system of (elastic) bodies within the universe (see GM VI 227–28, 440, 488–89).[122] It should be emphasized that while the conservation of mv^2 in the universe as a whole is absolute and without exception, Leibniz holds, in impact this only holds for perfectly elastic collisions, collisions in which no motion is lost to the smaller parts of bodies. Consider bodies A and B, with m_A the size of body A, and m_B the size of B. Then if A and B are not perfectly elastic, if in collision, motion is lost to their parts, it can happen after the collision that the sum "$m_A v^2 + m_B y^2$" is *less than* the sum "$m_A x^2 + m_B z^2$" because of force transmitted to the smaller parts of the two bodies; while such a collision does not result in a loss of total force in the universe, of course, force is not conserved in the motion of the bodies A and B (see ED, GM VI 230–31).

Next is what Leibniz calls the *conservation of respective speed*. Consider two bodies, A and B, moving on a straight line, body A with velocity v before collision and x after, and body B with velocity y before collision and z after.[123] (It is important to remember here that we are dealing with velocity, a signed (vector) quantity, and not speed; the sign, positive or negative, indicates the direction of the motion.) Then, Leibniz argues, the following equation holds for elastic bodies in collision:

$$v - y = z - x$$

Leibniz's reasoning here seems to be something like this. In colliding with one another, perfectly elastic bodies do not lose what Leibniz calls their respective force, their ability to act on one another.
Furthermore, Leibniz argues, this respective force depends only on
their relative velocity; if A approaches a resting B with velocity v,
from the point of view of impact it is the same as if B approached A
with that same speed. Now, let A and B be connected by means of an
elastic cord, so that they can act on one another even when moving
in opposite directions. In this circumstance, the two bodies can act
on one another either coming (through impact) or going (through the
cord). Here Leibniz argues that the respective force will be the same
when the relative speeds, either A and B approaching one another or
receding, are the same. And so, Leibniz argues, when A and B collide
elastically, their relative velocities must be the same before and after
the collision, otherwise their respective force would differ before
and after the collision.[124] It is important to note that as with the
conservation of absolute force, the conservation of respective speed
is limited to perfectly elastic collisions; when motion can be lost to
the smaller parts to make up A or B, then respective force can be lost
and this equation will not necessarily be satisfied.

In addition to these, Leibniz presents a third law, what he calls the
conservation of common progress. In accordance with this law, the
following equation holds for all bodies in collision:

$$m_A v + m_B y = m_A x + m_B z$$

This law, of course, is what has come to be called the conservation of momentum, though Leibniz never used the term. The
quantity, size times velocity that appears in this law must be
carefully distinguished from the Cartesian notion of quantity of
motion. According to Descartes and his followers, what is conserved in impact (and in the world as a whole) is size times *speed*,
a scalar quantity that does not involve direction. While Descartes
is concerned about what happens to directionality of motion in
impact, considerations of directionality don't enter into his conservation principle in any way; a body hitting another and rebound-
ing with the same speed has the exact same quantity of motion
before and after the collision.[125] In Leibniz's physics what is conserved is not size times speed, but size times *velocity*, a vector

quantity, speed together with direction; this he calls progressive or directional force, to distinguish it from the Cartesian notion of quantity of motion. And so, when a body reverses its motion after collision, its progressive or directional force is changed. Leibniz derives the conservation of common progress in the following way. He first argues that in a (closed) system of bodies, no collision among the bodies should change the speed or direction of the center of gravity of the aggregate, a conclusion that he takes to follow from the conservation of living force in the universe. And from this it follows, Leibniz argues, that in the aggregate, the totality of progressive or directional force must remain the same, whatever collisions there might be among the bodies in the aggregate. This law, it should be observed, holds for both elastic and nonelastic collisions; even if motion is lost to the smaller parts of larger bodies, the center of gravity of the aggregate should continue at the same speed in the same direction.[126]

These three laws are interconnected, Leibniz argues, and show how from any two the third can be derived (see ED, GM VI 228). Moreover, any two of them are sufficient for solving the problem of collision between two elastic bodies. Nevertheless, it is the conservation of absolute force, mv^2 in impact that Leibniz considers the most significant. In the beginning of the ED, Leibniz complains that many who have come to recognize the failure of the Cartesian conservation principle "have thrown themselves to the other extreme, and recognize no conservation of anything absolute that can take the place of the quantity of motion" (ED, GM VI 216). But, Leibniz says, in the conservation of mv^2 we have the conservation of an absolute, that is, a quantity that does not involve direction, unlike the conservation of respective speed or the conservation of common progress, which inevitably involve signed quantities. Leibniz writes in the ED, immediately following the exposition of the conservation of absolute force:

This equation has an excellent feature, that all of the variations in sign which can only come from the different direction of the speeds v, x, z, y, cease, because all of the letters which express these speeds are here raised to the square. For $-y$ and $+y$ have the same square, $+y^2$, so that all of the different directions mean nothing here. And it is also for this that this equation gives something absolute, independent of respective speeds or of the progress in a certain direction. We have only to estimate the different masses and speeds, without taking account of the direction of these speeds.

(GM VI 227–28)

While Leibniz is not explicit here, I suspect that his preference for an absolute conservation principle is connected with his own views on relations. For Leibniz, as we noted above in section 4.2, in connection with motion, something that is merely relative is not really real insofar as it cannot really have a subject. Absolute force, mv^2, though, is something that can be attributed to some one body; it is a present property of a body by virtue of which it has the ability to do work in the future.

Leibniz's arguments for the laws of motion all depend in one way or another on certain metaphysical principles, particularly the principle of the equality of cause and effect and the principle of continuity. Because of this, Leibniz argues, the laws of motion are contingent, and display the wisdom of God in choosing this best of all possible worlds.[127] Leibniz writes, for example, in the *Theodicy:*

I have discovered . . . that the laws of motion which are actually found in nature, and are verified by experience, are not in truth absolutely demonstrable, as a geometrical proposition would be. They do not derive entirely from the principle of necessity, but from the principle of perfection and order; they are an effect of the choice and the wisdom of God. I can demonstrate these laws in many ways, but it is always necessary to assume something which is not absolutely geometrically necessary.

(*Theodicy,* part I, par. 345 G VI 319; cf. *Discourse,* par. 21, G IV 446–47: AG 53–54)

But if the laws of motion are contingent in this way, how can Leibniz establish them by argument?

In his writings on physics, Leibniz simply assumes the metaphysical principles he needs and does the derivations from them, in essence simply assuming that the world we live in is a world created by a benevolent and wise God, who imposes such principles of order on his creation. This assumption is further supported by the fact that the laws so derived seem to be able to explain what actually happens in the world of bodies. And so, for example, when discussing with de Volder why the principle of the equality of cause and effect must be satisfied in our world, he remarks that a world "in which matter at rest obeys that which puts it in motion without any resistance" is both possible and imaginable, but, he notes, "such a world would be mere chaos." Leibniz continues:

And so, two things on which I always rely here, success in experience and the principle of order, brought it about that I later came to see that God created matter in such a way that it contains a certain repugnance to motion.
(Letter to De Volder, 24 March/3 April 1699, G II 170–71:AG 172)

Experience and our belief that the world is not a chaos then lead us away from the geometrical conception of the laws of motion Leibniz represents himself as having held in the TMA and the HPN, and toward the contingent laws he presents in his later writings; in this way we can have a kind of demonstration of the contingent truths which govern our mechanical world.

Leibniz sometimes argues in the other direction, using the empirical adequacy of the laws derived from metaphysical principles to argue for the existence of a wise and benevolent creator who laid down the metaphysical principles that govern motion. In the passage from the *Theodicy* quoted above Leibniz ends as follows:

These beautiful laws are a marvelous proof of an intelligent and free being [i.e., God], against the system of absolute and brute necessity of Straton and Spinoza.
(*Theodicy*, pt. I, par. 345, G VI 319; cf. *Principles of Nature and Grace*, par. 11, G VI 603: AG 211)

The dependence of the laws of motion on God's choice of the best of all possible worlds and the consequent contingency of the laws of motion are very important to Leibniz. For one, it provides a nice argument against those, like Spinoza, who see everything as necessary. Leibniz writes to Remond:

You are right, Sir, to judge that [my dynamics] is in good part the foundations of my system, because one learns there the difference between the truths whose necessity is brute and geometrical, and those truths which have their source in fitness and final causes.
(Letter to Remond, 22 June 1715, G III 645)

But also important to Leibniz was the fact that the contingency of the laws of motion brings God into the mechanical philosophy. He writes, for example, in the "*Tentamen Anagogicum*" of 1696:

This consideration gives us the middle term needed to satisfy both truth and piety . . . : all natural phenomena could be explained mechanically if we understood them well enough, but the principles of mechanics themselves cannot be explained geometrically, since they depend on more sublime principles which show the wisdom of the Author in the order and perfection of his work.   (G VII 272:L 478)

In this way, the laws of motion lead us to see more generally the importance of considering final causes in physics, as we shall later discuss.[128]

4.4 Atomism and elasticity

The new mechanical philosophy of the seventeenth century was closely connected with the revival of interest in ancient atomism in the late sixteenth and early seventeenth centuries. While there are a number of important figures connected with the revival of atomism, Pierre Gassendi is the most prominent. An editor, translator into Latin, and commentator on the Epicurean tracts preserved by Diogenes Laertius, Gassendi represented one of the main streams of early modern mechanist thought.[129] At the time Gassendi was producing his tomes in defense of an up-dated atomism, Descartes was working out a different conception of the mechanical philosophy. For the atomists, the world was made up of a void filled with atoms, small parts of matter that are perfectly hard, unsplittable, indestructible, at least by natural means. Descartes denied both. For him, the world was made up of matter infinitely divisible, and in some cases actually divided to infinity, that filled up all space.[130] Some, like Boyle, tried to set aside the debate and reject the question as to the infinite divisibility of matter or the existence of a real space, entirely empty of body.[131] But for most writing after Gassendi and Descartes, one had to make a choice.

Though Leibniz may intially have sided with Gassendi and the atomists, in his mature writings he clearly rejected atomism. We saw his rejection of the void in section 4.1. But Leibniz also had a variety of arguments directed against the existence of atoms. In some places he argues against the existence of atoms from his principle that no two things in the world can be perfectly similar. While the argument is not altogether clear, his idea seems to be that if there were only one kind of matter, and it was always perfectly hard,

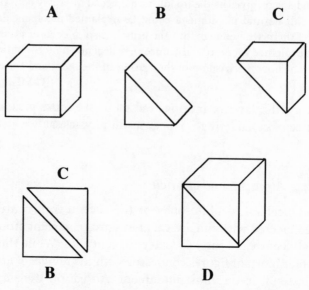

Figure 2

then there could be no physical features to distinguish pieces of it of the same volume (see e.g., "On Nature Itself," par. 13, G IV 514: AG 164; letter to De Volder, 20 June 1703, G II 250: AG 175; *New Essays*, Preface, A VI.vi: RB 57). In notes from October 1690, Leibniz formulated a different kind of argument, a kind of *reductio ad absurdum* of the idea of an atom. Assuming that atoms can come in all shapes, Leibniz hypothesizes a cubical atom, *A*, and two atoms in the shape of triangular prisms, *B* and *C*, that together make up a cube *D* of the same volume as *A* (see figure 2). When *B* and *C* come together to form *D*, then *D* is indistinguishable from *A*, Leibniz argues. And so, he claims, either *A* is made up of smaller parts, and is thus not an atom, or *D* is an atom, and is not made up of smaller parts, as hypothesized.[132] In the correspondence with Clarke, Leibniz suggests that it is the Principle of Sufficient Reason that undermines the hypothesis of atomism, since there can be no reason for stopping the divisibility (or, for that matter, the actual division) of matter at one place rather than another (see fourth letter to Clarke, Postscript, G VII 377–78: AG 332).

But there is one argument that Leibniz uses over and over, and returns to often, an argument from the principle of continuity. According to the principle of continuity, no change in nature happens through a leap. Now, Leibniz argues in part II of the SD:

If we were to imagine that there are atoms, that is, bodies of maximal hardness and therefore inflexible, it would follow that there would be a change through a leap, that is, an instantaneous change. For at the very moment of collision the direction of the motion reverses itself.
(SD, part II, par. 3, GM VI 248: AG 132; cf. G IV 398–99: AG 255; ED, GM VI 229; *Dynamica*, GM VI 491)

If bodies were perfectly hard, and had no "give" in them, then when they collided with one another, they would instantaneously change their direction and speed. And so, Leibniz argues, there can be no atoms, no perfectly hard and inflexible bodies in nature, on pain of violation of the principle of continuity.

This argument refutes the supposed existence of atoms, Leibniz thinks. But it also does a great deal more. From the general form of the argument one can establish not only that there are no atoms, but also that there are no bodies whatsoever that are inflexible. That is, as Leibniz writes again in the SD, "no body is so small that it is without elasticity" (SD, pt. II, par. 3, GM VI 249: AG 132; cf. *Dynamica*, GM VI 491).[133] But, Leibniz argues, if all bodies are elastic, then all bodies must be made up of smaller parts. Elasticity, for Leibniz as for his mechanist contemporaries, was not a basic property of matter, but one that was to be explained mechanically in terms of the configuration of parts that make up a given body. Leibniz writes in the ED, for example, that

Elasticity ought always to derive from a more subtle and penetrating fluid, whose movement is disturbed by the tension or by the change of the elastic body.
(ED, GM VI 228; cf. "On Nature Itself," par. 14, G IV 515: AG 165; letter to Burnett, 1699, G III 260: AG 289).[134]

Leibniz continues:

And since this fluid itself ought to be composed, in turn, of small solid bodies, themselves elastic, one well sees that this replication of solids and fluids goes to infinity.
(ED, GM VI 228; cf. SD, part II, par. 3, GM VI 248–49: AG 132–33)

From the principle of continuity, we reach the conclusion that the actual division of matter into smaller parts proceeds to infinity.

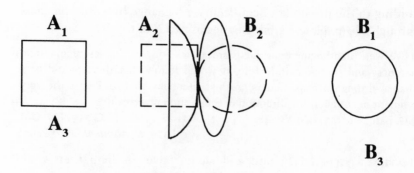

Figure 3

Leibniz draws another interesting consequence from the fact that everybody is elastic to some degree. Leibniz considers the case of two elastic bodies in collision. What happens, he says, is that in collision both bodies first become compressed and deformed; it is by virtue of their elasticity that they return to their original shapes, and in so doing, push themselves off from one another, so to speak (see fig. 3). And so, Leibniz concludes:

> The repercussion and bursting apart [of a body in impact] arises from the elasticity it contains, that is, from the motion of the fluid aetherial matter permeating it, and thus it arises from an internal force or a force existing within itself.
> (SD, part II, par. 5, GM VI 251: AG 135; cf. "New System," G IV 486: AG 145; "On Nature Itself," par. 14, G IV 515: AG 165; G IV 397, 399: AG 254, 255–56)

In this way, he writes,

> Bodies . . . always gain their motion in collision from their very own force, to which the impulse of another body provides only the occasion for acting and a limitation, so to speak.   (G IV 397: AG 254)

In this way, Leibniz claims in the "First Truths" paper of 1689, we have in nature an illustration of the metaphysical doctrine in accordance with which "no created substance exerts a metaphysical action or influx on any other thing" (C 521: AG 33).[135]

The doctrine of the elasticity of all body plays a central role in Leibniz's mature thought about the physical world. But it does have one odd and noteworthy feature. At the end of section 1, I discussed an important difference between Leibniz's early physics and the mature thought that emerged in the late 1670s. In the mature thought, metaphysical principles, like the principle of the equality of cause and effect, are woven into the basic fabric of the physical world, and made basic constraints on the activity of the corporeal substances that constitute the basis of Leibniz's physics. This is unlike the earlier treatment of such principles, which, if satisfied at all, were an *ad hoc* result of the state of the world; it is only because of the particular make-up of bodies in the HPN that a smaller body will lose motion when setting a larger resting body into motion, for example. But, I think, the doctrine of elasticity provides an interesting exception to this general tendency in Leibniz's later thought. For the doctrine that every body in the world must be elastic derives from the metaphysical (and contingent) principle of continuity; it is because the principle of continuity must be satisfied that bodies must be made up of smaller parts in such a way that they tend to restore themselves to their original state, when deformed. But that is to say that the metaphysical principle of continuity is satisfied in this world *only* because of the particular physical state of bodies in this world. In the doctrine of elasticity we see, as it were, a ghost of Leibniz's earlier thought.

5. GOD, MIND, AND THE MECHANICAL PHILOSOPHY

In the previous sections, I have outlined Leibniz's physics and its grounding in his program for dynamics. In this final section, I would like to address some larger questions about the place of Leibniz's physics in his system.

5.1 *God, final causes, and the world of physics*

The discussions earlier in this essay have shown the extent to which Leibniz's physics, his mechanical philosophy, and his dynamics are intimately intertwined with his conception of God, benevolent ruler of the world, who has chosen to create this best of all possible worlds, governed by the metaphysical principles that determine the laws of motion that bodies in the world obey. As Leibniz often puts it, everything within the world is explicable mechanistically but the laws themselves, which require appeal outside the world of the mechanical philosophy to a divine creator. In this way, Leibniz quite self-consciously reintroduces into physics the final cause that had been banished by earlier mechanists.

The final cause was, of course, a central notion in Aristotelian natural philosophy; indeed, for many, including perhaps Aristotle himself, it was the most important of the four causes.[136] But when the philosophy of the schools came under attack, so did final causes. Descartes, for example, argued in his *Principles of Philosophy:*

When dealing with natural things we will, then, never derive any explanations from the purposes which God or nature may have had in view when creating them and we shall entirely banish from our philosophy the search for final causes. For we should not be so arrogant as to suppose that we can share in God's plans.[137]

For Descartes, then, our ignorance of God's intentions prevents us from appealing to final causes in physics. Spinoza goes Descartes one better and denies that God has any intentions at all. He writes in his *Ethics:*

[There is] a widespread belief among men that all things in Nature are like themselves in acting with an end in view. Indeed, they hold it as certain that God himself directs everything to a fixed end; for they say that God has made everything for man's sake and has made man so that he should worship God. . . . There is no need to spend time in going on to show that Nature has no fixed goal and that all final causes are but figments of the human imagination. For I think that this is now quite evident [from discussions earlier in the *Ethics*] . . . that all things in Nature proceed from an eternal necessity and with supreme perfection.[138]

Not all mechanical philosophers followed Descartes and Spinoza in rejecting final causes, of course.[139] But final causes were clearly under attack, and Leibniz saw his role as defending them.

Leibniz's defense of final causes is, in a way, at the center of his metaphysics, and stands behind his whole account of contingency and divine freedom. But it also has a dimension that relates more specifically to his physics. We have already seen the way in which God's action reaches to the determination of the laws of motion; God creates substances in the world in such a way that they satisfy certain metaphysical principles like the principle of the equality of cause and effect and the principle of continuity, and because of that, they satisfy the sorts of conservation principles that Leibniz posits as basic in the world of bodies. But Leibniz sees final causes as more generally relevant for physics as well. Leibniz writes in the SD:

In general, we must hold that everything in the world can be explained in two ways: through the *kingdom of power*, that is, through *efficient causes*, and through the *kingdom of wisdom*, that is, through *final causes*, through God, governing bodies for his glory, like an architect, governing them as machines that follow the *laws of size* or *mathematics*, governing them, indeed, for the use of souls. . . . These two kingdoms everywhere interpenetrate each other without confusing or disturbing their laws, so that the greatest obtains in the kingdom of power at the same time as the best in the kingdom of wisdom.   (SD, part I, par. 14, GM VI 243: AG 126–27)

A special domain, as it were, within the kingdom of wisdom is what Leibniz calls the kingdom of grace. He writes in the *Monadology:*

Since earlier we established a perfect harmony between two natural kingdoms, the one of efficient causes, the other of final causes, we ought to note here yet another harmony between the physical kingdom of nature and the moral kingdom of grace, that is, between God considered as the architect of the mechanism of the universe, and God considered as the monarch of the divine city of minds. . . . This harmony leads things to grace through the very paths of nature. For example, this globe must be destroyed and restored by natural means at such times as the governing of minds requires it, for the punishment of some and the reward of others.
                    (*Monadology*, pars. 87–88, G VI 622: AG 224)

The world of the mechanical philosophy is in harmony with the kingdoms of wisdom and grace, Leibniz claims. Everything in the physical world that can be explained through God can be explained mechanically (assuming the laws of motion), and everything that can be explained mechanically can be explained through God as well. This amounts to saying that everything that the mechanical philosophy explains is a direct consequence of God's choice and design, not *just* the laws of mechanism, but *every particular* as well.[140] Leibniz writes in the *Discourse on Metaphysics:*

Anyone who sees the admirable structure of animals will find himself forced to recognize the wisdom of the author of things. And I advise those who have any feelings of piety and even feelings of true philosophy to keep away from the phrases of certain so-called free-thinkers, who say that we

see because it happens that we have eyes and not that eyes were made for
seeing.   (*Discourse*, par. 19, G IV 445: AG 52–53)

As a result, Leibniz suggests that we can appeal to God's wisdom in
dealing with specific problems in physics, where proceeding by way
of efficient causes is too complicated, particularly in optics (see SD,
part I, par. 14, GM 243: AG 126; G III 51–52: L 351; *Discourse*, par.
22, G IV 447–48: AG 54–55).[141] Furthermore, the harmony between the two kingdoms means that when God realizes his intentions in the world he created, he realizes them through mechanical
means; God has reasons for everything in his creation, but this
does not undermine the scope of Leibniz's mechanism. As Leibniz
suggests in the passage quoted above, even Noah's flood can be
explained mechanically.

But even though everything *can* be explained in terms of God,
Leibniz doesn't think that everything *should* be so explained. In the
May 1702 essay, Leibniz writes:

It is empty to resort to the first substance, God, in explaining the phenomena of his creatures, unless his means or ends are, at the same time, explained in detail, and the proximate efficient or even the pertinent final
causes are correctly assigned, so that he shows himself through his power
and wisdom.   (G IV 397–98:AG 254)

Everything can, of course, be explained in terms of God, Leibniz
holds. But unless specific details are given, the explanation is without content; to say that there was a universal deluge because God
willed it to be so is an explanation that can be used to explain
anything at all in the world. What we need to turn such an explanation into something with content is the specific reason that God had
for flooding the world when he did, and the means by which he
accomplished that end.

5.2 Soul, form, and gravity

In the *Theodicy*, Leibniz rehearsed an argument that he especially
liked:

M. Descartes wanted . . . to make a part of the action of the body depend on
the mind. He thought he knew a rule of nature which, according to him,
holds that the same quantity of motion is conserved in bodies. He did not

judge it possible that the influence of the mind could violate this law of bodies, but he believed, however, that the mind could have the power to change the direction of the motions which are in bodies . . . [but] two important truths on this subject have been discovered since M. Descartes. The first is that the quantity of absolute force which, indeed, is conserved, is different from the quantity of motion, as I have demonstrated elsewhere. The second discovery is that the same direction is conserved among all of those bodies taken together which one supposes to act on one another, however they may collide. If this rule had been known to M. Descartes, he would have rendered the direction of bodies as independent of the mind as their force. And I believe that this would have led him directly to the hypothesis of pre-established harmony, where these rules led me. Since beside the fact that the physical influence of one of these substances on the other is inexplicable, I considered that the mind cannot act physically on the body without completely disordering the laws of nature.

(*Theodicy*, pars. 60–61, G VI 135–36; cf. *Monadology*, par. 80, G VI 620–21: AG 223; letter to Arnauld, 30 April 1687, G II 94: AG 83–84; letter to Remond, 10 January 1714, G III 607: L 655; G IV 497–98; G VI 540: L 587.)

Seventeenth century philosophers grappled with the problem of understanding how it is that rational, sentient, creatures like us can fit into the world of the mechanical philosophy. This problem was especially difficult for those like Descartes and his followers who posited an immaterial, incorporeal mind or soul, attached to the human body, the source of its voluntary motions.[142] For Descartes, of course, the mind can directly cause changes in the body, and for his occasionalist followers, a volition in the mind can cause a bodily change with the intermediation of God. But this raises a problem for the mechanical philosophy. For if mind can be the cause of bodily change, either a direct cause or an occasional one, then the mind can cause violations in the laws of nature, it would seem. Leibniz attributes to Descartes the view that the mind can change the direction in which some part of the body is moving, but not its speed, thus allowing his conservation principle, the conservation of quantity of motion, to be satisfied even in the case of voluntary motion.[143] But, Leibniz remarks, with the Cartesian law overthrown, this is not possible. Among the laws that Leibniz proposes is what we called the conservation of common progress discussed in section 4.3, what we now call the conservation of momentum. This conservation law, which holds in both elastic and nonelastic collisions, would be violated were mind able to change the direction in which a body were moving. What we need, Leibniz thinks, is some way of preserving the laws of nature from violation while allowing for living creatures whose behavior is determined, at least in part, by something apparently outside of the material world. Leibniz's solution is pre-established harmony.

The doctrine of pre-established harmony is best known as a solution to the problem of mind-body interaction and to the problem of how it is that a mind could cause a change in a body (see, e.g., G IV 498–500: AG 147–49). But it is more than that; it is a solution to the problem of how to understand living creatures existing in a mechanical world. In presenting his views Leibniz, again, uses the image of two kingdoms, though somewhat differently than he uses it in connection with God above. Leibniz writes in the *Monadology:*

The soul follows its own laws and the body also follows its own; and they agree in virtue of the harmony pre-established between all substances, since they are all representations of a single universe. . . . Souls act according to the laws of final causes, through appetitions, ends, and means. Bodies act according to the laws of efficient causes or of motions. And these two kingdoms, that of efficient causes and that of final causes, are in harmony with each other. . . . According to this system, bodies act as if there were no souls (though this is impossible); and souls act as if there were no bodies; and both act as if each influenced the other.

(*Monadology,* pars. 78, 79, 81: G VI 620–21: AG 223; cf. "Antibarbarus physicus," G VII 344: AG 319; fifth letter to Clarke, par. 124, G VII 419: AG 345–56)

And so, Leibniz holds, what goes on in living creatures can be explained either mechanically, in terms of size, shape, and the laws of motion, or in accordance with the activity of the soul; the two, Leibniz claims, will always correspond. And so we have mind-body interaction of a sort, without any violation of the laws of nature.

It is important to remember here that this account holds quite generally for Leibniz, for, as we discussed above in sections 3.2 and 3.3, Leibniz holds that there are living things everywhere in his world. All body is grounded in corporeal substances that are composed of a unity of primitive active and primitive passive force. Or, since Leibniz identified the primitive active force with form or soul, and the primitive passive force with matter or body, these corporeal substances that ground the physical world can be thought of as Aristotelian substances, unities of form and matter that constitute living creatures, as we discussed above. And so, he argues, the world is filled with living creatures like us in having souls and bodies. Leibniz writes to Thomas Burnett in 1697:

> I believe that everything happens mechanically, as Democritus and Descartes hold . . . and that nevertheless everything also happens vitally and in accordance with final causes, everything being full of life and perceptions, contrary to the opinion of the Democriteans.
>
> (Letter to Burnett, 24 August 1697; G III 217)

Similarly, Leibniz wrote to Des Billettes in 1696:

> I believe that everything really happens mechanically in nature, and can be explained by efficient causes, but that, at the same time, everything also takes place morally, so to speak, and can be explained by final causes. These two kingdoms, the moral one of minds and souls and the mechanical one of bodies, penetrate each other and are in perfect accord through the agency of the Author of things, who is at the same time the first efficient cause and the last end.
>
> (Letter to Des Billettes, 4/14 December 1696, G VII 451: L 472; cf. letter to Conring, 19 March 1678, G I 199: L 190; G IV 559–60: L 577–78)

Not only can the voluntary activity of human beings be explained in terms of soul; *everything* in the world can be so explained, because at root, there are living creatures, souls attached to bodies *everywhere* in nature. Or, to put it equivalently, since these living creatures are corporeal substances, unities of matter and form, everything can be explained as the schoolmen do. But at the very same time, *everything* in nature can also be explained mechanically, even the voluntary motions of creatures like us.[144] In this way Leibniz quite self-consciously reconciles the philosophy of the schools with the most radically mechanistic philosophy of the moderns; both are correct, and the two pictures will always agree with one another. Leibniz writes in the *Discourse* that "the thoughts of the theologians and philosophers who are called scholastics are not entirely to be disdained. . . . [T]hey are not so distant from the truth or so ridiculous as the common lot of our new philosophers imagines" (*Discourse*, par. 11, G II 12: AG 43; par. 10, G IV 434: AG 42).

When dealing with human minds and bodies, we can and should explain particular voluntary actions in terms of the volition of the mind whenever we can. However, this is not so more generally when dealing with the animate corporeal substances that make up Leibniz's physical world. Though everything *can* be explained in terms of the forms Leibniz recognizes in nature, they should not be used to explain particulars; their proper function, Leibniz holds, is just to ground the general laws in terms of which particular phenomena *should* be explained. Leibniz explains in the *Discourse on Metaphysics:*

I agree that the consideration of these forms serves no purpose in the details of physics and must not be used to explain particular phenomena. That is where the Scholastics failed, as did the physicians of the past who followed their example, believing that they could account for the properties of bodies by talking about forms and qualities, without taking the trouble to examine their manner of operation. It is as if we were content to say that a clock has a quality of clockness derived from its form without considering in what all of this consists; that would be sufficient for the person who buys the clock, provided that he turns over its care to another.
(*Discourse*, par. 10, G IV 434: AG 42; cf. letter to Arnauld, 14 July 1686, G II 58; G IV 345–46; G IV 397–98: AG 254–5; "New System," G IV 479: AG 139; "Specimen Inventorum," G VII 317; SD, part I, par. 13; GM VI 242–43: AG 125–26)

Leibniz holds that the world of physics must be grounded in an Aristotelian world of corporeal substances, form and matter, tiny organisms, and that everything can be explained in those terms. But, he holds, while such explanations are always true, they are rarely informative, indeed, even more rarely than the appeal to God, and so while Leibniz holds that the Schoolmen are not to be despised, they are not to be followed either.

This is close to his attitude toward certain other dissidents from the new mechanical philosophy. Henry More, the Cambridge Platonist, among others, saw the mechanical philosophy as valuable, not primarily for the explanations that it gave, but for the explanations that it couldn't give; for More and his cohorts, by showing clearly what could be explained in physics, the mechanical philosophy showed clearly what couldn't and provided the best argument for the necessity of something outside of the mechanical world. Consequently, they posited a variety of immaterial substances to explain everything from ghosts and hauntings to gravity.[145] Leibniz objected in the SD:

However, even though I admit an active and, so to speak, vital principle superior to material notions everywhere in bodies, I do not agree with *Henry*

More and other gentlemen distinguished in piety and ability, who use an Archaeus (unintelligible to me) or hylarchic principle even for dealing with the phenomena, as if not everything in nature can be explained mechanically. . . . With these views, I say, I do not agree, and such a philosophy pleases me no more than that theology of certain men, who believed that Jupiter thundered and caused the snow to such an extent that they even defamed those who investigated more particular causes with the charge of atheism. In my opinion the middle way in which one satisfies both piety and knowledge is the best. That is, we acknowledge that all corporeal phenomena can be derived from efficient and mechanical causes, but we understand that these very mechanical laws as a whole are derived from higher reasons.

(SD, part I, par. 13, GM VI 242: AG 125–26; cf. "On Nature Itself," par. 2, G IV 505: AG 156; "Antibarbarus physicus," G VII 339–40: AG 314–15)

And so, while Leibniz agrees with More in rejecting the narrow mechanist ontology of extended substances, and adding active principles to nature, he doesn't think that they should be used for explaining particular phenomena, any more than the forms of the schoolmen should.[146]

It is in this context that we must understand Leibniz's reaction to Newton's theory of universal gravitation. In his *Principia*, Newton argued that all bodies in the universe attract one another by way of a force that varies inversely with the square of the distance. Leibniz certainly accepted this, at least with regard to what it is that keeps the planets in their orbits.[147] But in other regards he was decidedly hostile. While Newton's own attitude was not altogether clear on this, one could get the impression from Newton, and, indeed, one did get the clear view from some of his followers, that the universal gravitation of the *Principia* was intended to be a basic, irreducible, and inexplicable property of matter as such, something that one need not and could not explain mechanically.[148] It was this that Leibniz objected to and saw as a revival of the worst abuses of the scholastics. In an unpublished essay, the "Antibarbarus Physicus," Leibniz wrote:

It is, unfortunately, our destiny that, because of a certain aversion toward light, people love to be returned to darkness. We see this today, where the great ease for acquiring learning has brought forth contempt for the doctrines taught, and an abundance of truths of the highest clarity has led to a love for difficult nonsense. . . . It is permissible to recognize magnetic, elastic, and other sorts of forces, but only insofar as we understand that they are not primitive or incapable of being explained, but arise from motions and shapes. However, the new patrons of such things don't want this. And it has been observed that in our own times there was a real suggestion of this view among certain of our predecessors who established that the planets gravitate and tend toward one another. It pleased them to make the immediate inference that all matter essentially has a God-given and inherent attractive power and, as it were, mutual love. . . . [They argue] as if there were no room for mechanical explanations by which [the attraction] . . . could be accounted for through the motion of smaller pervading bodies. These same people threaten to give us other occult qualities of this sort, and thus, in the end, they may lead us back to the kingdom of darkness.

(G VII 337–38: AG 312, 313–14)

The particular kingdom of darkness Leibniz has in mind here is, of course, the natural philosophy of the Scholastics. For, if we allow the Newtonians their force of attraction, Leibniz argues in the preface to the *New Essays*, "I do not see what would prevent our Scholastics from saying that everything happens through faculties" (A VI.vi: RB 61). By implication, the Newtonian explanation of gravitation is as empty as the explanation of the properties of a time piece in terms of its innate clockness.

Leibniz sometimes adds another consideration, and argues that for God to impose such behavior on bodies as the Newtonians imagine he does would be miraculous. He writes in the correspondence with Clarke:

If God wanted to cause a body to move free in the aether round about a certain fixed center, without any other creature acting upon it, I say it could not be done without a miracle, since it cannot be explained by the nature of bodies. For a free body naturally recedes from a curve in the tangent. And therefore, I maintain that the attraction of bodies, properly so called, is a miraculous thing, since it cannot be explained by the nature of bodies.
(Third letter to Clarke, par. 17, G VII 366–67: AG 327; cf. fourth letter to Clarke, par. 45, G VII 377: AG 232; fifth letter to Clarke, pars. 35, 112–13, 118, G VII 417, 418: AG 336, 344, 345)

It would be a miracle for God simply to move bodies as the Newtonians claim he does. But, Leibniz thinks, it would be no miracle for him to structure the world in such a way that through mechanical causes, things in the world behaved as Newton described them. Interesting as this argument is, though, I am not sure that Leibniz is really entitled to it. For the Newtonians are not claiming that God simply moves bodies, but that God has given bodies such a nature that they attract one another in the appropriate way, and that such a nature directly gives rise to the Newtonian law of universal gravitation, without there being any mechanical cause. Their claim is not that the attraction of bodies for one another goes beyond their nature, but that their nature is something different than Leibniz (and other stricter mechanists) think it is.

Couldn't God have given bodies such a nature? Perhaps, but if so, then the mechanist's standard of intelligibility, explicability of everything in the world in terms of bodies colliding with one another in accordance with the laws of motion, must be wrong. And if it is wrong, then the world is forever unintelligible to us, Leibniz thought. Leibniz wrote to Herman Conring on 9 March 1678, at the very point at which his mature physics is beginning to emerge:

I recognize nothing in the world but bodies and minds . . . and [nothing] in bodies insofar as they are separated from mind but magnitude, figure, situation, and changes in these. Everything else is merely said, not understood; it is sounds without meaning. Nor can anything in the world be understood clearly unless it is reduced to these. . . . Unless physical things can be explained by mechanical laws, God cannot, even if he chooses, reveal and explain nature to us.   (G I 197: L 189)

Leibniz seems to have retained this attitude throughout his life. While he did his best to make peace with the schoolmen and reconcile his mechanism with their views, he was utterly unprepared for the reintroduction of specific innate tendencies into the world in the form of a Newtonian attractive force. By the time he died in 1716, the strict mechanism that had been so modern and so daring in his youth, the view around which he built his metaphysical physics, was well on its way to becoming an anachronism.[149]

NOTES

1 Unfortunately, space will not permit discussion of another important feature of Leibniz's physics, his use of the newly developed calculus in his work from the mid-1680s on. For a discussion of this, see Blay, *La naissance de la mécanique analytique*, pp. 113–52.

2 For representative developments of the foundations of Aristotelian natural philosophy, see, e.g., St. Thomas Aquinas' *De principiis naturae*,

translated in *Selected Writings of St. Thomas Aquinas*, ed. and trans., Goodwin; part III of Eustachius a Sancto Paulo's *Summa Philosophiae Quadripartita*, a popular textbook originally published in 1609, but often reprinted later; and Scipion Dupleix, *La physique*, originally published in 1603, also reprinted later, and now available in an edition edited by Roger Ariew, based on the 1640 edition. For modern accounts, see, e.g., Grant, *Physical Science in the Middle Ages* and Lindberg, ed., *Science in the Middle Ages.*

3 On the transmission of Aristotelian texts in the twelfth and thirteenth centuries, see, e.g., Dod, "Aristoteles Latinus," in Kretzmann, Kenny, and Pinborg, eds., *The Cambridge History of Later Medieval Philosophy*, pp. 45–79, and Lohr, "The Medieval Interpretation of Aristotle," in Kretzmann, Kenny, and Pinborg, *op. cit.*, pp. 82–98. For the thirteenth century condemnations, see Dod and Lohr *passim*, as well as Grant, "The Condemnation of 1277, God's Absolute Power, and Physical Thought in the Late Middle Ages," pp. 211–44. Attacks in the thirteenth century mostly came from conservative theologians whose more traditional ideas were in danger of being displaced by the new Aristotelian fashions. By the fifteenth and sixteenth centuries, Aristotelianism is the established philosophy, and the attacks come now from the innovators, from Humanists, sceptics, advocates of some variety of Platonism, Hermeticism, etc. See, e.g., Ingegno, "The New Philosophy of Nature," in Schmitt and Skinner, *The Cambridge History of Renaissance Philosophy*, pp. 236–63, and Menn, "The Intellectual Setting of Seventeenth-Century Philosophy," in *The Cambridge History of Seventeenth-Century Philosophy.* Despite later attacks, Aristotelian philosophy, including the Aristotelian natural philosophy, was central to the colleges and universities well into the seventeenth century. See Schmitt, *Aristotle and the Renaissance.*

4 For a survey of the mechanical philosophy, see Dijksterhuis, *The Mechanization of the World Picture*, and Westfall, *The Construction of Modern Science: Mechanisms and Mechanics.* For seventeenth century attempts to reconcile Aristotle and the new mechanical philosophy, with special reference to Leibniz, see especially Mercer, "The Seventeenth-Century Debate Between the Moderns and the Aristotelians: Leibniz and the Philosophia Reformata," in Marchlewitz and Heinekamp, eds., *Leibniz' Auseinandersetzung mit Vorgängern und Zeitgenossen*, and her *Leibniz's Metaphysics: Its Origins and Development.*

5 For Leibniz's earliest education, see Chap. 2 in this *Companion.*

6 Leibniz's own account of his turn toward the Moderns is found in his letter to Nicolas Remond, 10 January 1714, G III 606: L 654–55. This, though, is not to say that he abandoned the Aristotelian philosophy

altogether. Perhaps this moment is best seen as the point at which Leibniz embarked on the project of reconciling Aristotle with the Moderns. For an account of his early dealings with the mechanical philosophy, see Mercer, *Leibniz's Metaphysics.*

7 The earliest evidence is in a letter Leibniz wrote to his mentor Jakob Thomasius on 16/26 February, 1666, where Leibniz discussed a question raised by Thomasius as to why Anaxagoras spoke of the possibility of black snow, and showed some acquaintance with mechanist doctrines of perception. See A II.i 4–5. In *De arte combinatoria* of 1666, there are a number of references to Hobbes' materialistic tract *De corpore,* and a brief discussion of atomistic explanations, with reference to the atomistic tracts of Gassendi and J. C. Magnenus. See A VI.i 178, 183, 194, 216. In the theses for public disputation that Leibniz added to the work, he also included a claim that the four Aristotelian primary qualities, hot, cold, dry, and moist, could be reduced to density and rarity, in the style of the earlier seventeenth-century mechanist, Sir Kenelm Digby; see A VI.i 229, and Digby *Two Treatises in the one of which the Nature of Bodies in the other the Nature of Mans Soule is looked into in the way of discovery of the Immortality of Reasonable Soules* (Paris, 1644) bk. I, chap. III–IV. Leibniz's theological writings from the years immediately following also show an acquaintance with and a sympathy for the new mechanical philosophy. For example, in the *De transubstantiatione* (ca. 1668), Leibniz works within a framework within which the actions of mind are thought, and those of body are motion; see A VI.i 508–21: L 115–18). In the important *Confessio naturae contra atheistas* (1669), Leibniz gives an explicit endorsement of the mechanist program; see A VI.i 489: L 109–10.

8 See Garber, "Motion and Metaphysics in the Young Leibniz," in Hooker, ed., *Leibniz: Critical and Interpretative Essays;* Mercer, *Leibniz's Metaphysics;* and chap. 3 in this *Companion.* God's continual recreation of the world was the basic premise in one of the important arguments for occasionalism; see Garber, "How God causes Motion: Descartes, Divine Sustenance, and Occasionalism," pp. 567–80. Oddly enough, Leibniz identifies this as "a view that has never been heard of until now" (A II.i 23–24: L 102), suggesting that he was not well acquainted with the Cartesian literature. Leibniz's reaction to the doctrine of occasionalism will be discussed at greater length below in sec. 4.4.

9 See chap. 4 in this *Companion.*

10 This is the main theme of Mercer, *Leibniz's Metaphysics.*

11 The notes are found in A VI.ii 157–218; the HPN and TMA are found in that same volume. The HPN and TMA are also found in GM VI and G

IV, though there are some confusing differences in the numeration of the sections. The alternative title "Theoria motus Concreti" is not found on the title page of the HPN, but on the first page of the text.

12 For a fuller account of these writings, see Hannequin, *La première philosophie de Leibnitz*, vol. II, pp. 17–224, esp. pp. 59–148.

13 Loemker's otherwise fine translation should be treated with extreme caution in these passages. Leibniz is here especially indebted to Hobbes. See Kabitz, *Die Philosophie des jungen Leibniz* and Bernstein, "*Conatus*, Hobbes, and the Young Leibniz," pp. 25–37.

14 The account of collision is given on A VI.ii 268: L 142, sects. 20–24; the consequences are presented in a series of theorems that immediately follow (not translated in L).

15 According to Descartes' conservation principle, the sum over all bodies of size times speed (quantity of motion) is a quantity conserved by God; see Descartes, *Principles of Philosophy*, pt. II, sec. 36. For a discussion, see Garber, *Descartes' Metaphysical Physics*, chap. 7. It should be noted here that Descartes' principle differs from the conservation of momentum. Momentum is a vector quantity, size (mass) times *velocity*, and change of direction entails a change in momentum, even if the speed remains the same. Not so for Descartes' quantity of motion, which remains the same even if the direction is changed. Leibniz rejects Descartes' principle of the conservation of quantity of motion, though he adheres to a principle of the conservation of momentum; see sec. 4.3.

16 Descartes' creation story can be found in chap. 7 of *Le monde*, and in his *Principles*, pt. III, sec. 46. These two accounts differ somewhat; the initial state of the world in *Le monde* is a complete chaos, while in the *Principles*, Descartes imagines God to have created particles of approximately equal size. In the opening of Pt. V of the *Discourse on the Method*, Descartes outlines the whole program of deriving the present state of the world from creation; see Adam and Tannery, eds., *Oeuvres de Descartes*, VI 42ff.

17 For a more detailed discussion, see Hannequin *La première philosophie*, pp. 103–7.

18 Ibid., pp. 120–22.

19 For Wren's laws, see Wren, "Lex collisionis corporum," in *Philosophical Transactions of the Royal Society* (March 1669); they can also be found in Hall and Hall, eds., *The Correspondence of Henry Oldenburg*, vol. V, pp. 319–20 (Latin), 320–21 (English). Huygens' "Règles du mouvement dans la rencontre des corps" was published in the *Journal des sçavans*, 18 March 1669. It can also be found in *Oeuvres complètes de Christiaan Huygens*, vol. XVI, pp. 179–81. Huygens' main work on

bodies in impact was started as early as 1656, though not published until after his death; see "De motu corporum ex percussione," in *Oeuvres*, vol. XVI, pp. 29–168. On Huygens see Dijksterhuis, *The Mechanization of the World Picture*, pp. 373–76. On Huygens and Wren, see Westfall, *Force in Newton's Physics*, pp. 146–57 (on Huygens), and 203–5 (on Wren).

20 See the discussion of Leibniz's doctrine of substance in this period in chap. 4 in this *Companion*. Occasionalism briefly seems to resurface later in the decade in the *Pacidius Philalethi* of October 1676; see C 617, 624–25.

21 For accounts of Leibniz's work in physics during this period see Belaval, "Premières animadversions de Leibniz sur les *Principes* de Descartes," in *Mélanges Alexandre Koyré v. II: L'aventure de l'esprit*, pp. 29–56; Fichant, "La 'réforme' leibnizienne de la dynamique, d'après des textes inédits"; Fichant, "Les concepts fondamentaux de la mécanique selon Leibniz, en 1676"; Fichant, "Neue Einblicke in Leibniz' Reform seiner Dynamik (1678)," pp. 48–68; and Robinet, *Architectonique disjonctive, automates systèmiques et idéalité transcendentale dans l'oeuvre de G. W. Leibniz*, chap. 5.

22 The text is also given, together with a valuable commentary, in Belaval, "Premières animadversions."

23 Belaval, "Premières animadversions," p. 46.

24 This seems to be a change from the earlier writings, including the early notes on Descartes, referred to above, which seem to have been written at roughly the same time. It also seems to differ from the position taken in the "Propositiones" of 1672, where an important theme is that in the physics of the TMA, motion is lost in the world, unless there is a mind to add it; see A VI.iii 66–68, 72. See also A VI.ii 280.

25 Quoted in FC, p. LXIV. Unfortunately, Foucher de Careil gives no identifiable source for the quotation, and I have not been able to verify it in any more reliable source, so there is some uncertainty that attaches to the dating.

26 It is clear that this principle was much on Leibniz's mind as early as the mid-1670s; see A VI.iii 490ff, from 1 April 1676, where Leibniz discusses the principle at some length. See the discussion in Fichant "Les concepts fondamentaux," pp. 228f.

27 This is an argument that Leibniz repeated often later; see the discussion in sec. 4.3.

28 This manuscript and its history are discussed in Fichant "La 'réforme' "; see also Robinet *Architectonique disjonctive*, chap. 5.5. Fichant plans to publish the manuscript as a whole, with commentary, though at the time of this writing, it has not yet appeared.

29　See Fichant, "La 'réforme'," p. 199, 202–3.

30　It is difficult to know when exactly Leibniz came to this conclusion. Fichant, "La 'réforme'," p. 207, emphasizes that in the important document of January 1678 where Leibniz first asserts the conservation of mv^2, the question of the nature of body is entirely untouched.

31　See note 37 for some bibliographical remarks on this work.

32　An outline written by Leibniz for a book on the elements of physics, which the editors of the Academy edition securely date at 1678–82 on the basis of watermark evidence, is indicative of the range of Leibniz's scientific interests at this time; see VE III 649–53 (L 277–80). It is difficult to identify all of the sketches from the period from 1679 to 1686 or so that might be relevant; much remains to be published, and of the notes on physics that are available, the dating is often very problematic. For some notes relating to Leibniz's interests in the foundations of physics that the editors of the Academy edition also date in the period 1678–82, see VE III 625–48; VE VII 1666–79; and VE VIII 2035–45. It should be noted that these papers include only material that the editors deem to be of philosophical interest; the more technical papers remain largely unedited.

33　The text is given in GM VI 117–119, together with a later manuscript appendix on pp. 119–23 (L 296–301). This was not Leibniz's first scientific paper in the 1680s. But it is fair to say that the "Brevis Demonstratio" marks the real beginning of Leibniz's attempt to make public his mature program for physics.

34　For accounts of the controversy, see especially Iltis, "Leibniz and the *Vis Viva* Controversy," pp. 21–35; Costabel, "Contribution à l'offensive de Leibniz contre la philosophie cartésienne en 1691–1692," pp. 264–287; and Costabel, *Leibniz and Dynamics*.

35　Leibniz claims not to have seen the full text of Newton's *Principia* until he arrived in Rome in April 1689, and claims to have seen only a review in the *Acta Eruditorum* before that; see GM VI 189 and GM VII 329. For Leibniz's first reactions to Newton's work, see Leibniz, *Marginalia in Newtoni Principia Mathematica* (1687), ed., Fellmann; Meli, *The Development of Leibniz's Techniques and Ideas about Planetary Motion in the Years 1688 to 1690*; and Meli, "Leibniz's Excerpts from the *Principia Mathematica*," pp. 477–505. In *The Development*, p. 48ff Meli attempts to make the case that the set of Leibniz's notes on the *Principia* he discovered may date from before the Rome trip, casting some doubt on Leibniz's own account of his acquaintance with Newton's physics. But the argument looks indecisive to me, as "Leibniz's Excerpts," p. 478 suggests.

36　The text of the *Dynamica* was published for the first and only time in

GM VI 281–514. For a discussion of the Leibniz's plans to publish the book, see Robinet, *Architectonique disjonctive*, pp. 261 ff. Though the bulk of the work may have been completed in Italy, the prefatory "specimen" of arguments was probably written after January 1691; see AG 105–6.

37 The SD can be found in GM VI 234–54: AG 117–38. Gerhardt's text has been superseded by a new edition, edited and translated into German by Dosch, Most, and Rudolph, where the editors give a text with a full apparatus criticus, and the text of a previously unpublished preliminary version of part I. The editors number the paragraphs in their text, and so references to the SD will be given by part and paragraph number; in this chapter references are also given to Gerhardt's text. It should be noted that only part I was published by Leibniz; part II was left in manuscript and only published after Leibniz's death. For an account of the composition of the SD, see Most, "Zur Entwicklung von Leibniz' *Specimen Dynamicum*," pp. 148–163. Some of the most philosophically interesting content of the SD is repeated in an important essay dated May 1702, but unpublished in Leibniz's lifetime; see GM VI 98–106 or G IV 393–400: AG 250–256.

38 The text is given in GM VI 144–61; a second (unpublished) version is given in GM VI 161–87. For accounts of Leibniz's vortex theory, see Aiton, *The Vortex Theory of Planetary Motions*; Aiton, "The Mathematical Basis of Leibniz's Theory of Planetary Motion," pp. 209–25; and Meli, *The Development*.

39 Most notably smaller studies of the laws of motion (Costabel, *Leibniz and Dynamics* contains some such texts, and there are others in GM VI) and studies of optics in which Leibniz emphasizes that importance of reasoning from final causes. See especially "Unicum Opticae, Catoptricae, et Dioptricae Principium," *Acta Eruditorum*, June 1682, pp. 185–90; in Du III 145–51. Also, there are many technical papers on a wide variety of areas, including the barometer, chemistry, acoustics, magnetism, and clocks, as well as the papers that relate to the draining of the mines in the Harz Mountains. Excerpts are collected in vol. II pt. II of the Dutens edition of 1768 and in Gerland, *Leibnizens nachgelassene Schriften physikalischen, mechanischen und technischen Inhalts*; to the best of my knowledge, the transcription and publication of these manuscripts in the Academy edition is not yet even in progress.

40 On Newton's contribution in the Leibniz-Clarke exchange, see Koyré and Cohen, "Newton and the Leibniz-Clarke Correspondence," pp. 63–126.

41 This sentiment is repeated often in this period and afterwards. See, for example, *Discourse on Metaphysics*, par. 10, G IV 434–45: AG 42–43; Correspondence with Arnauld (1686–90), G II, 58, 78, 98; "On the Cor-

rection of Metaphysics" (1694), G IV 470: L 433; "On Body and Force, May 1702," G IV 393, 394–95, 398: AG 250, 251–52, 255; "Antibarbarus Physicus" (1710–16) G VII 343–44: AG 319.

42 See "On Body and Force, May 1702," G IV 394, 398: AG 251, 255 for this usage of the term "physics" and for the distinction between physics so understood and dynamics.

43 The threefold distinction I draw between mechanist physics proper, dynamics, or the science of force, and the metaphysical level of individual substance or monad corresponds reasonably closely to the account given in Gueroult, *Leibniz: Dynamique et Métaphysique*, pp. 203–8. Gale, "The Physical Theory of Leibniz," pp. 114–27, esp. p. 116 gives a different threefold categorization, distinguishing the metaphysical level (monads), the explanatory level (corporeal substance, primitive forces), and the observable level (body, derivative forces). McGuire, " 'Labyrinthus Continui': Leibniz on Substance, Activity, and Matter," in Machamer and Turnbull, eds., *Motion and Time, Space and Matter*, pp. 290–326, esp. pp. 307f gives a different threefold categorization still, distinguishing the levels of the ideal (space, time, motion), the phenomenal (phenomenal extension and change), and the real (substances and their attributes).

44 For a general account of Descartes' physics, see Garber, *Descartes' Metaphysical Physics*. For an account of physics among the Cartesians, see Mouy, *Le développement de la physique cartésienne: 1646–1712*.

45 For a good discussion of this argument, see Sleigh, *Leibniz and Arnauld: A Commentary on Their Correspondence*, pp. 112–14.

46 The exception to this rule is Gerauld de Cordemoy, who believed in both atoms and the void, but who considered himself to be a member of the Cartesian sect. The relevant texts can be found in Cordemoy, *Oeuvres philosophiques*, eds Clair and Girbal. See also Prost, *Essai sur l'atomisme et l'occasionalisme dans l'école cartésienne* and Battail, *L'avocat philosophe: Géraud de Cordemoy (1626–1684)*.

47 For other occurrences of the same basic argument, see, for example, "Notes on Fardella, March 1690," FC, pp. 319–20: AG 103; "New System," unpublished draft (ca. 1694), G IV 473; Response to Foucher (1695), G IV 492: AG 147; Letter to Jaquelot, 22 March 1703, G III 457; *Principles of Nature and Grace* (1714), par. 1; *Monadology* (1714), pars. 1–2. This argument is discussed in more detail in Garber, "Leibniz and the Foundations of Physics: the Middle Years," in Okruhlik and Brown, eds., *The Natural Philosophy of Leibniz* pp.27–130, esp. sec. I.

48 See the account of the BD argument in sec. 4.3.

49 See the discussion of this argument in Gueroult, *Leibniz: Dynamique et Métaphysique*, pp. 46–49.

50 See also versions of the argument in Letter to the *Journal des Savants*, June 1691, G IV 464–65; letter to Antonio Alberti, 1691?, G VII 447–48; SD, pt. I, par. 10–11, GM VI 240–41: AG 123–25; "On the Nature of Body and the Laws of Motion" (1690?), G VII 280–83: AG 245–50.

51 See the account of this argument in Garber, "Leibniz and the Foundations of Physics," pp. 78–79.

52 See, for example, Descartes' *Principles*, pt. II, secs. 40–44, where Descartes sets out his account of impact. For a discussion of the notion of force in Descartes, see Garber, *Descartes' Metaphysical Physics*, chap. 9, as well as Gueroult, "The Metaphysics and Physics of Force in Descartes," and Gabbey, "Force and Inertia in the Seventeenth Century: Descartes and Newton," both in Gaukroger, ed., *Descartes: Philosophy, Mathematics and Physics*, pp. 196–229 and 230–320 respectively.

53 For a discussion of the notion of force in the earlier part of the century, see Westfall, *Force in Newton's Physics*.

54 A very similar account is given in "On Body and Force, May 1702"; see G IV 395: AG 252.

55 Leibniz is referring here to an example he used earlier in the essay, where he examines the behavior of a ball in a hollow tube when the tube is rotating around an external center.

56 On passive force in Leibniz, see Bernstein, "Passivity and Inertia in Leibniz's *Dynamics*," pp. 97–113.

57 See "On Body and Force, May 1702," G IV 395: AG 252, where Leibniz makes the distinction more explicitly than he does in the SD.

58 Descartes is probably the first to have published the law that a body in motion remains in motion unless brought to rest by an external cause, though he was certainly not the first to have held it. See his *Principles*, pt. II, secs. 37–38, and Garber, *Descartes' Metaphysical Physics*, chap. 7. The principle, in fundamental opposition to Aristotelian physics, was characteristic of the new science of motion, and is found in many contemporaries and later figures. See, for example, Hobbes, *Leviathan*, chap. 2 (opening paragraph), and Spinoza, *Ethics*, pt. II, corollary to lemma 3 following prop. 13, and pt. III, prop. 6.

59 For a fuller development of this, see Garber, "Leibniz and the Foundations of Physics".

60 See Robinet, *Architectonique disjonctive*, where even finer distinctions are made.

61 See also Leibniz's comment to Bernoulli in his letter of 18 November 1698: "I hardly know how far the flint should be divided so that organic bodies (and therefore monads) might occur; but I readily declare that our ignorance on the matter has no effect on nature" GM III 552: AG 168.

62 But not without some difficulties. The bodies (matter) that unite with

the   souls (forms) to form corporeal substances in the metaphysical
writings are composed of further corporeal substances. But the matter
that Leibniz identifies with primitive passive force in the SD cannot be
construed in that way. For a discussion of this, see Garber, "Leibniz and
the Foundations of Physics," sec. II.
63 For a fuller development of this strain in Leibniz's thought, see Garber,
"Leibniz and the Foundations of Physics". See also Sleigh, *Leibniz and
Arnauld*, and Wilson, *Leibniz's Metaphysics: A Historical and Comparative Study*, who also discuss extensively the notion of corporeal
substance and the status of bodies on this conception.
64 For a fuller development of this conception of body in Leibniz, see Adams, "Phenomenalism and Corporeal Substance in Leibniz," in French,
Uehling, and Wettstein, eds., *Contemporary Perspectives on the History
of Philosophy*, pp. 217–57.
65 I take the simple substances in question to be the monads of the *Monadology*. See also letter to de Volder, 20 June 1703, G II 251: AG 175–76.
66 See also letter to Nicolas Remond, 11 February 1715, G III 636: L 659,
where Leibniz makes a similar comment about the inertia of bodies, a
derivative passive force.
67 The question of the possibility of there being real composite substance
in a world of monads is discussed at some length in connection with the
"substantial chain" or "*vinculum substantiale*." It is a matter of great
controversy just how committed Leibniz was to the doctrine. The term
"*vinculum substantiale*" first appears in Leibniz to Des Bosses, 5 February 1712, G II 435: AG 198, and appears regularly after that in their
correspondence, though it seems not to appear outside of that exchange.
On the *vinculum substantiale*, see Boehm, *Le "Vinculum substantiale"
chez Leibniz. Ses origines historiques*; Fremont, *L'être et la relation*;
and Robinet, *Architectonique disjonctive*.
68 The Latin in Gerhardt reads: "Consistit in potentia activa et passiva
primitivis . . . ." Hence Loemker's translation: "It consists of active and
passive power originally . . . ." Given that primitive active and passive
force (power) are well-established technical terms for Leibniz, it seems
clear to me that "primitivis" is a mistake in the manuscript or a misprint
in Gerhardt for "primitiva"; hence, the translation I give in the text.
69 This would raise a real problem for Leibniz, though; in his correspondence with de Volder, he emphasizes that we cannot have a derivative force without a corresponding primitive force. See, for example,
letter to de Volder, 20 June 1703, G II 251: AG 176. Perhaps the primitive forces should also have appeared in Leibniz's characterization of
semisubstances.

70 See Lennon, "Occasionalism and the Cartesian Metaphysic of Motion," pp. 29–40.

71 Clerselier to de la Forge, 4 December 1660, in Clerselier, *Lettres de M Descartes* [tome III], p. 642.

72 Cordemoy, *Oeuvres philosophiques*, p. 143.

73 Malebranche, *Recherche de la vérité* VI.II.III, in Malebranche, *Oeuvres*, ed., Rodis-Lewis, vol. I, p. 643: *The Search after Truth*, trans., Lennon and Olscamp, and *Elucidations of the Search after Truth*, trans., Lennon, p. 446.

74 Malebranche, *Oeuvres*, vol. I, pp. 643–46 (Lennon and Olscamp, pp. 446–48).

75 Malebranche, *Oeuvres*, vol. I, p. 649: Lennon and Olscamp, p. 450.

76 For a general discussion of Leibniz's rejection of occasionalism, see Brunner, *Études sur la Signification Historique de la Philosophie de Leibniz*, pp. 222–25 and Rutherford, "Natures, Laws, and Miracles," in Nadler, ed., *Causation in Early Modern Philosophy*, pp. 135–58.

77 For some important parts of the story, see Grant, "Place and Space in Medieval Physical Thought," in Machamer and Turnbull, *Motion and Time, Space and Matter*, pp. 137–67; Grant, "The Condemnation of 1277, God's Absolute Power, and Physical Thought in the Late Middle Ages," pp. 211–44; Grant, *Much Ado about Nothing: Theories of space and vacuum from the Middle Ages to the Scientific Revolution*; Duhem, *Medieval Cosmology*, ed. and trans., Ariew.

78 This position is strikingly held by Francesco Patrizi in the late sixteenth century, who was perhaps the first to step outside of the Aristotelian metaphysical framework and argue that space is neither substance nor accident, but *sui generis*, the container of all, God's first creation in which he placed all else, filling some places but leaving others empty. See Grant, *Much Ado*, pp. 199–206; Henry, "Francesco Patrizi da Cherso's Concept of Space and its Later Influence," pp. 549–75; Schmitt, "Experimental Evidence for and Against a Void: the Sixteenth-Century Arguments," pp. 352–66. Others, like Bruno, Telesio, and Campanella thought of space as a container independent of body, but never actually existing without body. See Grant, *Much Ado*, pp. 183–98.

79 See, e.g., Descartes' *Principles*, pt. II, secs. 5ff. See also the discussion in Garber, *Descartes' Metaphysical Physics*, chap. 5. An exception to this view among the Cartesians was Cordemoy; see the references cited in note 46.

80 For Gassendi's account of the vacuum, see his *Syntagma philosophicum*, pt. II, bk. II, chaps. 2–5, in his *Opera omnia*, vol. I. Much of the material, as it originally appeared in his earlier *Animadversiones in*

decimum librum Diogenis Laertii ... can be found in a more easily digestible form in Charleton, *Physiologia Epicuro-Gassendo-Charltoniana,* bk. I chaps. 3–5. For further discussion, see Grant, *Much Ado,* pp. 207–10, Bloch, *La philosophie de Gassendi: Nominalisme, matérialisme et métaphysique,* pp. 194–200, and Joy, *Gassendi the Atomist.* Pascal's views are found in *Expériences nouvelles touchant le vide* of October 1647, and the *Récit de la grande expérience de l'équilibre des liqueurs* of October 1648, along with an important exchange of letters with Father Etienne Noël; these can be found in Pascal, *Oeuvres complètes,* ed., Lafuma, pp. 195ff. For further discussion of Pascal's views, see, e.g., Fanton d'Andon, *Horreur du vide: Expérience et raison dans la physique pascalienne,* and Guenancia, *Du vide à Dieu.* For a discussion of the confrontation between Descartes and Pascal on the vacuum, see Garber, *Descartes' Metaphysical Physics,* chap. 5.

81 Newton, *Principia,* bk. I, Scholium to dfn VIII.

82 Newton, *Principia,* bk. III, General Scholium.

83 For a very illuminating account of Newton on absolute space, see Stein, "Newtonian Space-Time," in Palter, ed., *The Annus Mirabilis of Sir Isaac Newton,* pp. 258–84.

84 In the important April 1669 letter to Thomasius, for example, Leibniz writes that "space is a primary extended being or a mathematical body, which contains three dimensions and is the universal locus of all things. . . . So matter is a being which is in space or coextensive with space" A II.i 21: L 100.

85 See also Leibniz's account to Clarke as to how we acquire the concept of space, Leibniz's fifth letter, par. 47 (G VII 400–2:AG 337–39).

86 See also Leibniz to Des Bosses 29 May 1716, G II 515: AG 201. For more extensive discussions of Leibniz on space, see, e.g., Earman, "Was Leibniz a Relationist?," in French, Uehling, and Wettstein, eds., *Studies in Metaphysics,* pp. 263–76; Hartz and Cover, "Space and Time in the Leibnizian Metaphysic," pp. 493–519; and Wilson, *Leibniz's Metaphysics,* chap. 6.

87 See, e.g., Descartes, *Principles,* pt. II, secs. 16–19.

88 Leibniz seems to have a similar argument in mind in the SD of 1695; see SD, pt. II, par. 2, (GM VI 247–48: AG 130).

89 For a somewhat difficult exposition of this view, see "Conversation of Philarète and Ariste" (1712–15), Robinet, *Malebranche et Leibniz,* pp. 444–45:AG 262.

90 The same argument is also echoed in the introduction to the *New Essays* (1704); see A VI.vi: RB 57. Note that the "First Truths" paper, usually thought to date from the early or mid-1680s has recently been redated to 1689 on the basis of watermark evidence. See VE VIII 1998.

91 The same argument also comes up in the Leibniz-Clarke correspondence; see Leibniz's second letter, par. 2 (G VII 356: AG 322), Leibniz's third letter, par. 9, (G VII 365: AG 326), and especially Leibniz's fourth letter, Post Script (G VII 377–78: AG 332).

92 See Isaac Newton, *Principia Mathematica*, bk. I, scholium to the definitions.

93 Stein, "Newtonian Space-Time."

94 See also passages from earlier drafts of the SD given in the Dosch, Most, and Rudolph edition of the text, pp. 22–24, note to line 307 (AG 125, n. 173), p. 58, note to line 288 (AG 136, n. 188), and p. 74. On the relation between Leibniz and Huygens on this issue, see Bernstein, "Leibniz and Huygens on the 'Relativity' of motion," pp. 85–102.

95 There is not space to examine Leibniz's arguments in detail here. For discussion of Leibniz's complex position and the various tangled arguments he offered for it, see Stein, "Some Philosophical Prehistory of General Relativity," in Earman, Glymour, and Stachel, eds., *Foundations of Space-Time Theories*, pp. 3–49, esp. pp. 3–6, with notes and appendices, and Bernstein, "Leibniz and Huygens".

96 This is translated in Stein, "Some Philosophical Prehistory".

97 I would like to thank Richard Arthur for correcting my translation here. On Leibniz's attempts to use his doctrine of the equivalence of hypotheses in connection with the issue of Copernicanism and the Church, see Meli, "Leibniz on the Censorship of the Copernican System," pp. 19–42.

98 For a discussion of Leibniz and relations, see chap. 5 in this *Companion*.

99 In a sketch from 1677, Leibniz suggested that since motion is not a property of bodies taken individually, it must be a property of the world as a whole; see VE III 654. In that passage, though, Leibniz notes that "motum non in se formaliter, sed ratione causae considerando, posse attribui eius corpori a cujus contactu provenit mutatio."

100 In a fragment from 1678–82, there is a suggestion that in at least the case where a human being – itself a corporeal substance, if anything is – is the seat of the force, we can determine which body is genuinely in motion through the effort felt. See VE VII 1673–74. But this is no help at all in the general case in physics.

101 This, I think, is at least a good part of what Russell had in mind when he made his celebrated comment about the relations between Leibniz's physics and metaphysics: "Leibniz has acquired much credit for the vaunted interconnection of his views in these two departments, and few seem to have perceived how false his boast really is. As a matter of fact, the want of connection is, I think, quite one of the weakest points in his system." Russell, *A Critical Exposition of the Philosophy of Leibniz*, p. 89; see also pp. 86–87.

102 See, e.g., Descartes, *Principles*, pt. II, sec. 36. For a fuller account of Descartes' conservation principle, see Garber, *Descartes' Metaphysical Physics*, chaps. 7 and 9.

103 Though there is not sufficient space to enter into the question here, it should be noted that Leibniz owes a considerable debt in his laws of motion to other thinkers of the period. For a more detailed account of Leibniz's borrowings, and the way in which he transformed the work of others, see Gueroult, *Leibniz: Dynamique et Métaphysique*, chap. 4; Westfall, "The Problem of Force: Huygens, Newton, Leibniz," pp. 71–84, and Bos, "The Influence of Huygens on the Formation of Leibniz' Ideas," pp. 59–68.

104 For more detailed accounts of the complex disputes, see the references cited in note 34.

105 Leibniz outlines his strategy SD, pt. I, par. 15, (GM VI 243–44: AG 127–28).

106 See also the statement of the the the principle of the equality of cause and effect in the body of the *Dynamica*, GM VI 437.

107 This is a paraphrase of the argument in the BD, GM VI 117–19: L 296–98 and in *Discourse on Metaphysics*, par. 17 (G IV 442–43: AG 50). Gregory Brown, " 'Quod ostendendum susceperamus': What did Leibniz undertake to Show in the *Brevis Demonstratio*?," pp. 122–37, correctly notes, against Iltis and Wilson, that it is the main point of the BD argument to show simply that force is distinct from quantity of motion, and not that mv^2 is what is actually conserved in nature. However, it is important to point out that elsewhere Leibniz uses the basic argument form for other purposes, as we shall see.

The point is a rather important one for Leibniz. Leibniz thinks that the Cartesian conservation law is grounded in a mistake about what the proper measure of force is. Leibniz thinks that people generally agree that force is conserved, but he thinks that the only force generally known was dead force, as treated in statics, for example, and this force is proportional to size times speed. See BD, GM VI 117: L296; and SD, pt. I, par. 8, (GM VI 239:AG 122–23).

108 In the *Dynamica*, Leibniz argues for the conservation of the ability to do work (*potentia*) from the principle of the equality of cause and effect, both in the universe as a whole and in any closed system ("in quovis Systemate corporum cum aliis non communicantium"); see GM VI 440–41.

109 This argument is suggested in the opening paragraph of the BD, for example; see GM VI 117: L 296. It is important to remember here that the Cartesian quantity of motion, size times speed, is not the same as momentum, size (mass) times velocity, as discussed in this section.

The issue here is not the relatively trivial one as to whether one wants to take the conservation of living force, mv^2, or momentum as basic (though, as we shall later see, Leibniz does think that living force is more basic than momentum, whose conservation he also recognizes). Leibniz's point is that if the Cartesian law is satisfied, a system can lose the ability to do work; see the remarks to this effect in the SD, pt. I, par. 17, (GM VI 245–46: AG 129–30).

110 Such a machine is described, for example, in the *Specimen praelimi-nare* to the *Dynamica*, GM VI 289–90: AG 108–9. In that place, Leibniz is concerned not only to show that quantity of motion differs from force, but that quantity of motion is not conserved; he gives three different *a posteriori* arguments to that conclusion. See GM VI 288: AG 107 for a statement of the proposition proved, followed by three alternative demonstrations.

111 See Johann Bernoulli's comments to this effect in his letter to Leibniz, 8/18 June 1695, GM III 189.

112 Indeed, in the *Specimen praeliminare* of the *Dynamica*, he goes so far as to suggest that the equivalence of the two notions enables us to *demonstrate* Galileo's law of free fall! See GM VI 292: AG 111. Presumably what he has in mind is this. If the proper measure of force (the ability to do work) can be established *a priori*, then we can use the fact that in a given body, the force is proportional to the square of its speed to establish that the height to which a given body can raise itself then must be proportional to the square of its speed. From which it would follow by the principle of the equality of cause and effect that the speed it would acquire in free fall would be proportional to the square root of the distance fallen.

113 For more detailed discussions of the argument, see Gueroult, *Leibniz: Dynamique et Métaphysique*, pp 118–54, and Stammel, "Der Status der Bewegungsgesetze in Leibniz' Philosophie und die apriorische Methode der Kraftmessung," pp. 180–88. Gueroult, pp. 153–54 complains that were this argument to succeed (which he thinks it doesn't), then Leibniz would be in the position of holding that the conservation of mv^2 is necessary, in contradiction to his claim that the laws of motion are contingent, as we shall discuss below. This does not follow. What the argument would show, if successful, is that the proper measure of force is proportional to the square of speed. But the conservation of mv^2 requires the additional assumption that force is conserved in the world, an assumption that depends on the principle of the equality of cause and effect, which is contingent, for Leibniz, the result of God's wise choice.

114 Important here, of course is the work of Huygens and Wren; see the

references cited in note 19. Also important is the work of Mariotte; see his *Traité de la percussion ou choc des corps,* discussed in Westfall, *Force in Newton,* pp. 244–50.

115 Though note that Leibniz thought that in his account of impact, Malebranche fell prey to some of the same errors as Descartes did. See "Letter of Mr. Leibniz . . ." (1687), G III 53–54: L 352–53; Leibniz to Bayle, 9 January 1687, G III 46–47; and Mouy, *Les lois du choc d'après Malebranche.*

116 Descartes, *Principles,* pt. II, secs. 40–52. The measure of the "strength" of a body is implicit in the seven rules Descartes gives in secs. 46–52. For a discussion of Descartes' account of impact, see Gabbey, "Force and Inertia", and Garber, *Descartes' Metaphysical Physics,* chap.8.

117 Cf. Iltis, "Leibniz and the *Vis Viva* Controversy," p. 29.

118 Leibniz himself identifies this as the first published version of the principle in SD, pt. II, par. 4, (GM VI 249–50: AG 133).

119 These are Descartes' first and second rules of impact; see *Principles,* pt. II, secs. 46, 47.

120 It should be noted that Loemker's version of the diagram contains some mistakes. See also SD, pt. II, par. 4 (GM VI 249–51: AG 133–34).

121 For the sections of the *Dynamica* that relate to impact, see GM VI 488–514; the ED is found in GM VI 215–31.

122 "Absolute force" is the terminology Leibniz uses in the principal exposition of the conservation law in the ED, rather than "living force," the term he uses in the SD, though in at least one place (p. 219), he does refer to it as "la Force vive absolûe". Leibniz also talks about the conservation of "motive action." This is treated somewhat separately in the important ED; see GM VI 220f, and the account in Gueroult, *Leibniz: Dynamique et métaphysique,* pp. 50–55. However, motive action seems to be what he calls simply "action" in the context of the *a priori* derivation of the conservation of mv^2 as discussed above, and in the ED it is lumped together with living force ("force totale absolue") in giving the equation that expresses the conservation of mv^2 law on GM VI 227. And so, it will not get separate treatment here.

123 In the presentation in the ED, Leibniz measures the velocities with respect to the common center of gravity of the two bodies; see GM VI 226. But we should be able to take any reference point we like.

124 The principle is stated in the ED, GM VI 227; it is limited to elastic collisions on GM VI 330. The fuller argument is given in the *Dynamica;* for the definition of respective force, see GM VI 462; for the argument see GM VI 494–95, proposition 10. The argument I give in the text is a paraphrase of the first argument given in proposition 10. The device of the elastic cord connecting the two bodies is introduced

in the proof of proposition 7 on GM VI 492–93, where Leibniz argues
that respective force depends only on the relative velocity of two bodies, not the direction.

125 This is exactly the situation treated in Descartes' fourth rule of impact,
Principles, pt. II, sec. 49, where the smaller moving body rebounds from
the larger body at rest after collision, keeping its speed.

126 The principle is stated in the ED, GM VI 227; the notion of common progress is differentiated from the Cartesian notion of quantity of motion on
GM VI 216–17, and question of elasticity discussed on GM VI 230. The
argument for the principle is given in the *Dynamica*, GM VI 496f.

127 For an account of this feature of Leibniz's thought, see especially M.
Wilson, "Leibniz's Dynamics and Contingency in Nature," in Mach-
amer and Turnbull, eds., *Motion and Time, Space and Matter*; and Poser,
"Apriorismus der Prinzipien und Kontingenz der Naturgesetze. Das
Leibniz-Paradigma der Naturwissenschaft," pp. 164–179.

128 See sec. 5.1.

129 On Gassendi's atomism, see Bloch, *La philosophie de Gassendi: Nomi-
nalisme, matérialisme et métaphysique*; Brundell, *Pierre Gassendi,
From Aristotelianism to a New Natural Philosophy*; Joy, *Gassendi the
Atomist: Advocate of History in an Age of Science*; and Jones, *Pierre
Gassendi 1592–1655: An Intellectual Biography*.

130 See *Principles*, pt. II, secs. 1–23. Descartes claims that in certain circumstances matter is actually divided into indefinitely small pieces in
secs. 34–35.

131 For Boyle's attitude toward atomism, see his *Origin of Forms and
Qualities according to the Corpuscular Philosophy* (1666), in *The
Works of the Honorable Robert Boyle*, ed., Birch, vol. 3, p. 137. The
theoretical part can be found in *Selected Philosophical Papers of Robert
Boyle*, ed., Stewart. On Boyle's attitude on the nature of the vacuum,
see Shapin and Schaffer, *Leviathan and the Air-Pump*, chap. 2.

132 The argument is given in G VII 284–85, with some later reflections
given on 285–88. As Leibniz discovered very quickly, the argument is
not as straightforward as he originally thought, and to the best of my
knowledge, this ingenious argument does not appear anywhere else in
his writings.

133 On the role of elasticity in Leibniz's thought, see especially Breger,
"Elastizität als Strukturprinzip der Materie bei Leibniz," pp. 112–21.

134 Breger, "Elastizität," p. 120 n. 40 also gives a reference to a manuscript
from 1682–83 entitled: "Explicatio Mechanica Elastri . . .".

135 It is not clear here what Leibniz means by an illustration.

136 See, for example, Aristotle, *Physics* II.8; St. Thomas Aquinas, *De
principiis naturae* IV.25. See also Wallace, *Causality and Scientific Ex-*

planation, vol. I, pp. 73–80.

137 *Principles*, pt. I, sec. 28. Note that this includes material from the French version. See also Meditation IV, Adam and Tannery, eds., *Oeuvres de Descartes* VII. 55.

138 *Ethics*, pt. I, appendix, Spinoza, *Opera*, ed., Gebhardt vol. II, pp. 78–80.

139 See, e.g., Gassendi's objection to Descartes, Adam and Tannery VII 308–9; and Robert Boyle, *Disquisitions on the Final Causes of Natural Things* (1688), in Boyle, *Works*, vol. V, pp. 392–444.

140 This would seem to be a consequence of Leibniz's claim that "*everything* in the world can be explained in two ways . . .", though it appears to lead to obvious theological difficulties about God as the final cause of evil.

141 A specific example Leibniz refers to on a number of occasions is the "Unicum Opticae, Catoptricae, et Dioptricae Principium," *Acta Eruditorum*, June 1682, pp. 185–90; in Du, III, pp. 145–51.

142 See Watson, *The Breakdown of Cartesian Metaphysics*, for an account of some of the seventeenth century debate about Cartesian minds and bodies.

143 Actually, this view was not Descartes', though it was that of many of his followers. See Garber, "Mind, Body, and the Laws of Nature in Descartes and Leibniz," pp. 105–133 for this and a fuller account of Leibniz's argument.

144 We should remember, though, an implicit limitation Leibniz imposes on mechanical explicability, insofar as he holds that perception cannot be given a mechanical explanation. See *Monadology*, par. 17, G VI 609: AG 215.

145 See, for example, Henry More, *The Immortality of the Soul*, in his *A Collection of Several Philosophical Writings* (London, 1662), and Sir Kenelm Digby, *Two Treatises* (Paris, 1644). See also the discussion in Garber, "Soul and Mind," chap. V.1 of *The Cambridge History of Seventeenth-Century Philosophy*.

146 On Leibniz's reception of More and Cudworth on these questions, see C. Wilson, *Leibniz's Metaphysics*, pp. 160ff.

147 See the *Tentamen* and other works referred to in note 38.

148 See, e.g., Roger Cotes' introduction to the second edition of Newton's *Principia*; Newton, *Philosophiae naturalis principia mathematica*, eds., Koyré and Cohen, vol. I, p. 26. Leibniz gives this reading of Newton in a letter to Huygens, 1690, GM VI 189:AG 309.

149 I would like to thank Christia Mercer and Nicholas Jolley for very helpful comments on an earlier version of this essay.

10 Leibniz's ontological and cosmological arguments

> I believe . . . that almost all the methods which have been used to prove the existence of God are sound, and could serve the purpose if they were rendered complete.
>
> *(New Essays, A VI.vi: RB 438)*[1]

Few philosophers today would go this far. Even in a period that has witnessed a dramatic rebirth of Anglo-American philosophical theology, the typical strategy has been to embrace a favorite proof while criticizing others or to maintain, more cautiously, that a particular argument has not been refuted. Nevertheless, while most of these philosophers reject the claim that *all* the classic arguments can be rendered sound, they also dismiss as passé the once prevalent view that proving God's existence is a hopeless task.

Natural theology, then, is on the rise. At such a time, it is reasonable to review the arguments of Gottfried Leibniz, one of its most distinguished proponents. Because he thought deeply about many of the issues that now absorb us, an examination of his ideas is likely to illuminate contemporary concerns.

Leibniz gives his own versions of four traditional proofs of God's existence: the ontological argument, the cosmological argument, the argument from eternal truths, and the argument from design. According to the ontological argument, God's existence follows *a priori* from his definition as an absolutely perfect being. Since existence is more perfect than nonexistence, the very idea of God entails that he exists. The cosmological argument, on the other hand, begins with the fact that something exists and derives the existence of God via a causal principle. The proof from eternal truths asserts that since there are necessary truths (e.g., mathe-

353

matical ones), known *a priori*, they must exist "in an absolutely or metaphysically necessary subject, that is, in God" (G VII 305: L 488).[2] Finally, the argument from design claims that the degree of organization and order in the universe implies the existence of a divine being who designed things. Leibniz gives the argument a distinctive twist by purporting to show that the world consists of infinitely many monads which are perfectly coordinated with one another yet are utterly incapable of interaction. This infinite coordination, and the appearance of interaction to which it gives rise, involve a preestablished harmony that only God could have produced (e.g., *New Essays* IV.x, A VI.vi: RB 440; G IV 484–85: L 457–58).

In this essay, I discuss Leibniz's ontological and cosmological arguments. Although his other proofs are also important, I believe that these two contain his most enduring contributions to natural theology.

I

Leibniz formulates the ontological argument in several ways, each of which he seems to think expresses more or less the same idea.[3] Because the variations do not appear to be equivalent, it will be useful to examine the connections he sees between them. Even if we cannot justify his view that they come to the same thing, it makes sense to ask why he should think they do.

Two of these variations employ the concept of an absolutely perfect being.

OA1
1. God is by definition an absolutely perfect being.
2. Existence is a perfection.
3. Therefore, God exists.

OA2
1. God is by definition an absolutely perfect being.
2. Necessary existence is a perfection.
3. Therefore, God necessarily exists.

Leibniz also suggests that, by using the concept of a necessary being, one can construct the proof without mentioning the perfections. In that case, we would have:

OA3

1. A necessary being is by definition a being that necessarily exists.
2. But a being that necessarily exists, exists.
3. Therefore, a necessary being exists.[4]

To achieve theological significance for OA3, one must also prove that a necessary being is absolutely perfect. But Leibniz thinks he can do it. In his scheme, positive reality is the same thing as quantity of essence or degree of perfection. (e.g., G VI 613: L 646–47; G VII 261: L 267; G I 266: L 177) Furthermore, necessary existence is "absolute" existence and every absolute trait "expresses whatever it expresses without any limits" (G VII 261: L 267).[5] Therefore (swallowing hard!), we are led to the conclusion that a necessary being is a being with absolute perfection and conversely.[6]

For clarity, we should note that Leibniz distinguishes two modes of existence. Creatures exist contingently, i.e., their nonexistence is logically possible. God, on the other hand, exists necessarily, i.e., his nonexistence is logically impossible.[7] Leibniz also expresses this by saying that God is a necessary being (or that he has necessary existence) and that creatures are contingent beings (or that they have contingent existence).

Leibniz regards OA1–OA3 as incomplete rather than sophistical. Assuming that God is possible – or that his concept does not contain a contradiction – it follows that he exists. But what justifies that assumption? For all the proofs show, the idea of God might involve a hidden contradiction, as do the notions of a fastest possible speed and a greatest possible circle. If so, the the correct inference would be that God does not exist, since he is impossible (G IV 292 f., 401 ff., 405–6: D 141–46; New Essays IV.x, A VI.vi: RB 438).

The moral is that OA1–OA3 establish only this: if God is possible, God exists. In Leibniz's view, this is a very important result because it is the sole instance in which one can move from possibility to actuality (GIV 359: L386; GIV 294, 402: D141, 143; New Essays IV.x A VI.vi RB 438). The transition, however, requires that one prove that God is possible.

To this end, Leibniz offers two proofs, one defending the notion of an absolutely perfect being, the other justifying the concept of a necessary being. He also has what might be called a "fallback" position to the effect that, in the absence of proof, it is reasonable to presume that

God is possible. This presumption "may suffice for practical life, but it is not sufficient for a demonstration" (GIV 294: D 142).

We shall examine these proofs, together with the fallback position, later. First, however, I want to inquire why Leibniz treats OA1–OA3 as more or less equivalent. Unfortunately, since he does not explain this himself, I can merely offer a plausible conjecture.

It will be instructive to begin by asking why parallel reasoning won't prove the existence of other things, such as a perfect island. In other words, what justifies the claim that the ontological argument works only for God? Leibniz's answer, I believe, is that "perfect x" implies the actual existence of an x if and only if two conditions are satisfied: (1) "perfect x" is taken in a sense which entails "necessary x" and (2) "necessary x" is possible or non-contradictory. But, he thinks, condition (2) fails for anything except the concept of God.

Let us first ask why the idea of a perfect x entails x's existence only if "perfect x" entails "necessary x". As I noted, there are two modes of existence: the necessary and the contingent. Obviously, if "perfect x" does not entail "necessary x", it does not entail that x has necessary existence. But Leibniz argues that contingent existence cannot be inferred from *any* definition. Definitions, he says, are conditionals which state that if something answering to the definiendum should exist, it will be found to have the properties of the definiens (New Essays IV.xi 14, A VI.vi: RB 446–47). As such, coherent definitions always express necessary or eternal truths. Therefore, a thing's existence can be inferred from its definition only if its *necessary* existence can be inferred.

Why is "necessary x" contradictory for any concept other than that of God? This follows, I believe, from Leibniz's identification of reality with perfection. As we saw earlier, necessary existence is unlimited reality. But then unlimited reality is unlimited perfection, and a necessary being turns out to be one with all and only pure perfections. Thus, "necessary island" is contradictory because it means "island with all and only pure perfections," or "island with perfect knowledge, power, etc."[8] Clearly, on these assumptions, we will get a similar contradiction for the idea of anything except God.

This may explain why Leibniz lumps OA1–OA3 together, as though the differences between them were relatively insignificant.

Since he equates "necessary x" with "perfect x," he would naturally feel free to express the ontological argument using either concept. And, in the versions whose premises attribute necessary existence to God (OA2 and OA3), we can also see why the conclusion could be either that God necessarily exists (as in OA2) or simply that he exists (as in OA3). If the argument works at all, it proves that God necessarily exists, which of course entails that God exists.

But how can OA1, whose second premise says that existence is a perfection, differ only insignificantly from arguments which attribute necessary existence to God? Possibly Leibniz would take the following line. When one refers to existence *simpliciter* (as in OA1), or says merely that something "exists", one leaves it to the context to determine which mode of existence is intended. Now, Leibniz thinks it is fairly obvious that only necessary truths can be deduced from definitions and even more obvious that the conclusion of the ontological argument is not that God contingently exists.[9] In his view, to make existence part of something's definition is tacitly to attribute necessary existence to it. So perhaps he would say that a charitable reading of OA1 would construe it as amounting to OA2.

II

Let us now turn to the possibility of God. Leibniz's fallback position is that, in the absence of proof, one ought to assume that God is possible. This is because "there is always a presumption on the side of possibility; that is to say, everything is held to be possible until its impossibility is proved" (G IV 294, 405; D 142, 145; G IV 404; G III 444; *New Essays* IV.x, A VI.vi: RB 438). Possibility claims are, as it were, epistemically innocent until proven guilty. Thus we have:

The Presumptive Argument for God's Existence

1. If it is possible that God exists, then God exists.
2. In the absence of proof to the contrary, it is more reasonable to suppose that a statement of the form "It is possible that . . ." is true than that it is false.
3. There is no proof that "It is possible that God exists" is false.
4. Therefore, it is more reasonable to suppose that "It is possible that God exists" is true than that it is false.

5. Therefore, it is more reasonable to suppose that God exists than that God does not exist.

But premise 2 is much too strong, for it allows us to construct an equally good presumptive argument for atheism.[10] To see why, note first that, while Leibniz accepts 1, he would also accept:

1'. If it is possible that God does not exist, then God does not exist.

On Leibniz's definition, God is a necessary being, or one whose nonexistence is impossible. If it is nevertheless possible that God does not exist, then the very idea of his existence is contradictory and he is impossible. (This was the insight of Leibniz's critique of the ontological argument.) Until someone shows that God is possible, however, we are also entitled to:

3'. There is no proof that "It is possible that God does not exist" is false.

Given 1', 2, and 3', however, it follows that it is more reasonable to suppose that God does not exist than that he does.

It may be objected that Leibniz did not have anything quite so broad as premise 2 in mind. At one point, he distinguishes a presumption from what he calls a "supposition," arguing that "suppositions ought not to be admitted unless they are proved." But a presumption, "which is incomparably more than a simple supposition," should be admitted without proof (G III 444). The problem is that Leibniz does not indicate how to differentiate these notions and I, for one, have no plausible clue to offer on his behalf. Perhaps someone else can provide a defensible way of drawing this distinction.[11]

III

Presumptions aside, Leibniz thinks he can prove "with all imaginable accuracy" that God is possible (G IV 293: D 141). His most famous argument for this occurs in a paper he showed to Spinoza during a visit to the Hague, though the same idea is found in a couple of other essays apparently written at about the same time (1676) (G VII 261: A VI.ii: 578: L 167; A VI.iii 571–79; Cf. G IV 296 and *Monadology* par. 45, G VI 614: L 647). The argument rests on the definition of a perfection as a simple, absolutely positive property. It also presupposes that if "A perfect being is possible" is true, it is necessarily true and that every necessary truth is either an identity or reducible to an identity. The basic idea of the proof is this. Positive properties are always compatible, because things can exclude each other other only if one involves the negation of the other. Simple properties, on the other hand, are always irreducible, because reduction requires complexity. Consequently, for any two properties that are positive *and* simple, the proposition that they are incompatible neither is, nor is reducible to, an identity.

The Proof from Affirmative Simples

1. The concept of an absolutely perfect being is consistent if and only if the combination all perfections in one being is consistent.
2. The combination of all perfections in one being is consistent if and only if, for any two perfections, A and B, "A and B are incompatible" is not a necessary truth.
3. For any two perfections, A and B, "A and B are incompatible"is not a necessary truth if and only if this proposition neither is, nor is reducible to, an identity.
4. But, for any two perfections, A and B, "A and B are incompatible" is not an identity. For, if it were, A and B would express the negation of the other, which is contrary to the hypothesis that perfections are purely positive.
5. And, for any two perfections, A and B, "A and B are incompatible" is not reducible to an identity. For a reduction requires the resolution of at least one of the terms, which is contrary to the hypothesis that perfections are simple.
6. Hence, for any two perfections, A and B, "A and B are incompatible" is not a necessary truth.
7. Therefore, the concept of an absolutely perfect being is consistent.
8. If the concept of an absolutely perfect being is consistent, an absolutely perfect being is possible.
9. Therefore, an absolutely perfect being is possible.[12]

An objection to the second premise of this argument is that it does not follow from the fact that any *two* members of a set of properties can be consistently combined that *all* the members can be so combined. (Consider the set of properties: *married at t, happy at t, either unmarried or unhappy at t.*)

Leibniz would reply that although this does not follow in general, it does in the present instance. The combination of any two simple, positive properties yields a consistent property that is complex, but still purely positive. Since purely positive properties can never exclude one another, however, the new property can itself be consistently combined with any simple, positive property you like (and so forth ad infinitum).

The idea that the concept of God consists of simple properties is an instance of the more general notion that all complex concepts depend on simple elements (G VI 612: L 646; G I 143: L 199; G VII 293: L 230; G IV 425: L 293 and C 429–30). Furthermore, Leibniz identifies the simples (which he takes to be positive) with the primitive attributes of God (G IV 425: L 293; C 513: P 7; G VII 310: P 77). But while these assumptions may have felicitous consequences for the possibility of God, Leibniz worries whether they fit with his other views. He notes, for example, that on his account *all* positive properties are compatible *inter se* and this leads him to wonder what explains "the incompossibility of different things or how it is that different essences can be opposed to one another" (G VII 195: Russell, *Critical Exposition*, pp. 296–97). He is sure that the actualization of certain possibles excludes others, but if possibles consist solely of positive, and hence compatible, properties, how can this be? In the previous passage, he says that God alone knows the answer.[13]

Some may urge that the difficulty can be relieved by the addition of negative simples. Yet even on the doubtful premise that this idea is coherent, it destroys the proof of God's possibility. Or, at any rate, it does so given Leibniz's further view that simple concepts are the primitive attributes of God. Once negativity is added to the divine nature, the game is up, since the idea that all *positive* properties are compatible will then no longer entail that God is possible.

These issues are internal to Leibniz's system. Setting such matters aside, however, many would question the very idea of intrinsically simple properties.[14] Linguistic items, such as words or sentences, can be negative or positive, simple or complex, but what sense is there in simple properties or concepts? Leibniz seems to conflate linguistic and metaphysical entities by hypostatizing the former and projecting their features onto the latter. But even given this penchant, the case for a "true" set of simples that is not relative to any particular language is problematic, since it has often been noted that what is simple or positive in one language may be complex or negative in another.[15]

The charge of conflating language and metaphysical reality gains further credence when we note that the proof from affirmative simples says that any two perfections, *A* and *B*, are compatible just in case the *sentence* "A and B are incompatible" is neither an identity nor reducible to one. A sentence, moreover, is an identity, for Leibniz, when it is of a certain form (namely, "*A* is *A*," "*AB* is *A*," etc.). And it is reducible to an identity when one can be produced in a finite number of steps by substituting terms, on the basis of definitions, into the subject and/or predicate position of the sentence.[16] All of this makes a certain amount of sense when the entities and operations involved are linguistic, but little otherwise.

Leibniz's reply is that language represents concepts, which make up the content of significant discourse. If natural languages discriminate differently between simple and complex, negative and positive, or if there are inconsistencies within a single language, this means only that existing parlance does not adequately map the true conceptual order. But his ideas apply only to an *ideal* language, or one in which the form of a sentence corresponds to the form of the proposition it expresses and in which the substitutions that are possible in the former reflect parallel relationships in the latter.[17]

Yet if different languages suggest distinct mappings of the realm of concepts, how are we to know which mapping is correct or indeed whether there is any language-independent realm to be mapped? How, in fact, are we even to understand the claim that in an ideal language the form of a sentence corresponds to the form of the proposition it expresses? There are rules for identifying the form of a sentence, but none for determining the form of a proposition. So the basic problem remains.

Leibniz claims to have an infallible proof that there are simple concepts (G I 140: L 199; C 429; Cf. G VI 612: L 646).[18] If any concepts are conceived at all, they are either conceived through themselves or through other concepts. If they are conceived through themselves, they are incapable of analysis and hence are simple.[19] But nothing can be conceived thorough other concepts unless the sequence of concepts through which it is conceived terminates in ones conceived through themselves. Leibniz illustrates this point with an analogy. Suppose I give you a hundred dollars, which you are to receive from person A. A sends you on to B, B to C, and so on forever. In that case, you will never receive anything. Similarly, one cannot conceive a concept through others unless the sequence of concepts through which the first is conceived terminates in ones conceived through themselves (C 429–30: P 1–2; A VI.iii 514: L 160)[20] Therefore, since many concepts are in fact conceived, there are concepts which are conceived through themselves, i.e., ones that are simple.

Proof of the Existence of Simple Concepts

1. If any concepts are conceived, they are either conceived through themselves or through other ones.
2. If they are conceived through themselves, they are simple.
3. If they are conceived thorough other ones, then there must also be simple concepts, since the analysis of anything conceived through something else must terminate in concepts conceived through themselves.
4. Therefore, if any concepts are conceived, there are simple concepts.
5. But many concepts are conceived.
6. Therefore, there are simple concepts.

This argument should be intriguing to someone who accepts the assumption that there is a language-independent realm of concepts. But it does nothing to justify that assumption. Leibniz treats premise 1, for example, as axiomatic, and that axiom embodies the very intuition that we have been at pains to call into question.[21]

IV

Leibniz's next proof is a modal argument designed to defend the possibility of a necessary being. It turns on the following *a priori* premise: if a necessary being is not possible, no being is possible (G IV 406: D 147).[22] Leibniz defends this by claiming that contingent (or nonnecessary) beings *require* a necessary being to provide a sufficient reason for their existence.[23] On that assumption, if a necessary being is not possible, then neither a necessary nor a nonnecessary being is possible.

To derive "A necessary being is possible" from "If a necessary being is not possible, no being is possible" Leibniz needs only a premise to the effect that some being or other is possible. Most commentators have taken it for granted that he means to infer this *a posteriori* from the fact that something exists.[24] In that case, the proof of the possibility of God would be the first five steps of the following argument.

Modal Proof of the Existence of God

1. If a necessary being is not possible, no being is possible.
2. But something exists.

3. If something exists, some being is possible.
4. Therefore, some being is possible.
5. Therefore, a necessary being is possible.
6. If a necessary being is possible, a necessary being exists.
7. Hence, a necessary being exists.

Now this argument is valid and consists entirely of statements Leibniz accepts. So he would surely embrace it. Nevertheless, it does not complete the *ontological* argument, which, as he often points out, can include no *a posteriori* element. What we have here is a variation on the comological argument.

Did Leibniz lapse and complete the ontological argument cosmologically? That would be surprising, since he claims that his proof fills the gap "geometrically *a priori*," and the argument above glaringly fails to do so (G IV 405–6: D 145; Cf. G IV 403, 404; D 144; *New Essays* IV.x, A VI.vi: RB 438–39; G III 444; A VI.iii 583).

I think he had something else in mind. Leibniz holds that if the definition of a concept is noncontradictory, then the existence of something that exemplifies the concept is possible. This is true, moreover, whether or not the concept is complete, i.e., sufficiently complex to designate a possible individual. On his account, a "real" (as opposed to merely "nominal") definition is any one containing a proof that the thing defined is noncontradictory (G IV 424–25: L 293). Furthermore, he thinks there are many examples of such definitions, some of which we know to be "real" on *a priori* grounds. It would appear, then, that the desired premise could be supplied by choosing one of these definitions at random. Hence, the proof might run as follows:

Modal Proof of the Possibility of God
1. If a necessary being is not possible, no being is possible.
2. If the definition of a concept is noncontradictory, then a being that exemplifies the concept is possible.
3. But there are instances of definitions of concepts which are non-contradictory. (A circle, for example, is defined as a plane figure having all of its points equidistant from the center, and we know *a priori* that this definition is not contradictory.)
4. Therefore, a being that exemplifies the concept of a circle is possible.
5. Therefore, some being is possible.
6. Therefore, a necessary being is possible.

Some may object that Leibniz's basis for premise 3 is *a posteriori*. He would agree that a circle, and other such things, are possible, but only because he has experienced examples of these things, not because he knows their possibility *a priori*. Consequently, the only version of the proof he would accept is unfit to complete the ontological argument.

But that is mistaken. In some notes on the definition of God, Leibniz begins by stating that if the existence of a thing is to follow from its essence, it must be conceivable *a priori* that the thing is possible. He then adds emphatically:

A priori, I say: that is, not from experience but from the very nature of the thing, just as we would conceive that the number three, a circle and other things of that kind are possible even if we had never experienced that they actually exist or, at any rate, had taken no account of this experience.

(A VI.iii 583)

In this passage, Leibniz does not say how to show *a priori* that a circle is possible. But, in general, he describes two *a priori* ways of establishing a thing's possibility: one involves pushing the analysis of its definition back to primitive notions, the other (which he calls "causal") involves describing a method for generating the thing (GIV 450: L 319). And he indicates elsewhere that he would use the *a priori* causal method in the case of a circle.[25] So there is no doubt that he thinks he can establish the possibility of a circle without resorting to experience.

Obviously, this proof also depends on its first premise, which, as I noted, rests on a thesis supported in the cosmological argument. I turn to the cosmological argument now.

V

Leibniz bases his cosmological argument on the famous principle of sufficient reason.[26] In paragraph 32 of the *Monadology*, he expresses this as follows:

No fact can be real or existent, nor any proposition true, without there being a sufficient reason why it is so rather than otherwise. (G VI 612: L 646)

Likewise, he tells Samuel Clarke that there must be "a sufficient reason for anything to exist, for any event to occur, for any truth to obtain" (G VII 419: L 717).[27]

For Leibniz, P is a sufficient reason for Q just in case P fully accounts for Q. Put slightly differently: P is a sufficient reason for Q if and only "P is true" gives a full and definitive answer to "Why is Q the case?" Sometimes Leibniz says simply that nothing is without a reason and at other times that everything has a cause. But he often uses "reason" and "cause" synonymously, taking "cause" in a broad Aristotelian sense.[28] So, these formulations probably come to the same thing, to wit: there is a full explanation of everything.

Leibniz regards the principle of sufficient reason as a corollary of his predicate-in-subject principle. The latter asserts that there is an *a priori* connection, or relation of inclusion, between the predicate and subject concepts of every true proposition, and this guarantees that there is a full reason for the proposition's truth (G VII: 300–1: L 226–27; G VI 612: L 646; C 518–19: L 267–68; G IV 436–38: L 310–11; C 513: P 8; G VII 309; P 75). In the case of contingent truths, we humans cannot discover the connection *a priori*, though it is always there and known to God.

When it comes to existing individuals, the principle implies that there is an answer to the question why there is anything at all and, more particularly, why things should be as they are rather than otherwise. On this view, if one knows that Q exists because R brought it about, and that R exists because S brought it about etc., but one does not know why there should have been anything at all, or why this sequence of things exists rather than some other, then one does not have a full answer to why Q, R, or S exist. In general, if an individual's existence does not settle these questions, then, whatever it may explain, it does not give a *sufficient* reason for anything.

With this in mind we can give a quick overview of Leibniz's version of the cosmological argument. If there were no necessary being, there would be no answer to the question: Why does the world exist? For the world is a series of contingent things and no such series contains a sufficient reason for its existence. Therefore, there must be a necessary being to provide a sufficient reason for the contingent ones.

Leibniz fills in the details of the argument in slightly different ways in different places (G VII 302–3: L 486–87; G VI 602, 612–13, 106: L 639, 646, H 127; G VII 310: P 76–77; Cf. C 533–34: P 145; C 519: L 268; G IV 106–7: L 110–11). But since there is a single idea running through these texts, a couple of substantial citations will provide enough material for our discussion. Here is a copious statement of the argument, taken from *The Ultimate Origination of Things* (1697).

> Besides the world or aggregate of finite things, there is a certain One dominant being which . . . not only rules the world but fabricates or makes it . . . and hence is the ultimate reason for things. For a sufficient reason for existence cannot be found merely in any one individual thing or even in the whole aggregate and series of things. Let us imagine the book on the *Elements of Geometry* to have been eternal, one copy always being made from another; then it is clear that though we can give a reason for the present book based on the preceding book from which it was copied, we can never arrive at a complete reason, no matter how many books we may assume in the past, for one can always wonder why such books should have existed at all times; why there should be books at all, and why they should be written in this way. What is true of books is true also of the different states of the world; every subsequent state is somehow copied from the preceding one (although according to certain laws of change). No matter how far we may have gone back to earlier states, therefore, we will never discover in them a full reason why there should be a world at all, and why it should be such as it is. Even if we should imagine the world to be eternal, therefore, the reason for it would clearly have to be sought elsewhere, since we would still be assuming nothing but a succession of states in any one of which we can find no sufficient reason, nor can we advance the slightest toward establishing a reason, no matter how many of these states we assume. . . . The reasons for the world therefore lie in something extramundane . . . which has absolute or metaphysical necessity. . . . Therefore, . . . since there is no reason for an existing thing except in an existing thing, there must necessarily exist some one being of metaphysical necessity . . . which is distinct from the plurality of beings or from the world.
>
> (G VII 302–3: L 486–87)

We should observe that Leibniz says that some sort of an account of the existence of the members of the series can be found within the series itself: "We can give *a reason* for the present book based on the preceding book from which it was copied." But he stresses that no sequence of such explanations, however long, gives a "complete" or "sufficient" reason for any of the books: "We can never arrive at *a complete reason* [for the present book], no matter how many books we may assume in the past; for one can always wonder . . . why there should be books at all, and why they should be written in this way."

Why can't anything in the world answer these questions? Leibniz's reply is that the world as a whole and everything in it are contingent. Nothing contingent, however, can contain a sufficient reason for its own existence or that of anything else. Here is a shorter statement of the argument (taken from *The Monadology*, 1714) which brings this point out more clearly than the previous citation:

> A sufficient reason must . . . be found in the case of contingent truths . . . that is to say, in the case of the sequence of things distributed through the universe of creatures, whose analysis into particular reasons could proceed into unlimited detail. . . . As all this detail includes other earlier or more detailed contingent factors, each of which in turn needs a similar analysis to give its reason, one makes no progress, and the sufficient or final reason will have to be outside the sequence or series of these detailed contingent factors, however infinite they may be. Thus, the final reason of things must be in a necessary substance in which the detail of the changes can be contained only eminently as in their source. It is this substance that we call God.   (G VI 612–13:L 646)

Once again, Leibniz identifies the sufficient reason for a thing with its final (or complete) reason and he locates "the sufficient or final reason" outside the series of contingent things. Although the members of this series are linked by "particular reasons," their sufficient reason is in God.[29]

Perhaps the following reconstruction captures what is essential in these passages.

The Cosmological Argument

1. If anything exists, there must be a sufficient reason why it exists.
2. But this world exists and it is a series of contingent beings.
3. Therefore, there must be a sufficient reason why this series of contingent beings exists.
4. But nothing contingent – and, in particular, neither the existing series as a whole nor any of its members – can contain a sufficient reason why this series exists.
5. A sufficient reason for any existing thing can only be in an existing thing, which is itself either necessary or contingent.
6. Therefore, a sufficient reason why this series exists must be in a necessary being that lies outside the world.
7. Therefore, there is a necessary being that lies outside the world.

The passages quoted earlier also contain a very important argument for step 4.

Proof of Step 4

A. If each member of a series of beings is contingent, the series as a whole is contingent.

B. But each member of the existing series is contingent. (Second conjunct of premise 2)

C. Therefore the existing series as a whole and each of its members is contingent.

D. Nothing contingent can contain a sufficient reason for its own existence or that of anything else.

E. Therefore, nothing contingent – and, in particular, neither the existing series as whole nor any of its members – can contain a sufficient reason why this series exists.

Leibniz stresses that we cannot get around this by supposing that the series is infinitely old and that a reason for each of its members can be found in preceding ones. Even if that were so, there would be no *sufficient* reason for the series, since nothing contingent, no matter how old or complex, can explain why there is anything at all or why this series exists rather than another one.

VI

In this section, I consider objections that do not purport to deny the principle of sufficient reason. One such criticism attacks premise 2. Obviously, the world exists, but how does Leibniz know that it consists of nothing but contingent beings? Maybe something within it is necessary.

Some would say that we observe things come into being and expire and thus know *a posteriori* that they are contingent. But that would not assure us that *everything* in the world is contingent, since there is far too much that we have not observed. Possibly, for example, all the composite things we perceive are contingent and destructible, but their basic elements are necessary.

As we saw in section I, however, Leibniz's identification of reality with perfection entails that a necessary being must have all and only pure perfections. And this, together with the identity of indiscernibles, implies that there is only *one* necessary being.[30]

This raises the question how Leibniz can be sure that the world itself is not the necessary being. Even if we grant that any series of contingent substances is contingent, one might still deny premise 2 by holding, with Spinoza, that the world is a single necessary substance.

Against this there is the intuition that the world might not have existed. That seems possible. But, in this context, it is not clear how much weight to assign this intuition, since it also seems possible (to me, anyway) for absolutely nothing to exist. Yet this contradicts the idea that there is a necessary being. If I'm wrong in thinking that it is possible for nothing whatsoever to exist, perhaps my intuition that the world is contingent is also mistaken.[31]

Perhaps. Yet Leibniz might answer that when one weighs up the number of deep intuitions that Spinozism sacrifices, it is far less costly, and therefore far more plausible, to believe that the world is a collection of contingent things than that it is a single necessary substance.

According to necessitarianism, for example, everything that is possible occurs in the actual world and nothing could have been otherwise. But this is ludicrous, says Leibniz, since what is related in any self-consistent novel or story is possible. Are we therefore to imagine

that there are certain poetic regions in the infinite extent of space and time where we might see wandering over the earth King Arthur of Great Britain, Amadis of Gaul, and the fabulous Dietrich von Bern invented by the Germans?   (FC 178–79: L 263)[32]

Likewise, Leibniz thinks it flies in the face of good sense to suppose that nothing could have been otherwise.

A stubborn Spinozist might answer that the fabulous von Bern and his friends can't be found wandering in outer space, but they aren't really possible either. He might also insist that Leibniz is begging the question by just asserting that things could have been otherwise. These replies, however, don't increase the plausibility of the Spinozist's view. Surely we must agree with Leibniz that necessitarianism is counterintuitive.

Unfortunately, it is not clear that his own theory avoids this result. In every true proposition, he says, the concept of the predicate is contained in that of the subject. But, if so, how can any true proposition fail to be necessary? Leibniz struggled mightily with this question, and I shall not try to judge his answers here.[33] Nevertheless, the force of the question is evident.

Leibniz would also be likely to point out that a further cost of Spinozism is its counterintutive doctrine that each individual is really but a mode of God. He accepts the *cogito* and thinks it shows that he is a true individual substance, not a property of something else. A Spinozist could answer that we are each *self-conscious* modes of God and that Leibniz can therefore know his own existence without being a substance. But, although this might explain one's knowledge of one's own existence, it would not increase the appeal of the claim that you and I are just modes.

A modified Spinozist could deal with these last issues and also raise other problems. He conceives of the universe as an eternal series of substances, including self-conscious ones who can know their own existence via the cogito. In his scheme, each substance is brought into existence by previous ones and each eventually expires, leaving others which remain. Because of the constitution of things, however, each substance *must* have exactly the properties it actually has: the time when it arises, the attributes it expresses, and the moment of its demise are fixed necessarily by the order of nature. Now the universe exists just in case at least one of its members does.[34] But since each member must exist at its appointed time, and since it is always true that at least one member exists, the universe is a necessary being: it cannot fail to be and it has its reason for being in the eternal order of its components.[35] Accordingly, each component substance of the universe also has a sufficient reason, not in itself nor in any finite sequence of other substances, but in the infinite sequence, taken as a whole, that leads up to it. This metaphysics seems to preserve the Spinozistic challenge without sacrificing either the cogito or our individual substancehood.

Which part of the cosmological argument would the modified Spinozist deny? To answer this, note first that the substances described above are contingent. A necessary being is eternal, because it is logically impossible that it should *ever* fail to exist (*New Essays* II.xvii, A VI.vi: RB 159; Gr 302–3; G I 140, 146, 149: L 197, 202–3). So our substances aren't necessary. And, since Leibniz defines a contingent being as one that is not necessary, it follows that these substances are contingent. But in that case the modified Spinozist is in a good position to deny 4A: as he has set things up, the series of contingent beings is necessary. This, of course, also undermines 4, which assumes that the series as a whole is contingent.

On Leibniz's definition, anything that exists only some of the time is contingent. The problem, from his opponent's perspective, is that this does not entail that if something is contingent, it might never have existed at all. Leibniz just *assumes* that. Given the assumption, 4A may be defensible: if each member of a series is such that it is logically possible that it should not have existed at all, it is plausible to suppose that it is logically possible that the entire series should not have existed. Yet Leibniz's assumption can be denied, as the modified Spinozist's substances illustrate.

It will do no good for Leibniz to assert that since these substances are only hypothetically necessary, each of them is such that it might never have existed. Taken by itself, that claim doesn't justify the assumption, it simply reexpresses it. Nor will it suffice to change the definition of "contingent being" from "nonnecessary being" to "thing that might not have existed at all." This would merely turn the opponent's attack against the idea that the world is a series of contingent things (i.e., against the second half of 2). The modified Spinozist's view, after all, is that no substance is such that it might never have existed.

A better tactic would be to concede that the disputed assumption does not follow from the definition of "contingent being" and to defend 4A in terms of the unacceptable consequences of denying it. The objection to 4A was just that the modified Spinozist scheme might be true. But while that scheme eliminates *some* of the most implausible features of standard Spinozism (namely, those having to do with the cogito and our own individual substancehood), it does not eliminate all of them. It still implies, for example, that everything that is possible occurs in the actual world and that nothing could have been otherwise – a position that Leibniz regards as patently absurd. Although he may overstate his point, it does seem to sully the critique of 4A.

Another response uses premises 4D and 5 to argue that the modified Spinozist violates the principle of sufficient reason. 4D, we will recall, asserts that nothing contingent can contain a sufficient reason for its own existence or that of anything else. 5 says that a sufficient reason for an existing thing can only be in an existing thing. If every component of the universe is contingent, however, then there is nowhere to locate a sufficient reason for any substance. The modified Spinozist concedes that the reason cannot be either in the substance itself or in any finite sequence of its companions, since all of these are contingent. His view is rather that each substance "has a sufficient reason, not in itself nor in any finite sequence of other substances, but in the infinite sequence, *taken as a*

whole, that leads up to it." But even if we count this sequence as a
"thing," it is not, taken as a whole anyway, an *existing* thing. At any
moment, at most a *part* of the relevant sequence exists, a part which
is contingent and hence incapable of supplying a sufficient reason
for anything at all.[36] So, in fact, Leibniz would say, *no* substance in
this system has a sufficient reason.

Possibly Leibniz's adversary could find a plausible way of continuing the dialogue. But I shall not attempt to do so, since the modified
Spinozist has already served my purposes.[37]

In the final section, I consider arguments for and against premise 1.

VII

Some believe that the principle of sufficient reason involves an incoherent conception of explanation.[38] On their view, one can explain
something only by appealing to something else. Thus, one might
explain why the water boiled by referring to the fire that heated it or
why the roof collapsed by mentioning the unusually heavy object
that fell upon it, but in no case would it make sense to say that
something explained itself. Yet, as Leibniz employs the idea, there
can be a sufficient reason for the existence of something only if there
is a *self-explaining* being. Therefore, premise 1 is absurd.

As it stands, this argument is inconclusive. Leibniz could concede
that ordinary explanations work as described, but insist that his
critic just *asserts* that there cannot be a case of an extraordinary
explanation. What proof is there that every possible explanation is of
the garden variety?[39]

I should also mention a criticism of 1 which, for lack of space, I
cannot explore here. Kant attacks the ontological argument by claiming that existence is not a predicate.[39] This thesis, moreover, has
been taken to imply that the very concept of a necessary being is
incoherent, because many construe a necessary being as one that has
the predicate of existence necessarily. But if the idea of a necessary
being is incoherent, then so is the principle of sufficient reason: for
on Leibniz's understanding, there is no sufficient reason for the existence of anything unless there is a necessary being.[40]

The time has long since past, however, when one could sum-
marily dismiss the idea of a necessary being on Kantian grounds. A
number of philosophers now argue that existence *is* a predicate and

many others hold that, though existence is not a predicate, *neces-sary existence* is. (Leibniz himself takes the first line in some passages and the second in others.) It may yet be that Kant's view, or something like it, is correct, but the critic must work to show it.[41]

The next tactic is not so much a refutation of 1 as a criticism of 4, but since it leads to a problem with 1, I consider it here.

Many commentators charge that the cosmological argument erroneously assumes that the series of contingent things is something over and above its constituents. They would locate this error in the proof of step 4, which contrasts the members of the series with the series as a whole.[42] Leibniz states that there could be a reason within the series for each of its members without that constituting a reason for the series as a whole. Yet there isn't any difference here: the series *is* the totality of its members, and so if each member has a reason, the series *ipso facto* has one. Thus, the argument rests on a distinction without a difference.

I cannot see that Leibniz makes this mistake, however. He distinguishes *each* member of the series from the series as a whole, but that's impeccable. He also says there can be a reason for each of the members without that constituting a sufficient reason for the series. But that isn't because he distinguishes the series from its members; it's because he distinguishes *a reason* from a *sufficient reason*. As he insists, the presence of a reason, or contingent cause, for each thing in the series doesn't explain why this series exists and therefore does not provide a sufficient reason for anything. The critic supposes that there is a distinction without a difference because he focuses on the wrong distinction.

This reply, however, is very likely to raise suspicions about premise 1. Part of the appeal of the premise, I suspect, is that many people assume that there must be a causal explanation of all events in terms of ones that precede them, and they unwittingly confuse this with the presence of a sufficient reason for everything. But once one sees the difference, one can easily doubt premise 1 and question whether there is a truly *sufficient* reason for anything. What proof is there that there is an explanation of why this world exists rather than a different one or none at all?

Leibniz tries to answer this by giving arguments for the principle of sufficient reason. He deduces it *a priori*, for example, from his definition of truth. A proposition is true, he says, just in case the concept of the predicate is contained in that of the subject, and this entails that whatever is true has a sufficient reason (C 519: L 268; C 401–2: P 93; C 11: P 172).[43] Likewise, in a famous passage supporting the principle, Leibniz tells Arnauld that either truth¹ is concept containment, "Or else I do not know what truth is" (G II 56: L 337).[44]

This obviously invites the question why we should identify truth with concept containment. And it is very tempting to suppose that Leibniz's real motivation for this is his desire to be able to prove the principle of sufficient reason *a priori!*[45]

Leibniz also gives a proof that whatever exists has a sufficient reason using definitions of a sufficient reason and a requisite (A VI ii 483. Cf. Gr 263, 267; G VII 393: L 698; A VI. ii 118). His claim is that whatever exists must have all of its necessary conditions (or requisites) posited and that the complete set of a thing's necessary conditions *is* its sufficient reason. Therefore, whatever exists has a sufficient reason.

Proof that Whatever Exists Has a Sufficient Reason

Definition 1: A sufficient reason is something which, if it has been posited, the thing exists.

Definition 2: A requisite is something which, if it has not been posited, the thing does not exist.

1. If a requisite of a thing has not been posited, the thing does not exist. (By Definition 2)
2. Therefore, whatever exists has all of its requisites posited.
3. If a thing does not exist, some requisite or other of it has not been posited.
4. Therefore, if all the requisites of a thing have been posited, the thing exists. (By contraposition of 3)
5. Therefore, all the requisites of a thing constitute a sufficient reason for it. (By Definition 1)
6. Therefore, whatever exists has a sufficient reason.

The argument is faulty on two counts. First, as Sleigh points out, step 3 begs the question: this claim does not follow from either of Leibniz's definitions.[46] Second (and more pertinent to the cosmological argument), the proof does not show in particular that the set of a thing's requisites must include something to answer the question: Why does this series exist rather than another or nothing at all?[47] As we know, however, Leibniz thinks a sufficient reason *must* answer these questions.

Next, Leibniz thinks that the principle has *a posteriori* support, because no one has ever produced an event that lacks a reason.

I have often defied people to . . . produce any one uncontested example in which [the principle of sufficient reason] fails. But they have never done it, nor ever will. Yet there is an infinite number of instances in which it succeeds, or rather it succeeds in all the known cases in which it has been employed. From which one may one may reasonably judge that it will also succeed in unknown cases . . . according to the method of experimental philosophy which proceeds a posteriori, even if it were not also justified by pure reason, or a priori.   (G VII 420: L 717)

Leibniz's point seems to be that since a cause has always turned up in known cases, there probably is one in unknown cases. Let's grant this for the sake of argument. How does it support the principle of sufficient reason? Even if we have found *a reason* for everything we have investigated, we have not found a *sufficient reason* for anything; for surely we haven't discovered empirically why this world exists rather than an entirely different one or none at all. Is Leibniz forgetting his distinction between a reason and a sufficient reason? Or is he leaping from causal relations between events to a sufficient reason for the very fact of existence?

Another suggestion is that he is merely arguing that no one is likely to cast doubt on the principle of sufficient reason by finding an event without a cause. On this weaker reading, however, the argument does not even attempt to support the thesis that concerns us, namely, that there is an explanation of why there is anything at all and of why this world in particular exists.

Finally, Leibniz attempts to vindicate the principle pragmatically by arguing that it is indispensible to our epistemic pursuits. He says, for example, that much of physics and ethics rests on it and that there can be no inductive arguments without it, nor any conclusions drawn in civil matters. Ultimately, he thinks "whatever is not of mathematical necessity . . . must be sought [in the principle of sufficient reason] entirely" (G VII 301: L 227). However clear this may have seemed to Leibniz, it would certainly require a wholesale defense today.

Rationalist that he was, Leibniz thought the truth of the principle of sufficient reason should be evident to anyone who reflects carefully about it. In moments of frustration, he would even declare that the principle is so obvious that it doesn't need proof (G VII 419:L 717). Yet, as we know, it is a thesis which many thoughtful and intelligent people have rejected.

I close with an observation about the connection between this topic and Leibniz's modal proof. Leibniz sought to justify the concept of a necessary being by recourse to the principle of sufficient reason. But what is uncertain about the former is also uncertain about the latter, namely, whether it makes sense for anything to contain its own reason for existence. To prove the possibility of a necessary being, then, one cannot take the principle of sufficient reason for granted: one must prove it. And that is something that neither Leibniz nor anyone else has ever done.

NOTES

1 I wish to thank Robert Almeder, Holly Thomas, and Donald Rutherford for suggestions about the issues in this paper. The notes contain an English translation (where I know of one) following a reference to an edition of the original text. Translations are from the cited English translation, though possibly with some changes. Where no English edition is cited, the translation is mine.

2 This proof was also a favorite of St. Augustine, from whom Leibniz derived it.

3 The ontological argument was first proposed by St. Anselm of Canterbury (1033–1109) and was subsequently embraced by Descartes, Leibniz, and Spinoza, to name only a few. Unlike the others, Spinoza used it to support the heretical view that God is actually the universe itself, which he regarded as a single, all-encompassing substance with infinite attributes. The ontological argument has been criticized by a host of philosophers, including Gaunilo (a cohort of Anselm), Aquinas, Gassendi, and Kant. Gaunilo attempted to reduce it to absurdity by claiming that the reasoning would work as well for a perfect island. The most famous criticism, however, is Kant's, who objected that existence is not a real predicate. "X exists," he said, does not add anything to the concept of x. It merely "posits" an x, i.e., says there is something that exemplifies the concept of x. One can therefore never establish a thing's existence a priori via its concept or definition. Though Kant's criticism has convinced many, the ontological argument still has distinguished defenders. Some have replied, for example, that Kant's point does not hold for necessary existence, the special kind of existence possessed only by God. For references and discussion, see Plantinga, The Ontological Argument.

4 Leibniz very frequently uses OA1 to formulate the argument. But his extensive remarks on a letter from Jaquelot make clear that he also regards OA2, OA3, and other variations as acceptable reconstructions (G III 442–54). Sometimes he expresses a preference for versions which do not mention the perfections, though he doesn't make much of it (G IV 358–59: L 386). Cf. G IV 405: D 145.

5 In other words, necessary existence is existence in the highest possible degree.

6 In connection with the cosmological argument, Leibniz also gives other proofs of the perfection of a necessary being (G VI 602 and 106: L 639 and H 127).

7 This distinction corresponds to Leibniz's definition of a necessary truth as one whose opposite implies a contradiction and a contingent truth as one that is not necessary (G III 400: AG 193; G VI 612: L 646; G VII 108ff; G VI 106: H 127).

8 At G IV 402: D 143, Leibniz rejects the idea of a perfect body because "a body being limited by its essence cannot include all perfections."

9 Leibniz would have agreed with Hartshorne that the contingent existence of God is senseless. Since God is supposed to be a necessary being, the proposition that he exists is either a necessary truth or a contradiction.

10 This is noted by Adams, "Presumption and the Necessary Existence," p. 21.

11 Reasons for skepticism about this, however, can be found in Adams, "Presumption."

12 My reconstruction most closely mirrors Leibniz's statement of the proof at A.VI.iii 572. In the Hague version, in place of "an identity" Leibniz uses the equivalent notion of a proposition "known per se" (per se nota) (G VII 261: A.VI.iii 578: L 167).

13 How Leibniz finally meant to analyze compossibility is still disputed among scholars.

14 For example, van Inwagen, "Ontological Arguments", p. 382; Mates, "Leibniz on Possible Worlds," p. 346; Philosophy of Leibniz, pp. 61–62; Malcolm, "Anselm's Ontological Arguments," p. 59; and Wittgenstein and Quine, passim.

15 As if matters were not bad enough, Mates points out that even in a single language, a sentence that is atomic may seem synonymous with one that is not (e.g., "Zeus is bald" and "Zeus does not have hair on his head"). Mates, "Leibniz on Possible Worlds," p. 346.

16. Leibniz assumes that sentences that are not of the subject/predicate form can converted into equivalent ones that are.

17 For an excellent discussion of Leibniz's conception of an ideal language, see chap. VIII.

18 Although Leibniz is sure that there are simple concepts, he often expresses uncertainty about whether we humans can discover any of them (G IV 423–25: L 292–93; C 513: p. 7. But cf. G III 582: L 664).

19 A concept is "conceived through" the ones that make it up, or are part of its analysis. The concept, *man*, for example, is conceived through the concepts, *rational* and *animal*, which are each part of its analysis. If a concept is conceived through itself, it has no "parts" and it is therefore simple.

20 Cf. the material quoted at Mates, "Leibniz on Possible Worlds," p. 58, where the analogy is to explaining the meaning of a word by reference to a series of other words, none of which the speaker understands. As Couturat points out, however, Leibniz later gives up such analogies. C 430n. For more on this topic, see my next note.

21 It is also important to mention that Leibniz eventually rejects step 3 of his "infallible" argument. According to his later views, the analysis of every contingent proposition involves an infinite, and hence nonterminating, sequence of steps. Nevertheless, he does not abandon the idea that complex concepts are constituted from simples. Instead, after about 1686, he maintains that the analysis of necessary truths terminates in primitive ideas, whereas that of contingent truths "converges" upon them. For he still takes it as evident that the complex presupposes the simple, even where analysis cannot reach the latter in a finite number of steps.

22 What Leibniz says, specifically, is: "If being of itself is impossible, then all beings by others are too." But since he equates being of itself with necessary being, and beings by others with nonnecessary beings, he would take this principle to be equivalent to the one stated in main text. Using the latter reduces technical terminology and simplifies the exegesis.

23 His proof that only a necessary being could provide a sufficient reason for contingent ones is contained in his cosmological argument, which I explore in section V. (Note that this part of the cosmological argument is *a priori*.)

24 Russell, *Critical Exposition*, p. 173; Rescher, *Philosophy of Leibniz*, pp. 66–67; and Craig, *The Cosmological Argument from Plato to Leibniz*, p. 277 n. 3.

25 G III 452: "The possibility of a circle is proved through its cause, viz., by the movement in a plane of a straight line one point of which remains at rest." G VII 294: L 230: "The concept of a circle set up by Euclid, that of a figure described by the motion of a straight line in a plane about a fixed end, affords a real definition, for such a figure is evidently possible."

26 Many different kinds of cosmological argument have been given, including ones by Aristotle, Aquinas, Descartes and others. Aristotle argued

from the observed fact of movement to the need for an unmoved mover. Aquinas, relying on Aristotle, reasoned that there must be an unmoved mover and an uncaused cause, which he identified with God. Aquinas based another proof on the existence of contingent, perishable beings. Whatever is capable of perishing, he said, at some time does perish. If *all* things were like this, however, there would have been a time at which they all perished. But then there would have been nothing to cause the things that now exist. So there must be an imperishable, necessary being. Descartes noted that his idea of God represents (i.e., mentally depicts) an infinite degree of reality. But, he argued, since the cause of an idea must possess at least as much reality as the idea represents, the idea of God can only be caused by God himself. He also offered a variation on this, which begins with his famous cogito – "I think, therefore I exist" – and concludes that God is the cause of Descartes's existence. Descartes's cosmological proofs occur in his third *Meditation*. Relevant selections from Aristotle and Aquinas, along with references and commentary, are in Burrill, *The Cosmological Arguments*. For detailed discussion of a wide variety of cosmological proofs, see Craig, *The Cosmological Argument*.

27 Other references are: C 533: P 145; G VII 309: P 75; G II 56: L 337; G VII 301; L 226–27; C 519: L 268: G VI 127, 413–14: H 147, 419.

In the *Monadology* and elsewhere we are told that even the existence of God has a sufficient reason, though a necessary being "has its reason for its existence in itself" (G VI 614: L 647). Also see G VI 602: L 639 and G VII 310: P 77. But cf. G VII 303: L 487.

28 C 533: P 145: "A cause is simply a real reason." Gr 269: "Nothing is without a reason is understood of the efficient, material, formal and final cause." Although Leibniz often equates "reason" with "cause," he sometimes treats a cause as a special kind of reason which is external to the thing and which produces it. On this usage, eternal truths, like those of mathematics and the existence of God, have reasons but not causes. For instructive discussion, see Parkinson, *Logic and Reality*, pp. 62–67 and Mates, *The Philosophy of Leibniz*, pp. 158–60.

29 Some other passages in which Leibniz distinguishes a reason from a sufficient (full, final, complete) reason are G VII 310: P 77 and G IV 107: L 111. Cf. Gr 267.

30 Leibniz usually proves this point in a different way. Typically, he takes it for granted that all worldly things are contingent and reasons from their interconnectedness to the extramundane existence of a single necessary being (G VI 613: L 646 and G VII 305: L 489). Obviously, however, that won't meet the objection we have just considered. The argument in the main text, on the other hand, *does* meet the objection (and perhaps

occurs at G VII 310: P 77). But unfortunately it rests on some uninviting neoplatonic ideas, which contemporary defenders of the cosmological proof may wish to avoid.

31 To be sure, Leibniz attacks Spinoza's proof that the world is necessary. But the question now is not so much whether Spinoza has proved this as whether Leibniz has ruled it out.

32 Dietrich von Bern is an important figure in German epic literature. Hailed for victories over his rival, Siegfried, Dietrich also battles a series of giants, dwarfs, and water sprites, and gloriously serves Queen Virginal. Discerning and judicious, yet dauntless in the execution of vengeance, Dietrich has been called "the heroic ideal of the twelfth and thirteenth centuries." Robertson and Reich, *A History of German Literature*, pp. 67–68.

33 I have discussed some of his most important answers in Blumenfeld, "Superessentiaism, Counterparts, and Freedom"; "Leibniz on Contingency and Infinite Analysis"; "Necessity, Contingency, and Things Possible in Themselves."

34 Plantinga, *God and Other Minds*, pp. 19–20.

35 Of course, the universe is not a necessary *substance*, because it isn't a substance at all, only a vast collection of them. The problem, however, is that it is apparently a *necessary* collection.

36 Granted, "The universe exists" is always true. But for any substance, s, "The infinite sequence leading up to s exists" is always false!

37 I use the imaginary opponent only as a foil, not to test the limits of his resources. Anyone who thinks I have given him short shrift, may of course carry on the defense.

38 Flew, *God and Philosophy*, p. 83 and Russell, "A Debate on the Existence of God," p. 173.

38 Many philosophers say that it is obvious that all explanation is irreflexive. But if they wish to establish their point, they will have to do a lot more than that. (Along the way, incidentally, they will need to cope with recent arguments against their view by Robert Nozick, *Philosophical Explanation*, pp. 116–21.)

40 Kant, *Critique of Pure Reason*, pp. 504–5. For a brief explanation of Kant's point, see note 3.

41 The following gives some indication of the variety of contemporary positions on the relevant issues. Nathan Salmon, "Existence," holds that existence is a predicate, though he rejects the ontological argument on other grounds. Malcolm, "Anselm's Ontological Arguments," and Hartshorne, *Man's Vision of God*, support the argument by distinguishing existence from necessary existence, whereas Alston, "The Ontological Argument Revisited," takes a modified Kantian position.

Van Inwagen, "Ontological Argument," on the other hand, argues "that anyone who wants to claim either that [the ontological argument] is sound or that it is unsound faces grave difficulties."

42 A particularly nice statement of this kind of objection, together with some good responses, is in Edwards, "The Cosmological Argument," pp. 113–20.

43 At G VI 414: H 419, Leibniz says that the principle of sufficient reason is "contained in the definition of the true and the false" and "that it is even necessary that that which has no sufficient reason should not exist."

44 The statement is a classic case of leading with one's chin.

45 This is argued by Mondadori, "Reference, Essentialism, and Modality in Leibniz's Metaphysics," p. 90 n14. Cf. Couturat, *La Logique*, pp. 208–18. Robert Sleigh, on the other hand, thinks the theory of truth is grounded in Leibniz's conviction that it is needed to account for the identity of substances over time. Sleigh, *Leibniz and Arnauld*, p. 90. If Sleigh is correct, then the defense of the principle of sufficient reason that we are now considering rests on whether Leibniz's theory of truth really is required to explain the identity of individuals.

46 Sleigh, "Leibniz on the Two Great Principles of All our Reasonings," p. 203.

47 Of course, if something occurs, everything required for it occurs. But is it required that anything provide a full (final, complete, sufficient) explanation? That is the question.

11 Perfection and happiness in the best possible world

Since all possible things have a claim to existence in God's understanding in proportion to their perfections, the result of all these
claims must be the most perfect actual world which is possible.

(Leibniz, G VI 603:L 639)

Candide, stunned, stupefied, despairing, bleeding, trembling, said
to himself: – If this is the best of all possible worlds, what are the
others like?[1]

(Voltaire)

Few philosophical theses are so renowned as Leibniz's illustrious
claim that this is the best of all possible worlds. Ironically, the doctrine's great fame is due more to the ridicule it received in *Candide*
than to broad public familiarity with Leibniz's ideas. Even among
philosophers well acquainted with Leibnizian texts, the subject of
God's standards of perfection has only recently begun to receive
detailed discussion.[2] Yet these standards are essential to the meaning of the best possible world doctrine, and the place of humanity in
the divine scheme is at the heart of Leibniz's treatment of the problem of evil. Consequently, it behooves us to ask what canons God
invokes when he compares possible worlds, and in what ways these
standards affect the prospects for human well-being.

When we examine these questions, however, we find a number of
different perspectives of varying degrees of clarity, which Leibniz
often leaves to his reader to harmonize. In this paper, I attempt to
elucidate and unify these perspectives. Where I am unable to do so, I
point out the ambiguities, gaps, and shifts in Leibniz's point of view.

Since the route to our destination is neither smooth nor direct, it
may help to chart the course in advance. In section I, I examine
Leibniz's claim that perfection is determined by variety and simplic-

382

ity. After inquiring what this means and how it fits with the thesis that God creates the greatest number of things, I seek in section II to tie it to several other Leibnizian dicta (e.g., that perfection derives from quantity of essence, monadic clarity, etc.). In section III, I discuss the idea that the actual world is the best possible one judged from a moral perspective. In doing so, I document some dramatic changes in Leibniz's attitude toward the place of happiness in the divine scheme.

I. VARIETY AND SIMPLICITY

Before delineating the canons of divine choice, it is important to note that Leibniz thinks these canons are objective. Issues of good and evil rest on God's intellect rather than his will, and it is with reference to fixed and eternal standards that God makes his infallible choice of the best possible world. In Leibniz's opinion, the objectivity of goodness is essential to true religion and, in fact, is dictated by the principle of sufficient reason. "Every act of will," Leibniz says, "implies some reason for willing and . . . this reason naturally precedes the act of will itself" (G IV 428: L 304).

The criteria of perfection, then, are objective. But what are these criteria? Leibniz frequently answers by citing two factors: variety and simplicity. In a typical passage, for example, he says: "God has chosen that world which is the most perfect, that is to say, which is at the same time the simplest in its hypotheses [i.e., laws] and the richest in phenomena" (G IV 43: L 306; Cf G VI 238, 241: H 254–5, 257; G VI 603: L 639). Let us refer to this thesis as "the variety/ simplicity criterion."

The variety/simplicity criterion generates a number of difficult problems. One would like to know (a) exactly how it is to be interpreted, (b) why it is the test of worldly excellence, and (c) how it coheres with other indices of value that Leibniz acknowledges. Question (c) is the subject of later sections and question (a) requires extended treatment. I therefore begin with (b).

Leibniz identifies perfection with harmony, which he defines in classical fashion as "unity within variety." There are many terminological variations on this theme: harmony is said to be "agreement in . . . variety," "similarity in variety or diversity balanced by identity," and order (regularity, uniformity, etc.) within plurality (Gr 12,

267; G W 171–72: AG 233–34; A VI.iii 116, G VI 616; L 648). But these variations are evidently intended to signify the same thing, namely, a certain order that unifies diversity. The specific kind of order that determines harmony, however, is the one expressed by the variety/simplicity criterion.

To see why, note first that Leibniz thinks that order, in its most general sense, applies to any conceivable series of things. In the *Discourse on Metaphysics*, for example, he tells us that it is not even possible to imagine events that are irregular or do not exhibit some uniformity, however complex or baroque it might be (G IV 431: L 306).[3] Since any series is ordered, but not every one is equally harmonious, the degree of harmony must depend upon the extent to which the series embodies an ideal kind of order.

This order is the kind that best satisfies reason by unifying a manifold in the simplest and most beautiful way, i.e., the one that does the most with the least, or produces the maximum desired effect by the most efficient means (Gr 12, 267–68, 285–87; G IV 430: L 306). Harmony, so construed, delights the intellect and gives pleasure to a rational being. Indeed, in *The Philosopher's Confession* (1672–73), Leibniz tells us that to be delighted just *is* to feel harmony and that "in fact nothing is pleasing to the mind besides harmony" (A VI.iii 116). Elsewhere, he explains that the experience of harmony delights perception because it "makes it easier, and extricates it from confusion."

Consonances please, since agreement is easily observable in them. . . . Agreement is sought in variety, and the more easily it is observed there, the more it pleases; and in this consists the feeling (*sensus*) of perfection. Moreover, the perfection a thing has is greater, to the extent that there is more agreement in greater variety, whether we observe it or not. Therefore, this is what order and regularity come to. (GW 171: AG 233)

Though every series has some sort of order, then, the most *harmonious* order involves the greatest variety of phenomena regulated by the simplest laws. It follows that God, who wishes to maximize harmony, will choose the world that fulfills the variety/simplicity criterion.

Turning to question (a), it may help to cite some analogies by which Leibniz seeks to illuminate his criterion. In section 5 of the *Discourse*, he likens God to an excellent geometrician who knows how to find the best constructions of a problem; or a good architect who makes the most advantageous use of the space and the capital intended for a building, leaving nothing which offends or which lacks the beauty of which it is capable; or a good family head who makes such use of his holdings that there is nothing uncultivated and barren; or a skilled machinist who produces his work by the easiest process that can be chosen; or a learned author who includes the greatest number of subjects in the smallest possible volume.

As for simplicity,

this is shown especially in the means which he uses, whereas the variety, opulence, and abundance appears in regard to the ends or results. The one thus ought to be in equilibrium with the other, just as the funds intended for a building should be proportional to the size and beauty one requires in it. It is true that nothing costs God anything, even less than it costs a philosopher to build the fabric of his imaginary world out of hypotheses, since God has only to make his decrees in order to create a real world. But where wisdom is concerned decrees or hypotheses are comparable to expenditures, in the degree to which they are independent of each other, for reason demands that we avoid multiplying hypotheses or principles, somewhat as the simplest system is always preferred in astronomy.

(G IV 430–31: L 305–7; Cf. G VII 303–4: L 487; G VI 603: L 639)

Leibniz goes on to say that his comparisons "portray an imperfect semblance of the divine wisdom" and he claims to use them only to "lift our spirit to some conception of what cannot well be expressed."

Setting mystical apologies aside, we must ask: To what conception is our spirit being lifted? Nicholas Rescher has given a plausible answer. On his interpretation, the variety/simplicity criterion

can be illustrated in somewhat oversimplified form by minimax-problems in the differential calculus; for example, by considering the choice-situation depicted in a diagram of the following sort:

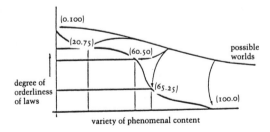

We suppose here that the merit function is of the simplest additive sort:

merit index = (variety index) + (orderliness).[4]

Since orderliness represents simplicity, the criterion of a world's perfection is the sum of its variety and nomic simplicity.

Rescher also argues that the best possible world embodies the ideal trade-off of variety and simplicity, which he takes to be in conflict with each other.

The immediately striking feature of the [variety/simplicity] criterion is that the two factors are *opposed* to one another and pull in opposite directions. On the one hand, a world whose only metal is (say) copper, or whose only form of animal life is the amoeba, will obviously have a simpler structure of laws because of this impoverishment. On the other hand, a world whose laws are more complex than the rules of the astrologers demands a wider variety of occurrences for their exemplification. Clearly, the less variety a world contains – the more monotonous and homogeneous it is – the simpler its laws will be; and the more complex its laws, the greater the variety of its phenomena must be to realize them. Too simple laws produce monotony; too varied phenomena produce chaos.[5]

The actual world therefore embodies the maximally efficient trade-off of the two determinants of perfection. Rescher's graph nicely depicts this: the best world is higher on the variety index than some of its competitors, lower than others; and the same holds for the orderliness (or simplicity) index. Nevertheless, that world is best on the whole because the sum of its two values is higher than that of any other world .[6]

Despite its initial plausibility, however, I believe that the trade-off idea is mistaken. For Leibniz says repeatedly that the actual world is the richest one and that it contains the greatest conceivable variety of phenomena. Throughout his career, but especially in his maturity, he insists on the unsurpassable richness of things: in the *Discourse*, for example, he says that the world is "the richest in phenomena"; in the *Principles of Nature and Grace* he declares that it has "the greatest variety together with the greatest order"; and in the *Monadology* he asserts flatly that it has "the greatest variety possible." All of this indicates that God is not required to trade-off variety in his selection of the best possible world (G IV 431: L 306;

G VI 603: L 639; G VI 616: L 648; Cf. Gr 285; G VII 290: P 146; G IV
524: L 496–97).[7]

Leibniz also believes that the world with the most variety has
the largest number of individuals. He states this in numerous
works and in 1686 he even goes so far as to define "the existent" as
"that which is compatible with the most things" (C 360, 376: PLP
51, 65; Cf. G I 331: L 211; V E 6 1141, VE 8 2036; Gr 17; G VII 194:
Russell, *Critical Exposition*, p. 296). We should observe that he
sometimes suggests that the world has the maximum number of
phenomenal entities, on other occasions, that it has the most
monads. The explanation is simply that he holds both views and
regards the former diversity as founded on the latter.[8] At the phenomenal level, he says, there is a vast continuum of species –
plants, animals, men, and endless others – which form a "single
chain" whose links are so closely united that it is impossible for
the senses and imagination to fix the precise point where any one
begins or ends.[9] Likewise, although he believes that many worlds
have infinite members,[10] he assures us that, at the phenomenal
level, the actual world contains infinities of things within infinities
of things *ad infinitum*. So great is the number and diversity of
phenomenal things that "every small part of the universe contains
a world with an infinite number of creatures" (C 522: L 270).[11] This
incomparable variety, moreover, arises from the perceptual activity
of the largest number of underlying monads.[12]

In order to reconcile the claim that this world has the greatest
conceivable variety with the demand for simplicity, some may suggest the following interpretation: the actual world has the greatest variety of phenomena governed by the simplest laws that are
compatible with maximum variety. Although more complex laws
would accommodate as much diversity, by choosing the simplest
ones that do so, God maximizes harmony without trading-off any
variety at all.

The following text, moreover, supports this interpretation. Having
said that all the actions of God conform to general rules, Leibniz adds:

Just as there is no line freely drawn by hand, however irregular it may seem,
which cannot be reduced to a rule or definition, likewise the whole series of
God's actions makes up a certain entirely regular disposition without any
exception. And . . . it is the most perfect one possible or the simplest, just as

of all the lines that can pass through the same points, one is the simplest. (Robinet, *Malebranche et Leibniz*, p. 222)

This suggests that God could have maximized variety using more complex laws, but chose instead to do it in the simplest and most perfect way.[13]

Unfortunately, the passage conflicts with other important Leibnizian doctrines. Taken at face value, for example, it implies not only that more complex laws are compatible with phenomena as rich as ours, but that such laws are compatible with qualitatively the *same* phenomena. (For it speaks of different lines passing through the same points.) This violates the identity of indiscernibles by implying that there is at least one other possible world that differs from ours in its laws, but not in any purely qualitative respect.

Perhaps we shouldn't take the passage at face value. Maybe Leibniz means no more than what the present interpretation suggests, namely, that more complex laws are consistent with phenomena as rich, though not exactly the same, as ours. If so, however, at least one other possible world will have as much variety as ours, which contradicts the claim that ours is the richest of all.[14]

Some may reply that in claiming that our world is richest, Leibniz might mean only that no world is richer in phenomena.[15] But there are just too many places where he says that this world is *the* richest to permit this way out (E.g. G IV 431: L 306; G VI 603, 616: L 639, 648; G III 573: L 662; Gr 285; G VII 290: P 146). Furthermore, as we have seen, he defines the existent as whatever is compatible with the most things, and he lets "the most things" refer to either monads or phenomenal entities. But letting it refer to the latter would be self-defeating if he thought there were more than one world with the most phenomena, since in that case his definition would not pick out a unique set of individuals. (We may note that his definition also creates a further difficulty for the trade-off view: if there were worlds with more phenomenal entities, as that view implies, then our world wouldn't qualify as existent.)

A final problem is that Leibniz indicates that simplicity is the *means* to variety and that achieving the most diversity therefore *requires* using the simplest laws of nature. In 1679, for example, he tells Malebranche that if God had not used simple laws, he would have been unable to create as many things as he did.

God makes the most things he can and what obliges him to seek simple laws is the need to find a place for as many things as can be put together; if he made use of other laws, it would be like trying to make a building with round stones, which make us lose more space than they occupy.

(G I 331: L 211)

In another early text, he says:

The necessary being acts in the simplest ways. For among the infinite possible ways there are certain simplest ones, but the simplest are the ones which offer the most.   (Gr 267; Cf 285f.)

And essentially the same idea comes up in the *Theodicy* (1710), where he explains that "intricate processes take up too much ground, too much space, too much place, too much time that might have been better employed" (G VI 241: H 257).[16]

Leibniz's thesis in these places is that simplicity is productive: God's decision to maximize phenomena required him to use the simplest laws because they alone would produce it. This contradicts the idea that there are worlds that have as much variety as ours, but more complex laws. It also conflicts with the trade-off view, which has it that simplicity and variety "pull in opposite directions."

In light of all this, we must attribute to Leibniz a more radical position than the ones we have considered. Ultimately, he thinks the best world contains the most diverse phenomena *and* the simplest laws of nature;[17] indeed, he believes that the greatest number and variety of things is unobtainable apart from such laws. I shall dub this doctrine "the harmony of variety and simplicity."

The harmony of variety and simplicity may seem to be an astonishing thesis, even from someone like Leibniz, whose philosophy is a profusion of unexpected harmonies. The paradox, however, is less dramatic than it seems; for, when Leibniz says that simplicity is the means to variety, he is not suggesting that *fewer* laws bring greater diversity, but only that *simpler* ones do so. In fact, as we shall see, he thinks the best world has "a multitude" of natural laws.

We can state Leibniz's view more perspicuously by drawing a few distinctions. Possible laws differ in degree of internal complexity: some are very complex and convoluted, others quite simple. Let us refer to a law as "maximally simple" just in case it governs the type of phenomena it covers in the simplest way possible. When discussing the number of such laws in a world, let us speak of the world's "simplicity index": the greater the number of maximally simple laws, the higher the simplicity index. Now Leibniz thinks maximally simple laws are maximally productive. So his thesis, expressed in our terms, is that the highest simplicity index is the means to the greatest variety.

Our next task is to determine what Leibniz's criteria for simplicity are and why he thinks the highest simplicity index is the means to the greatest variety. One mark of simplicity is the extent to which a law approaches perfect universality, i.e., freedom from exceptions. Exceptions occur when two laws conflict and one restricts the other or both give way to a third (G VI 315: H 328; Cf. GW 163: AG 231). Since exceptions make a law more complex, a necessary condition for maximum simplicity, is that the law be strictly universal, or exception-free.

Leibniz accordingly treats exceptions to a law as imperfections, which a God who values simplicity will seek to avoid as far as reason permits.[18] "The ways of God," we learn, "are the most simple and uniform: for he chooses rules that least restrict one another" (G VI 241: H 257). In fact, apart from the exceptions to natural law required by miracles, the best world involves a set of perfectly universal principles, rather than a system of conflicting laws in which higher-order ones govern "gaps" in lower-order ones.[19]

Leibniz also treats universality as a mark of regularity and claims that a multitude of regularities (i.e., universal laws) produces variety.

One can say that that which is more perfect is that which is more regular, that is, that which admits of more observations, namely, more general observations. And so my view is expressed more distinctly in this way, for the term "observation" is commonly used even for exceptions. However, a multitude of regularities brings forth variety. Thus are uniformity, that is, generality, and variety obtained [conciliantur].

(Letter dated 1715, GW 163: AG 231)

In this passage, Leibniz does not explain why a multitude of regularities brings forth variety. One suggestion might be that a large set of universal laws yields many phenomena because different universal laws cover different phenomena. But this can't be the whole story. That a large set of universal laws produces variety does not in itself show that any such set produces the greatest possible variety. And even if it did show this, it still wouldn't establish that simplicity is required for the most variety. If a multitude of simple, universal laws can generate the maximum diversity, why couldn't a multitude of complex laws do so too?

The resolution of these issues lies in another criterion for simplicity, which Leibniz articulates elsewhere. A maximally simple law is not only universal: it is also "architectonic," or so structured that it makes the most efficient use of whatever aspect of being it covers. The most efficient way of achieving an end, moreover, is always the simplest one, because the simplest just *is* whatever does the most with the least (Gr 285f.).[20]

On this account, architectonicness – or maximum efficiency – is both necessary and sufficient for a law to be maximally simple.[21] Thus, although a multitude of complex and inefficient laws would produce variety, an equally great multitude of simple and efficient ones would produce even more variety. And only the largest system of maximally efficient laws could produce the greatest possible variety.

It is no surprise, then, that Leibniz should say that God uses architectonic laws of nature exclusively (G VII 273, 278, 302: L 479, 484, 487). Furthermore, because God wants to create as abundantly as possible, he selects as many architectonic laws as are needed to produce the greatest conceivable diversity. In *The Ultimate Origination of Things*, Leibniz asserts that God works by laws "through which the greatest amount of essence or possibility is brought into existence" and that each law dictates "that a maximum effect should be achieved with a minimum outlay." Where time and space are the outlay, and the number and variety of things is the end to be maximized, Leibniz compares the problem of creation to

certain games in which all the spaces on a board are to be filled according to definite rules, but unless we use a certain device, we find ourself at the end blocked from the difficult spaces and compelled to leave more spaces vacant than we needed or wished to. Yet there is a definite rule by which a maximum number of spaces can be filled in the easiest way.

(G VII 303: L 487).[22]

Analogously, the most productive way of filling the universe with phenomena is through architectonic laws of nature.[23] Moreover, since God gives the actual world architectonic laws for every aspect of reality (space, time, motion, qualities, etc.), it will have the largest consistent set of such laws and the greatest conceivable variety.[24]

We can conclude that the "multitude of regularities" which "brings forth variety" is the largest system of architectonic principles. Likewise, because architectonic rules are maximally simple, we can say that this system embodies the highest simplicity index. Most importantly, we can now see why this index is the means to the greatest variety.

Some will object that this conflicts with Leibniz's acceptance of the principle of parsimony. After all, he tells us specifically that God avoids multiplying hypotheses (G IV 430: L 306). So how can he also maintain that God chooses the *largest* number of simple laws?

The following passage gives the answer.

> The general rule which the nominalists frequently use is that entities must not be multiplied beyond necessity. This rule is frequently opposed by others as violating the divine opulence, which is generous rather than parsimonious and takes pleasure in the variety and abundance of things. But those who raise this objection have not, I think, grasped the meaning of the nominalists, which, though more obscurely stated, reduces to this: the simpler a hypothesis is, the better it is. And in accounting for the causes of phenomena, that hypothesis is most successful which makes the fewest gratuitous assumptions. Whoever acts differently by this very fact accuses nature, or rather God, its author, of an unfitting superfluity. (G IV 158: L 128)

Leibniz thinks that God avoids multiplying *gratuitous* hypotheses, or ones that involve more than is necessary to achieve his ends. But since the highest simplicity index is *required* to maximize variety, choosing it satisfies the principle of parsimony.[25]

Our analysis of harmony so far has focused on laws of phenomena. We should not forget, however, that phenomenal laws are the products of an underlying noumenal harmony: all natural laws, as well as the data they govern, result from infinitely coordinated principles of monadic development. These monadic laws, moreover, literally generate the entire phenomenal realm, since they are forces, or tendencies, which bring forth all monadic activity (e.g., G IV 391: L 409). Finally, like the phenomenal laws to which they give rise, noumenal laws are architectonic principles.

> The state of the soul ... is ... a tendency ... to change its thoughts ... in the simplest and most uniform way which its state permits. ... And the reason for the change of thoughts in the soul is the same as that of the change of things in the universe which it represents. The mechanical rea-

sons which are developed in the bodies are united . . . in the souls . . . indeed, they have their source there. . . . [Monads] are always images of the universe. They are . . . worlds in abridged form, fruitful simplicities, substantial unities, but virtually infinite by the multitude of their modifications, centers which express an infinite circumference.

(G IV 562: L 579. Cf. G IV 524, L 497)

The variety and simplicity of the phenomenal world therefore supervene on the greatest noumenal harmony, one which arises when the largest number of monads is driven by simplest developmental laws.[26]

We have already established that the highest simplicity index is the means to the greatest variety. It is now clear, however, that at a deeper level the mechanism responsible for this index is a perfect accommodation between the noumenal laws-of the largest system of monads. Therefore, in the *Monadology*, Leibniz is also able to state that the mutual accommodation of "the infinite multiplicity of simple substances" is "the means of obtaining the greatest variety possible, but with the greatest possible order" (G VI 616: L 648). The harmony above rests on the harmony below.

II. VARIANT ACCOUNTS OF PERFECTION

Leibniz does not always define perfection in terms of variety and simplicity. In fact, he says many things about the sources of value whose relation to our interpretation still needs clarification. He asserts, for example, that possible beings have different degrees of internal perfection, which God takes into account in assessing a possible world. He also holds that a monad's perfection is a function of the distinctness of its perceptions and of its degree of action rather than passion. How, one wishes to know, do these claims relate to one another and to the variety/simplicity criterion? Furthermore, Leibniz says that "perfection is nothing but quantity of essence," or, positive reality (e.g., G VII 303: L 487; G I 266: L 177; G VI 613: L 646–47). Yet he also identifies perfection with universal observability and with affirmative intelligibility, thus leading us to ask how these conceptions connect to all the others.

There are dozens of places at which Leibniz assembles assorted pieces of this puzzle, but nowhere, as far as I know, where he puts them all together. We must therefore take the various pieces and construct from them the most complete picture we can. Let us begin with quantity of essence and join it to what we have already organized.

This piece fits in fairly neatly. Leibniz equates a world's perfection, or harmony, with its quantity of essence, and he thus understandably regards the best world as the one with the greatest quantity of essence. But he also thinks the world with the most harmony has the largest number of phenomenal things and the largest number of monads. It follows that the most harmonious world is at once the one with the most phenomenal entities, the most monads, and the greatest quantity of essence. This brings together in a simple way a variety of Leibnizian theses: the best possible world = the most harmonious one = the one that satisfies the variety/simplicity criterion = the one with the most phenomenal individuals and the most monads = the one with the most reality, or essence.[27]

The next element is the degree of universal observability. This is determined by the number of universal laws in a world, because, obviously, the more such laws there are, the larger the number of universal observations that are possible. Leibniz claims, moreover, that the world with the most harmony must be the one with the most universal observability. But why? The answer, I believe, is that universal laws cover their phenomena in a perfectly regular way, and different universal laws cover *different* phenomena. So the world with the most universal laws will have the greatest variety of phenomena governed in the most regular fashion. Thus, he tells Wolff that "Nothing is more regular than the divine intellect, which is the source of all rules, and produces the most perfect system of the world, the system that is as harmonious as possible and thus contains the greatest number of universal observations" (GW 171: AG 233).

Leibniz also identifies perfection, or positive reality, with affirmative intelligibility and he claims that the latter is equivalent to universal observability. Since we have seen that the most universal observability involves the most harmony and regularity, an account of affirmative intelligibility should enable us to forge several more links in our chain of equivalences.

On inquiring in 1715 about Leibniz's definition of perfection, Christian Wolff received this reply:

The perfection about which you ask is the degree of positive reality, or what comes to the same thing, degree of affirmative intelligibility, so that something more perfect is something in which more things worthy of observation [*notatu digna*] are found. . . . When I say that something in which more is worthy of observation is more perfect, I understand general observations or rules. . . . The more there is worthy of observation in a thing, the more universal properties, the more harmony it contains. . . . [Likewise, the more regular] is that which provides more universal rules or universal observations.

(GW 161, 170–71: AG 230, 232–33)[28]

Leibniz holds that the real, in its most general sense, is the intelligible;[29] hence, "positive reality" and "affirmative intelligibility" are but two names for the same thing. A world is intelligible, moreover, to the degree that it contains "things worthy of observation," by which he means things subject to universal laws, or ones that are regular and harmonious. All of which implies that the world with the most positive reality, or quantity of essence = the one with the most affirmative intelligibility = the one with the most universal observability = the one with the greatest regularity and the most harmony.

Finally, Leibniz thinks the simplest way of producing a desired effect is the most beautiful one, and he says that harmony is the very kind of order from which beauty arises (VE 1 37; G VII 87: L 426). Consequently, the world with the greatest simplicity, harmony, and other traits we have discussed above will also have the greatest conceivable beauty.

Until now I have concentrated on the perfection of an entire world. Before turning to the determinants of an individual monad's perfection, however, I will consider a series of questions whose answers bring our picture into sharper focus.

The first question concerns the claim that perfection is nothing but quantity of essence. This may seem to conflict with things Leibniz says about simplicity, for he indicates that, in addition to being the means to variety, simplicity has *intrinsic* value.[30] If so, how can perfection be "nothing but" quantity of essence?

The question mistakenly assumes that quantity of essence is tallied independently of simplicity. A world's quantity of essence is the same thing as its degree of harmony, and the latter is determined by variety and simplicity. Thus, there is no problem in simplicity contributing *per se* to degree of essence.[31]

This may appear to damage the argument that the best world has the greatest variety of phenomena. If worldly perfection is not measured solely by variety, what assurance is there that the best world has the most variety?

The answer is that a world with less variety could be better than one with more only if the former had simpler laws. But simplicity is the means to variety, and this entails that the best world has both the greatest simplicity *and* the greatest variety.

One might now ask how Leibniz knows that there is only *one* world with the greatest simplicity and variety. Even if simplicity is the means to variety, how can he prove, for example, that there are not two worlds with maximally efficient laws and maximally varied phenomena?

His reply is that if there were two or more such worlds, they would be equally worthy of choice. God would then be without a sufficient reason for deciding between them, and, like Buridan's ass, he would choose nothing. But God has in fact chosen this world. So there is exactly one best possible world (G VI 107: H 128).[32]

We can now consider Leibniz's remarks about the perfection of an individual monad. In this instance, he tells us that a monad's quantity of essence = its degree of perfection, that its degree of perfection = its degree of distinctness, and that its distinctness = its degree of action. Here, however, I am content to explicate the link between action and distinctness and merely raise questions about their connection to perfection, or harmony. As it turns out, Leibniz's account of the latter is far less developed, and therefore less certain, than his account of the former.

The first issue is how action can be attributed to created beings at all. Action involves causation, and, strictly speaking, finite substances are incapable of interaction (G VI 607: L 643; G II 57: MP 65). In what sense, therefore, can they act on one another?

Leibniz responds by distinguishing the strict sense of action from another one. Although created substances are metaphysically independent, it is possible for the state of monad A to express that of monad B more distinctly than B's state expresses A's. Under these conditions, B's state is more easily inferable from A's than conversely, and A's state better represents the reason for the mutual relations between the two monads. This creates the appearance of interaction and provides a sense in which we say that A acts on B.

In a letter of 1686 to Arnauld, Leibniz explains that the independence of monads does not prevent "commerce" between substances:

For as all created substances are a continual production of the same sovereign being in accordance with the same plans, and are an expression of the same universe and the same phenomena, they harmonize exactly among themselves and that causes us to say that one acts upon the other, because one is a more distinct expression than the other of the cause of or reason for the changes, more or less as we attribute motion to the vessel rather than to the whole sea, and rightly so, although speaking abstractly one might uphold another hypothesis of motion, since motion in itself, disregarding the cause, is always relative. This is how, in my opinion, one must understand the commerce between created substances.

(G II 57–58: MP 64–65; Cf. G II 47, 69–70: MP 53, 84–85).

Likewise, in the *Monadology*, he states that we attribute action to a created being "insofar as it has distinct perceptions" and that one monad acts on another if we find in it "that which will supply a reason *a priori* for what happens in the other" (G VI 615: L 647–48; Cf. G IV 440–41: L 313; G VI 138–39: H 158–59).

Despite the absence of metaphysical interaction, then, we say that monad A acts on B if A supplies the reason for what happens in B. But the degree to which a monad provides such reasons is the same as the degree to which it has distinct perceptions. Hence, degree of action = degree of distinctness.

In the passage just quoted Leibniz also states that a monad acts outwardly "insofar as it has perfection," thus indicating that degree of action equals degree of perfection. Since all perfection is harmony, however, it follows that a monad's action and distinctness are each equal to its harmony.

But the basis of the connection is not obvious: What is the link between harmony on the one hand and action and distinctness on the other?[33] It won't do to reply that a monad's distinctness equals its quantity of essence, which is the same thing as its degree of harmony. That only prompts one to ask what justifies equating distinctness with quantity of essence. To answer these questions, Leibniz would need to explicate the fit between the notion of harmony (i.e., simplicity within variety) and that of monadic distinctness.

In fact, he makes some intriguing first steps along these lines. As we saw at the end of section II, Leibniz says that every monad undergoes a series of changes which unfold in the simplest way its state permits. He also says that even the slightest thought contains variety and represents a multitude in unity (G VI 608–9: L 644). The former statement suggests that a monad's overall distinctness can be explained as a relation of variety and simplicity. The latter suggests that there is a degree of harmony in every perception which is equivalent to the perception's distinctness.

These ideas raise a host of important questions. Exactly how does the variety/simplicity criterion apply to the slightest thought? Does its application yield a harmony value which corresponds to the distinctness of each perception? If so, is the harmony of each monad definable in terms of the distinctness of its perceptions, and the harmony of the world in terms of the distinctness of its monads? In each case, what are the details of the analysis?

Unfortunately, I know of nowhere where he answers these questions. Although some possible answers come to mind, my present textual basis is too slim to support them adequately. Therefore, I shall not hazard a guess as to how the various harmonies should be played out, or attempt to complete a score which Leibniz apparently left unfinished.

III. MORAL PERFECTION AND HUMAN HAPPINESS

In addition to its other resplendent features, the actual world is "the most perfect morally" (G VII 306: L 489). Yet this thesis, which Leibniz regards as certain, has struck generations of his critics as incredible. For it seems to entail not only that the world contains as much happiness as possible, but that any difference in the total history of the universe, together with all of its consequences, would have yielded a morally inferior result.

In this section, I focus on what Leibniz's theory implies about happiness vis-à-vis other values that might be thought to compete with it. The principal issues are: (a) whether the morally best world must contain the greatest happiness (b) if so, whether the universe was made exclusively for that purpose and (c) how important the happiness of spirits is in comparison to that of lower beings, who are incapable of it.[34] As we shall see, Leibniz's views on some of these issues undergo important changes.

To understand Leibniz's position one must first ask what he takes moral perfection to be. We may approach this issue by considering how he classifies types of imperfection, or evil. Basically, he adopts the old Scholastic view that evil is a limitation, i.e., a privation of being, or perfection. Furthermore,

Evil may be taken metaphysically, physically and morally. Metaphysical evil consists in mere imperfection, physical evil in suffering, and moral evil in sin.   (G VI 115: H 136)

This account of metaphysical evil accords with his identification of perfection with quantity of essence, or positive reality. From the other definitions, one can infer that physical perfection is the opposite of suffering and moral perfection the opposite of sin. Moral perfection, however, requires justice, which Leibniz says entails a loving concern for the happiness of all those one can affect (G III 386–87: L 421; Gr 579; A VI.iii 116f.). Since he defines happiness as a state of lasting joy, it follows that God cares about the lasting joy of all spirits (G VII 43; Gr 579, 582; G VII 86: L 425; *New Essays*, II.xx, A VI.vi: RB 163).

The idea that God's moral nature implies his loving concern for our happiness is a persistent theme in Leibniz's writings. In the opening pages of *The Philosopher's Confession* (1673), he defines a just person as one who loves everyone, or who is delighted by the happiness of others (A VI.iii 117).[35] By arguing that all happiness is harmony, and that all awareness of harmony is delight, he is able to conclude that:

All happiness is pleasing to God. Therefore, (by the definition of love posited a little while ago) God loves everyone, and consequently (by the definition of justice already set out) God is just.   (A VI.iii 117)

Although Leibniz here deduces God's justice from his love, it is clear that he could have argued in the opposite direction, as he does, for example, in the *Discourse* (G IV 460–61: L 326). The view that divine goodness entails love and respect for the happiness of spirits appears throughout the remainder of Leibniz's life.

Nevertheless, God has other important values, such as his abiding concern for variety and order. It is therefore of great concern to us to know how much he cares about our welfare and what weight he attaches to his other objects of interest.

The answer is also important for assessing Voltaire's claim that the amount of unhappiness makes it ludicrous to believe that this is the best possible world. This assumes that Leibniz thinks the best world contains the greatest happiness. But the thesis that God cares about us does not entail this, since it leaves it open that he may care about other things more. If we learn, for example, that metaphysical values are more significant than moral ones and that God trades off our happiness to secure the most variety and order, this would deflect the attack. For then the idea that this is the best possible world would have far less auspicious implications for us than Voltaire imagines. Indeed, in that case, Leibniz would be an ontological, but not a full-blown moral, optimist.[36]

The assumption that the actual world contains the most happiness has a firm textual basis, however. In an early paper, Leibniz asserts that God creates "the greatest possible happiness" and that "everything is made for the sake of the pleasure of souls" (VE 8 2042f. [Ca. 1678–82]).[37] Leibniz repeats these ideas in many other places in his early and middle years, but nowhere does he articulate them so fully as in the last three sections of the *Discourse*, where he claims that God enters into a republic with spirits and makes their happiness his principal aim. Leibniz leaves no doubt, moreover, about the degree of importance which the ruler of the divine republic places on its citizens. Intelligent substances, he says,

must be infinitely nearer to [God] than all other things, which can pass only for the instruments of spirits. So we see that all wise persons value man infinitely more highly than all other things, no matter how precious. . . . And just as we would praise a king who prefers to save the life of one man above that of his rarest and most precious animal, so we cannot doubt that the most enlightened and most just of all monarchs is of the same opinion.

(G IV 461: L 326; Cf. VE 8 2043 [1678–82])

Leibniz preaches of the intimacy of the relationship between God and his most cherished creatures. Spirits are "of [God's] lineage or like the children of his household. . . . One single spirit is worth a whole world." So dear to him are the members of his republic that "the greatest possible felicity of its inhabitants becomes his highest law." And in a passionate closing passage, Leibniz praises Jesus Christ, who has revealed the laws of heaven and made us see:

how much God loves us and with what exactness he has provided for all that concerns us; how God who cares for the sparrows will not neglect the reasonable creatures who are infinitely more dear to him ... how God has more concern for the least of these intelligent souls than for the whole world mechanism. (G IV 461–63: L 327)

These passages not only involve moral optimism, they assign infinitely greater intrinsic value to happiness than to purely metaphysical good. But, despite the disproportionate weighting, Leibniz thinks that omnipotence can maximize *both* kinds of value, for he frequently states that the world contains the greatest metaphysical perfection as well as the most happiness. This makes him a moral *and* an ontological optimist. I shall refer to this double optimism as "the harmony of variety and happiness."

Leibniz subscribes to the harmony of variety and happiness in a large number of texts. In the *Discourse* (1686), however, he states it this way:

If the highest principle ruling the existence of the physical world is the decree which gives it the greatest perfection possible, the highest purpose in the moral world, or the City of God which is the noblest part of the universe, should be to spread in it the greatest possible happiness. (G IV 462: L 327; Cf. GM VI 243; L 44)

In the period around 1686, then, Leibniz embraces the following three theses:

(T1) Each spirit's happiness is of infinitely greater importance than any other kind of thing.
(T2) The happiness of spirits is God's principal end.
(T3) The world contains the greatest variety and order and also the greatest conceivable happiness. (The harmony of variety and happiness.)

In the *Discourse*, Leibniz supports T1 on the grounds that spirits express God "better beyond all comparison than anything else." They alone express him "with a knowledge of what they are doing" and with an awareness of "the great truths about God and the universe." Only a spirit can "enter into a conversation, so to speak, and even a society" with God, thereby coming to love and freely serve him. Consequently, God "derives infinitely more glory from them than from all other beings" (G IV 460–62: L 326–27).

Sometimes Leibniz deduces T2 from T1, arguing that if the happiness of spirits is infinitely more valuable than other things, God will have no higher end (G IV 462: L 327). At other thimes, he infers T2 from a different, and far weaker thesis, namely:

(T1') Spirits have more value than any other kind of thing (G IV 430; L 306; cf. G VII 291: P 147).[38]

So we might say that Leibniz has a stronger and a weaker approach to T2.

What are Leibniz's grounds for T3? This question deserves far more space than we have here, but perhaps the following sketch will suffice.[39] We know that perfection is harmony and that happiness is just a spirit's awareness of harmony. So the world with the most harmony offers the greatest potential for happiness, a potential, we may add, which will be realized provided that this world contains enough spirits who love God and are deserving of happiness. But spirits incorporate the most perfection in the smallest space and their existence least obstructs the existence of other things (G IV 430: L 306; cf. G VII 291: P 147; A VI.iii 472: L 157; C 530: L 169). Consequently, the world with the greatest perfection will contain the largest number of the best spirits which are compossible with one another (cf. GVI 407: H 412). Therefore, the world with the greatest harmony will also contain the greatest possible happiness.

Finally, Leibniz maintains:

(T4) The universe is made only for spirits.

But he is ambivalent about it. On the one hand, he plainly asserts T4 in a number of prominent texts, often suggesting that it follows from T1. In the *Discourse* (1686), he says that rational souls "must be infinitely nearer to [God] than all other things, which can pass only for the instruments of spirits" (G IV 461: L 326). Likewise, in a letter of 1687 to Arnauld, after stating that God forms a community with spirits, and that his relation to them is "infinitely more exalted" than it is to anything else, he concludes that "the whole universe was created only so as to contribute to the embellishment and happiness of that city of God" (G II 125: MP 160). Later, in the *New System* (1695), he says that spirits have "incomparably more perfection" than other things, and again infers that "all the rest is made only for them" (G IV 480: L 455; cf. G IV 485: L 458). On the other hand, Leibniz also *denies* T4, stating in the *Discourse* that it is self-deception to think God "had in view only one particular thing" and that it is "a great abuse to believe that God made the world only for us" (G IV 445: L 316).

The theses we have been discussing involve some serious problems. Consider T4, for example. If all other things are merely "instruments of spirits" and if the universe is made *only* for them, then it is difficult to see how anything else could have a value *per se*. This contradicts Leibniz's view that everything has an intrinsic value proportional to its quantity of essence. It may also conflict with T2, which suggests that God has other ends, albeit subordinate ones. We have seen, moreover, that Leibniz infers T4 from T1, and if this inference holds, T1 should be problematic as well. So the ideas of this period call for considerable straightening out.

The *Theodicy* tells a very different story about these matters. By the time of its publication in 1710, Leibniz had developed a single-minded attitude toward T4 and reconciled the other conflicts noted above. The changes are evident in a long critique of Bayle's maxim that God's only aim in creation is to produce the happiness of intelligent creatures. Though Bayle is the announced adversary, the issue is plainly T4 – and Leibniz now comes to final terms with it.

I grant that the happiness of intelligent creatures is the principal part of God's design, for they are most like him; but nevertheless I do not see how one can prove that to be his sole aim.   (G VI 168: H 188)

Here Leibniz still accepts T2, deducing it in effect from T1'. But he unequivocally rejects T4.[40] His reasons involve a repudiation of some notions that were important in the *Discourse:*

It is true that the realm of nature must serve the realm of grace; but . . . there is no reason to suppose that God, for the sake of some lessening of moral evil, would reverse the whole order of nature. Each perfection or imperfection in the creature has its value, but there is none that has infinite value. Thus the moral or physical good and evil of rational creatures does not infinitely exceed the good and evil which is simply metaphysical, namely that which lies in the perfection of other creatures; and yet one would be bound to say this if the present maxim were strictly true.

The passage continues:

No substance is absolutely contemptible or absolutely precious before God . . . God sets greater store by a man than a lion; nevertheless it can hardly be said with certainty that God prefers a single man in all respects to the whole of lion-kind. Even should it be so, it would by no means follow that the interest of a certain number of men would prevail over the considerations of a general disorder diffused through an infinite number of creatures.

(G VI 168–69: H 188; cf. G VI 377–78: H 379)

Leibniz argues that T4 presupposes T1, which he now renounces on the grounds that it would entail an unacceptable degree of disorder. T1 also elevates rational creatures too high: although other beings are much less precious than we, our value is not infinitely greater than theirs.

What is his attitude toward T3? Certainly the *Theodicy* is far more sober and less anthropocentric than the *Discourse*.[41] Pressed to explain the amount of unhappiness in the world, Leibniz forswears the infinite gap between created spirits and other beings, and stresses instead how the need for order and the good of other creatures can interfere with our desires.

This may suggest that he gives up the harmony of variety and happiness by compromising his moral optimism. But while his position in the *Theodicy* is complex and sometimes ambiguous, the claims that appear to cast doubt on T3 usually turn out to be compatible with it.[42] More significantly, his most definite pronouncements on the issue in his final years affirm T3. In an appendix to the *Theodicy*, for example, he says that God

chooses not only to create men, but to create men as happy as it is possible to be in this system. . . . [Moreover] we can reason concerning the whole world just as we have reasoned concerning the human race. God resolved to create a world, but he was bound by his goodness at the same time to choose such a world as should contain the greatest possible order, regularity, virtue, happiness.   (G VI 426: H 431; cf. G VI 182–83, 406: H 201–2, 411)

Leibniz says much the same in section 10 of *The Principles of Nature and Grace* (1714):

It follows from the supreme perfection of God that he has chosen the best possible plan in producing the universe, a plan which combines the greatest variety together with the greatest order; with situation, place, and time arranged in the best possible way; with the greatest effect produced by the simplest means; with the most power, the most knowledge, the greatest happiness and goodness in created things which the universe could allow.

Later, in section 15, he declares that the world contains

as much virtue and happiness as is possible. And this takes place, not by a
dislocation of nature ... but by the very order of natural things itself, by
virtue of the harmony preestablished ... between the realms of nature and
grace ... in such a way that nature leads to grace, and grace perfects nature
by using it.   (G VI 603, 605: L 639f.)

It is clear, then, that Leibniz altered his position on happiness
considerably: he shifted from the unstable view of the *Discourse*,
which included T1 and T4, to the more carefully conceived doctrine
of the *Theodicy*, which dispensed with these ideas. In doing so, he
resolved conflicts born of his earlier excessive claims about spirits.
But he did not give up the harmony of variety and happiness or
fundamentally denature his moral optimism. In fact, he remained
both a moral and an ontological optimist right to the end.

NOTES

1 Voltaire, *Candide, or Optimism*, p. 12.
   I am grateful to Martha Gibson, Nicholas Jolley, Jeffrey Tlumak, and
   Robert Sleigh, Jr., for helpful comments on various parts of this paper. I
   am also especially indebted to Donald Rutherford for lengthy conversations on all of this material.
   The notes contain a citation of an English translation (where I know of
   one) plus a reference to an edition of the original text. Translations in
   the paper are from the cited English edition, though sometimes with
   changes. Where no English edition is cited, the translation is my own.
2 Some recent discussions are: Gale, "Did Leibniz Have a Practical Philosophy of Science?," "On What God Chose: Perfection and God's Freedom";
   Rescher, *Leibniz's Metaphysics of Nature*; Brown, "Compossibility, Harmony, and Perfection in Leibniz," "Leibniz and the Confluence of
   Worldly Goods."
3 Take any random distribution of points on a piece of paper, he says, and
   it will be possible to find an uninterrupted curve that passes through all
   the points in precisely the order in which they were drawn. If the rule
   generating the curve is complex, the line is commonly said to be irregular, but, strictly speaking, it is as regular as a curve whose rule is easy for
   the ordinary person to grasp. Cf. G VI 262: H 277; G VII 312, p 78–79;
   Robinet, *Malebranche et Leibniz*, p. 222.
4 Rescher, "Logical Difficulties in Leibniz's Metaphysics," pp. 184–85.
5 Rescher, *Leibniz's Metaphysics of Nature*, p. 11.
6 Gale, ("Did Leibniz . . . ?," "What God Chose . . . ,") who also holds the
   trade-off view, represents perfection as the ratio of variety to simplicity

rather than as their sum. Cf. Brown, "Compossibility," "Leibniz's Theodicy."

7 Some may object that in section 5 of the *Discourse* Leibniz says the simplicity of the means must be in balance with the richness of the effects, thus apparently suggesting a trade-off. Note, however, that two factors are "in balance" when they stand in the most felicitous relationship to one another – one which may, but does not necessarily, involve a compromise between them. As I subsequently verify, Leibniz thinks the most felicitous relationship between simplicity and variety is something quite different from a trade-off.

8 This also explains, I think, why he is sometimes unclear about whether "the most things" refers to monads or phenomenal entities. Since he believes both propositions, he allows his definition of the existent to refer to either kind of entity and is not always careful about drawing a distinction.

9 Langley, *New Essays*, pp. 712–13 [Guhrauer, *Leibniz: Eine Biographie*: Notes to the second volume 32]. Cf. *New Essays*, III.vi, A VI.vi: RB 307.

10 In fact, he says there is an infinity of such worlds. See G VI 252: H 167–68.

11 Cf. G VI 618: L 650. "Each part of matter can be thought of as a garden full of plants or as a pond full of fish. But each branch of the plant, each member of the animal, each drop of its humors, is also such a garden or such a pond."

12 I must report that Leibniz's *proof* that the world has the most things appears to have a hole. If there is to be a reason for existence, he says, then every possible individual must have a "claim" ("demand," "right") to exist which is proportional to its degree of perfection. In that case, he maintains, the largest collection of compossible individuals will have the greatest claim to exist and therefore will be actualized by God. G VII 194: Russell, *Critical Exposition*, p. 296; VE 6 1141; G VII 303–4; L 487–88). Now if each possible substance had an equal amount of perfection, this inference would hold, for then the largest collection of them would certainly have the largest claim to exist. But, in fact, Leibniz denies that all possible individuals are equally perfect, thus apparently leaving it open for a smaller group of individuals to have more perfection than a larger one. In note 26, I pursue this problem a little farther.

13 To avoid a possible confusion, I should point out that Leibniz distinguishes between natural laws, to which miracles are exceptions, and the exception-free, supernatural law referred to above. My focus here is on *natural* laws, not the supernatural principle that governs them. But note that the quoted passage still supports the interpretation at hand, since Leibniz takes it that a more complex supernatural law would generate more complex natural laws.

14 The interpretation given in the last paragraph also involves this problem.

15 I made this suggestion in Blumenfeld, "Leibniz's Theory of the Striving Possibles," and also mistakenly took Leibniz's claim that the best world has "the most things" to cover only types of phenomena.

16 We shall also encounter this attitude in other passages, which are discussed below.

17 G IV 430: L 306: "God has chosen that world which is . . . at the same time the simplest in its hypotheses and the richest in phenomena." G VI 603: L 639: "[God] has chosen . . . a plan which combines the greatest variety together with the greatest order." Cf. Gr 267, 285f.

18 GW 163: AG 231: "Imperfections are exceptions, which disturb the rules, that is, the *universal observations*. If there were many exceptions to a rule, there would be nothing worthy of observation, but only chaos."

19 Miracles, in the strict sense, always involve exceptions to natural law. G VI 241, 265: H 257, 280. But while these exceptions derive from a higher-order, supernatural basis, there is no similar hierarchy among natural laws themselves, which are otherwise universal. (This idea, for which I give further evidence later, is derived from Garber, "Mind, Body, and the Laws of Nature in Descartes and Leibniz," pp. 120–22).

In view of the premium on exception-free principles, one wonders how there can be miracles at all. Although the supernatural law that grounds them is beyond our ken, Leibniz proudly notes that the pre-established harmony banishes all *superfluous* miracles, thus keeping exceptions to the bare minimum required by faith. G VI 241: 257.

20 In some contexts, Leibniz describes the simplest laws as the "most determined" or "unique" ways that nature can follow. For helpful discussion of these terms, see Gale, "Did Leibniz . . . ?," pp. 156–60.

21 Since maximal simplicity entails universality, it follows that all architectonic laws are universal.

22 Cf. Gr 12: "[Nature acts so that there can be] more bodies in a given space, more motion in a given time, more forms in a given portion of matter, more qualities in a given subject."

23 Leibniz provides a number of examples of these laws, usually without much explanation of how they help to maximize variety. See G VII 303f., 270–79: L 487f., 477–84; G III 51–55: L 351–53. Often his point seems clear enough, however, as when he cites the principle that there are no discontinuities, or gaps, in nature or when he claims that if nothing more determines the route, a motion between two points will always follow the shortest path. Gaps (among forms, for instance) would thwart the greatest variety, whereas the shortest path maximizes the activities that can occur in a given time and space.

24 *The Ultimate Origination of Things* implies, but does not explicitly state, that the world has the largest number of architectonic laws. At GW 171: AG 233, however, Leibniz says that the world "contains the greatest number of universal observations [or, laws]" and, given his insistence that God uses only architectonic laws, this is a virtually direct statement of our thesis.

25 Note too that although the world has a multitude of laws, it has extremely few relative to the variety of its phenomena. In fact, because all of its laws are maximally productive, no possible world can have a smaller number of laws relative to the degree of its diversity. In this sense, it is consistent for Leibniz to say, as he occasionally does, that there are "few hypotheses to explain phenomena" or to refer approvingly to Malebranche's view that God uses "only a very small number of natural laws to produce a very great number of admirable works." E.g., G II 40: AG 71; Robinet, *Malebranche et Leibniz*, p. 96.

26 This raises a question which is a variation on a theme from note 12. Can Leibniz rule out the possibility of an equally numerous system of monads with *more complex* developmental laws and a *less perfect* phenomenal order? If not, then he can't describe the best world simply as the one with the most monads.

There may be an answer. He argues that the world with the simplest natural laws is the one with the most phenomena on the grounds that phenomenal simplicity is the means to phenomenal diversity. But he also holds that the world with the simplest developmental laws is the one with the most monads. So perhaps he thinks, analogously, that developmental simplicity is the means to maximum compossibility. This would solve the problem stated above and also plug the hole (see note 12) in his proof that the best world has the most things. For if maximum compossibility requires developmental simplicity, then a world with more complex developmental laws cannot have as many monads as ours. Likewise, if the largest set of monads must have the simplest developmental laws, it follows that it will have the most phenomena, the most harmony, and the greatest claim to existence. Admittedly, though, I am conjecturing here, not explicating text.

27 Gregory Brown, "Compossibility," p. 201, and "Leibniz's Theodicy," p. 588f., claims that Leibniz eventually abandoned the view that the best world has the most individuals. His only direct textual evidence, however, is a letter of 1715 which states that one can regard perfection as degree of essence "if essence is calculated from harmonious properties." GW 172: AG 234. Brown takes this to mean that when God chose the world with the most essence, he picked the one with the most harmony, but not necessarily the one with the most individuals. Yet, prior to 1715,

Leibniz had held that the world with the most harmony *is* the one with the most individuals. So I do not think this passage is evidence of a change of mind.

28 In the quotation, I have spliced together complementary material from two letters.

29 G I 272: "Reality is nothing other than thinkability." In fact, the idea of reality in Leibniz has several aspects, or senses, that tend to cluster around this one. For example, a real possibility, is simply one that is conceivable, or intelligible; one entity is said to be "more real" than another insofar as it contains more essence, or more of what is distinctly conceivable; and the real (i.e., actually existing) world is the one that contains the most of what is distinctly conceivable. For some other relevant discussion, see Mates, "Leibniz on Possible Worlds," pp. 47f., especially note 3.

30 G VI 241: H 257: "The wisest mind so acts, as far as it is possible, that the *means* are also in a sense *ends*, that is, they are desirable not only on account of what they do, but on account of what they are." Cf. *Malebranche et Leibniz*, p. 418. At H 257 Leibniz also remarks that if one assumed that there were a world with more complex laws and greater variety, our world might still be more perfect due to its greater simplicity. Note, however, that the assumption is counterfactual, not only because our world has the greatest possible variety, but also because simplicity is the means to variety.

31 Cf. Rescher, *Leibniz's Metaphysics of Nature*, p. 11 and Brown, "Compossibility," p. 203.

32 This strategy also rules out the worry that one possible universe may be better than another unto infinity. G VI 232, 364: H 249, 372.

33 Cf. Brown, "Compossibility," p. 201n.

34 Spirits (i.e., beings capable of reason and science) are the only ones with the capacity for happiness. Beasts have feelings but lack reflection, which true happiness requires. G VII 317: P 85; G VI 611–12: L 645–46; VE 1 39: L 218; G VI 600: L 637–38.

35 Leibniz's standard definition of justice is the charity, or benevolence, of a wise person. See, e.g., G III 386: L 421; Gr 622.

36 As I use the terms, a full-blown moral optimist thinks the world contains the greatest possible happiness, a full-blown ontological optimist that it contains the greatest possible metaphysical value. (Obviously, one could also define less inflated forms of optimism, but these species serve the purposes at hand.)

37 Cf. the material from 1686 translated in Sleigh, *Leibniz and Arnauld*, p. 197, which states that the republic of spirits is "the most perfect and the most felicitous possible."

38 At G IV 461: L 326, Leibniz deduces T2 from the claim that spirits are "the most perfectible of substances."

39 Fortunately, much of the work on this subject has already been done by Brown, "Leibniz's Theodicy." Although my sketch deviates from his account in important respects, I wish to acknowledge how much I have profited from his fine essay.

40 Cf. G VI 232: H 248: "We find in the universe some things that are not pleasing to us; but let us be aware that it is not made for us alone." Also see, Robinet, *Malebranche et Leibniz*, *(Jan. 1712)*, p. 418.

41 To cite only a few examples: in the *Discourse* Leibniz describes God as a father who is infinitely solicitous of the needs of his children, but in the *Theodicy* he warns us not to view God as "a mother . . . whose almost only care concerns . . . the happiness of [her child]." G VI 176–77: H 196. In the *Discourse*, even the humblest spirit is worth more than the whole world mechanism, but in the *Theodicy* it is not clear that a spirit is worth the whole of lion-kind. Likewise, at G VI 243: H 259, we learn that to change the order of the universe is something of infinitely greater consequence than the prosperity of a good man.

42 Given the amount Leibniz wrote on this subject, it would be surprising if he managed to be entirely consistent about it. But it is worth noting that two texts that have been thought to conflict blatantly with T3 are, in fact, compatible with it. I have been told, for example, that G VI 324: H 337, which says that "there is no reason why there should not be worlds happier than ours," conclusively rejects T3. The context, how-ever, suggests that Leibniz is talking about planets rather than possible worlds! C. Wilson, "Leibnizian Optimism," p. 776, on the other hand, claims that the following statement (G VI 244: H 260) contradicts T3: "God can follow a simple, productive, regular plan; but I do not believe that the best and the most regular is always opportune for all creatures simultaneously." Yet this entails only that it is false that *every* spirit's happiness is maximized, not that there is a possible world with greater happiness. So it too is consistent with T3.

12 Leibniz's moral philosophy

More than twenty years ago, Carl J. Friedrich offered this rather deflationary assessment of Leibniz's significance as a legal and political philosopher – that he was not "a thinker of the first rank on law and politics; no basically novel insight can be attributed to him."[1] Indeed, it must be admitted that Leibniz followed a traditional Christian reading of the divisions of natural law expounded in the *Institutes* of Justinian's Code (completed in 529 and revised in 534). It is also true that he resisted the trend toward independent sovereign states in favor of a return to a unified *respublica christiana*, to be achieved by revitalizing that practically defunct offspring of the medieval marriage of church and state, the Holy Roman Empire. But it must also be said that he developed a profound and inventive philosophical underpinning for the conventional legal wisdom. This is nowhere more apparent than in his attempt to reconcile the view of Grotius that human society was founded upon a faculty of sociability inherent in the nature of man, and the view of Hobbes that "all society . . . is either for gain, or for glory; that is, not so much for love of our fellows, as for the love of ourselves."[2] Leibniz's reconciliation was based upon his notion of "disinterested love," which in many ways anticipated Bishop Butler's later response to the egoist. His notion of distinterested love enabled Leibniz to reconcile egoism with the possibility of altruism and to develop a theory of obligation which did not make obligation dependent, as it seemed to be in Hobbes, Pufendorf, Locke, and others of the period, on threat of punishment or the command of a superior. Moreover, he developed a theory of virtue, happiness, and human good which had as practical consequences that it was a primary obligation of individuals and states alike to promote the education of *all* men in the arts and

411

sciences. He also insisted that rational beings had a special moral value, that good men sought their perfection and happiness as ends in themselves and never simply as means to some further end, and that they were all, by virtue of their reason, citizens of the "kingdom of grace," or the "City of God"; this, of course, was an idea that Kant was later to appropriate and make famous in his notion of the "kingdom of ends."

In the *Discourse on Metaphysics* (1686), Leibniz explained that the actual world was founded on two decrees of God, "the first free decree of God, which leads him always to do what is most perfect, and on the decree which God has made about human nature (following the primary one), which is that man shall always do, though freely, that which appears best to him" (*Discourse* §13, G IV 438: L 311). Thus "the object of the will is the apparent good, and nothing is desired by us except under the form of an apparent good" (C 25). Consequently, a deliberate act of will presupposes a judgment that something is good: "To will," Leibniz wrote in a revisionary note (ca. 1697–1700) to his *Nova methodus discendae docendaeque jurisprudentiae* (1667), "is nothing but the striving arising from thought, or to strive for something which our thinking recognizes as good" (A VI.i 284: L 91, n. 11). Unlike Spinoza, then, who notoriously held that "we neither strive for, nor will, neither want, nor desire anything because we judge it to be good," but "judge something to be good because we strive for it, will it, want it, and desire it,"[3] and Hobbes, who similarly held that "whatsoever is the object of any man's Appetite or Desire; that is it, which he for his part calleth *Good*,"[4] Leibniz agreed with Aristotle who held that "desire is consequent on opinion rather than opinion on desire; for the thinking is the starting-point."[5]

The good itself Leibniz defined variously. Sometimes he defined it as "what contributes to pleasure" (Gr 11; cf. Gr 513, 519, 532, 541, 603, 639; C 474), or "what contributes more to [a creature's] joy than to its sorrow" (Gr 604). And thus in a list of definitions from ca. 1701–1705, he wrote that "the good of each thing is what contributes to its felicity" (Gr 667). But he also defined "the good" as "what contributes to perfection" (G VII 195), the "true good" as "that which serves in the perfection of intelligent substances" (M 48: R 50), and the "general good" as "the advancement toward perfection of men" (K X 11: R 105). These different characterizations of the good are related through Leibniz's definition of pleasure, according to which it is "the perception of perfection" (G VII 73: W 568; cf. G II 581; G VII 86: L 425; G VII 112; G VII 291: P 147; GW 172; Du IV iii 313: L 424; M 60: R 57; M 62: R 59; Gr 395, 579: R 83; Gr 582, 584, 639; C 475, 491; New Essays II.xxi.42, A VI.vi 194: RB 194; Theodicy §33, G VI 122: H 142).[6] Thus, what "serves in the perfection of intelligent substances" will also contribute to their pleasure.[7]

Although Leibniz characterized the good generally as what contributes to the perfection, and hence to the pleasure, of intelligent substances, it must be noted that he was an earnest advocate of a theory of motivation that has since come to be known as psychological egoism. For example, in the preface to his *Mantissa codicis iuris gentium diplomaticus* (1700), and against those who held "that it is more perfect so to submit yourself to God that you are moved by his will alone and not by your own delight," Leibniz argued:

> We must recognize that this conflicts with the nature of things, for the impulse to action arises from a striving toward perfection, the sense of which is pleasure, and there is no action or will on any other basis. Even in our evil purposes we are moved by a certain perceived appearance of good or perfection, even though we miss the mark, or rather pay for a lesser good, ill sought, by throwing away a greater. Nor can anyone renounce (except merely verbally) being impelled by his own good, without renouncing his own nature.
> (L 424; cf. A.I.vi 198; A.VI.i 461: L 134; E 790: W 565)

As we shall see, it was one of Leibniz's great achievements that he found a way of reconciling his psychological egoism with the possibility of altruism.

NATURAL LAW

The idea of natural law was central to Leibniz's moral and political theory. "There are *fundamental Maxims*," he wrote in the *New Essays*, "which constitute the very law itself; they make up the actions, defences, replications etc. which, when they are taught by pure reason and do not come from the arbitrary power of the state, constitute natural law" (*New Essays*, IV.vii.19, A VI.vi 425: RB 425).

Because he distinguished between positive and natural law, Leibniz was anxious to expose "the error of those who have made justice dependent on power." This error he attributed to a "confounding [of] right and law":

Right cannot be unjust, it is a contradiction; but law can be. For it is power which gives and maintains law; and if this power lacks wisdom or good will, it can give and maintain quite evil laws.   (M 47: R 50)

The main target of Leibniz's remarks was Hobbes, "who is noted for his paradoxes [and] has wished to uphold the same thing as Thrasymachus: for he holds that God has the right to do everything, because he is all-powerful. This is a failure to distinguish between right and fact. For what one can do is one thing, what one should do, another" (M 43: R 47). Indeed in the *Leviathan* (1651), after he had enumerated nineteen "Lawes of Nature," Hobbes immediately added that they are only properly called laws "if we consider [them] as delivered in the word of God, that by right commandeth all things."[8] But in a later discussion of the kingdom of God, at *Leviathan*, II, 31, Hobbes explained that "the Right of Nature, whereby God reigneth over men, and punisheth those that break his Lawes, is to be derived . . . from his *Irresistible Power*"; his conclusion was finally that irresistible power rules by nature.[9] Against this, Leibniz argued that justice, or right, was to be founded in wisdom and goodness (M 48: R 50; cf. R 216).

In his insistence that power must be distinguished from right, Leibniz was merely restating the antivoluntarist sentiments that had earlier been expressed by the great Dutch natural lawyer, Hugo Grotius – "the incomparable Grotius," as Leibniz often called him (e.g., see Du IV 276: R 65; *Theodicy*, Preliminary Dissertation §6, G VI 53: H 77; *New Essays* IV.xvi.10, A VI.vi 467: RB 467). In an infamous passage from the preface to his *De iure belli ac pacis* (1625) – a passage that Leibniz was later explicitly to cite and enthusiastically to endorse (for example, see Du IV.iii 279–80: R 71; *Theodicy* §183, G VI 266: H 243) – Grotius had maintained that the principles of natural law would remain valid "even if we should concede that which cannot be conceded without the utmost wickedness, that there is no God, or that the affairs of men are of no concern to Him."[10] Grotius believed this because he believed that the laws of nature were necessary truths, following from facts about human nature, and therefore independent of God's will.[11] Similarly, in the *Theodicy* Leibniz wrote:

One is . . . justified in saying that the precepts of natural law assume the reasonableness and justice of that which is enjoined, and that it would be man's duty to practise what they contain even though God should have been so indulgent as to ordain nothing in that respect. Pray observe that in going back without visionary thoughts to that ideal moment when God has yet decreed nothing, we find in the ideas of God the principles of morals under terms that imply an obligation [*nous trouvons dans les idées de Dieu les principes de morale sous des termes qui emportent une obligation*]. We understand these maxims as certain, and derived from the eternal and immutable order. . . . You would not dare to deny that these truths impose upon man a duty in relation to all acts which are in conformity with strict reason. . . . Now since by the very nature of things, and before the divine laws, the truths of morality impose upon man certain duties [*puisque par la nature même des choses, et anterieurement aux loix divines, les veritez de morale imposent à l'homme certains devoirs*], Thomas Aquinas and Grotius were justified in saying that if there were no God we should nevertheless be obliged to conform to natural law.

(*Theodicy* §183, G VI 226: H 243; cf. M 47: R 49–50, Du IV.iii: 280: R 71–72)

So in his *Opinion of the Principles of Pufendorf* (1706), Leibniz argued that the "efficient cause [of natural law] in us is the light of eternal reason, kindled in our minds by the divinity" (Du IV.iii 282: R 75). But we have already seen that in his theory of motivation, Leibniz was a psychological egoist. Thus when Leibniz says that "the efficient cause of [natural] law" is found "in the nature of things and in the precepts of right reason which conform to it, which emanate from the divine understanding [*in rerum natura, rectaeque secundum hanc rationis praeceptis, a divina mente emanantibus*]" (Du IV.iii 279: R 70) and that "virtue is the habit of acting according to wisdom [*l'habitude d'agir selon la sagesse, habitus agendi secundum sapientiam*]" (Gr 579: R 83, Gr 581, 640), or that it is "the habit of acting reasonably [*l'habitude d'agir raisonnablement, habitus agendi cum ratione*]" (G III 425: R 197, K X 11: R 105, Gr 609), or finally that it is "a habit of the soul of following right reason [*habitus animi rectam rationem sequentis*]" (Gr 612), it must be borne in mind that it was Leibniz's position that "wisdom . . . is the knowledge of our own good [*la sagesse ... est la connaissance de notre propre bien*]" (M 58: R 57) and that

> The right reason for our actions is the same as prudence [*Ratio ... recta agendorum cum prudentia idem sit*]. It follows, therefore, that there can be no justice without prudence. Prudence, furthermore, cannot be separated from our own good. . . . There is no one who deliberately does anything except for the sake of his own good, for we seek the good also of those whom we love for the sake of the pleasure which we ourselves get from their happiness. . . . It follows from this . . . that no one can be obligated to do evil to himself. What is more, no one can be obligated except for his own good [*nec nisi in bonum suum obligari quenquam*]. For since justice is something of which a prudent man can be convinced, and since no one can be convinced of anything except for reasons of his own utility, it follows that every duty must be useful . . . that every duty (or injustice) is useful (or harmful).
>
> (A VI.i 461: L 134)

Implicitly at work in this argument, of course, is something like the principle that "ought" implies "can". If men cannot act except for the sake of what they perceive to be their own good, natural law cannot reasonably be regarded as binding unless it can be shown that acting in accordance with its principles is beneficial to the agent and that acting in violation of its principles is harmful to the agent. In attempting to show that "every duty (or injustice) is useful (or harmful)," Leibniz was attempting to show that the demands of morality were not only not in conflict with the demands of rational self-interest, but that the demands of the former were actually coincident with the demands of the latter.

Grotius had assumed that men were moved to act in accordance with natural law by "an impelling desire for society [*appetitus societatis*]."[12] Thus, as Richard Tuck has observed, Grotius

> simply assumed that men want to be responsible and social beings even though they may suffer as individuals for those wants in the short term, and that the law of nature obliges them to follow their natural bent. No special explanation of why it is rational for individuals to do so seemed necessary to Grotius.[13]

But others among his contemporaries were not as sanguine as Grotius was about the natural sociability of human beings. The English jurist, John Selden (1584–1654), for example, repudiated the Grotian psychological assumptions and opted for a prudential theory of obligation, as did that group of this followers who came to be known as the Tew Circle.[14] Tuck has argued that Selden's *De iure naturali et gentium iuxta disciplinam Ebraeorum* (1640) "constitutes the first example of the English interest in the nature of moral obligation, and of the scepticism found in many later seventeenth-century English philosophers over whether there can be an account of obligation distinct from one of motivation."[15] More notorious than Selden or any of his Tew Circle followers was Hobbes who also came to reject the Grotian assumptions about sociability and to adopt a prudential theory of obligation. In *De cive* (1642), Hobbes had remarked that "the greatest part of those men who have written aught concerning commonwealths, either suppose, or require us or beg of us to believe, that man is a creature born fit for society," but his own view was that "all society . . . is either for gain, or for glory; that is, not so much for love of our fellows, as for the love of ourselves."[16] So much for *appetitus societatis*. Moreover, in holding, notoriously, that in the state of nature – where there is no common power to enforce the peace and consequently a "warre of every man against every man" – "nothing can be Unjust" and "the notions of Right and Wrong, Justice and Injustice [can] have . . . no place,"[17] Hobbes put himself at odds with that tradition of natural law which had culminated in the work of Grotius.

It is against this background that we must understand the intrusion of a theory of motivation into Leibniz's theory of obligation, as well as his concern to establish that the rationally self-interested man is bound by natural law. In a letter of 1696, Leibniz suggested "that the positions of Grotius and Hobbes are easily reconciled," declaring that while he did "not doubt but that Grotius would have been ready to say certain things against the opinions of Hobbes, had he been alive at the right time," neither did he doubt "but that he would have been prepared to turn something from Hobbes to his own use" (Gr 655).[18] And so, in his *Opinion on the Principles of Pufendorf*, Leibniz argued that even if one should grant that God does not exist, "care for one's own preservation and well-being certainly lays on men many requirements about taking care of others, as even Hobbes perceives in part" (Du IV.iii 280: R 71; cf. Du IV.iii 281: R 73). Much of Leibniz's *Meditation on the Common Concept of Justice* (ca. 1702–1703) is given over to an attempt to establish that the same reasons that would lead a prudent man to act in accordance with the lowest level of natural law, *ius strictum*, which is founded upon the principle *neminem laedere* (to harm no one), must also lead him to act in accordance with the principle of equity, "which orders that we give each his due: *suum cuique tribuere.*" In his *Codex iuris gentium* (1693), Leibniz explained that whereas the *ius strictum* aims only at "the conservation of peace" and the avoidance of misery, equity "tends toward happiness, but only such as is possible in this life" (G III 388: R 173). Moreover, whereas *ius strictum* "does not take account of differences among men," at the level of equity "merits are weighed, and thus privileges, rewards and punishment have their place" (G III 388: R 172). As Leibniz explained it in the *Meditation*, what is due to each at the level of equity

is determined by the rule of equity or equality: *quod tibi non vis fieri, aut quod tibi vis fieri, neque aliis facito aut negato* [what you do not wish to be done to you, or what you do wish to be done to you, do not do to others, or do not deny to others]. This is the rule of reason and of our Lord. Put yourself in the place of another, and you will have the true point of view for judging what is just or not.   (M 57: R 56)

Hobbes himself had cited the golden rule as a sort of shorthand formula from which all the laws of nature could be derived, to be used by those lacking either the subtlety or the time to follow his own deduction.[19] But Leibniz thought that by appealing to this rule he could obtain stronger results than Hobbes had.[20] In the *Meditation*, Leibniz advanced what he called a nominal definition of justice, that it is "a constant will to act in such a way that no one has a reason to complain of us" (M 53: R 53). Leibniz expected that everyone would be able to accept this definition, but he also recognized that this would not in itself yield a common concept of justice unless there was agreement about what constitutes a reason for complaint. While most would readily grant that one has reason to complain if he is harmed by another, some would grant no more than that. The problem Leibniz set for himself was to show that there is reason for complaint not only when one is harmed by another, but also when one is not helped to obtain a great good by another who could do so without significant loss to himself; in sum, that justice requires not only that one refrain from harming others, but also that one be charitable.

The argument Leibniz offered for this in the *Meditation* is of some interest because it makes appeal to selfish motives alone and does not assume that the good of others is something that can be desired and sought for its own sake. So although Leibniz suggested that "one can give more than one reason for this," *viz.*, refraining from doing evil to others, he maintained that "the most pressing will be the fear that someone will do the same to us" (M 55: R 54). But by the same token, Leibniz argued that he must fear reprisal who refuses to prevent evil to others when he can do so without significant loss to himself; so the same reason that would lead selfish men to refrain from harming others must lead them also to prevent evil to others, if they can do so without significant loss to themselves. To bridge the gap between this conclusion and the claim that the same reason must also lead the selfish man to be charitable, Leibniz considered two intermediate cases: the prudent man would not refuse to relieve the ills of others and remove impediments to their obtaining a good – "at least in so far as they can without inconveniencing themselves"[21] – since such a one would complain if others were to refuse him the same. Having gotten this far, what remained, Leibniz thought, would be easy: "You could make me happy and you do not do it: I complain; you would complain in the same situation; thus I complain with justice" (M 56–57: R 55). Consequently,

one can say . . . that justice, at least among men, is the constant will to act, so far as possible, in a way such that no one can complain of us, if we would not complain of others in a similar case. From which it is evident that, since it is impossible to act so that the whole world is content, one must try to content people as much as possible, and thus that whatever is just, conforms to the charity of the wise.   (M 58: R 56–57)

"Charity of the wise" became Leibniz's standard definition of justice. But he defined wisdom as "the knowledge of our own good," and it is that which "brings us to justice, that is to a reasonable advancement of the good of others" (M 58: R 57). But we must remember that thus far we have been exploring what natural law requires on that wicked hypothesis, that God does not exist. But in his *Opinion on the Principles of Pufendorf*, Leibniz insisted that "a natural law based on this source alone," i.e., upon "care for one's preservation and well-being" apart from a consideration of God's existence, "would be very imperfect" (Du IV.iii 280: R 71),[22] indeed, "only a regard for God and immortality makes the obligations of virtue and justice absolutely binding" (*New Essays* II.xxx.55, A VI.vi 201: RB 201). Thus against both Hobbes and Pufendorf, who were extremely reluctant to bring considerations of God and an afterlife into their accounts of natural law, Leibniz argued vigorously that any complete account of natural law, which he often called "universal justice" (see, for example, M 17, M 64: R 60, Du IV.iii 278: R 69, G III 389: R 174), must include such considerations. In a passage remarkable for its studied rejection of any Platonic assumptions about the value of justice apart from a consideration of external rewards, Leibniz wrote:

One cannot doubt, in fact, that the ruler of the universe, at once most wise and most powerful, has allotted rewards for the good and punishments for the wicked, and that his plan will be put into effect in a future life, since in present life many crimes remain without punishment and without recompense. Therefore, to set aside . . . the consideration of the future life, which is inseparably connected to divine providence, and to be content with an inferior degree of natural law, which can even be valid for atheists . . . , would mean cutting off the best part of the science [of law], and suppressing many duties in this life as well. Why, indeed, would someone risk riches, honors and his very existence on behalf of his dear ones, or his country or of justice, when, by the ruin of others, he could think only of himself, and live amidst honors and riches? Indeed, to put off [the enjoyment of] actual and tangible goods simply for the immortality of one's name and for posthumous fame – for the voices of those whom one can no longer hear – what would this be if not magnificent folly? More sublime and perfect is the theory of natural law according to Christian doctrine . . . , or rather of the true philosophers, [namely] that not everything should be measured by the goods of this life. In fact, unless someone is born or educated to find an intense pleasure in virtue, and pain in vice (which is not true of everybody), there will be no more arguments which can dissuade him from committing great crimes, which can gain very great goods for him with impunity: *Sit spes fallendi, miscebit sacra profanis* [Horace, *Epistolae* I, 16, v. 54: "So long as there is hope of successful deceit, he will mix sacred with profane"]
(Du IV.iii 276–77: R 67)

In the *Meditation*, Leibniz explained that the "best part of the science [of law]," as he referred to it in the preceding passage, is "stamped with the supreme precept: *honeste* (*hoc est probe, pie*) *vivere*" (M 64: R 60). And in the same place he argued that by revealing himself to men, "as he has done through the eternal light of reason which he has given us, and through the wonderful effects of his power, of his wisdom and of his infinite goodness," God has given to everyone a motive to be just; for the fact that there exists an omniscient, omnipotent, and perfectly just being, entails that every act of justice will be rewarded and that every injustice will be punished (M 61–62: R 58–59; cf. K X 10: R 105; G VI 605: L 640; G VI 622: L 652; G III 389: R 173). Thus, when it is understood that "justice conforms to the will of a sage whose wisdom is infinite and whose power is proportioned to it, they find that they would not be wise at all (that is, prudent) if they did not conform themselves to the will of such a sage" (M 63: R 59). In the *Codex iuris gentium*, we are told that *ius strictum* and equity "can be interpreted as limited to the relations within mortal life," whereas at the level of piety "we ought to hold this life itself and everything that makes it desirable inferior to the great advantage of others, and that we should bear the greatest pains for the sake of those near us" (G III 388: R 173). But, again, this could not reasonably be done if God did not exist and the soul were not immortal. Thus God's existence and the immortality of the soul are not required simply in order to given men a reason to act in accordance with strict right and equity when they could get away with doing otherwise to their own advantage, but also to make it reasonable for men of faith to risk everything in this life for the sake of the common good.

Thus far we have been considering the reasons Leibniz was able to offer the selfish man for acting in accordance with justice. But it must be borne in mind that Leibniz did not think that anyone who acted in accordance with the principles of justice merely out of hope of reward or fear of punishment – which Leibniz regarded as calculating and mercenary motives – could be truly just. It is worth remarking, then, that for Leibniz no action could be truly just unless it proceeded from appropriate motives; and no agent could be truly just unless that agent acted from appropriate motives. In his *Opinion on the Principles of Pufendorf*, Leibniz went out of his way to fault Pufendorf for having suggested "that that which remains hidden in the soul, and does not appear externally, is not pertinent to natural law" (Du IV iii 277: R 68). For one thing, Leibniz argued that unless one is tutored to act for the right reasons, there remains a great risk that such a one will eventually fail in his duty. The motives of hope and fear, for example, will cease to be effective in the case of a person who believes he has nothing (external) to lose or who believes that he can act unjustly without being caught. Consequently,

> While it is possible that someone, by hope or by fear, will repress wicked thoughts, so that they do no harm (a thing which is, however, hard to attain), nonetheless he will never succeed in making them useful. Therefore whoever is not well-intentioned will often sin, at least by omission. Thus the author's hypothesis about a soul which is internally corrupt and outwardly innocent is not very safe and not very probable.
>
> (Du IV.iii 278: R 69)

But beyond this, Leibniz believed, against those mystics who regarded God's infinite perfections as beyond all human comprehension, that divine justice and human justice must be defined by the same rules (see M 45–46: R 48–49). And therefore, since even Pufendorf allowed that God has an interest in internal motives, and since "the rules which are common [to divine and human justice] certainly enter into the science [of natural law], and ought to be considered in universal jurisprudence," natural law ought not to exclude "the consideration of internal probity [*interna probitas*]" (Du IV.iii 278, 279: R 69, 70). Consequently, "not only external acts, but also all of our sentiments are regulated by a certain rule of law; thus those who are worthy of being philosophers of law [must] consider not only concord among men, but also friendship with God, the possession of which assures us of an enduring felicity" (Du IV.iii 281: R 73): "he who obeys God from fear is not yet the friend of God," but "every wise man is a friend of God" (E 670: W 569).

The question that finally remains, then, is what, according to Leibniz, is the motive to right action in the truly virtuous man. Leibniz thinks that the answer to this can be discovered by considering what could constitute such a motive in God, who is, after all, a morally perfect being. In the *Meditation*, Leibniz argued that since God is omnipotent he cannot be motivated to act out of hope or fear. Indeed,

> One cannot envisage in God any other motive than that of perfection, or, if you like, of his pleasure; supposing (according to my definition) that pleasure is nothing but a feeling of perfection, he has nothing to consider outside himself; on the contrary everything depends on him. But his goodness would not be supreme, if he did not aim at the good and at perfection so far as is possible.
>
> (M 60: R 57)

But Leibniz argued furthermore that "this same motive has a place in truly virtuous and generous men, whose supreme function is to imitate divinity, in so far as human nature is capable of it." Since virtue is "perfection of the will" and vice is "imperfection" of the will, such a man "would find the greatest pleasure in virtue and the greatest evil in vice," and he would "find so much pleasure in the exercise of justice and so much ugliness in unjust actions, that other pleasures and displeasures [would be] obliged to give way" (M 61: R 58). Leibniz regarded the agent's pleasure in acting as justice demands as so important to determining the moral value of the agent and his act that he was willing to say that "he who acts well, not out of hope or fear, but by an inclination of his soul, is so far from not behaving justly that, on the contrary, he acts more justly than all others, imitating, in a certain way, as a man, divine justice" (Du IV.iii 280: R 72).[23]

LOVE OF GOD: THE FOUNTAIN OF TRUE JUSTICE

Around 1678 Leibniz wrote a series of four dialogues on religion; in the first of these, he declared that "whoever truly loves God above all things will not fail to do what he knows to conform to his commands. This is why it is necessary to begin with this love, since charity and justice are its inescapable results" (L 213). Against the suggestion that love of God is not necessary for salvation because "penitence bestowed through fear of punishment suffices, along with the sacrament of absolution" (L 214), Leibniz argued that "since God has commanded us to love him above all things, it is very clear that whoever does not is in a state of mortal sin" (L 214). Kant, of course, would argue that there is implicit in this a violation of the principle that "ought" implies "can," since "love out of inclination," not being subject to the will, "cannot be commanded."[24] Leibniz would doubtless have agreed that such love is not directly subject to the will, but he would also have insisted that it is at least indirectly so. Leibniz regarded it to be one of our duties "to seek knowledge of God" (C 517), and he certainly thought that that was something we could choose to do. But knowledge of God, according to Leibniz, is both a necessary and a sufficient condition for loving God. "To love," Leibniz held, "is to find pleasure in the perfection of another" (Gr 579: R 83),[25] so it is fairly obvious that on Leibniz's account "one cannot love God without knowing his perfections" (Gr 580: R 84). But because "His perfections are infinite and cannot end, [so that] the pleasure which consists in the feeling of his perfections is the greatest and most durable which can exist," it is equally clear that "one cannot know God as one ought without loving him above all things" (M 62: R 59; cf. G VI 605: L 641). So "it is not enough," Leibniz wrote in his *Opinion on the Principles of Pufendorf,*

that we be subject to God just as we would a tyrant; nor must he be only feared because of his greatness, but also loved because of his goodness: which right reason teaches, no less than the Scriptures. To this lead the best principles of universal jurisprudence, which collaborate also with wise theology and bring about true virtue.   (Du IV.iii 280: R 72)

But how does love of God bring about true virtue? Sometimes Leibniz argued that it does so directly, on the simple ground that one's love of God will result in taking the greatest pleasure in willing what God wills, i.e., the common good (or what is the same, his own glory [see M 8; G III 261: R 191; K X 10: R 105]). "We cannot benefit God," Leibniz argued, because he is already perfect; but "we do something similar when we try to fulfill his presumptive will" (M 37). Thus, in his *Meditation on the Common Concept of Justice,* following the passage considered earlier in which he cited the rewards and punishments of God as sufficient motives to right action in the prudent man, Leibniz wrote eloquently of a motive of a different kind:

What Cicero said allegorically of ideal justice is really true in relation to this substantial justice: that if we could see this justice, we would be inflamed by its beauty. One can compare the divine monarchy to a kingdom whose sovereign would be a queen more intelligent and more wise than Queen Elizabeth; more judicious, more happy and, in a word, greater than Queen Anne; more clever, more wise, and more beautiful than the Queen of Prussia: in short, as accomplished as it is possible to be. Let us imagine that the perfections of this queen make such an impression on the minds of her subjects, that they take the greatest pleasure in obeying her and in pleasing her: in this case everyone would be virtuous and just by inclination. It is this which happens literally, and beyond everything one can describe, with respect to God and those who know him. It is in him that wisdom, virtue, justice, and greatness are accompanied by sovereign beauty. One cannot know God as one ought without loving him above all things, and one cannot love him thus without willing what he wills. His perfections are infinite and cannot end, and this is why the pleasure which consists in the feeling of his perfections is the greatest and most durable which can exist. That is, the greatest happiness, which causes one to love him, causes one to be happy and virtuous at the same time.   (M 62–63: R 59)

But to secure the good of others because it pleases us to please God must, on Leibniz's view of the matter, still involve calculating and mercenary motives. For in this case the good of others will be desired, not as an end in itself, but as a means to pleasing God, which in turn pleases us. In a relatively early work, *Elementa iuris naturalis* (1670–71), Leibniz explained:

There is in justice a certain respect for the good of others, and also for our own, but not in the sense that one is the end of the other. Otherwise it may follow that it will be just to abandon some wretched person in his agony, though it is in our power to deliver him from it without much difficulty, merely because we are sure there is no reward for helping him. Yet everyone abominates this as criminal, even those who find no reason for a future life; not to mention the sound sense of all good people which spurns so mercenary a reason for justice.   (A VI.i 464: L 136)

But now the problem for Leibniz is fairly obvious: By his own psychological assumptions, no one can act except for his own perceived good; but in order to act in a truly just way, one cannot act on mercenary motives. It would thus appear that no one can ever act in a truly just way. That is the problem; "the answer," Leibniz held, "certainly depends on the nature of love" (A VI.i. 464: L 136).

We have already seen that to love, on Leibniz's view, is to find pleasure in the perfections of another. But for Leibniz, it is a sufficient sign that we desire something for its own sake that we take immediate pleasure in it. If we did not desire the good of another for its own sake, with no further end in view, we would not take pleasure in his obtaining that good, contrary to the nature of love. "For whatever produces pleasure immediately through itself," Leibniz wrote in a letter of 1697, "is also desired for itself, as constituting (at least in part) the end of our wishes, and as something which enters into our own felicity and gives us satisfaction" (G II 577: W 564–65). And in his *Elementa iuris naturalis* he concluded that "we can therefore readily understand how we not only can achieve the good of others without our own but can even seek it in itself; namely, insofar as the good of others is pleasant to us. A true definition of love can be built from this. For we *love* him whose good is our delight" (A VI.i 464: L 137; cf. L 424, G II 578, 581: W 565, 566–67). It is this kind of love that Leibniz called "disinterested," or "true pure," love; it is "independent of hope, of fear, and of regard for any question of utility. In truth, the happiness of those whose happiness pleases us turns into our own happiness, since things which please us are desired for their own sake" (G III 387: R 171). This is the kind of love that is borne toward God by him who is "the friend of God" (G VII 74: W 569), and it is the kind of love that, borne toward men, constitutes charity (see G II 577: W 564). It is thus the kind of love that is borne toward other men by those who are truly just: "a good man is one who loves everybody, in so far as reason permits" (G III 386: R 171). We recall that Leibniz's standard definition of justice was the "charity of the wise." But "charity is a universal benevolence, and benevolence the habit of loving or of willing the good" (G III 387: R 171), so that justice is finally "a habit of loving conformed to wisdom" (Gr 579: R 83). It was thus by means of his notion of disinterested love that Leibniz was able to reconcile the apparently egoistic psychology of Hobbes with the possibility of altruism implied in Grotius's assumption of a natural sociability in human beings. The love that the good man bears towards others is *not* selfless according to Leibniz, so it is consistent with egoistic psychological assumptions; and such love is not mercenary, so it is consistent with the sociability postulated by Grotius.[26]

Justice, then, demands that we love others disinterestedly and not seek their good solely as a means, even as a means to pleasing God. "Reason and Scripture both tell us that we must love God above all things," but also "our neighbor as ourself" (L 214, 216). But love of neighbor is no more subject to command than is love of God. But just as we have seen that love of God can be at least indirectly subject to the will (since we can will to seek knowledge of God, which will naturally result in love for God), so love of neighbor can be indirectly subject to the will in precisely the same way. For, again, "one cannot love God without knowing his perfections"; but "one cannot know God without loving one's brother" (Gr 580, 581: R 84); so one cannot love God without loving one's brother, or "he who loves God loves all men" (G VII 75: W 569), but to the degree that reason permits. But why cannot one know God without loving one's brother? Perhaps the best place to begin to look for an answer to this question is in the following passage from *Elementa iuris naturalis:*

Everything which is loved is beautiful, that is, delightful to a sentient being, but not . . . everything beautiful is loved. For we do not really love non-rational beings, since we do not seek their good in itself, except those who make the popular mistake of imagining that there is some reasonable element – I know not what – in animals which they call sense. Since justice, therefore, demands that we seek the good of others in itself, and since to seek the good of others in itself is to love them, it follows that love is of the nature of justice.   (A VI.i 464–65: L 137)

Minds, or rational souls "which are capable of knowing God and discovering eternal truths" (G II 124: MP 159) are uniquely loveable, Leibniz suggests, precisely because they are rational; and it is precisely in virtue of being rational that minds are said by Leibniz to be "images of divinity" (*Monadology* §83, G IV 621: L 651; cf. *Principles* §14, G VI 604: L 640) or a "little divinity" (*Monadology* §83, G VI 621: L 651; cf. G II 125: MP 159). "God, in giving [man] intelligence, has presented him with an image of the Divinity" (*Theodicy* §147, G VI 197: H 215). Thus, created minds, in Leibniz's view, "differ from God only in degree, from finite to infinite" (G II 125: MP 160), "since he is himself a mind and as it were one amongst us" (G II 125: MP 159).[27] The preeminent status of minds – which "express God rather than the world" – in relation to other creatures – which "express the world rather than God" (G II 124: MP 159; cf. *Principles* §14, G VI 604: L 640; *Monadology* §83, G VI 621: L 651; *Discourse* §35, G IV 460: L 326) – was a constant theme in Leibniz's writings. "The spirit not only has a perception of the works of God," Leibniz wrote in *The Principles of Nature and of Grace, Based on Reason* (1714),

but is even capable of producing something which resembles them, though in miniature. For not to mention the wonders of dreams in which we invent, without effort but also without will, things which we should have to think a long time to discover when awake, our soul is architectonic also in its voluntary actions and in discovering the sciences according to which God has regulated things (by weight, measure, number, etc.). In its own realm and in the small world in which it is allowed to act, the soul imitates what God performs in the great world.
(*Principles* §14, G VI 604: L 640; cf. *Monadology* §83, G VI 621: L 651, G VI 507: L 552)

Indeed, it is precisely in discovering the divine sciences that we come to know God:

> Since we can know [God] only in his emanations, these are two means of seeing his beauty, namely in the knowledge of eternal truths . . . and in the knowledge of the Harmony of the universe (in applying reasons to facts). That is to say, one must know the marvels of reason and the marvels of nature.   (Gr 580–81: R 84)

As we come to recognize the perfection of God through the scientific study of the cosmos, which reveals the order and beauty in God's works, we also come to recognize the perfection of the rational soul which imitates God: God has produced order and beauty in the universe, but the rational soul can imitate that creative act by discovering and coming to understand scientific theories which mirror the order exhibited in the natural world. It is reason, Leibniz told Sophia Charlotte in a letter of 1702, that "makes us resemble God in miniature not only through our knowledge of order but also through the order which we can ourselves impart to the things within our grasp, in imitation of that which God imparts to the universe. It is in this, also, that our *virtue* and perfection consist, as our *felicity* consists in the pleasure we take in it" (G VI 507: L 552; cf. G VII 89: L 427, L 218–19). Virtue consists in the perfection of the intellect and the will (M 18). Reason perfects the intellect by imposing order upon phenomena through the creation of scientific theories (L 280); reason perfects the will by governing and ordering the passions (C 517, M 8). In each case there is an imitation of the way in which God has ordered the world in accordance with wisdom. Knowing God leads us to see the perfection of God in man. "But the perfection of God," Leibniz held, "is somehow transferred into us by being understood and loved" (M 17), and "thus he who loves God, i.e., he who is wise, will love all men, but each one more the more distinct traces of the divine virtue shine forth in him" (M 8), which is precisely the degree of love that reason permits.[28]

So in the end, Leibniz's answer to Pufendorf, who had maintained that obligation derives from the command of a superior, was that

> whoever, indeed, does good out of love for God or of his neighbor, takes pleasure precisely in the action itself (such being the nature of love) and does not need any other incitement, or the command of a superior, for that man

the saying that the law is not made for the just is valid. To such a degree is it repugnant to reason to say that only the law or constraint make a man just.

(Du IV.iii 280: R 72)

But Leibniz again added that "it must be conceded that those who have not reached this point of spiritual perfection are susceptible of obligation only by hope or fear; and that the prospect of divine vengeance, which one cannot escape even by death, can better than anything else make apparent to them the absolute and universal necessity to respect law and justice" (Du IV.iii 280–81: R 72–73).[29] Moreover, Leibniz made it clear that he thought that true justice was beyond the power of most men:

One can say that this serenity of spirit, which would find the greatest pleasure in virtue and the greatest evil in vice, that is, in the perfection or imperfection of the will, would be the greatest good of which man is capable here below. . . . But it must . . . be admitted that it is difficult to arrive at this disposition, that the number of those who have attained it is small, and the majority of men are insensible to this motive, great and beautiful as it is.

(M 61: R 58)

The "spiritual disposition" that Leibniz refers to here is so difficult to arrive at partly because he makes it so heavily dependent upon intellectual achievement – i.e., upon a fairly deep scientific understanding of the harmony of the physical world, upon which a true love of God, and hence a universal love of man, supervenes. As we shall see, the intellectualist bent in Leibniz's ethics led him to view education as being as central to the ethical life as Plato did – and with the same result, namely, that true justice seems to become the privilege of a very small elite.[30] "I assume," the "honorable" Poliander of Leibniz's dialogue piously announces, "that God is truly loved"; to which Theophile would respond: "The assumption you make is a great one and very rare here below. What, Poliander! Do you really think that God is loved above all things? I maintain that few people know what the love of God is" (L 214).

PRACTICAL BENEVOLENCE AND THE ORIGIN AND FUNCTION OF THE STATE

Against Hobbes who held that men formed societies to avoid harm from others, and against Aristotle who held that men were by nature made for the polis, Leibniz argued that the Huron and Iroquois Indians of North America

have shown, by their surprising conduct, that entire peoples can be without magistrates and without quarrels, and that as a result men are neither taken far enough by their natural goodness nor forced by their wickedness to provide themselves with a government and to renounce their liberty. But the roughness of these savages shows that it is not so much necessity as the inclination to advance to a better [condition], and to arrive at felicity through mutual assistance, which is the foundation of societies and of states. But it must be granted that security is the most essential point in this.

(G III 424: R 196; cf. *New Essays* III.i.1, A VI.vi 273–74; RB 273–74)

Leibniz grants to Hobbes that security is the most essential function of the state, but not because it is the ultimate end of the state; it is rather because the ultimate end of the state, which is the happiness of its citizens, cannot be attained without providing for the security of its citizens (see K IX 143: Gr 613). "The end of politics," Leibniz wrote in a letter of 1699 to Thomas Burnett, "after virtue, is the maintenance of abundance, so that men will be in a better position to work in common concert for that sound knowledge which causes the sovereign author to be admired and loved" (G III 261: R 191). But "that sound knowledge which causes the sovereign author to be admired and loved" is precisely that "knowledge of the Harmony of the Universe" (Gr 581: R 84) which is the object of natural science. In his work *On the Elements of Natural Science* (ca. 1682–84), Leibniz argued that "the knowledge of bodies is . . . most important on two grounds – first to perfect our mind through an understanding of the purposes and causes of things; second, to conserve and nurture our body . . . by furthering what is wholesome for it and reducing what is harmful" (L 280). Since the knowledge that perfects the mind depends upon "an understanding of the purposes and causes of things," Leibniz followed Aristotle in holding that theoretical knowledge plays a central role in the good life for man:

Of those two applications of [natural] science [i.e., to the perfection of our mind and the conservation of our body], the former can be sought only in theoretical physics, the latter in empirical physics as well. . . . For though all science increases our power over external things provided a proper occasion arises for using it, there is nonetheless another use which depends on no such occasion, namely the perfection of the mind itself. By understand-

ing the laws or the mechanisms of divine invention, we shall perfect ourselves far more than by merely following the constructions invented by
men. For what greater master can we find than God, the author of the
universe?   (L 280)

The pursuit of theoretical science turns out to constitute the most
perfect form of worship and to generate the most profound love of
God:

And what more beautiful hymn can we sing to him than one in which the
witness of things themselves expresses his praise? But the more one can
give reasons for his love, the more one loves God. To find joy in the perfection of another – this is the essence of love. Thus the highest function of our
mind is the knowledge or what is here the same thing, the love of the most
perfect being, and it is from this that the maximum or the most enduring
joy, that is, felicity, must arise.   (Ibid.)

We are thus reminded that it is knowledge of God's perfections that
is, according to Leibniz, the source of our happiness. Unlike Aristotle who suggested that "it is to be expected that those who know
will pass their time more pleasantly than those who inquire,"[31] Leibniz maintained that our happiness consists in the continuous search
for, and discovery of, things previously unknown: "all new knowledge is an increase of our perfection, and therefore all distinct perceptions which show us something new are accompanied with pleasure" (G VII 113). But since minds can never perish on Leibniz's
view, their perpetual happiness depends upon their having an inex-
haustible object of knowledge; and only an infinite being can be
such an object: "It is true that the supreme happiness (with whatever *beatific vision* or knowledge of God it may be accompanied)
cannot ever be full, because God, being infinite, cannot ever be
known entirely. Thus our happiness will never consist, and ought
never to consist in complete joy, which leaves nothing to be desired
and which would stupefy our spirit, but in a perpetual progress to
new pleasures and new perfections" (*Principles* §18, G VI 606: L 641;
cf. *New Essays* II.xxi. 36, 41, : A VI.vi 189, 194: RB 189, 194).

    Natural science is important both for the perfection of the mind,
"which consists in the knowledge of truth and the exercise of virtue" (L 219), and for the discovery of things that can improve the
material conditions of human life.[32] And since perfection of the
mind and preservation of the body are necessary for human happi-

ness,[33] states are obligated to support the sciences, and scientific minds are obligated to contribute to knowledge and invention:

The greater his talent, the greater his obligation. For in my opinion an Archimedes, a Galileo, a Kepler, a Descartes, a Huygens, a Newton are more important with respect to the goal of the human race than great military men, and they are at least on a par with those esteemed legislators whose aim has been to lead men to what is truly good and solid.

(G III 261: R 191)

Given that the happiness of its citizens is the goal of the state, and given the connection that exists in Leibniz's theory between our happiness and our knowledge of God's perfections, or, what is the same, our scientific knowledge of nature, it is not surprising that Leibniz maintained that the state ought to promote the sciences.[34] But we recall that Leibniz implied that virtue was the first end of politics: "The end of politics, after virtue, is the maintenance of abundance, so that men will be in a better position to work in common concert for that sound knowledge which causes the sovereign author to be admired." But our earlier discussion shows that virtue itself must also be augmented by the increase of that scientific knowledge which causes God to be loved; for again, love of God brings about universal benevolence.

"The greatest and most efficacious means of attaining all these things," Leibniz wrote in his *Memoir for Enlightened Persons*, "and of augmenting the general welfare of men, while enlightening them, while turning them toward the good and while freeing them from annoying inconveniences, in so far as this is feasible, would be to persuade great princes and [their] principal ministers to make extraordinary efforts to procure such great goods and to allow our times to enjoy advantages which, without this [extraordinary effort], would be reserved for a distant posterity" (K X 14: R 107). Because the state was so important for securing the happiness and security of its citizens, Leibniz was not inclined to leave the selection of a sovereign in the hands of the people. Against Hobbes and Locke, who held that all men were equal in the state of nature, Leibniz argued that men differed significantly in their natural abilities. Thus "it seems that Aristotle is more correct here than Mr. Hobbes. [For] following natural reason, government belongs to the wisest" (G III 264: R 192). By nature government belongs to the wisest because "the end of political science with regard to the doctrine of forms of commonwealths, must be to make the empire of reason flourish" (G III 277: R 193). Given this end of politics, the end of the ideal government, of whatever form, is the establishment of a sovereign who seeks wisdom and the common good: "The end of monarchy is to make a hero of eminent wisdom and virtue reign. . . . The end of aristocracy is to give the government to the most wise and most expert. The end of democracy, or polity, is to make the people themselves agree to what is good for them. And if one could have all at once: a great hero, very wise senators, and very reasonable citizens, that would constitute a mixture of the three forms" (G III 277: R 193). "To make the empire of reason flourish" more than the security of the citizens is required. For the latter can be maintained, *à la* Hobbes, by means of arbitrary power; but "arbitrary power is opposed to the empire of reason" (ibid.).

Leibniz did not, of course, hold that it was the state alone that was obliged to serve the common good; nor that such an obligation fell only on individuals who were especially gifted in science: "Each must fulfill his duty without reference to others" (K X 15: R 108). We have seen that a good action is one that contributes to the common good, or to the perfection of minds; and because Leibniz believed the world to be governed by a perfect monarch, he believed, as we have also seen, that every good action would be rewarded and every evil action punished. This has the "practical" result, Leibniz tells us, that "the more minds have good will and are brought to contribute to the glory of God, or (what is the same thing) to the common good, the more they participate in happiness themselves" (K X 10: R 105). It is wonderfully clear from this just what Leibniz thinks the person who is wise must do:

Every enlightened person must judge that the true means of guaranteeing forever his own individual happiness is to seek his satisfaction in occupations which tend toward the general good. . . . Now this general good, in so far as we can contribute to it, is the advancement toward perfection of men, as much by enlightening them so that they can know the marvels of the sovereign substance, as by helping them to remove the obstacles which stop the progress of our enlightenment.

To contribute truly to the happiness of men, one must enlighten their understanding; one must fortify their will in the exercise of virtues, that is, in the habit of acting according to reason; and one must, finally, try to remove the obstacles which keep them from finding the truth and following true goods.   (K X 10–11: R 105)

In this best of all possible worlds, virtue will produce its own reward: By increasing the knowledge and virtue of others, the truly virtuous man will increase his own happiness; for the truly virtuous man loves all others and hence will take pleasure in their increased perfection.

NOTES

1 Friedrich, "Philosophical Reflections of Leibniz on Laws, Politics, and the State," in Frankfurt, ed., *Leibniz*, p. 48.
2 Hobbes, *De Cive*, I 2 in Gert, ed., Hobbes: *Man and Citizen*, pp. 112–13.
3 Spinoza, *Ethics* III Prop. 9 Scholium in Gebhardt ed) *Opera* II 148; Curley, ed., *Collected Works* I 500.
4 Hobbes, *Leviathan* I. 6, Macpherson, ed., p. 120.
5 Aristotle, *Metaphysics* 1072a 28–9.
6 Leibniz also defined pleasure as the "perception of *increasing* perfection" (M 7, my emphasis; cf. M 17; L 218; G VII 73: W 568; G VII 197; Gr 603), and this has led John Hostler to conclude straightaway that "when he speaks of pleasure as being an awareness of perfection, what Leibniz means is that one perceives an increase of perfection" (Hostler, *Leibniz's Moral Philosophy*, p. 23). But some analysis seems to be called for here. In the tract on *Felicity* (ca. 1694–98), Leibniz declared that "pleasure is a knowledge or feeling of perfection, not only in ourselves, but also in others, *for in this way some further perfection is aroused in us*" (Gr 579: R 83, my emphasis). This is clarified somewhat by what Leibniz says in the following passage from the tract *On Wisdom* (1690's?): "*Pleasure* is the feeling of a perfection or an excellence, whether in ourselves or in something else. For the perfection of other beings also is agreeable, such as understanding, courage, and especially beauty in another human being, or in an animal or even in a lifeless creation, a painting or a work of craftsmanship, as well. For the image of such perfection in others, impressed upon us, causes some of this perfection to be implanted and aroused within ourselves. Thus there is no doubt that he who consorts much with excellent people or things becomes himself more excellent" (G VII 86: L 425).
    This passage suggests that the reason Leibniz sometimes defined pleasure as the perception or knowledge of perfection is because the perception of perfection in other things is a cause of an increase in our own perfection. This is also suggested by Leibniz's remark that "the perfection of God is somehow transferred into us by being understood and loved" (M 17). But it must be borne in mind that "the perfections of

others sometimes displease us – as for example, the understanding or the courage of any enemy, the beauty of a rival, or the luster of another's virtue which overshadows or shames us" (G VII 86: L 425). Still, Leibniz maintained that "this is not because of the perfection itself but because of the circumstance which makes it inopportune for us, so that the sweetness of our first perception of this perfection in someone else is exceeded and spoiled by the consequent bitterness of our afterthoughts" (ibid.). In general, as we shall discuss in detail below, Leibniz held that it is only in the perfection of those whom we love that we take pleasure.

7   Sometimes, too, Leibniz defined pleasure as "the perception of harmony [*perceptio harmoniae*]" (A VI.i: 484), or as "the sense of harmony [*sensus harmoniae*]" (G I 73: L 150). But that is because he identified perfection with harmony: "*pleasure*," Leibniz declared in a letter to Wolff of 18 May 1715, "is the feeling of perfection. *Perfection* is the harmony of things, or the observability of universals, or concord or identity in variety; then too you can say that it is degree of thinkability [*gradum considerabilitatis*]" (GW 172). I have elsewhere (see "Compossibility, Harmony," and "Leibniz's Theodicy," discussed Leibniz's account of perfection and harmony in detail, but it is worth remarking here that in his *Résumé of Metaphysics* (ca. 1697), Leibniz declared that "an intelligent being's *pleasure* is simply the perception of beauty, order and perfection" (G VII 290: P 146), that is, harmony. Since this world is the best of all possible worlds, "that series [of things] has prevailed through which there arises the greatest amount of what is distinctly thinkable" (ibid.), that is, that series which is most orderly and perfect in the sense that it "is at the same time simplest in hypotheses and the richest in phenomena" (*Discourse* §6 G IV 431: L 306). Because "distinct cogitability gives order to a thing and beauty to a thinker . . . , it . . . follows in general that the world is a cosmos, full of ornament; that is, that it is made in such a way that it gives the greatest satisfaction to an intelligent being" (G VII 290: P 146). It follows finally, therefore, that "the first cause is of the highest *goodness*, for whilst it produces as much perfection as possible in things, at the same time it bestows on minds as much pleasure as possible, since *pleasure* consists in the perception of perfection" (G VII 291: P 147).

8   *Leviathan* I.15, pp. 216–17.

9   Ibid., II. 31, p. 397. Cf. *De Cive* XV. 5. p. 292.

10 *Classics of International Law*, ed., Scott, III.ii. 13.

11 In *De iure belli ac pacis*, Grotius explained that "the law of nature . . . is unchangeable – even in the sense that it cannot be changed by God. Measureless as is the power of God, nevertheless it can be said that there are certain things over which that power does not extend; for things of which this is said are spoken only, having no sense corresponding with

THE CAMBRIDGE COMPANION TO LEIBNIZ

reality and being mutually contradictory. Just as even God, then, cannot cause that two times two should not make four, so He cannot cause that which is intrinsically evil be not evil" (*De iure belli ac pacis*, I.i.10.5, *Classics of International Law*, ed., Scott, III.i 5; III.ii 40).

Moreover, as he later explained in a letter to his brother, "God was at full Liberty not to create Man. The Moment he is determined to create Man, that is, a Nature endowed with Reason, and formed for a Society of an excellent Kind, he necessarily approves of such Actions as are suitable to that Nature, and as necessarily disapproves of those which are contrary to it. But there are several other Things which he commands or prohibits, because he thought fit to do so, and not because he could not act otherwise" (as quoted in Tuck, *National Rights Theories*, p. 76).

12 *De iure belli ac pacis*, par. 6, *Classics of International Law*, ed., Scott III.ii 11.

13 Tuck, *Natural Rights Theories*, p. 68.

14 For a succinct account of Selden's place in the history of natural rights theories, as well as the place of his followers in the Tew Circle, see Tuck, *Natural Rights Theories*, Chaps. 4–5.

15 Tuck, *Natural Rights Theories*, p. 90.

16 *De Cive* I. 2. pp. 110, 112–13.

17 *Leviathan* I.13, p. 188.

18 Leibniz's contemporary, the great German political philosopher, Samuel Pufendorf (1632–94), was similarly engaged in an attempt to reconcile Hobbes and Grotius. In the end, however, Pufendorf was led to repudiate both Grotius and Hobbes (see Tuck, *Natural Rights Theories*, Chap. 8). Leibniz did not think much of Pufendorf, as is clear from the discussion in his *Opinion on the Principles of Pufendorf* (Du IV.iii 275–83: R 64–75). As the following passage indicates, Leibniz believed that Pufendorf had erred grievously on the side of Hobbes: "He [Pufendorf] . . . does not find [the efficient cause of natural law] in the nature of things and in the precepts of right reason which conform to it, which emanate from the divine understanding, but (what will appear to be strange and contradictory) in the command of a superior. . . . This paradox, brought out by Hobbes above all, who seemed to deny to the state of nature, that is [a condition] in which there are no superiors, all binding justice whatsoever . . . , is a view to which I am astonished that anyone could have adhered" (Du IV.iii 279: R 70).

19 See *Leviathan* I. 15, p. 214.

20 It is perhaps significant that Hobbes presented only a negative formulation of the rule: "*Do not that to another, which thou wouldest not have done to thy selfe*" (*Leviathan*, I, 15, p. 214). On the other hand, we have seen that Leibniz formulated the rule in such a way that it had both

negative and positive import: "*quod tibi non fieri, aut quod tibi vis fieri, neque aliis facito aut negato*" (M 57: R: 56). It should also be remarked that while Hobbes argued that the laws of nature always "oblige *in foro interno;* that is to say, they bind to a desire they should take place: but *in foro externo;* that is, to the putting them in act, not alwayes" (*Leviathan*, I, 13, p. 215). In particular, where there is no security, as in the state of nature, the laws do not bind *in foro externo*. Needless to say, Leibniz subscribed to no such distinction.

21 Parenthetically, Leibniz immediately added that "I do not examine now how far this inconvenience may go" (M 56: R 55). It is thus clear that Leibniz thought it might go some distance, but that it should, at some point, have gone too far. This view, that what one has a moral right to demand from another depends on how much the other person must sacrifice in order to meet the demand, has not met with universal acceptance. For example, in her famous article on abortion, Judith Jarvis Thomson argued that "it's rather a shocking idea that anyone's rights should fade away and disappear as it gets harder and harder to accord them to him" (Thomson, "A Defense of Abortion," p. 61).

22 In his *Opinion on the Principles of Pufendorf*, Leibniz was commenting on the following passage from the preface to Pufendorf's *De officio hominis et civis:* "The decrees of natural law are adapted only to the human forum, which does not extend beyond this life, and they are wrongly applied in many places to the divine forum, which is the especial care of theology" (*Classics of International Law* ed., Scott, X.ii vii; and see Du IV.iii 276: R 66).

23 Leibniz's position, that the moral worth of an action or an agent depends upon the pleasure the agent takes in acting, was, of course, turned utterly on its head by Kant, who maintained, to the contrary, that insofar as an action proceeded from inclination, and not simply from "reverence for the [moral] law," it had no moral worth, and the agent deserved no moral credit for performing it (see Kant, *Gesammelte Schriften VI* 397–401; Kant, *Groundwork of the Metaphysic of Morals*, ed., Paton, 65–69).

24 *Gesammelte Schriften*, p. 399. *Groundwork*, p. 67.

25 Alternatively, Leibniz suggested that "to love is to delight in the happiness of another" (C 516; cf. G III 387: R 171, G VI 605: L 641). But as John Hostler has remarked (*Leibniz's Moral Philosophy*, p. 49), this definition is "misleading" because it obscures the fact that what delights us, on Leibniz's view, is not really the happiness of those we love, but their perfections, which bring about their happiness as well as our own: "to love," Leibniz wrote, "is to have an affection which makes us find pleasure *in what conduces to [dans ce qui convient à]* the happiness of the beloved object" (G II 581: W 567; my emphasis).

26 Leibniz went so far as to hold that there is in men a natural inclination to love their fellows and a natural instinct to do what reason commands. For example, in the *New Essays* Leibniz wrote: "Since morality is more important than arithmetic, God has given to man instincts which lead, straight away and without reasoning, to part of what reason commands. Similarly we walk in conformity with the laws of mechanics without thinking about them; and we eat not only because it is necessary for us to, but also and much more because eating gives us pleasure. But these instincts do not irresistibly impel us to act: our passions lead us to resist them, our prejudices obscure them, and contrary customs distort them. Usually, though, we accede to these instincts of conscience, and even follow them whenever stronger feelings do not overcome them. . . . Nature instils in man and even in most of the animals an affection and gentleness towards the members of their own species" (*New Essays* I.ii.9, A VI.vi 92–93: RB 92–93).

Similarly, in his remarks on Shaftesbury's *Characteristics of Men, Manners, Opinions, Times* (1712), Leibniz observed that "our natural affections produce our contentment: and the more natural one is, the more he is led to find his pleasure in the good of others, which is the foundation of universal benevolence, of charity, of justice. . . . Wisdom ordains that this benevolence have its degrees: and as the air, though it extends all around our globe, to a great height, has more body and density near us than has that which is in the high regions of our atmosphere, one can say as well that the charity which bears upon those who most nearly touch us, must have more intensity and more force" (G III 428–29: R 198: L 632–33). These passages suggest that while there is some natural inclination to love all men and an instinct to obey the command of reason, our love of others is often too weak or too inconstant to generate in men a truly universal benevolence. As we shall see, Leibniz held that the way to a universal love of man was through a love of God; and the love of God itself was to be generated by the scientific study and understanding of nature.

27 As a consequence of this, Leibniz says that minds "enter by virtue of reason and the eternal truths into a kind of society with God and are members of the City of God, that is to say, the most perfect state, formed and governed by the greatest and best of monarchs" (*Principles* §15, G VI 604: L 640).

28 It is standard Leibnizian doctrine, of course, that God is the source of the perfections in things, while their imperfections are due to their limited natures. See, for example, *Monadology* §42, G VI 613: L 647; *Theodicy* §31, G VI 121: H 141–42.

29 It should be noted here that even for those who have reached the state of "spiritual perfection," an afterlife would still be required in order that

they might have time to rejoice in their virtue. "If God did not exist," Leibniz wrote in his *De tribus iuris naturae et gentium gradibus*, "the wise would not be obligated to charity beyond what would be in conformity with their own advantage, and not to true virtue, unless by reason of its own perfection, for which one could not have sufficient reason in this brief life, if the soul were not immortal" (M 17).

30 On the other hand, Leibniz sometimes wrote as though he thought that knowledge was relatively unimportant to the ethical life. We have already seen (see note 26, for example, that he held that men have a natural inclination to love their fellows and that they are led by "instincts of conscience" to do what reason commands. He also wrote that "I am of the opinion that justice can be most succinctly and effectively defined as the charity of the wise, namely, universal love or benevolence, which would certainly have to be in the most wise, if any of such a kind were to be found among humans. I regard it in this way not because it is as if it is necessary that the just or good man excel in the knowledge of things and understand the first causes of equity and goodness, but because in those things which concern charity, that same thing is to be done which the wise man would do or command. Therefore, the just man himself will be accustomed to act with the highest reason, or at least he will be ready to obey the wise man, which suffices here" (M 35).

We have seen that Leibniz was prepared to lay considerable stress upon the importance of scientific knowledge to the acquisition of a knowledge, and thence to a love, of God. We have also seen that Leibniz was prepared to suggest that such love was necessary for the development of a nonmercenary love of all men, which love was itself required as the motive of any truly just action. But the present passage seems to downplay the role of such knowledge in the making of "the just or good man," who is here not required to "excel in the knowledge of things." For it is here enough "to obey the wise man" – the need to be motivated by a nonmercenary love is not mentioned at all. And because Leibniz expresses some doubt about whether there is any who are truly wise among humans, he goes on to argue that it remains for us to model our action upon God's (see M 37). This is reminiscent of a passage in *The Common Concept of Justice* in which Leibniz argues that "one can say absolutely that justice is goodness conformed to wisdom, even in those who have not attained to this wisdom. . . . [For] as soon as they consider that justice conforms to the will of a sage whose wisdom is infinite and whose power is proportioned to it, they find that they would not be wise at all (that is, prudent) if they did not conform themselves to the will of such a sage" (M 63: R 59). Leibniz's entire scheme of a "City of God," of a community of imperfectly rational, and hence imperfectly just, souls who are ruled by God's supreme wisdom (see, for example, *Principles* §15, G VI 605: L 640, *Monadology* §§85–86, G VI 621–22: L 651–52) invites the obvious comparison with Plato's ideal state, a community of imperfectly rational, and hence imperfectly just, citizens who are ruled by the collective reason of supremely enlightened philosopher kings.

31 *Nicomachean Ethics* 10.7, 1177a, 25–27.

32 Leibniz always made a point of stressing the importance of both the theoretical results and the practical applications of scientific research. Thus in his *Memoir for Enlightened Persons of Good Intention* (ca. 1695), Leibniz wrote that "to make men as happy as possible, one must seek the means of preserving their health, and of giving them the conveniences of life. Thus one must inquire into the nature of bodies in the universe, as much to recognize therein the marvelous traces of divine wisdom, as to notice the respects in which they can be useful to our preservation and even to our greater perfection. Thus the advancement of natural science and of the fine arts is of great importance" (K X 12: R 106–7). And in a remarkable passage from his *Meditation on the Common Concept of Justice*, Leibniz makes the following remarks about the importance of funding research involving the microscope: "Now, as nothing better reconfirms the incomparable wisdom of God, than the structure of the works of nature, above all the structure which appears when looking at them more closely with a microscope; it is for this reason, as well as because of the great lights which could be thrown on bodies for the use of medicine, food, and mechanical ends, that it is most necessary that one advance knowledge with [the use of] microscopes. . . . This is why I have more than once hoped that one could bring great princes to make arrangements for this and to support men who worked at it. . . . It is for great princes to arrange this for the public utility, in which they are the most interested. . . . For myself, I have no other motive in recommending this research, than that of advancing the knowledge of truth and the public good, [which is] strongly interested in the augmentation of the treasure of human knowledge" (M 52–53: R 53).

33 Leibniz defined happiness, or felicity, as "a lasting joy, which is obtained through the perfection of the body and the mind" (C 527). Thus "present joy does not make happy if it has no *permanence*; indeed, he is rather unhappy who falls into a long wretchedness for the sake of brief joy" (G VII 86: L 425). But permanent joy depends on knowledge and virtue, so that "it is reason and will that leads us towards happiness, whereas sensibility and appetite lead us only towards pleasure" (*New Essays*, II.xxi.41, A VI.vi: 194: RB 194). Moreover, in the tract *On Wisdom*, Leibniz presented this further account of the source of permanent joy: "Now when the soul feels within itself a great harmony, order, freedom, power, or

perfection, and hence feels pleasure in this, the result is joy. . . . Such joy is permanent and cannot deceive, nor can it cause a future unhappiness if it arises from knowledge and is accompanied by a light which kindles an inclination to the good in the will, that is virtue. But when pleasure and joy are directed toward satisfying the sense rather than the understanding, they can as easily lead us to unhappiness as to bliss, just as food which tastes good can be unwholesome. . . . But the pleasure which the soul finds in itself through understanding is a present joy such as can serve our joy for the future as well" (G VII 88: L: 426).

Again, in the tract on *Felicity*, Leibniz had this to say: "The confused perception of some perfection constitutes the pleasure of sense, but this pleasure can be [productive] of greater imperfections which are born of it, as a fruit with a good taste and good odor can conceal a poison. This is why one must shun the pleasures of sense, as one shuns a stranger, or, sooner, a flattering enemy" (Gr 579–80: R 83). On the other hand, "one need not shun at all pleasures which are born of intelligence or of reasons, as one penetrates the reason of the reasons of perfections, that is to say as one sees them flow from their source, which is the absolutely perfect being" (Gr 580: R 83–84). Leibniz thus kept company with Plato and Aristotle in holding that the intellectual pleasures, associated with the perfection of one's mind in knowledge, were the pleasures which led to happiness, the ones which were "the most valuable" (*New Essays* II.xxi.41, A VI.vi 194: RB 194).

34 It is well known that Leibniz himself often lobbied the powerful in Europe to support the establishment of scientific societies, and he succeeded in founding (in 1700) and serving as the first president of what was to become the Berlin Academy of Sciences. It is worth noting, in light of our earlier discussion, that Leibniz went out of his way to fault already established scientific societies, like those in Paris and London, for not pursuing practical applications for scientific discoveries. As for the society in Berlin, Leibniz explicitly recommended that it should serve not only to promote pure science, but also to promote the application of science to manufacturing and commerce.

13 The reception of Leibniz in the eighteenth century

Leibniz claimed to be proud of the fact that, during his lifetime, he had no school, no disciples, and no popularizers. He despised, he said, the sectarian spirit which he associated with the Cartesians. Whether this attitude did not hide a kind of disappointment in the end is open to question. Leibniz was widely admired as a diplomat, a man of learning, and as a mathematician. But he was not, during his lifetime and long afterwards, considered a great philosopher, and after the deaths of Sophie Charlotte, the Queen of Prussia, in 1705, and her mother, the Electress Sophie, in 1714, no one showed an intense interest in his metaphysical theories. The dispute with Newton and the Royal Society, followed by the increasingly agitated argument with Newton's representative Samuel Clarke, threw a pall over Leibniz's last two years. Newton, never a gracious opponent, is said to have boasted that he killed Leibniz. This is hardly true; Leibniz had outlived most of his contemporaries and had been unwell for a long time, but his exit from the world was certainly agitated rather than peaceful. He was out of favor with his employer, the Elector of Hanover Brunswick, who became George I of England in 1714, for having failed to bring the royal family's history beyond the year 1005. Shortly after Leibniz's death, rumors and gossip about his religious insincerity were spread through France and Germany by the clergyman Christian Matthaeus Pfaff.

To a large extent, the story of the reception of Leibniz's philosophy in the eighteenth century and the controversies it inspired was determined by the order in which his works were collected, edited, and released. Most of what Leibniz had published during his lifetime had appeared in journals: the Leipzig *Acta Eruditorum*, whose readers he addressed in the Scholastic style, and the Paris *Journal des*

442

savants, whose readers he addressed in the Cartesian style. As time
went on, these papers became increasingly inaccessible. The *Theodicy*, which appeared in 1710 with numerous editions thereafter,
was widely read, but Leibniz did not regard the book as a very full or
adequate expression of his thoughts, and he seemed to have hoped
that someone else would assume the burden of collecting his scattered writings after his death so as to make him better understood
(see, e.g., letters to Remond, 14 July 1714, G III 618; 26 August 1714,
G III 624). The *Monadology*, a collection of theses addressed specifically to Prince Eugene, more generally "to those who are not yet too
accustomed" to the styles of the Schools and the Cartesians, he
regarded as the best summary of his philosophy: the Latin edition
appeared in 1721. But it was a brief document, enigmatic and ellipti-
cal and not well-suited as a general introduction. In 1737, more than
twenty years after Leibniz's death, C. G. Ludovici, who complained
that the omission of Leibniz from a recent history of philosophy was
like the omission of Jupiter from a list of the Gods, or Alexander
from a history of the Greeks, published an excellent catalog of Leibniz's known works.[1] Ludovici listed 269 printed works, nineteen
unprinted, and six drafts; this did not include the notes and loose
papers of Leibniz's *Nachlass* which amounted, according to his secretary J. G. Eckhart, to over a million pages. Until 1765 when Raspe
published his two-volume collection, which included the *New Essays*,[2] and Dutens his six-volume collection in 1768, understanding
Leibniz was based on (in addition to the *Theodicy* and Pierre Bayle's
entry on the theory of pre-established harmony in his *Historical and
Critical Dictionary*) Pierre des Maizeaux's *Recueil des pièces diverses*[3] of 1720 (which included the Leibniz-Clarke correspondence),
Leibniz's late letters to Remond, some reflections on Locke's *Essay*,
short papers on "enthusiasm," Shaftesbury, and Bayle – as well as a
treatise on fatalism which was not by Leibniz. Besides the *Monadology*, the *New System* and the *Principles of Nature and Grace*
went through several editions, and the *Protogaea* was finally published in 1749.[4] The main source of biographical information was
Eckhart's account of Leibniz's life – full of errors according to
Ludovici – , which served as the basis of Fontenelle's *Eloge* written
for the French Academy in 1717.[5]

This essay will concentrate mainly on Leibniz's reception in Germany, with only brief mention of France, for it is only in Germany

that there is anything like a continuous story to tell. In England, Leibniz became, after his death, little more than a name and a symbol – a threat to the honor of Newton and to the national honor as well. In France, there was little sustained interest in Leibniz among philosophers, as opposed to *littérateurs*.[6] The excellent study of W. H. Barber concludes that, despite the presence of a polemical literature, French interest in Leibniz in the eighteenth century was largely restricted to a brief flurry between 1740 and 1750, corresponding to the excitement over Alexander Pope's optimistic *Essay on Man*, Christian Wolff's continental expansion, and the efforts of Mme. du Chatelet.[7] Thereafter, it collapsed. The *lumières* of the second half of the eighteenth century were hostile to Leibniz: insofar as they had a philosophy, it was anticlerical, antiabstraction, and sensualistic-sensationalistic. It is, thus, important to distinguish, following Belaval, between the German *Aufklärung* and the French *siècle des lumières*.[8] The French weapon against dogma and dogmatism was mockery and a pointed insouciance. The Germans had their mockers and scoffers, but they insisted on the difference between "true" and "false" enlightenment, between libertinism and responsible reform. Conservative, academic philosophy never lost favor in Germany, and the philosophy of the *Aufklärung* was, in the first instance, school-philosophy.[9]

I. THE LEIBNIZ-WOLFF PHILOSOPHY

The first phase of Leibniz's reception involved the creation of the body of doctrine which came to be known as the Leibniz-Wolff philosophy, attacked and defended in various forms through the time of Kant. As late as the nineteenth century, Leibniz was sometimes regarded as a mere forerunner of the great metaphysician Christian Wolff (1679–1754) who had taken the scattered theses of Leibniz – his claim that this is the best of all possible worlds, his principle of sufficient reason, and his theory of pre-established harmony – and erected on that basis the world's first strictly reasoned system of knowledge. The detachment of Leibniz from Wolff was an achievement of the last quarter of the eighteenth century; the idea that Leibniz too had a "system" seems to have been an even later development, for when Leibniz was first redeemed by the Romantics, it was his unsystematic character that appealed to them.

Wolff, who was trained as a mathematician, did not think of himself as substantially influenced by Leibniz, and Leibniz did not think of him in this way either. Wolff had come to the older man's attention in 1704 when Leibniz had received a copy of his Inaugural Dissertation, *De philosophia practica universalia methodo mathematica conscripta*, and the two carried on a correspondence on mathematical, physical, and chemical subjects, which barely touched on metaphysical issues, until Leibniz's death. Wolff, not particularly suited to the role of disciple in Leibniz's eyes, surprised his colleagues when he began to venture outside the mathematics faculty at the University of Halle after Leibniz's death to give philosophical lectures. Between 1720 and 1725, he issued German editions of his great set of textbooks, the *Vernuenfftige Gedancken*, and between 1728 and 1753 produced Latin versions; both sets "crushingly outnumbered"[10] Leibniz's works.

In his autobiography, Wolff explained that he had been motivated to study philosophy and to bring to bear on it the certain and reliable proof-procedures of mathematics because of his distress at the unending conflict between Protestants and Catholics. He named Descartes, Malebranche, Spinoza, and Tschirnhaus as his inspirations, and he was unhappy to find his name linked closely with Leibniz's; the term "Leibniz-Wolffian" was coined by his contemporary G. B. Bilfinger. Wolff wrote in numbered paragraphs referring to previously established results in a manner loosely reminiscent of Spinoza, but even more loosely of Euclid; the notion that philosophy was a body of deductively related propositions, able to be elucidated from primitive definitions and axioms, served Wolff more as an ontological vision of the order of the sciences than as a model for philosophical discourse, although the gulf between form and content was not as great in his case as in Leibniz's. For although Leibniz generally approved of axiomatic presentations, he had never tried to present his own philosophy in that form, and he was doubtful about the advantages doing so would bring. Wolff, however, outlined in his textbooks a full system of "world wisdom," as philosophy was conventionally called, which covered such subjects as the power of human knowledge, God, the world and the soul of man, moral action, the purposes of creatures and the uses of their bodily parts, and "everything in general." These subjects all *methodo scientifica pertractata*. His reputation as a rigid deductivist notwithstanding,

Wolff believed fervently in the use of hypotheses; he believed that the general form of scientific method was hypothetico-deductive, and he analyzed the triumph of Copernicanism – his favorite example of scientific progress – in these terms.[11] Leibniz's pre-established harmony of body and soul, he believed, fell into this category; it was a hypothesis which should not be regarded as anything more than highly probable.

Wolff believed in a certain version of monadology, accepting Leibniz's claim that if there are complex things, there must be simple things – Wolff never used the term "monad" – which are more like unextended points than like physical atoms. These simple things, he states, cannot come into being in any understandable way or over the course of time, as complex things do. Once they exist, their subsequent development unfolds in a law-like fashion; they possess appetition in Leibniz's sense, but he refuses to assign to them the power of perception; they are not Leibniz's living mirrors of the universe. Where Leibniz had seen psychology as dictating categories to ontology, with the indestructibility of the "I" serving as a model for the indestructibility of simple substances, Wolff saw psychology as a special science and so never arrived at Leibniz's panpsychism. The ontological study of simple substances is prior to the special study of souls with their representing faculties. There are nevertheless clear echoes of the *Monadology* in Wolff:

Because all complex things in the world are connected to one another and the simple things with other simples, so as to make together with them a complex thing, we must take the inner condition of a particular simple thing to be according to that of all complex things which are around it as a midpoint. And so every simple thing is in harmony with the whole world; from which the perfection of the world arises.[12]

In his youth, Wolff had written a treatise on gears, *De Rotis Dentatis*, and his general view of nature could be described not simply as "mechanistic," but as "machinistic";[13] his commitment to the idea of a fixed order of nature was even more extreme than Leibniz's. He cites with approval Spinoza's remark that a miracle is an event whose reasons common people do not understand, and his treatment of the subject suggests a good familiarity with the Leibniz-Clarke correspondence. A miraculous event exceeds the natural powers of things and can only be construed as a display of power and not of wisdom on

God's part. The principle of sufficient reason implies that miracles cannot be insulated from the course of nature; whoever tinkers with the hands of a clock has thrown it off for good. "Whether the disturbing of the order of nature through a miracle can serve to the improvement of nature" is, he says, a question which "will be passed over in silence."[14]

Wolff recognized that his doctrine of "connection," his commitment to the theory of pre-established harmony, and his belief in the universal reign of the principle of sufficient reason threatened to automate the mind. "A machine through mere movement," he concedes, "could perform exactly what the soul does through her spiritual force."[15] This possibility had been noted earlier by Leibniz, whose notion of the *automaton spirituale* implies that thoughts and experiences – including the activity of reasoning – insofar as they involve physiological events and processes, are produced mechanically and, at the same time, pneumatically, from the dispositions of the incorporeal soul. Leibniz had certainly believed that a machine could, in principle, construct demonstrations, make logical inferences. He did not share Descartes's view that "reason" was a kind of supramechanical power of the soul, and he was hopeful about the possibility of actually constructing reasoning machines. But at least at the time of the *New Essays*, he had seemed inclined, after all, to reserve certain special functions to the soul; he suggests, for example, that it is only the incorporeal "I" which has a true identity and is capable of philosophically confirming it (cf. *New Essays* II xxvii, A VI.vi; RB 236–37), and that this "I" has a distinctive role in the discovery of innate notions.[16] Wolff, by contrast, seemed unthreatened by the looming spectre of Locke's materialism and was more consistent and serene in his psycho-physical parallelism. Where Leibniz had aroused nothing more than the suspicion that he was a fatalist and a necessitarian in the psychological as well as the physical realm, Wolff now ensured his own persecution by drawing out the full implications of Leibniz's views on law, miracles, and sufficient reason. In doing so, he intensified the worries about what sort of philosopher Leibniz himself had been and heightened the stakes of Leibniz-interpretation considerably.

Wolff captured something of Leibniz's spirit and doctrine not only in his general metaphysical position, but in his epistemology. In the beginning of his *Vernuenfftige Gedancken von den Kraeften des menschlichen Verstands*, he acknowledges the impact on himself of Leibniz's long-neglected "Meditations on Knowledge, Truth and Ideas," which he found in an old number of the Leipzig *Acta Eruditorum*. He extracted from that paper the idea later so vehemently attacked by Kant, that sensation and intellection lie on a continuum, with sensation a kind of "darkened" intellectual presentation. Leibniz's distinctions between symbolic and intuitive understanding, and between clear and confused (even if "distinct") ideas, were noted and developed. Wolff was, in the first instance, a teacher of philosophy as Leibniz was not, and he assumed the responsibility of changing, improving, and indeed liberating his students. He was not, as is often assumed, simply an unimaginative pedant; his unprecedented philosophical output notwithstanding, he asserts, with some justification, that "the philosopher is not just a windbag." What seems at first a fatiguing insistence on proof, demonstration, and order serves the same purpose in Wolff that it had in Spinoza; these are antidogmatic instruments. To hew to method was to resist the blandishments as well as the threats of all nonrational authorities: to refuse to allow oneself to be intimidated. Wolff believed that in contests between method and dogma, dogma would simply have to give way: this was the lesson he extracted from the progress of astronomy between Galileo and Newton and the triumph of Copernicanism.[17]

In his book on the purposes of natural things, Wolff threw himself eagerly into the only theology really available to one of his convictions – the physico-theology imported from England through northern Germany, whose roots reach back to Browne, More, and Ray. The wisdom and existence of God were to be revealed through a consideration of the details and adaptations of the Creation, and Wolff's anthropomorphism here reaches extremes undreamed of by Leibniz. He is a master of the counterfactual conditional, and if he is Panglossian and absurd in this book, it does not, for that reason, lack a certain warmth and charm.[18] Wolff was a graceful, clear, and organized writer, and it was no doubt the combination of the grand vision and the homely example which endeared him to his students. It is easy to understand the reaction of one like Gottsched who described his dreary student days in Scholastic Koenigsberg where he was made to read Aristotle, the Cartesians, Locke, Christian Thomasius, and Geulincx, before finally happening on two books which spoke to his conditions: Leibniz's *Theodicy* and Wolff's *German Metaphysics*. "It was as though I had come out of a wild sea of contradictory opinions into a safe harbour and after many waves and buffetings finally came to stand on solid ground."[19] In making something of Leibniz which could be, strange as this might seem, ground under one's feet, Wolff had cut off metaphysics from its Leibnizian substructure, the problems of force and materiality on one hand, concepts and truths on the other. The moral message might be clear, but the metaphysics itself was increasingly perceived as artificial and arbitrary. Wolff anticipated some of the difficulties which Kant's *Critique* would address under the heading of the limits of the understanding; he admits – though he seems untroubled by the problem of the composition of the continuum which so puzzled Leibniz – that we may have difficulty in understanding the generation of complex, extended substances from simple, unextended ones, and that we cannot understand the origin of simple substances at all. His solution is to say that, as such, substances are not material, we cannot understand them through the imagination but only intellectually: "Just as they can only be grasped through the understanding, so must their coupling with each other be only intelligible. We cannot try to imagine the inner and outer condition of simple things and their connection with each other."[20] In retrospect this renaming of the unintelligible as the intelligible seems an obvious ploy; such was the power of the eighteenth century critique of reason which Wolff encouraged without being in a position to benefit from it.

II. THE WOLFF AFFAIR AND ITS REPERCUSSIONS ON LEIBNIZ

As soon as his books began to appear in the mid-1720s, Wolff was attacked vigorously by a group of opponents who came from the dominant group of pietist theologians at the University of Halle. He and his supporters replied to these offensives, generating a polemical literature in which Leibniz's name appears frequently, but usually as no more than a stick for beating Wolff. A typical one of these, C. Lanhausen's *Streitschriften* of 1724, seems to sum up the main issue: *De necessitate omnium, quae existunt, absoluta, in theodicea G. G. Leibnitii, cui Wolffianum Metaphysicae systema super structum est, asserta.*

The Halle pietists were opposed to what they regarded as the overloading of religion with intellectual concepts and theoretical distinctions; disagreements in theology should be solved by returning to the literal sense of the Bible, not by definitions and analysis. What they understood under the heading of theology was not in any case the study of the philosophical puzzles religious doctrine seems to generate, but the problem of the religious destiny of the individual, and they had a strong sense of sin, allied naturally enough with a passionate belief in free will and mind-body causal interaction, and a generally "pessimistic" world-view.[21] The attacks of their ringleader, Joachim Lange (1670–1744), a grammarian and church historian, are understood by the Leibniz-sympathizer Hartmann as due to their "disgusted horror, revulsion, and antipathy in the face of reason and philosophy," which Lange considered a "lewd whore" parading in the dress of virtue, or true Christianity.[22] The "causa remota" of metaphysics, Lange thought, was none other than the devil.

Wolff was especially easy to resent because he was popular; though his subject-matter might have been abstract and at times highly formal, he delivered his lectures in a "lively, clear, thorough, pleasant manner" which seems to have enraged his colleagues. Even the Jesuits liked Wolff's books; he could soon boast that they were being used in Ingolstadt, Vienna, and even Rome. As a nineteenth-century commentator describes the situation, "in the University and the pulpit there were sad and numerous evidences of decline. Perhaps no system of philosophy has ever penetrated the masses as did this of Wolff, for no one has been more favoured with champions who aimed to indoctrinate the unthinking."[23] The pace of change seemed too fast: "Everything that had age on its side was rejected because of its age. Even the titles of books were fraught with copious definitions."[24]

What finally brought about Wolff's expulsion from Halle by order of Friedrich Wilhelm I, the King of Prussia, was a public lecture on Confucian morality. Like Leibniz who had once stated that the Europeans had surpassed the Chinese in the industrial arts and contemplative sciences while remaining backward in morals and practical philosophy,[25] Wolff was a Sinophile. He was indeed a better Sinophile, for while Leibniz approached Chinese metaphysics and theory of religion in the hope of finding confirmation for his views on immaterial substances, God, and immortality,[26] Wolff was able to concentrate on the moral meaning of Confucianism, which he praised as an alternative to Christian ethics. An atheist, he had stated in his so-called *Institutiones Morales*, is fully capable of living virtuously even if his virtue is less perfect than that of the theist. For it is reason which dictates the moral law, and the reasonable man is one who gives laws to himself.[27] Wolff denied that atheism is a motive for evil deeds, although he felt he should concede that it might remove a motive for goodness – a concession only somewhat at odds with his scorn for the idea of heaven and hell as ethically motivating inevitabilities.

The terms of the invective employed against Wolff partly set the stage for the great conflicts of the 1780s and '90s over reason, religion, and philosophical method.[28] The notion of sufficient reason, as it had been stated in Leibniz's fifth letter to Clarke and elevated by Wolff to a position of supreme importance, played a key role in this conflict under its formal aspect as well as its ontological aspect. Formally, the principle was understood as identifying the essential feature of a philosophical system: a Euclidean deductive structure. Materially, the principle was taken as implying the impossibility of free will or providential action on God's part. Under its formal interpretation, it presented theology with the following dilemma; either deny the demonstrability of religious dogma, thus losing the weapon of reason against the sceptic, or make the human intellect equal to the mysteries of the faith. Under its material aspect, the principle implied, at best, a pagan-stoical morality of resignation and adaptation, rather than a Christian one of personal transformation. As a result, the believer was left with only three real alternatives. He might: (1) retain, as Mendelssohn would, the old-fashioned commitment to the demonstrability of the existence and nature of God through the power of human reason; or (2) make a rational leap of faith as Jacobi recommended, on the basis of an inner feeling of conviction but admittedly without the force of demonstration – a leap which could be seen as having its own self-authenticating religious value; or (3) follow the anti-method "method" of Kant's *Transzendentale Methodenlehre*, which performed a kind of methodological twist by means of which God, as a source of ethical motivation, was put out of reach of demonstration, but not of "thought."[29]

In his anti-Wolff treatises, Lange made the following points which are further witness to the uneasy relations between metaphysics and theology in the period. The question of God's existence is not a problem for logic to solve, but a universal dogma of the human race. Religion is damaged rather than strengthened by attempted proofs of an abstract nature. Human liberty is "the first requisite of a sound theology and morals," and the machine of the world is therefore not fully determined but allows for interruptions and interventions through the human and divine wills. The theory of pre-established harmony is inadequate to explain self-control, the action of God or demons on the human body, or even the learning of artistic skills. Human beings must therefore consist of a soul and a body "metaphysically and really united." Leibniz's efforts to show that the sequence of events in the world can be said to be both logically contingent and morally determined at the same time, Lange dismisses as wholly unconvincing. Leibnizian necessity *ex hypothesi* he thinks is just necessity and is identical with Spinoza's.[30]

Lange was suspicious of the *Theodicy*, which he regarded as a *lusus philosophi*, in which Leibniz had played the game of reconciling a deterministic, optimistic system with revealed religion, without real commitment or success in either. The theologian Pfaff had even claimed to be in possession of a letter from Leibniz in which the latter had confessed this to him. Pfaff stirred up high expectations with his repeated announcement that he was on the verge of publishing the letter, but he always found some excuse not to – though he eventually printed an "excerpt."[31] The *Theodicy* had, in any case, its enemies as well as its admirers. As Ludovici saw it, many people, "when they can tear the signs of victory won by diligence, hard work and intelligence out of the hands of a learned hero do not hesitate to do so." By 1737 there was, as a result, radical uncertainty about how to read the work, which, according to a lengthy four-part review in the Jesuit-run *Mémoires de Trevoux*, had on its appearance "divided learned and Christian Europe." Was the work optimistic or pessimistic? An occasional piece for currying favor or a serious contribution? Was the writer a friend of religion or a Spinozist in disguise? Did not the writer's attempt to reconcile all opinions, variations, and even heresies issue in a sort of relativism? Was not the attribution of perfection to this world a denial of Paradise? The *Journal* spent a good many pages trying to establish the Spinozistic character of the work, paying special attention to the theory of combinatorial creation.[32] Leibniz's professional experience as a diplomat was always mentioned or implied in this and succeeding discussions of what the *Theodicy* really meant, and the question of Leibniz's underlying seriousness was raised repeatedly in the course of the century. Gottsched, for example, grew restless in the safe harbour of the *Theodicy* and began to wonder whether the system of pre-established harmony was not another *lusus*,[33] and later Lessing and Eberhard would agree, despite their differences, that Leibniz had an "esoteric" philosophy in addition to his popular "exoteric" one.

III. INCIDENTAL CRITICISM OF LEIBNIZIAN DOCTRINES

The Wolff affair ended officially in 1744, with Wolff's triumphant recall to Halle at the invitation of the new Emperor. Townspeople lined the streets to welcome him home, and even Dr. Lange was on hand to wish him well. Meanwhile, interest in Leibniz had focused on other issues besides his alleged fatalism, and he was not without a few exegetes and defenders. The most adequate of these was probably G. B. Bilfinger, who was, as noted, responsible for the term "Leibniz-Wolffian," but who had clearly gone back to the original. His understanding of Leibniz seems to have been more precise than Wolff's. He delivered and published a defense of the "reasonable and innocent" system of pre-established harmony as his Inaugural Dissertation in 1721,[34] placed on the index in 1734, and in his *Dilucidationes philosophicae de deo, anima humana et generalibus rerum affectionibus* of 1725, he addressed such relatively obscure Leibnizian topics as the infinite analysis of contingent truths, the striving of possibles towards existence, and the ontological status of the laws of motion, along with more popular subjects such as the origin of evil. The problem of soul-body relations was much debated in the *Streitschriften* with the scholastic system of causal influx enjoying new favor, despite the Wolffian's effort.[35] Other literature focused on the monads and on the idealistic implications of the monadology. By 1756 both Berkeley's *Principles of Human Knowledge* and Arthur Collier's *Clavis Universalis*, which denied the existence of an external material world, had been translated into German. Both Leibniz and Wolff had tried to employ the notion of the "well-foundedness" of the phenomena of materiality in simple substances to escape the difficult implications of an immaterial atomism, but, as had been the case in the dispute over the necessitarian aspects of their systems, enunciated distinctions tended to be "unmasked" by the critic.[36]

As Wolff's European reputation spread on the basis of his Latin works, the reaction to them assumed organized form when Maupertuis (1698–1759), who had been given the task of rehabilitating what had become a lackluster institution, assumed the Presidency of the Prussian Academy of Sciences in Berlin in 1746. Maupertuis took quick stock of the situation, determining that the chemistry in the Academy was the best in Europe, the mathematics competitive, the astronomy improving, whereas philosophy and *belles lettres* were in such a sorry state due to the influence of Wolff that they could not be helped. Maupertuis regarded Wolff's philosophy as "scholastic barbarism" and disapproved of the effort to introduce mathematical rigor into philosophy which he thought made it more shadowy and dubious than ever.[37] Between 1747 and 1763, the Academy sponsored a set of essay competitions on Leibnizian themes: monadology, optimism, and the use of the mathematical method in metaphysics and theology.[38] These contests were normally entered by the educated public – clergymen, teachers, lawyers – in addition to academicians and professors, indicating that the Leibniz-Wolff philosophy had indeed become diffuse and popular, whether this was the cause or the effect of the stagnation Maupertuis had perceived. But after his death in 1759, the Academy relaxed its stance and in 1768 graciously offered a prize for the best essay in defense of Leibniz.[39]

Maupertuis's hostility to Wolff was almost certainly enhanced by his priority dispute with the dead Leibniz over the Law of Least Action. Maupertuis presented himself in 1746 as the discoverer of the Law, which he regarded not simply as a regulative or heuristic principle, but as a proof for the existence of God. Although his statement of it was elaborated in better detail than Leibniz's remarks on the importance of maximum and minimum quantities in physics, Leibniz had clearly anticipated Maupertuis in a published paper of 1682 and in numerous statements thereafter, including the *Specimen Dynamicum*, the first part of which had been published in 1695, where he argued that the "architectonic" qualities of theories provided evidence of a divine architect and a realm of final causes. The unsuccessful Academy applicant, Samuel Koenig, on the basis of another secret letter said to have been written by Leibniz and containing an identical statement of the Law, accused Maupertuis of plagiarism, and the quarrel dragged on until Maupertuis's death, with Koenig, who was unable to produce the letter, accused in turn of plagiarism.[40] Meanwhile Leibniz's name achieved some brief and reflected glory, even in France, thanks to the physicist Mme. du Châtelet, Voltaire's friend, who based her *Institutions de Physique* of 1740 on Wolff's Latin works, and to J. L. S. Formey, who survived somehow as Secretary of the Berlin Academy while publishing the six-volume digest for ladies and others requiring a lighter mode of presentation, *La Belle wolffienne*, from 1741 to 1753. But these results were short-lived; Condillac's *Treatise of systems* of 1749 summarized and consolidated the anti-metaphysical mood of the mid-century with what W. H. Barber calls "the severest attack on speculative metaphysics which the century produced."

Condillac took a different tack from the theologically-motivated Halle critics; he was less offended by the contents of Leibniz's philosophy or even by the implied attempt to talk about God as Euclid had talked about circles and triangles than he was amused and bemused by its conceptual apparatus. What interested him as a reader of Locke, and as a strict advocate of the view that all ideas have their basis in sensory experience was the status of the main Leibnizian theoretical entities. He began his critique of systems by inviting the reader to consider the systems of divination and astrology practiced in superstitious ages in which results that speak directly to human hopes and fears are extracted from a set of principles which, springing from the imagination, are lacking in any correspondence to reality. "The images which a mirror reflects," he says, "represent exactly their objects, and in the same way one comes to believe that the images in our minds conform exactly to things outside it. One gives these images the names of ideas, notions, archetypes . . . and one ends by regarding them as real things which express, so to speak, things outside."[41] The systems of Descartes, Malebranche, Spinoza and Leibniz are so many dream worlds, the productions of *bels esprits* gifted with beautiful and curious thoughts. We don't really know what to make of Leibniz's talk of perception, mirroring, and representation in monads, he thinks; we can attach no definite idea to the notion of a simple substance endowed with force. "This philosopher . . . never employed, on this subject, anything but metaphors; finally, he got lost in the infinite."[42] Locke, who Condillac admits had neither wisdom, nor method, nor style and was not a *bel esprit*, is a better, more instructive philosopher.

This was also the sentiment of Voltaire, who found himself in the predicament of having to respond politely to the enthusiasm of the Crown Prince Frederick (later Frederick II) for Wolff in the late 1730s, and tolerantly to his friend and fellow experimentalist Mme. du Châtelet's interest, encouraged by Koenig, in Leibnizian forces and Wolffian ontology. Voltaire did not like Leibniz, but he could not help being puzzled and intrigued by the issues of determinism and optimism. Where Leibniz himself was concerned, he recognized in him both the widely read, broadly experienced diplomat and the exact mathematician, and, at the same time, the author of an isolated, divisive, fantastic system. The difficulty of fusing these images into one seems to have been the source of the irritation which led him to regard Leibniz as a popular charlatan. Voltaire owned the main eighteenth-century editions of Leibniz's works and certainly read, or read in, the *Theodicy* as well as the Leibniz-Clarke correspondence and the *Monadology*, and the references in his letters make it clear that he sees Leibniz and Wolff as distinct, though equally unsympathetic, personalities.[43]

It is often said or implied that Voltaire's distaste for metaphysics and especially for metaphysical discursiveness, made it impossible for him to meet Leibniz on his own ground, thus depriving his criticisms of much force. Certainly, as with his observation that the pre-established harmony is like one man preaching and the other making the gestures, he knew how to be quick and funny at Leibniz's expense. But he sometimes tried – in a surprisingly conventional way – to refute Leibniz on the grounds of inconsistency, and he returned over and over to tease and worry the problem of evil, convinced at the same time that philosophy had no rational solution to offer. Voltaire devoted three stories to the problem: *Zadig* (1747), *Memnon, ou la Sagesse humaine* (1749), and *Candide* (1759), as well as a poem on the Lisbon earthquake of 1755 published only a month after the event. Each story juxtaposes the narration of a sequence of disasters with the pronouncements of a metaphysician – Dr. Pangloss in the best-known story *Candide* – to the effect that everything is for the best, and it is sometimes "shown," that these disasters are necessary preconditions of future benefits. But the suffering described is just as absurd as the pronouncements of Pangloss are absurd, so that the

story seems to show not the inability of suffering to touch metaphysics, or metaphysics to touch suffering, but the absurd effect of trying
to treat metaphysics and suffering in the same story. If this was not a
direct refutation of the *Theodicy*, it still did not allow Leibnizian
optimism to emerge unscathed.

Both Voltaire and Condillac had thus insisted on the artificial, cut-
off character of metaphysical reasoning, a form of criticism echoed
in the modern positivist idea that metaphysics and poetry, as products of the imagination, stand opposed to science, the latter forming
a sort of condensed register of sensory experiences. This criticism
was made more precise and was brought into philosophy in Kant's
analysis of the failure of metaphysical concepts to reach their intended referents.

An adequate study of Kant's reaction to Leibniz would have to
determine to what extent Kant tried to grapple directly with Leibniz's available writings, which were not in his own library, and to
what extent he obtained his knowledge from Wolff and the textbook
writer Baumgarten, and from the opposing forces of eclectic philosophers, pietists, and Academy members. According to Wundt, the
material of the Kantian antinomies can be found in Lange's polem-
ics, and, despite the fact that the section on the "amphibolies of Pure
Reason" in Kant's first *Critique* is often identified as a decisive
Leibniz-refutation, there is little evidence that it emerged from any
sustained effort to understand its subject. Its connection to Leibniz's
actual epistemological doctrine is not easy to determine.

But whatever the state of Kant's first-hand acquaintance with Leibniz, the topics with which he concerned himself beginning in the
mid-1740s, were strongly conditioned by the Wolff affair. Kant wrote
on monadology (*Monadologica physica*, 1756); on optimism (*Versuch einiger Betrachtungen ueber den Optimismus*, 1759); on the
principles of contradiction and sufficient reason (*Nova Dilucidatio*,
1755); on the *vis viva* controversy (*Gedancken von der wahren
Schaetzung der lebendigen Kraefte*, 1746); on demonstrations for
the existence of God and physico-theology (*Der einzig moegliche
Beweisgrund zu einer Demonstration des Daseins Gottes*, 1763) and
on the mathematical method in its application to morals and theology for the Academy essay contest (*Untersuchung der Deutlichkeit
der Gruendsaetze der natuerlichen Theologie und der Moral*, 1764),
and finally, in the *Traeume eines Geistersehers* of 1765, on the

pseudo-science of pneumatology, treating the metaphysical study of the soul as equivalent to the study of ghosts and precognition. By 1765, Kant had also discovered incongruent counterparts (*Von dem ersten Grunde des Unterschieds der Gegenden im Raume*) which he initially used to argue that Leibniz must have been wrong in thinking that space was a purely a matter of relations. In his essay on negative quantities of 1763, he argued that the real force of repulsion which keeps bodies separated is something other than the logical principle of noncontradiction, emphasizing the differences between concept and object which he so often returns to in his criticisms of Leibniz.[44] Thus, although his early attitude towards Leibniz would have to be described as generally negative – Kant was never, at any stage of his career, a Leibnizian – and as mock-respectful, there is no sign of any organized program of attack.

Kant had participated in the Academy essay contest of 1763, but it was perhaps Lambert who impressed on him the idea of a methodological renewal in metaphysics which would be based on the proper understanding of the nature of mathematical knowledge. "If ever a science needs methodical reconstruction and cleansing," Lambert wrote to Kant in 1766, "it is metaphysics."[45] His chief complaint about Leibniz and Wolff was that they had misused mathematical methods by employing merely nominal definitions rather than real ones. Locke had done better in recognizing that the simple elements of knowledge cannot be found through conceptual analysis but are given in immediate sense-experience, or intuition, like space and time. "The universal, which is supposed to reign in [metaphysics] leads us to suppose ourselves omniscient, and thus we venture beyond the limits of possible human knowledge," Lambert explains, "If we want to avoid omissions, premature inferences, and circular reasoning, we had better work piecemeal, demanding to know at every step only what is capable of being known."[46]

Lambert called Kant's attention to the opening pages of Euclid's *Elements*, which he thought supported the Lockean idea of the dependence of reasoning on sensory intuitions: Euclid had not tried to define, for example, "space," but had begun with actual examples of angles and lines and had proceeded from there. This explained, Lambert suggested, both the referential link of mathematics and the progress within the discipline.[47] The Wolffians paid lip-service to Euclid's conception of demonstration with their tedious principles and deductions, but they had missed the essential element and so their metaphysics was both empty and stationary. The interpretation of Euclid was highly congenial to Kant; the notion of "construction" based on intuitions of figures and manipulative processes involving them, which he announces in the introduction to his own *Critique of Pure Reason* and develops in the section on "Transcendental Method," is his main weapon against a metaphysics which allegedly deduces its theorems and so achieves knowledge of supersensible objects which could not be attained through experience. His analysis of the "logic of illusion," and his subsequent restriction of the subject matter of metaphysics to exclude knowledge of the properties of the soul, or God, or the world taken as a whole are disavowals of Wolff's project; here, at least, Kant decisively met his target, as he perhaps did not meet Leibniz.

What Kant incorporated into his philosophy, the notions of the limited epistemological subject and the unlimited moral subject, were as important as what he left out. A second important anti-Leibnizian whose influence on Kant in this respect has been relatively little studied[48] was Christian August Crusius, who published an essay against the principle of sufficient reason in 1743. Crusius, who also knew something of Locke and who was eager to stress the idea of the limits of possible human knowledge brought the moral-theological objections to Wolff of the sort raised by the pietists to a much higher philosophical level. He repeated, it is true, most of the arguments of Lange's generation, claiming that Wolff had drawn out the fatalistic, deterministic, compromising, intolerant, abstruse, and Spinozistic implications of Leibniz's philosophy, but his piece on the use and limits of the principle of sufficient reason,[49] which argued that the principle was ambiguous in the first place and only useful in certain isolated departments of life, has a kind of fresh Austinian flavor to it. Philosophy should not be understood as the science of possible things, as Wolff had defined it, Crusius said, and its task is not the discovery of the reasons behind the order of external events; rather, it is a study of the human condition within the limits of human knowledge. Unhealthy philosophy is based upon a "falsche Spitzfindigkeit" – a deceptive exactness, a subtlety which actually supports superstition (the superstitions of atheism, fatalism, etc.) It is "thelematology," or the theory of forces, among which the human will must be reckoned, which has a bearing on the practical conduct of life. Belief in God is a duty which requires the exercise of the human will in the face of uncertainty and intellectual indemonstrability,[50] and the ideas of faith and duty are what is missing in the intellectual systems of Leibniz and Wolff. For Crusius, the fact of human freedom makes optimism untenable; he pictures the world as a free clash of forces, a battleground of angels and demons. The practical turn of Kant's own philosophy, which culminates in the presentation of the noumenal world as a focus of moral obligation rather than a realm for intellectual exploration, has, in turn, clear affinities with Crusius's point of view, though Kant certainly did not share the latter's biblico-prophetic theology.

IV. THE EBERHARD-LESSING CONTROVERSY

As theologians sought to make religion more universal, rational, and anti-autocratic, the general problem of Leibniz interpretation flared up again, this time in connection with the problem of eternal damnation, a doctrine that seemed more appropriate to a religion of fear and coercion than Christianity ought to be. In the *Theodicy*, Leibniz had mentioned a rare book by one Daniel Soner, which had attempted to show that eternal damnation is a false teaching on the grounds that no finite sin can merit an infinite punishment (*Theodicy*, pars. 266 ff., G VI 275 ff.). Leibniz presents himself as having an answer to Soner which will save the dogma – the damned continue to sin while in hell, thus generating their own infinite punishment recursively from a finite sin. What was puzzling in this connection was that Leibniz also mentions that he had earlier planned to reissue Soner's book with a critical preface by himself. In the cat-and-mouse game of seventeenth-century publishing, this remark would tend to establish that he was actually in sympathy with Soner's position and wanted to give it a hearing while protecting himself.[51]

In 1772, the theologian J. A. Eberhard, who was interested in the theme of pagan virtue, had claimed in his *Apologie des Sokrates* that Leibniz, like the ancient philosophers, had possessed both an exoteric popular doctrine and an esoteric private one. He was driven to this position by his sense that Leibniz's optimism was incompatible with the doctrine of eternal punishment of the damned. Certainly it was possible to work out a reply to Soner – as Leibniz had done. But can it really be supposed, he asked, that Leibniz regarded his scheme for infinite recursive sin as realized in the best of all possible worlds? Leibniz's real belief, he thought, being in sympathy with this position himself, was that the world is constantly increasing in perfection, asymptotically rising towards a state of absolute perfection, as he had suggested in his letter to Bourguet of 1714. Seeking universal acceptance for his philosophy, however, he had tried to represent his theories as advantageous for all disputing parties. "He took their dogmas as presuppositions, and gave them a tolerable sense by bringing them into alignment with his system, without obligating himself."[52] Eberhard observed that Leibniz had often offered up his philosophy as a solution to someone else's problem: he had shown Des Bosses, for example, how to account for transsubstantiation on monadological principles, even though he, Leibniz, was a Lutheran consubstantialist who did not face the problem of disappearing substances.[53]

So Eberhard attempted to enlist Leibniz as an ally, arousing the irritation of Lessing, who thought that it was presumptuous to ascribe an opinion at variance with what he had explicitly stated to a philosopher of Leibniz's caliber. Was it not the case, he argued, that Leibniz had tried to force the dogma into line with his philosophy rather than vice-versa? Leibniz, he thought, never insincerely endorsed a doctrine he privately disagreed with, but he shook and worried a dogma until he could make something satisfactory out of it, and in doing so he did obligate himself. Lessing conceded that Leibniz had treated the theory of eternal damnation "extremely exoterically" and that he would have expressed himself privately in a different manner. He understood him as taking heaven and hell to be states of the individual rather than actual locations, and he argued that there was less conflict between his optimism and his belief in eternal hell in this sense, than between his supposed secret allegiance to the doctrine of universal salvation and his belief that every action carries with it an effect resounding into infinity.[54]

Lessing took the idea of a world ever increasing in perfection with utmost seriousness. He argued, however, that this improvement was not to be understood in terms of individual achievement or progress towards salvation, but as a wider phenomenon involving the whole race of men. In his celebrated paper on the "bringing up" or "education" of mankind (*Die Erziehung des Menschengeschlechts*, 1780) he looks forward to a period of moral perfection in which the terrors of hell and the delights of heaven no longer play a coercive role in human actions,[55] a Wolffian sentiment, though Lessing, who regarded Wolff as an irrational philosopher trying unsuccessfully to become a rational Christian, was hardly in a position to acknowledge it as such.

V. THE EFFECT OF THE *NEW ESSAYS*

The lack of an immediate collective reaction to the *New Essays* on their appearance in 1765, which Tonelli has documented,[56] is well exemplified in Hamann's remarks to Herder on the publication of Raspe's edition. "The writer shows himself in the same light as ever: his scholastic chatter has never been to my taste . . . I doubt this publication will improve Leibniz's posthumous reputation. . . . A certain marketcryerish and boastful personality is too much in the spotlight."[57] But even if the reaction was deferred, it came. The *New Essays* freed Leibniz from his association with Wolff and his entrapment in the *Streitschriften*. They helped to organize anti-Kantian sentiment in the last quarter of the eighteenth century, and Kant himself who had paid little or no attention to the book on its first release was to find himself swept up in the Leibniz-renaissance of the late 1780s and '90s. If Wolff made himself the German philosopher of the Enlightenment, the new Leibniz was made into the German philosopher of the counter-Enlightenment, for what now seemed the dead systematicity and ultramechanical world view of Wolff could be held up against the unfinished journey into the infinitely complex self which the *New Essays* offered.

The pietist movement with its emphasis on original sin and the keen self-scrutiny which this implied was both developed and countered by the cult of passion and feeling stimulated in Germany by the aesthetic and moral theories developed in England and Scotland. It was extended in the sense that in both movements the experience of the individual was valued over the intellectual mastery of nature; it was countered in that it implicitly endorsed dangerous emotions. The rise of the novel, attacked by theologians as morally destructive, defended by readers as educational and uplifting, is a striking characteristic of the period. Even the Berlin Academy revived the *belles lettres* Maupertuis had scorned and proposed as the prize essay subject for 1776 the questions, what were the powers of thinking and feeling, how were they dependent on one another or interacted with one another, and how one could judge genius and character from the grade and strength of these powers and their relations? As the winning essay observed, "The fine arts received, from that time on, even in the eyes of philosophers, a dignity and a usefulness which one had only dimly perceived in them up to then."[58]

The Kantian position on the Academy question was, of course, that thinking and feeling were entirely distinct: feeling and perceiving were a matter of being affected, while thinking was a matter of manipulating concepts. Conceptual confusion was a state of affairs entirely different from unclear perception, and Kant reproached Leibniz with a failure to understand that categorical difference here. "The conditions of sensible intuition, which carry with them their own differences, he did not regard as original, sensibility being for him only a confused mode of representation, and not a separate source of representations. . . . In a word, Leibniz *intellectualized* appearances."[59] In the new aesthetics-driven context, however, there was strong interest in the suggestion that thinking and feeling lie along a kind of continuum and are subject to mutual influence, and Leibniz's notions of unconscious experience, of clear-but-confused perception, and of the I-know-not-what of aesthetic experience found a broad field of application.

The chief architect of the reconstruction of Leibniz on the basis of the *New Essays* was the Halle theologian and "popular philosopher," compiler of a famous dictionary of synonyms, J. A. Eberhard, whom we have already introduced as Lessing's opponent. Eberhard's reputation has suffered perhaps unnecessarily from Kant's having thought him a fool: he edited a not-too-successful journal, the *Philosophisches Magazin*, later the *Philosophisches Archiv*, whose *raison d'être* was the publication of articles hostile to Kant, especially those which argued that Leibniz had anticipated all that was worthwhile in Kant's critical philosophy. Eberhard had reviewed the *New Essays* directly after its appearance and had rewritten Eckhart's biography of Leibniz to depict his subject for the first time as an authentic German genius. Effectively, Eberhard moved Leibniz out of the schools and freed him from the leveling effect of disputations. He created for the philosophical genius an agenda – the study of human beings, especially their passions and emotions, and he romanticized the whole idea of the philosopher in a way which was wholly new, providing him with a temperament – sensitive, melancholy, and a venue – lonely valleys, the isolation of the cloister, the dark cabinet of Malebranche, or alternatively, a sunny Greek landscape full of mirth and laughter – Plato's Athens before its collapse. "For Aristotle [read Wolff] there soon remained no more than the task of bringing exactness, clarity and methodicality into his writings."[60]

Eberhard was drawn to the theory of unconscious and "confused" perceptions and to the idea that motivation and character are tied somehow to these dimmed and darkened mental contents. He is interested at the same time in the extremes of experience – the passion of the lover or the nun, the unsilenceable inner voices of the murderer, the Eureka! of the inventor, and so on. He sees the mind as possessing a single fundamental force, a drive to have presentations, analogous to the physical *Grundkraft* of nature; the one manifests itself in feeling and thinking, the other in light, warmth, and electricity.[61] He explains the passivity of the passions, the puzzling combination of energy and helplessness which they induce in terms of Leibniz's discovery that a feeling may be a confused or indistinct representation, and yet still clear, as when a revolving coal produces the vivid impression of a circle of fire.[62] Passions thus correspond to confused representations of actual states of affairs. Writing in 1776, Eberhard would have had before him the great model of the passions, Werther, from Goethe's novel of 1774, whose vivid but confused representations drive him to suicide. In his essay on the value of sensitivity, *Ueber den Wert der Empfindsamkeit, besonders in Ruecksicht auf die Romane* of 1786, Eberhard criticized novels as a bad influence on young people, which promoted by example the values of confusion and inappropriate action, but, having made these points, he went on to argue in the Appendix to the work that sensitivity, which the novel exemplifies, depicts, and promulgates, was the real foundation of ethics, which is based on empathy with one's fellow creatures and merciful action towards them.[63] Eberhard thought that Leibniz was correct in maintaining that all action must pass through a stage of motivation which is emotive rather than purely cognitive. These views alone would have brought him into conflict with Kant, whose philosophy was a strong reaction against moral sense theory, and who would have been appalled by the idea that the study of pathological states of emotion might in some way furnish a clue to the springs of morality.

Eberhard anticipated the role that a theory of unconscious perception might play in aesthetics. Leibniz's characterization of harmony as the binding of a multiplicity of perceptions into a unity, and his famous description of music as "unconscious mathematics" in the *Principles of Nature and of Grace* are reflected in Eberhard's description of aesthetic experience as the search, carried out at an unconscious level, for a unified form. We hear a tune as we perceive a beautiful, unlined face – as a whole, not as a collection of parts.[64] The Leibnizian I-know-not-what, the surface manifestation of countless unidentifiable *petites perceptions* is given a romantic thrust, and Eberhard explains with its help the disillusion which follows possession of a longed-for object. The good we have not yet enjoyed is indeterminate and attracts the free play of the imagination, but once obtained, "the confusion of the representation is resolved and passion drains away."[65] Eberhard was clearly no ordinary product of Halle, and his habit of treating religion as a sentiment must have been as unsettling even to liberal theologians as Wolff's intellectualizing had been to the Pietists. What other eighteenth-century writers identify as "theopathy," a powerful emotional devotion to God or to the idea of God, began to appear in the light of a diagnosis, as a personality-characteristic and nothing more.[66] The method-critique of mid-century had established a problem of reference for whole systems of thought and for metaphysical terms such as God and the soul for which intuitions or perceptions were lacking – but obviously it was counter-productive to tie religious language exclusively to inner experience, as Kant, for one, was acutely aware.

VI. THE SEARCH FOR SOURCES

Wundt has argued that the positive reception of Leibniz in the last years of the eighteenth century was tied to a rediscovery of Plato and a corresponding devaluation of school-philosophy with its "Aristotelian" stamp.[67] It was also assuredly the case that the rapid rehabilitation of Spinoza stimulated by Lessing and the acceptance and development of pantheistic ideas were responsible for increased attention to Leibniz, whose relationship to Spinoza was always considered a vexed question. There was, nevertheless, no general agreement in the period that Leibniz was a major philosophical figure. J. G. Buhle, for example, in his influential history of philosophy written at the turn of the nineteenth century, held to the old view that Leibniz's achievement was that of a polyhistor and "polypragmon" and not the product of free independent speculation as Dèscartes's was. But Buhle accepted the premise that originality in philosophy was possible and desirable. The notion – and the allied notion that philosophy was a progressive discipline – was itself something new, and demanded a different form of historiography. Where the older historian had assumed the existence of certain fixed schools – Democritean, Aristotelian, Stoic, etc. – and had tended to understand the modern philosopher as a reviver of one or the other tradition, the new historian saw philosophy as a whole as moving forward in some definite direction.[68] This meant, in turn, showing its dependence on its origins and the path of its evolution. Kant, for example, who read the history of philosophy avidly, was concerned to find a general framework within which his own system could appear as the ultimate stage of metaphysics and so constructed a scheme of thesis, antithesis, and synthesis. The dogmatic philosophy of Wolff, he argued, confronted by the skeptical philosophy of Hume, had reached a standstill, which could be broken through only by his own critical philosophy. This last phase of metaphysics was to restore a rational basis to science on one hand and religion and morals on the other, but confine their scope within the limits of the healthy human understanding. This was the theme of what is arguably Kant's most substantive treatment of Leibniz, the essay of 1790 on the progress of metaphysics in Germany since the time of Leibniz and Wolff.[69]

Better worked out, from the historical point of view, though distinctively biased, was Tiedemann's *Geist der spekulativen Philosophie*. Ludovici had once planned to write an account of Leibniz's philosophy which would trace its roots back to Platonic and Chinese thought; Tiedemann went further in arguing for the influence of Cabbalism, Jakob Boehme, and the German mystical tradition, arguing that the central notion in Leibniz's philosophy was that of "inner sense" (not sufficient reason).[70] To some critics, this search for roots seemed to have gone too far and was damaging to the worth of the individual philosopher. Dutens had stressed the importance of innate ideas in Leibniz in the preface to his 1768 edition by comparing him to Plato and Descartes; he was attacked by Hissmann, who wrote a long article for the *Teutsche Merkur* to prove that Leibniz's innatism was *sui generis* and had nothing to do with either Platonic reminiscence or with Cartesianism; innate ideas are not etched by the finger of God, but present as potentialities of the "idea-forming force" of the soul.[71] Hissmann invoked the distinction between philosophical genius and mere scholarship, arguing that the great philosophers – among whom he included Newton and Buffon as well as Leibniz in a way which was not untypical – had scarcely read their predecessors and had certainly not been influenced by them to any appreciable degree.

VII. THE ROMANTIC RECEPTION OF LEIBNIZ

The eighteenth century did not settle all or even most of the interpretive problems it was able to raise, but this fact alone helped to distinguish Leibniz from Wolff, whose work had never been viewed as requiring any particular hermeneutical strategies. Sometimes appreciation for Leibniz seemed based in a kind of aestheticism – the *Theodicy* was already for the Swiss Charles Bonnet in 1748 a kind of toy or ornament, rather than a truth-bearing philosophical apparatus. He describes it as "a kind of telescope, which showed me another universe, which presented to me an enchanted perspective . . . almost magical." J. G. Herder (1744–1803) too saw Leibniz's genius as residing in his ability to give us another world: Newton's division of the sunray, Descartes's analysis of light, and Leibniz's resolution of experience into the sum of *petites perceptions* are, he thinks, the great moments of philosophy, for they show us the world as it is and as it is not.[72] And as the great physical scientist is one who feels through a kind of empathy the powers and divisions of the *Grundkraefte*, the philosopher is one who reaches down to an understanding of love and hate and all the fundamental forces of the soul.[73] Herder saw Leibniz through his metaphors – the "sparks" or "living fires" in the soul, the veins of marble in the uncut statue; it is the *witzig* element in Leibniz – the clever, spirited, inventive element which interests him.[74] Herder is disapproving of the ludic "anthropopathy" of the *Theodicy*: "God does not play with worlds as children play with soap bubbles, until one pleases him and he singles it out." Yet he is fascinated by Leibniz's analogy between the divine production of the world and the artist's creation of his object.[75] The metaphysician is an artist too, the *Monadology* is a poem. Wolff, with his "arbitrary" and "disgustingly repeated" definitions, with his schoolteacher's mind, understood nothing of this: that truth lies not in what is clear and distinct, but in the shadows.

It was with apparent relief that many of the literary minds at the end of the century could turn away from Kant to Leibniz as their philosopher, from the difficulties of Kant's prose and his logic, and his "hypermoralism" to the graceful, urbane constructions and the long, pleasing perspectives opened up by Leibniz. Schelling (1775–1854) praised Leibniz's theory of the self-production of experiences at the expense of the Kantians: "There is nothing from which Leibniz could have been more remote than the speculative chimera of a world of things-in-themselves which, known and intuited by no mind yet affects us and produces all our ideas."[76] F. W. Schlegel (1772–1829), found the *Theodicy* important as an ethical and aesthetic document; it was to be understood not in terms of historical teleology, but as a statement of the infinite beauty of the world. Like most of his contemporaries, he admired above all Leibniz's theory of unconscious perception. It constituted, he says, "at least the first approach towards the penetration of the secret workshop of the soul . . . as the night stars instruct us about the light of day and its true progress."[77] There was, perhaps, a certain tension in his assessment of Leibniz as, on one hand, an artist whose talent was so pure that "he knew as little of what he was doing as the beaver does of its art," on the other, a great politician of the philosophical world. The pre-established harmony Schlegel takes for a clever piece of artificiality, and the *Theodicy*, he thinks, "turns aside the question of evil in the world with the clever dexterity of the practiced diplomat." "In religious belief," he determines, developing the conclusions of the earlier Lessing-Eberhard controversy, "Leibniz remained with one foot in, one foot out, and the reason for this was the inner incompleteness of his apparently immeasurable understanding."[78] His highest and best idea – developed by Lessing – is the idea of a world ever increasing in perfection, which is the true meaning of the Christian doctrine of revelation by contrast with the Mosaic idea of the ultimate display of purely divine power. "The more clearly and decidedly we see the grounds of a true Christian philosophy in him, the more regrettable it is that this ground remained unperfected, and that his intelligence could not entirely raise itself above the abstract concepts of his time and surroundings to living knowledge."[79] Schlegel extends this charge of spiritual defectiveness to Leibniz's theory of space and time: the philosopher saw only the order of consecutive or proximate things in space and not "the infinite ensouled showplace of the realization of the eternal," as he failed to see in time "the living pulsebeats in the spiritual sea of eternal love." "So dead and mute concepts tread ever more on the place of true and real feeling in everything which is most suited for lifting men above the sensory world."[80] Leibniz's teachings, he thought, had become scholastic philosophy through the intervention of Wolff and had there met the fate, common to Aristotle, Descartes, and Kant, of being reduced to dead formula.

Commenting on the problem of Leibniz-interpretation, Yvon Belaval observed some years ago that, according to an unfortunate law of diffusion and confusion, information is lost over time as communication increases in complexity. A thought is refracted, distorted, inverted, in a way that makes it impossible to trace its actual history, so that "one ends by wondering whether the worst way of understanding the history of philosophy is not to become an expert."[81] The history of philosophy is, he concludes, a continuous creation: Leibniz is invented and re-invented by each historian and through the collective pool of readings and misreadings which he draws upon. Still, it is not only a case of invention but of discovery too; for Leibniz works upon the minds of his readers in ways in which their minds would not have worked upon themselves. These claims are borne out by the present study. It is true both that the order of publication and dissemination of Leibniz's work was generally controlling of Leibniz-interpretation in the eighteenth century – had the *New Essays* not been published, the late eighteenth century Leibniz renaissance could hardly have taken place. But the history of Leibniz-reception provides ample evidence for the motto "Seek and ye shall find." Leibniz's work was used to support polemical undertakings and power struggles, to develop an introspective psychology of passion and feeling which he would have found foreign to his own intentions, and, finally, to enhance the self-understanding of the philosophers who read him. Both Kant[82] and Schelling made statements to the effect that only their age had been able to understand and restore the real Leibniz; they meant not so much to boast about their own powers of interpretation as to confess their own difficulties in comprehending him. The young Schelling was, of all Leibniz's end-of-century readers, perhaps the most convinced by the *Mo-*

nadology. His tribute, from the *Ideas for a Philosophy of Nature*, is simple but unmatched: "His mind despised the fetters of the schools; small wonder that he has survived among us only in a few kindred spirits and among the rest has long become a stranger. He belonged to the few who treat science as a free activity. He had in himself the universal spirit of the world, which reveals itself in the most manifold forms, and, where it enters, life expands."[83]

NOTES

1   Ludovici, *Ausfuehrlicher Entwurf einer vollstaendigen Historie der Leibnizischen Philosophie zum Gebrauch seiner Zuhoerer herausgegeben.*
2   Raspe, *Oeuvres philosophiques latines et françoises de feu M. Leibnitz*, 7 vols.
3   des Maizeaux, *Receuil des pieces diverses sur la philosophie, la religion naturelle, l'histoire, les mathematiques, etc.*
4   Other early collections included: Feller, *Otium hanoveranum sive Miscellanea, ex ore et schedis illustris viri*; C. Kortholt, *G. G. Leibniz, Epistolae ad diversos, theologici, iuridici, medici, philosophici, matematici, et philologici argumenti.* For complete bibliographical information, see Ravier, *Bibliographie des oeuvres de Leibniz.*
5   de Fontenelle, *Eloge de M. Leibnitz*, in *Eloges des academiciens avec l'histoire de l'Academie royale des sciences en MDCXCIX.*
6   See Heinekamp, *Einleitung, Beiträge zur Wirkungs-und Rezeptionsgeschichte von G.W. Leibniz*, p. viii.
7   See Barber, *Leibniz in France from Arnauld to Voltaire: A Study in French Reactions to Leibnizianism, 1670–1760*, esp. pp. 137–62.
8   Belaval, *Etudes leibniziennes*, p. 243.
9   See Wundt, *Die Deutsche Schulphilosophie im Zeitalter der Aufklärung*; Saine, *Von der Kopernikanischen bis zur Französischen Revolution: die Auseinandersetzung der deutschen Aufklärung mit der neuen Zeit*; and Schneiders, *Die wahre Aufklärung, zum Selbstverständnis der deutschen Aufklärung.*
10 Tonelli, "Leibniz on Innate Ideas and the Early Reactions to the Publication of the *Nouveaux Essais (1765)*," pp. 437–54, esp. p. 444.
11 See, for example, his *Preliminary Discourse on Philosophy in General*, pp. 67–70. On Wolff, see the recent collection, *Christian Wolff: Interpretationen zu seiner Philosophie und deren Wirkung*, ed. Schneiders.
12 Wolff, *Vernuenfftige Gedancken von Gott, der Welt, und der Seele des Menschens, auch allen Dingen Ueberhaupt, (Deutsche Metaphysik)*, (1720) p. 152.

13 See Philipp, *Das Werden der Aufklärung in theologiegeschichtlicher Hinsicht*, p. 130.

14 Wolff, *Deutsche Metaphysik*, §639, p. 390.

15 Ibid., §781, p. 487.

16 Faced with Locke's own parallelist suggestion that men are machines with consciousness attached, Leibniz appears uneasy; in response, he tends to emphasize the special knowledge-acquiring capacity of the (incorporeal) mind, though he insists (*New Essays*, A VI.vi: RB 77) that his theory of innate ideas is not in conflict with his own theory of pre-established harmony.

17 Wolff, "On the Freedom to Philosophize," in *Preliminary Discourse*, tr. Blackwell, p. 112ff.

18 "If anyone would rightly impress on his mind," Wolff says in the *Vernünfftige Gedancken von den Absichten der natürlichen Dinge* (1724), "the great advantages which he derives from the sun, let him imagine himself living [without it] only one month, and see where he would be with all his undertakings if it were not day but night. . . . From the sun we learn to recognize when it is midday and . . . we can get our clocks right . . . and generally speaking, we should have no sundials if we had no sun." Quoted by W. James, *Varieties of Religious Experience*, p. 372. On Wolff's physico-theology, see esp. Phillip, *Das Werden der Aufklärung*, p. 133; on Kant's criticisms of this "purposiveness," see the *Critique of Judgement*, pt. II, §.63ff.

19 Quoted by Wundt, *Deutsche Schuiphilosophie*, p. 121.

20 Wolff, *Deutsche Metaphysik*, §604, p. 372f.

21 For a general characterization see Wundt, *Deutsche Schulphilosophie*, p. 7ff.

22 Hartmann, *Anleitung zur Historie der Leibnitzisch-Wolffischen Philosophie 1737*, p. 624.

23 Hurst, *A History of Rationalism*, p. 107.

24 Ibid.

25 *The Preface to Leibniz's Novissima Sinica* (1699), tr. Lach, p. 69.

26 According to Rosemont and Cook, tr. and ed., *Discourse on the Natural Philosophy of the Chinese*. For a full treatment, see Mungello, *Leibniz and Confucianism: the Search for Accord*.

27 Wolff, *Institutiones juris naturae et gentium*, §675, p. 508.

28 On the dilemma and its management, see the recent book of Beiser, *The Fate of Reason: German Philosophy from Kant to Fichte*.

29 For some of the difficulties with this move, see C. Wilson, "Subjektivität und Form: Zum Problem der Transzendentalen Methodenlehre," in Gabriel and Schildknecht, *Literarische Formen der Philosophie*, pp. 139–54.

30 Lange, *Kontroversschriften gegen die Wolffische Metaphysik*, 1723, Preface, p. 1–14. See also Hartmann, *Anleitung*, p. 650ff.

31 Ludovici, *Ausfuehrlicher Entwurf*, p. 476.

32 As Barber observes, the same ideas "which might have been welcomed, with the *Theodicée*, as defending the Christian view of God against the Manichaean ideas propounded by Bayle, now incurred censure for their failure to emphasize the specifically Christian doctrine of the incarnation." *Leibniz in France*, p. 116.

33 Ludovici, *Ausfuerhlicher Entwurf*, p. 409.

34 Bilfinger, *De harmonia animi et corporis humani maxime praestabilita: ex mente illustris Leibnitii commentatio hypothetica*, 1723.

35 For a list of pro- and anti-Leibnizian works and selections, see C. G. Ludovici, *Ausfuehrlicher Entwurf*, p. 345ff.; *Sammlung und Auszuege der saemmtlichen Streitschrifften wegen der Wolffischen Philosophie;* and Hartmann, *Anleitung*, p. 650ff.

36 A typical title is Weissmuller, *L'analyse des êtres simples & reéls ou la monadologie de feu Mr. le baron de Leibniz demasqué & l'idealisme renversée*, 1736.

37 Harnack, *Geschichte der Königlich preussischen Akademie der Wissenschaften zu Berlin*, ll 276.

38 The monadology contest was won by Justi, a lawyer; the optimism contest by Rheinhard, a pupil of the pessimistic Crusius. The method contest, on the question, "Whether the truths of metaphysics in general, and especially the first principles of natural theology and morals, are just as amenable to proof as geometrical truths, and, if they are not amenable to such proof, what the true nature of their certainty is, and what degree of certainty they can be held to possess, and whether this degree is sufficient for full conviction," was won by Mendelssohn, who took a more compromising stance. For a full discussion, see Tonelli, "Der Streit über die mathematische Methode in der ersten Hälfte des 18. Jahrhunderts," *Archiv für Philosophie*, pp. 37–66.

39 Won by the astronomer J. S. Bailly for his *Eloge de Leibniz*.

40 For details see Harnack, *Geschichte der preussischen Akademie*, II 292f.

41 *Traité des systèmes*, in vol. 2 of *Oeuvres complètes de Condillac*. For an overview, see Barber, *Leibniz in France*, pp. 155–56.

42 Condillac, *Traité des systèmes*, p. 67.

43 "This man," Voltaire wrote to Maupertuis in 1741, referring to Wolff, "has brought to German all the horrors of scholasticism, overlaid with sufficient reason, monads, indiscernibles, and all the scientific absurdities which Leibniz introduced into the world for reasons of vanity and which the Germans study just because they are Germans." Letters to Maupertuis, 10 August 1741, in *Voltaire's Correspondence*, ed. Bester-

man, XI:182. For full discussion of Voltaire's assessments of Leibniz, see Barber, *Leibniz in France*, pt. III; Wade, *The Intellectual Development of Voltaire*, pt. IV, chap. 1, and the papers of Pomeau and Ferenczi in Brockmeier et al., eds., *Voltaire und Deutschland*.

44 *Versuch den Begriff der negativen Groessen in die Weltweisheit einzufuehren*, 1763, A70; cf. *Metaphysical Foundations of Natural Science*, A33.

45 Letter to Kant, 3 February 1766 in Zweig, tr. and ed., Kant, *Philosophical Correspondence*, p. 50.

46 Ibid.

47 Ibid., p. 53.

48 Though see Tonelli's introduction to C. A. Crusius, *Die Philosophischen Hauptwerke*, eds. Tonelli, Carboncini, and Finster; and Carboncini, "Christian August Crusius und die Leibniz-Wolffische Philosophie," pp. 110–25. On Kant and the Königsberg milieu, see Tonelli, "Conditions in Königsberg and the Making of Kant's Philosophy," in Bucher, et al., eds., *Bewusst sein. Gerhart Funke zu eigen*, pp. 126–44.

49 *Dissertatio de usu et limitibus principium rationis determinantis vulgo sufficientis*, 1752.

50 See Crusius, "Anweisungen venuenftig zu leben" in *Die Philosophischen Hauptwerke*, I 413ff. Cf. Kant, *Critique of Pure Reason*, A829/B857.

51 Leibniz was a strong proponent of censorship for dangerous books (see Harnack, *Geschichte der preussischen Akademie*, II 95). Thus, he would probably not have re-issued a work whose conclusions he found abhorrent, even with an attached refutation.

52 J. C. Eberhard, *Neue Apologie des Sokrates oder Untersuchung der Lehre von der Seligkeit der Heiden*, II 415.

53 Ibid., II 492.

54 Lessing, *Leibniz von den ewigen Strafen*, in *Werke*, VII 298.

55 Lessing, *Werke*, VIII 508.

56 "If," according to Tonelli, "a reading of the NE really affected Kant's 1769 philosophical revolution, it cannot be considered as an effect of a positive collective reaction to the NE because, for a long time after 1769, this reaction simply did *not*, occur." "Early Reactions," p. 453.

57 Quoted by Luserke, "Die Ordnung der Dinge und das Triktrak philosophischer Sprache. Zur Genese des Leibniz-Bildes bei J. G. Herder," p. 497.

58 Eberhard, *Allgemeine Theorie des Denkens und Empfindens*, p. 10.

59 Kant, *Critique of Pure Reason*, A270/B326.

60 Eberhard, *Allgemeine Theorie*, p. 139ff.

61 Ibid., p. 32f.

62 Ibid., p. 77f. Cf. Leibniz, "Meditations on Knowledge, Truth, and Ideas," G IV 424.

63 *Ueber den Wert der Empfindsamkeit, Nachschrift.*
64 Eberhard, *Allgemeine Theorie*, pp. 80–81.
65 Ibid., p. 58.
66 Leibniz had a kind of instinct for this danger; he mistrusted the excesses of theopathy and disapproved of the oversubjectivization of religion. (See his "Reply to Bayle", G IV 570.) For him, as for Wolff, physico-theology gave religion its referential link.
67 Wundt, *Die Deutsche Schulphilosophie*, p. 319.
68 See Zimmerli, "Von der Verfertigung einer philosophiehistorischen Grösse: Leibniz in der Philosophiegeschichteschreibung des 18. Jahrhunderts," pp. 148–67. Cf. Buhle, *Geschichte der neueren Philosophie seit der Epoche der Wiederherstellung der Wissenschaft.*
69 *Critique of Pure Reason*, A856/B884. See Kant's essay *What Real Progress has Metaphysics made in Germany since the time of Leibniz and Wolff?*, tr. and ed. Humphrey.
70 Tiedemann, *Geist der spekulativen Philosophie*, VI:347ff.
71 *Teutsche Merkur*, October 1777, pp. 22–52, p. 43.
72 Herder, "Wahrheiten aus Leibniz," *Sämtliche Werke*, XXXII 211.
73 Herder, "Vom Erkennen und Empfinden," 1778, *Sämtliche Werke*, VIII 170.
74 Ibid., p. 196. See Dreike, *Herders Naturauffassung in ihrer Beeinflussung durch Leibniz' Philosophie*, pp. 7–39.
75 Herder, "Gott, Ein Gespraech," 1787, *Sämtliche Werke*, XVI 481.
76 Schelling, *Ideas for a Philosophy of Nature*, tr. Harris and Heath, p. 16.
77 Schlegel, *Geschichte der alten und neuen Literatur*, 1815, in *Sämtliche Werke*, II 174. See Bertoletti, "Friedrich Schlegel über Leibniz," pp. 240–67.
78 *Geschichte der alten und neuen Literatur*, *Sämtliche Werke*, II 175.
79 Ibid., p. 176.
80 Ibid.
81 Belaval, *Etudes leibniziennes*, p. 221.
82 See Kant's anti-Eberhard polemic, "On a Discovery According to which any Critique of Pure Reason has been made Superfluous by an Earlier One." In *The Kant-Eberhard Controversy*, ed. Allison. Here Kant tries to attach a sense to the monadology and the pre-established harmony and claims that the *Critique of Pure Reason* can be understood as "a genuine apology for Leibniz," which recognized, beyond what the philosopher actually said, what he meant to say, p. 160.
83 Schelling, *Ideas for a Philosophy of Nature*, p. 16.

BIBLIOGRAPHY

TEXTS AND EDITIONS

(Note: Works cited in the Abbreviations list are not included.)

Alexander, H. G., ed. *The Leibniz-Clarke Correspondence.* Manchester: Manchester University Press, 1956.

Cassirer, E., ed. *G. W. Leibniz: Hauptschriften zur Grundlagen der Philosophie.* Translated by A. Buchenau, 2 vols. Leipzig. Felix Meiner, 1924. Reprinted Hamburg: Meiner, 1966.

Des Maizeaux, P. *Recueil des pieces diverses sur la philosophie, la religion naturelle, l'histoire, les mathematiques etc.* Amsterdam, 1720.

Feller, J. F. *Otium hanoveranum sive Miscellanea, ex ore et schedis illustris viri.* Leipzig, 1718.

Fellmann, E. A. *G.W. Leibniz: Marginalia in Newtoni Principia Mathematica.* Paris: Vrin, 1973.

Foucher de Careil, A. *Refutation inédite de Spinoza.* Paris: 1854.

———. *Leibniz, la philosophie juive et la cabale. Trois lectures . . . avec les manuscrits inédits de Leibniz.* Paris: Auguste Durand, 1861.

Gerland, E. *Leibnizens nachgelassene Schriften physikalischen, mechanischen und technischen Inhalts.* Leipzig: B. G. Teubner, 1906.

Klopp, O., ed. *Correspondenz von Leibniz mit der Prinzessin Sophie.* Hannover: Klindworth's Verlag, 1873.

Kortholt, C. *G. G. Leibniz: Epistolae ad Diversos, Theologici, Iuridici, Medici, Philosophici, Historici et Philologici Argumenti.* Leipzig: 1734–42.

Lach, D. F. *The Preface to Leibniz' Novissima Sinica.* Honolulu: University of Hawaii Press, 1957.

Lestienne, H., ed. *G. W. Leibniz: Discours de Métaphysique.* Paris: Vrin, 1907.

Raspe, R. E. *Oeuvres philosophiques latines et françoises de feu M. Leibnitz.* 7 vols. Amsterdam, 1765.

Robinet, A. *Malebranche et Leibniz: relations personnelles.* Paris: Vrin, 1955.

———. *G. W. Leibniz. Principes de la nature et de la grace fondés en raison. Principes de la philosophie ou Monadologie.* 3rd ed. Paris: Presses Universitaires de France, 1986.

Rosemont, H., and D. Cook, trans. and eds. *G. W. Leibniz: Discourse on the Natural Theology of the Chinese.* Honolulu: University of Hawaii Press, 1977.

Scheidt, L., ed. *G. W. Leibniz: Protogea.* Göttingen, 1749.

Schmidt, F., trans. and ed. *G. W. Leibniz: Fragmente zur Logik.* Berlin: Akademie-Verlag, 1960.

Waterman, J. T., trans. *Leibniz and Ludolf on Things Linguistic: Excerpts from their Correspondence (1688–1703).* Berkeley: University of California Press, 1978.

TEXTS AND EDITIONS: OTHER
PRE-TWENTIETH-CENTURY WRITERS

Allison, H. E., ed. *The Kant-Eberhard Controversy.* Baltimore: Johns Hopkins University Press, 1973.

Aquinas, St. Thomas, *Selected Writings,* edited and translated by R. P. Goodwin. Indianapolis: Bobbs-Merill, 1965.

Arnauld, A. *The Art of Thinking.* Translated by J. Dickoff and P. James. Indianapolis: Bobbs-Merrill, 1964.

———. *Des Vraies et des Fausses Idées.* Paris, 1683.

Bailly, J. S. *Eloge de Leibniz.* Berlin, 1768.

Bayle, P. *Historical and Critical Dictionary: Selections.* Edited and translated by R. H. Popkin. Indianapolis: Bobbs-Merrill, 1965.

Bilfinger, G. B. *De Harmonia animi et corporis humani maxime praestabilita ex mente illustris Leibnitii commentatio hypothetica.* Tübingen, 1723.

Bossuet, J. B. *Correspondance.* Edited by C. Urbain and E. Levesque. *Nouvelle Edition.* Paris: Hachette, 1912.

Boyle, R. *Selected Philosophical Papers.* Edited by M. A. Stewart. Manchester: Manchester University Press, 1979.

———. *Works.* 6 vols. Edited by T. Birch. London, 1772.

Buhle, J. G. *Geschichte der neuren Philosophie seit der Epoche der Wiederstellung der Wissenschaft.* Göttingen, 1800–03.

Charleton, W. *Physiologia Epicuro-Gassendo-Charltoniana.* London, 1654.

Clerselier, C. *Lettres de Mr. Descartes,* vol. III. Paris, 1667.

Condillac, E. *Oeuvres complètes.* 2 vols. Paris: Badouin, 1827.

Cordemoy, G. de. *Oeuvres philosophiques.* Edited by P. Clair and F. Girbal. Paris: Presses Universitaires de France, 1968.

Crusius, C. A. *Die Philosophischen Hauptwerke.* Edited by G. Tonelli, S. Carboncini, and R. Finster. Hildesheim: Olms, 1969–.

Descartes, R. *Oeuvres.* Edited by C. Adam and P. Tannery. 12 vols. Paris: Cerf, 1897–1913. Reprinted, Paris: Vrin/CNRS, 1964–76.

———. *Philosophical Writings.* Translated by J. Cottingham, R. Stoothoff, and D. Murdoch. 2 vols. Cambridge University Press, 1985.

———. *Philosophical Letters.* Translated by A. Kenny. Minneapolis: University of Minnesota Press, 1970.

———. *Discourse on Method, Optics, Geometry and Meterology.* Edited by P. J. Olscamp. Indianapolis: Bobbs-Merrill, 1965.

Dillmann, E. *Eine neue Darstellung der Leibnizschen Monadenlehre auf Grund der Quellen.* Leipzig, 1881. Reprinted, Hildesheim: Olms, 1974.

Eberhard, J. A. *Neue Apologie des Sokrates oder Untersuchung der Lehre von der Seligkeit der Heiden.* 2 vols. Berlin, 1772–78. Reprinted, Brussels: Culture et Civilisation (Aetas Kantiana), 1968.

———. *Allgemeine Theorie des Denkens und Empfindens.* Berlin, 1776.

Eberhard, J. A., and J. G. Eckhart. *Leibniz Biographien.* Hildesheim: Olms, 1982.

Erdmann, J. *Versuch einer wissenschaftlichen Darstellung der neuren Philosophie.* Fromann-Holzboog: Stuttgart-Bad Cannstatt, 1977.

Fontenelle, B. de. *Eloge de M. Leibnitz.* In *Eloges des academiciens avec l'Histoire de l'Academie royale des sciences en MDCXCIX.* Hague, 1731. Reprinted, Brussels: Culture et Civilisation, 1969.

Gassendi, P., *Opera Omnia*, 6 vols. Lyons, 1658.

———. *Selected Works,* edited by C. B. Brush. New York: Johnson Reprint Corp., 1972.

Guhrauer, G. E. *Gottfried Wilhelm Freiherr von Leibniz: Eine Biographie.* 2 vols. Breslau, 1842. Reprinted, Hildesheim: Olms, 1966.

Hartmann, G. V. *Anleitung zur Historie der Leibnitzisch-Wolffischen Philosophie* (1737). Hildesheim: Olms, 1973.

Herder, J. G. *Sämtliche Werke.* Edited by B. Suphen. 33 vols. Berlin: Weidemann, 1877–1913.

Hobbes, T. *Leviathan.* Edited by C. B. MacPherson. Harmondsworth: Penguin, 1968.

———. *Man and Citizen.* Edited by B. Gert. Garden City, New York: Anchor, 1972.

Hurst, J. F., *A History of Rationalism.* New York: Nelson and Philips, 1865.

Huygens, C., *Oeuvres Complètes,* 22 vols. The Hague: Martinus Nijhoff, 1888–1950.

Kant, I. *Critique of Pure Reason.* Translated by N. Kemp Smith. London: MacMillan, 1958.

————. *What Real Progress Has Metaphysics made in Germany since the Time of Leibniz and Wolff?* Translated and edited by T. Humphrey. New York: Abaris, 1983.

————. *Philosophical Correspondence.* Translated and edited by A. Zweig. Chicago: University of Chicago Press, 1957.

Lange, J. *Kontroversschriften gegen die Wolffische Metaphysik* (1723). Hildesheim: Olms 1986.

Lessing, G. *Werke.* 7 vols. Munich: Karl Hanser, 1972–76.

Ludovici, C. G. *Ausfuehrlicher Entwurf einer vollstaendigen Historie der Leibnizschen Philosophie zum Gebrauch seiner Zuhoerer herausgegeben.* Leipzig, 1737. Reprinted, Hildesheim, Olms 1966.

Mackie, J. N. *Life of Godfrey William von Leibnitz.* Boston: Gould, Kendall and Lincoln, 1845.

Malebranche, N., *Oeuvres,* edited by G. Rodis-Lewis. Paris: Gallimard, 1979.

————. *The Search After Truth.* Translated and edited by T. M. Lennon and P. J. Olscamp. Columbus, Ohio: Ohio State University Press, 1980.

Newton, I. *Philosophiae naturalis principia mathematica.* Edited by A. Koyré and I. B. Cohen. Cambridge, Mass.: Harvard University Press, 1972.

Oldenburg, H. *Correspondence.* 13 vols. Edited by A. R. Hall and M. B. Hall. Madison: University of Wisconsin Press, 1965–.

Pascal, B. *Oeuvres complètes.* Edited by L. Lafuma. Paris: Editions du Seuil, 1963.

Schelling, F. W. J. *Ideas for a Philosophy of Nature.* Translated by E. E. Harris and P. Heath. Cambridge: Cambridge University Press, 1988.

Schlegel, F. W. *Sämtliche Werke.* 15 vols. Vienna, 1846.

Scott, J. B., ed. *The Classics of International Law.* 22 vols. New York: Oceana, 1911–50.

Spinoza, B. de. *Opera.* 4 vols. Edited by C. Gebhardt. Heidelberg: Winters, 1925. Reprinted 1972.

————. *Collected Works.* Vol. 1. Edited and translated by E. Curley. Princeton: Princeton University Press, 1985.

Spitzel, T. *De Atheismo eradicando ad Virum praeclarissimum Dn. Antonium Reiserum Augustanum Epistola.* 1669

Stein, L., *Leibniz und Spinoza.* Berlin: Reimer: 1890.

Sturm, J. *Philosophia Eclectica.* Altdorf, 1686.

Tiedemann, D. *Geist der Spekulativen Philosophie.* 6 vols. Marburg, 1791–97.

Voltaire. *Candide.* Translated by J. Butt. Penguin: Harmondsworth, 1947.

————. *Candide, or Optimism,* translated by R. M. Adams. New York: Norton, 1966.

———. *Correspondence.* 107 vols. Edited by T. Besterman. Geneva: Institut et Musée Voltaire Les Delices, 1953–67.

Weigel, E. *Analysis Aristotelica ex Euclide restituta* (1658).

Wolff, C. *Vernuenfftige Gedancken von Gott, der Welt und der Seele des Menschens, auch allen Dingen Ueberhaupt.* Deutsche Metaphysik, 1720.

———. *Preliminary Discourse on Philosophy in General.* Translated by R. J. Blackwell. Indianapolis: Bobbs-Merrill, 1963.

———. *Institutiones juris naturae et gentium.* Hildesheim: Olms, 1969.

BOOKS PUBLISHED AFTER 1900

Aarsleff, H. *From Locke to Saussure: Essays on the Study of Language and Intellectual History.* Minneapolis: University of Minnesota Press, 1982.

Aiton, E. J. *The Vortex Theory of Planetary Motions.* London: MacDonald, 1972.

———. *Leibniz: A Biography.* Bristol and Boston: Adam Hilger, 1985.

Austin, J. L. *Philosophical Papers.* Oxford: Oxford University Press [Clarendon], 1961.

Barber, W. H. *Leibniz in France from Arnauld to Voltaire: A Study in French Reactions to Leibnizianism, 1670–1760.* Oxford: Oxford University Press (Clarendon), 1955.

Battail, J. F. *L'avocat philosophe: Géraud de Cordemoy (1626–84).* The Hague: Martinus Nijhoff, 1973.

Beiser, F. *The Fate of Reason: German Philosophy from Kant to Fichte.* Cambridge, Mass.: Harvard University Press, 1987.

Belaval, Y. *Leibniz critique de Descartes.* Paris: Gallimard, 1960.

———. *Leibniz: Initiation à sa philosophie.* Paris: Vrin, 1962.

———. *Etudes leibniziennes.* Paris: Gallimard, 1976.

Blay, M., *La naissance de la mécanique analytique.* Paris: Presses Universitaires de France, 1992.

Bloch, O. *La philosophie de Gassendi: Nominalisme, matérialisme et métaphysique.* The Hague: Martinus Nijhoff, 1971.

Boehm, A. *Le "Vinculum Substantiale" chez Leibniz.* Paris: Vrin, 1962.

Bohatec, J. *Die Cartesianische Scholastik in der Philosophie und reformierten Dogmatik des 17 Jahrhunderts.* Leipzig, 1912. Reprinted Hildesheim: Olms, 1966.

Broad, C. D. *Leibniz: An Introduction.* Cambridge: Cambridge University Press, 1975.

Brockliss, L. W. B. *French Higher Education in the Seventeenth and Eighteenth Centuries.* Oxford: Oxford University Press (Clarendon), 1987.

Brockmeier, P., ed. *Voltaire und Deutschland.* Stuttgart: Metzler, 1979.

Brown, S. *Leibniz*. Brighton: Harvester Press, 1984.

Brundell, B., *Pierre Gassendi: From Aristotelianism to a New Natural Philosophy*. Dordrecht: Reidel, 1987.

Brunner, F. *Etudes sur la Signification de la Philosophie Historique de Leibniz*. Paris: Vrin, 1951.

Burrill, D. R., ed. *The Cosmological Arguments: A Spectrum of Opinion*. Garden City, New York: Doubleday, 1967.

Cassirer, E. *Leibniz' System in seinen wissenschaftlichen Grundlagen*. Marburg, 1902. Reprinted Hildesheim: Olms, 1962.

———. *The Philosophy of Symbolic Forms*. Vol. I: Language. Translated by R. Mannheim. New Haven: Yale University Press, 1953.

Costabel, P. *Leibniz and Dynamics*. Ithaca, New York: Cornell University Press, 1973.

Couturat, L. *La Logique de Leibniz, d'après des documents inédits*. Paris: Alcan, 1901. Reprinted Hildesheim: Olms, 1961.

Craig, W. L. *The Cosmological Argument from Plato to Leibniz*. London: Macmillan, 1980.

Dascal, M. *La Sémiologie de Leibniz*. Paris: Aubier-Montaigne, 1978.

———. *Leibniz: Language, Signs and Thought: A Collection of Essays*. Amsterdam and Philadelphia: John Benjamins, 1987.

Dijksterhuis, E. J. *The Mechanization of the World Picture*. Oxford: Oxford University Press, 1961.

Duhem, P. *Medieval Cosmology*. Translated by R. Ariew. Chicago: University of Chicago Press, 1985.

Fanton d'Andon, J. P. *Horreur du Vide: Expérience et raison dans la physique pascalienne*. Paris: Editions du Centre National de la Recherche Scientifique, 1978.

Flew, A. *God and Philosophy*. New York: Harcourt, Brace, and World, 1966.

Frankfurt, H. G., ed. *Leibniz: A Collection of Critical Essays*. New York: Doubleday Anchor, 1972.

Fremont, C. *L'être et la rélation*. Paris: Vrin, 1981.

Friedmann, G. *Leibniz et Spinoza*. Paris: Gallimard, 1962.

Garber, D. *Descartes' Metaphysical Physics*. Chicago: University of Chicago Press, 1992.

Goodman, A., and A. Mackay, eds. *The Impact of Humanism in Western Europe*. London: Longman, 1990.

Gracia, J. J. *Introduction to the Problem of Individuation in the Early Middle Ages*. Washington: Catholic University of America Press, 1984.

Grafton, A. *Defenders of the Text: The Tradition of Scholarship in an Age of Science, 1450–1800*. Cambridge, Mass.: Harvard University Press, 1991.

Grafton, A., and A. Blair. *The Transmission of Culture in Early Modern Europe*. Philadelphia: University of Pennsylvania Press, 1990.

Grant, E. *Physical Science in the Middle Ages.* New York: John Wiley and Sons, 1971.

———. *Much Ado About Nothing: Theories of Space from the Middle Ages to the Scientific Revolution.* Cambridge: University Press, 1981.

Guenancia, P. *Du vide à Dieu.* Paris: François Maspero, 1976.

Gueroult, M., *Leibniz: Dynamique et Métaphysique.* Paris: Aubier-Montaigne, 1967.

Hampshire, S. *The Age of Reason.* New York: New American Library, 1956.

Hannequin, A. *La première philosophie de Leibnitz,* in Hannequin, *Etudes d'histoire des sciences et d'histoire de la philosophie.* Paris: Alcan, 1908.

Harnack, A. *Geschichte der Königlich preussischen Akademie der Wissenschaften zu Berlin.* 3 vols. Berlin: Reichsdruckerei, 1900.

Hartshorne, C. *Man's Vision of God.* Hamden, Conn.: Harper and Row, 1964.

Hooker, M., ed. *Leibniz: Critical and Interpretive Essays.* Minneapolis: University of Minnesota Press, 1982.

Hostler, J. *Leibniz's Moral Philosophy.* London: Duckworth, 1975.

Ishiguro, H. *Leibniz's Philosophy of Logic and Language.* London: Duckworth, 1972.

James, W. *Varieties of Religious Experience.* Cambridge, Mass.: Harvard University Press, 1902.

Jolley, N. *Leibniz and Locke: A Study of the New Essays on Human Understanding.* Oxford: Oxford University Press (Clarendon), 1984.

Jones, H. *Pierre Gassendi 1592–1655: an Intellectual Biography.* Nieuwkoop: De Graaf, 1981.

Joy, L. *Gassendi the Atomist.* Cambridge: Cambridge University Press, 1987.

Kabitz, W. *Die Philosophie des jungen Leibniz.* Heidelberg: Carl Winter, 1909.

Kenny, A. *The God of the Philosophers.* Oxford: Oxford University Press (Clarendon), 1979.

Kneale, W. and M. *The Development of Logic.* Oxford: Oxford University Press (Clarendon), 1962.

Knowlson, J. *Universal Language Schemes in England and France 1600–1800.* Toronto/Buffalo: University of Toronto Press, 1975.

Koyré, A. *La philosophie de Jacob Boehme.* New York: Franklin, 1929; reprinted 1968.

Kripke, S. *Naming and Necessity.* Revised ed. Oxford: Blackwell, 1980.

Kristeller, P. O. *The Classics and Renaissance Thought.* Cambridge, Mass.: Harvard University Press, 1955.

———. *Studies in Renaissance Thought and Letters.* Rome: Edizione di storia e letteratura, 1956.

482   Bibliography

Kulstad, M. *Leibniz on Apperception, Consciousness, and Reflection*. Munich: Philosophia Verlag, 1991.

Lewis, D. *On the Plurality of Worlds*. Oxford: Blackwell, 1986.

Lindberg, D.C., eds. *Science in the Middle Ages*. Chicago: University of Chicago Press, 1978.

Loeb, L. E. *From Descartes to Hume: Continental Metaphysics and the Development of Modern Philosophy*. Ithaca: Cornell University Press, 1981.

McRae, R. *Leibniz: Perception, Apperception, and Thought*. Toronto: University of Toronto Press: 1976.

Martin, G. *Leibniz: Logic and Metaphysics*. Translated by K. J. Northcott and P. G. Lucas. New York: Barnes and Noble, 1967.

Mates, B. *The Philosophy of Leibniz: Metaphysics and Language*. New York: Oxford University Press, 1986.

Meli, D. B., *The Development of Leibniz's Techniques and Ideas about Planetary Motion in the Years 1688 to 1690*. Cambridge: unpublished Ph.D. thesis, 1988.

Mercer C. *Leibniz's Metaphysics: Its Origins and Development*. Forthcoming, Cambridge: Cambridge University Press.

Moll, K. *Der junge Leibniz*. 2 vols. Stuttgart-Bad Cannstatt: Fromann-Holzboog, 1978.

Mouy, P. *Les lois du choc d'après Malebranche*. Paris: Vrin, 1917.

———. *Le développement de la physique Cartésienne 1646–1712*. Paris: Vrin, 1934.

Muller, K., and G. Kronert. *Leben und Werk von Gottfried Wilhelm Leibniz: eine Chronik*. Frankfurt am Main: Klostermann, 1969.

Mungello, D. *Leibniz and Confucianism: the Search for Accord*. Honolulu: University of Hawaii Press, 1977.

Nozick, R. *Philosophical Explanations*. Cambridge, Mass.: Belnap Press of Harvard University Press, 1981.

Parkinson, G. H. R. *Logic and Reality in Leibniz's Metaphysics*. Oxford: Oxford University Press, 1965.

———. *Leibniz on Human Freedom, Studia Leibnitiana, Sonderheft 2*. Wiesbaden: Franz Steiner, 1970.

Peterson, P. *Geschichte der Aristotelischen Philosophie im Protestantischen Deutschland*. Stuttgart-Bad Cannstatt: Fromann-Holzboog, 1964.

Philipp, W. *Das Werden der Aufklärung in theologiegeschichtliche Hinsiicht*. Göttingen: Vandenhoeck and Ruprecht, 1957.

Plantinga, A., ed. *The Ontological Argument*. Garden City, New York: Doubleday and Co., 1965.

———. *God and Other Minds*. Ithaca: Cornell University Press, 1967.

———. *The Nature of Necessity*. Oxford: Oxford University Press (Clarendon), 1974.

Pombo, O. *Leibniz and the Problem of a Universal Language.* Münster: Nodus Publikationen, 1987.

Popkin, R. *The History of Scepticism from Erasmus to Spinoza.* Berkeley: Univeristy of California Press, 1979.

Prost, J. *Essai sur l'atomisme et l'occasionalisme dans l'école Cartésienne.* Paris: Paulin, 1907.

Ravier, E., *Bibliographie des Oeuvres de Leibniz.* Paris, 1937; reprinted Hildesheim: Olms, 1966.

Rescher, N. *The Philosophy of Leibniz.* Englewood Cliffs: Prentice Hall, 1967.

———. *Leibniz: An Introduction to his Philosophy.* Lanham, Maryland: University Press of America, 1979.

Robertson, J. G. and Reich, D., *A History of German Literature.* Elmsford, New York: London House and Maxwell, 1970.

Robinet, A. *Architectonique disjonctive, automates systémiques et idealité transcendentale dans l'oeuvre de G. W. Leibniz.* Paris: Vrin, 1986.

Russell, B. *A Critical Exposition of the Philosophy of Leibniz,* 2nd ed. London: Allen and Unwin, 1937.

Saine, T. *Von der Kopernikanischen bis zur Französischen Revolution; die Auseinandersetzung der deutschen Aufklärung mit der neuen Zeit.* Berlin: Schmidt, 1987.

Schmitt, C. *Aristotle and the Renaissance.* Cambridge, Mass.: Harvard University Press, 1983.

———. *John Case and Aristotelianism in Renaissance England.* Montreal: McGill-Queen's University Press, 1983.

Schneiders, W. *Die wahre Aufklärung: zum Selbstverständnis der Deutschen Aufklärung.* Freiburg: K. Alber, 1974.

Schneiders, W., ed. *Christian Wolff: Interpretationen zu seiner Philosophie und deren Wirkung.* Hamburg: F. Meiner, 1983.

Schulenburg, S. *Leibniz als Sprachforscher.* Frankfurt: Klostermann, 1973.

Shapin, S., and S. Shaffer. *Leviathan and the Air-Pump.* Princeton: Princeton University Press, 1985.

Slaughter, M. M. *Universal Languages and Scientific Taxonomy in the Seventeenth Century.* Cambridge: Cambridge University Press, 1982.

Sleigh, R. C., Jr. *Leibniz and Arnauld: A Commentary on their Correspondence.* New Haven: Yale University Press, 1990.

Tuck, R. *Natural Rights Theories.* New York: Cambridge University Press, 1979.

Wade, I. O. *The Intellectual Development of Voltaire.* Princeton: Princeton University Press, 1969.

Wallace, W. *Causality and Scientific Explanation.* 2 vols. Ann Arbor: University of Michigan Press, 1972.

Watson, R. A. *The Breakdown of Cartesian Metaphysics.* Atlantic Highlands, N. J.: Humanities Press International, 1987.
Westfall, R. S. *Force in Newton's Physics.* New York: American Elsevier, 1971.
———. *The Construction of Modern Science: Mechanisms and Mechanics.* New York: Wiley, 1971.
Wilson, C. *Leibniz's Metaphysics: A Comparative and Historical Study.* Princeton: Princeton University Press, 1989.
Witt, C. *Substance and Essence in Aristotle: An Interpretation of Metaphysics VII–IX.* Ithaca, New York: Cornell University Press, 1989.
Wundt, M. *Die Deutsche Schulphilosophie im Zeitalter der Aufklärung.* Tübingen, 1945. Reprinted Hildesheim: Olms, 1964.
———. *Die Philosophie an der Universität Jena.* Jena, 1932.

ARTICLES

Aarsleff, H. "Leibniz on Locke on Language." *American Philosophical Quarterly* 1 (1964):165–88. Reprinted in *From Locke to Saussure.*
———. "The Study and Use of Etymology in Leibniz."*Studia Leibnitiana Supplementa* 3 (1969):173–89. Reprinted in *From Locke to Saussure.*
———. "Schulenburg's *Leibniz als Sprachforscher,* with some Observations on Leibniz and the Study of Language." *Studia Leibnitiana* 7 (1975): 122–34.
———. "The Eighteenth Century Including Leibniz." In *Current Trends in Linguistics,* edited by T. A. Seboek, 383–479. The Hague: Mouton, 1975.
Adams, R. M. "Phenomenalism and Corporeal Substance in Leibniz." In *Contemporary Perspectives on the History of Philosophy,* edited by P. A. French, T. E. Uehling, and H. K. Wettstein. *Midwest Studies in Philosophy* 8 (1983):217–57.
———. "Predication, Truth, and Transworld Identity in Leibniz." In *How Things Are: Studies in Predication and the History of Philosophy and Science,* edited by J. Bogen and J. E. McGuire, 235–83. Dordrecht: Reidel, 1985.
———. "Presumption and the Necessary Existence of God." *Nous* 22 (1988): 19–32.
Aiton, E. J. "The Mathematical Basis of Leibniz's Theory of Planetary Motion." *Studia Leibnitiana Sonderheft* 13 (1984):209–25.
Alston, W. P. "The Ontological Argument Revisited." *Philosophical Review* 69 (1960):452–74. Reprinted in *The Ontological Argument,* edited by Plantinga, 86–110. Garden City, New York: Doubleday and Co., 1965.
Ariew, R. "Descartes and Scholasticism: The Intellectual Background to

Descartes' Thought." In *The Cambridge Companion to Descartes*, edited by J. Cottingham, 58–90. Cambridge: Cambridge University Press, 1992.

Belaval, Y. "Premières Animadversions de Leibniz sur les *Principes* de Descartes." In *Mélanges Alexandre Koyré*, vol. II, *L'aventure de l'esprit*, 29–56. Paris: Hermann, 1964.

Bernstein, H. "*Conatus*, Hobbes, and the Young Leibniz." *Studies in History and Philosophy of Science* 11 (1980):25–37.

———. "Passivity and Inertia in Leibniz's Dynamics." *Studia Leibnitiana* 13 (1981):97–113.

———. "Leibniz and Huygens on the 'Relativity' of Motion." *Studia Leibnitiana Sonderheft* 13 (1984):85–102.

Bertoletti, S. F. "Friedrich Schlegel über Leibniz." *Studia Leibnitiana Supplementa* 26 (1986):240–67.

Blumenfeld, D. "Leibniz's Modal Proof of the Possibility of God." *Studia Leibnitiana* 4 (1972):132–40.

———. "Leibniz's Theory of the Striving Possibles." *Studia Leibnitiana* 5 (1973):163–77.

———. "Superessentialism, Counterparts, and Freedom." In *Leibniz: Critical and Interpretive Essays*, edited by M. Hooker, 103–23. Minneapolis: University of Minnesota Press, 1982.

———. "Leibniz on Contingency and Infinite Analysis." *Philosophy and Phenomenological Research* 45 (1985):483–514.

———. "Necessity, Contingency, and Things Possible in Themselves." *Philosophy and Phenomenological Research* 49 (1988):81–101.

Bos, J. M. "The Influence of Huygens on the Formation of Leibniz's Ideas." *Studia Leibnitiana Supplementa* 17 (1978): 59–68.

Breger, H. "Elastizität als Strukturprinzip der Materie bei Leibniz." *Studia Leibnitiana Sonderheft* 13 (1984):112–21.

Brekle, H. "Die Idee einer Generativen Grammatik in Leibnizens Fragmenten zur Logik." *Studia Leibnitiana* 3 (1971):141–49.

Brockliss, L. W. B. "Aristotle, Descartes, and the New Science: Natural Philosophy at the University of Paris, 1600–1740." *Annals of Science* 38 (1981):33–69.

Brown, G. " '*Quod ostendendum susceperamus*': What did Leibniz undertake to Show in the *Brevis Demonstratio?*" *Studia Leibnitiana Sonderheft* 13 (1984):122–37.

———. "Compossibility, Harmony, and Perfection in Leibniz." *The Philosophical Review* 96 (1987):173–203.

———. "Leibniz's Theodicy and the Confluence of Worldly Goods." *Journal of the History of Philosophy* 26 (1988):571–91.

Brown, S. "Leibniz and More's Cabbalistic Circle." In *Henry More: Tercentenary Studies*, edited by S. Hutton, 77–95. Dordrecht: Kluwer, 1985.

Carboncini, S. "Christian August Crusius und die Leibniz-Wolffische Philosophie." *Studia Leibnitiana Supplementa* 26 (1986):110–25.

Cohen, L. J. "On the Project of a Universal Character." *Mind* 63 (1954): 49–63.

Cook, D. "Leibniz and Hegel on the Philosophy of Language." *Studia Leibnitiana Supplementa* 15 (1972):229–38.

Costabel, P. "Contribution à l'offensive de Leibniz contre la philosophie cartésienne en 1691–92." *Revue Internationale de Philosophie* 20 (1966):264–87.

Coudert, A. "Some Theories of Natural Language from the Renaissance to the Seventeenth Century." *Studia Leibnitiana Sonderheft* 7 (1978):56–114.

Cover, J. A. "Relations and Reduction in Leibniz." *Pacific Philosophical Quarterly* 70 (1989):185–211.

Dascal, M. "About the Idea of Generative Grammar." *Studia Leibnitiana* 3 (1971):272–90. Reprinted in *Leibniz, Language, Signs, and Thought*, 125–44.

———. "Language and Money: A Simile and its Meaning in 17th Century Philosophy of Language." *Studia Leibnitiana* 8 (1976):187–218. Reprinted in *Leibniz, Language, Signs, and Thought*, 1–29.

———. "Universal Language Schemes in England and France: Comments on James Knowlson." *Studia Leibnitiana* 14 (1982):98–109.

Dod, B. G. "Aristoteles Latinus." In *The Cambridge History of Later Medieval philosophy*, edited by N. Kretzmann, A. Kenny, and J. Pinborg, 45–79. Cambridge: Cambridge University Press, 1982.

Drecke, B. M. "Herders Naturauffassung in ihrer Beeinflussung der Leibniz' Philosophie." *Studia Leibnitiana Supplementa* 10 (1973):7–39.

Duchesneau, F. "Leibniz on the Classificatory Function of Language." *Synthese* 75 (1988):163–81.

Earman, J. "Perception and Relations in the Monadology." *Studia Leibnitiana* 9 (1977):212–30.

———. "Was Leibniz a Relationist?" *Midwest Studies in Philosophy* 4 (1979):263–76.

Edwards, P. "The Cosmological Argument." In *The Rationalist Annual for the Year 1959*. 101–23. Reprinted in *The Cosmological Arguments: A Spectrum of Opinion*, edited by D. R. Burrill. Garden City, New York: Doubleday and Co., 1967.

Fichant, M. "La 'réforme' leibnizienne de la dynamique, d'après des textes inédits." *Studia Leibnitiana Supplementa* 13 (1974):195–214.

———. "Les concepts fondamentaux de la mécanique selon Leibniz, en 1676." *Studia Leibnitiana Supplementa* 17 (1978):219–32.

———. "Neue Einblicke in Leibniz' Reform seiner Dynamik (168)." *Studia Leibnitiana* 22 (1990):48–68.

Fouke, D. C. "Leibniz's Opposition to Cartesian Bodies during the Paris Period (1672–76)." *Studia Leibnitiana* 23 (1991):195–206.

———. "Spontaneity and the Generation of Rational Beings in Leibniz's Theory of Biological Reproduction." *Journal of the History of Philosophy* 29 (1991):33–45.

———. "Metaphysics and the Eucharist in the Early Leibniz." *Studia Leibnitiana* 24 (1992):145–59.

———. "Dynamics and Transubstantiation in Leibniz's *Systema Theologicum.*" *Journal of the History of Philosophy* 32 (1994):45–61.

———. "Emanation and the Perfection of Being: Divine Causation and the Autonomy of Nature in Leibniz." Forthcoming, *Archiv für Geschichte der Philosophie.*

Friedrich, C. J., "Philosophical Reflections of Leibniz on Laws, Politics and the State." In *Leibniz: A Collection of Critical Essays,* edited by Frankfurt, 47–68.

Furth, M. "Monadology." *The Philosophical Review* 76 (1967):169–200. Reprinted in *Leibniz: A Collection of Critical Essays,* edited by Frankfurt, 99–135.

Gabbey, A. "Force and Inertia in the Seventeenth Century: Descartes and Newton." In *Descartes: Philosophy, Mathematics, and Physics,* edited by S. Gaukroger. Brighton: Harvester Press, 1980.

Gale, G. "The Physical Theory of Leibniz." *Studia Leibnitiana* 2 (1970): 114–27.

———. "Did Leibniz Have A Practical Philosophy of Science?" Proceedings of the Second International Leibniz Congress. *Studia Leibnitiana Supplementa* 13, vol. ii:151–60. Wiesbaden: Franz Steiner 1974.

———. "On What God Chose: Perfection and God's Freedom." *Studia Leibnitiana* 8 (1976):69–87.

Garber, D., "Motion and Metaphysics in the Young Leibniz." In *Leibniz: Critical and Interpretative Essays,* edited by M. Hooker, 160–84. Minneapolis: University of Minnesota Press, 1982.

———. "Mind, Body, and the Laws of Nature in Descartes and Leibniz." In *Contemporary Perspectives on the History of Philosophy,* edited by P. A. French, T. E. Uehling, and H. K. Wettstein. *Midwest Studies in Philosophy* 8 (1983):105–33.

———. "Leibniz and the Foundations of Physics: The Middle Years." In *The Natural Philosophy of Leibniz,* edited by K. Okruhlik and J. R. Brown, 27–130. Dordrecht: Reidel, 1985.

———. "How God Causes Motion: Descartes, Divine sustenance, and Occasionalism." *Journal of Philosophy* 84 (1987):567–80.

————. "Descartes, the Aristotelians and the Revolution that did not Happen in 1637." *The Monist* 71 (1988):471–86.

————. Review of R. C. Sleigh. *Leibniz and Arnauld, Journal of Philosophy* 89 (1992):151–65.

————. "Soul and Mind." *Cambridge History of Seventeenth-Century Philosophy.* Cambridge: Cambridge University Press, forthcoming.

Gensini, S. "Variety and Unity of Linguistic Inquiries: Leibniz's Theory of Meaning." Proceedings of the Vth International Leibniz-Kongress, Hannover. In *Leibniz: Tradition und Aktualität.* 1988:297–304.

Gerhardt, C. I. "Uber neu gefundene Manuscripte von Leibniz." *Sitzungsberichte der Königlich Preussischen Akademie der Wissenschaften zu Berlin.* Phil.Hist. Klasse, 1885:19–23, 133–43.

Grant, E. "Place and Space in Medieval Physical Thought." In *Motion and Time: Space and Matter,* edited by P. Machamer and R. G. Turnbull 37–67. (Columbus, Ohio: Ohio State University Press, 1976).

————. "The Condemnation of 1277, God's Absolute Power, and Physical Thought in the Late Middle Ages." *Viator* 10 (1979):211–44.

Gueroult, M. "The Metaphysics and Physics of Force in Descartes." In *Descartes: Philosophy, Mathematics, and Physics,* edited by S. Gaukroger, 196–229. Brighton: Harvester Press, 1980.

Hacking, I. "Leibniz and Descartes: Proof and Eternal Truths." *Proceedings of the British Academy* 59 (1973):1–16.

————. "Locke, Leibniz, Language and Hans Aarsleff." *Synthese* 75 (1988): 135–53.

Hartz, G., and J. A. Cover. "Space and Time in the Leibnizian Metaphysic." *Nous* 22 (1988):493–519.

Heinekamp, A. "Ars Characteristica und natürliche Sprache bei Leibniz." *Tijdschrift voor Filosofie* 34 (1972):446–88.

————. "Natürliche Sprache und Allgemeine Charakteristik bei Leibniz." *Studia Leibnitiana Supplementa* 15 (1975): 257–86.

————. "Sprache und Wirklichkeit nach Leibniz." In *History of Linguistic Thought and Contemporary Linguistics,* edited by H. Parret, 518–70. Berlin/New York: de Gruyter, 1976.

————. Einleitung. *Beiträge zur Wirkungs- und Rezeptions-geschichte von G. W. Leibniz, Studia Leibnitiana Supplementa* 26. Wiesbaden: F. Steiner, 1986.

Henry, J. "Francesco Patrizi da Cherso's Concept of Space and its Later Influence." *Annals of Science* 36 (1979):549–75.

Iltis, C. "Leibniz and the *Vis Viva* Controversy." *Isis* 62 (1971):21–35.

Ingegno, A. "The New Philosophy of Nature." In *The Cambridge History of Renaissance Philosophy,* edited by C. Schmitt and Q. Skinner, 236–63. Cambridge: Cambridge University Press, 1988.

Jolley, N. "Leibniz and Phenomenalism." *Studia Leibnitiana* 18 (1986): 38–51.

Kabitz, W. "Leibniz und Berkeley." *Sitzungsberichte der Preussischen Akademie der Wissenschaften.* Phil. Hist. Klasse (Berlin), 24 (1932):623–36.

Kayser, W. "Böhmes Natursprachenlehre und ihre Grundlagen." *Euphorion* 31 (1924):521–62.

Kneale, W. "Leibniz and the Picture Theory of Language." *Revue Internationale de Philosophie* 20 (1966):204–15.

Koyré, A. and Cohen, I. B. "Newton and the Leibniz-Clarke Correspondence." *Archives internationales d'histoire des sciences* 15 (1962):63–126.

Kulstad, M. A. "Leibniz's Conception of Expression." *Studia Leibnitiana* 9 (1977):55–76.

———. "A Closer Look at Leibniz's Alleged Reduction of Relations." *Southern Journal of Philosophy* 18 (1980):417–32.

———. "Causation and Pre-established Harmony in the Early Development of Leibniz's Philosophy." In *Causation in Early Modern Philosophy,* edited by S. Nadler, 93–117. University Park: Pennsylvania State University Press, 1993.

Lennon, T. "Occasionalism and the Cartesian Metaphysic of Motion." *Canadian Journal of Philosophy.* Supplementary Vol. 1 (1974):29–50.

Lewis, D. "Counterpart Theory and Quantified Modal Logic." *Journal of Philosophy* 65 (1968):113–26.

Loemker, L. E. "A Note on the Origin and Problem of Leibniz's Discourse of 1686." *Journal of the History of Ideas* 8 (1947):449–66.

———. "Boyle and Leibniz." *Journal of the History of Ideas* 16 (1955):22–43.

———. "Leibniz and the Herborn Encyclopedists." *Journal of the History of Ideas* 22 (1961):323–38. Reprinted in *The Philosophy of Leibniz and the Modern World,* edited, by I. Leclerc, 276–97. Nashville: Vanderbilt University Press, 1973.

Lohr, C. H. "The Medieval Interpretation of Aristotle." In *The Cambridge History of Later Medieval Philosophy,* edited by N. Kretzmann, A. Kenny, and J. Pinborg, 80–98. Cambridge: Cambridge University Press, 1982.

McCullough, L. "Leibniz and Traditional Philosophy." *Studia Leibnitiana* 10 (1978):254–70.

McGuire, J. E. " 'Labyrinthus continui': Leibniz on Substance, Activity and Matter." In *Motion and Time; Space and Matter: Interrelations in the History of Philosophy and Science,* edited by P. Machamer and R. Turnbull, 291–326. Columbus, Ohio: Ohio State University Press, 1976.

McRae, R. "Locke and Leibniz on Linguistic Particles." *Synthese* 75 (1988): 155–81.

Malcolm, N. "Anselm's Ontological Arguments." *The Philosophical Re-*

view 69 (1960):41–62. Reprinted in *The Ontological Argument*, edited by Plantinga, 132–59.

Mates, B. "Leibniz on Possible Worlds." In *Logic, Methodology, and Philosophy of Science*, edited by B. van Rootselaar and J. F. Stahl, 507–29. Amsterdam: North Holland Publishing Company, 1968. Reprinted in *Leibniz: A Collection of Critical Essays*, edited by Frankfurt, 335–64.

———. "The Lingua Philosophica." *Studia Leibnitiana Sonderheft* 8 (1979): 59–66.

———. "Nominalism and Evander's Sword." *Studia Leibnitiana Supplementa* 21 (1980):213–35.

Meli, D. B. "Leibniz on the Censorship of the Cartesian System." *Studia Leibnitiana* 20 (1988):19–42.

———. "Leibniz's Excerpts from the *Principia Mathematica*." *Annals of Science* 45 (1988):477–505.

Menn, S. "The Intellectual Setting of Seventeenth-Century Philosophy." In *The Cambridge History of Seventeenth-Century Philosophy*. Cambridge: Cambridge University Press, forthcoming.

Mercer, C. "The Seventeenth-Century Debate between the Moderns and the Aristotelians: Leibniz and *Philosophia Reformata*." *Studia Leibnitiana Supplementa* 27 (1990):18–29.

———. "The Vitality and Importance of Early Modern Aristotelianism," in *The Rise of Modern Philosophy*, edited by T. Sorell, 33–67. Oxford: Oxford University Press (Clarendon), 1993.

———. "Mechanizing Aristotle: Leibniz and Reformed Philosophy." Forthcoming, *Oxford Studies in the History of Philosophy*.

Merchant, C. "The Vitalism of Anne Conway: Its Impact on Leibniz's Concept of the Monad." *Journal of the History of Philosophy* 17 (1979):255–69.

Monadadori, F. "Reference, Essentialism, and Modality in Leibniz's Metaphysics." *Studia Leibnitiana* 5 (1973):74–101.

Most, G. W. "Zu Entwicklung von Leibniz' *Specimen Dynamicum*." *Studia Leibnitiana Sonderheft* 13 (1984):148–63.

Mugnai, M. "Der Begriff der Harmonie als metaphysische Grundlage der Logik und Kombinatorik bei Johann Heinrich Bisterfeld und Leibniz." *Studia Leibnitiana* 5 (1973):43–73.

———. "A Systematical Approach to Leibniz's Theory of Relations and Relational Sentences." *Topoi* 9 (1990):61–81.

O'Neill, E. "Influxus Physicus." In *Causation in Early Modern Philosophy*, edited by S. Nadler, 27–55. University Park: Pennsylvania State University Press, 1993.

Parkinson, G. H. R. "Leibniz's *De Summa Rerum*: A Systematic Approach." *Studia Leibnitiana* 18 (1986):132–51.

Pombo, O. "Leibnizian Strategies for the Semantic Foundations of a Universal Language." In *Leibniz: Tradition und Aktualität,* Proceedings of the Vth International Leibniz Kongress, Hannover. 753–60.

Popkin, R. "Leibniz and the French Sceptics." *Revue internationale de philosophie* 20 (1966):228–48.

———. "The Third Force in Seventeenth-Century Thought: Scepticism, Science, and Millenarianism." In *The Prism of Science,* edited by E. Ullmann-Margalit, 21–50. Dordrecht: Reidel, 1986.

———. "The Religious Background of Seventeenth-Century Philosophy." *Journal of the History of Philosophy* 25 (1987):35–50.

Poser, H. "Apriorismus der Prinzipien und Kontingenz der Naturgesetze. Das Leibniz-Paradigma der Naturwissenshaft." *Studia Leibnitiana Sonderheft* 13 (1984):164–79.

Putnam, H. "The Meaning of 'Meaning'." In *Mind, Language, and Reality: Philosophical Papers,* vol. 2, 215–71. Cambridge: Cambridge University Press, 1975.

Rescher, N. "Logical Difficulties in Leibniz's Metaphysics." *Studia Leibnitiana Supplementa* (1968):253–65. Reprinted in *The Philosophy of Leibniz and the Modern World,* edited by I. Leclerc, 176–88. Nashville: Vanderbilt University Press, 1973.

———. "Leibniz and the Evaluation of Possible Worlds." *Studies in Modality.* Oxford: Blackwell, 1974. Reprinted in *Leibniz's Metaphysics of Nature,* 1–19. Holland/Boston: Reidel, 1981.

Ross, G. M. "The Demarcation between Metaphysics and Other Disciplines in the Thought of Leibniz." In *Metaphysics and the Philosophy of Science in the Seventeenth and Eighteenth Centuries,* edited by R. S. Woolhouse, 133–63. Cambridge: Cambridge University Press, 1988.

Rossi, P. "The Twisted Roots of Leibniz' Characteristic." In *The Leibniz Renaissance,* 271–89. Florence: Olschki, 1989.

Russell, B., "A Debate on the Existence of God." In *The Existence of God,* edited by J. Hick, 167–91. New York: Macmillan, 1964.

Rutherford, D. "Truth, Predication, and the Complete Concept of an Individual Substance." *Studia Leibnitiana Sonderheft* 15 (1988):130–44.

———. "Leibniz's 'Analysis of Multitude and Phenomena into Unities and Reality.' " *Journal of the History of Philosophy* 28 (1990):525–52.

———. "Phenomenalism and the Reality of Body in Leibniz's Later Philosophy." *Studia Leibnitiana* 22 (1990):11–28.

———. "Natures, Laws and Miracles: The Roots of Leibniz's Critique of Occasionalism." In *Causation in Early Modern Philosophy,* edited by S. Nadler, 135–58. University Park: Pennsylvania State University Press, 1993.

———. "Leibniz and the Problem of Monadic Aggregation." Forthcoming, *Archiv für Geschichte der Philosophie.*

Salmon, N. "Existence." In *Philosophical Perspectives: Metaphysics*, edited by J. Tomberline, 49–109. Atascardero, Calif.: Ridgeview Press, 1987.

Schepers, H. "Leibniz' Arbeiten zu einer Reformation der Kategorien." *Zeitschrift für philosophische Forschung* 20 (1966):539–67.

———. "Begriffsanalyse und Kategorialsynthese Zur Verflechtung von Logik und Metaphysik." *Studia Leibnitiana Supplementa* 3 (1969):34–49.

Schmitt, C. "Experimental Evidence for and Against a Void: the Sixteenth-Century Arguments." *Isis* 58 (1967):352–66.

———. "Towards a Reassessment of Renaissance Aristotelianism." *History of Science* 11 (1973);159–93.

Schrecker, P. "Une Bibliographie de Leibniz." *Revue Philosophique de la France et de l'Etranger* 63 (1938):324–46.

Singer, T. C. "Hieroglyphs, Real Characters, and the Idea of a Natural Language in English Seveneteenth-Century Thought." *Journal of the History of Ideas* 50 (1989):49–70.

Sleigh, R. C., Jr. "Leibniz on the Two Great Principles of All our Reasonings." In *Contemporary Perspectives on the History of Philosophy*, edited by P. A. French, T. E. Uehling, and H. K. Wettstein. *Midwest Studies in Philosophy* 8 (1983):193–216.

———. "Leibniz on Malebranche on Causality." In *Central Themes in Early Modern Philosophy*, edited by J. A. Cover and M. Kulstad, 161–94. Indianapolis: Hackett, 1990.

Spade, P. V. "The Semantics of Terms." In *The Cambridge History of Later Medieval Philosophy*, edited by N. Kretzmann, A. Kenny, and J. Pinborg, 188–96. Cambridge: Cambridge University Press, 1982.

Stammel, H. "Der Status der Bewegungsgesetze in Leibniz' Philosophie und die apriorische Methode der Kraftmessung." *Studia Leibnitiana Sonderheft* 13 (1984):180–88.

Stein, H. "Some Philosophical Prehistory of General Relativity." In *Foundations of Space-Time Theories*, edited by J. Earman, C. Glymour, and J. Stachel, 3–49. *Minnesota Studies in the Philosophy of Science*, vol. viii. Minneapolis: University of Minnesota Press, 1977.

———. "Newtonian Space-Time." In *The Annus Mirabilis of Sir Isaac Newton*, edited by R. Palter, 258–74. Cambridge, Mass.: MIT Press, 1970.

Strange, S. K. "Plotinus, Porphyry, and the Neoplatonic Interpretation of the 'Categories'." In *Aufstieg und Niedergang der romischen Welt*, edited by H. Temporini and W. Haase, Teil II, 36.1, 955–74. Berlin: de Gruyter, 1972.

Thomson, J. J. "A Defense of Abortion." *Philosophy and Public Affairs* 1 (1971):47–66.

Tonelli, G. "Der Streit über die mathematische Methode in der ersten Hälfte des 18 Jahrhunderts." *Archiv für Philosophie* 9 (1959):37–66.

———. "Leibniz on Innate Ideas and the Early Reactions to the Publication of the *Nouveaux Essais* (1765)." *Journal of the History of Philosophy* 12 (1974):437–54.

———. "Conditions in Königsberg and the Making of Kant's Philosophy." In *Bewusst sein: Gerhard Funke zu eigen*, edited by A. J. Bucher, H. Drue, T. M. Seebohm, 126–44. Bonn: Bouvier, 1975.

Trentman, J. "Scholasticism in the Seventeenth Century." In *The Cambridge History of Later Medieval Philosophy*, edited by N. Kretzmann, A. Kenny, and J. Pinborg, 818–37. Cambridge: Cambridge University Press, 1982.

van Inwagen, P. "Ontological Arguments." *Nous* 11 (1977):375–95.

Walker, D. P., "Leibniz and Language." *Journal of the Warburg and Courtauld Institutes* 35 (1972):294–307.

Westfall, R. S. "The Problem of Force: Huygens, Newton, Leibniz." *Studia Leibnitiana Sonderheft* 13 (1984):71–84.

Wilson, C. "Leibnizian Optimism." *Journal of Philosophy* 80 (1983):765–83.

———. "Subjektivität und Form: Zum Problem der Transzendentalen Methodenlehre." In *Literarische Formen der Philosophie*, edited by G. Gabriel and C. Schildknecht, 139–54. Stuttgart: Metzler, 1990.

Wilson, M. "Leibniz's Dynamics and Contingency in Nature." In *Motion and Time, Space and Matter: Interrelations in the History and Philosophy of Science*, edited by P. Machamer and R. Turnbull, 264–89. Columbus: Ohio State University Press, 1976.

———. "The Phenomenalisms of Leibniz and Berkeley." In *Essays on the Philosophy of Berkeley*, edited by E. Sosa, 3–22. Dordrecht: Reidel, 1987.

Wohrmann, K. R. "Die Unterscheidung von Exoterik und Esoterik bei Leibniz." *Studia Leibnitiana Supplementa* 21 (1980):72–82.

Zimmerli, W. C. "Von der Verfertigung einer philosophiehistorischen Grösse: Leibniz in der Philosophiegeschichteschreibung." *Studia Leibnitiana Supplementa* 26 (1986):148–67.

INDEX